PHILIP'S

Ordnance Survey®

STREET ATLAS

Berkshire

First published in 1990 by

Philip's, a division of
Octopus Publishing Group Ltd
2–4 Heron Quays, London E14 4JP

Second colour edition 2000
Third impression with revisions 2002

ISBN 0-540-07676-7 (hardback)
ISBN 0-540-07677-5 (spiral)

Printed and bound in Spain
by Cayfosa-Quebecor

Contents

III **Key to map symbols**

IV **Key to map pages**

VI **Route planning**

VIII **Administrative and Postcode boundaries**

1 **Street maps** at 3½ inches to 1 mile

154 **Index** of towns and villages

155 **Index** of streets, hospitals, industrial estates, railway stations, schools, shopping centres and universities

Digital Data

The exceptionally high-quality mapping found in this atlas is available as digital data in TIFF format, which is easily convertible to other bit mapped (raster) image formats.

The index is also available in digital form as a standard database table. It contains all the details found in the printed index together with the National Grid reference for the map square in which each entry is named.

For further information and to discuss your requirements, please contact Philip's on 020 7531 8439 or george.philip@philips-maps.co.uk

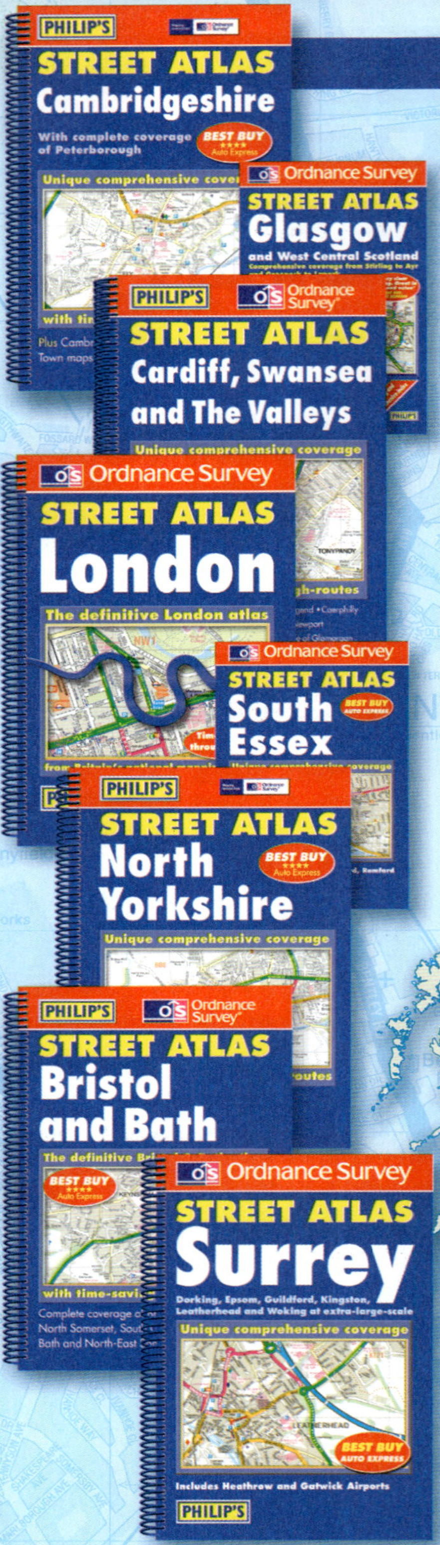

PHILIP'S
STREET ATLAS
Cambridgeshire
With complete coverage of Peterborough
BEST BUY
Auto Express
Ordnance Survey
STREET ATLAS
Glasgow
and West Central Scotland
STREET ATLAS
Cardiff, Swansea and The Valleys
Unique comprehensive coverage
STREET ATLAS
London
The definitive London atlas
STREET ATLAS
South Essex
STREET ATLAS
North Yorkshire
Unique comprehensive coverage
STREET ATLAS
Bristol and Bath
STREET ATLAS
Surrey
Dorking, Epsom, Guildford, Kingston, Leatherhead and Woking at extra-large scale
Unique comprehensive coverage
Includes Heathrow and Gatwick Airports

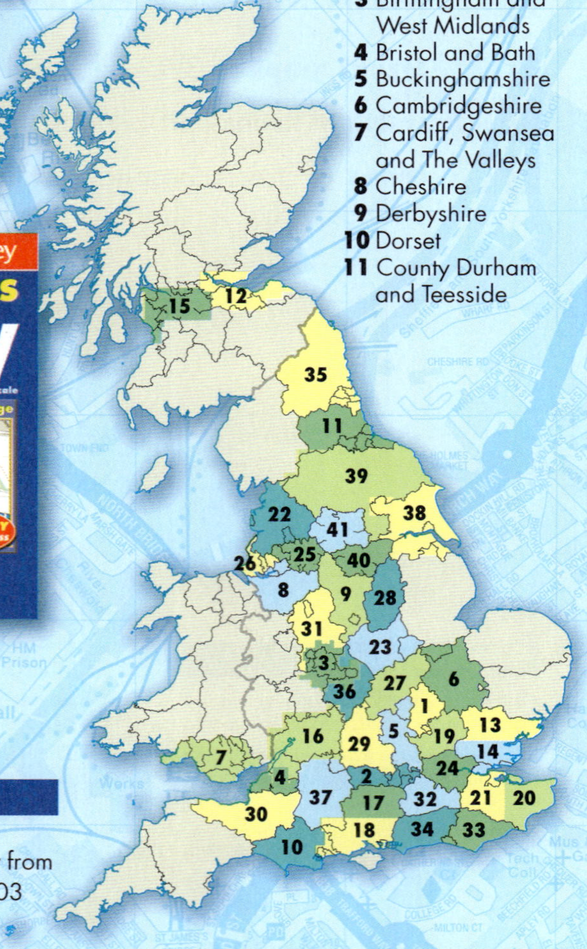

22a	**Motorway** with junction number
	Primary route - dual carriageway and single
	A road - dual carriageway and single
	B road - dual carriageway and single
	Minor road - dual carriageway and single
	Other minor road - dual carriageway and single
	Road under construction
	Pedestrianised area
DY7	**Postcode boundaries**
	County and Unitary Authority boundaries
	Railway
	Tramway, miniature railway
	Rural track, private road or narrow road in urban area
	Gate or obstruction to traffic (restrictions may not apply at all times or to all vehicles)
	Path, bridleway, byway open to all traffic, road used as a public path
	The representation in this atlas of a road, track or path is no evidence of the existence of way
126 / 94	**Adjoining page indicators**

Allot Gdns	**Allotments**	Meml	**Memorial**
Acad	**Academy**	Mon	**Monument**
Cemy	**Cemetery**	Mus	**Museum**
C Ctr	**Civic Centre**	Obsy	**Observatory**
CH	**Club House**	Pal	**Royal Palace**
Coll	**College**	PH	**Public House**
Crem	**Crematorium**	Recn Gd	**Recreation Ground**
Ent	**Enterprise**	Resr	**Reservoir**
Ex H	**Exhibition Hall**	Ret Pk	**Retail Park**
Ind Est	**Industrial Estate**	Sch	**School**
Inst	**Institute**	Sh Ctr	**Shopping Centre**
Ct	**Law Court**	TH	**Town Hall/House**
L Ctr	**Leisure Centre**	Trad Est	**Trading Estate**
LC	**Level Crossing**	Univ	**University**
Liby	**Library**	Wks	**Works**
Mkt	**Market**	YH	**Youth Hostel**

Walsall	**Railway station**
	London Underground station
	Private railway station
	Bus, coach station
	Ambulance station
	Coastguard station
	Fire station
	Police station
	Accident and Emergency entrance to hospital
H	**Hospital**
+	**Places of worship**
i	**Information Centre** (open all year)
P	**Parking**
P&R	**Park and Ride**
PO	**Post Office**
	Camping site
	Caravan site
	Golf course
	Picnic site
Prim Sch	**Important buildings, schools, colleges, universities and hospitals**
River Medway	**Water name**
	Stream
	River or canal - minor and major
	Water
	Tidal water
	Woods
	Houses
House	**Non-Roman antiquity**
VILLA	**Roman antiquity**

■ The dark grey border on the inside edge of some pages indicates that the mapping does not continue onto the adjacent page

■ The small numbers around the edges of the maps identify the 1 kilometre National Grid lines

The scale of the maps is 5.52 cm to 1 km
3½ inches to 1 mile 1: 18103

0 ¼ ½ ¾ 1 mile

0 250 m 500 m 750 m 1 kilometre

Key to map pages

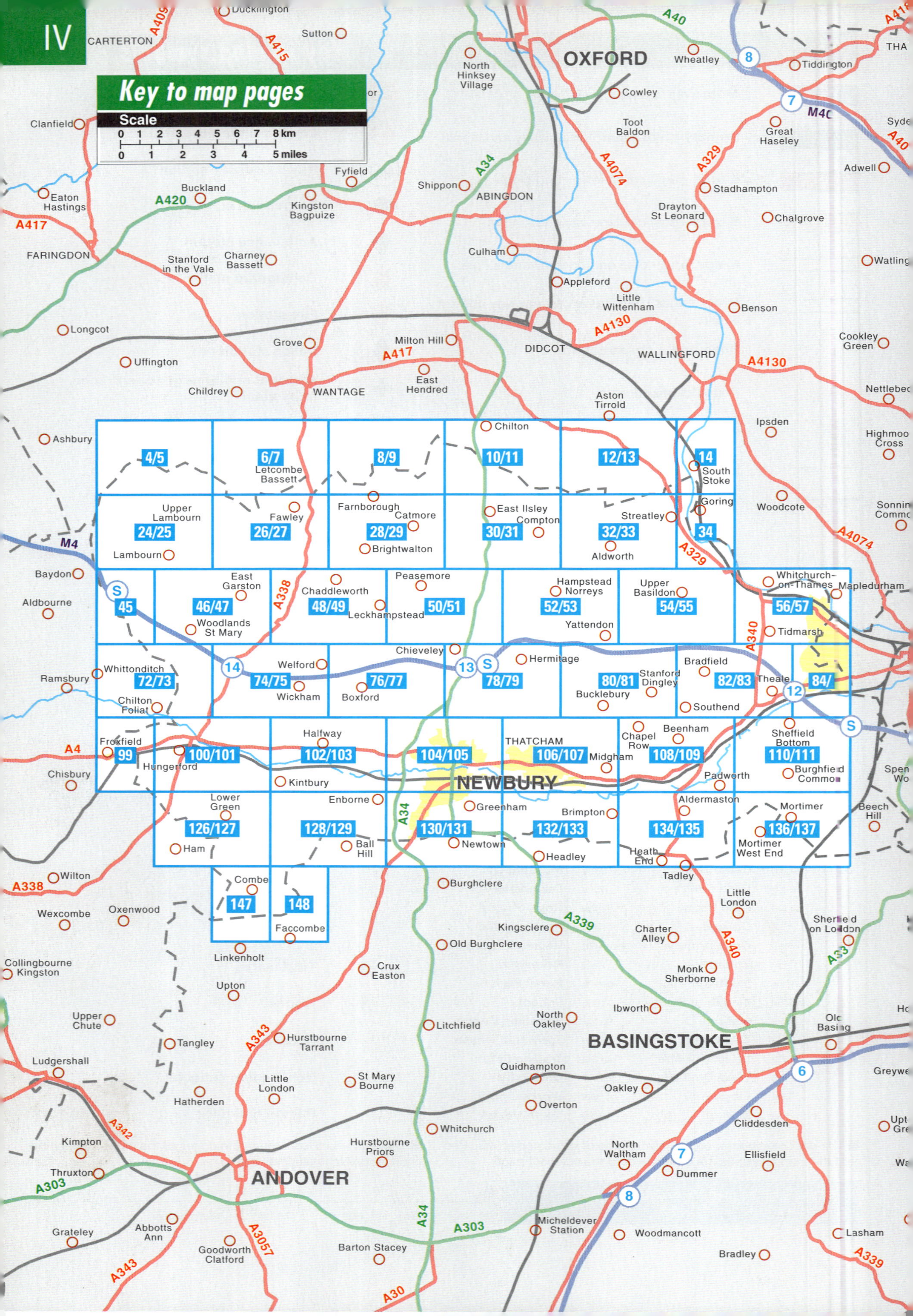

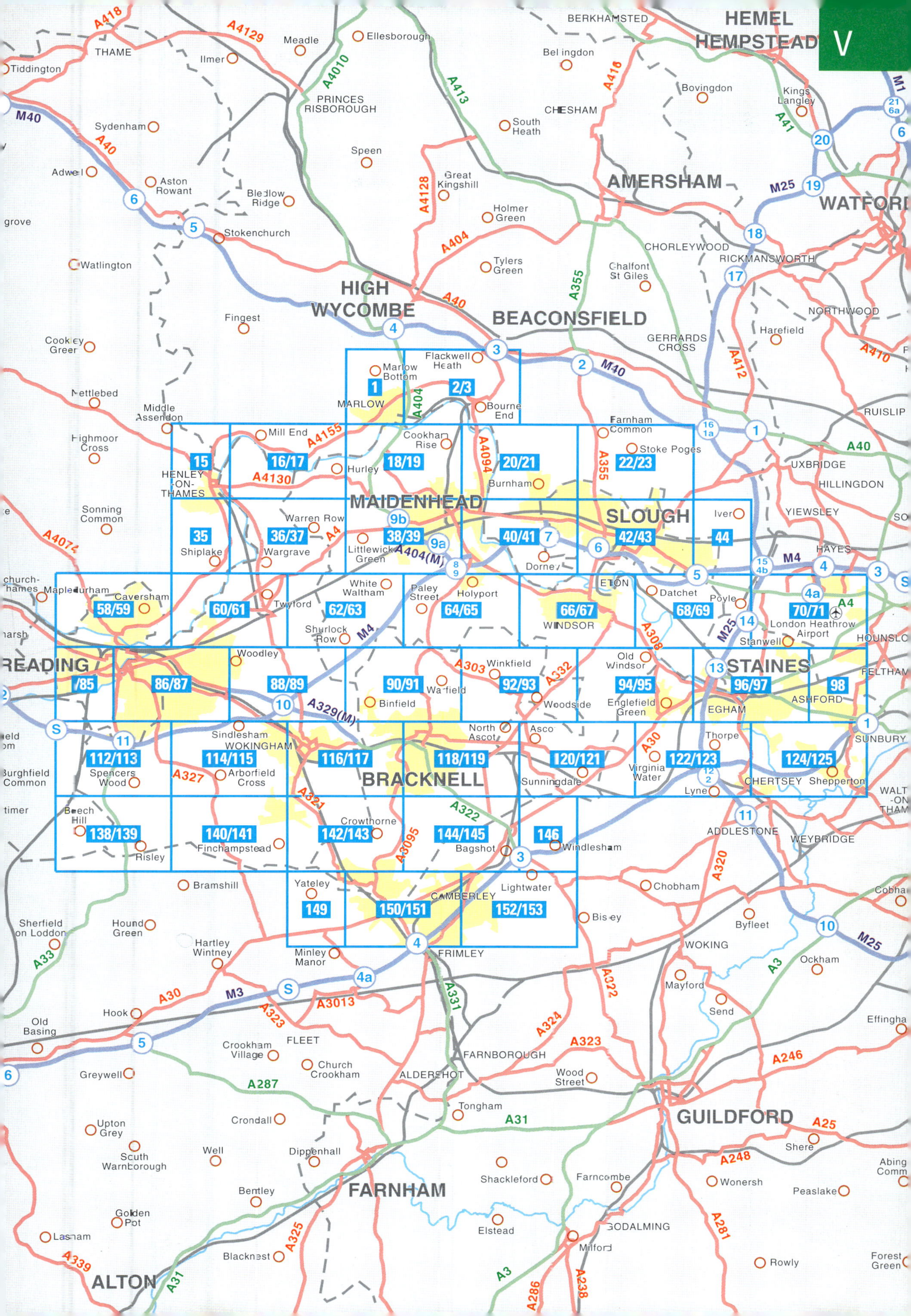

V
HEMEL HEMPSTEAD
BERKHAMSTED
THAME
Tiddington
Meadle
Ellesborough
Ilmer
A418
A4129
A4010
A413
A416
Bellingdon
Bovingdon
Kings Langley
M1
21 6a
6
20
19
A41
PRINCES RISBOROUGH
CHESHAM
South Heath
M40
Sydenham
A40
Speen
Adwell
Aston Rowant
Bledlow Ridge
Great Kingshill
A4128
AMERSHAM
M25
WATFORD
grove
6
5
Stokenchurch
Holmer Green
A404
18
CHORLEYWOOD
RICKMANSWORTH
Watlington
Tylers Green
Chalfont St Giles
A355
17
HIGH WYCOMBE
A40
BEACONSFIELD
Fingest
4
NORTHWOOD
Cookley Green
3
GERRARDS CROSS
Harefield
A412
A4010
2
M40
Flackwell Heath
Marlow Bottom
1
2/3
Nettlebed
MARLOW
A404
Bourne End
Middle Assendon
Farnham Common
16 1a
1
RUISLIP
Highmoor Cross
Mill End
A4155
Cookham Rise
A4094
A355
Stoke Poges
A40
15
16/17
18/19
20/21
22/23
UXBRIDGE
HENLEY-ON-THAMES
A4130
Hurley
Burnham
HILLINGDON
MAIDENHEAD
SLOUGH
Sonning Common
Warren Row
9b
Iver
YIEWSLEY
A4074
35
36/37
A4
38/39
9a
40/41
7
6
42/43
44
Shiplake
Wargrave
Littlewick Green
A404(M)
8 9
Dorney
HAYES
M4
15 4b
5
4
3
Church Thames
Mapledurham
Caversham
ETON
White Waltham
Paley Street
Holyport
Datchet
Poyle
4a
A4
58/59
60/61
Twyford
62/63
64/65
66/67
68/69
70/71
London Heathrow Airport
WINDSOR
A308
14
M25
Stanwell
HOUNSLOW
Shurlock Row
M4
READING
Woodley
A303
Winkfield
A332
Old Windsor
13
STAINES
FELTHAM
/85
86/87
88/89
90/91
Warfield
92/93
94/95
96/97
98
10
A329(M)
Binfield
Woodside
Englefield Green
EGHAM
ASHFORD
S
North Ascot
Ascot
A30
Thorpe
1
SUNBURY
11
Sindlesham
WOKINGHAM
112/113
114/115
116/117
118/119
120/121
122/123
124/125
Spencers Wood
A327
Arborfield Cross
BRACKNELL
Sunningdale
Virginia Water
12 2
CHERTSEY
Shepperton
Burghfield Common
A321
Lyne
WALTON-ON-THAMES
Beech Hill
A322
Crowthorne
11
ADDLESTONE
WEYBRIDGE
138/139
140/141
142/143
144/145
146
Windlesham
A3095
Risley
Finchampstead
Bagshot
3
A320
Bramshill
Yateley
Lightwater
Chobham
Cobham
CAMBERLEY
149
150/151
152/153
Sherfield on Loddon
Hound Green
Bisley
Byfleet
Hartley Wintney
4
Minley Manor
FRIMLEY
WOKING
10
M25
A33
4a
S
A3
Ockham
A30
M3
A331
A322
Mayford
Hook
A3013
A323
Send
Old Basing
FLEET
Effingham
5
Crookham Village
A324
A323
FARNBOROUGH
A246
Greywell
Church Crookham
ALDERSHOT
Wood Street
A287
Tongham
A31
GUILDFORD
A25
Upton Grey
Crondall
South Warnborough
Well
Dippenhall
Shackleford
Farncombe
A248
Shere
Abinger Common
Wonersh
Bentley
FARNHAM
Peaslake
Golden Pot
Lasham
A325
Elstead
GODALMING
A281
A339
Blacknest
Milford
A3
Rowly
Forest Green
ALTON
A31
A286
A238

Route planning

Scale
0 1 2 3 4 5 6 7 8 km
0 1 2 3 4 5 miles

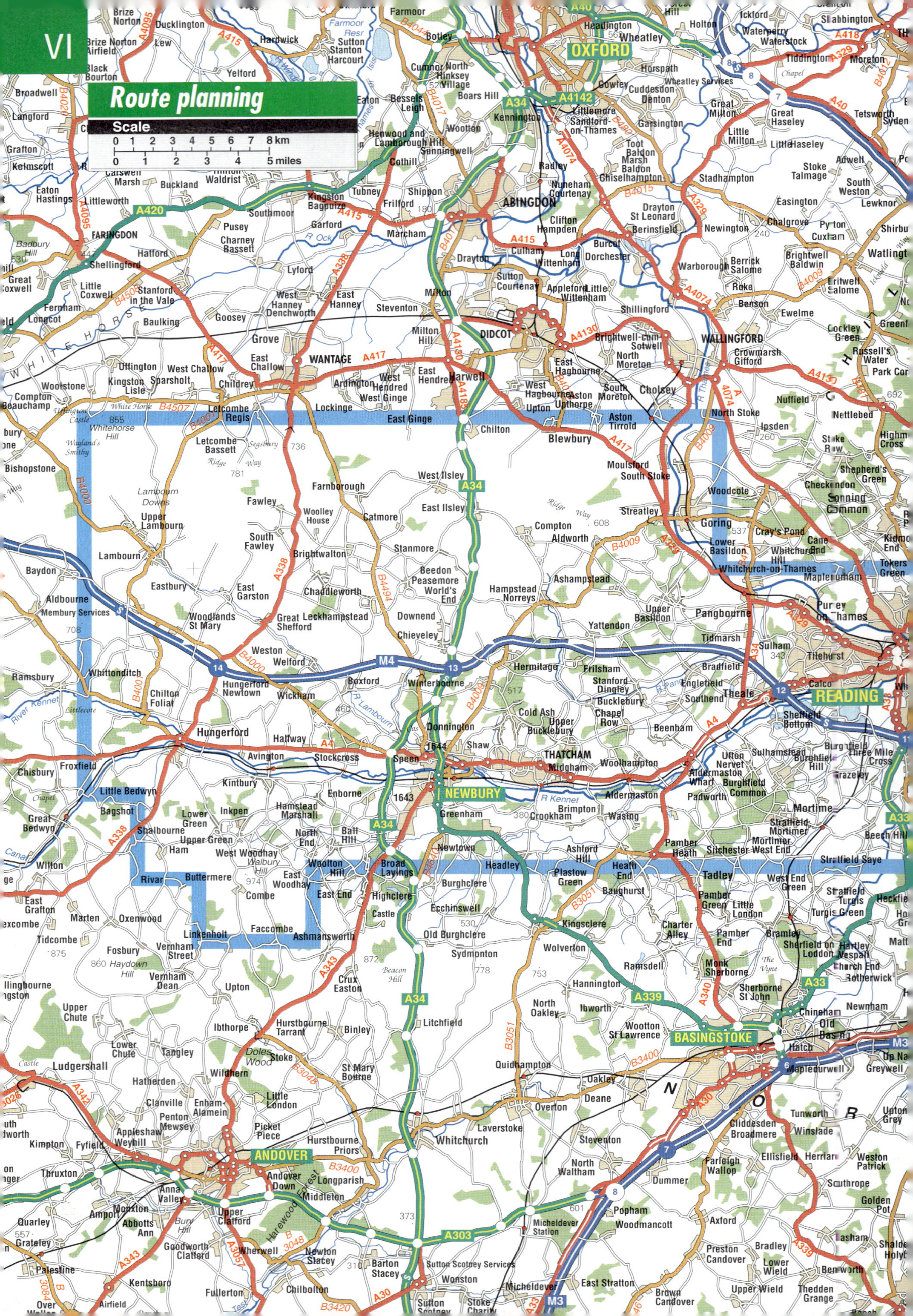

THAME
HEMEL HEMPSTEAD
PRINCES RISBOROUGH
AMERSHAM
CHESHAM
WATFORD
CHORLEYWOOD
RICKMANSWORTH
HIGH WYCOMBE
BEACONSFIELD
MARLOW
MAIDENHEAD
SLOUGH
UXBRIDGE
HILLINGDON
HAYES
HENLEY-ON-THAMES
READING
WINDSOR
ETON
London Heathrow Airport
STAINES
FELTHAM
ASHFORD
SUNBURY
EGHAM
WOKINGHAM
BRACKNELL
ADDLESTONE
CHERTSEY
WEYBRIDGE
WALTON-ON-THAMES
CAMBERLEY
FRIMLEY
WOKING
FLEET
FARNBOROUGH
ALDERSHOT
GUILDFORD
FARNHAM
GODALMING
ALTON
Windsor Forest
GREAT PARK
Chobham Common
Royal Military Academy
M40
M4
M25
M3
M1
A404(M)
A329(M)
Grand Union Canal

Major administrative and Postcode boundaries

- County and unitary authority boundaries
- Postcode boundaries
- Area covered by this atlas

Scale: 0, 5, 10, 15 km; 0, 5, 10 miles

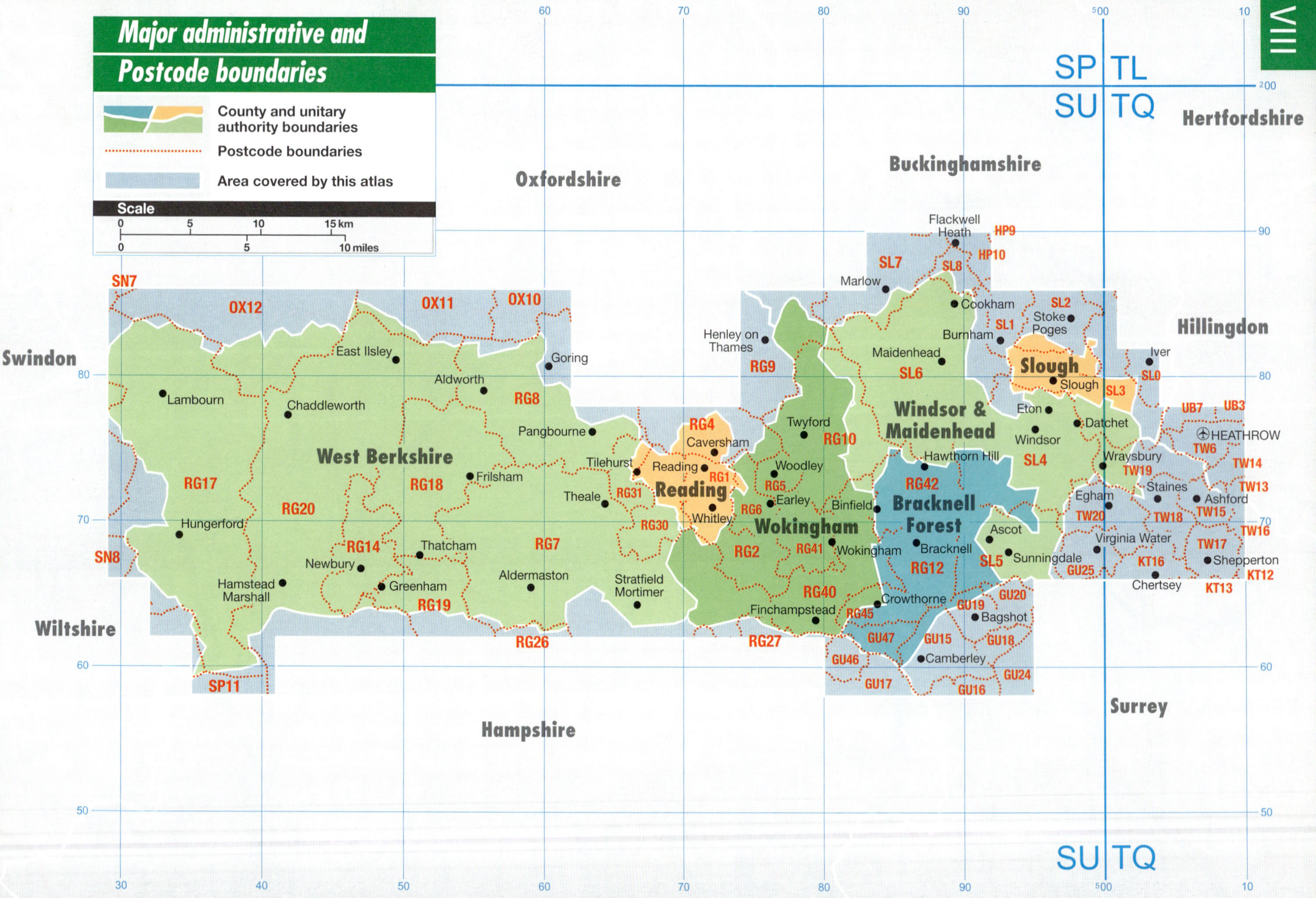

2

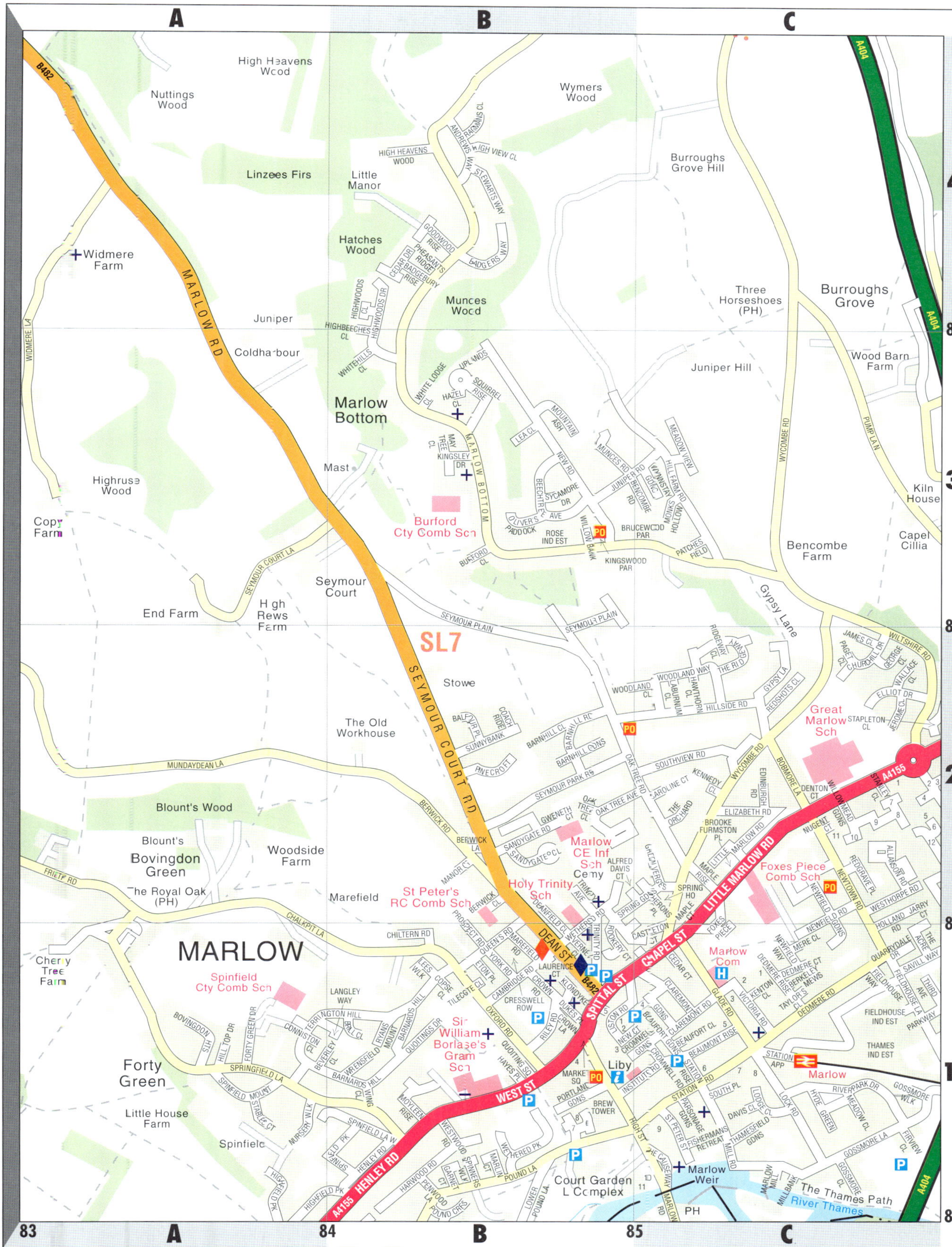

B1
1 BRAEMAR CT
2 CHISWICK LODGE
3 LISTON CT
4 LIME BARN
5 MORRIS PL
6 BARLEY WAY
7 MALTHOUSE WAY
8 PORTLANDS MEWS

18

C1
1 BEECH CT
2 VICTORIA CT
3 GLADE HO
4 ST JAMES CTYD
5 LEIGHTON HO
6 MONKSWOOD CT
7 LITTLE BOLTONS
8 PENN CT
9 TEMPLARS PL

2

10 TIERNEY CT
11 DUNSTABLE HO
C2
1 EASTWOOD CT
2 WILTSHIRE RD
3 MILE ELM
4 BEECHINGSTOKE
5 BUTLER CT
6 BYRON CL
7 MEAD CL
8 WILLOWMEAD RD
9 WILLOWMEAD SQ
10 WILLOWMEAD CL
11 ROMNEY CT
12 SHELLEY RD

1

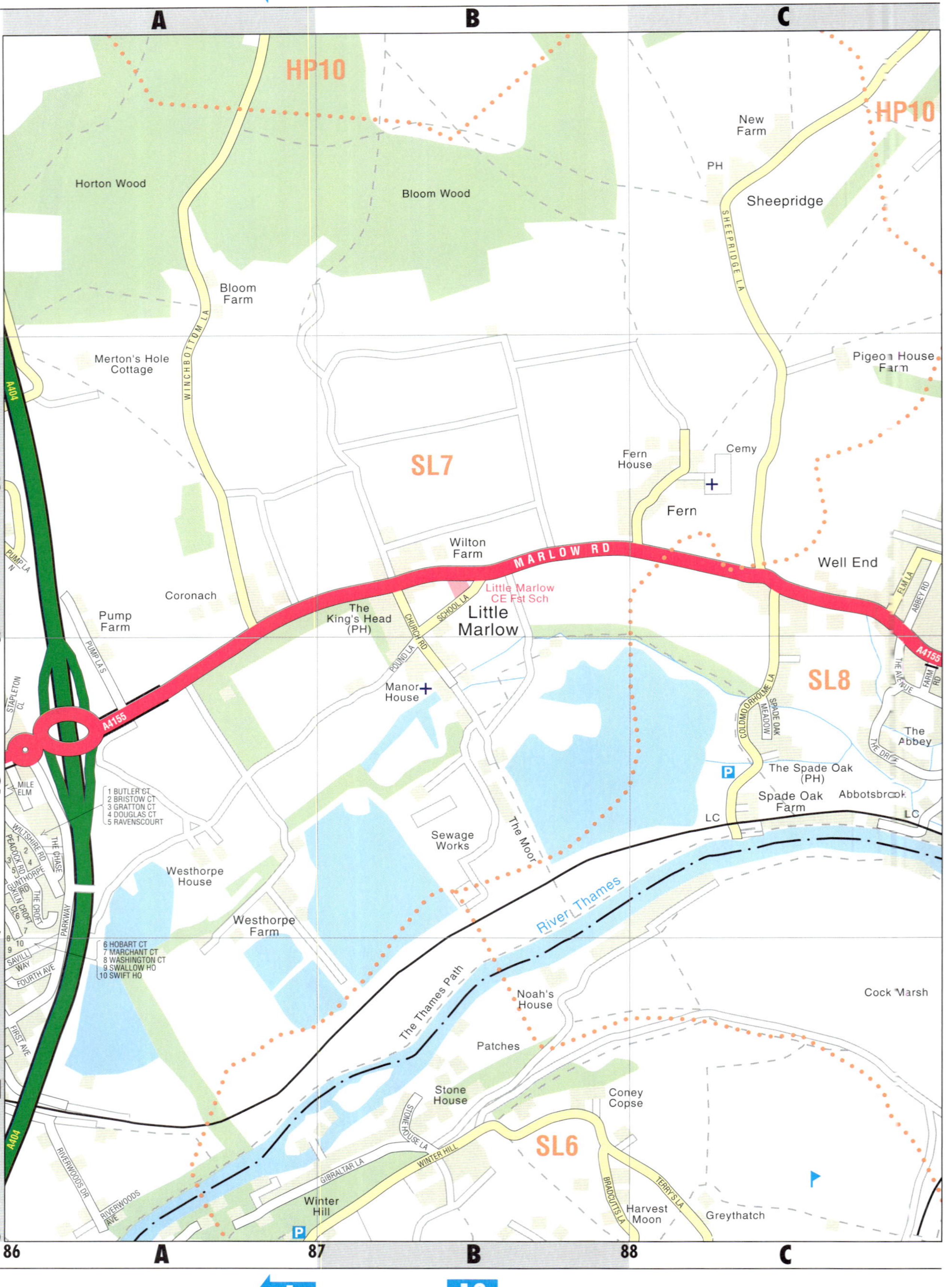
HP10
Horton Wood
Bloom Wood
Bloom Farm
New Farm
PH
Sheepridge
SHEEPRIDGE LA
WINCHBOTTOM LA
Merton's Hole Cottage
Pigeon House Farm
SL7
Fern House
Cemy
Fern
Wilton Farm
MARLOW RD
Well End
Coronach
Pump Farm
The King's Head (PH)
Little Marlow CE Fst Sch
Little Marlow
A4155
SL8
Manor House
The Abbey
The Spade Oak (PH)
Spade Oak Farm
Abbotsbrook
LC
1 BUTLER CT
2 BRISTOW CT
3 GRATTON CT
4 DOUGLAS CT
5 RAVENSCOURT
Sewage Works
The Moor
Westhorpe House
Westhorpe Farm
River Thames
6 HOBART CT
7 MARCHANT CT
8 WASHINGTON CT
9 SWALLOW HO
10 SWIFT HO
The Thames Path
Noah's House
Cock Marsh
Patches
Stone House
Coney Copse
SL6
Winter Hill
Harvest Moon
Greythatch
A404
PUMP LA
PUMP LA S
SCHOOL LA
CHURCH RD
POUND LA
COLDMOORHOLME LA
SPADE OAK MEADOW
ELM LA
ABBEY RD
FARM RD
THE AVENUE
THE DRIVE
STAPLETON CL
MILE ELM
WILTSHIRE RD
PEACOCK RD
GUNTHORPE RD
KILN CROFT
THE CHASE
THE CROFT
PARKWAY
SAVILL WAY
FOURTH AVE
FIRST AVE
RIVERWOODS DR
RIVERWOODS AVE
GIBRALTAR LA
STONE HOUSE LA
WINTER HILL
BRADCUTTS LA
TERRY'S LA
A B C
86 87 88
4 89 3 88 2 87 1 86

1
19

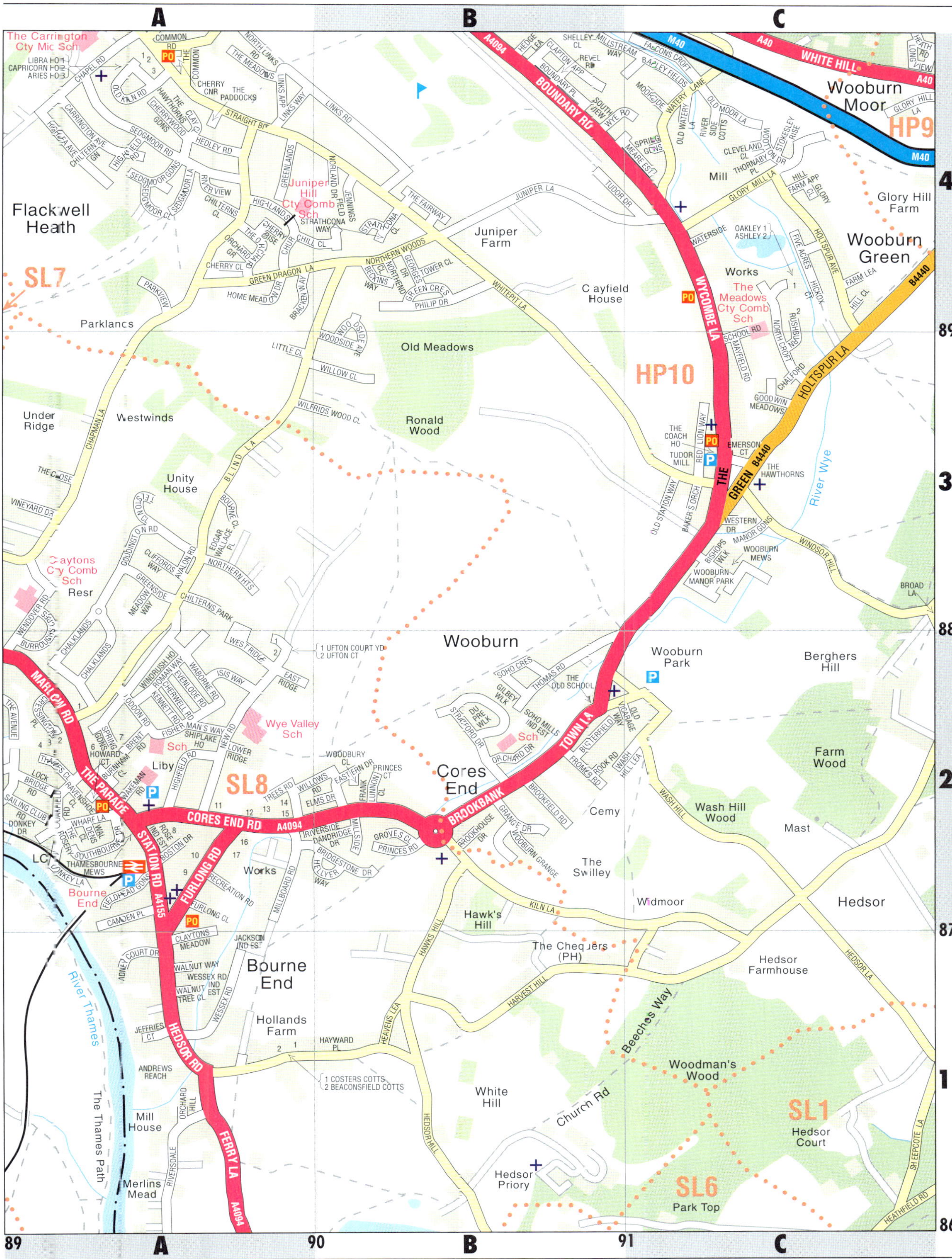

A2
1 ROWAN HO
2 COKERS CT
3 RUSSELL HO
4 RAY HO
5 GRANT HO
6 ORCHARD HO
7 BAILEY HO
8 BOURNE END BSNS CTR
9 EGHAMS CT
10 HYLAND HO
11 FARRIER CT
12 MOUNT PLEASANT COTTS
13 SYCAMORE CL
14 THE WILLOWS
15 THE MAPLES
16 MEADOW BANK
17 THE COURTYARD

20

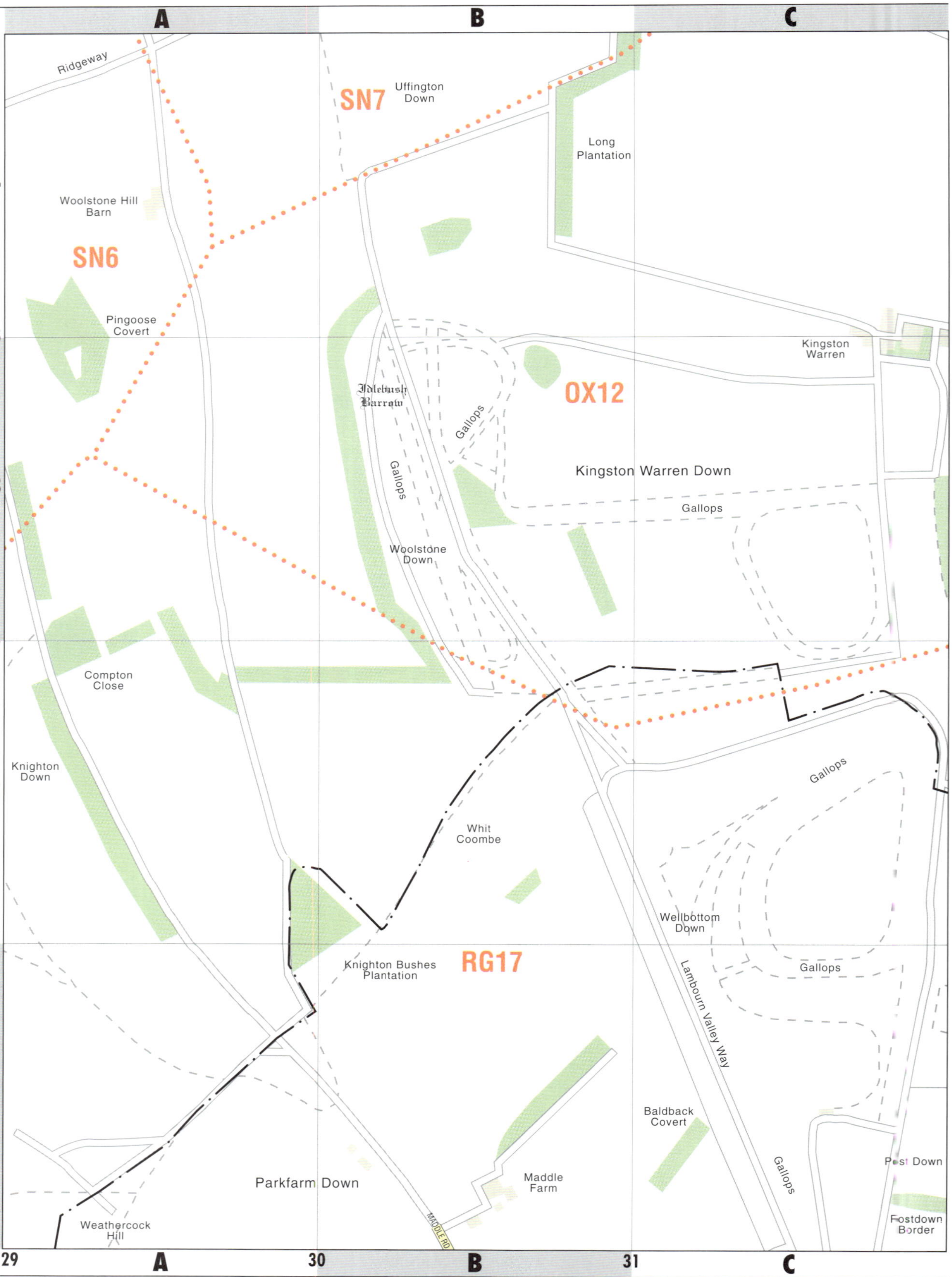
A
B
C
Ridgeway
SN7
Uffington Down
Long Plantation
4
Woolstone Hill Barn
SN6
Pingoose Covert
85
Kingston Warren
Idlebush Barrow
OX12
Gallops
Gallops
3
Kingston Warren Down
Gallops
Woolstone Down
84
Compton Close
Knighton Down
2
Gallops
Whit Coombe
Wellbottom Down
83
Knighton Bushes Plantation
RG17
Gallops
Lambourn Valley Way
1
Baldback Covert
Gallops
Post Down
Maddle Farm
Parkfarm Down
MADDLE RD
Weathercock Hill
Fostdown Border
82
29
A
30
B
31
C

24

6

A
B
C
Hillbarn Clump
Ridgeway
Rubblepit Plantation
Old Plantation
Pigtrough Bottom
B4001
Hill Barn
Down Barn
Gallops
Hackpen Hill
Mast
Radio Station
OX12
Sparsholt Firs
Scary Hill
Sparsholt Down
Gallops
Moss Hill
Gallop
Green Down
Faringdon Down Gallop
Eastmanton Down
Crog Hill
Westcot Down
Boundary Covert
Long Barrow
Pit Down
Old Warren
Sevenbarrows House
Seven Barrows
Gallops
Gallops
RG17
Faringdon Road Down
Long Covert
Post Down
Crow Down
Postdown Farm
Sheepdrove Farm
Croker's Hole
Wormhill Bottom
B4001
4
85
3
84
2
83
1
82
32
33
34

25

6

5

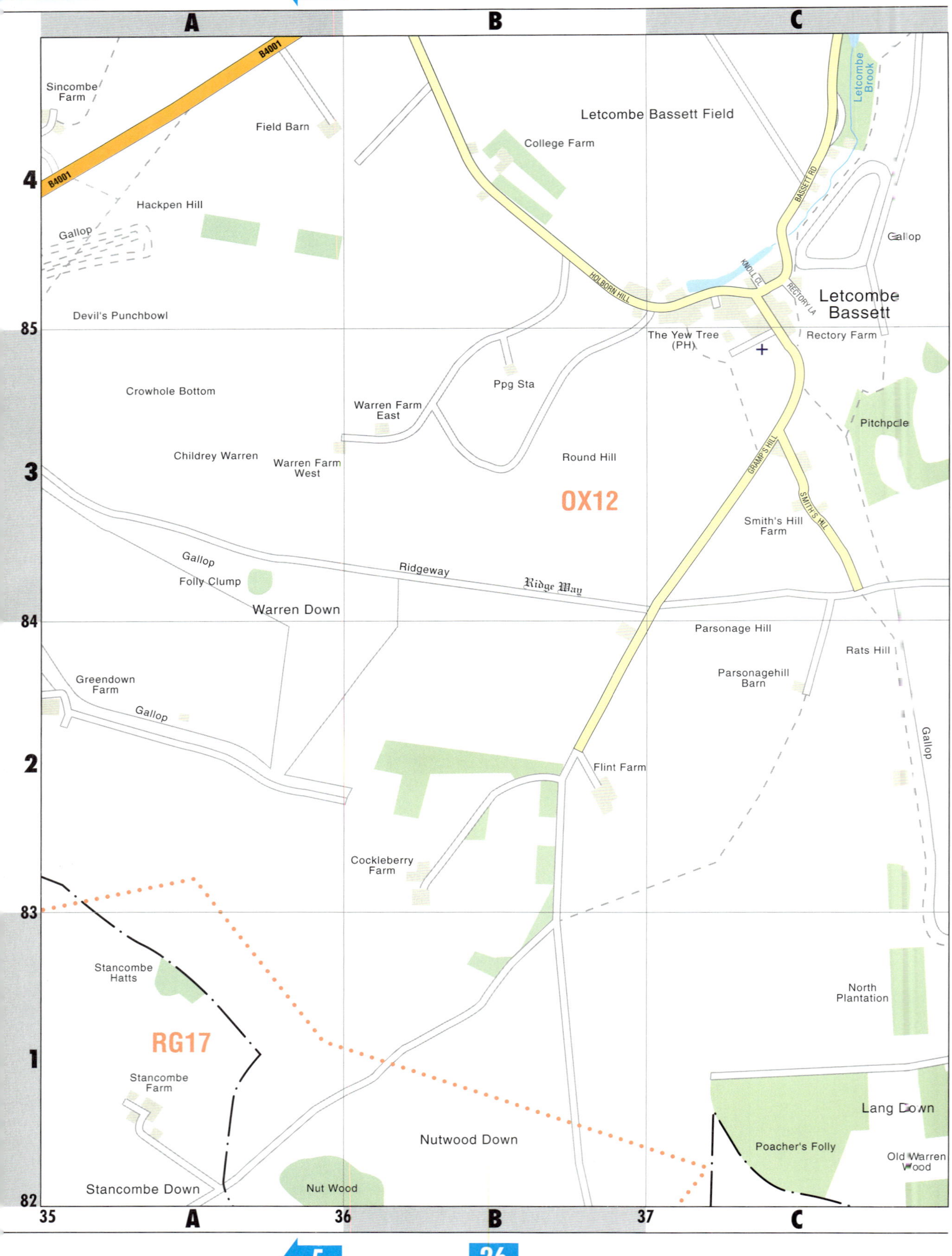
A
B
C
Sincombe Farm
B4001
Field Barn
Letcombe Bassett Field
College Farm
Letcombe Brook
BASSETT RD
Hackpen Hill
Gallop
HOLBORN HILL
KNOLL CL
RECTORY LA
Letcombe Bassett
Devil's Punchbowl
The Yew Tree (PH)
Rectory Farm
Crowhole Bottom
Ppg Sta
Warren Farm East
Pitchpole
Childrey Warren
Warren Farm West
Round Hill
GRAMP'S HILL
OX12
SMITH'S HILL
Smith's Hill Farm
Gallop
Ridgeway
Ridge Way
Folly Clump
Warren Down
Parsonage Hill
Rats Hill
Greendown Farm
Parsonagehill Barn
Gallop
Flint Farm
Cockleberry Farm
Stancombe Hatts
North Plantation
RG17
Stancombe Farm
Lang Down
Nutwood Down
Poacher's Folly
Old Warren Wood
Stancombe Down
Nut Wood
4
85
3
84
2
83
1
82
35
36
37

5
26

8

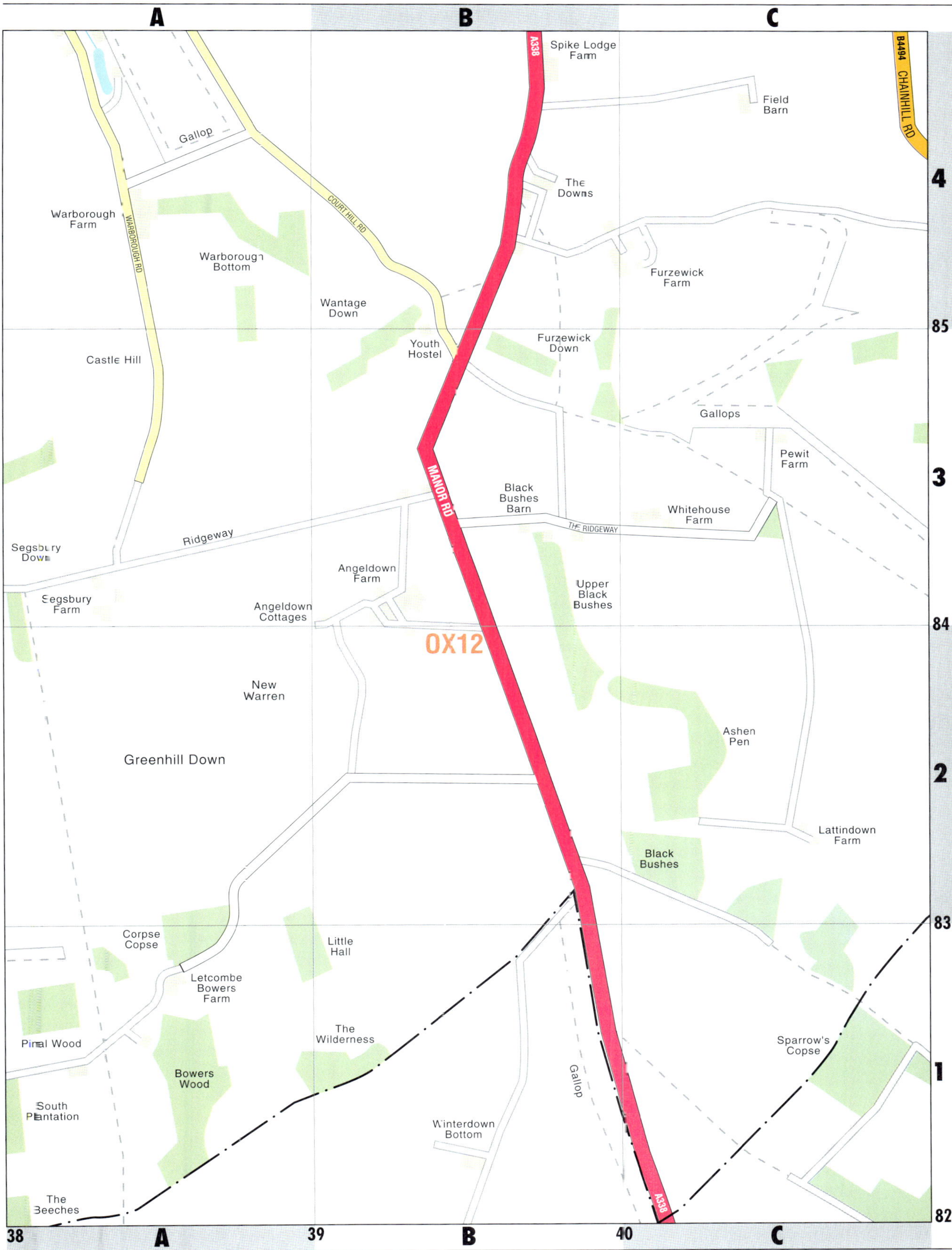
A
B
C
A338
Spike Lodge Farm
B4494 CHAINHILL RD
Field Barn
Gallop
4
The Downs
Warborough Farm
WARBOROUGH RD
COURT HILL RD
Warborough Bottom
Furzewick Farm
Wantage Down
85
Youth Hostel
Furzewick Down
Castle Hill
Gallops
Pewit Farm
MANOR RD
3
Black Bushes Barn
Whitehouse Farm
THE RIDGEWAY
Ridgeway
Segsbury Down
Angeldown Farm
Upper Black Bushes
Segsbury Farm
Angeldown Cottages
84
OX12
New Warren
Ashen Pen
Greenhill Down
2
Lattindown Farm
Black Bushes
83
Corpse Copse
Little Hall
Letcombe Bowers Farm
The Wilderness
Sparrow's Copse
Pinal Wood
1
Bowers Wood
Gallop
South Plantation
Winterdown Bottom
The Beeches
A338
82
38
39
40

27

8

7

A
B
C
4
85
3
84
2
83
1
82
41
42
43
Droveway Hill
Coldharbour Road
Chalkhill Barn
Resr
Long Valley Down
Corsica Pine Wood
Jew's Harp
The Sycamores
Ardington Down
Midsummer Wood
Resr
B4494
Goddard's Road
Gallop
BITHAM RD
CHAINHILL RD
Ridgeway
Ridgeway Down
Monument
Middlehill Down
Wether Down
Old Street
Betterton Down
P
Yew Down
OX12
Mead Platt
The Warren
Lattin Down
Triangle Wood
Betterton Copse
Mast
Lockinge Kiln Farm
Farnborough Furze Down
Lockinge Down
Little Coombe Farm
Moonlight Barn
Coombe Down
Coombe Lodge
Farnborough
Hall
COPPERAGE RD
B4494

7
28

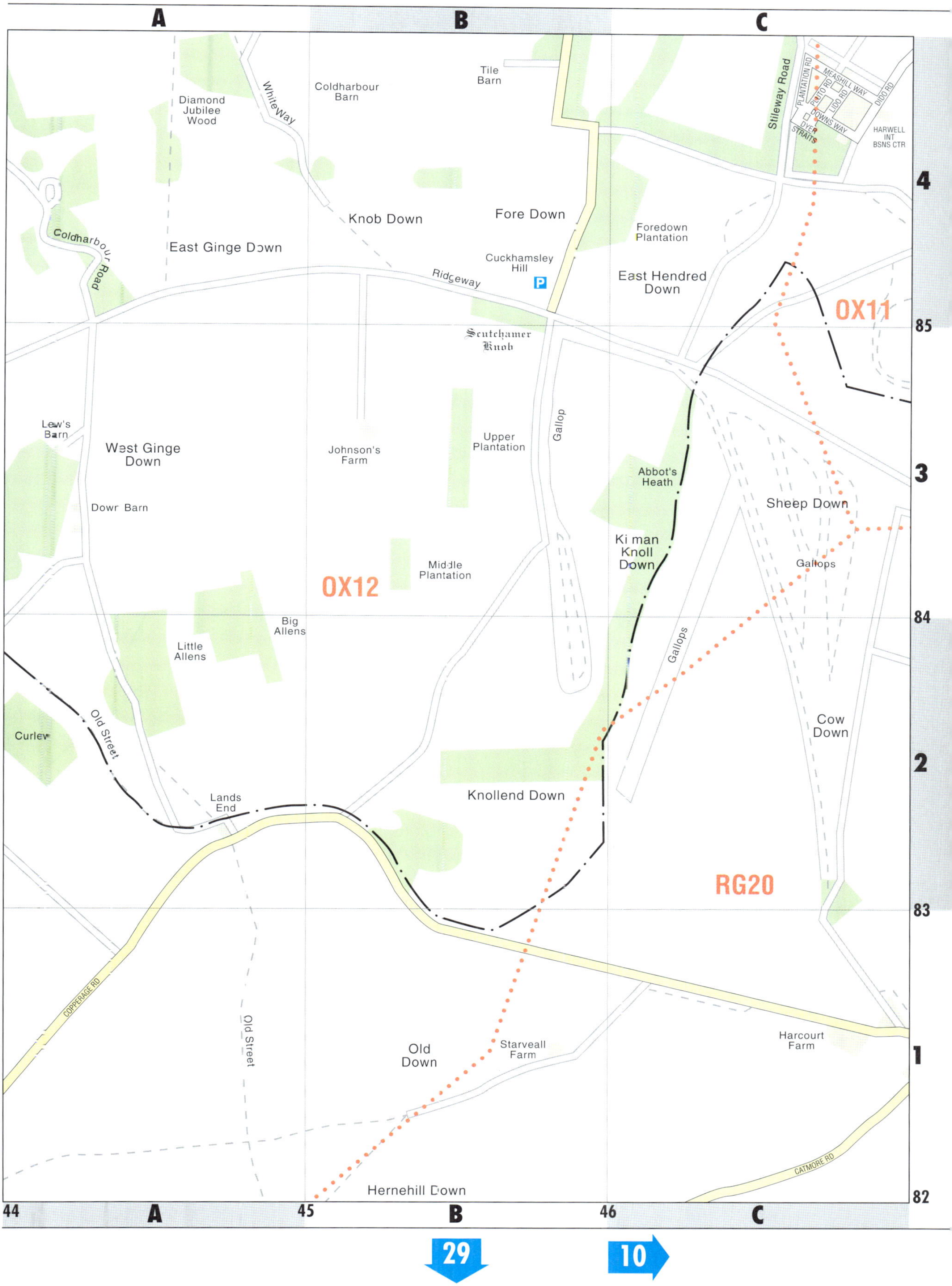
10
A
B
C
Diamond Jubilee Wood
Whiteway
Coldharbour Barn
Tile Barn
Stileway Road
PLANTATION RD
MEASHILL WAY
PLUTO RD
LIDO RD
DIDO RD
DOWNS WAY
DYER STRAITS
HARWELL INT BSNS CTR
Knob Down
Fore Down
Foredown Plantation
Coldharbour Road
East Ginge Down
Cuckhamsley Hill
Ridgeway
East Hendred Down
OX11
Scutchamer Knob
Lew's Barn
West Ginge Down
Johnson's Farm
Upper Plantation
Gallop
Abbot's Heath
Sheep Down
Down Barn
Kilman Knoll Down
Gallops
Middle Plantation
OX12
Big Allens
Little Allens
Old Street
Curlew
Cow Down
Lands End
Knollend Down
RG20
COPPERAGE RD
Old Street
Old Down
Starveall Farm
Harcourt Farm
CATMORE RD
Hernehill Down
4
85
3
84
2
83
1
82
44
45
46
29
10

9

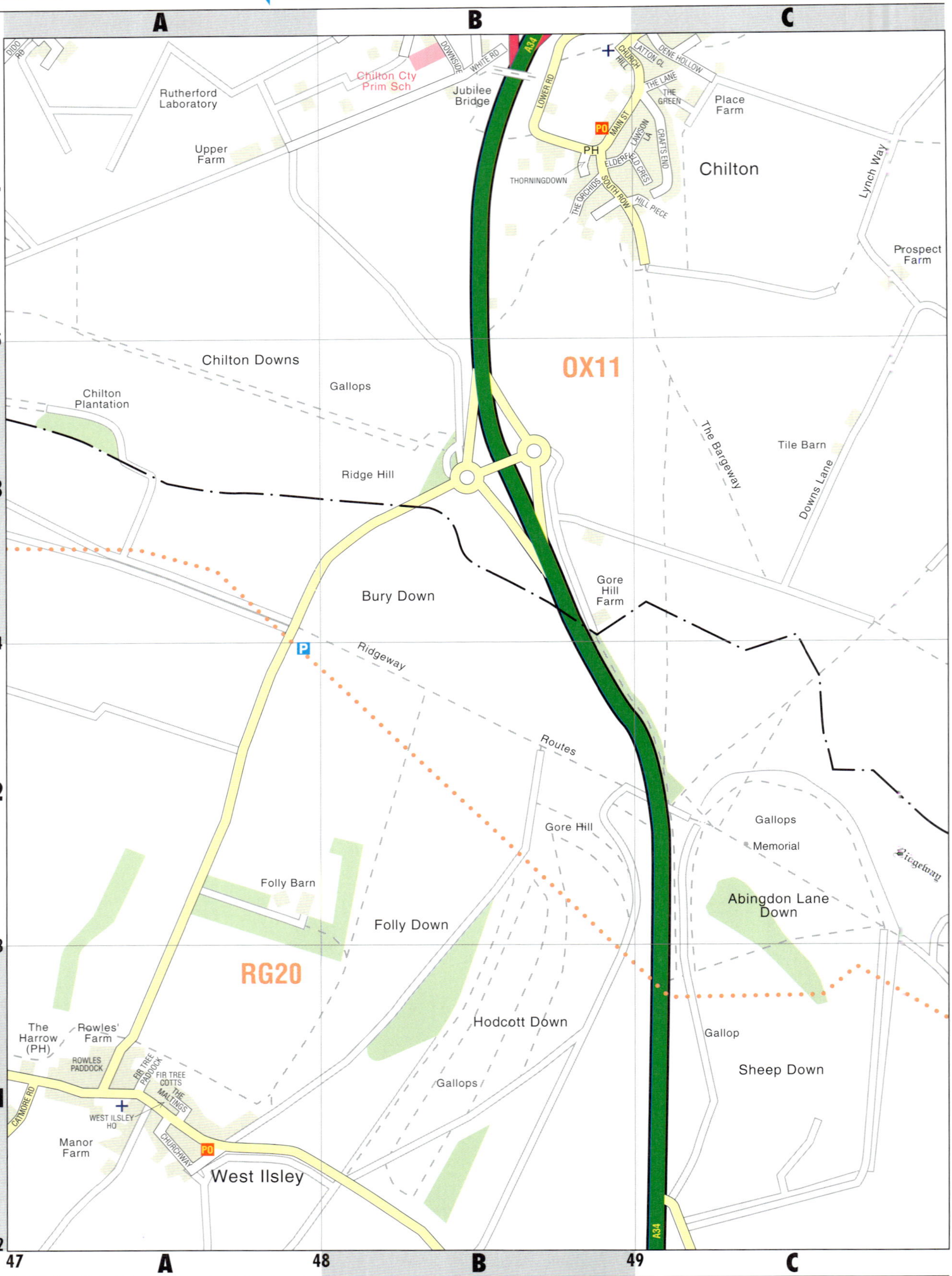

Rutherford Laboratory
Chilton Cty Prim Sch
Jubilee Bridge
Upper Farm
Place Farm
Chilton
Prospect Farm
Lynch Way
THORNINGDOWN
OX11
Chilton Downs
Gallops
Chilton Plantation
Ridge Hill
The Bargeway
Tile Barn
Downs Lane
Bury Down
Gore Hill Farm
Ridgeway
Routes
Gore Hill
Gallops
Memorial
Folly Barn
Folly Down
Abingdon Lane Down
RG20
Hodcott Down
Gallop
Sheep Down
The Harrow (PH)
Rowles' Farm
Gallops
Manor Farm
West Ilsley
A34

9
30

12

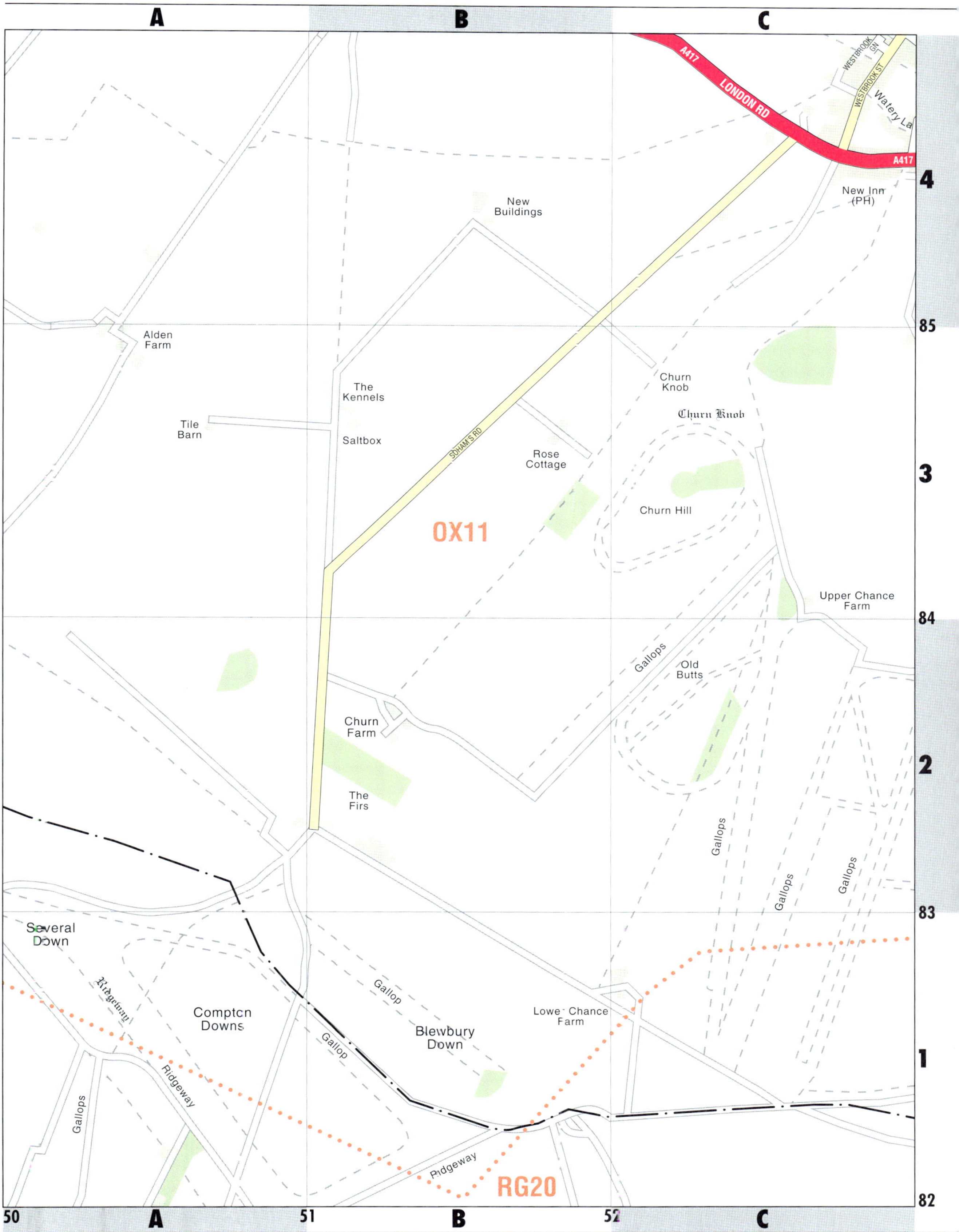
A
B
C
A417
LONDON RD
WESTBROOK GN
WESTBROOK ST
Watery La
A417
4
New Inn (PH)
New Buildings
85
Alden Farm
Churn Knob
The Kennels
Churn Knob
Tile Barn
Saltbox
SOHAM'S RD
Rose Cottage
3
Churn Hill
OX11
Upper Chance Farm
84
Gallops
Old Butts
Churn Farm
2
The Firs
Gallops
Gallops
Gallops
83
Several Down
Ridgeway
Gallop
Compton Downs
Gallop
Blewbury Down
Lower Chance Farm
1
Ridgeway
Gallops
Ridgeway
RG20
82
50
A
51
B
52
C

31

12

11

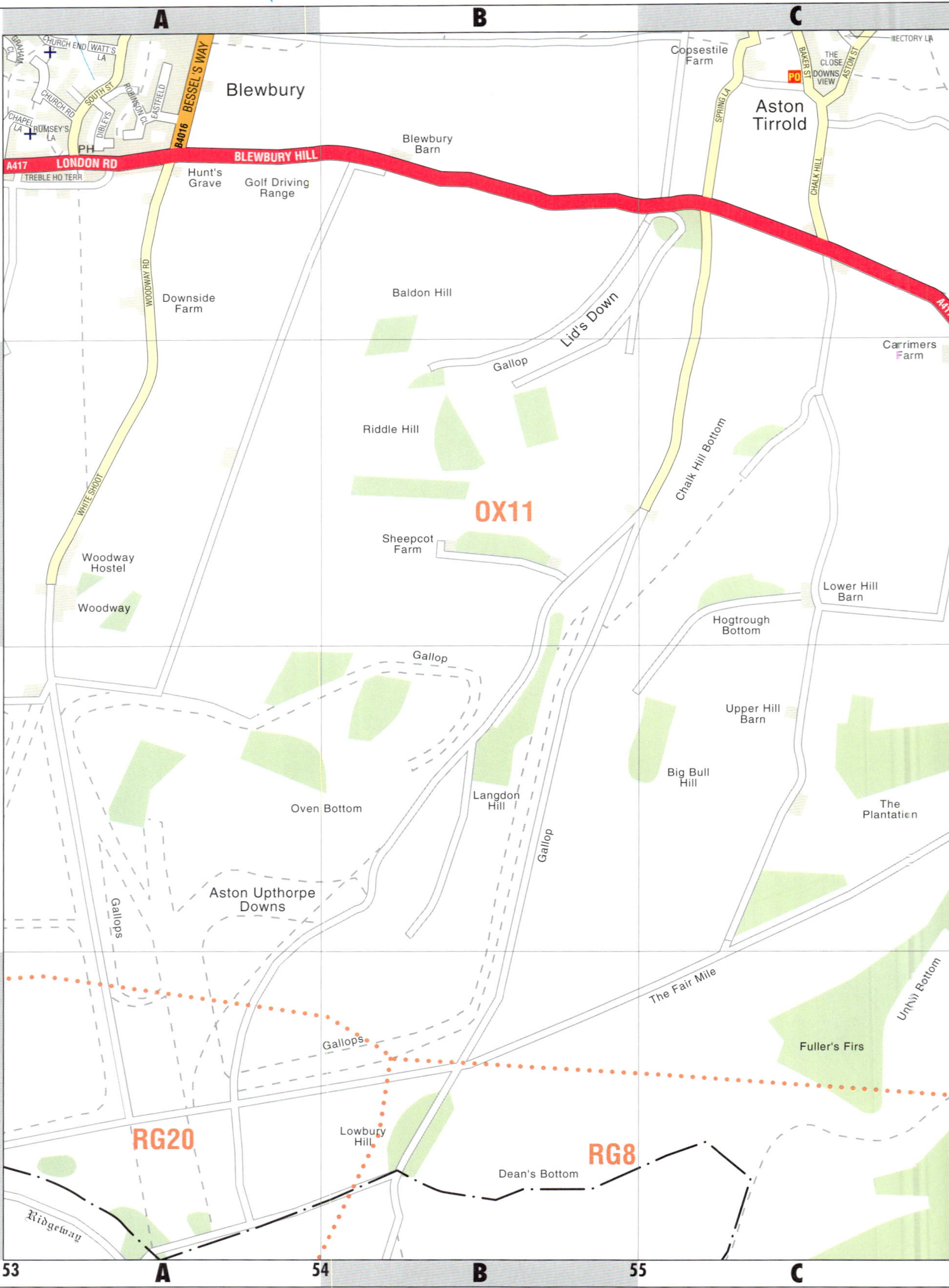
A
B
C
Blewbury
Aston Tirrold
Copsestile Farm
PO
BAKER ST
THE CLOSE
DOWNS VIEW
ASTON ST
RECTORY LA
SPRING LA
CHURCH END
WATT'S LA
GRAHAM CL
SOUTH ST
CHURCH RD
ROBINSON CL
EASTFIELD
BESSEL'S WAY
B4016
CHAPEL LA
RUMSEY'S LA
DIBLEYS
PH
A417
LONDON RD
BLEWBURY HILL
TREBLE HO TERR
Hunt's Grave
Golf Driving Range
Blewbury Barn
CHALK HILL
Downside Farm
WOODWAY RD
Baldon Hill
Lid's Down
Gallop
Carrimers Farm
Riddle Hill
Chalk Hill Bottom
WHITE SHOOT
OX11
Sheepcot Farm
Woodway Hostel
Woodway
Lower Hill Barn
Hogtrough Bottom
Gallop
Upper Hill Barn
Big Bull Hill
Langdon Hill
Oven Bottom
The Plantation
Gallop
Aston Upthorpe Downs
Gallops
The Fair Mile
Unhill Bottom
Gallops
Fuller's Firs
RG20
Lowbury Hill
RG8
Dean's Bottom
Ridgeway
4
85
3
84
2
83
1
82
53
54
55

11
32

14

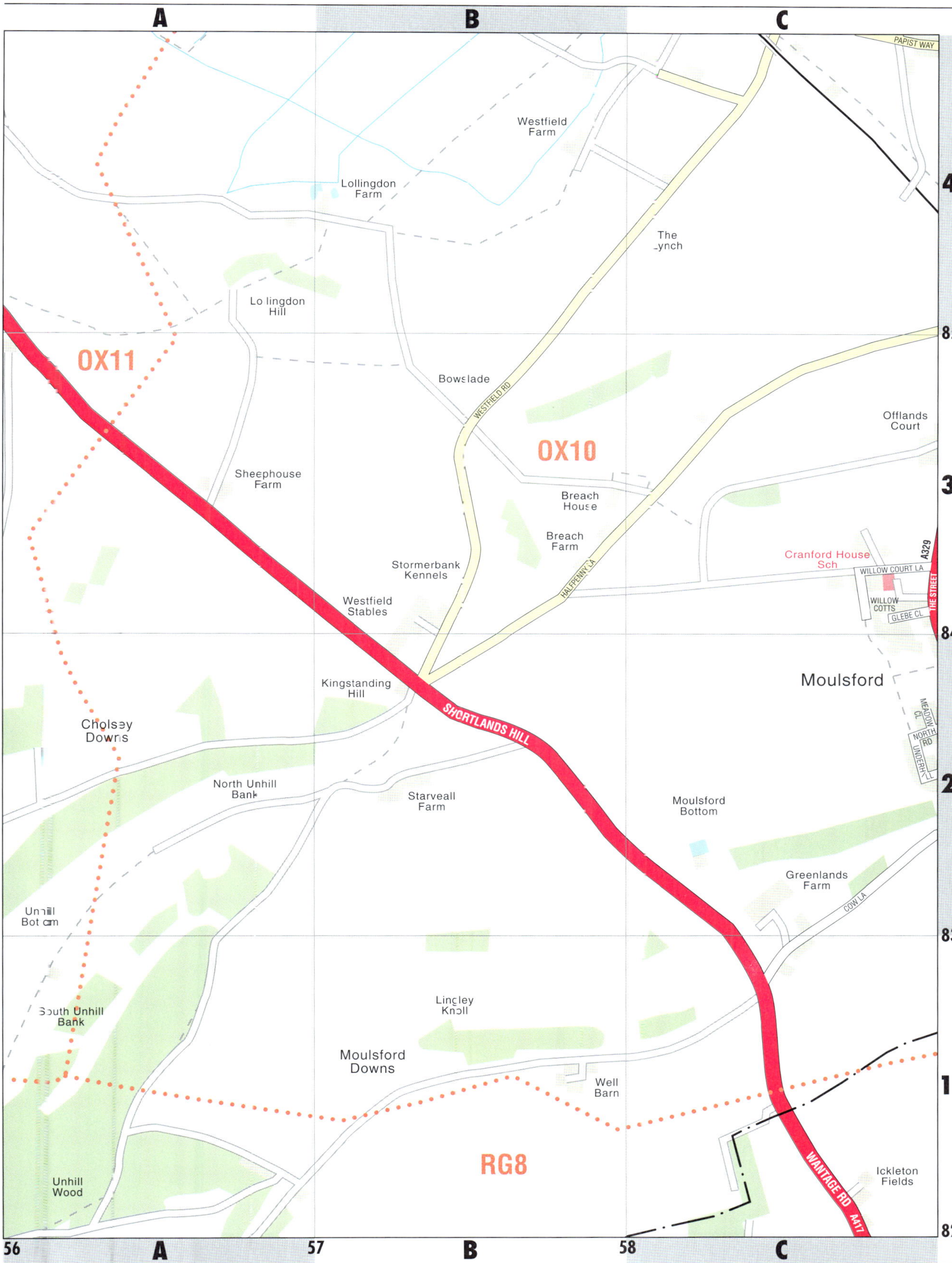
A
B
C
PAPIST WAY
Westfield
Farm
Lollingdon
Farm
The
Lynch
Lollingdon
Hill
OX11
85
Bowslade
WESTFIELD RD
Offlands
Court
OX10
Sheephouse
Farm
3
Breach
House
Breach
Farm
A329
Cranford House
Sch
WILLOW COURT LA
Stormerbank
Kennels
HALFPENNY LA
Westfield
Stables
WILLOW
COTTS
GLEBE CL
THE STREET
84
Kingstanding
Hill
Moulsford
Cholsey
Downs
SHORTLANDS HILL
MEADOW
CL
NORTH
RD
UNDERHILL
North Unhill
Bank
Starveall
Farm
Moulsford
Bottom
2
Unhill
Bottom
Greenlands
Farm
COW LA
83
Lingley
Knoll
South Unhill
Bank
Moulsford
Downs
Well
Barn
1
RG8
Unhill
Wood
Ickleton
Fields
WANTAGE RD
A417
82
56
A
57
B
58
C

33

14

13

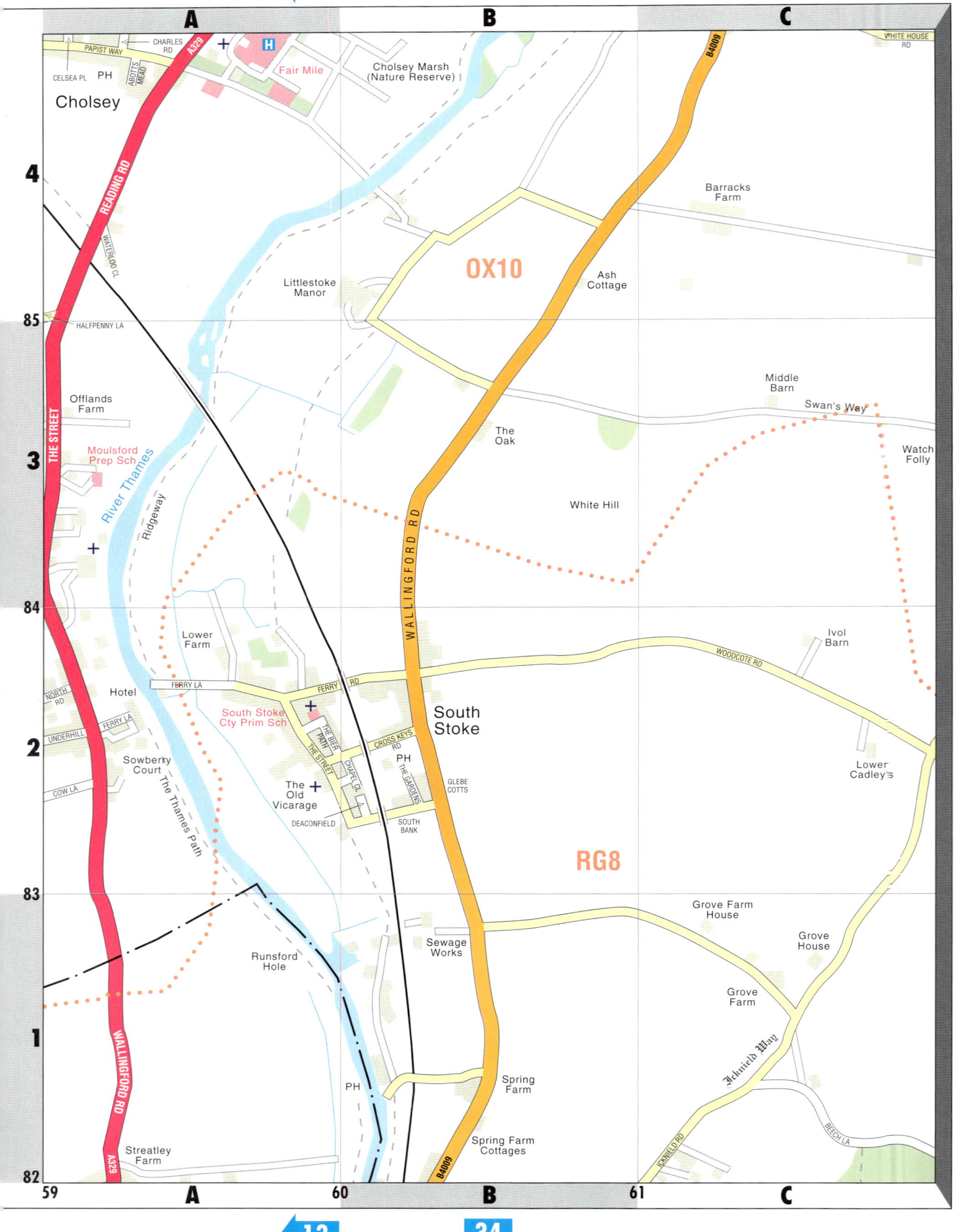
A
B
C
4
85
3
84
2
83
1
82
59
60
61
Cholsey
PAPIST WAY
CHARLES RD
CELSEA PL
PH
ABOTTS MEAD
A329
Fair Mile
Cholsey Marsh
(Nature Reserve)
B4009
WHITE HOUSE RD
READING RD
WATERLOO CL
Barracks
Farm
Littlestoke
Manor
OX10
Ash
Cottage
HALFPENNY LA
Offlands
Farm
THE STREET
Middle
Barn
Swan's Way
The
Oak
Watch
Folly
Moulsford
Prep Sch
River Thames
Ridgeway
White Hill
WALLINGFORD RD
Ivol
Barn
Lower
Farm
WOODCOTE RD
FERRY LA
FERRY RD
NORTH RD
Hotel
South Stoke
Cty Prim Sch
South
Stoke
FERRY LA
UNDERHILL
THE BIER PATH
CROSS KEYS RD
THE STREET
PH
Sowberry
Court
CHAPEL CL
THE GARDENS
GLEBE COTTS
Lower
Cadleys
COW LA
The Thames Path
The
Old
Vicarage
DEACONFIELD
SOUTH BANK
RG8
Grove Farm
House
Sewage
Works
Runsford
Hole
Grove
House
Grove
Farm
Icknield Way
WALLINGFORD RD
Spring
Farm
PH
BEECH LA
Spring Farm
Cottages
ICKNIELD RD
Streatley
Farm
A329
B4009

13
34

16

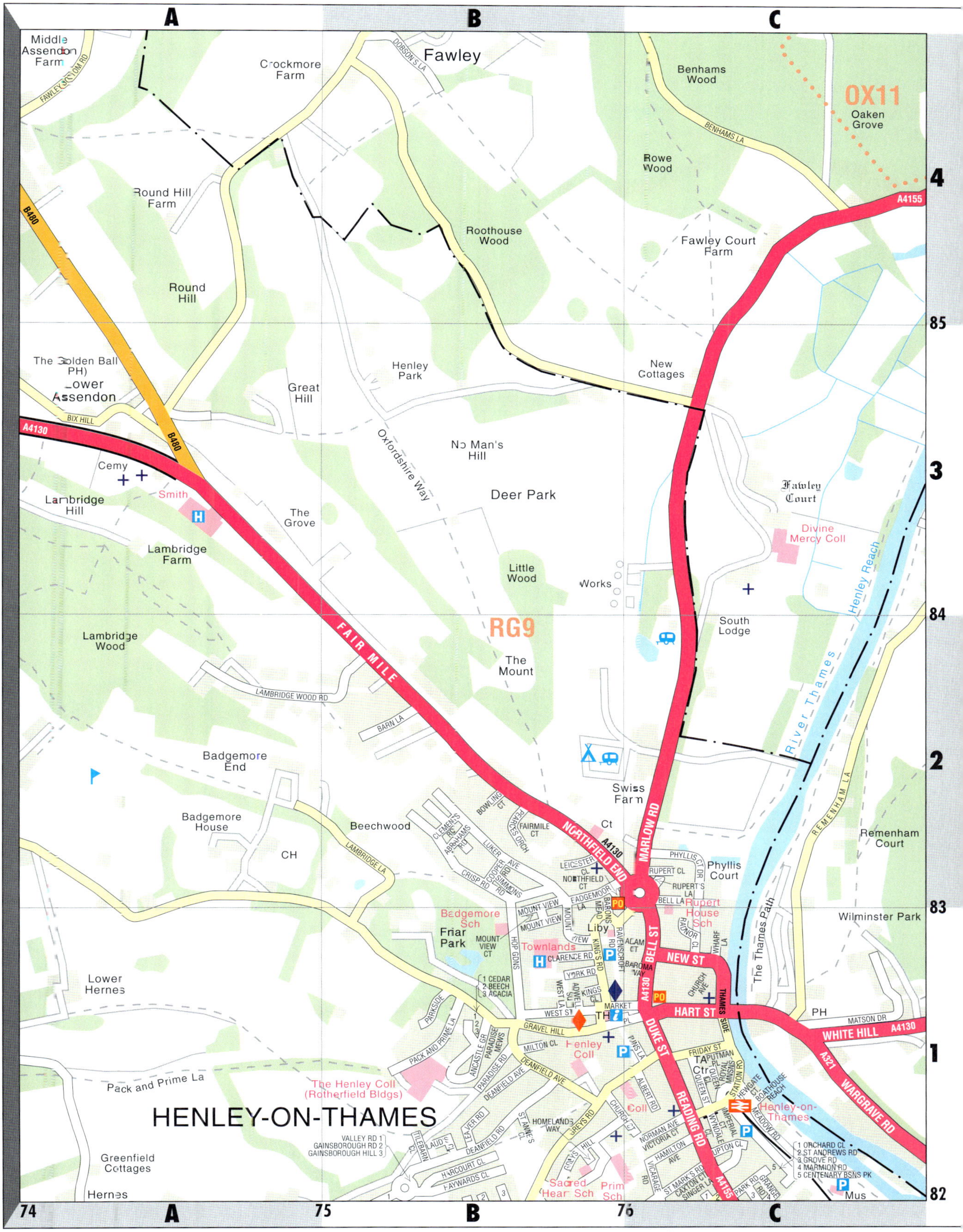
A
B
C
Fawley
Crockmore Farm
Middle Assendon Farm
Benhams Wood
OX11
Oaken Grove
Rowe Wood
Round Hill Farm
Roothouse Wood
Fawley Court Farm
Round Hill
A4155
4
85
The Golden Ball (PH)
Lower Assendon
Henley Park
Great Hill
New Cottages
A4130
B480
No Man's Hill
Oxfordshire Way
Cemy
Lambridge Hill
Smith
Deer Park
The Grove
Fawley Court
Divine Mercy Coll
3
Lambridge Farm
Little Wood
Works
South Lodge
Henley Reach
84
Lambridge Wood
RG9
FAIR MILE
The Mount
River Thames
LAMBRIDGE WOOD RD
BARN LA
Badgemore End
2
Swiss Farm
Badgemore House
Beechwood
NORTHFIELD END
MARLOW RD
Remenham Court
CH
Phyllis Court
REMENHAM LA
Badgemore Sch
Rupert House Sch
83
Friar Park
Libby
Townlands
Wilminster Park
BELL ST
NEW ST
HART ST
The Thames Path
Lower Hernes
PH
WHITE HILL
A4130
DUKE ST
A321
WARGRAVE RD
1
Henley Coll
Pack and Prime La
The Henley Coll (Rotherfield Bldgs)
TA Ctr
READING RD
Henley-on-Thames
HENLEY-ON-THAMES
Coll
Greenfield Cottages
Sacred Heart Sch
Prim Sch
Hernes
Mus
82
74
75
76

35

16

15

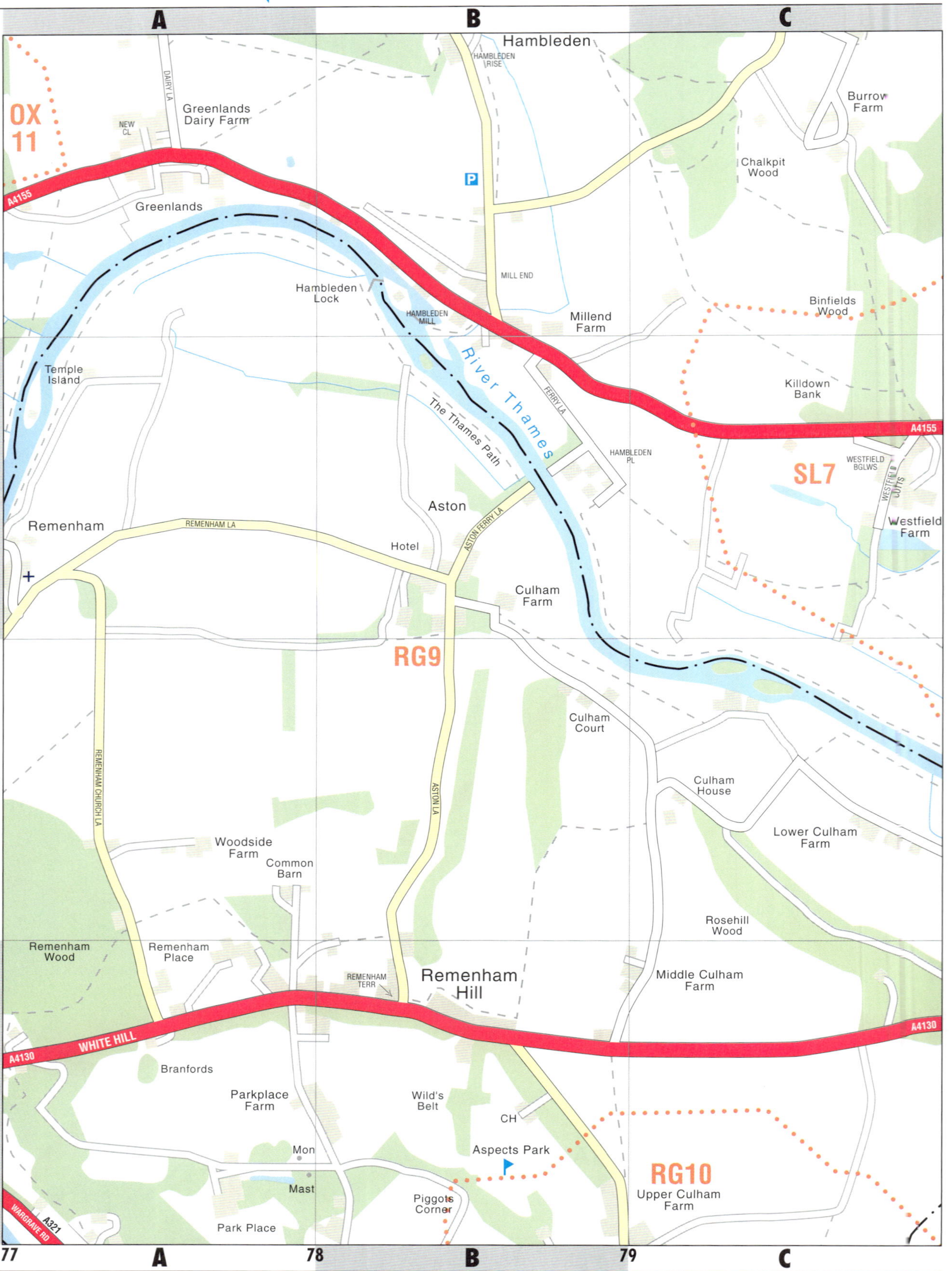

A
B
C
4
85
3
84
2
83
1
82
77
78
79
OX 11
SL7
RG9
RG10
Hambleden
HAMBLEDEN RISE
DAIRY LA
NEW CL
Greenlands Dairy Farm
Burrow Farm
Chalkpit Wood
A4155
Greenlands
MILL END
Hambleden Lock
HAMBLEDEN MILL
Millend Farm
Binfields Wood
Temple Island
River Thames
The Thames Path
FERRY LA
Killdown Bank
HAMBLEDEN PL
WESTFIELD BGLWS
WESTFIELD COTTS
Westfield Farm
Aston
Remenham
REMENHAM LA
ASTON FERRY LA
Hotel
Culham Farm
Culham Court
REMENHAM CHURCH LA
ASTON LA
Culham House
Lower Culham Farm
Woodside Farm
Common Barn
Rosehill Wood
Remenham Wood
Remenham Place
REMENHAM TERR
Remenham Hill
Middle Culham Farm
A4130
WHITE HILL
Branfords
Parkplace Farm
Wild's Belt
CH
Mon
Aspects Park
Mast
Piggots Corner
Upper Culham Farm
Park Place
WARGRAVE RD
A321

15
36

18

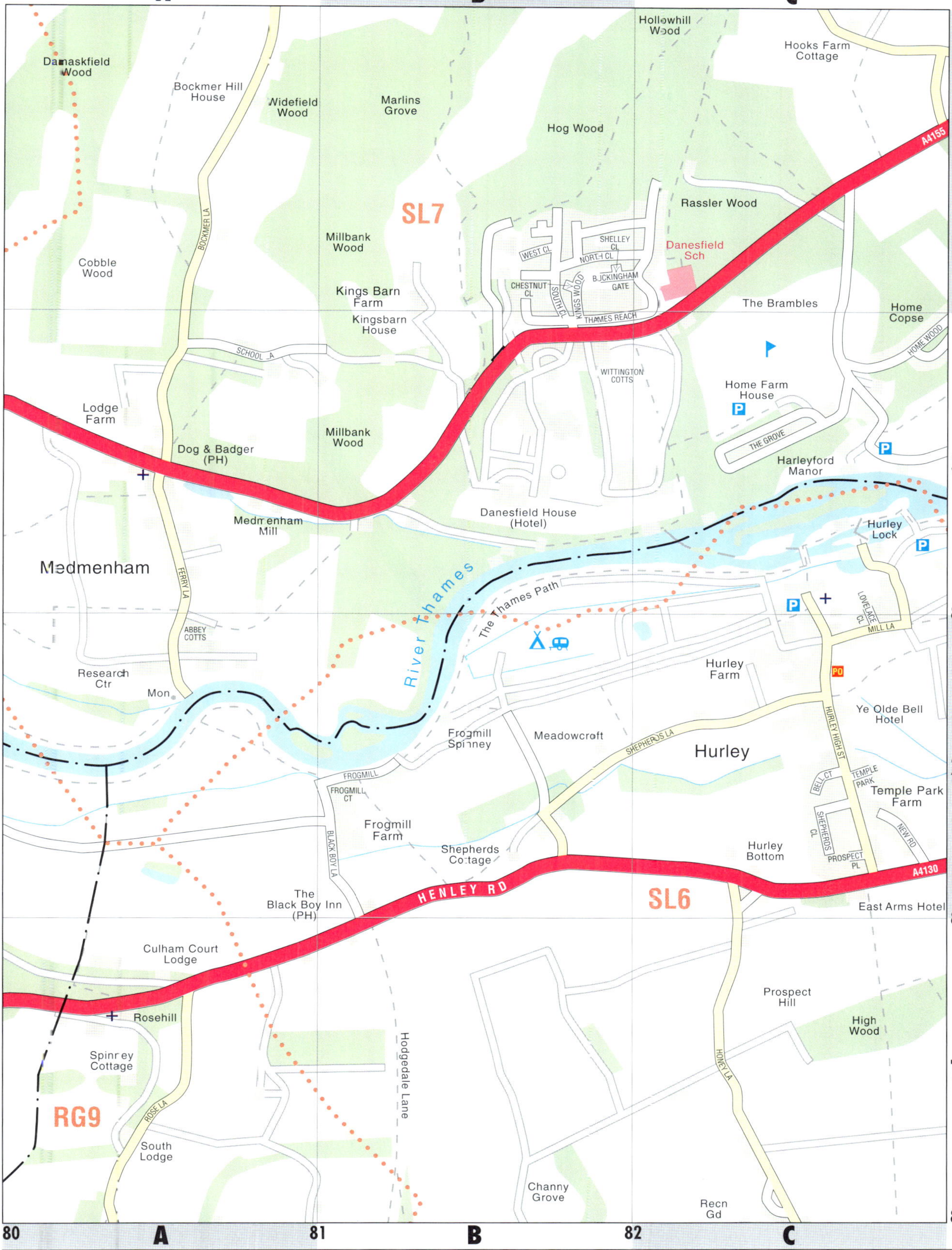
A
B
C
Damaskfield Wood
Bockmer Hill House
Widefield Wood
Marlins Grove
Hollowhill Wood
Hooks Farm Cottage
Hog Wood
A4155
4
Rassler Wood
SL7
Millbank Wood
Cobble Wood
BOCKMER LA
WEST CL
SHELLEY CL
NORTH CL
Danesfield Sch
BUCKINGHAM GATE
CHESTNUT CL
SOUTH CL
KINGS WOOD
Kings Barn Farm
THAMES REACH
The Brambles
Home Copse
85
Kingsbarn House
HOME WOOD
SCHOOL LA
WITTINGTON COTTS
Home Farm House
Lodge Farm
Millbank Wood
THE GROVE
Dog & Badger (PH)
Harleyford Manor
3
Danesfield House (Hotel)
Medmenham Mill
Hurley Lock
Medmenham
River Thames
The Thames Path
FERRY LA
LOVELACE CL
84
ABBEY COTTS
MILL LA
Research Ctr
Hurley Farm
PO
Mon
Ye Olde Bell Hotel
Frogmill Spinney
Meadowcroft
SHEPHERDS LA
Hurley
2
FROGMILL
HURLEY HIGH ST
FROGMILL CT
BELL CT
TEMPLE PARK
Temple Park Farm
Frogmill Farm
SHEPHERDS CL
NEW RD
BLACK BOY LA
Shepherds Cottage
Hurley Bottom
PROSPECT PL
A4130
HENLEY RD
The Black Boy Inn (PH)
SL6
East Arms Hotel
83
Culham Court Lodge
Prospect Hill
Rosehill
High Wood
Spinney Cottage
Hodgedale Lane
1
HONEY LA
RG9
ROSE LA
South Lodge
Channy Grove
Recn Gd
82
80
81
82

37
18

17
1

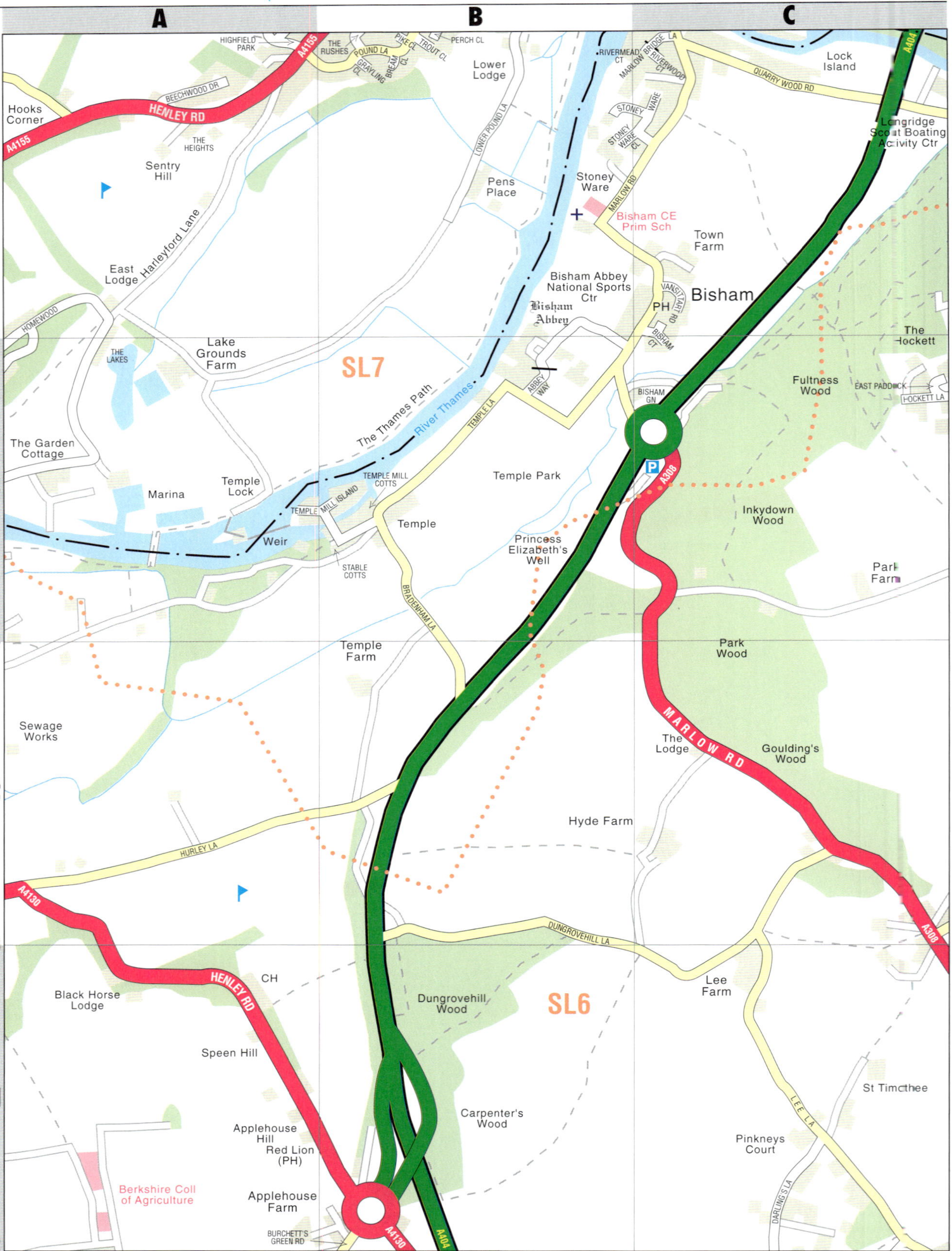
A
B
C
4
85
3
84
2
83
1
82
83
84
85
Hooks Corner
HENLEY RD
A4155
BEECHWOOD DR
HIGHFIELD PARK
THE RUSHES
POUND LA
PIKE CL
TROUT CL
PERCH CL
GRAYLING CL
BREAM CL
Lower Lodge
THE HEIGHTS
Sentry Hill
LOWER POUND LA
Pens Place
RIVERMEAD CT
MARLOW BRIDGE LA
RIVERWOOD CT
QUARRY WOOD RD
Lock Island
STONEY WARE
STONEY WARE CL
Longridge Scout Boating Activity Ctr
Stoney Ware
MARLOW RD
Bisham CE Prim Sch
Town Farm
A404
Harleyford Lane
East Lodge
Bisham Abbey National Sports Ctr
Bisham Abbey
VANSITTART RD
PH
Bisham
BISHAM CT
HOMEWOOD
THE LAKES
Lake Grounds Farm
SL7
The Hockett
Fulthess Wood
EAST PADDOCK
HOCKETT LA
ABBEY WAY
BISHAM GN
The Thames Path
River Thames
TEMPLE LA
The Garden Cottage
Temple Park
P
A308
Marina
Temple Lock
TEMPLE MILL COTTS
TEMPLE MILL ISLAND
Temple
Weir
Inkydown Wood
Princess Elizabeth's Well
STABLE COTTS
Park Farm
BRADENHAM LA
Temple Farm
Park Wood
Sewage Works
MARLOW RD
The Lodge
Goulding's Wood
Hyde Farm
HURLEY LA
A4130
DUNGROVEHILL LA
CH
Black Horse Lodge
HENLEY RD
Dungrovehill Wood
SL6
Lee Farm
Speen Hill
St Timothee
LEE LA
Carpenter's Wood
Applehouse Hill
Red Lion (PH)
Pinkneys Court
Berkshire Coll of Agriculture
Applehouse Farm
BURCHETT'S GREEN RD
DARLING'S LA

17
38

2
20

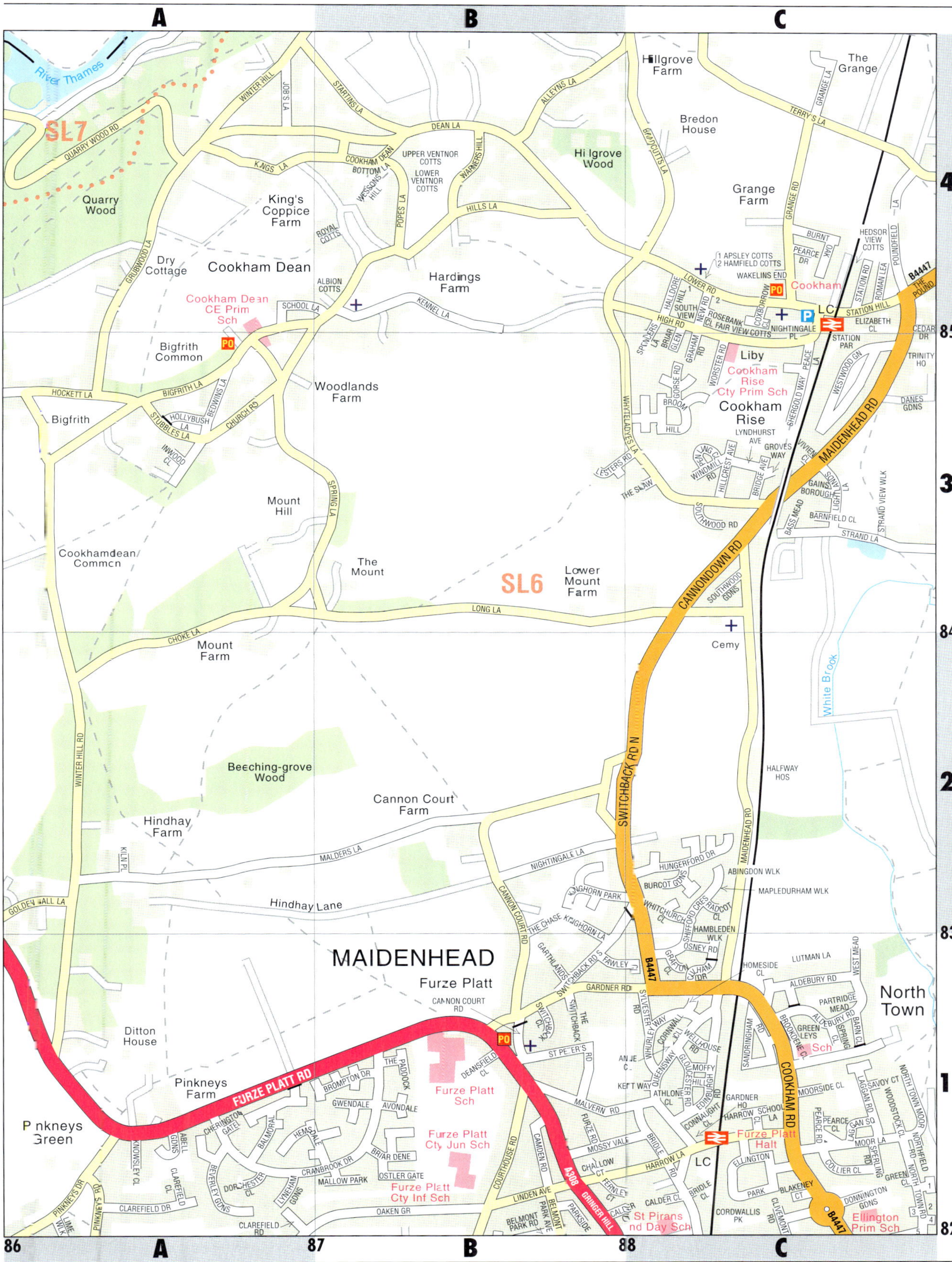

39
20

C1
1 NORTH TOWN CL
2 ALYSON CT
3 NORTH GN
4 NORTH TOWN MEAD
5 NORTHDEAN

19
3

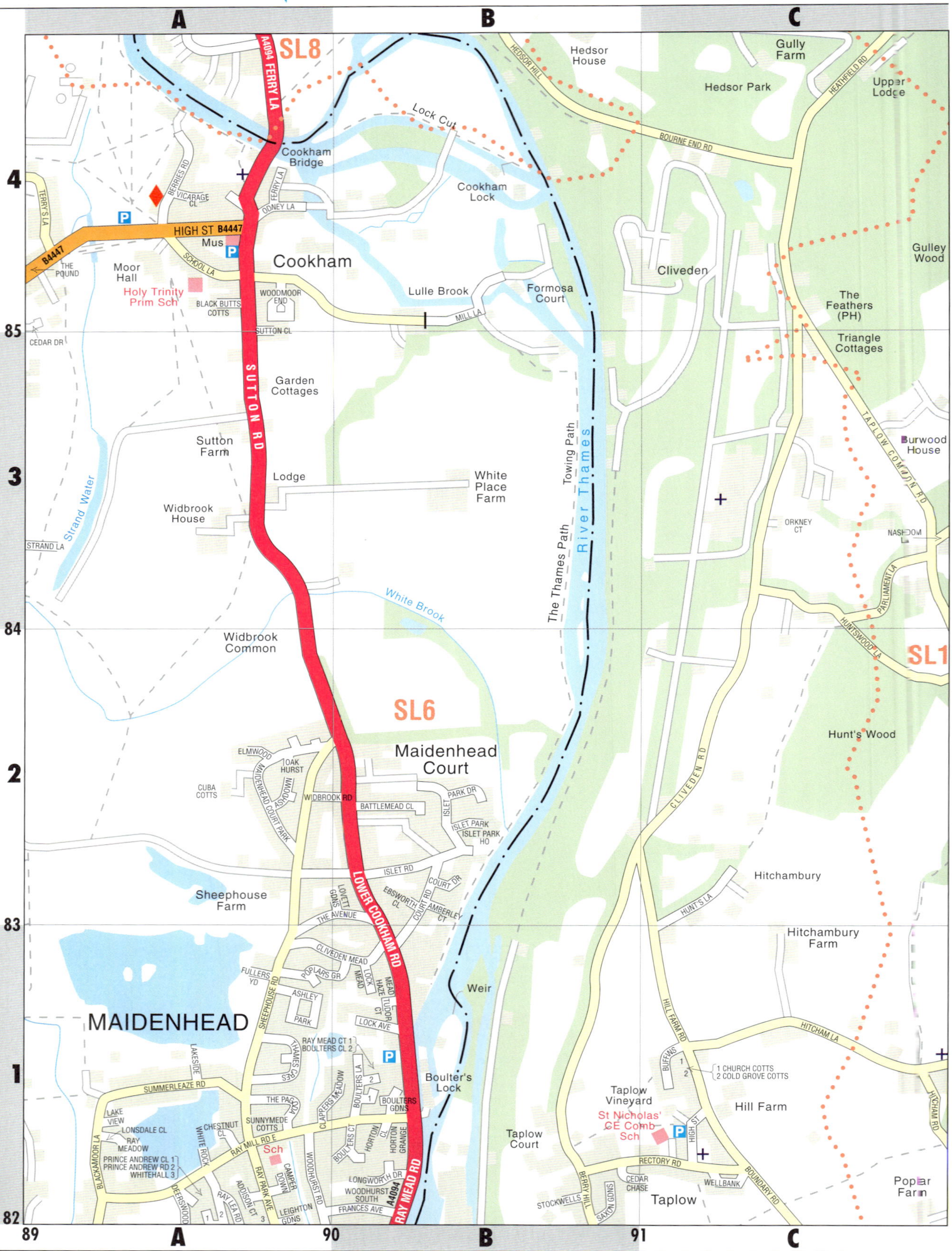
A
B
C
4
85
3
84
2
83
1
82
89
90
91
SL8
SL6
SL1
A4094 FERRY LA
Cookham Bridge
Lock Cut
Hedsor House
Hedsor Park
Gully Farm
Upper Lodge
HEDSOR HILL
BOURNE END RD
HEATHFIELD RD
Cookham Lock
TERRY'S LA
BERRIES RD
VICARAGE CL
FERRY LA
ODNEY LA
HIGH ST B4447
B4447
Mus
Cookham
THE POUND
Moor Hall
SCHOOL LA
Holy Trinity Prim Sch
BLACK BUTTS COTTS
WOODMOOR END
SUTTON CL
Lulle Brook
MILL LA
Formosa Court
Cliveden
Gulley Wood
The Feathers (PH)
Triangle Cottages
CEDAR DR
SUTTON RD
Garden Cottages
Sutton Farm
Lodge
White Place Farm
Towing Path
River Thames
The Thames Path
Burwood House
TAPLOW COMMON RD
ORKNEY CT
NASHDOM
Strand Water
Widbrook House
STRAND LA
PARLIAMENT LA
White Brook
HUNTSWOOD LA
Widbrook Common
SL6
Hunt's Wood
ELMWOOD
OAK HURST
Maidenhead Court
CUBA COTTS
MAIDENHEAD COURT PARK
ASHDOWN
WIDBROOK RD
BATTLEMEAD CL
PARK DR
ISLET
ISLET PARK
ISLET PARK HO
CLIVEDEN RD
ISLET RD
COURT DR
Hitchambury
Sheephouse Farm
LOVETT GDNS
EBSWORTH CL
COURT RD
AMBERLEY CT
THE AVENUE
HUNT'S LA
LOWER COOKHAM RD
Hitchambury Farm
CLIVEDEN MEAD
FULLERS YD
POPLARS GR
LOCK MEAD
HAZE CL
MEAD
TUDOR CT
SHEEPHOUSE RD
ASHLEY PARK
Weir
LOCK AVE
MAIDENHEAD
HILL FARM RD
HITCHAM LA
RAY MEAD CT 1
BOULTERS CL 2
LAKESIDE
THAMES CRES
BUFFINS
1 CHURCH COTTS
2 COLD GROVE COTTS
Boulter's Lock
SUMMERLEAZE RD
THE PAGODA
CLAPPERS MEADOW
BOULTERS LA
BOULTERS GDNS
Taplow Vineyard
Hill Farm
LAKE VIEW
CHESTNUT CL
SUNNYMEDE COTTS
St Nicholas' CE Comb Sch
HIGH ST
HITCHAM RD
LONSDALE CL
RAY MEADOW
WHITE ROCK
RAY MILL RD E
BOULTERS CT
HORTON CL
HORTON GRANGE
Taplow Court
BLACKAMOOR LA
PRINCE ANDREW CL 1
PRINCE ANDREW RD 2
WHITEHALL 3
Sch
CAMPER DOWN
WOODHURST RD
LONGWORTH DR
A4094
RAY MEAD RD
RECTORY RD
CEDAR CHASE
WELLBANK
BOUNDARY RD
Poplar Farm
DEERSWOOD
RAY LEA RD
ADDISON CT
RAY PARK AVE
LEIGHTON GDNS
WOODHURST SOUTH
FRANCES AVE
BERRY HILL
STOCKWELLS
SAXON GDNS
Taplow

19
40

22

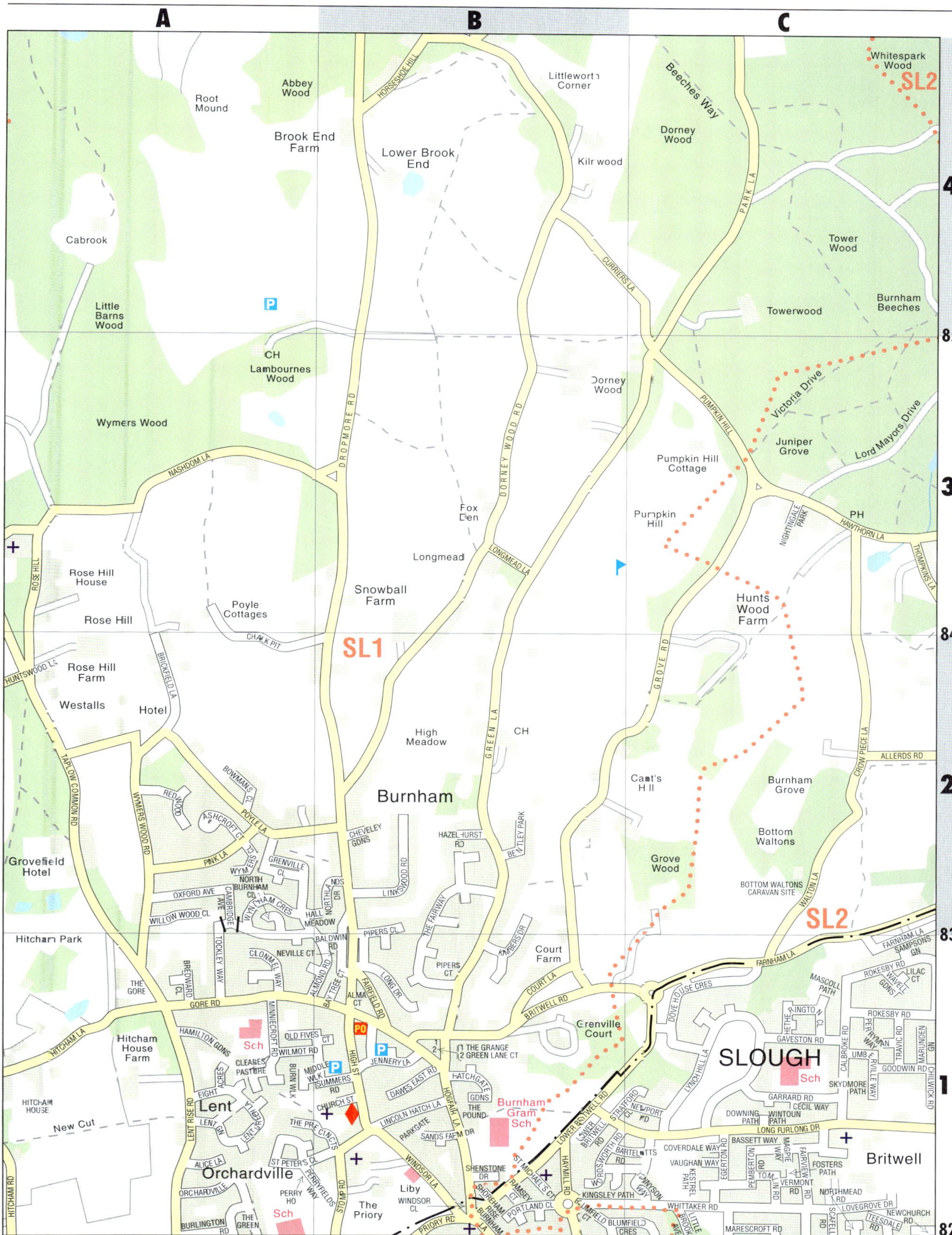

A
B
C
Root Mound
Abbey Wood
Brook End Farm
Lower Brook End
Littleworth Corner
Kiln wood
Beeches Way
Dorney Wood
Whitespark Wood
SL2
PARK LA
Tower Wood
Cabrook
Little Barns Wood
CURRIERS LA
Towerwood
Burnham Beeches
CH
Lambournes Wood
Wymers Wood
DROPMORE RD
Dorney Wood
PUMPKIN HILL
Victoria Drive
Juniper Grove
Lord Mayors Drive
NASHDOM LA
DORNEY WOOD RD
Pumpkin Hill Cottage
Pumpkin Hill
PH
HAWTHORN LA
Fox Den
Longmead
LONGMEAD LA
NIGHTINGALE PARK
THOMPKINS LA
ROSE HILL
Rose Hill House
Snowball Farm
Poyle Cottages
Rose Hill
Hunts Wood Farm
CHALK PIT
SL1
HUNTSWOOD LA
Rose Hill Farm
BRICKFIELD LA
GROVE RD
Westalls
Hotel
High Meadow
GREEN LA
CH
ALLERDS RD
CROW PIECE LA
TAPLOW COMMON RD
WYMERS WOOD RD
Burnham
Cant's Hill
Burnham Grove
Bottom Waltons
Grovefield Hotel
BOTTOM WALTONS CARAVAN SITE
WALTON LA
Grove Wood
SL2
Hitcham Park
Court Farm
FARNHAM LA
GORE RD
BRITWELL RD
Grenville Court
HITCHAM LA
Hitcham House Farm
Sch
HIGH ST
SLOUGH
Sch
New Cut
Lent
Burnham Gram Sch
Orchardville
Sch
The Priory
Liby
Britwell
LONG FURLONG DR
92
93
94
4
85
3
84
2
83
1
82

41

22

21

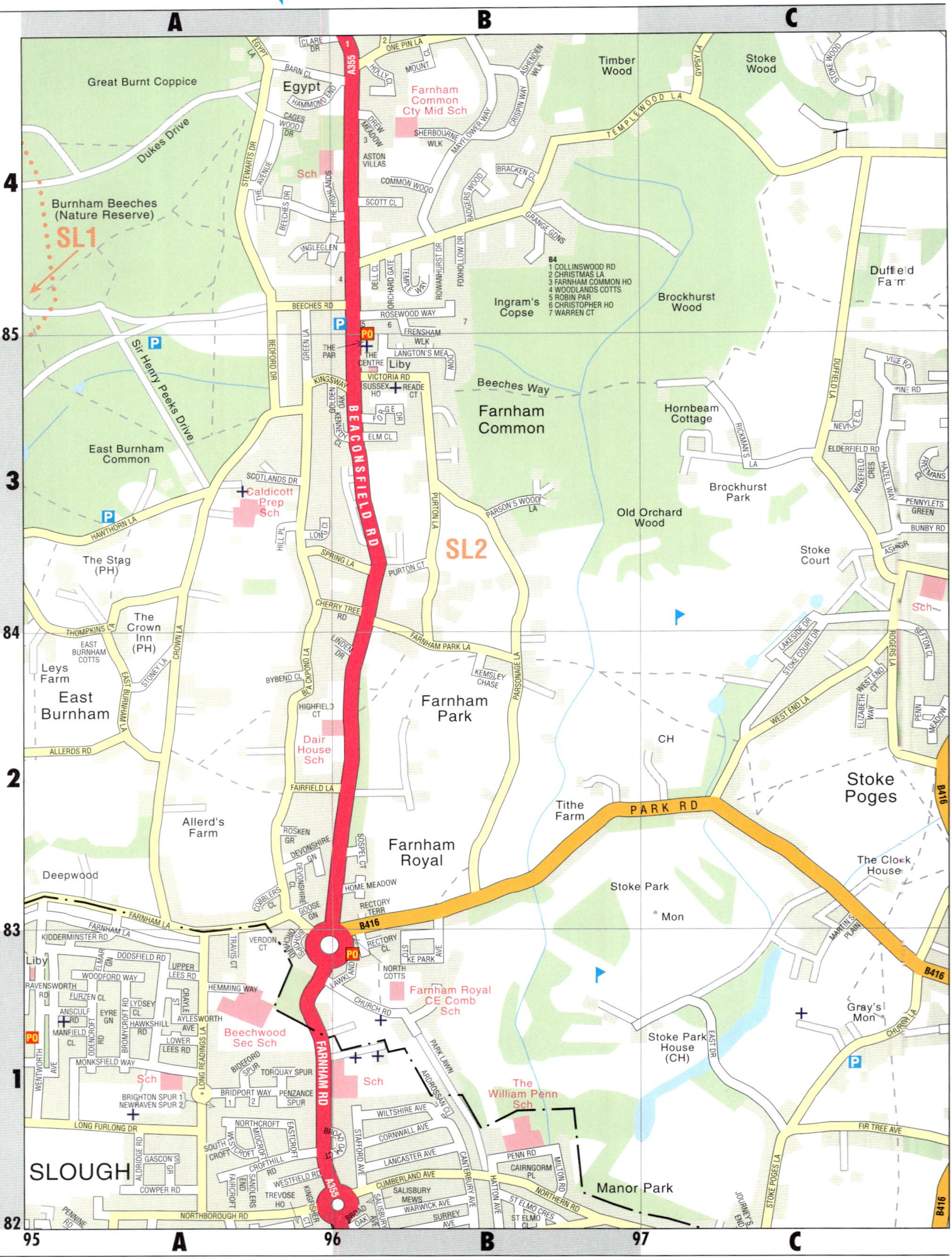

A
B
C
4
85
3
84
2
83
1
82
95
96
97
Great Burnt Coppice
Dukes Drive
Burnham Beeches (Nature Reserve)
SL1
Egypt
Farnham Common Cty Mid Sch
Timber Wood
Stoke Wood
TEMPLEWOOD LA
GYPSY LA
STEWARTS DR
THE AVENUE
BEECHES DR
THE HIGHLANDS
Sch
ASTON VILLAS
COMMON WOOD
SCOTT CL
INGLEGLEN
SHERBOURNE WLK
MAYFLOWER WAY
CRISPIN WAY
ASHENDEN WLK
BRACKEN CL
GRANGE GDNS
BADGERS WOOD
FOXHOLLOW DR
ROWANHURST DR
ORCHARD GATE
DELL CL
TEMPLE WAY
B4
1 COLLINSWOOD RD
2 CHRISTMAS LA
3 FARNHAM COMMON HO
4 WOODLANDS COTTS
5 ROBIN PAR
6 CHRISTOPHER HO
7 WARREN CT
Ingram's Copse
Brockhurst Wood
Duffield Farm
BEECHES RD
ROSEWOOD WAY
FRENSHAM WLK
LANGTON'S MEADOW
Sir Henry Peeks Drive
PO
THE PAR
THE CENTRE
Liby
VICTORIA RD
SUSSEX HO
READE CT
KINGSWAY
GOLDEN OAK
KENNEDY CL
FORGE DR
ELM CL
BEACONSFIELD RD
A355
Beeches Way
Farnham Common
Hornbeam Cottage
RICKMAN'S LA
DUFFIELD LA
NEVILLE CL
ELDERFIELD RD
WAKEFIELD CRES
HAZELL WAY
PENNYLETS GREEN
BUNBY RD
East Burnham Common
SCOTLANDS DR
Caldicott Prep Sch
HAWTHORN LA
BEDFORD DR
GREEN LA
HILL PL
LONG CL
SPRING LA
PURTON CT
PURTON LA
PARSON'S WOOD LA
SL2
Brockhurst Park
Old Orchard Wood
Stoke Court
The Stag (PH)
The Crown Inn (PH)
THOMPKINS LA
CROWN LA
EAST BURNHAM COTTS
STONEY LA
EAST BURNHAM LA
Leys Farm
East Burnham
CHERRY TREE RD
LINDEN DR
FARNHAM PARK LA
KEMSLEY CHASE
PARSONAGE LA
BYBEND CL
BLACKPOND LA
HIGHFIELD CT
Dair House Sch
Farnham Park
LAKESIDE DR
STOKE COURT DR
WEST END LA
WEST END CT
ELIZABETH WAY
ROGERS LA
SEFTON CL
PENN MEADOW
CH
ALLERDS RD
FAIRFIELD LA
Stoke Poges
B416
Allerd's Farm
Tithe Farm
PARK RD
ROSKEN GR
DEVONSHIRE GN
DEVONSHIRE CL
SOSPEL CT
Farnham Royal
HOME MEADOW
Deepwood
Stoke Park
Mon
The Clock House
COBBLERS CL
GOOSE GN
RECTORY TERR
MARTINS PLAIN
FARNHAM LA
KIDDERMINSTER RD
TRAVIS CT
VERDON CT
BISHOPS ORCHARD
RECTORY CL
STOKE PARK AVE
NORTH COTTS
Liby
DODSFIELD RD
UPPER LEES RD
ELMAR GN
WOODFORD WAY
HEMMING WAY
LAWKLAND
RAVENSWORTH RD
FURZEN CL
LYDSEY CL
CRAYLE ST
Farnham Royal CE Comb Sch
CHURCH RD
ANSCULF RD
EYRE GN
HAWKSHILL RD
AYLESWORTH AVE
Beechwood Sec Sch
Gray's Mon
CHURCH LA
MANFIELD CL
ODENCROFT RD
BROMYCROFT RD
LOWER LEES RD
FARNHAM RD
Stoke Park House (CH)
EAST DR
MONKSFIELD WAY
BIDEFORD SPUR
TORQUAY SPUR
PARK LAWN
ARDROSSAN CL
WENTWORTH AVE
LONG READINGS LA
BRIGHTON SPUR 1
NEWHAVEN SPUR 2
BRIDPORT WAY
PENZANCE SPUR
The William Penn Sch
WILTSHIRE AVE
LONG FURLONG DR
NORTHCROFT
MIDCROFT
EASTCROFT
WESTCROFT
SOUTHCROFT
BROAD OAK CT
CORNWALL AVE
STAFFORD AVE
FIR TREE AVE
SLOUGH
ALDRIDGE RD
GASCON'S GR
CROFTHILL RD
LANCASTER AVE
CANTERBURY AVE
PENN RD
MILTON RD
CAIRNGORM PL
FAIRCROFT
SANDLERS END
WESTFIELD RD
TREVOSE HO
KINGFISHER CT
CUMBERLAND AVE
SALISBURY MEWS
SALISBURY AVE
WARWICK AVE
SURREY AVE
HATTON AVE
NORTHERN RD
ST ELMO CRES
ST ELMO CL
Manor Park
JOURNEY'S END
STOKE POGES LA
COWPER RD
PENNINE RD
NORTHBOROUGH RD
BROAD OAK

21

42

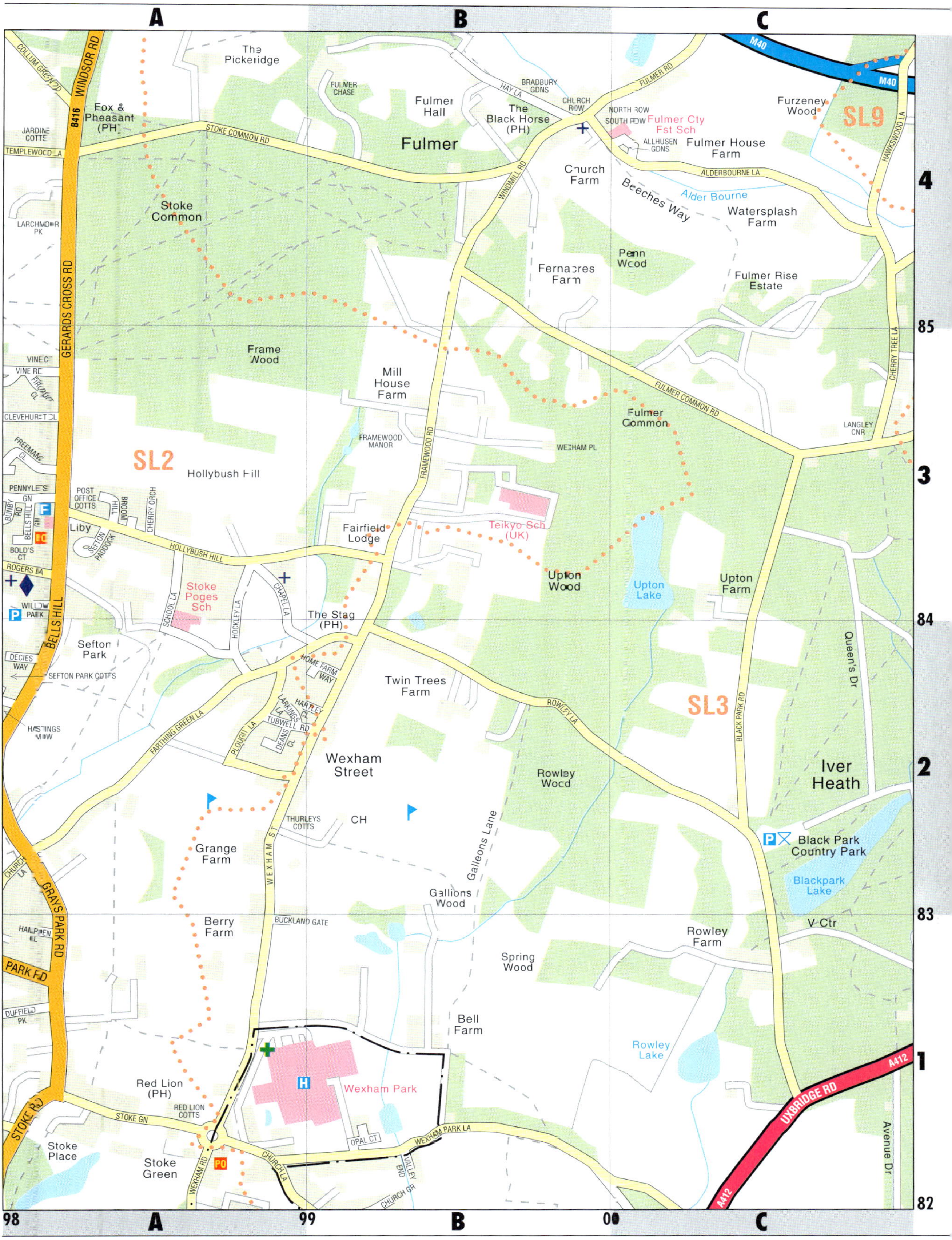
A
B
C
The Pickeridge
Fulmer Chase
Fulmer Hall
Hay La
Bradbury Gdns
Church Row
Fulmer Rd
M40
Collum Green Rd
Windsor Rd
B416
Fox & Pheasant (PH)
Jardine Cotts
Templewood La
Stoke Common Rd
The Black Horse (PH)
Fulmer
North Row
South Row
Fulmer Cty Fst Sch
Allhusen Gdns
Fulmer House Farm
Furzeney Wood
SL9
Hawkswood La
Windmill Rd
Church Farm
Alderbourne La
Beeches Way
Alder Bourne
Watersplash Farm
Stoke Common
Larchmoor Pk
Penn Wood
Fernacres Farm
Fulmer Rise Estate
Gerrards Cross Rd
Vine Cl
Vine Rd
Firecroft Cl
Frame Wood
Mill House Farm
Fulmer Common Rd
Cherry Tree La
Clevehurst Cl
Fulmer Common
Langley Cnr
Freeman Cl
Framewood Manor
Framewood Rd
Wexham Pl
SL2
Hollybush Hill
Pennylets Gn
Bunby Rd
Bells Hill Gn
Post Office Cotts
Broom Hill
Cherry Orch
Teikyo Sch (UK)
Liby
Fairfield Lodge
Sefton Paddock
Bold's Ct
Rogers La
Hollybush Hill
Stoke Poges Sch
Chapel La
School La
Hockley La
Upton Wood
Upton Lake
Upton Farm
Willow Park
The Stag (PH)
Bells Hill
Sefton Park
Decies Way
Sefton Park Cotts
Home Farm Way
Twin Trees Farm
Queen's Dr
Rowley La
Black Park Rd
SL3
Hastings Mdw
Farthing Green La
Larkings La
Hartley Cl
Tubwell Rd
Deans Cl
Plough La
Wexham Street
Rowley Wood
Iver Heath
Thurleys Cotts
CH
Galleons Lane
Black Park Country Park
Church La
Grange Farm
Wexham St
Blackpark Lake
Grays Park Rd
Gallions Wood
Hampden Cl
Berry Farm
Buckland Gate
V Ctr
Rowley Farm
Park Rd
Spring Wood
Duffield Pk
Bell Farm
Rowley Lake
A412
Red Lion (PH)
Wexham Park
Uxbridge Rd
Stoke Rd
Stoke Gn
Red Lion Cotts
Wexham Park La
Opal Ct
Stoke Place
Stoke Green
Wexham Rd
PO
Church La
Valley End
Church Gr
Avenue Dr
98
99
00
82
83
84
85
1
2
3
4

43

4

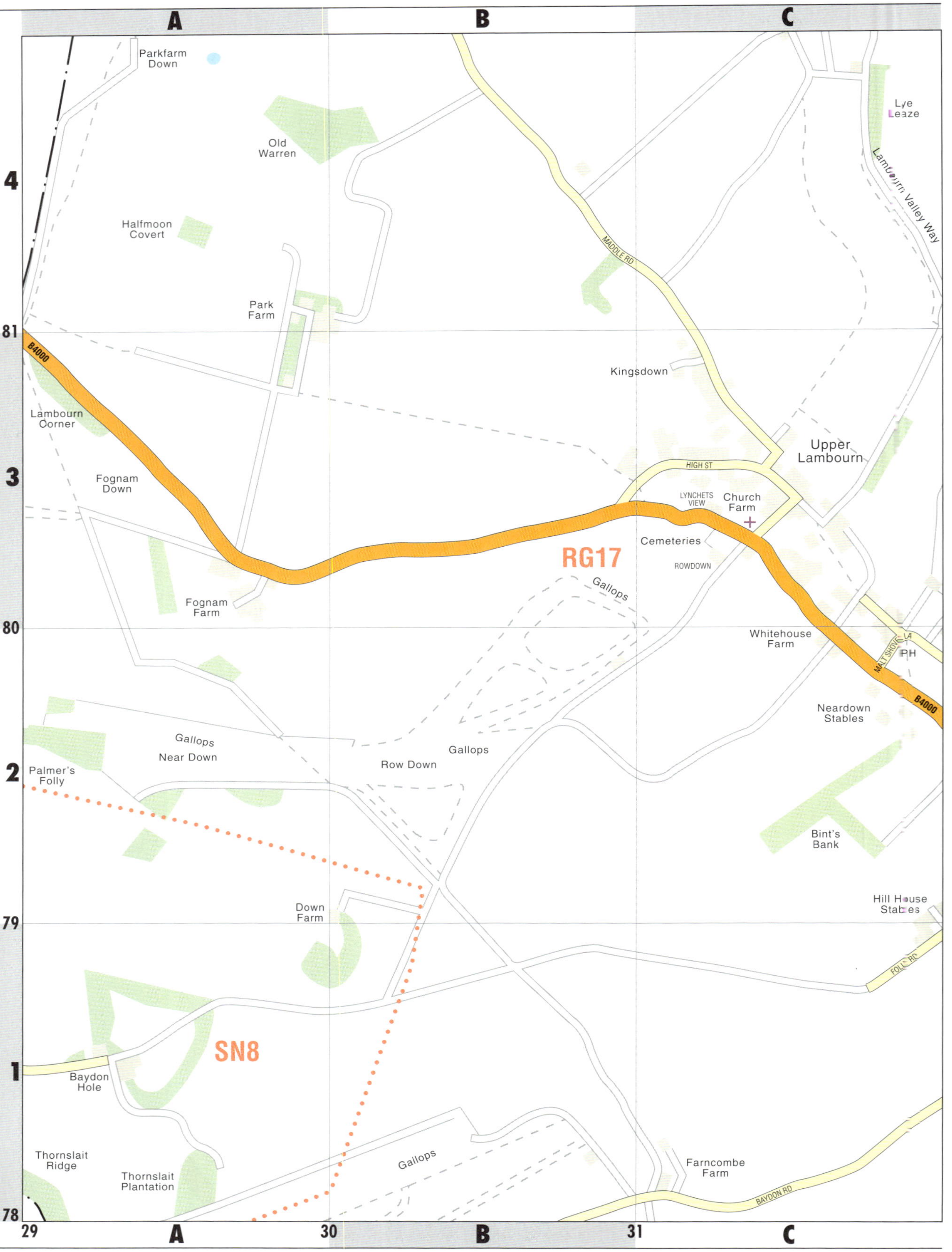

A
B
C
Parkfarm Down
Old Warren
Lye Leaze
Lambourn Valley Way
Halfmoon Covert
MADDLE RD
Park Farm
B4000
Kingsdown
Lambourn Corner
Upper Lambourn
HIGH ST
Fognam Down
LYNCHETS VIEW
Church Farm
Cemeteries
RG17
ROWDOWN
Gallops
Fognam Farm
Whitehouse Farm
MALT SHOVEL LA
PH
Neardown Stables
Gallops
Near Down
Gallops
Row Down
Palmer's Folly
Bint's Bank
Hill House Stables
Down Farm
FOLLY RD
SN8
Baydon Hole
Thornslait Ridge
Thornslait Plantation
Gallops
Farncombe Farm
BAYDON RD
4
3
2
1
81
80
79
78
29
30
31

45

5
26

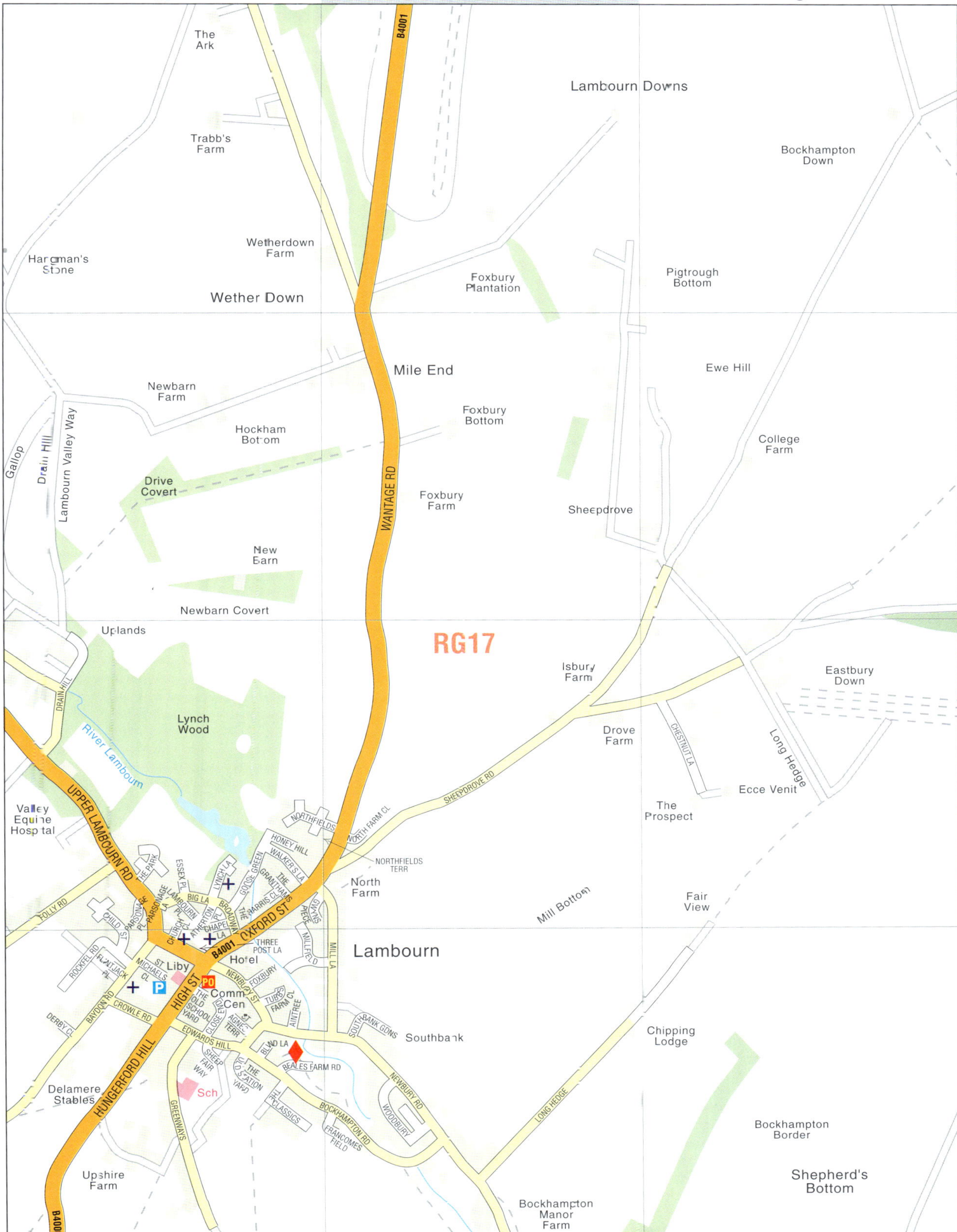
A
B
C
The Ark
Trabb's Farm
Lambourn Downs
Bockhampton Down
Hangman's Stone
Wetherdown Farm
Wether Down
Foxbury Plantation
Pigtrough Bottom
Mile End
Newbarn Farm
Ewe Hill
Foxbury Bottom
Hockham Bottom
College Farm
Drive Covert
Foxbury Farm
Sheepdrove
Gallop
Drain Hill
Lambourn Valley Way
New Barn
Newbarn Covert
Uplands
RG17
Isbury Farm
Eastbury Down
Lynch Wood
River Lambourn
Drove Farm
Long Hedge
Ecce Venit
Valley Equine Hospital
UPPER LAMBOURN RD
WANTAGE RD
B4001
SHEEPDROVE RD
CHESTNUT LA
The Prospect
North Farm
Mill Bottom
Fair View
Lambourn
Hotel
Comm Cen
Southbank
Chipping Lodge
Delamere Stables
Sch
Upshire Farm
Bockhampton Border
Shepherd's Bottom
Bockhampton Manor Farm
HUNGERFORD HILL
HIGH ST
OXFORD ST
NEWBURY RD
LONG HEDGE
B4000
4
81
3
80
2
79
1
78
32
33
34

46
26

25
6

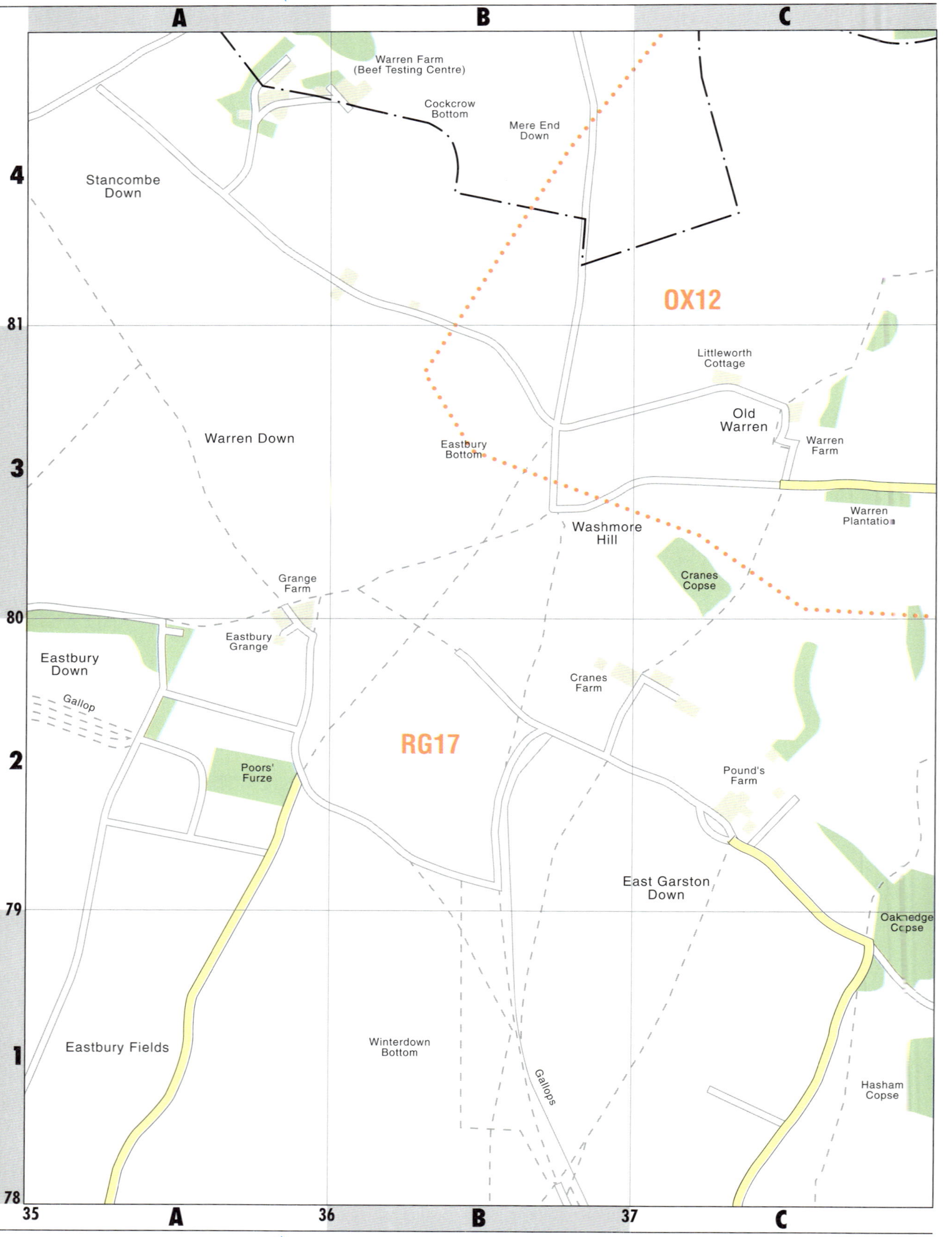
A
B
C
Warren Farm
(Beef Testing Centre)
Cockcrow
Bottom
Mere End
Down
Stancombe
Down
OX12
Littleworth
Cottage
Old
Warren
Warren
Farm
Warren Down
Eastbury
Bottom
Warren
Plantation
Washmore
Hill
Cranes
Copse
Grange
Farm
Eastbury
Grange
Eastbury
Down
Gallop
Cranes
Farm
RG17
Poors'
Furze
Pound's
Farm
East Garston
Down
Oakhedge
Copse
Eastbury Fields
Winterdown
Bottom
Gallops
Hasham
Copse
4
81
3
80
2
79
1
78
35
36
37

25
47

7
28

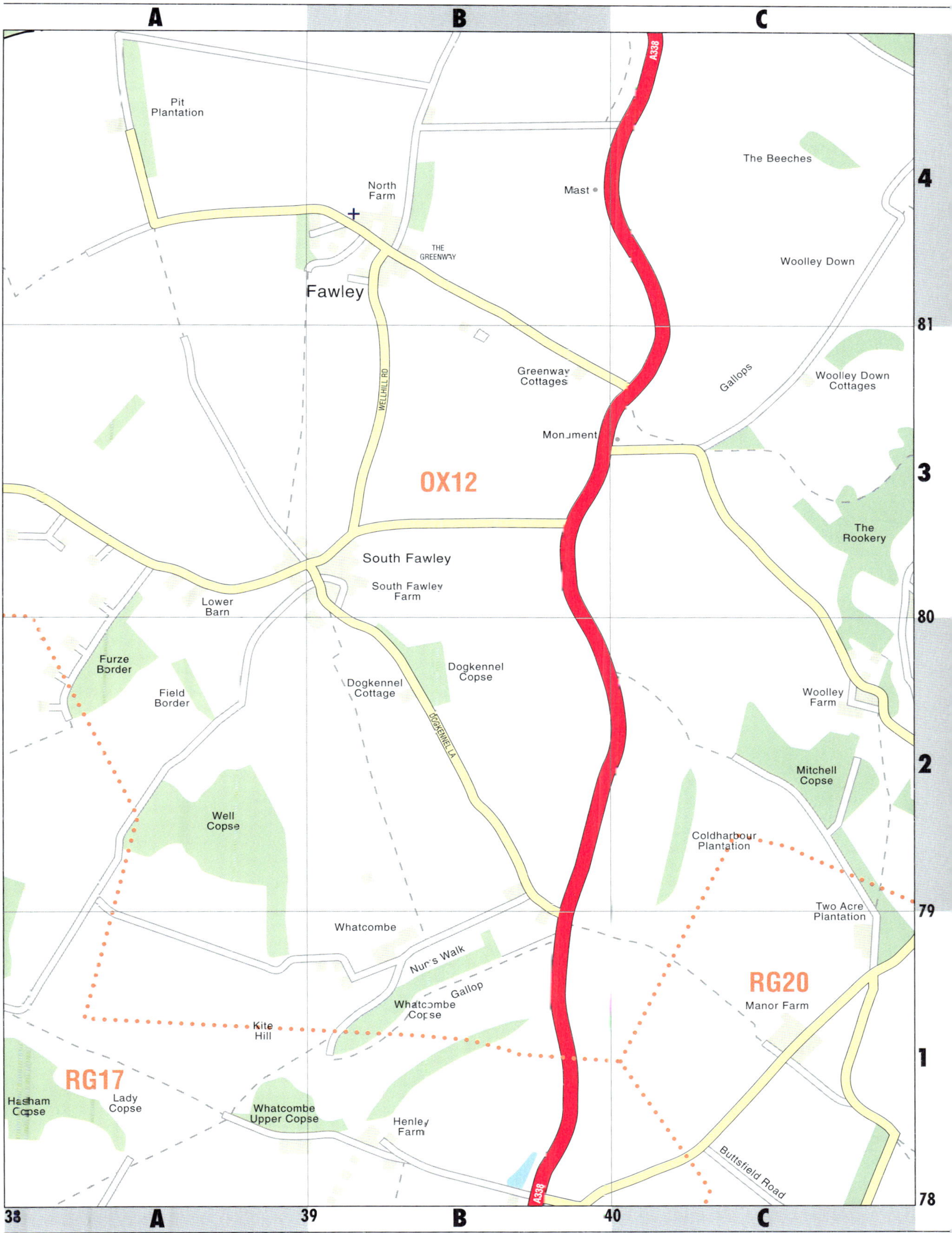
A
B
C
4
3
2
1
81
80
79
78
38
39
40
A338
Pit Plantation
North Farm
THE GREENWAY
Fawley
Mast
The Beeches
Woolley Down
Greenway Cottages
Gallops
Woolley Down Cottages
Monument
OX12
WELLHILL RD
The Rookery
South Fawley
South Fawley Farm
Lower Barn
Furze Border
Field Border
Dogkennel Cottage
Dogkennel Copse
DOGKENNEL LA
Woolley Farm
Mitchell Copse
Well Copse
Coldharbour Plantation
Two Acre Plantation
Whatcombe
Nun's Walk
Gallop
Whatcombe Copse
RG20
Manor Farm
Kite Hill
RG17
Hasham Copse
Lady Copse
Whatcombe Upper Copse
Henley Farm
Buttsfield Road

48
28

27 8

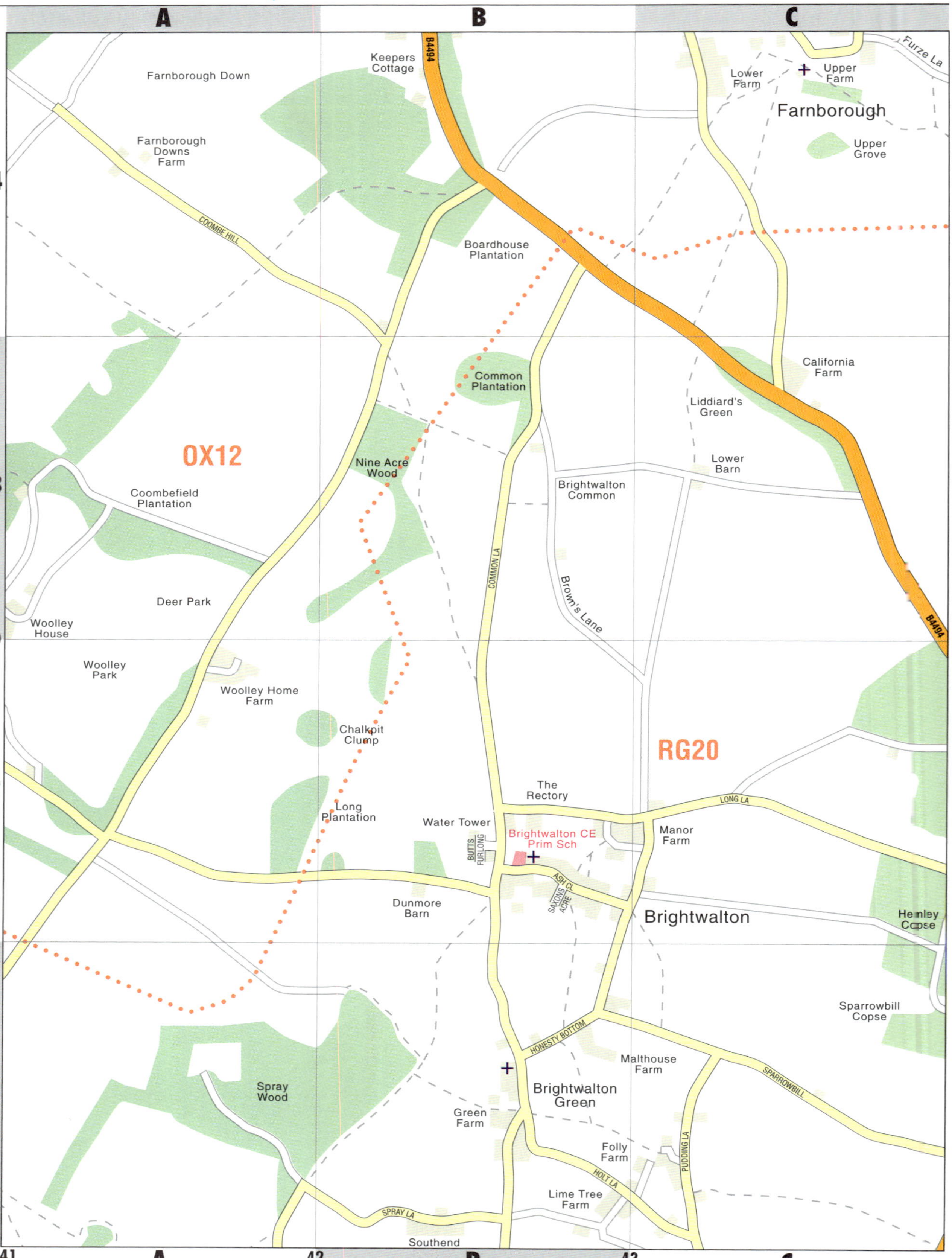
A
B
C
4
81
3
80
2
79
1
78
41
42
43
Farnborough Down
Keepers Cottage
B4494
Lower Farm
Upper Farm
Furze La
Farnborough
Upper Grove
Farnborough Downs Farm
COOMBE HILL
Boardhouse Plantation
California Farm
Common Plantation
Liddiard's Green
Lower Barn
OX12
Nine Acre Wood
Brightwalton Common
Coombefield Plantation
COMMON LA
Brown's Lane
Deer Park
Woolley House
Woolley Park
Woolley Home Farm
Chalkpit Clump
RG20
The Rectory
LONG LA
Long Plantation
Water Tower
Brightwalton CE Prim Sch
Manor Farm
BUTTS FURLONG
ASH CL
SAXONS ACRE
Dunmore Barn
Brightwalton
Henley Copse
Sparrowbill Copse
HONESTY BOTTOM
Malthouse Farm
SPARROWBILL
Spray Wood
Brightwalton Green
Green Farm
Folly Farm
PUDDING LA
HOLT LA
Lime Tree Farm
SPRAY LA
Southend

27 49

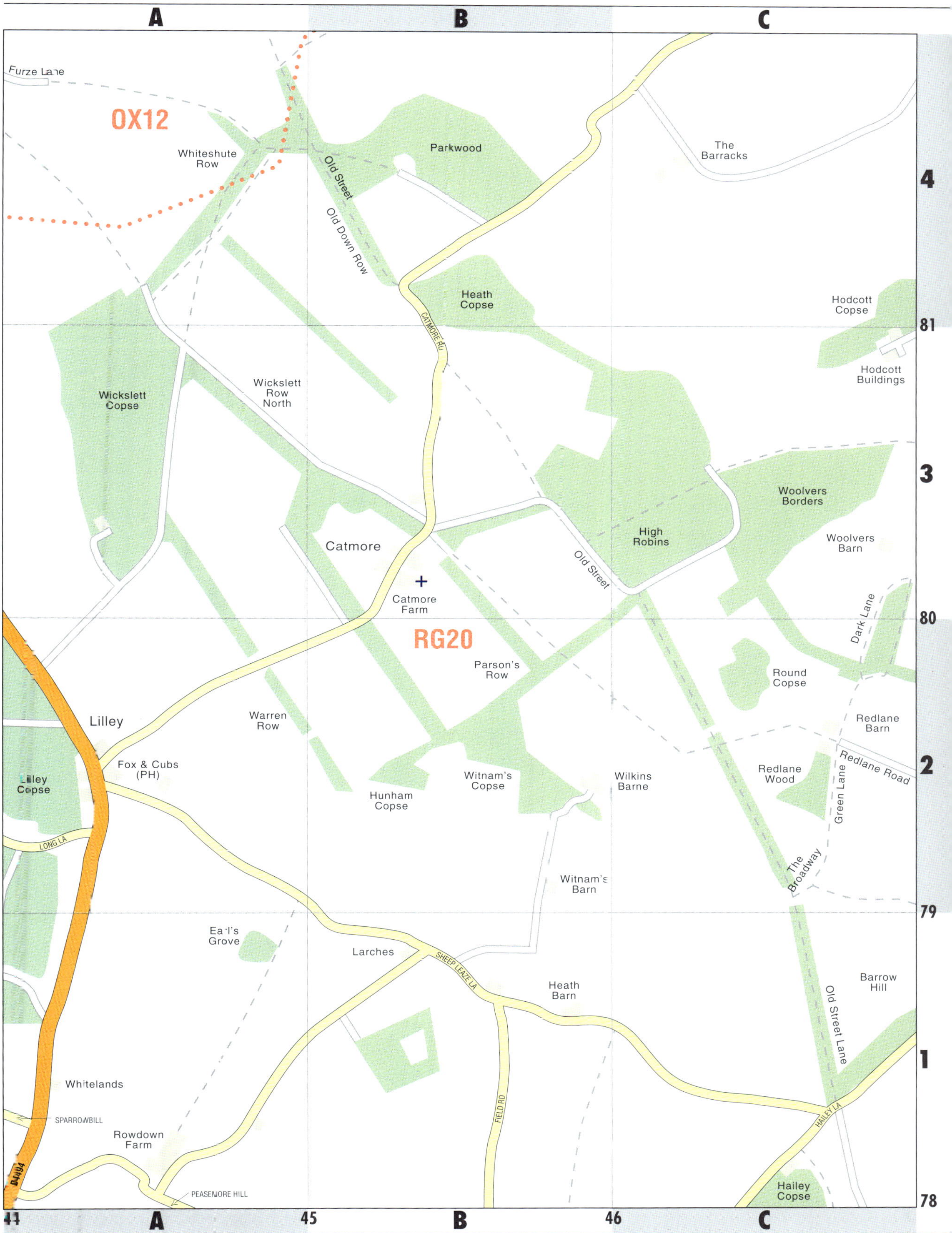
A
B
C
Furze Lane
OX12
Whiteshute Row
Old Street
Old Down Row
Parkwood
The Barracks
4
Heath Copse
CATMORE RD
Hodcott Copse
81
Hodcott Buildings
Wickslett Row North
Wickslett Copse
3
Woolvers Borders
High Robins
Catmore
Woolvers Barn
Old Street
Catmore Farm
Dark Lane
80
RG20
Parson's Row
Round Copse
Lilley
Warren Row
Redlane Barn
Fox & Cubs (PH)
Redlane Road
2
Lilley Copse
Witnam's Copse
Wilkins Barne
Redlane Wood
Green Lane
Hunham Copse
LONG LA
Witnam's Barn
The Broadway
79
Earl's Grove
Larches
SHEEP LEAZE LA
Heath Barn
Barrow Hill
Old Street Lane
1
Whitelands
FIELD RD
SPARROWBILL
HAILEY LA
Rowdown Farm
A4494
PEASEMORE HILL
Hailey Copse
78
44
A
45
B
46
C

29
10

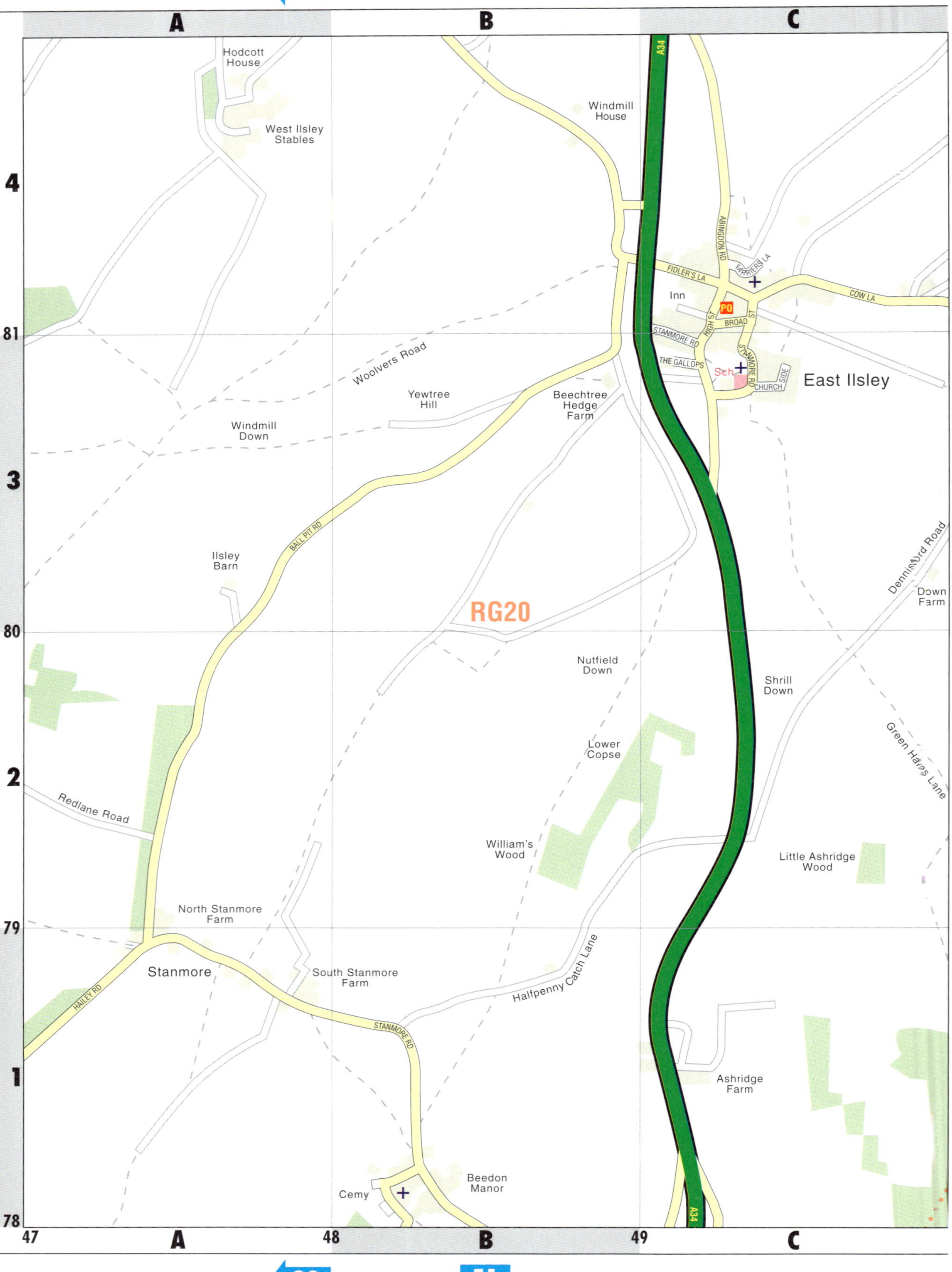
A
B
C
4
81
3
80
2
79
1
78
47
48
49
Hodcott House
West Ilsley Stables
Windmill House
A34
ABINGDON RD
FIDLER'S LA
FARRIERS LA
COW LA
Inn
PO
BROAD
HIGH ST
STANMORE RD
THE GALLOPS
Sch
CHURCH
SIDE
East Ilsley
Woolvers Road
Yewtree Hill
Beechtree Hedge Farm
Windmill Down
BALL PIT RD
Ilsley Barn
RG20
Nutfield Down
Shrill Down
Down Farm
Green Hares Lane
Lower Copse
Redlane Road
William's Wood
Little Ashridge Wood
North Stanmore Farm
Stanmore
HAILEY RD
South Stanmore Farm
Halfpenny Catch Lane
STANMORE RD
Ashridge Farm
Beedon Manor
Cemy

29
51

11
32

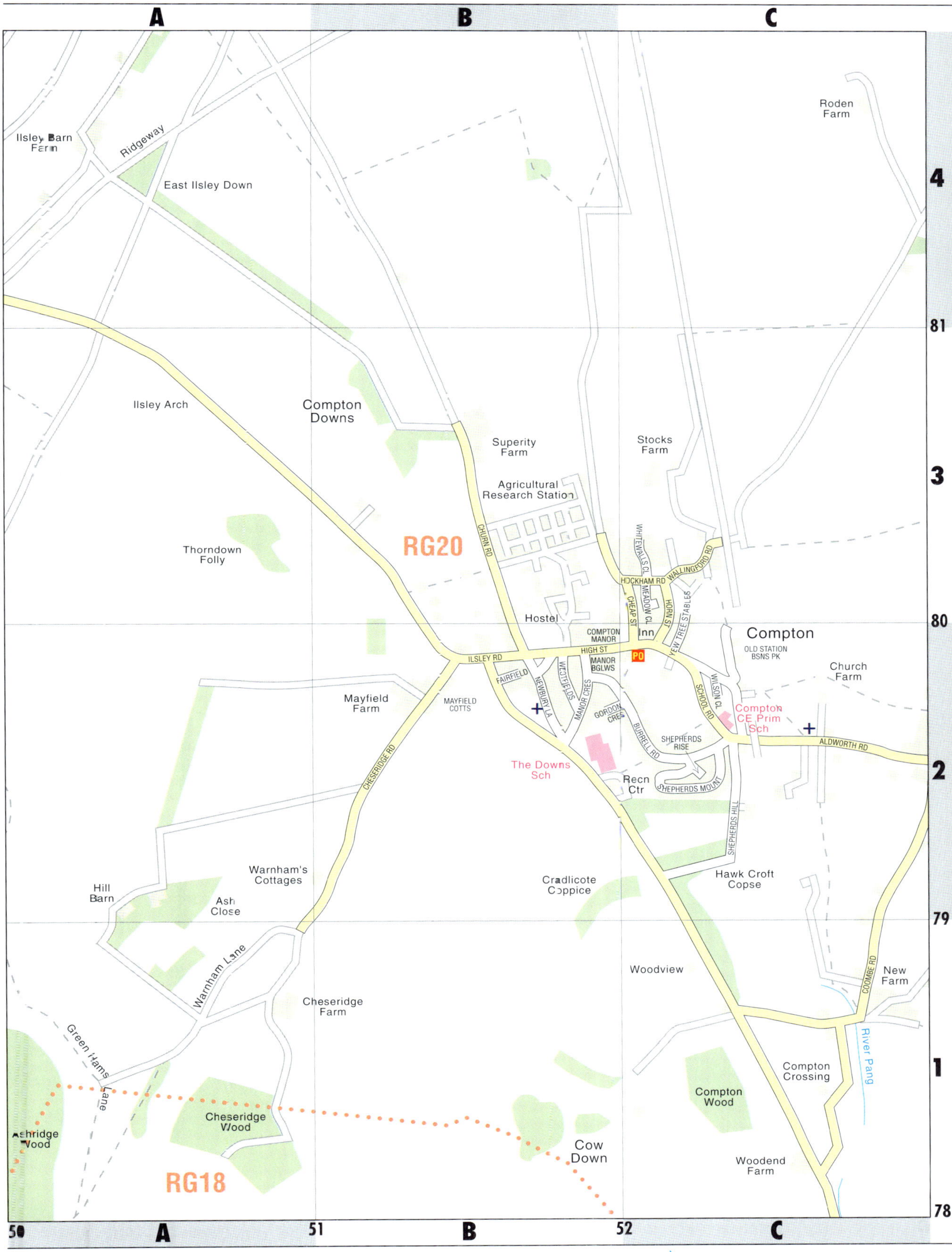
A
B
C
4
81
3
80
2
79
1
78
50
51
52
Ilsley Barn Farm
Ridgeway
East Ilsley Down
Roden Farm
Ilsley Arch
Compton Downs
Superity Farm
Stocks Farm
Agricultural Research Station
Thorndown Folly
RG20
CHURN RD
WHITEWALLS CL
WALLINGFORD RD
HOCKHAM RD
MEADOW CL
CHEAP ST
HORN ST
YEW TREE STABLES
Hostel
COMPTON MANOR
Inn
Compton
OLD STATION BSNS PK
Church Farm
ILSLEY RD
HIGH ST
PO
MANOR BGLWS
FAIRFIELD
NEWBURY LA
WESTFIELDS
MANOR CRES
GORDON CRES
BURRELL RD
SCHOOL RD
WILSON CL
Compton CE Prim Sch
SHEPHERDS RISE
ALDWORTH RD
Mayfield Farm
MAYFIELD COTTS
CHESERIDGE RD
The Downs Sch
Recn Ctr
SHEPHERDS MOUNT
SHEPHERDS HILL
Warnham's Cottages
Hill Barn
Ash Close
Cradlicote Coppice
Hawk Croft Copse
Warnham Lane
Woodview
New Farm
COOMBE RD
Cheseridge Farm
Green Hams Lane
River Pang
Compton Crossing
Compton Wood
Cheseridge Wood
Cow Down
Woodend Farm
RG18

52
32

31 12

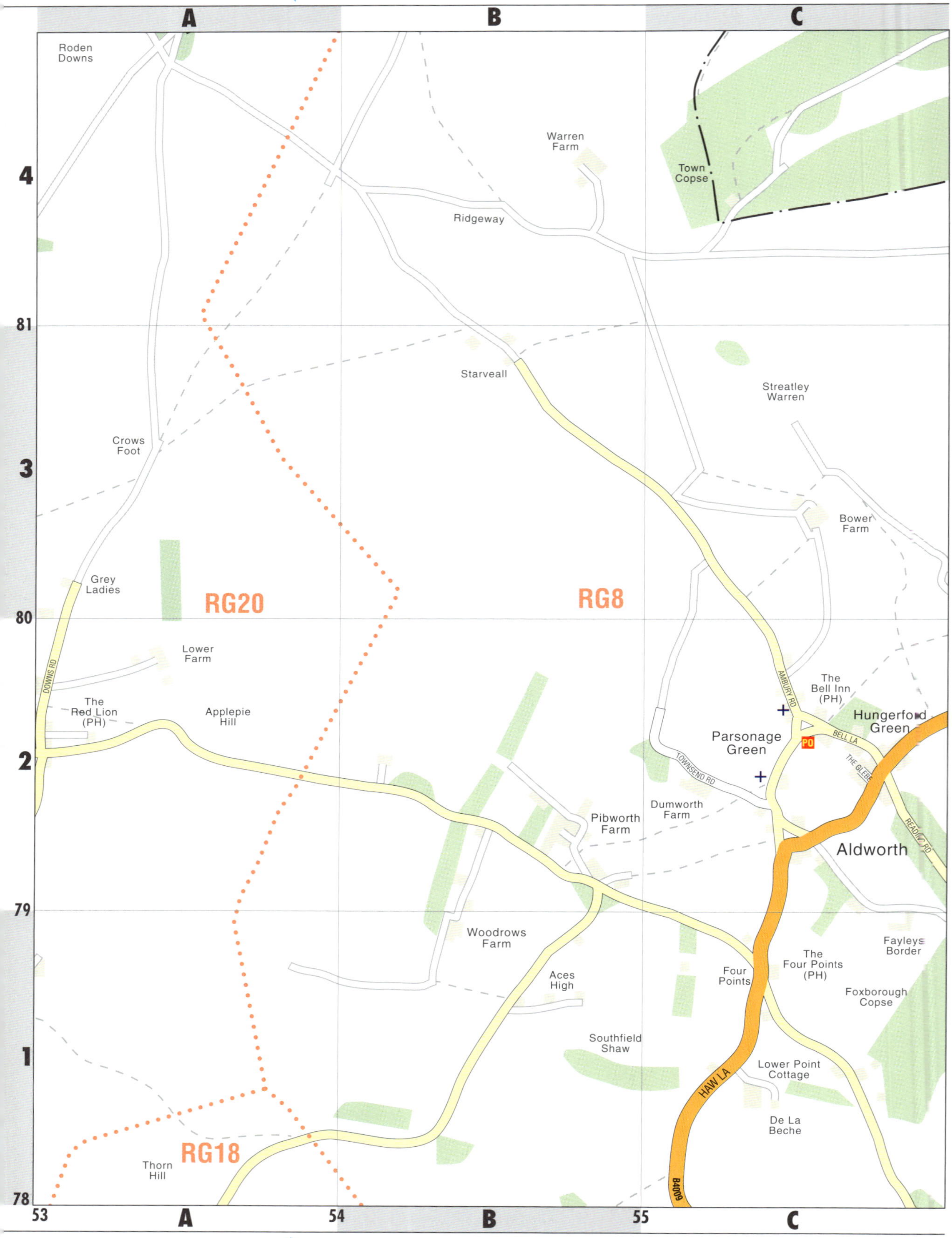
A
B
C
Roden Downs
Warren Farm
Town Copse
Ridgeway
4
81
Starveall
Streatley Warren
Crows Foot
3
Bower Farm
Grey Ladies
RG20
RG8
80
Lower Farm
DOWNS RD
The Red Lion (PH)
Applepie Hill
AMBURY RD
The Bell Inn (PH)
Hungerford Green
Parsonage Green
BELL LA
PO
THE GLEBE
TOWNSEND RD
2
Dumworth Farm
Pibworth Farm
READING RD
Aldworth
79
Woodrows Farm
Fayleys Border
The Four Points (PH)
Aces High
Four Points
Foxborough Copse
Southfield Shaw
1
Lower Point Cottage
HAW LA
De La Beche
RG18
Thorn Hill
B4009
78
53
54
55

31 53

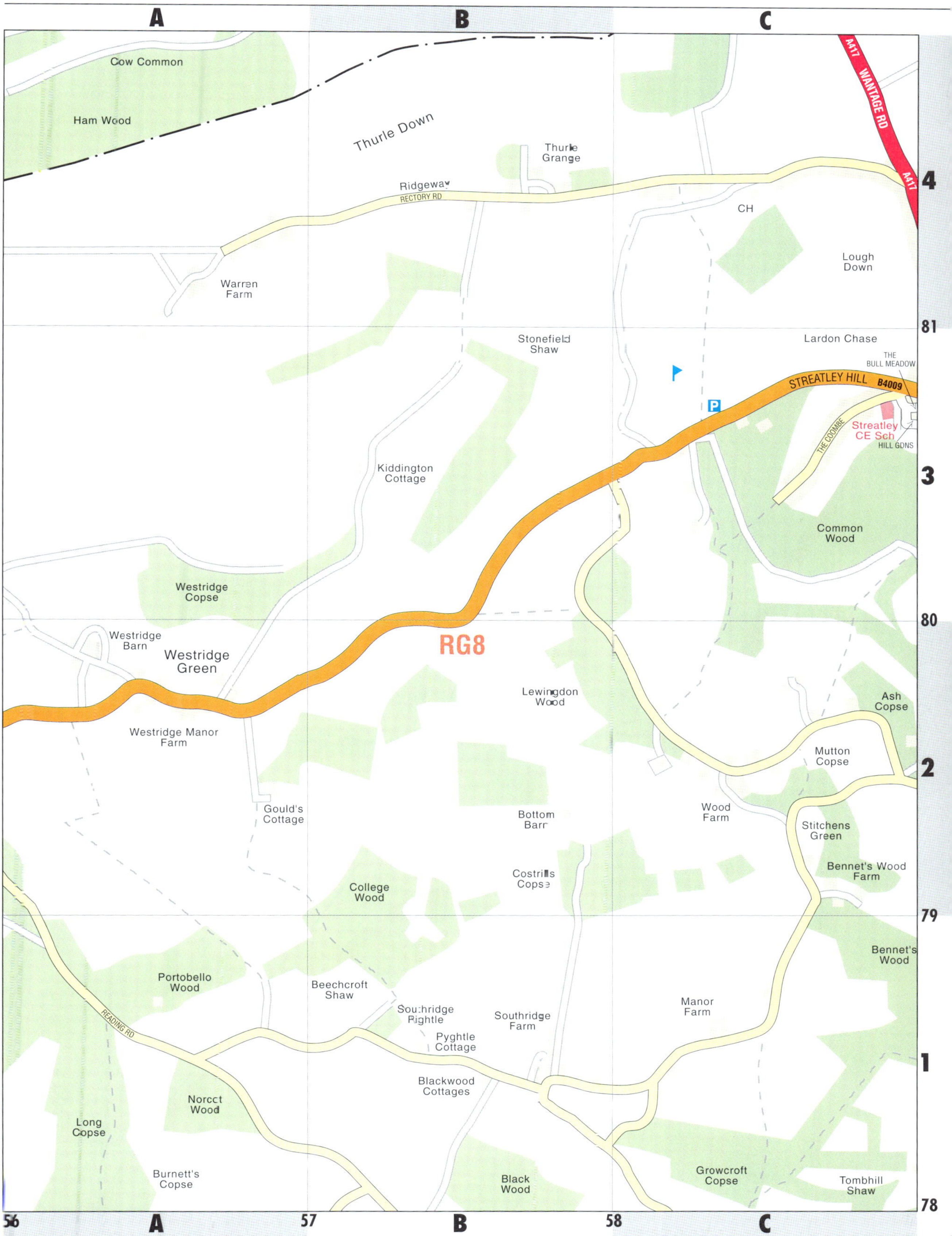
A
B
C
Cow Common
Ham Wood
Thurle Down
Thurle Grange
Ridgeway
RECTORY RD
A417
WANTAGE RD
CH
Lough Down
Warren Farm
Stonefield Shaw
Lardon Chase
THE BULL MEADOW
STREATLEY HILL
B4009
Streatley CE Sch
THE COOMBE
HILL GDNS
Kiddington Cottage
Common Wood
Westridge Copse
Westridge Barn
Westridge Green
RG8
Lewingdon Wood
Ash Copse
Westridge Manor Farm
Mutton Copse
Gould's Cottage
Bottom Barn
Wood Farm
Stitchens Green
Bennet's Wood Farm
College Wood
Costrills Copse
Bennet's Wood
Portobello Wood
Beechcroft Shaw
Southridge Pightle
Southridge Farm
Manor Farm
READING RD
Pyghtle Cottage
Blackwood Cottages
Norcot Wood
Long Copse
Burnett's Copse
Black Wood
Growcroft Copse
Tombhill Shaw
4
81
3
80
2
79
1
78
56
57
58

33
14

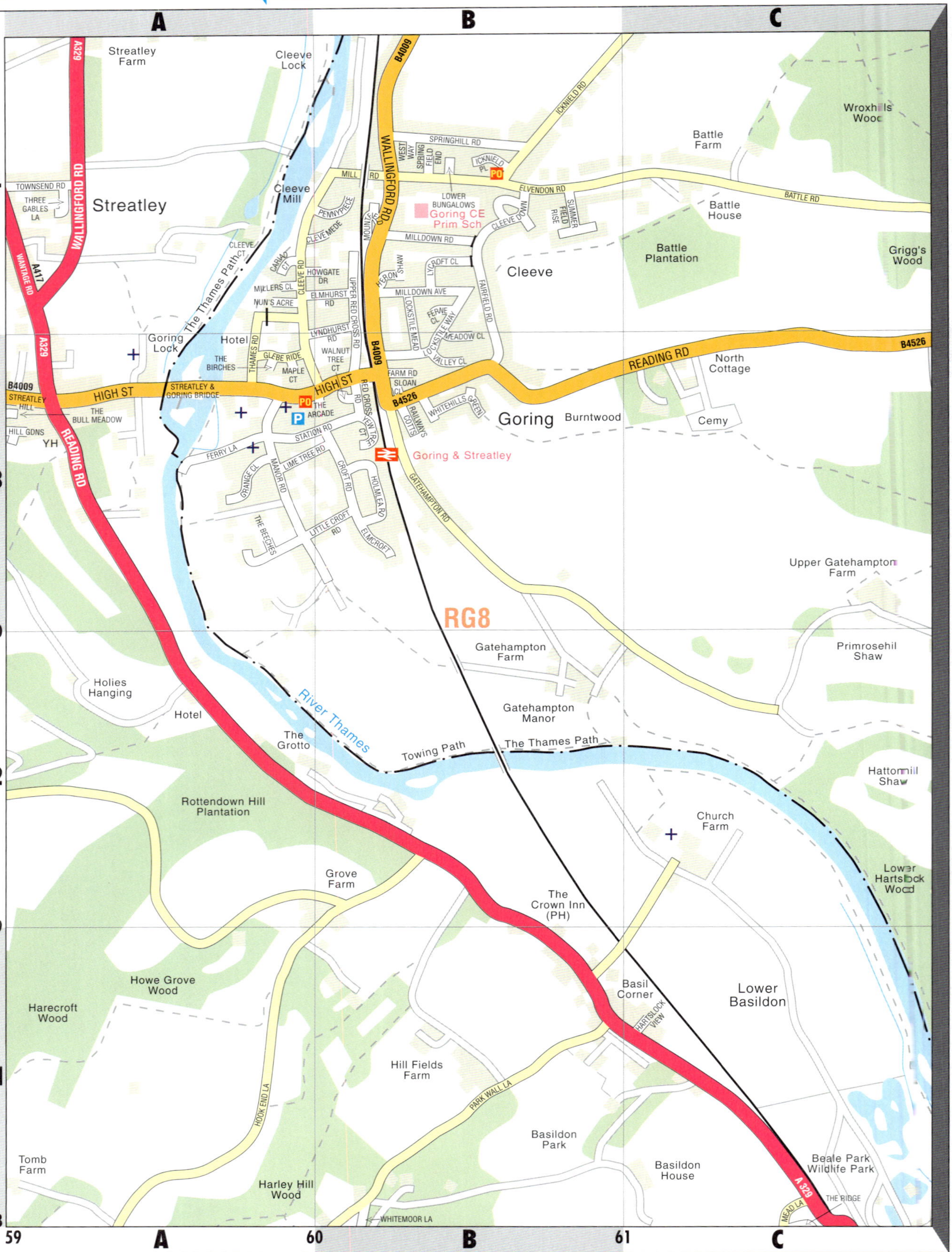
A
B
C
4
81
3
80
2
79
1
78
59
60
61
Streatley Farm
Cleeve Lock
Streatley
Cleeve Mill
TOWNSEND RD
THREE GABLES LA
WALLINGFORD RD
A329
A417
WANTAGE RD
The Thames Path
CLEEVE CT
Goring Lock
Hotel
THE BIRCHES
THAMES RD
GLEBE RIDE
MAPLE CT
WALNUT TREE CT
HIGH ST
B4009
STREATLEY HILL
STREATLEY & GORING BRIDGE
THE BULL MEADOW
HILL GDNS
YH
READING RD
PO
THE ARCADE
STATION RD
FERRY LA
GRANGE CL
MANOR RD
LIME TREE RD
CROFT RD
HOLMLEA RD
THE BEECHES
LITTLE CROFT RD
ELMCROFT
CLEEVE RD
MILLERS CL
NUN'S ACRE
HOWGATE DR
ELMHURST RD
LYNDHURST RD
UPPER RED CROSS RD
RED CROSS RD
YEW TREE CT
PENNYPIECE
CLEEVE MEDE
MILL RD
MOUNTFIELD
WALLINGFORD RD
SPRINGHILL RD
WEST WAY
SPRING FIELD END
ICKNIELD PL
ICKNIELD RD
LOWER BUNGALOWS
Goring CE Prim Sch
MILLDOWN RD
MILLDOWN AVE
HERON SHAW
LYCROFT CL
LOCKSTILE MEAD
FERNE CL
LOCKSTILE WAY
MEADOW CL
VALLEY CL
FAIRFIELD RD
CLEEVE DOWN
ELVENDON RD
SUMMER FIELD RISE
Cleeve
FARM RD
SLOAN CL
B4526
RAILWAY COTTS
WHITEHILLS GREEN
Goring
Burntwood
Goring & Streatley
GATEHAMPTON RD
READING RD
North Cottage
Cemy
Battle Farm
Battle House
BATTLE RD
Battle Plantation
Wroxhills Wood
Grigg's Wood
Upper Gatehampton Farm
RG8
Gatehampton Farm
Gatehampton Manor
Primrosehill Shaw
Holies Hanging
Hotel
The Grotto
River Thames
Towing Path
The Thames Path
Hattonmill Shaw
Rottendown Hill Plantation
Church Farm
Lower Hartslock Wood
Grove Farm
The Crown Inn (PH)
Howe Grove Wood
Harecroft Wood
Basil Corner
HARTSLOCK VIEW
Lower Basildon
Hill Fields Farm
HOOK END LA
PARK WALL LA
Basildon Park
Tomb Farm
Harley Hill Wood
Basildon House
Beale Park Wildlife Park
THE RIDGE
MEAD LA
WHITEMOOR LA
A 329

33
55

15 36

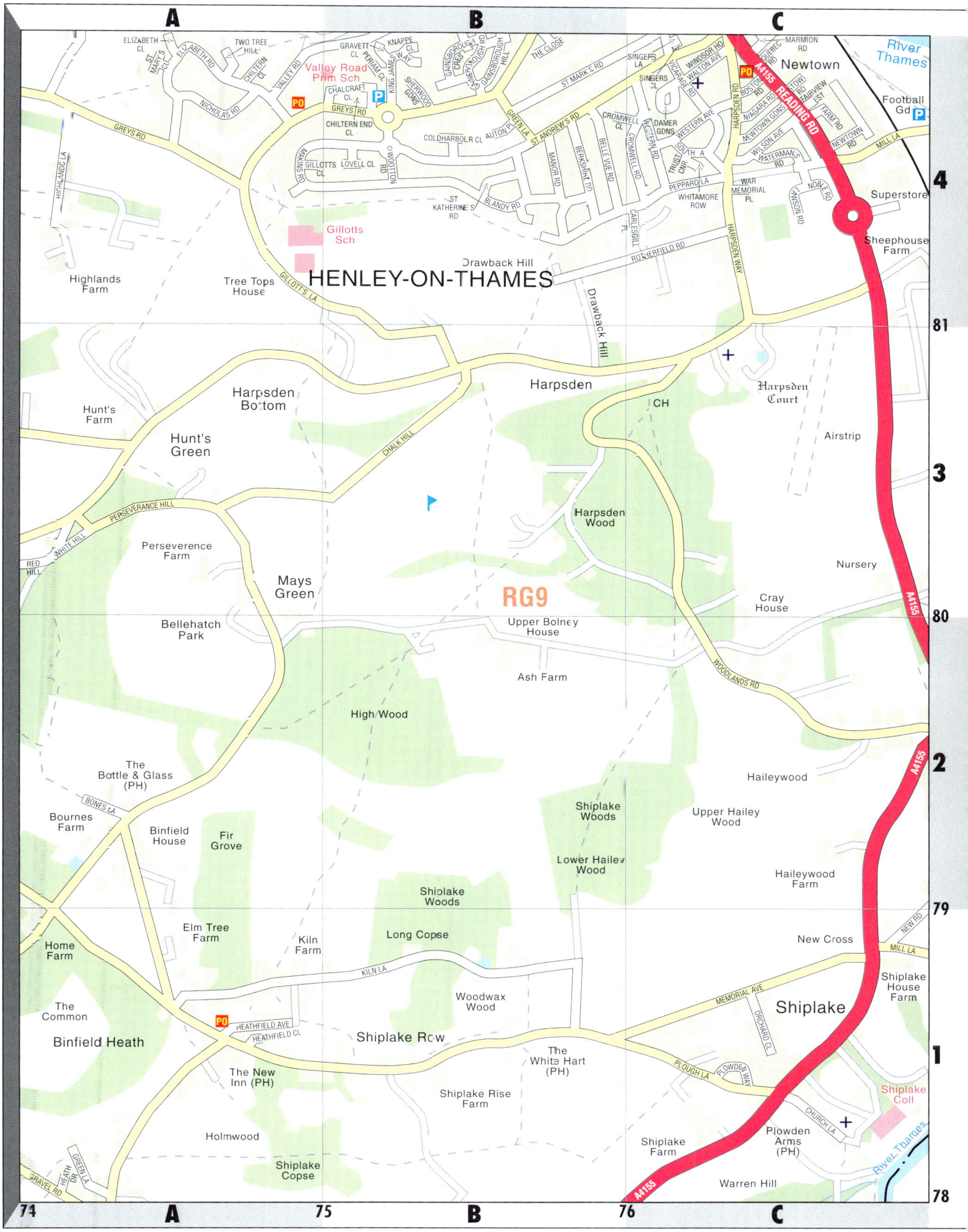

A
B
C
Valley Road Prim Sch
Newtown
River Thames
Football Gd
GREYS RD
NICHOLAS RD
VALLEY RD
CHILTERN END CL
COLDHARBOUR CL
ST MARK'S RD
ST ANDREW'S RD
GREEN LA
READING RD
A4155
HARPSDEN RD
WESTERN AVE
PEPPARD LA
WHITAMORE ROW
WAR MEMORIAL PL
MILL LA
Superstore
Sheephouse Farm
HIGHLANDS LA
Gillotts Sch
Drawback Hill
HENLEY-ON-THAMES
Highlands Farm
Tree Tops House
GILLOTT'S LA
ROTHERFIELD RD
HARPSDEN WAY
Harpsden
Harpsden Court
Airstrip
CH
Harpsden Bottom
Hunt's Farm
Hunt's Green
CHALK HILL
PERSEVERANCE HILL
WHITE HILL
RED HILL
Perseverence Farm
Harpsden Wood
Mays Green
RG9
Nursery
Cray House
Bellehatch Park
Upper Bolney House
Ash Farm
WOODLANDS RD
High Wood
The Bottle & Glass (PH)
BONES LA
Bournes Farm
Haileywood
Shiplake Woods
Upper Hailey Wood
Binfield House
Fir Grove
Lower Hailey Wood
Haileywood Farm
Shiplake Woods
Elm Tree Farm
Home Farm
Kiln Farm
Long Copse
New Cross
NEW RD
KILN LA
Woodwax Wood
MEMORIAL AVE
Shiplake House Farm
Shiplake
The Common
HEATHFIELD AVE
HEATHFIELD CL
Binfield Heath
Shiplake Row
The White Hart (PH)
ORCHARD CL
PLOUGH LA
The New Inn (PH)
Shiplake Rise Farm
Shiplake Coll
CHURCH LA
Plowden Arms (PH)
Holmwood
Shiplake Farm
River Thames
Shiplake Copse
Warren Hill
GRAVEL RD
HEATH DR
GREEN LA
4
81
3
80
2
79
1
78
74
75
76

60 36

35
16

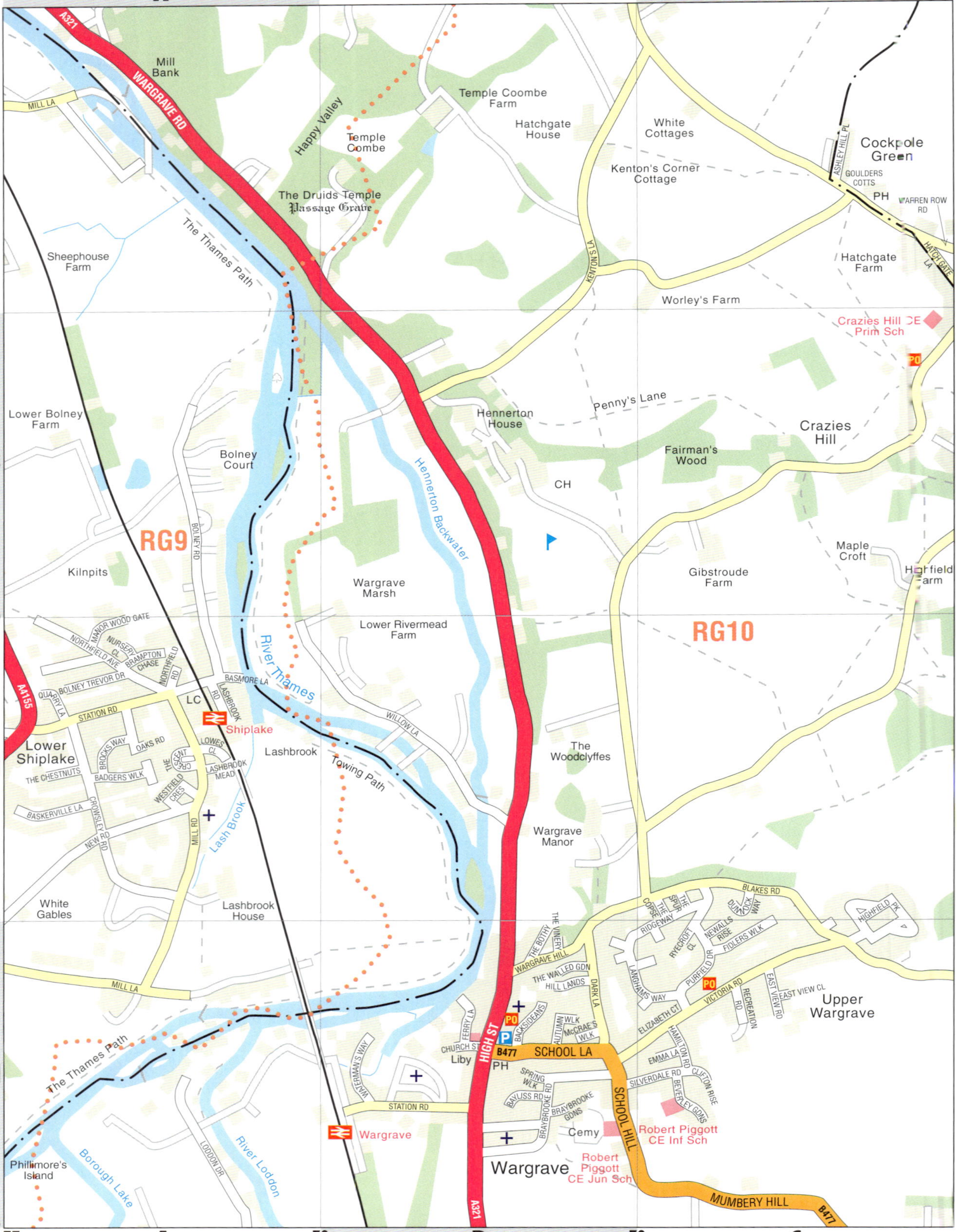
A
B
C
4
81
3
80
2
79
1
78
77
78
79
Mill Bank
MILL LA
WARGRAVE RD
A321
Happy Valley
Temple Coombe Farm
Hatchgate House
White Cottages
Cockpole Green
ASHLEY HILL PL
GOULDERS COTTS
PH
WARREN ROW RD
HATCHGATE LA
Temple Combe
Kenton's Corner Cottage
The Druids Temple
Passage Grave
Sheephouse Farm
The Thames Path
KENTON'S LA
Hatchgate Farm
Worley's Farm
Crazies Hill CE Prim Sch
PO
Lower Bolney Farm
Hennerton House
Penny's Lane
Crazies Hill
Bolney Court
Fairman's Wood
CH
Hennerton Backwater
RG9
BOLNEY RD
Maple Croft
Kilnpits
Wargrave Marsh
Gibstroude Farm
Highfield Farm
Lower Rivermead Farm
RG10
MANOR WOOD GATE
NURSERY CL
NORTHFIELD AVE
BRAMPTON CHASE
NORTHFIELD RD
BOLNEY TREVOR DR
BASMORE LA
River Thames
A4155
QUARRY LA
STATION RD
LC
LASHBROOK RD
Shiplake
WILLOW LA
Lower Shiplake
BROCKS WAY
OAKS RD
THE CRESCENT
LOWES CL
Lashbrook
Towing Path
The Woodclyffes
THE CHESTNUTS
BADGERS WLK
LASHBROOK MEAD
WESTFIELD CRES
BASKERVILLE LA
CROWSLEY RD
NEW RD
MILL RD
Lash Brook
Wargrave Manor
White Gables
Lashbrook House
BLAKES RD
COPSE
THE SPUR
THE RIDGEWAY
DUNNOCK WAY
HIGHFIELD PK
THE BOTHY
THE VINERY
RYECROFT CL
NEWALLS RISE
FIDLERS WLK
WARGRAVE HILL
THE WALLED GDN
HILL LANDS
DARK LA
LANDHAMS WAY
PURFIELD DR
VICTORIA RD
EAST VIEW RD
EAST VIEW CL
MILL LA
Upper Wargrave
RECREATION RD
ELIZABETH CT
BACKSIDEANS
AUTUMN WLK
McCRAE'S WLK
FERRY LA
HIGH ST
P
B477
SCHOOL LA
HAMILTON RD
EMMA LA
CHURCH ST
Liby
PH
SPRING WLK
SILVERDALE RD
CLIFTON RISE
BEVERLEY GDNS
The Thames Path
WATERMAN'S WAY
BAYLISS RD
BRAYBROOKE RD
BRAYBROOKE GDNS
STATION RD
SCHOOL HILL
Cemy
Robert Piggott CE Inf Sch
Wargrave
Phillimore's Island
Borough Lake
LODDON DR
River Loddon
Wargrave
Robert Piggott CE Jun Sch
MUMBERY HILL

35
61

17
38

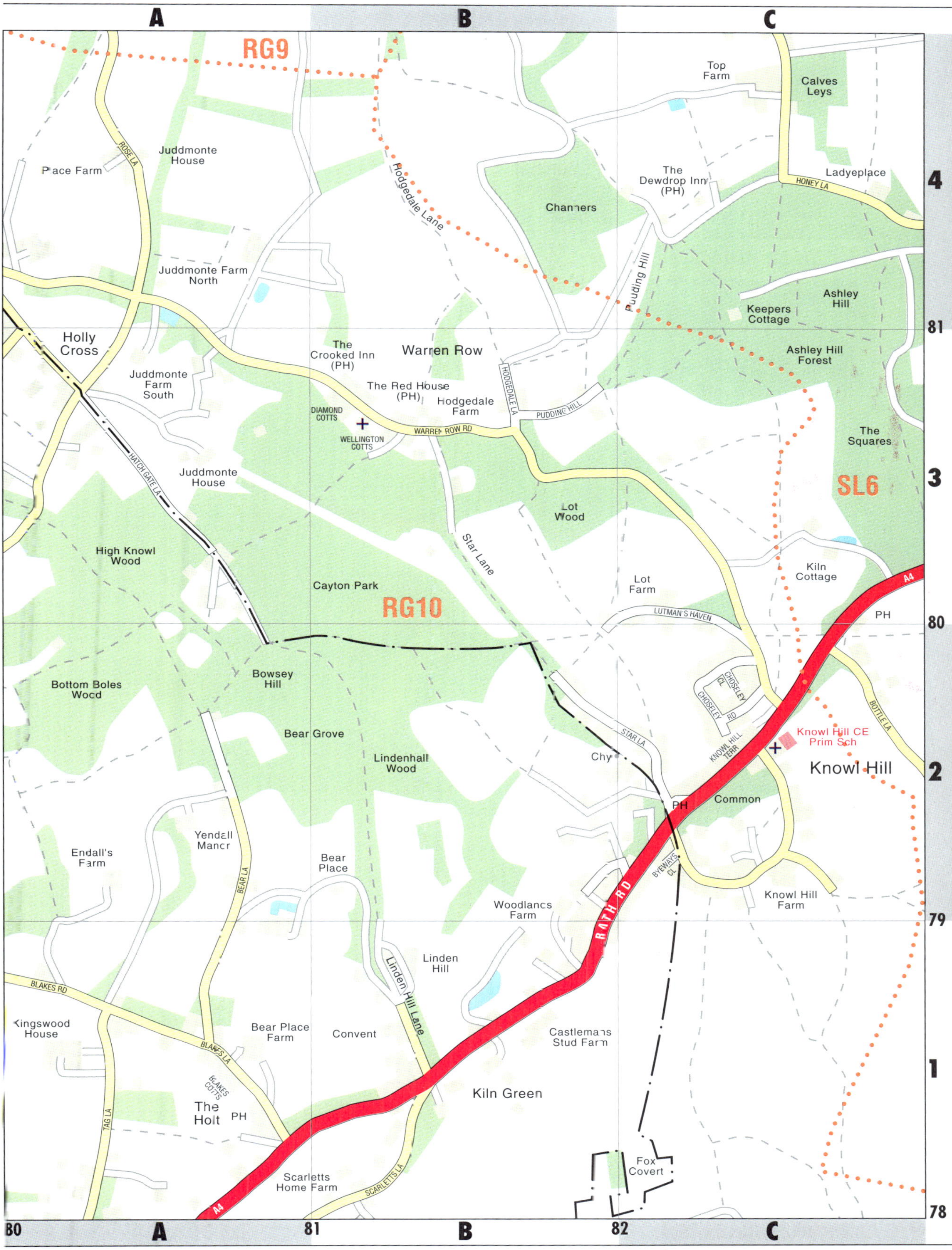
A
B
C
RG9
RG10
SL6
Place Farm
Juddmonte House
Juddmonte Farm North
Holly Cross
Juddmonte Farm South
Juddmonte House
High Knowl Wood
Bottom Boles Wood
Bowsey Hill
Bear Grove
Cayton Park
The Crooked Inn (PH)
Warren Row
The Red House (PH)
Hodgedale Farm
DIAMOND COTTS
WELLINGTON COTTS
WARREN ROW RD
Hodgedale Lane
HODGEDALE LA
PUDDING HILL
Pudding Hill
Channers
The Dewdrop Inn (PH)
Top Farm
Calves Leys
Ladyeplace
HONEY LA
Keepers Cottage
Ashley Hill
Ashley Hill Forest
The Squares
Lot Wood
Star Lane
Lot Farm
LUTMAN'S HAVEN
Kiln Cottage
A4
PH
CHOSELEY CL
CHOSELEY RD
KNOWL HILL TERR
Knowl Hill CE Prim Sch
Knowl Hill
Common
BOTTLE LA
STAR LA
Chy
PH
BYEWAYS CL
Lindenhall Wood
Endall's Farm
Yendall Manor
BEAR LA
Bear Place
Woodlands Farm
Knowl Hill Farm
BATH RD
Linden Hill
Linden Hill Lane
BLAKES RD
Kingswood House
BLAKES LA
BLAKES COTTS
Bear Place Farm
Convent
Castlemans Stud Farm
Kiln Green
The Holt
PH
TAG LA
Scarletts Home Farm
SCARLETTS LA
Fox Covert
A4
4
81
3
80
2
79
1
78
80
81
82

62
38

37
18

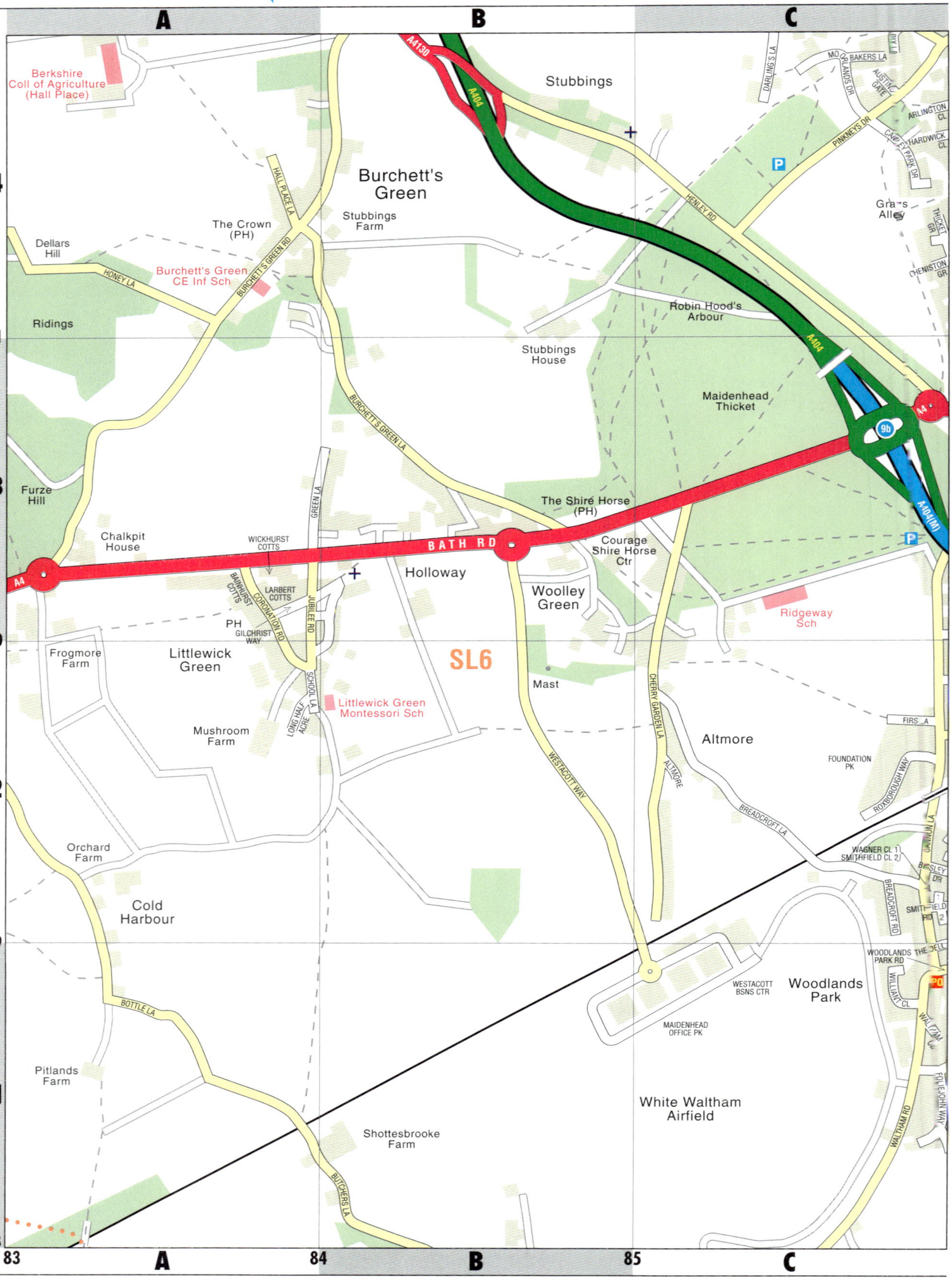
A
B
C
4
81
3
80
2
79
1
78
83
84
85
Berkshire Coll of Agriculture (Hall Place)
Stubbings
Burchett's Green
Stubbings Farm
The Crown (PH)
Dellars Hill
HONEY LA
HALL PLACE LA
BURCHETT'S GREEN RD
Burchett's Green CE Inf Sch
Ridings
Robin Hood's Arbour
Stubbings House
Maidenhead Thicket
HENLEY RD
PINKNEYS DR
DARLING'S LA
BAKERS LA
ORLANDS DR
AUSTIN GATE
ARLINGTON CL
HARDWICK CL
CAREY PARK DR
Grass Alley
THICKET GR
CHENISTON GR
A4130
A404
A404(M)
A4
9b
BURCHETT'S GREEN LA
Furze Hill
Chalkpit House
WICKHURST COTTS
GREEN LA
BATH RD
The Shire Horse (PH)
Courage Shire Horse Ctr
Holloway
Woolley Green
BAINHURST COTTS
LARBERT COTTS
CORONATION RD
JUBILEE RD
PH
GILCHRIST WAY
Frogmore Farm
Littlewick Green
SL6
Mast
Ridgeway Sch
SCHOOL LA
LONG HALF ACRE
Littlewick Green Montessori Sch
Mushroom Farm
CHERRY GARDEN LA
WESTACOTT WAY
ALTMORE
Altmore
FIRS LA
FOUNDATION PK
ROXBOROUGH WAY
BREADCROFT LA
WAGNER CL 1
SMITHFIELD CL 2
Orchard Farm
Cold Harbour
WESTACOTT BSNS CTR
Woodlands Park
WOODLANDS PARK RD
THE DELL
WILLIANT CL
MAIDENHEAD OFFICE PK
BOTTLE LA
Pitlands Farm
White Waltham Airfield
WALTHAM RD
Shottesbrooke Farm
BUTCHERS LA
P
PO

37
63

C4
1 HIGH ST MALL
2 WHITE HART RD
3 QUEENS WLK MALL
4 KINGS WLK
5 NICHOLSONS CTR
6 BROADWAY MALL
7 BROCK LA MALL
8 QUEEN'S LA
9 REGENT CT
10 OLD POST OFFICE LA

39 20

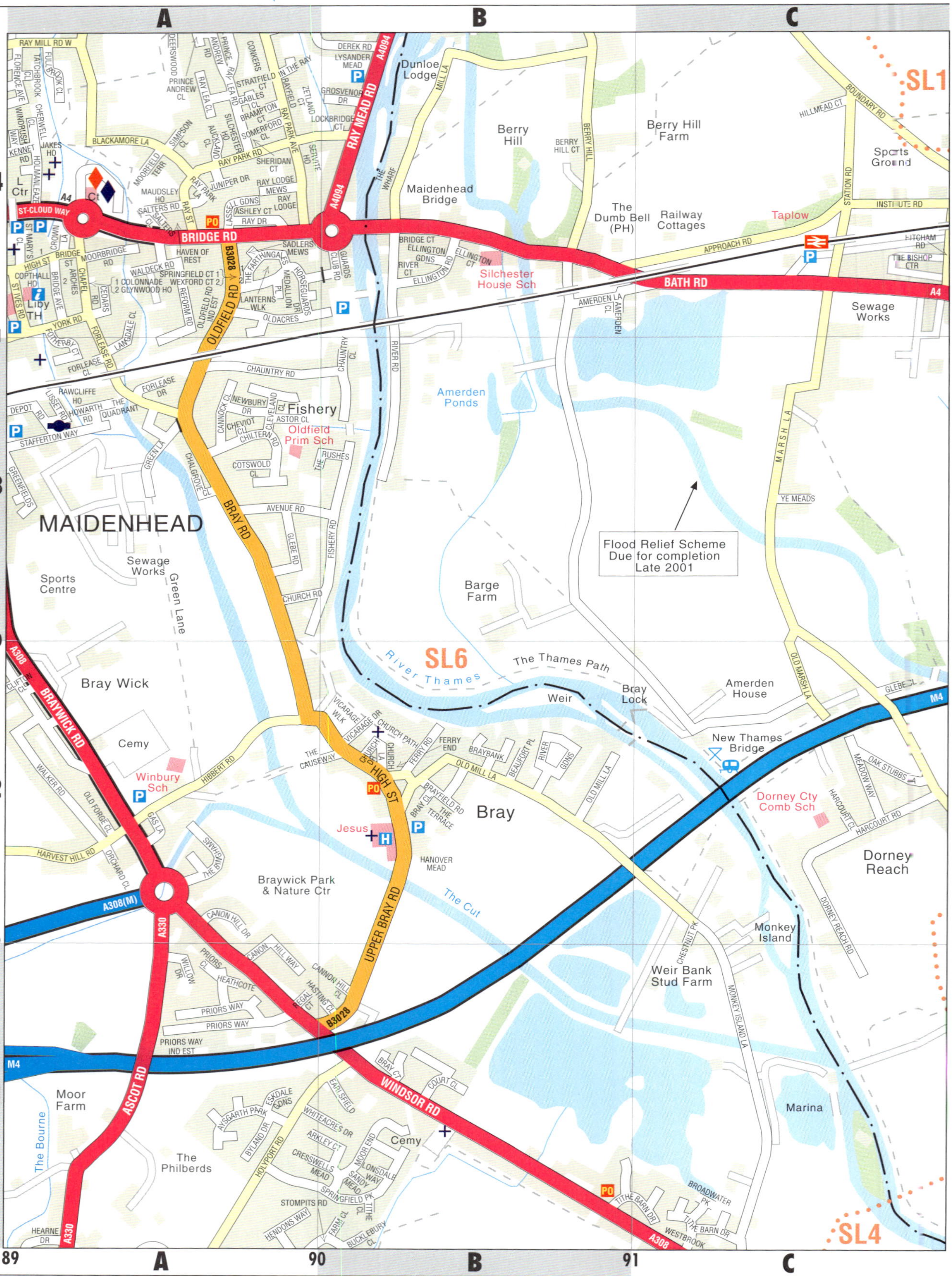
A
B
C
4
3
2
1
81
80
79
78
89
90
91
SL1
SL6
SL4
MAIDENHEAD
Bray
Bray Wick
Dorney Reach
Monkey Island
Marina
Berry Hill
Berry Hill Farm
Dunloe Lodge
Maidenhead Bridge
The Dumb Bell (PH)
Railway Cottages
Taplow
Sports Ground
Sewage Works
Silchester House Sch
Amerden Ponds
Fishery
Oldfield Prim Sch
Flood Relief Scheme
Due for completion
Late 2001
Barge Farm
River Thames
The Thames Path
Weir
Bray Lock
Amerden House
New Thames Bridge
Dorney Cty Comb Sch
Sports Centre
Sewage Works
Green Lane
Cemy
Winbury Sch
Jesus
Braywick Park & Nature Ctr
The Cut
Weir Bank Stud Farm
Moor Farm
The Bourne
The Philberds
Cemy
Liby
TH
L Ctr
Ct
BRIDGE RD
BATH RD
A4
A4094
RAY MEAD RD
OLDFIELD RD
B3028
BRAY RD
HIGH ST
UPPER BRAY RD
BRAYWICK RD
A308
A308(M)
A330
ASCOT RD
WINDSOR RD
M4
OLD MILL LA
MARSH LA
OLD MARSH LA
STATION RD
BOUNDARY RD
HILLMEAD CT
INSTITUTE RD
APPROACH RD
MONKEY ISLAND LA
ST-CLOUD WAY
BLACKAMORE LA
CHAUNTRY RD
AVENUE RD
HARVEST HILL RD
PRIORS WAY
PRIORS WAY IND EST
HOLYPORT RD
STOMPITS RD
HEARNE DR

39 65

21
42

C3
1 SHERIDAN CT
2 SELWYN PL
3 BOWER CT
4 LEWINS FARM CT
5 WATERMAN CT
6 BIDDLES CL
7 MOLYNS MEWS

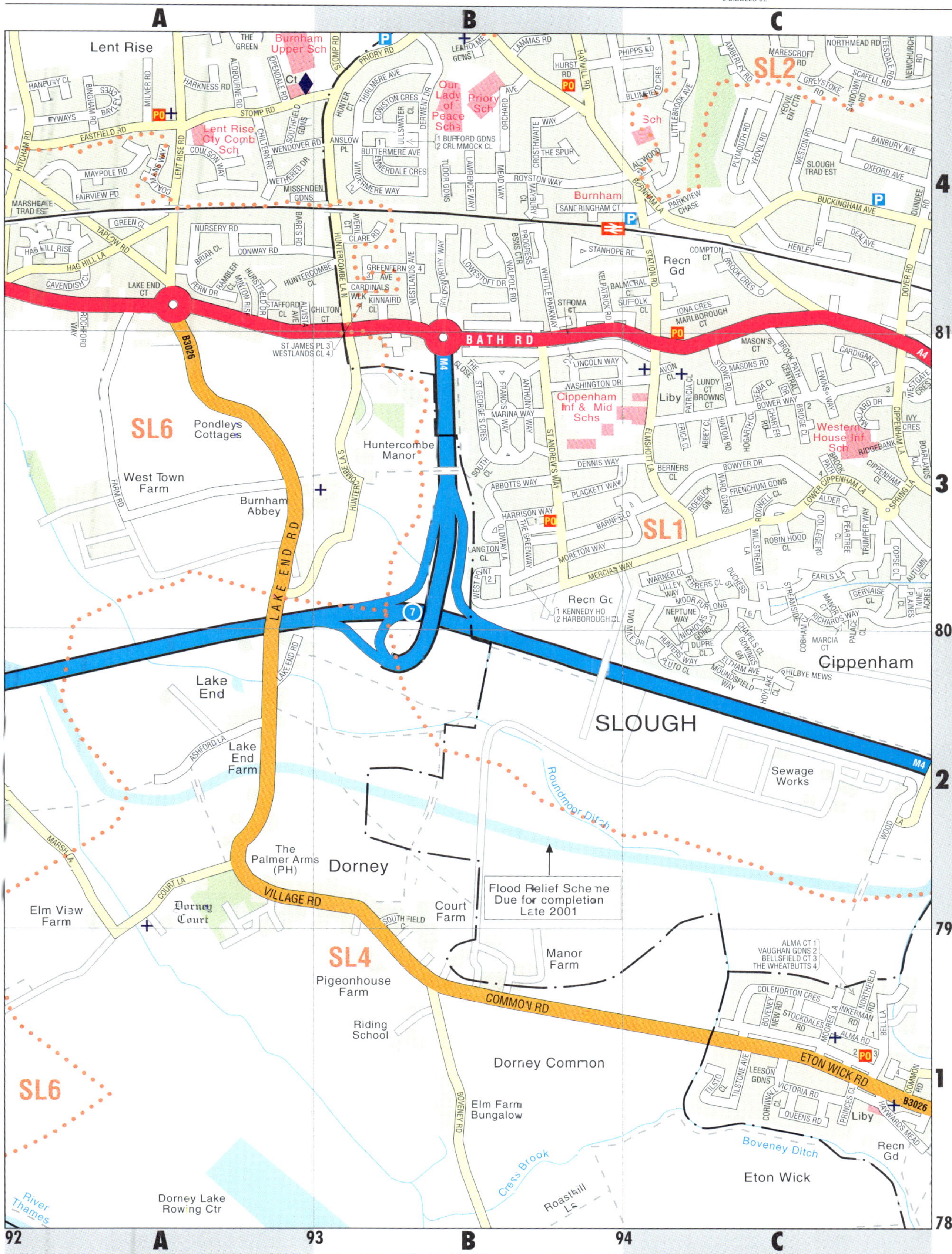

66
42

41 22

41 67

C2
1 BURLINGTON CT
2 BURLINGTON RD
3 HILPERTON RD
4 TOWER HO
5 ASHBOURNE HO
6 SHAFTESBURY CT
7 MOORSTOWN CT
8 PRUDENTIAL BLDGS
9 MACKENZIE ST
10 MACKENZIE MALL
11 OLD CROWN
12 BUCKINGHAM GDNS
13 THE VILLAGE SH CTR
14 LEOPOLD MALL
15 CURZON MALL
16 CHANDOS MALL
17 TOWN SQ
18 VICTORIA ST
19 BISHAM CT
20 BEMBRIDGE CT
21 STEPHENSON CT
22 ETON WLK
23 ST ANDREWS CT
24 LINCOLN CT
25 LOCKSLEY CT
26 SPRUCE CT
27 DARTMOUTH CT
28 ALBERT CL
29 MANOR CT

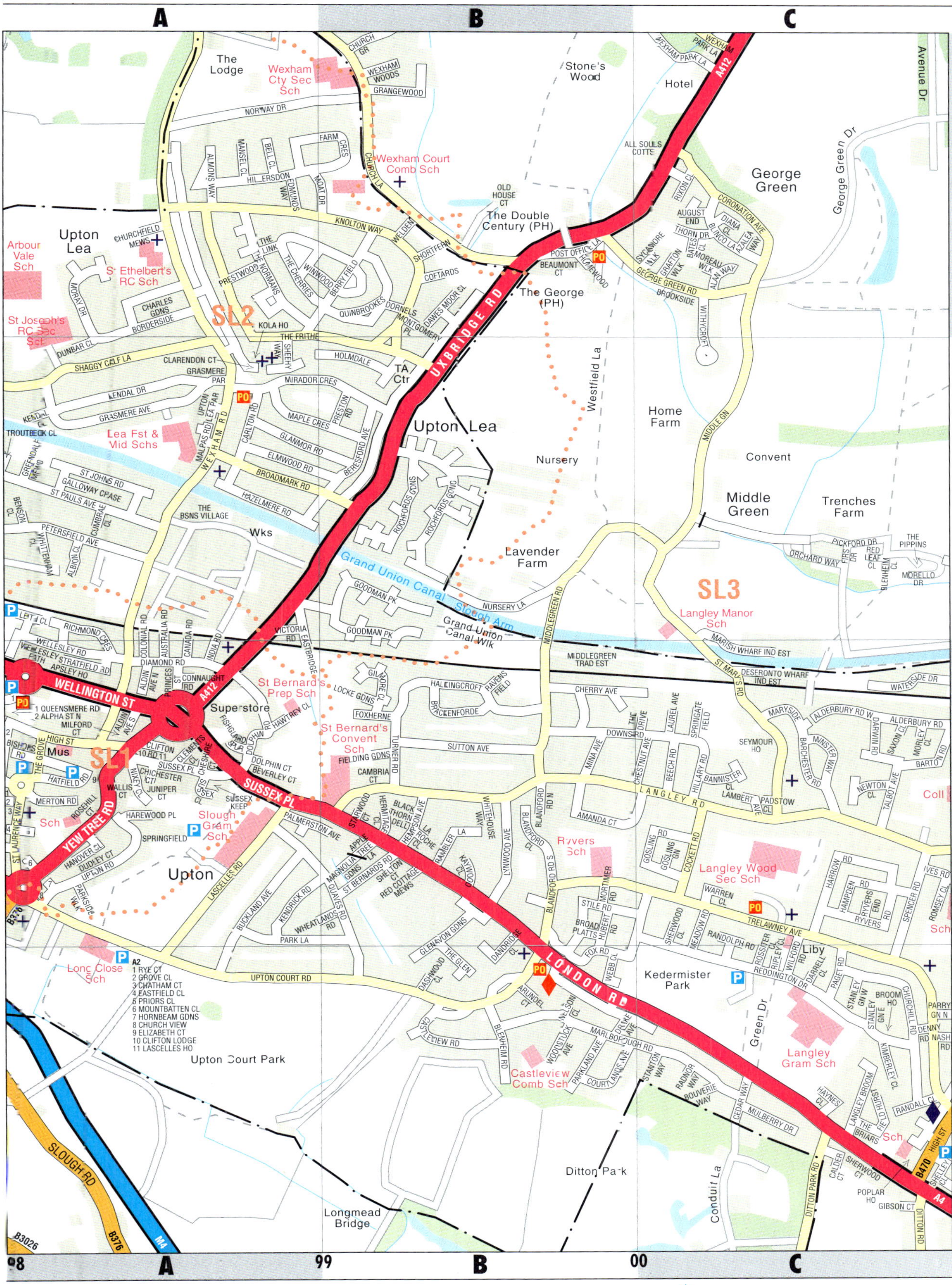
A
B
C
The Lodge
Wexham Cty Sec Sch
Stone's Wood
Hotel
A412
NORWAY DR
Wexham Court Comb Sch
CHURCH LA
George Green
George Green Dr
Avenue Dr
ALL SOULS COTTS
OLD HOUSE CT
The Double Century (PH)
Upton Lea
Arbour Vale Sch
St Ethelbert's RC Sch
St Joseph's RC Sec Sch
KNOLTON WAY
CORONATION AVE
GEORGE GREEN RD
BROOKSIDE
POST OFFICE LA
BEAUMONT CT
The George (PH)
SL2
UXBRIDGE RD
SHAGGY CALF LA
KOLA HO
THE FRITHE
CLARENDON CT
GRASMERE PAR
HOLMDALE
TA Ctr
MIRADOR CRES
KENDAL DR
GRASMERE AVE
Westfield La
Home Farm
MIDDLE GN
Lea Fst & Mid Schs
WEXHAM RD
MAPLE CRES
GLANMOR RD
ELMWOOD RD
BROADMARK RD
HAZELMERE RD
Upton Lea
Nursery
Convent
Middle Green
Trenches Farm
ST JOHNS RD
GALLOWAY CHASE
ST PAULS AVE
THE BSNS VILLAGE
Wks
PETERSFIELD AVE
Lavender Farm
Grand Union Canal
Slough Arm
Grand Union Canal Wlk
NURSERY LA
SL3
Langley Manor Sch
MIDDLEGREEN RD
MIDDLEGREEN TRAD EST
MARISH WHARF IND EST
DESERONTO WHARF IND EST
ST MARY'S RD
ORCHARD WAY
PICKFORD DR
THE PIPPINS
MORELLO DR
WATERSIDE DR
WELLINGTON ST
A412
Superstore
St Bernard's Prep Sch
St Bernard's Convent Sch
SUSSEX PL
SL1
Mus
CHERRY AVE
SUTTON AVE
LANGLEY RD
ALDERBURY RD
Coll
YEW TREE RD
Slough Gram Sch
Upton
Sch
Ryvers Sch
Langley Wood Sec Sch
TRELAWNEY AVE
LONDON RD
Kedermister Park
Liby
Long Close Sch
UPTON COURT RD
A2
1 RYE CT
2 GROVE CL
3 CHATHAM CT
4 EASTFIELD CL
5 PRIORS CL
6 MOUNTBATTEN CL
7 HORNBEAM GDNS
8 CHURCH VIEW
9 ELIZABETH CT
10 CLIFTON LODGE
11 LASCELLES HO
Upton Court Park
Castleview Comb Sch
Langley Gram Sch
Green Dr
Ditton Park
Conduit La
Longmead Bridge
SLOUGH RD
B3026
B376
M4
B470
A4
HIGH ST
98
99
00
4
81
3
80
2
79
1
78

43

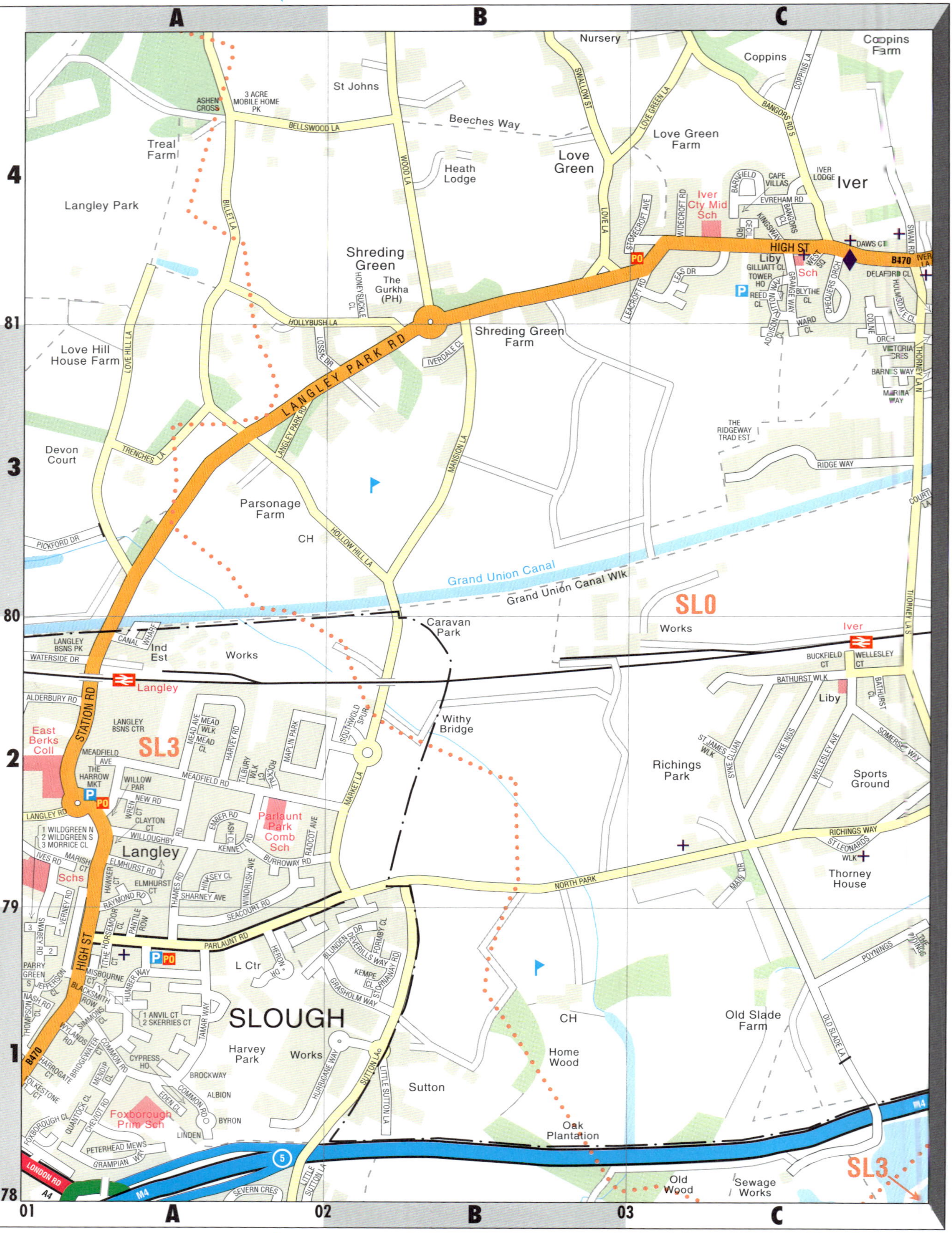

Nursery
Coppins
Coppins Farm
St Johns
Beeches Way
BELLSWOOD LA
3 ACRE MOBILE HOME PK
ASHEN CROSS
Treal Farm
Langley Park
Heath Lodge
Love Green
Love Green Farm
Iver
Iver Cty Mid Sch
HIGH ST
B470
Shreding Green
The Gurkha (PH)
HOLLYBUSH LA
LANGLEY PARK RD
Shreding Green Farm
Love Hill House Farm
Devon Court
Parsonage Farm
CH
THE RIDGEWAY TRAD EST
RIDGE WAY
Grand Union Canal
Grand Union Canal Wlk
SL0
Works
Caravan Park
Ind Est
Langley
Withy Bridge
East Berks Coll
SL3
Richings Park
Sports Ground
Parlaunt Park Comb Sch
NORTH PARK
RICHINGS WAY
Thorney House
SLOUGH
Harvey Park
L Ctr
Sutton
Home Wood
Old Slade Farm
Foxborough Prim Sch
Oak Plantation
Old Wood
Sewage Works
M4
A4
LONDON RD

43

69

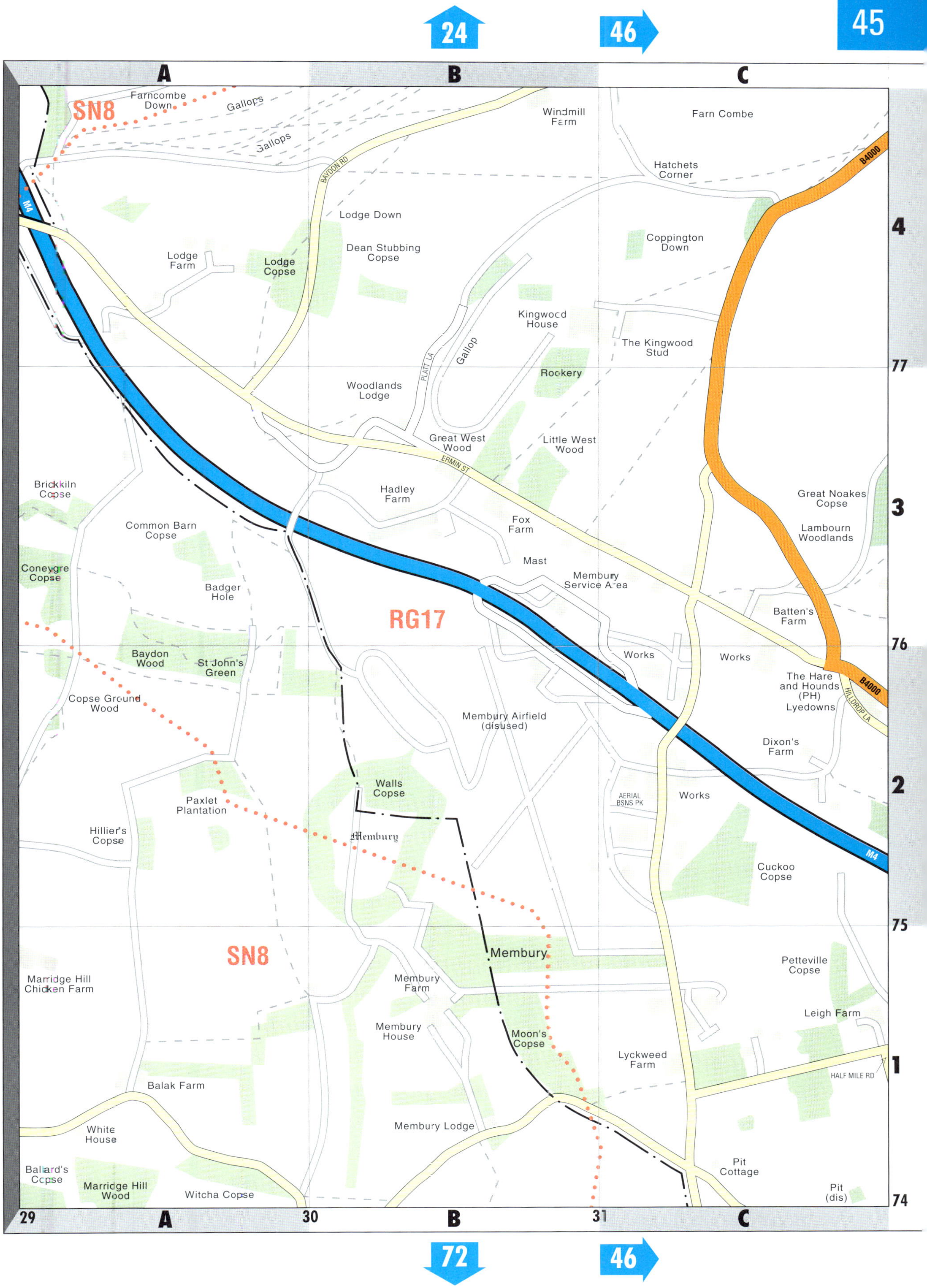
24
46
A
B
C
SN8
Farncombe Down
Gallops
Gallops
Windmill Farm
Farn Combe
Hatchets Corner
B4000
BAYDON RD
M4
Lodge Down
Dean Stubbing Copse
Lodge Farm
Lodge Copse
Coppington Down
4
Kingwood House
The Kingwood Stud
Gallop
PLATT LA
Rockery
77
Woodlands Lodge
Great West Wood
Little West Wood
ERMIN ST
Brickkiln Copse
Hadley Farm
Great Noakes Copse
3
Common Barn Copse
Fox Farm
Lambourn Woodlands
Mast
Coneygre Copse
Membury Service Area
Badger Hole
RG17
Batten's Farm
Baydon Wood
St John's Green
Works
Works
76
The Hare and Hounds (PH)
Lyedowns
B4000
HILLDROP LA
Copse Ground Wood
Membury Airfield (disused)
Dixon's Farm
Walls Copse
2
Paxlet Plantation
AERIAL BSNS PK
Works
Hillier's Copse
Membury
M4
Cuckoo Copse
75
SN8
Membury
Petteville Copse
Marridge Hill Chicken Farm
Membury Farm
Leigh Farm
Membury House
Moon's Copse
Lyckweed Farm
1
HALF MILE RD
Balak Farm
White House
Membury Lodge
Ballard's Copse
Marridge Hill Wood
Witcha Copse
Pit Cottage
Pit (dis)
74
29
A
30
B
31
C
72
46

45
25

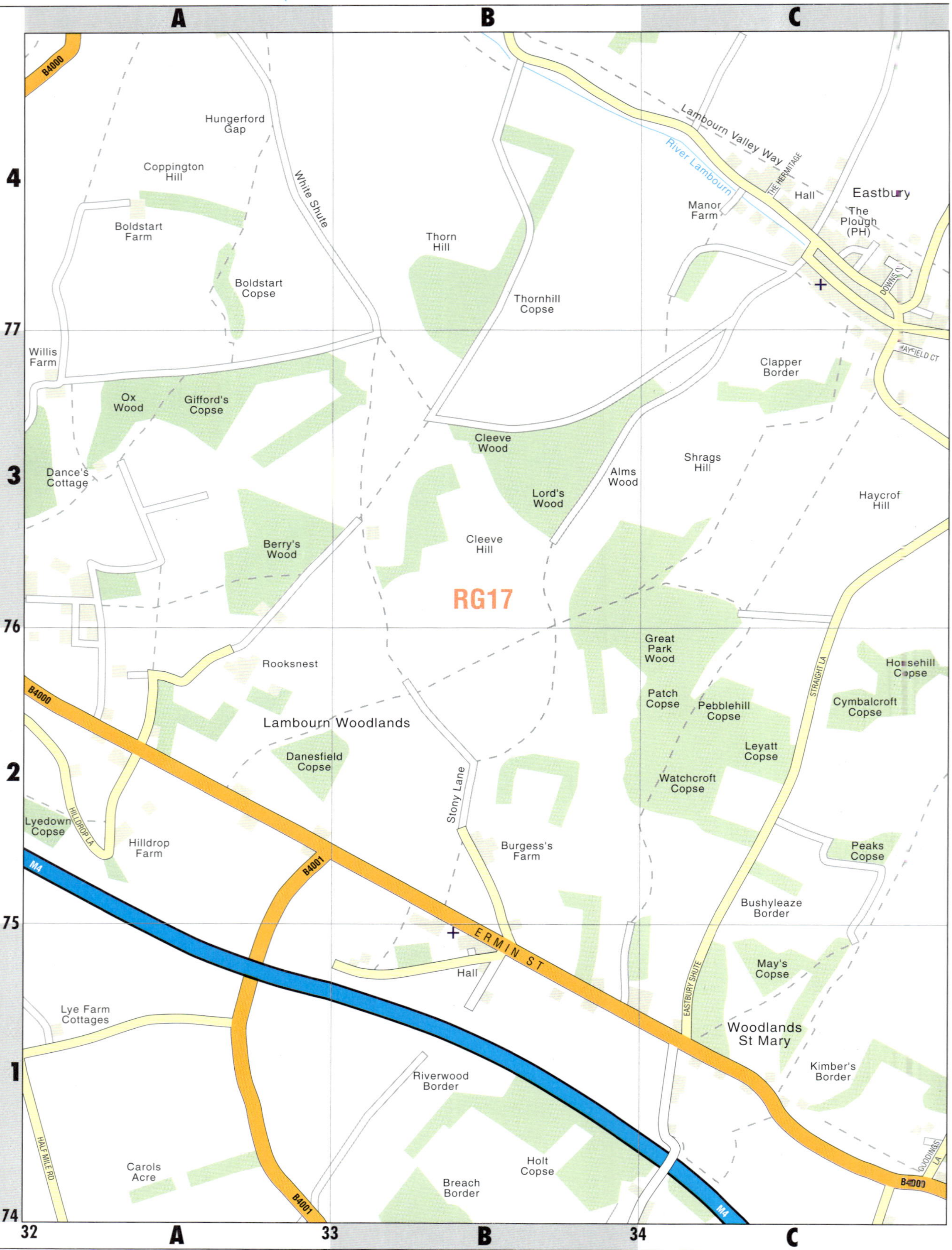
A
B
C
4
77
3
76
2
75
1
74
32
33
34
B4000
Hungerford Gap
Coppington Hill
White Shute
Boldstart Farm
Boldstart Copse
Willis Farm
Ox Wood
Gifford's Copse
Dance's Cottage
Berry's Wood
Thorn Hill
Thornhill Copse
Cleeve Wood
Lord's Wood
Cleeve Hill
Alms Wood
RG17
Lambourn Valley Way
River Lambourn
THE HERMITAGE
Manor Farm
Hall
Eastbury
The Plough (PH)
DOWNS CL
HAYFIELD CT
Clapper Border
Shrags Hill
Haycrof Hill
Great Park Wood
Patch Copse
Pebblehill Copse
Leyatt Copse
Watchcroft Copse
STRAIGHT LA
Horsehill Copse
Cymbalcroft Copse
Rooksnest
Lambourn Woodlands
Danesfield Copse
Stony Lane
Lyedown Copse
HILLDROP LA
Hilldrop Farm
Burgess's Farm
Peaks Copse
Bushyleaze Border
M4
B4001
ERMIN ST
Hall
May's Copse
EASTBURY SHUTE
Woodlands St Mary
Kimber's Border
Lye Farm Cottages
Riverwood Border
HALF MILE RD
Carols Acre
Holt Copse
Breach Border
GOODINGS LA
B4000

45
73

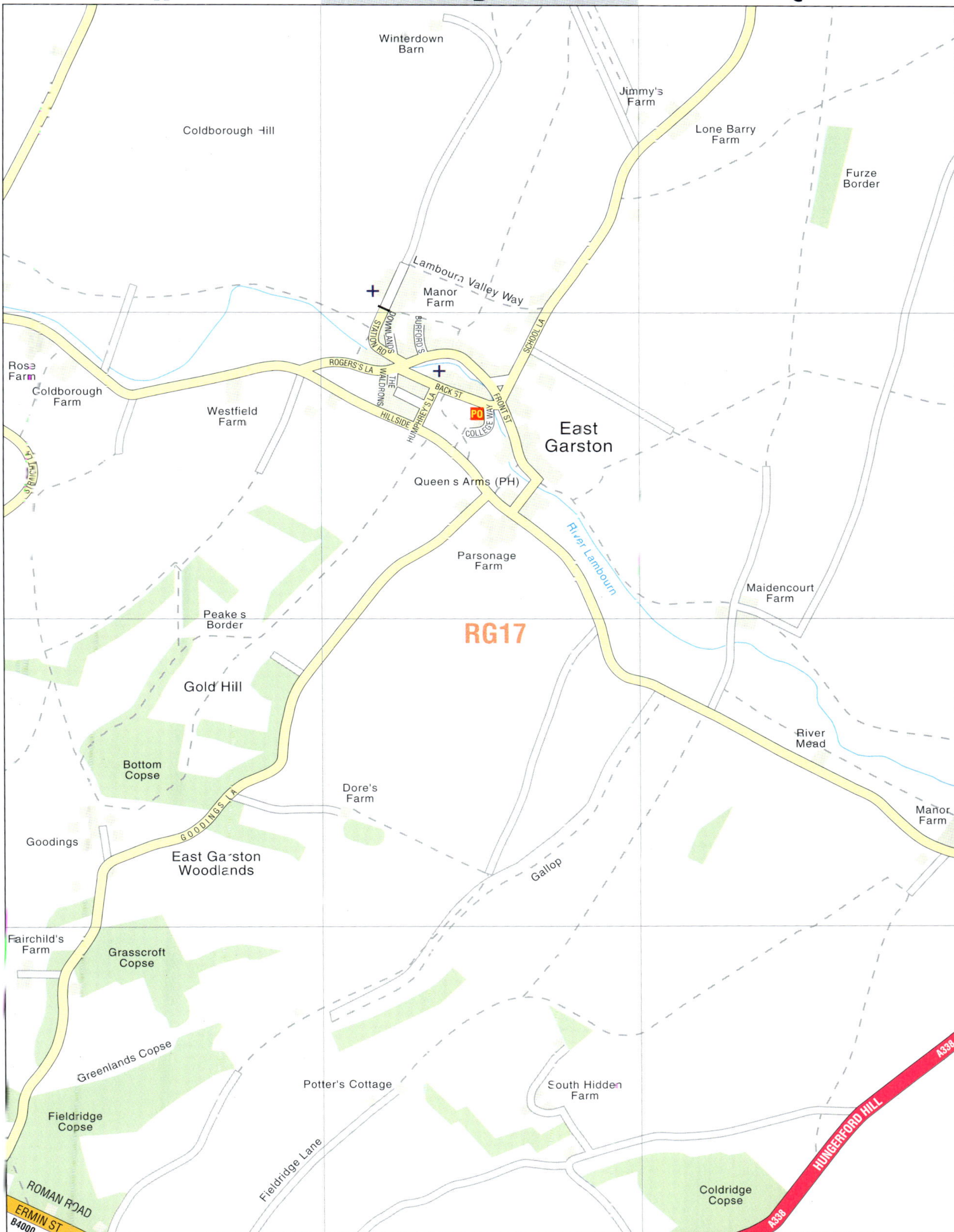
A
B
C
4
3
2
1
77
76
75
74
35
36
37
Winterdown Barn
Coldborough Hill
Jimmy's Farm
Lone Barry Farm
Furze Border
Lambourn Valley Way
Manor Farm
DOWNLANDS
STATION RD
BURFORD S
SCHOOL LA
ROGERS'S LA
WALDRONS
THE
BACK ST
FRONT ST
HILLSIDE
HUMPHREY'S LA
PO
COLLEGE WAY
Rose Farm
Coldborough Farm
Westfield Farm
East Garston
Queen s Arms (PH)
River Lambourn
Parsonage Farm
Maidencourt Farm
Peake s Border
RG17
Gold Hill
River Mead
Bottom Copse
Dore's Farm
Manor Farm
GOODINGS LA
Goodings
East Garston Woodlands
Gallop
Fairchild's Farm
Grasscroft Copse
Greenlands Copse
Potter's Cottage
South Hidden Farm
A338
HUNGERFORD HILL
Fieldridge Copse
Fieldridge Lane
Coldridge Copse
ROMAN ROAD
ERMIN ST
B4000
A
B
C

47
27

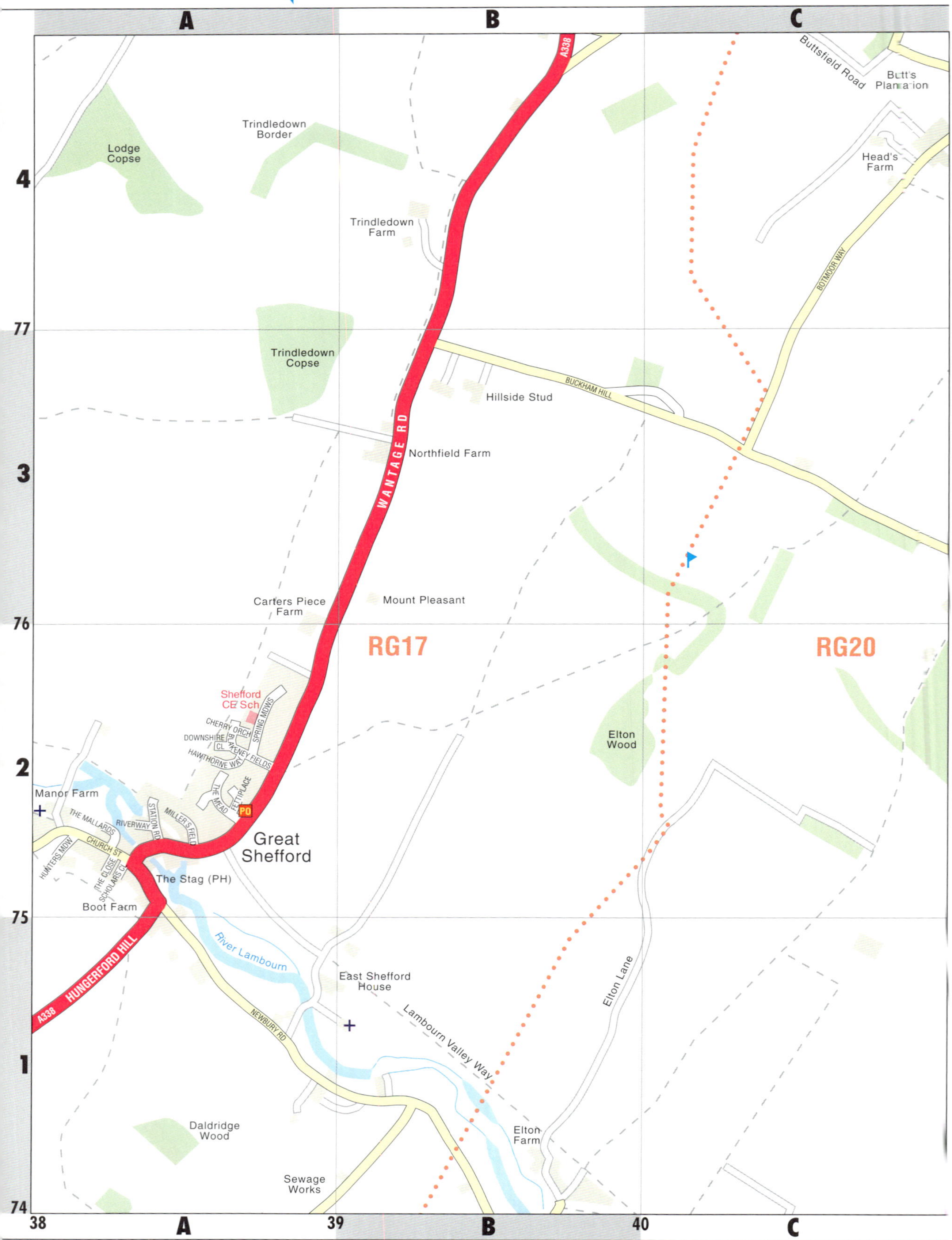
A
B
C
4
77
3
76
2
75
1
74
38
39
40
A338
Buttsfield Road
Butt's Plantation
Lodge Copse
Trindledown Border
Head's Farm
Trindledown Farm
BOTMOOR WAY
Trindledown Copse
BUCKHAM HILL
Hillside Stud
WANTAGE RD
Northfield Farm
Carters Piece Farm
Mount Pleasant
RG17
RG20
Shefford CE Sch
SPRING MDWS
CHERRY ORCH
DOWNSHIRE CL
BLAKENEY FIELDS
HAWTHORNE WAY
Elton Wood
Manor Farm
THE MEAD
FETTIPLACE
PO
THE MALLARDS
RIVERWAY
STATION RD
MILLER'S FIELD
Great Shefford
CHURCH ST
HUNTERS MDW
THE CLOSE
SCHOLARS CL
The Stag (PH)
Boot Farm
River Lambourn
HUNGERFORD HILL
East Shefford House
Elton Lane
NEWBURY RD
Lambourn Valley Way
Daldridge Wood
Elton Farm
Sewage Works

47
75

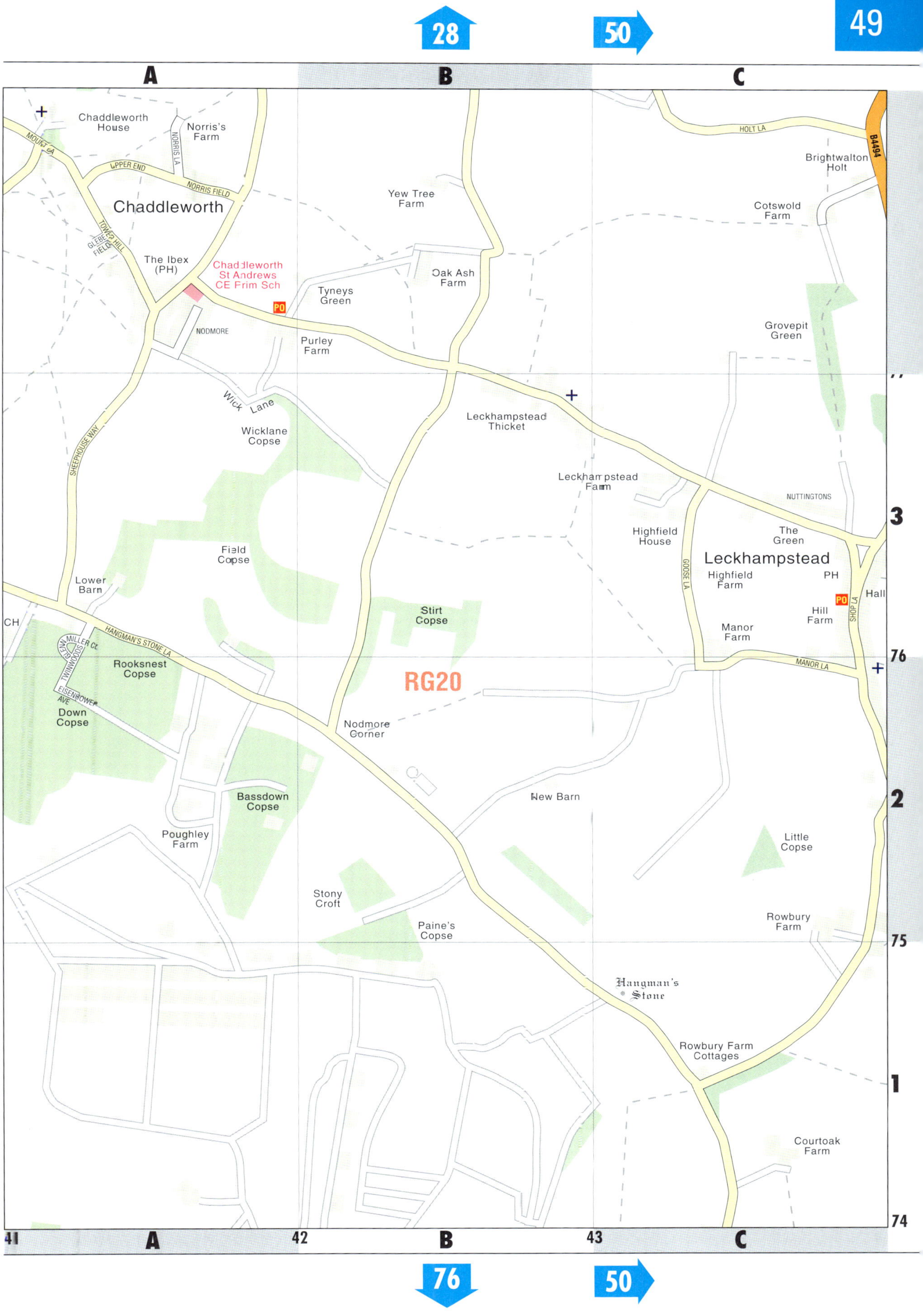
28
50
A
B
C
Chaddleworth House
Norris's Farm
MOUNT LA
UPPER END
NORRIS LA
NORRIS FIELD
Chaddleworth
TOWER HILL
GLEBE FIELD
The Ibex (PH)
Chaddleworth St Andrews CE Prim Sch
PO
NODMORE
Yew Tree Farm
Oak Ash Farm
Tyneys Green
Purley Farm
HOLT LA
B4494
Brightwalton Holt
Cotswold Farm
Grovepit Green
Wick Lane
Wicklane Copse
SHEEPHOUSE WAY
Leckhampstead Thicket
Leckhampstead Farm
NUTTINGTONS
Highfield House
The Green
Leckhampstead
Highfield Farm
PH
GOOSE LA
Field Copse
Lower Barn
Stirt Copse
Hill Farm
SHOP LA
Hall
Manor Farm
MANOR LA
CH
HANGMAN'S STONE LA
MILLER CL
TWINWOODS
EISENHOWER AVE
Rooksnest Copse
Down Copse
RG20
Nodmore Corner
Bassdown Copse
New Barn
Poughley Farm
Little Copse
Stony Croft
Paine's Copse
Rowbury Farm
Hangman's Stone
Rowbury Farm Cottages
Courtoak Farm
3
76
2
75
1
74
41
42
43
76
50

49
29

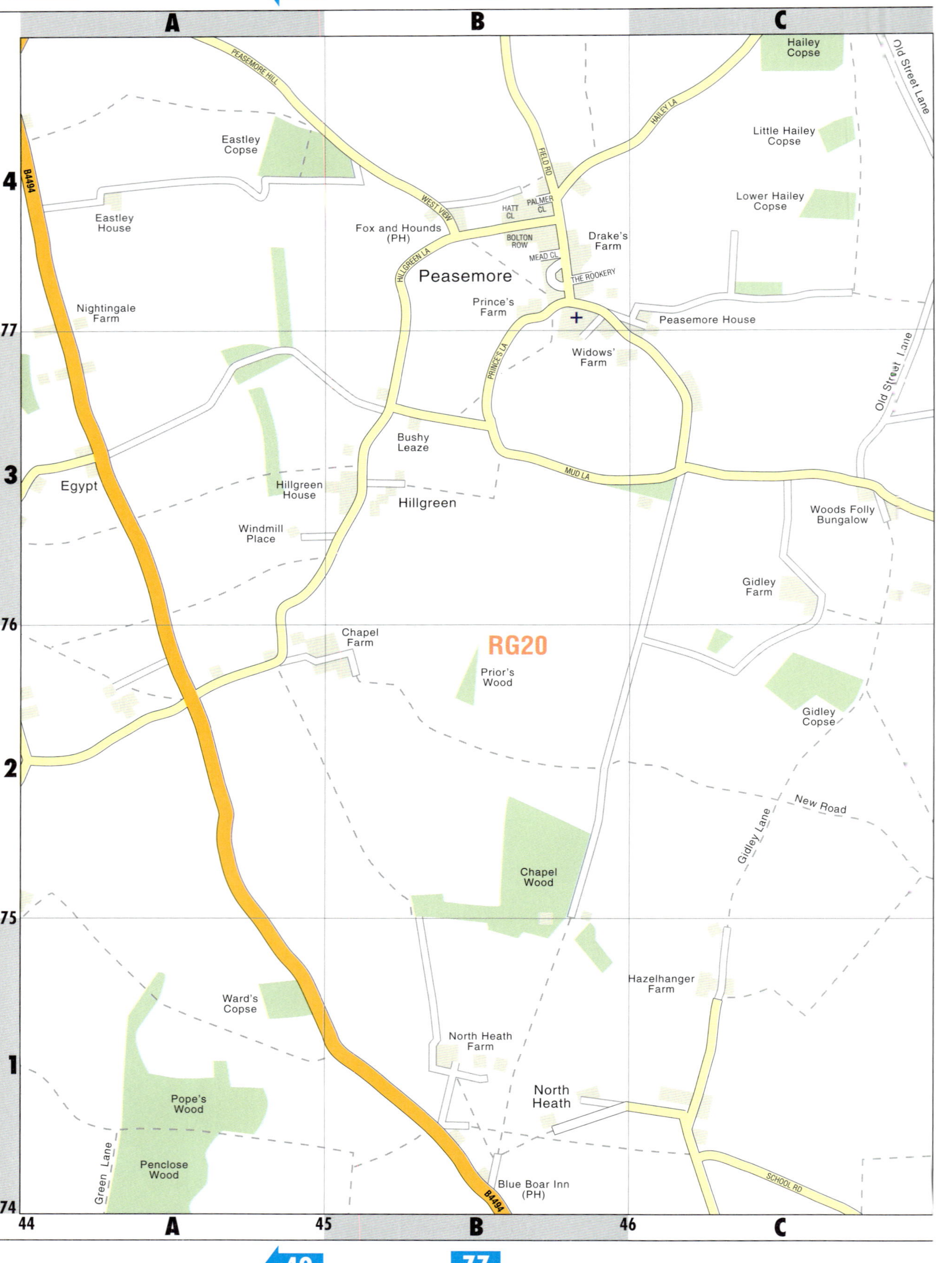
A
B
C
Hailey Copse
Old Street Lane
PEASEMORE HILL
HAILEY LA
Little Hailey Copse
Eastley Copse
FIELD RD
B4494
4
Lower Hailey Copse
WEST VIEW
HATT CL
PALMER CL
Eastley House
Fox and Hounds (PH)
BOLTON ROW
Drake's Farm
MEAD CL
HILLGREEN LA
Peasemore
THE ROOKERY
Prince's Farm
Nightingale Farm
Peasemore House
77
PRINCE'S LA
Widows' Farm
Old Street Lane
Bushy Leaze
3
MUD LA
Egypt
Hillgreen House
Hillgreen
Woods Folly Bungalow
Windmill Place
Gidley Farm
76
Chapel Farm
RG20
Prior's Wood
Gidley Copse
2
New Road
Gidley Lane
Chapel Wood
75
Hazelhanger Farm
Ward's Copse
North Heath Farm
1
North Heath
Pope's Wood
Green Lane
Penclose Wood
SCHOOL RD
Blue Boar Inn (PH)
B4494
74
44
45
46

49
77

30
52

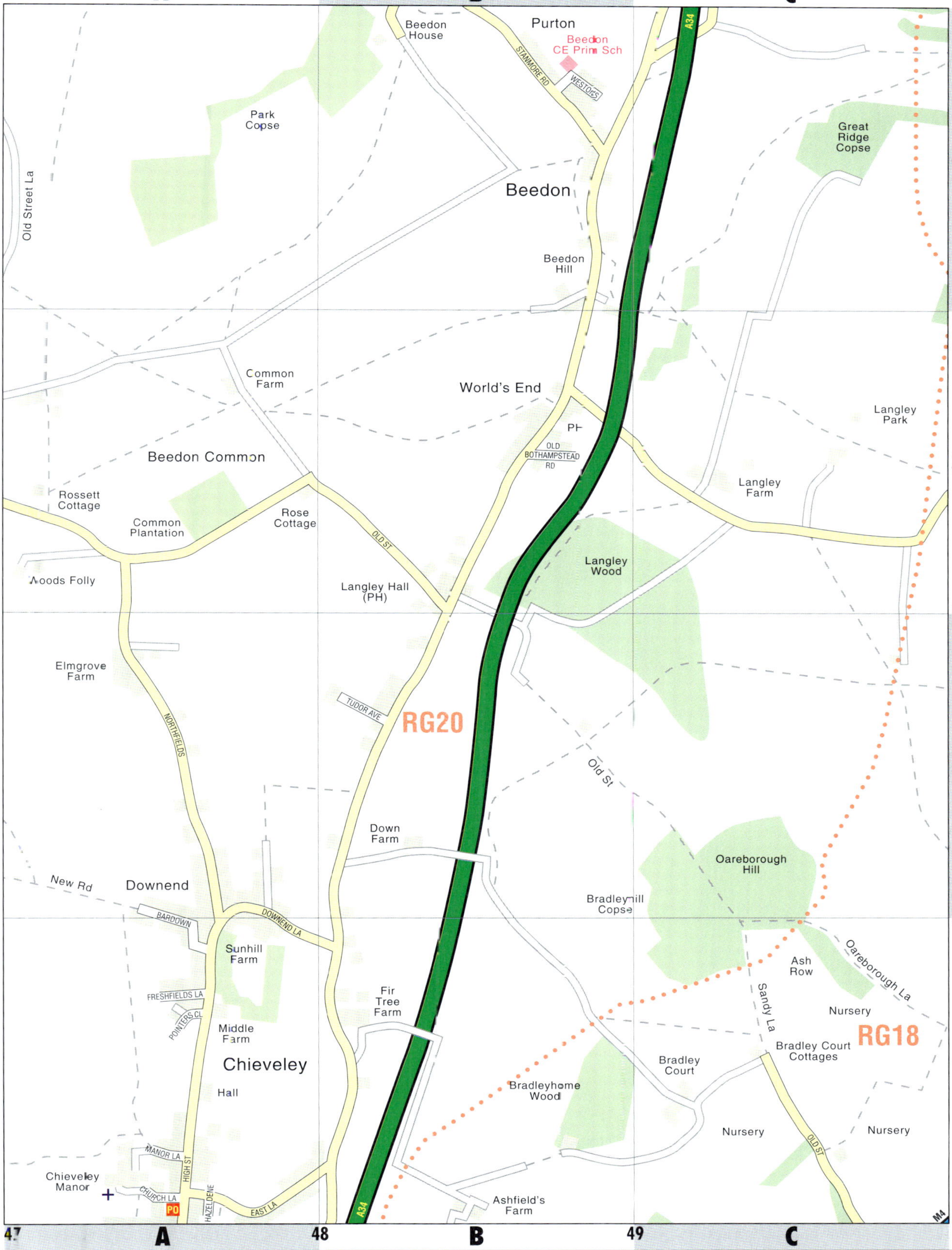
A
B
C
Beedon House
Purton
Beedon CE Prim Sch
STANMORE RD
WESTONS
A34
Park Copse
Great Ridge Copse
Old Street La
Beedon
Beedon Hill
4
77
Common Farm
World's End
PH
OLD BOTHAMPSTEAD RD
Langley Park
Beedon Common
3
Rossett Cottage
Common Plantation
Rose Cottage
Langley Farm
OLD ST
Woods Folly
Langley Wood
Langley Hall (PH)
76
Elmgrove Farm
TUDOR AVE
RG20
NORTHFIELDS
Old St
2
Down Farm
Oareborough Hill
New Rd
Downend
Bradleyhill Copse
BARDOWN
DOWNEND LA
75
Sunhill Farm
Ash Row
Oareborough La
Fir Tree Farm
Sandy La
Nursery
FRESHFIELDS LA
POINTERS CL
Middle Farm
RG18
Bradley Court Cottages
Chieveley
Bradley Court
1
Hall
Bradleyhome Wood
Nursery
Nursery
MANOR LA
HIGH ST
Chieveley Manor
CHURCH LA
HAZELDENE
EAST LA
PO
Ashfield's Farm
M4
74
47
48
49

78
52

51
31

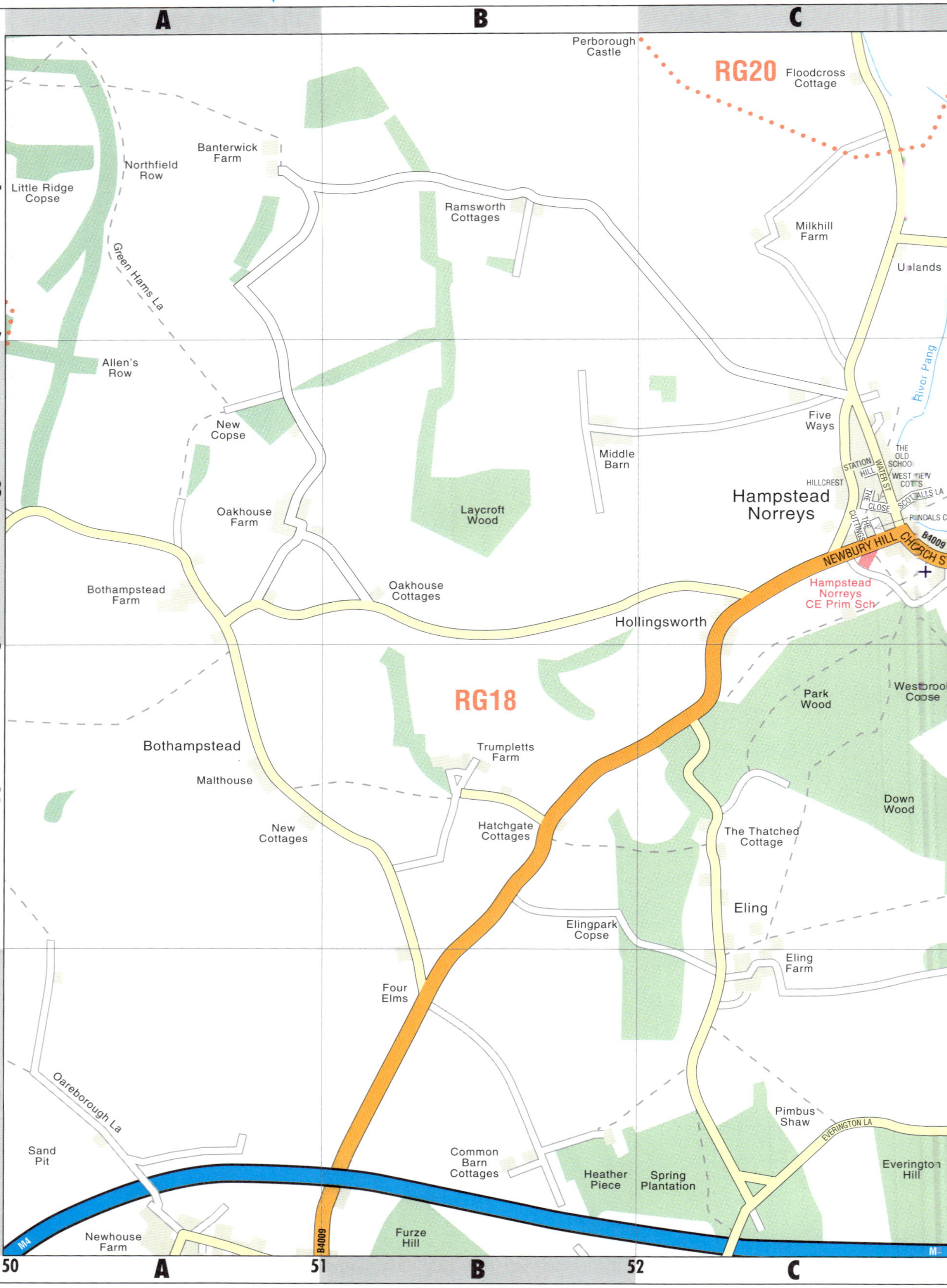
A
B
C
4
77
3
76
2
75
1
74
50
51
52
Perborough Castle
RG20
Floodcross Cottage
Banterwick Farm
Northfield Row
Little Ridge Copse
Ramsworth Cottages
Milkhill Farm
Uplands
Green Hams La
Allen's Row
River Pang
Five Ways
New Copse
Middle Barn
Laycroft Wood
Oakhouse Farm
Hampstead Norreys
STATION HILL
WATER ST
HILLCREST
THE CLOSE
THE CUTTINGS
THE OLD SCHOOL
WEST VIEW COTTS
SCOTTALLS LA
RANDALS CL
B4009
NEWBURY HILL
CHURCH ST
Hampstead Norreys CE Prim Sch
Bothampstead Farm
Oakhouse Cottages
Hollingsworth
RG18
Park Wood
Westbrook Copse
Bothampstead
Trumpletts Farm
Malthouse
Down Wood
New Cottages
Hatchgate Cottages
The Thatched Cottage
Eling
Elingpark Copse
Eling Farm
Four Elms
Oareborough La
Pimbus Shaw
EVERINGTON LA
Sand Pit
Common Barn Cottages
Heather Piece
Spring Plantation
Everington Hill
M4
Newhouse Farm
Furze Hill

51
79

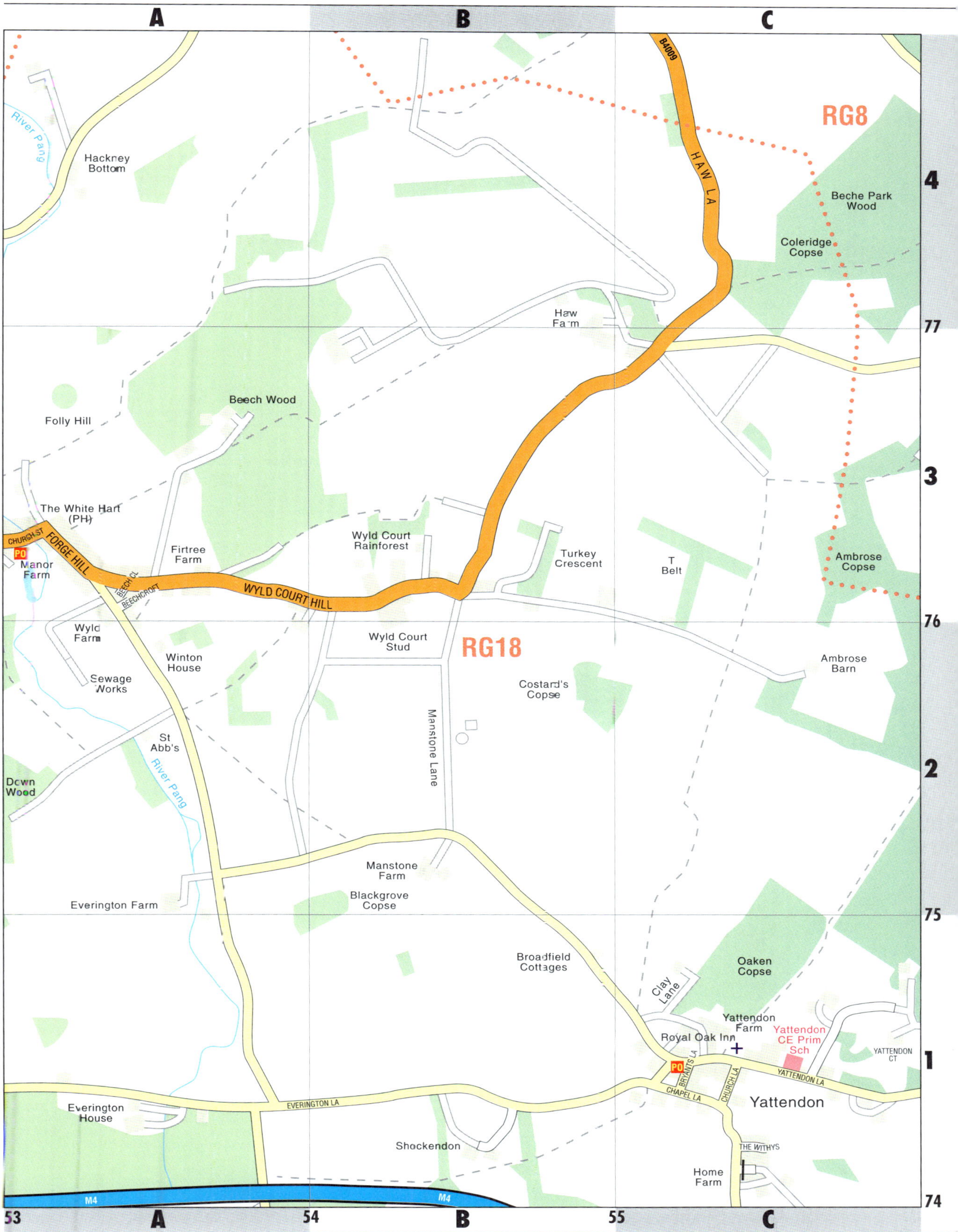
A
B
C
4
77
3
76
2
75
1
74
53
54
55
RG8
RG18
B4009
HAW LA
Hackney Bottom
River Pang
Beche Park Wood
Coleridge Copse
Haw Farm
Beech Wood
Folly Hill
The White Hart (PH)
CHURCH ST
FORGE HILL
PO
Manor Farm
Firtree Farm
BEECH CL
BEECHCROFT
WYLD COURT HILL
Wyld Court Rainforest
Turkey Crescent
T Belt
Ambrose Copse
Wyld Farm
Wyld Court Stud
Winton House
Sewage Works
Ambrose Barn
Costard's Copse
Manstone Lane
St Abb's
Down Wood
Manstone Farm
Blackgrove Copse
Everington Farm
Broadfield Cottages
Clay Lane
Oaken Copse
Yattendon Farm
Royal Oak Inn
Yattendon CE Prim Sch
YATTENDON CT
BRYANTS LA
CHURCH LA
YATTENDON LA
CHAPEL LA
Yattendon
EVERINGTON LA
Everington House
Shockendon
THE WITHYS
Home Farm
M4

53
33

A
B
C
Hartridge Farm
Hartridge Cottages
Tombhill Row
Hare Green
The Row
Broom Wood
Bullard's Copse
HATTON HILL
Eastfield Wood
Grim's Ditch
Bowler's Copse
Dark Copse
Ashampstead Green
Hartridge Lye Wood
CHAPEL LA
NOAKES HILL
PO
Longcroft Shaw
DOG LA
Ashampstead
CHURCH LA
FLOWERS PIECE
HOLLY LA
White Hill
Drift Hill
Rushdown Farm
Drift Farm
Hill Corner
Rush Down
James's Copse
Stubbles
Hanging Close Row
CAPTAINS GORSE
Westcroft Shaw
PALMER'S HILL
New Inn (PH)
WHITEMOOR LA
TENAPLAS DR
Pinfold Lane
Clayhanger Farm
Factory
KILN RIDE
Quick's Green
Greenaway's Copse
Flower's Copse
Pyt House
RG8
Captain's Gorse
Lay Fields
Young Plantation
Sodom Lane
Lye Wood
PYKE'S HILL
Pinfold Lane
Calvesleys Farm
Child's Court Farm
Mumsgrove Copse
SUCK'S LA
Home Copse
Ashampstead Common
Old Park
RG18
Bushy Copse
Gravelpit Copse
Challengehook Plantation
YATTENDON LA
Slade Gate
Clack's Copse
Yattendon Park
Mapletons
Burnthill Common
Burnt Hill
The Nut & Bolt (PH)
Strouds
Withy Copse
Burnthill House
Broomhill Copse
Upperlands Copse
4
77
3
76
2
75
1
74
56
57
58

53
81

34
56

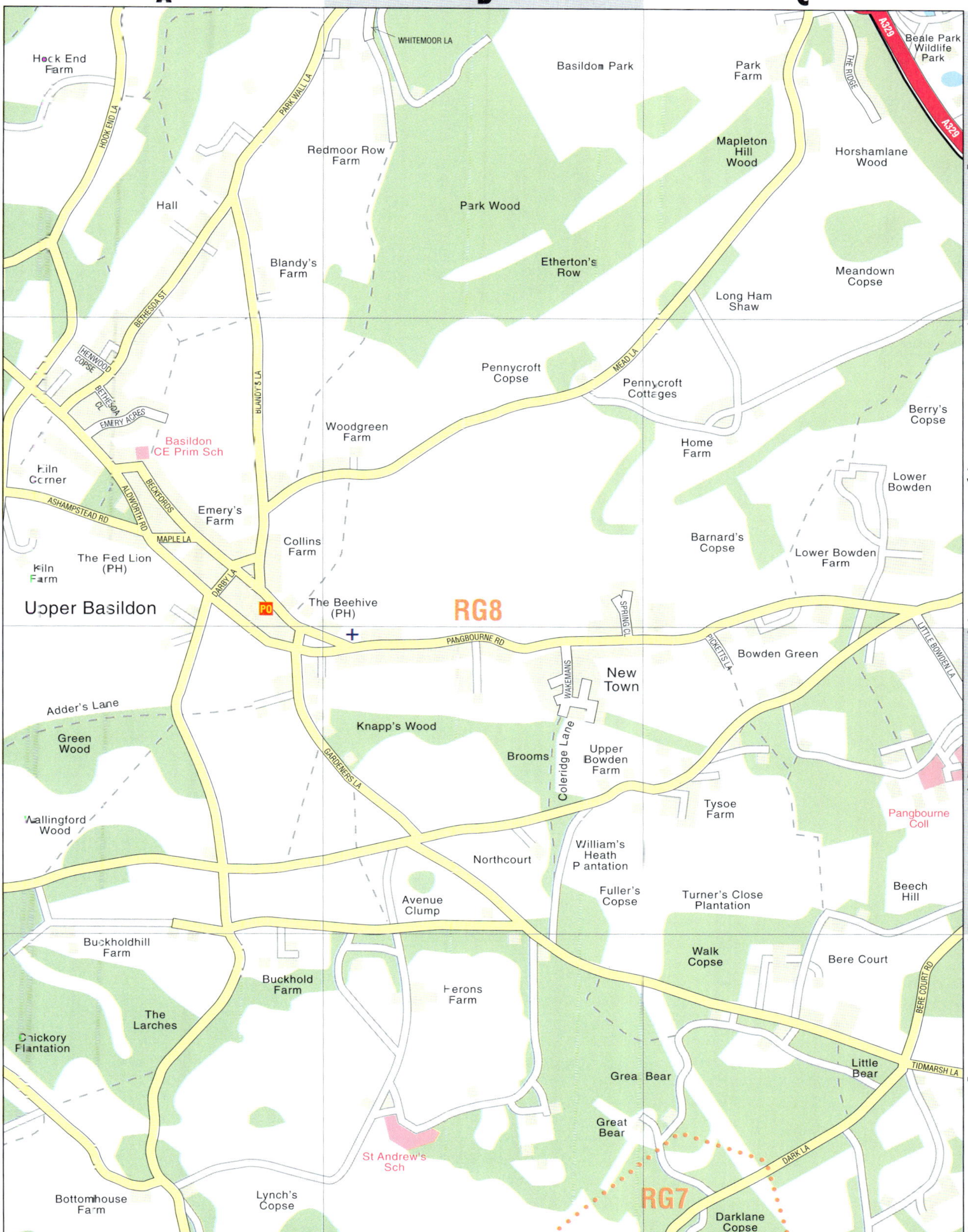
A
B
C
Hook End Farm
WHITEMOOR LA
Basildon Park
Park Farm
THE RIDGE
A329
Beale Park Wildlife Park
HOOK END LA
PARK WALL LA
Redmoor Row Farm
Mapleton Hill Wood
Horshamlane Wood
4
Hall
Park Wood
Blandy's Farm
Etherton's Row
Meandown Copse
BETHESDA ST
Long Ham Shaw
77
HENWOOD COPSE
BETHESDA CL
EMERY ACRES
BLANDY'S LA
Pennycroft Copse
MEAD LA
Pennycroft Cottages
Berry's Copse
Woodgreen Farm
Basildon CE Prim Sch
Home Farm
Kiln Corner
3
Lower Bowden
ASHAMPSTEAD RD
ALDWORTH RD
BECKFORDS
Emery's Farm
MAPLE LA
Collins Farm
Barnard's Copse
Lower Bowden Farm
The Red Lion (PH)
Kiln Farm
DARBY LA
Upper Basildon
PO
The Beehive (PH)
RG8
SPRING CL
76
PANGBOURNE RD
PICKETTS LA
Bowden Green
LITTLE BOWDEN LA
WAKEMANS
New Town
Adder's Lane
Knapp's Wood
Green Wood
Coleridge Lane
Brooms
Upper Bowden Farm
GARDENERS LA
2
Tysoe Farm
Pangbourne Coll
Wallingford Wood
William's Heath Plantation
Northcourt
Fuller's Copse
Turner's Close Plantation
Beech Hill
Avenue Clump
75
Buckholdhill Farm
Walk Copse
Bere Court
Buckhold Farm
Herons Farm
BERE COURT RD
The Larches
Chickory Plantation
Little Bear
TIDMARSH LA
1
Great Bear
Great Bear
DARK LA
St Andrew's Sch
Bottomhouse Farm
Lynch's Copse
RG7
Darklane Copse
74
59
60
61

82
56

55

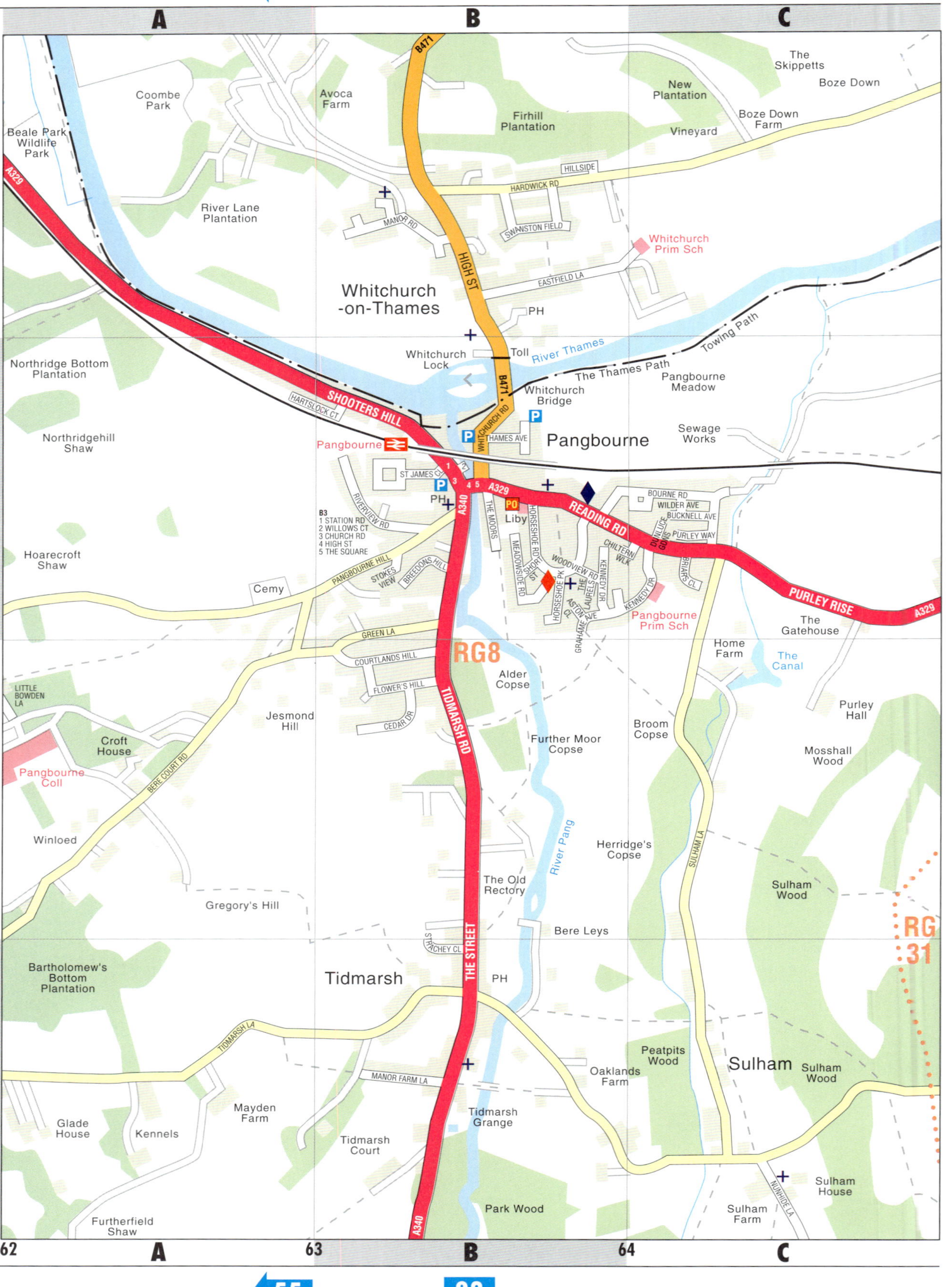
A
B
C
4
77
3
76
2
75
1
74
62
63
64
Coombe Park
Avoca Farm
Beale Park Wildlife Park
A329
Firhill Plantation
The Skippetts
Boze Down
New Plantation
Boze Down Farm
Vineyard
B471
HILLSIDE
HARDWICK RD
River Lane Plantation
MANOR RD
SWANSTON FIELD
Whitchurch Prim Sch
HIGH ST
EASTFIELD LA
Whitchurch -on-Thames
PH
Towing Path
River Thames
Toll
Whitchurch Lock
The Thames Path
Pangbourne Meadow
Northridge Bottom Plantation
Whitchurch Bridge
SHOOTERS HILL
HARTSLOCK CT
WHITCHURCH RD
Northridgehill Shaw
Pangbourne
THAMES AVE
Sewage Works
ST JAMES CL
A329
READING RD
BOURNE RD
WILDER AVE
BUCKNELL AVE
PURLEY WAY
B3
1 STATION RD
2 WILLOWS CT
3 CHURCH RD
4 HIGH ST
5 THE SQUARE
RIVERVIEW RD
A340
THE MOORS
PO
Liby
HORSESHOE RD
MEADOWSIDE RD
SHORT ST
WOODVIEW RD
CHILTERN WLK
DUNLUCE GDNS
BRIARS CL
Hoarecroft Shaw
PANGBOURNE HILL
STOKES VIEW
BREEDONS HILL
HORSESHOE PK
THE LAURELS
ASTON CL
KENNEDY DR
GRAHAME AVE
Cemy
Pangbourne Prim Sch
PURLEY RISE
A329
The Gatehouse
GREEN LA
RG8
Home Farm
The Canal
COURTLANDS HILL
FLOWER'S HILL
Alder Copse
LITTLE BOWDEN LA
Jesmond Hill
CEDAR DR
TIDMARSH RD
Broom Copse
Purley Hall
Croft House
Further Moor Copse
Mosshall Wood
Pangbourne Coll
BERE COURT RD
Winloed
River Pang
Herridge's Copse
SULHAM LA
The Old Rectory
Gregory's Hill
Sulham Wood
Bere Leys
STRACHEY CL
THE STREET
RG 31
Bartholomew's Bottom Plantation
Tidmarsh
TIDMARSH LA
Peatpits Wood
Oaklands Farm
Sulham
Sulham Wood
MANOR FARM LA
Mayden Farm
Glade House
Kennels
Tidmarsh Grange
Tidmarsh Court
Sulham House
NUNHIDE LA
Sulham Farm
Furtherfield Shaw
Park Wood

55

83

58

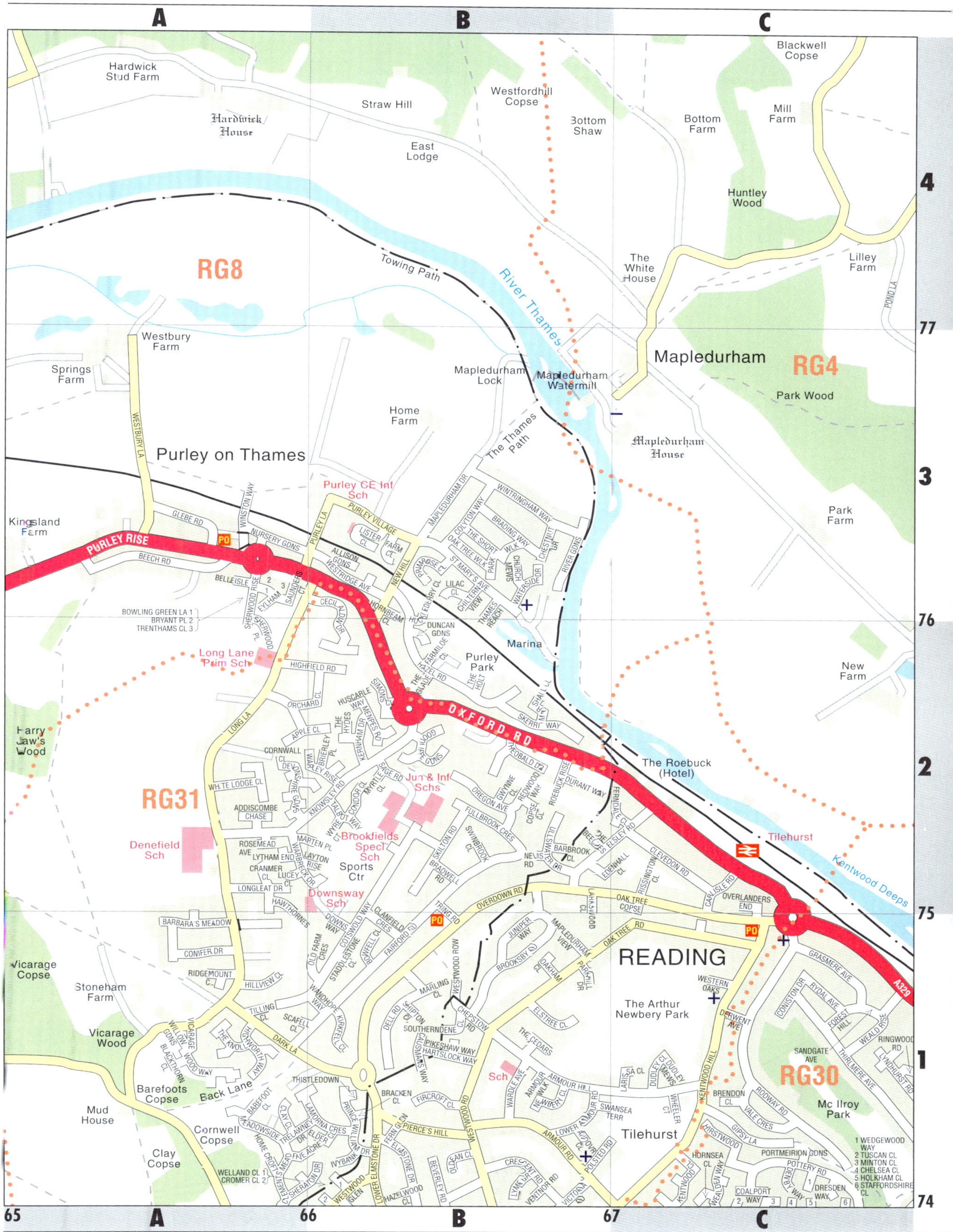
A
B
C
Hardwick Stud Farm
Hardwick House
Straw Hill
Westfordhill Copse
Bottom Shaw
Bottom Farm
Blackwell Copse
Mill Farm
East Lodge
Huntley Wood
RG8
Towing Path
River Thames
The White House
Lilley Farm
POND LA
Westbury Farm
Springs Farm
Mapledurham Lock
Mapledurham Watermill
Mapledurham
RG4
Park Wood
Home Farm
WESTBURY LA
Purley on Thames
The Thames Path
Mapledurham House
Purley CE Inf Sch
Park Farm
Kingsland Farm
PURLEY RISE
PO
GLEBE RD
BEECH RD
BELLEISLE
NURSERY GDNS
WINSTON WAY
PURLEY LA
PURLEY VILLAGE
LISTER CL
FARM CL
ALLISON GDNS
WESTRIDGE AVE
NEW HILL
MAPLEDURHAM DR
COLYTON WAY
WINTRINGHAM WAY
BRADING WAY
THE SHORT
OAK TREE WLK
ST MARY'S AVE
CHESTNUT GR
RIVER GDNS
LILAC CL
CHILTERN VIEW
THAMES REACH
CHURCH MEWS
WATERSIDE DR
BOWLING GREEN LA 1
BRYANT PL 2
TRENTHAMS CL 3
SHERWOOD RISE
EYLHAM
SAUNDERS CT
CECIL ALDIN DR
HORNBEAM CL
DUNCAN GDNS
FARMILOE CL
HAZEL RD
Marina
Purley Park
THE HOLT
Long Lane Prim Sch
HIGHFIELD RD
ORCHARD CL
HUSCARLE WAY
SIMONS LA
MEMPES RD
KERNHAM DR
THE HYDES
SKERRIT WAY
OXFORD RD
LONG LA
Harry Law's Wood
APPLE CL
CORNWALL CL
DEVONSHIRE GDNS
WARLEY RISE
BRIERLEY PL
GOODRICH GDNS
Jun & Inf Schs
THEOBALD DR
GWYNNE CL
REDWOOD WAY
ROEBUCK RISE
DURANT WAY
FERNDALE CL
The Roebuck (Hotel)
RG31
WHITE LODGE CL
ADDISCOMBE CHASE
KNOWSLEY RD
OREGON AVE
FULLBROOK CRES
Tilehurst
Kentwood Deeps
Denefield Sch
ROSEMEAD AVE
LYTHAM END
MARTEN PL
LAYTON RISE
Brookfields Specl Sch
Sports Ctr
CRANMER CL
LUCEY CL
LONGLEAT DR
SKILTON RD
SWINBROOK CL
NEVIS RD
BARBROOK CL
ELSLEY RD
CLEVEDON RD
LEDENHALL CL
RISSINGTON CL
CARLISLE RD
OVERLANDERS END
HAWTHORNES
Downsway Sch
BRADWELL RD
OVERDOWN RD
OAK TREE COPSE
BARBARA'S MEADOW
DOWNS WAY
CLANFIELD CRES
TRING RD
OAK TREE RD
CONIFER DR
OLD FARM CRES
COTSWOLD WAY
FAIRFORD RD
JUNIPER WAY
MAPLEDURHAM VIEW
Vicarage Copse
RIDGEMOUNT CL
HILLVIEW CL
STADDLESTONE CL
WESTWOOD ROW
BROOKSBY RD
OAKHAM CL
PARKHILL DR
READING
WESTERN OAKS
GRASMERE AVE
A329
Stoneham Farm
WANDHOPE WAY
KIRKFELL CL
MARLING CL
CHEPSTOW RD
The Arthur Newbery Park
CONISTON DR
RYDAL AVE
FOREST HILL
WEALD RISE
TILLING CL
SCAFELL CL
DELL RD
SOUTHERNDENE CL
ELSTREE CL
DERWENT AVE
Vicarage Wood
THE KNOLL
HIGHWORTH WAY
DARK LA
PIKESHAW WAY
HARTSLOCK WAY
THE CEDARS
RINGWOOD RD
SANDGATE AVE
LYNDHURST RD
THIRLMERE AVE
WOODGAMS WAY
Sch
ARMOUR HILL
LARISSA CL
DUDLEY MEWS
KENTWOOD HILL
RG30
Barefoots Copse
Back Lane
THISTLEDOWN
BRACKEN CL
FIRCROFT CL
WARDLE AVE
NEWBERY CL
SWANSEA TERR
WHEELER CT
BRENDON CL
RODWAY RD
Mc Ilroy Park
Mud House
BAREFOOT CL
CLAY CL
LAMORNA CRES
PRINCE WILLIAM DR
FERN GLEN
PIERCE'S HILL
WESTWOOD RD
ARMOUR RD
LOWER ARMOUR RD
Tilehurst
VALE CRES
GIPSY LA
Cornwall Copse
MEADOWSIDE
HOME CROFT
TRELAWNEY DR
ELDER CL
FIVE ACRE
IVYBANK
ELMSTONE DR
HIRSTWOOD
HORNSEA CL
PORTMEIRION GDNS
POTTERY RD
1 WEDGEWOOD WAY
2 TUSCAN CL
3 MINTON CL
4 CHELSEA CL
5 HOLKHAM CL
6 STAFFORDSHIRE CL
Clay Copse
WELLAND CL 1
CROMER CL 2
SHERATON DR
WESTWOOD GLEN
LOWER ELMSTONE DR
HAZELWOOD CL
BEVERLEY RD
OLDEAN CL
CRESCENT RD
VENTNOR RD
VICTORIA RD
POLSTED RD
KENTWOOD CL
WEALDON WAY
COALPORT WAY
DRESDEN WAY
4
77
3
76
2
75
1
74
65
66
67

84
58

57

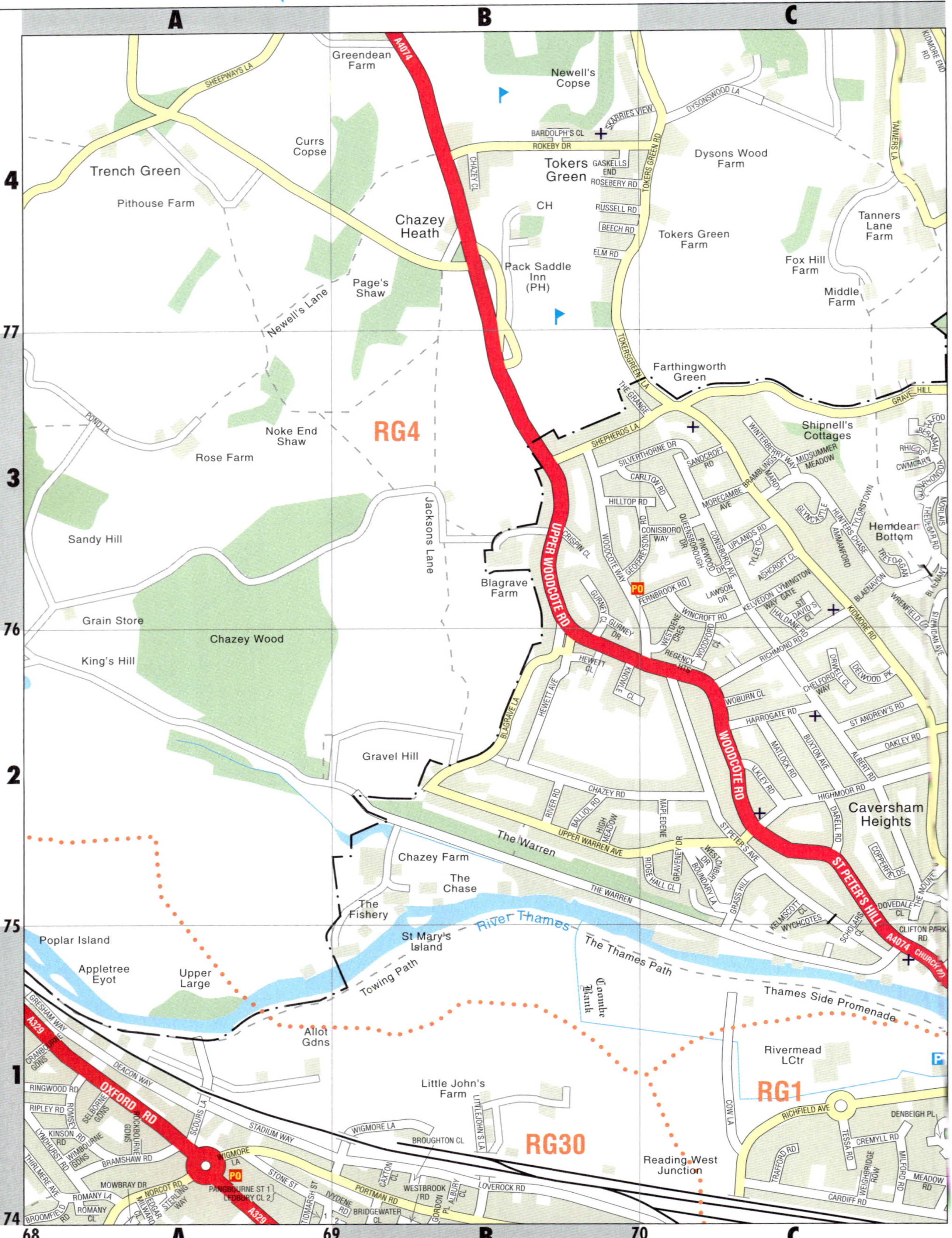
A
B
C
4
77
3
76
2
75
1
74
68
69
70
A4074
Greendean Farm
Newell's Copse
Sheepways La
Dysonswood La
Kidmore End Rd
Tanners La
Skarries View
Bardolph's Cl
Rokeby Dr
Curs Copse
Trench Green
Pithouse Farm
Chazey Cl
Tokers Green
Gaskells End
Rosebery Rd
Tokers Green Rd
Dysons Wood Farm
CH
Russell Rd
Beech Rd
Elm Rd
Chazey Heath
Tokers Green Farm
Tanners Lane Farm
Fox Hill Farm
Pack Saddle Inn (PH)
Page's Shaw
Newell's Lane
Middle Farm
Tokersgreen La
Farthingworth Green
The Grange
Grave Hill
Pond La
Shipnell's Cottages
Noke End Shaw
RG4
Shepherds La
Silverthorne Dr
Sandcroft Rd
Winterberry Way
Midsummer Meadow
Rose Farm
Carlton Rd
Brambling Mardy
Hilltop Rd
Morecambe Ave
Glyncastle
Tylorstown
Sandy Hill
Jacksons Lane
Upper Woodcote Rd
Crispin Cl
Woodcote Way
Geoffreyson Rd
Conisboro Way
Queensborough Dr
Conisboro Ave
Pinewood Dr
Uplands Rd
Tyler Cl
Hunters Chase
Ammanford
Hemdean Bottom
Ashcroft Cl
Lymington Gate
Treforgan
Blaenavon
Blagrave Farm
PO
Fernbrook Rd
Lawson Dr
Kelvedon Way
St David's Cl
Wrenfield Dr
Grain Store
Gurney Cl
Gurney Dr
Westdene Cres
Wincroft Rd
Haldane Rd
Kidmore Rd
Chazey Wood
Woodford Cl
Regency Hts
Richmond Rd
King's Hill
Hewett Cl
Knowle Cl
Orwell Cl
Delwood Pk
Hewett Ave
Woburn Cl
Chelford Way
St Andrew's Rd
Blagrave La
Harrogate Rd
Oakley Rd
Woodcote Rd
Matlock Rd
Buxton Ave
Albert Rd
Gravel Hill
Ilkley Rd
Chazey Rd
River Rd
Balliol Rd
High Meadow
Mapledene
Highmoor Rd
Caversham Heights
Darell Rd
The Warren
Upper Warren Ave
St Peter's Ave
St Peter's Hill
Chazey Farm
Ridge Hall Cl
Gravelly Dr
Westonbirt Dr
Boundary La
Copperfield
The Chase
The Warren
Grass Hill
Dovedale Cl
The Mount
The Fishery
Kelmscott Cl
Wychcotes
Scholars Cl
Clifton Park Rd
River Thames
Poplar Island
St Mary's Island
The Thames Path
A4074
Church Rd
Appletree Eyot
Upper Large
Towing Path
Coombe Bank
Thames Side Promenade
Gresham Way
A329
Allot Gdns
Rivermead LCtr
Granby Gdns
Deacon Way
Oxford Rd
Ringwood Rd
Little John's Farm
RG1
Ripley Rd
Romsey Rd
Selborne Gdns
Rockbourne Gdns
Scours La
Richfield Ave
Denbeigh Pl
Kinson Rd
Wimborne Gdns
Stadium Way
Littlejohn's La
Cow La
Tessa Rd
Cremyll Rd
Lyndhurst Rd
Bramshaw Rd
Wigmore La
Broughton Cl
RG30
Trafford Rd
Weighbridge Row
Milford Rd
Thirlmere Ave
Mowbray Dr
Norcot Rd
Stone St
Caxton Cl
Reading West Junction
Meadow Rd
Romany La
Sterling Way
Pangbourne St
Ledbury Cl
Portman Rd
Westbrook Rd
Albury Cl
Loverock Rd
Cardiff Rd
Broomfield Rd
Romany Cl
Edgar Milward Cl
Tidmarsh St
Ivydene Rd
Bridgewater Cl
Gordon Pl
P

57

85

60

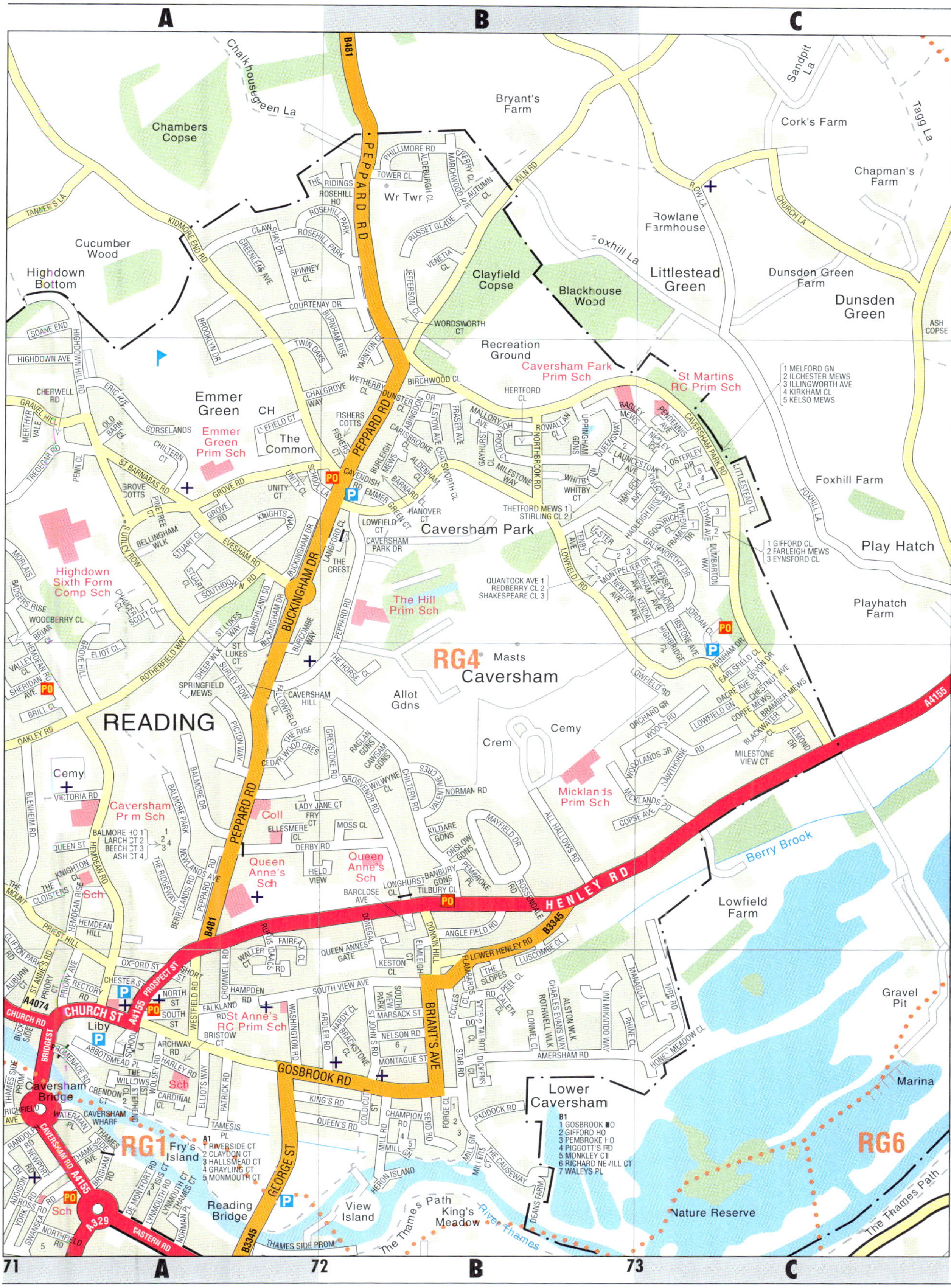
READING
Caversham
Caversham Park
Emmer Green
Littlestead Green
Dunsden Green
Lower Caversham
RG4
RG1
RG6
PEPPARD RD
BUCKINGHAM DR
HENLEY RD
CHURCH ST
GOSBROOK RD
GEORGE ST
BRIANT'S AVE
River Thames
The Thames Path
Caversham Bridge
Reading Bridge
View Island
Fry's Island
King's Meadow
Nature Reserve
Marina
Berry Brook
Lowfield Farm
Play Hatch
Playhatch Farm
Foxhill Farm
Cork's Farm
Chapman's Farm
Bryant's Farm
Rowlane Farmhouse
Chambers Copse
Cucumber Wood
Clayfield Copse
Blackhouse Wood
Highdown Bottom
Recreation Ground
Highdown Sixth Form Comp Sch
Emmer Green Prim Sch
Caversham Park Prim Sch
St Martins RC Prim Sch
The Hill Prim Sch
Micklands Prim Sch
Caversham Prim Sch
Queen Anne's Sch
St Anne's RC Prim Sch
Gravel Pit

86
60

59
35

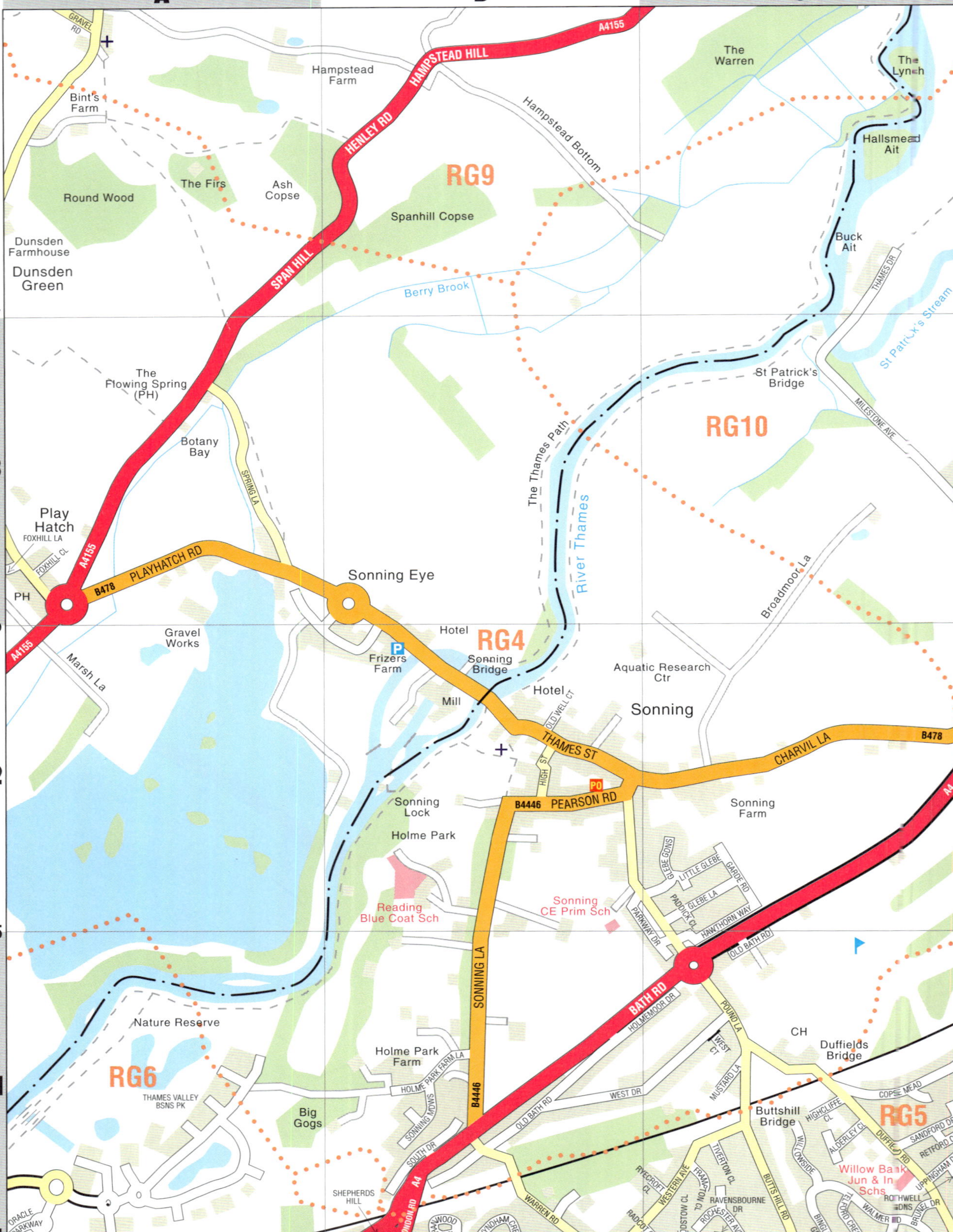
A
B
C
4
3
2
1
77
76
75
74
Hampstead Farm
HAMPSTEAD HILL
A4155
HENLEY RD
SPAN HILL
Bint's Farm
Round Wood
The Firs
Ash Copse
Spanhill Copse
RG9
Dunsden Farmhouse
Dunsden Green
Berry Brook
Hampstead Bottom
The Warren
The Lynch
Hallsmead Ait
Buck Ait
THAMES DR
St Patrick's Stream
St Patrick's Bridge
MILESTONE AVE
RG10
The Flowing Spring (PH)
Botany Bay
SPRING LA
The Thames Path
River Thames
Play Hatch
FOXHILL LA
FOXHILL CL
PLAYHATCH RD
B478
PH
Sonning Eye
Broadmoor La
Gravel Works
Marsh La
Hotel
RG4
Frizers Farm
Sonning Bridge
Mill
Hotel
OLD WELL CT
Aquatic Research Ctr
Sonning
THAMES ST
HIGH ST
CHARVIL LA
PO
B4446
PEARSON RD
Sonning Lock
Holme Park
Sonning Farm
A4
GLEBE GDNS
LITTLE GLEBE
GARDE RD
PADDICK CL
GLEBE LA
HAWTHORN WAY
PARKWAY DR
OLD BATH RD
Reading Blue Coat Sch
Sonning CE Prim Sch
SONNING LA
BATH RD
HOLMEMOOR DR
POUND LA
Nature Reserve
CH
Duffields Bridge
WEST CT
RG6
THAMES VALLEY BSNS PK
Holme Park Farm
HOLME PARK FARM LA
SONNING MDWS
WEST DR
MUSTARD LA
Buttshill Bridge
COPSE MEAD
HIGHCLIFFE CL
RG5
ALDERLEY CL
Big Gogs
SOUTH DR
OLD BATH RD
WILLOWSIDE
SANDFORD DR
RETFORD CL
Willow Bank Jun & Inf Schs
UPPINGHAM DR
SHEPHERDS HILL
WARREN RD
RYECROFT CL
WESTERN AVE
FRAMPTON CL
TIVERTON CL
BUTTS HILL RD
RAVENSBOURNE DR
ROTHWELL GDNS
WALMER RD
BRUNEL DR
ORACLE PARKWAY
LONDON RD
HAWOOD CL
WYNDHAM CRES
RADCOT CL
GODSTOW CL
ROCHESTER AVE
BINGLEY GR
ELFORD CRES
74
75
76

59
87

36
62

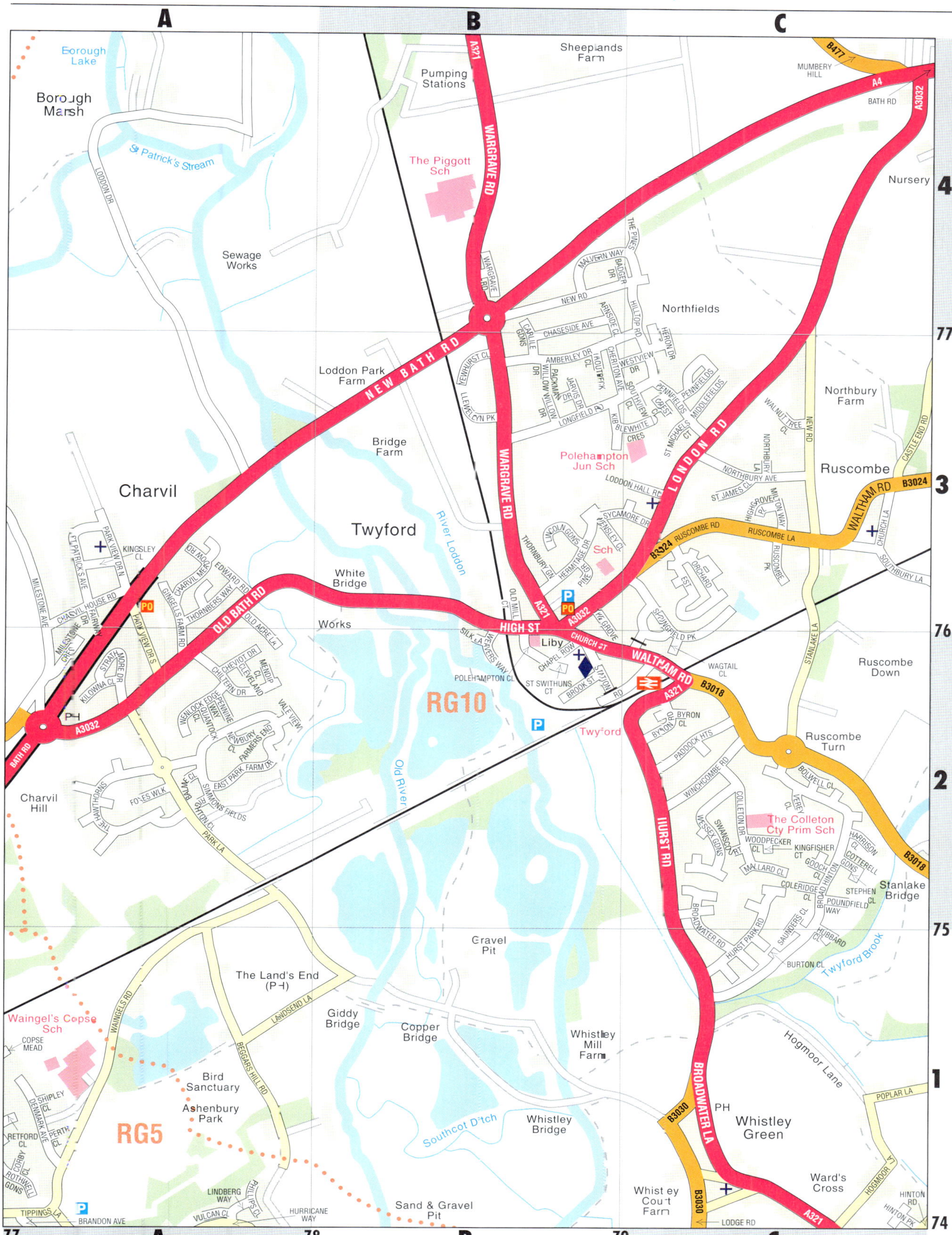

A
B
C
4
77
3
76
2
75
1
74
77
78
79
Borough Lake
Borough Marsh
St Patrick's Stream
Sewage Works
Pumping Stations
Sheeplands Farm
The Piggott Sch
Mumbery Hill
B477
A4
BATH RD
A3032
A321
WARGRAVE RD
Nursery
Northfields
NEW BATH RD
Loddon Park Farm
Bridge Farm
Charvil
Twyford
River Loddon
White Bridge
Works
HIGH ST
CHURCH ST
WALTHAM RD
LONDON RD
Polehampton Jun Sch
Northbury Farm
Ruscombe
RUSCOMBE RD
RUSCOMBE LA
WALTHAM RD
B3024
B3018
Ruscombe Down
Ruscombe Turn
RG10
Twyford
OLD BATH RD
Charvil Hill
Old River
HURST RD
The Colleton Cty Prim Sch
Stanlake Bridge
Twyford Brook
Gravel Pit
The Land's End (PH)
Giddy Bridge
Copper Bridge
Whistley Mill Farm
Hogmoor Lane
Waingel's Copse Sch
Bird Sanctuary
Ashenbury Park
RG5
Southcot Ditch
Whistley Bridge
BROADWATER LA
B3030
PH
Whistley Green
Ward's Cross
Whistley Court Farm
Sand & Gravel Pit
WAINGELS RD
BEGGARS HILL RD
LANDSEND LA
PARK LA
STANLAKE LA
NEW RD
MALVERN WAY
NEW RD
CHASESIDE AVE
AMBERLEY DR
LONGFIELD RD
NORTHBURY AVE
LODDON HALL RD
SYCAMORE DR
ST JAMES CL
HERMITAGE DR
STATION RD
BROOK ST
ST SWITHUNS CT
POLEHAMPTON CL
KINGSLEY CL
PARK VIEW DR N
HOUSE RD
EDWARD RD
OLD ACRE LA
CHEVIOT DR
CHILTERN DR
FARMERS END
EAST PARK FARM DR
FOXES WLK
SIMMONS FIELDS
WINCHCOMBE RD
PADDOCK HTS
BYRON CL
COLLETON DR
WOODPECKER CL
KINGFISHER CT
MALLARD CL
COLERIDGE CL
POUNDFIELD WAY
HURST PARK RD
SAUNDERS CL
HUBBARD CL
BURTON CL
POPLAR LA
LODGE RD
HINTON RD
HINTON PK
LINDBERG WAY
VULCAN CL
HURRICANE WAY
TIPPINGS LA
BRANDON AVE
SHIPLEY CL
DENMARK AVE
PERTH CL
RETFORD CL
COPSE MEAD
ROTHWELL GDNS

88
62

61
37

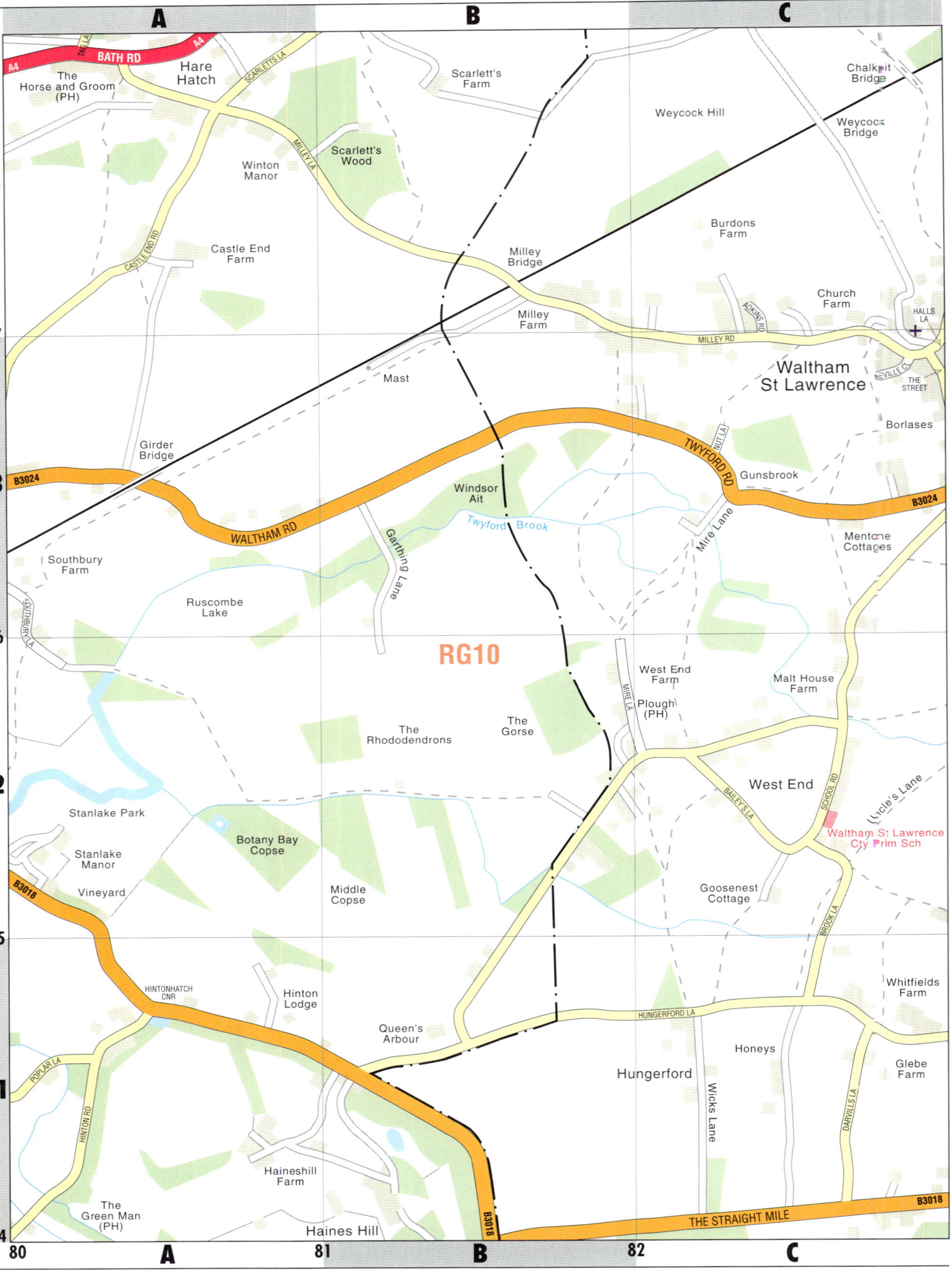
A
B
C
4
77
3
76
2
75
1
74
80
81
82
BATH RD
A4
TAG LA
The Horse and Groom (PH)
Hare Hatch
SCARLETTS LA
Scarlett's Farm
Weycock Hill
Chalkpit Bridge
Weycock Bridge
MILLEY LA
Scarlett's Wood
Winton Manor
Burdons Farm
CASTLE END RD
Castle End Farm
Milley Bridge
Church Farm
ADKINS RD
Milley Farm
HALLS LA
MILLEY RD
Mast
Waltham St Lawrence
THE STREET
Borlases
NUT LA
Girder Bridge
TWYFORD RD
Gunsbrook
B3024
Windsor Ait
Twyford Brook
WALTHAM RD
Mire Lane
Mentone Cottages
Southbury Farm
Garthing Lane
SOUTHBURY LA
Ruscombe Lake
RG10
West End Farm
Malt House Farm
MIRE LA
Plough (PH)
The Rhododendrons
The Gorse
West End
SCHOOL RD
BAILEY'S LA
Stanlake Park
Botany Bay Copse
Waltham St Lawrence Cty Prim Sch
Stanlake Manor
B3018
Vineyard
Middle Copse
Goosenest Cottage
BROOK LA
HINTONHATCH CNR
Hinton Lodge
Whitfields Farm
HUNGERFORD LA
Queen's Arbour
Honeys
POPLAR LA
Glebe Farm
Hungerford
Wicks Lane
HINTON RD
DARVILLS LA
Haineshill Farm
The Green Man (PH)
Haines Hill
THE STRAIGHT MILE

61
89

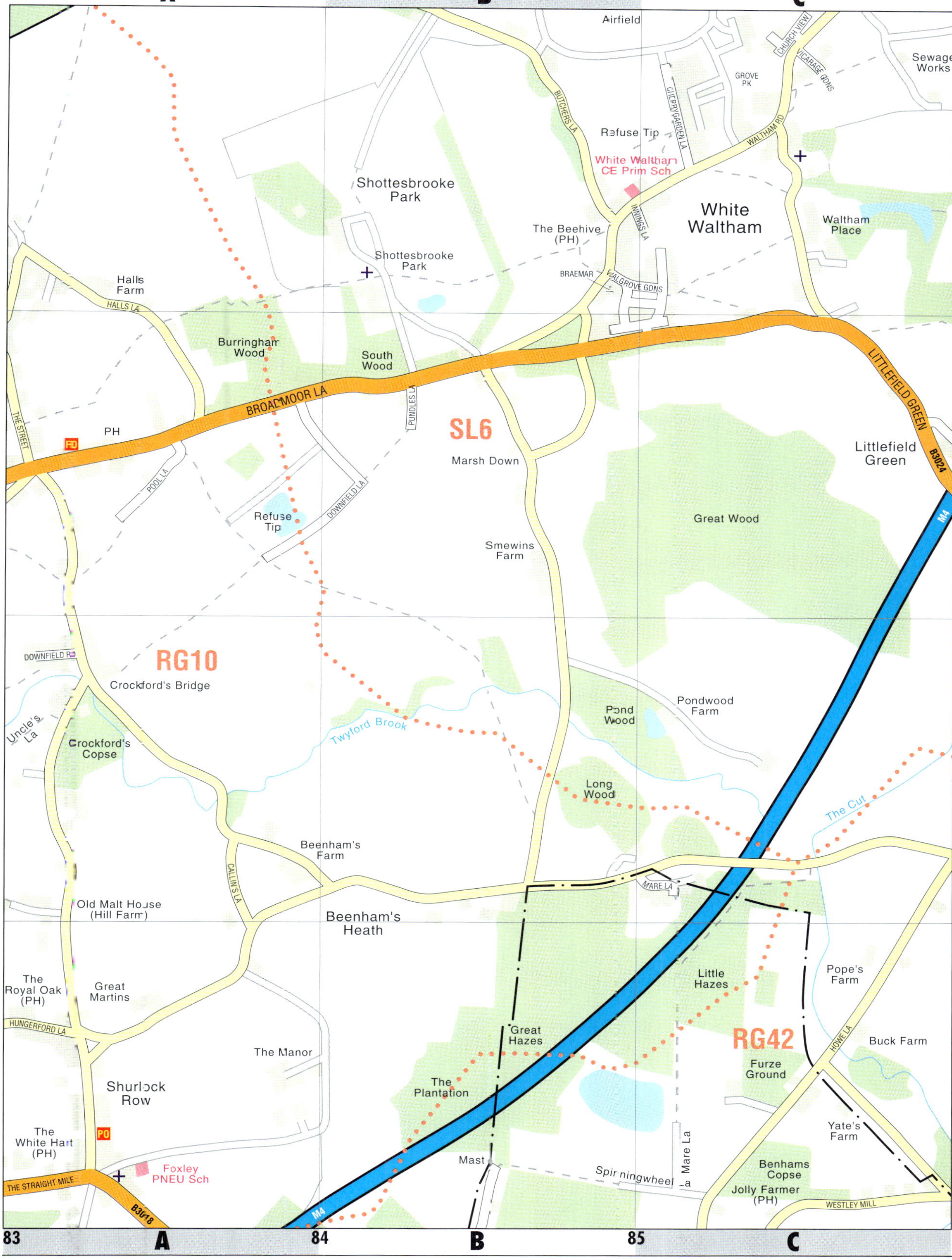
A
B
C
Airfield
Sewage Works
GROVE PK
CHURCH VIEW
VICARAGE GDNS
BUTCHERS LA
GILCHRIST GARDEN LA
Refuse Tip
WALTHAM RD
White Waltham CE Prim Sch
Shottesbrooke Park
White Waltham
Waltham Place
The Beehive (PH)
INNINGS LA
Shottesbrooke Park
BRAEMAR
WALGROVE GDNS
Halls Farm
HALLS LA
Burringham Wood
South Wood
BROADMOOR LA
LITTLEFIELD GREEN
PUNDLES LA
SL6
THE STREET
PH
PO
Marsh Down
Littlefield Green
B3024
POOL LA
Refuse Tip
DOWNFIELD LA
Great Wood
M4
Smewins Farm
DOWNFIELD RD
RG10
Crockford's Bridge
Pond Wood
Pondwood Farm
Uncle's La
Twyford Brook
Crockford's Copse
Long Wood
The Cut
Beenham's Farm
CALLIN'S LA
MARE LA
Old Malt House (Hill Farm)
Beenham's Heath
Little Hazes
Pope's Farm
The Royal Oak (PH)
Great Martins
HUNGERFORD LA
Great Hazes
RG42
HOWE LA
Buck Farm
The Manor
Furze Ground
Shurlock Row
The Plantation
Yate's Farm
The White Hart (PH)
PO
Mare La
Mast
Spinningwheel La
Benhams Copse
THE STRAIGHT MILE
Foxley PNEU Sch
Jolly Farmer (PH)
B3018
M4
WESTLEY MILL
83
84
85
74
75
76
77
1
2
3
4

63
39

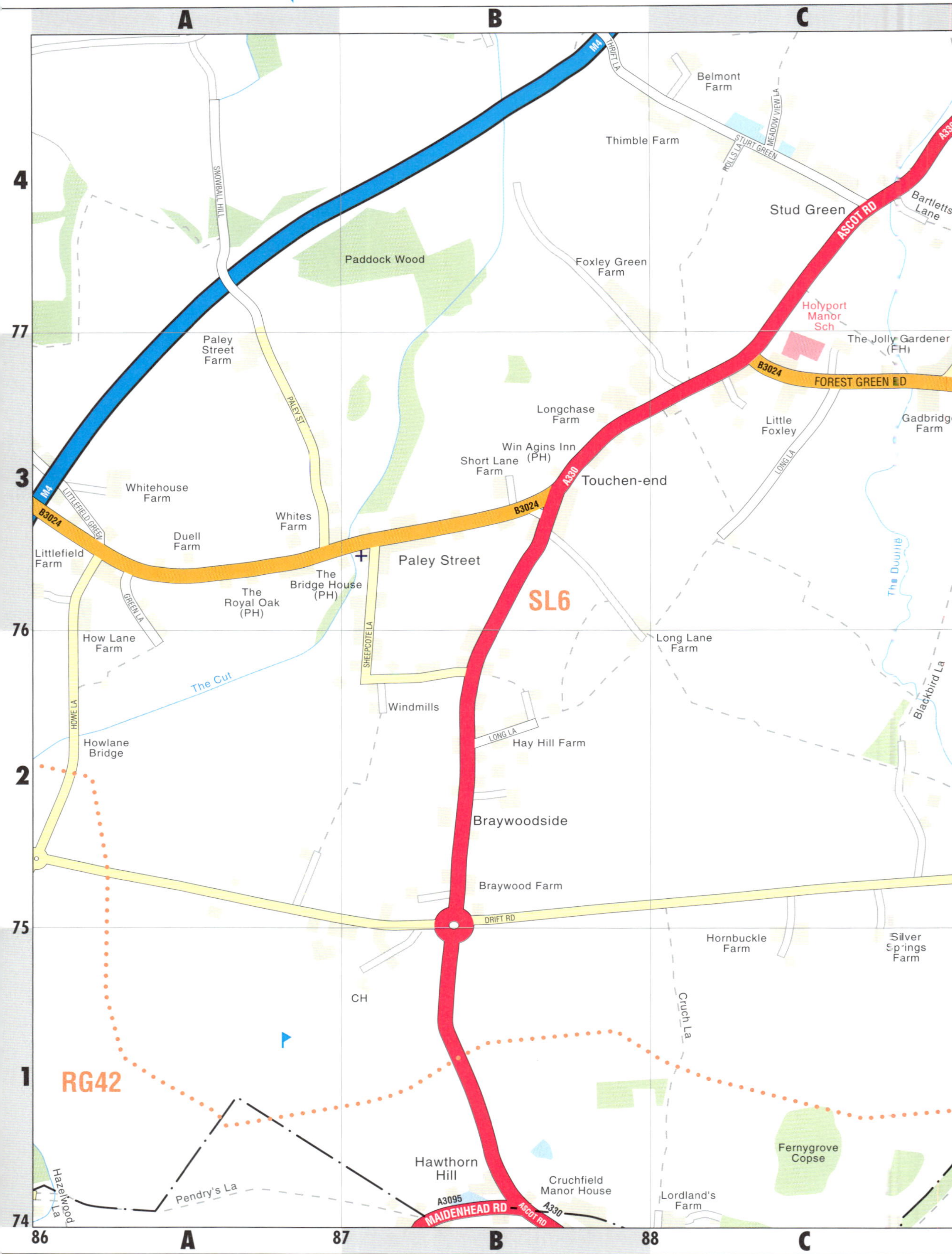
A
B
C
4
77
3
76
2
75
1
74
86
87
88
M4
Thrift La
Belmont Farm
Meadow View La
Sturt Green
Rolls La
Thimble Farm
A330
Ascot Rd
Stud Green
Bartletts Lane
Snowball Hill
Paddock Wood
Foxley Green Farm
Holyport Manor Sch
The Jolly Gardener (PH)
B3024
Forest Green Rd
Paley Street Farm
Paley St
Longchase Farm
Little Foxley
Gadbridge Farm
Win Agins Inn (PH)
Short Lane Farm
Long La
Touchen-end
Whitehouse Farm
Littlefield Green
Whites Farm
Duell Farm
Littlefield Farm
Paley Street
The Bridge House (PH)
The Royal Oak (PH)
Green La
SL6
Sheepcote La
How Lane Farm
Long Lane Farm
The Cut
Windmills
Howe La
Long La
Hay Hill Farm
Howlane Bridge
Blackbird La
Braywoodside
Braywood Farm
Drift Rd
Hornbuckle Farm
Silver Springs Farm
CH
Cruch La
RG42
Fernygrove Copse
Hawthorn Hill
Cruchfield Manor House
Lordland's Farm
Hazelwood La
Pendry's La
A3095
Maidenhead Rd
Ascot Rd
A330

63
91

40
66

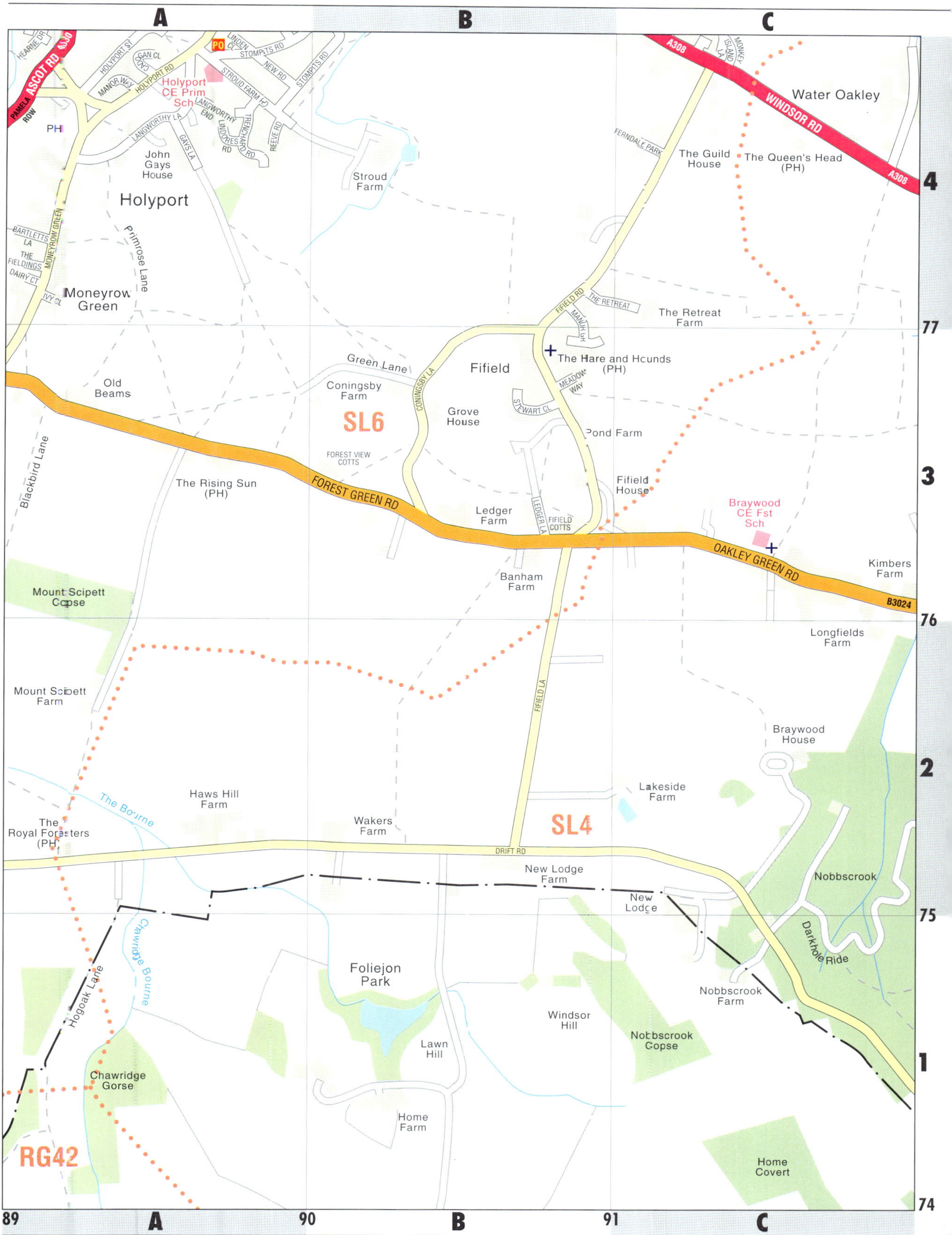
A
B
C
Holyport
Holyport CE Prim Sch
John Gays House
Moneyrow Green
Primrose Lane
Stroud Farm
Water Oakley
WINDSOR RD
A308
ASCOT RD
A330
PAMELA ROW
HEARNE DR
HOLYPORT ST
GAN CL
MANOR WAY
HOLYPORT RD
LINDEN CL
STOMPITS RD
NEW RD
STROUD FARM RD
LANGWORTHY END
LANGWORTHY LA
GAYS LA
LINDORES RD
TRENCHARD RD
REEVE RD
MONKEY ISLAND LA
BARTLETTS LA
THE FIELDINGS
DAIRY CT
IVY CL
MONEYROW GREEN
FERNDALE PARK
The Guild House
The Queen's Head (PH)
FIFIELD RD
THE RETREAT
The Retreat Farm
MANOR LA
The Hare and Hounds (PH)
MEADOW WAY
STEWART CL
Fifield
Green Lane
Coningsby Farm
CONINGSBY LA
Grove House
Pond Farm
Old Beams
SL6
FOREST VIEW COTTS
Blackbird Lane
The Rising Sun (PH)
FOREST GREEN RD
Ledger Farm
LEDGER LA
FIFIELD COTTS
Fifield House
Braywood CE Fst Sch
OAKLEY GREEN RD
B3024
Kimbers Farm
Banham Farm
Mount Scipett Copse
Longfields Farm
Mount Scipett Farm
FIFIELD LA
Braywood House
Haws Hill Farm
Lakeside Farm
The Bourne
The Royal Foresters (PH)
Wakers Farm
SL4
DRIFT RD
New Lodge Farm
Nobbscrook
New Lodge
Darkhole Ride
Chawridge Bourne
Foliejon Park
Hogoak Lane
Nobbscrook Farm
Windsor Hill
Nobbscrook Copse
Lawn Hill
Chawridge Gorse
Home Farm
RG42
Home Covert
4
77
3
76
2
75
1
74
89
90
91

92
66

65
41
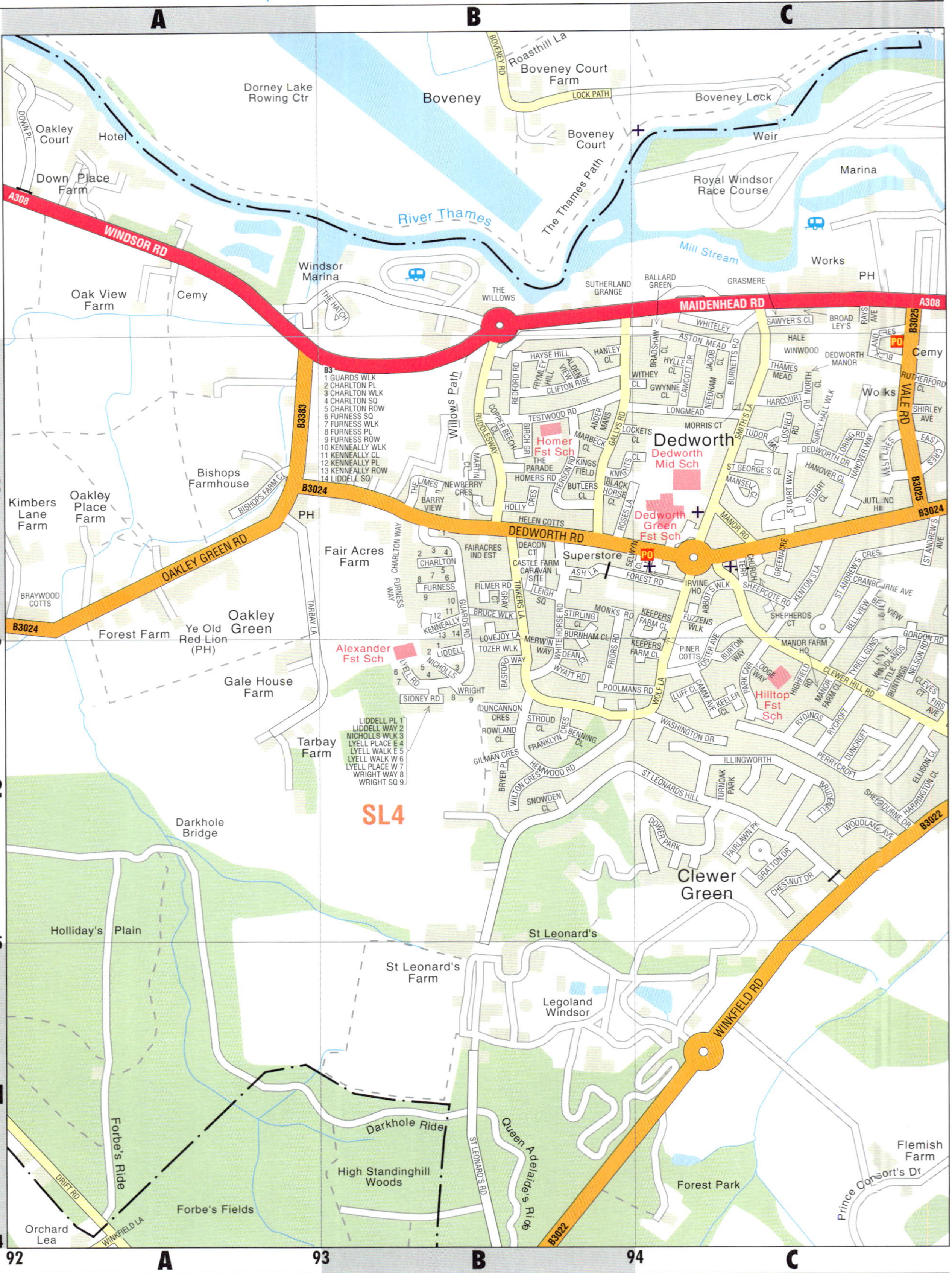
Boveney
Dorney Lake Rowing Ctr
Boveney Court Farm
Boveney Court
Boveney Lock
Weir
Marina
Royal Windsor Race Course
River Thames
The Thames Path
Mill Stream
Works
PH
Oakley Court
Hotel
Down Place Farm
WINDSOR RD
A308
Windsor Marina
THE WILLOWS
SUTHERLAND GRANGE
BALLARD GREEN
GRASMERE
MAIDENHEAD RD
Oak View Farm
Cemy
B3383
Bishops Farmhouse
Kimbers Lane Farm
Oakley Place Farm
B3024
OAKLEY GREEN RD
BRAYWOOD COTTS
PH
Fair Acres Farm
Oakley Green
Forest Farm
Ye Old Red Lion (PH)
Gale House Farm
Alexander Fst Sch
Tarbay Farm
Willows Path
1 GUARDS WLK
2 CHARLTON PL
3 CHARLTON WLK
4 CHARLTON SQ
5 CHARLTON ROW
6 FURNESS SQ
7 FURNESS WLK
8 FURNESS PL
9 FURNESS ROW
10 KENNEALLY WLK
11 KENNEALLY CL
12 KENNEALLY PL
13 KENNEALLY ROW
14 LIDDELL SQ
LIDDELL PL 1
LIDDELL WAY 2
NICHOLLS WLK 3
LYELL PLACE E 4
LYELL WALK E 5
LYELL WALK W 6
LYELL PLACE W 7
WRIGHT WAY 8
WRIGHT SQ 9
Dedworth
Dedworth Mid Sch
Dedworth Green Fst Sch
Homer Fst Sch
DEDWORTH RD
Superstore
FOREST RD
Hilltop Fst Sch
Cemy
VALE RD
B3025
CLEWER HILL RD
WASHINGTON DR
ST LEONARDS HILL
SL4
Darkhole Bridge
Clewer Green
St Leonard's
St Leonard's Farm
Legoland Windsor
Holliday's Plain
WINKFIELD RD
B3022
Darkhole Ride
High Standinghill Woods
Forbe's Ride
Forbe's Fields
Queen Adelaide's Ride
ST LEONARD'S RD
Forest Park
Flemish Farm
Prince Consort's Dr
Orchard Lea
DRIFT RD
WINKFIELD LA
A
B
C
4
77
3
76
2
75
1
74
92
93
94
65
93

42
68

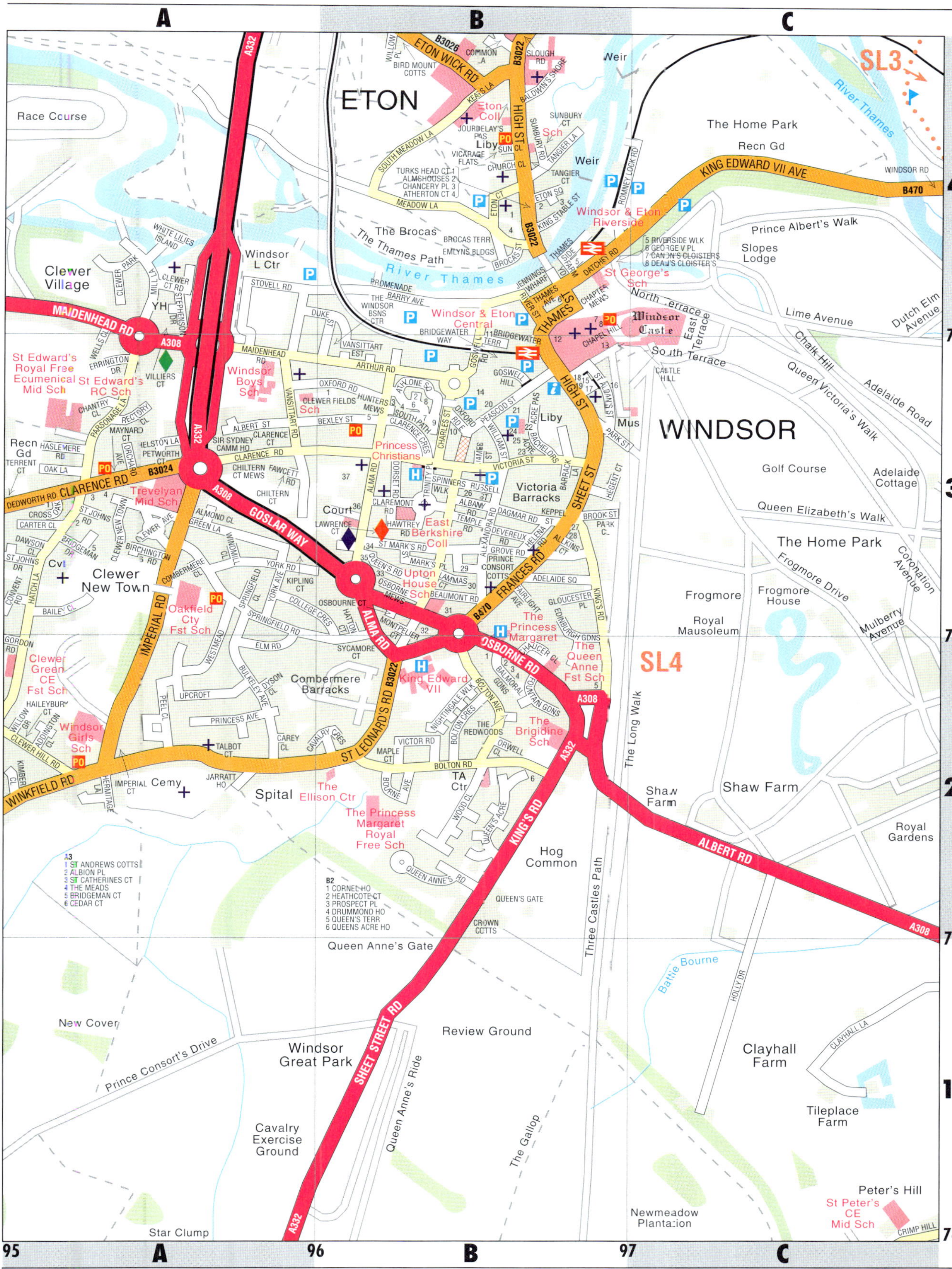

A3
1 ST ANDREWS COTTS
2 ALBION PL
3 ST CATHERINES CT
4 THE MEADS
5 BRIDGEMAN CT
6 CEDAR CT

B2
1 CORNEL HO
2 HEATHCOTE CT
3 PROSPECT PL
4 DRUMMOND HO
5 QUEEN'S TERR
6 QUEENS ACRE HO

B3
1 BEAUMONT COTTS
2 CAMBRIDGE HO
3 WARD ROYAL PAR
4 CHRISTIAN SQ
5 CRESCENT VILLAS
6 WARD ROYAL
7 BOWES-LYON CL
8 MOUNTBATTEN SQ
9 CHARLES HO
10 QUEEN ANNE'S CT
11 CASTLEVIEW HO
12 HORSESHOE CLOISTERS
13 LODGINGS OF THE MILITARY KNIGHTS
14 KING EDWARD CT
15 CHURCH ST
16 ST ALBANS CL
17 CHURCH LA
18 MARKET ST
19 QUEEN CHARLOTTE ST
20 AMBERLEY PL
21 PEASCOD PL
22 ROYAL FREE CT
23 ELLISON HO
24 SUN PAS
25 HIBBERT'S ALLEY
26 GARFIELD PL
27 KING'S ROAD HO
28 COACHMAN'S LODGE
29 ST LEONARD'S AVE
30 LAMMAS AVE
31 CROSSWAYS CT
32 KNIGHTS PL
33 HOUSTON CT
34 WARWICK CT
35 CHELMSFORD CT
36 CAMPERDOWN HO
37 VISCOUNT CT

94
68

67
43

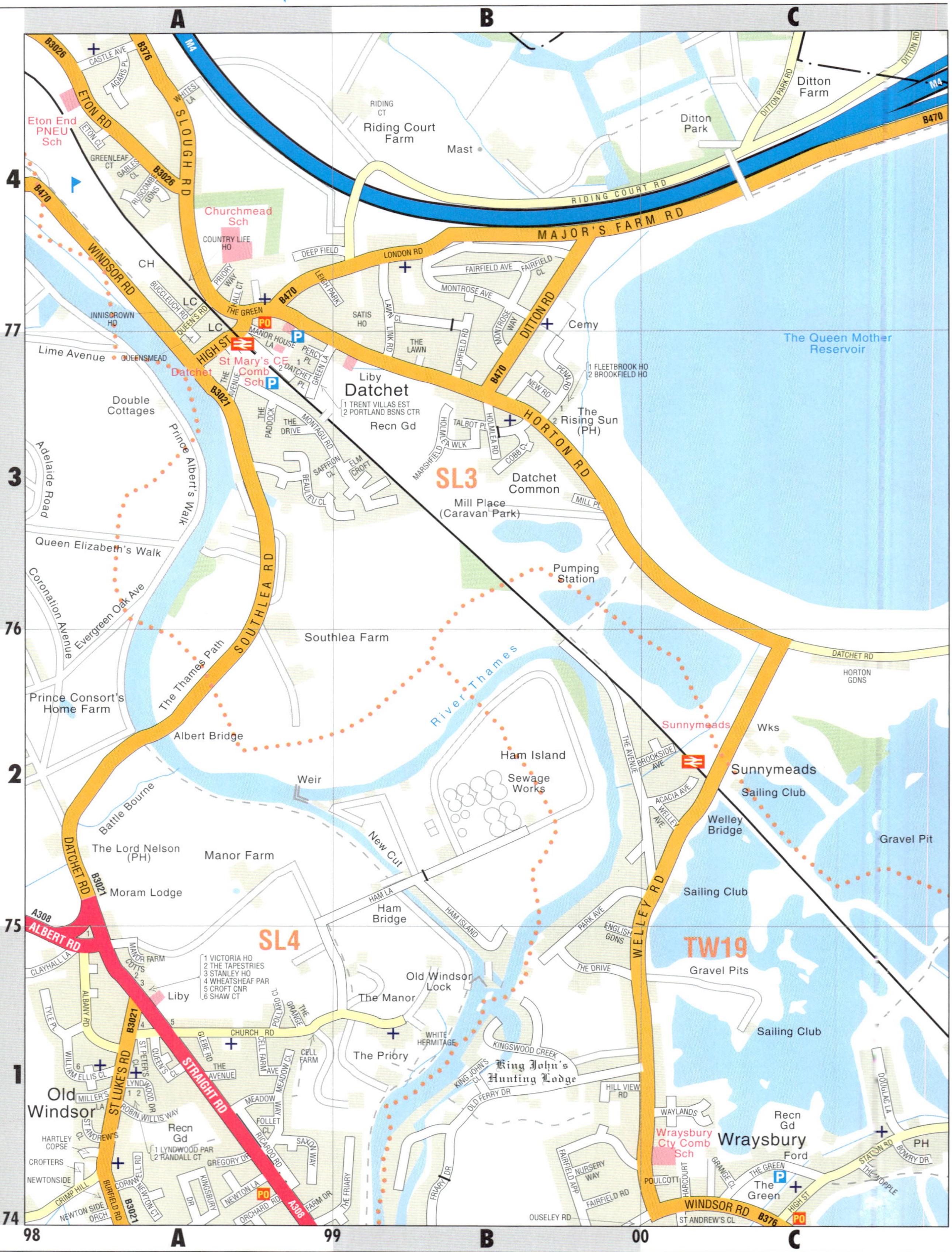
A
B
C
4
77
3
76
2
75
1
74
98
99
00
M4
B3026
B376
B470
B3021
A308
Eton End PNEU Sch
ETON RD
ETON CL
GREENLEAF CT
GABLES CL
RUSCOMBE GDNS
CASTLE AVE
AGARS PL
WHITES LA
SLOUGH RD
Churchmead Sch
COUNTRY LIFE HO
PRIORY WAY
HALL CT
WINDSOR RD
CH
BUCCLEUCH RD
QUEEN'S RD
LC
THE GREEN
PO
HIGH ST
MANOR HOUSE LA
PERCY PL
DATCHET PL
GREEN LA
St Mary's CE Comb Sch
INNISCROWN HO
Lime Avenue
QUEENSMEAD
Datchet
Double Cottages
Prince Albert's Walk
Adelaide Road
Queen Elizabeth's Walk
Coronation Avenue
Evergreen Oak Ave
Prince Consort's Home Farm
The Thames Path
Albert Bridge
SOUTHLEA RD
Southlea Farm
Battle Bourne
DATCHET RD
The Lord Nelson (PH)
Manor Farm
Moram Lodge
RIDING CT
Riding Court Farm
Mast
RIDING COURT RD
MAJOR'S FARM RD
DEEP FIELD
LEIGH PARK
LONDON RD
FAIRFIELD AVE
FAIRFIELD CL
MONTROSE AVE
MONTROSE WAY
DITTON RD
SATIS HO
LAWN CL
LINK RD
THE LAWN
LICHFIELD RD
Cemy
Liby
Datchet
1 TRENT VILLAS EST
2 PORTLAND BSNS CTR
Recn Gd
THE AVENUE
THE PADDOCK
THE DRIVE
MONTAGU RD
SAFFRON CL
ELM CROFT
BEAULIEU CL
MARSHFIELD
HOLM CL
TALBOT PL
WALK
HOLMLEA RD
COBB CL
NEW RD
PENN RD
1 FLEETBROOK HO
2 BROOKFIELD HO
The Rising Sun (PH)
HORTON RD
SL3
Datchet Common
Mill Place (Caravan Park)
MILL PL
Pumping Station
Ditton Farm
Ditton Park
DITTON PARK RD
DITTON RD
The Queen Mother Reservoir
DATCHET RD
HORTON GDNS
River Thames
Sunnymeads
Wks
Sunnymeads
Sailing Club
Welley Bridge
Gravel Pit
Sailing Club
THE AVENUE
BROOKSIDE AVE
ACACIA AVE
WELLEY AVE
WELLEY RD
Ham Island
Sewage Works
Weir
New Cut
HAM LA
Ham Bridge
HAM ISLAND
PARK AVE
ENGLISH GDNS
THE DRIVE
TW19
Gravel Pits
Sailing Club
ALBERT RD
CLAYHALL LA
MANOR FARM COTTS
SL4
1 VICTORIA HO
2 THE TAPESTRIES
3 STANLEY HO
4 WHEATSHEAF PAR
5 CROFT CNR
6 SHAW CT
Liby
POLLARD CL
THE GRANGE
Old Windsor Lock
The Manor
TYLE PL
ALBANY RD
CHURCH RD
GLEBE RD
CELL FARM AVE
MEADOW CL
CELL FARM
The Priory
WHITE HERMITAGE
KINGSWOOD CREEK
King John's Hunting Lodge
KING JOHN'S CL
OLD FERRY DR
HILL VIEW RD
WILLIAM ELLIS CL
ST LUKE'S RD
ST PETER'S CL
QUEEN'S CL
LYNDWOOD DR
THE AVENUE
STRAIGHT RD
Old Windsor
MILLER'S LA
ROBIN WILLIS WAY
ST ANDREW'S CL
HARTLEY COPSE
CROFTERS
NEWTONSIDE
CRIMP HILL
NEWTON SIDE ORCH
BURFIELD RD
CORNWALL CL
NEWTON CT
Recn Gd
1 LYNDWOOD PAR
2 RANDALL CT
GREGORY DR
KINGSBURY DR
MEADOW WAY
FOLLET CL
RICARDO RD
SAXON WAY
NEWTON LA
ORCHARD RD
FARM DR
THE FRIARY
FRIARY DR
FAIRFIELD APP
NURSERY WAY
FAIRFIELD RD
OUSELEY RD
WAYLANDS
Wraysbury Cty Comb Sch
POULCOTT
HARCOURT
GRANGE CL
Wraysbury
Recn Gd
Ford
THE GREEN
The Green
HIGH ST
WINDSOR RD
ST ANDREW'S CL
B376
DOUGLAS LA
STATION RD
THE WOPPLE
BOWRY DR
PH

67
95

44
70

A
B
C
SL0
Gravel Pit
Brands Hill
M4
B470
A4
LONDON RD
COLNBROOK BY-PASS
The Crown (PH)
Colnbrook
Brook Farm
The Greyhound (PH)
The Queen Mother Resr
Mildridge Farm
HIGH ST
Colnbrook CE Prim Sch
Poyle Cty Fst Sch
Poyle
SL3
Horton Lodge
Colne Valley Way
Colne Brook
Poyle Lodge
Manor Farm
Rectory
Ashgood Farm
Berkyn Manor Farm
The Five Bells (PH)
Horton
STANWELL RD
HORTON RD
A3113
AIRPORT WAY
M25
Wraysbury River
TW19
Wraysbury Resr
Stanwell Manor
Gravel Pit
Sailing Club
River Colne
Whitehall Nurseries
STATION RD
Wraysbury
Stanwell Moor
Lower Mill Farm
King George VI Resr
4
77
3
76
2
75
1
74
01
02
03

96
70

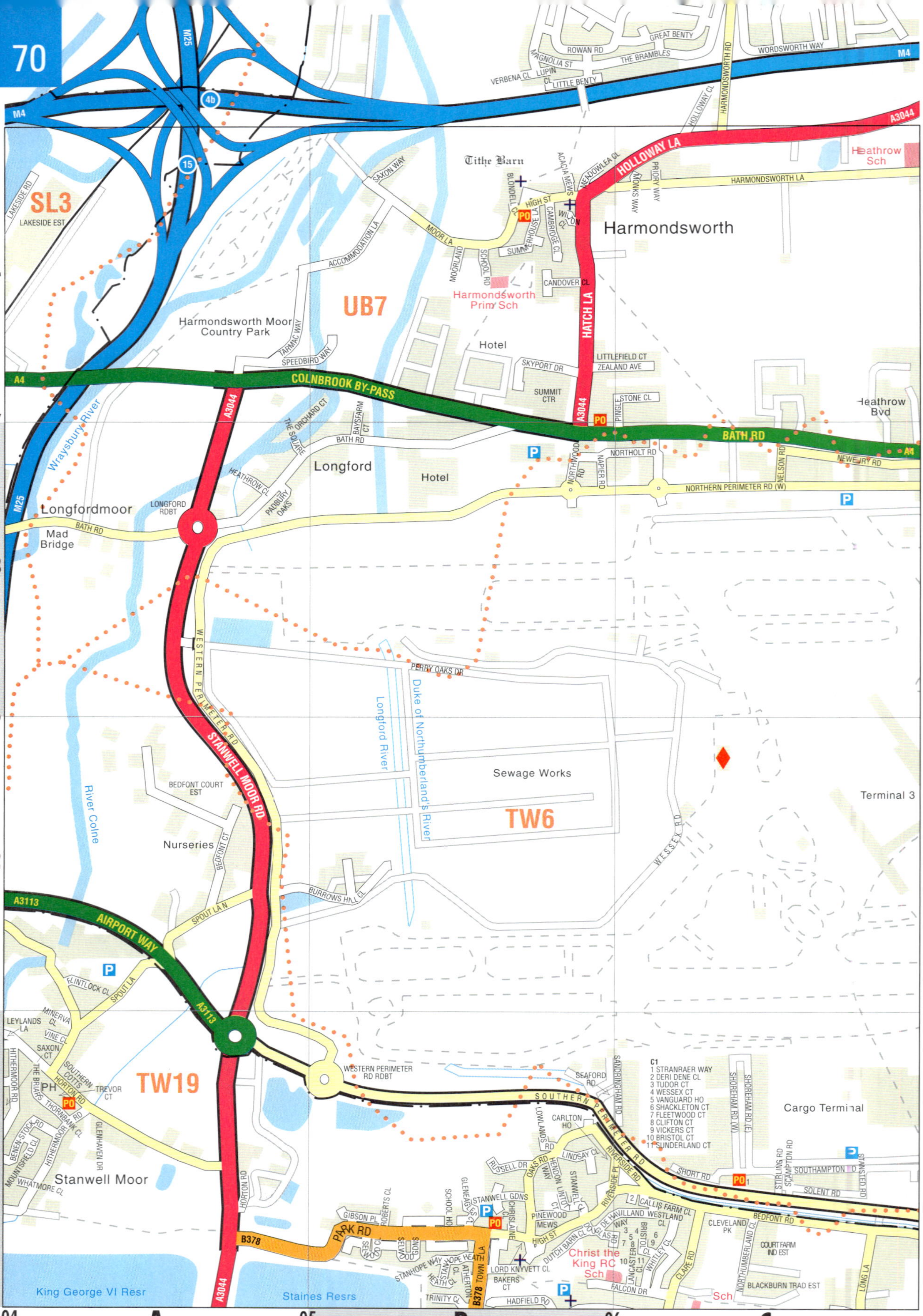
M25
M4
4b
15
SL3
LAKESIDE RD
LAKESIDE EST
ROWAN RD
GREAT BENTY
MAGNOLIA ST
THE BRAMBLES
WORDSWORTH WAY
HARMONDSWORTH RD
VERBENA CL
LUPIN CL
LITTLE BENTY
HOLLOWAY CL
A3044
Tithe Barn
Heathrow Sch
SAXON WAY
BLONDELL CL
ACACIA MEWS
MEADOWLEA CL
HOLLOWAY LA
MONKS WAY
PRIORY WAY
HARMONDSWORTH LA
HIGH ST
PO
CAMBRIDGE CL
WILTON CL
Harmondsworth
MOOR LA
ACCOMMODATION LA
MOORLAND
SCHOOL RD
CANDOVER CL
Harmondsworth Prim Sch
UB7
HATCH LA
Harmondsworth Moor Country Park
TARMAC WAY
SPEEDBIRD WAY
Hotel
SKYPORT DR
LITTLEFIELD CT
ZEALAND AVE
SUMMIT CTR
A4
COLNBROOK BY-PASS
ORCHARD CT
THE SQUARE
BAYSFARM CT
STONE CL
PINGLE
Heathrow Bvd
Wraysbury River
BATH RD
NORTHOLT RD
Longford
Hotel
HEATHROW CL
NORTHWOOD RD
NAPIER RD
NELSON RD
NEWBURY RD
NORTHERN PERIMETER RD (W)
Longfordmoor
LONGFORD RDBT
PADBURY OAKS
Mad Bridge
WESTERN PERIMETER RD
PERRY OAKS DR
Longford River
Duke of Northumberland's River
STANWELL MOOR RD
Sewage Works
BEDFONT COURT EST
River Colne
Terminal 3
TW6
Nurseries
BEDFONT CT
WESSEX RD
BURROWS HILL CL
A3113
AIRPORT WAY
SPOUT LA N
FLINTLOCK CL
SPOUT LA
MINERVA CL
LEYLANDS LA
VINE CL
SAXON CT
SOUTHERN COTTS
HORTON RD
TREVOR CT
TW19
WESTERN PERIMETER RD RDBT
SEAFORD RD
SANDRINGHAM RD
C1
1 STRANRAER WAY
2 DERI DENE CL
3 TUDOR CT
4 WESSEX CT
5 VANGUARD HO
6 SHACKLETON CT
7 FLEETWOOD CT
8 CLIFTON CT
9 VICKERS CT
10 BRISTOL CT
11 SUNDERLAND CT
SHOREHAM RD (W)
SHOREHAM RD (E)
Cargo Terminal
HITHERMOOR RD
THE BRIARS
PH
THORNBANK CL
GLENHAVEN DR
SOUTHERN PERIMETER RD
LOWLANDS RD
CARLTON HO
RIVERSIDE RD
BENEN-STOCK RD
MOUNTSFIELD CL
Stanwell Moor
WHATMORE CL
HORTON RD
RUSSELL DR
OAKS RD
HENDON WAY
LINDSAY CL
STANWELL CL
SHORT RD
STIRLING RD
SCAMPTON RD
SOUTHAMPTON RD
STANSTED RD
SOLENT RD
ROBERTS CL
SCHOOL HO
GLENEAGLES CL
STANWELL GDNS
CHRISLAINE CL
PINEWOOD MEWS
RIVERSIDE PL
CALLIS FARM CL
DE HAVILLAND WAY
WESTLAND CL
BEDFONT RD
CLEVELAND PK
NORTHUMBERLAND CL
GIBSON PL
PARK RD
B378
A3044
HIGH ST
DUTCH BARN CL
Christ the King RC Sch
LANCASTER CL
BRISTOL CL
WHITLEY CL
CLARE RD
COURTFARM IND EST
STANHOPE WAY
HEATH CL
ATHERTON PL
TOWN LA
LORD KNYVETT CL
BAKERS CT
BLACKBURN TRAD EST
LONG LA
King George VI Resr
Staines Resrs
TRINITY CL
HADFIELD RD
FALCON DR
Sch
4
77
3
76
2
75
1
74
04
A
05
B
06
C

69
97

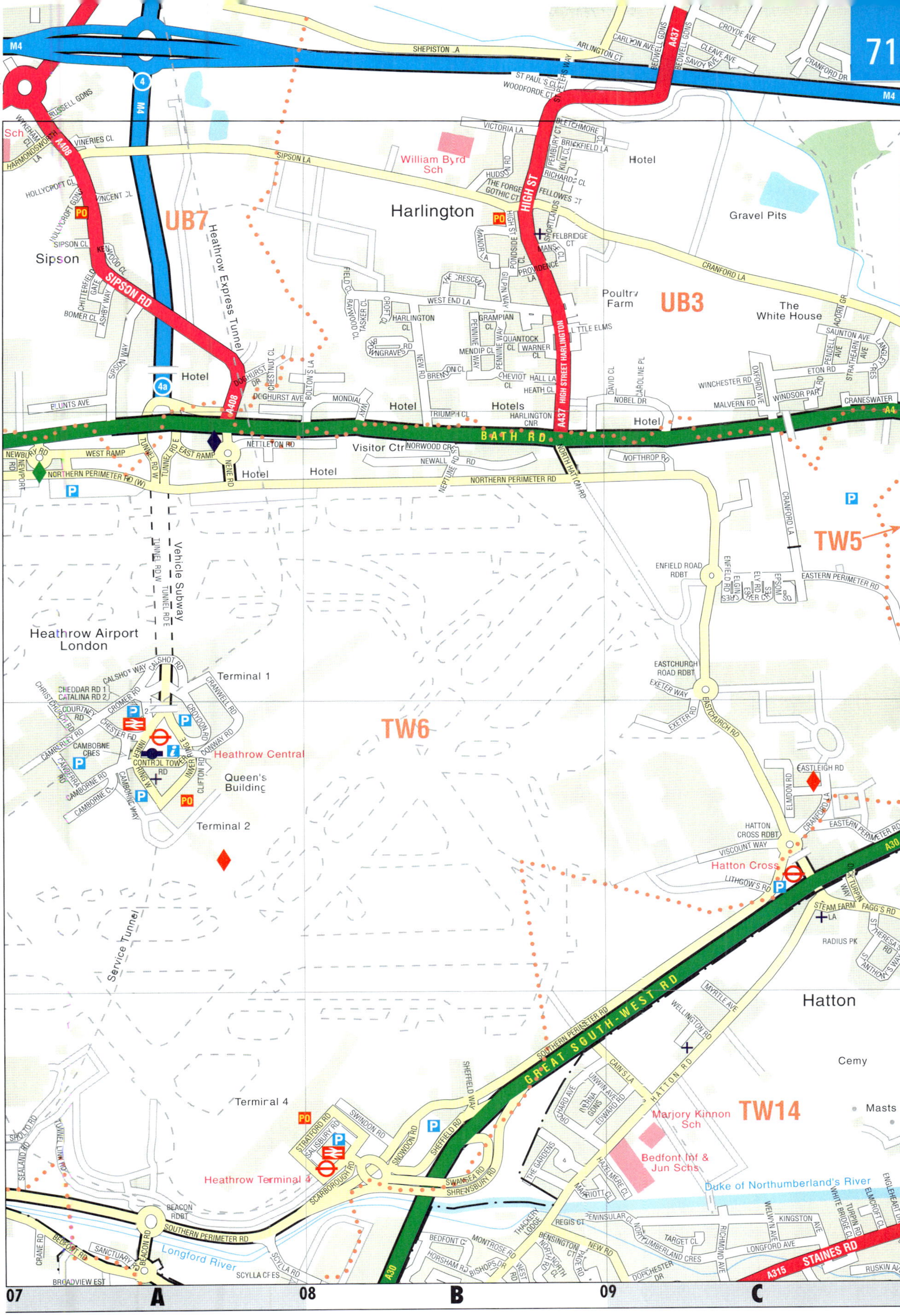
M4
SHEPISTON LA
ARLINGTON CT
CARLTON AVE
BEDWELL GDNS
A437
CROYDE AVE
CLEAVE AVE
SAVOY AVE
CRANFORD DR
ST PAUL'S CL
WOODFORDE CT
ST PETERS WAY
RUSSELL GDNS
WYKEHAM CL
HARMONDSWORTH LA
A408
VINERIES CL
Sch
VICTORIA LA
BLETCHMORE CL
BRICKFIELD LA
PEMBURY CT
KILN CL
William Byrd Sch
SIPSON LA
Hotel
HOLLYCROFT CL
HOLLYCROFT GDNS
VINCENT CL
PO
UB7
Heathrow Express Tunnel
Harlington
HUDSON RD
THE FORGE
GOTHIC CT
HIGH ST
RICHARDS CL
FELLOWES CT
Gravel Pits
SIPSON CL
Sipson
KENWOOD CL
SIPSON RD
FELBRIDGE CT
MANSE CL
PROVIDENCE LA
CRANFORD LA
CHITTERFIELD GATE
ASHBY WAY
BOMER CL
THE CRESCENT
WEST END LA
FIELD CL
RAYMOOD CL
TASKER CL
CROFT CL
HARLINGTON CL
GRAMPIAN CL
PENNINE WAY
QUANTOCK CL
WARNER CL
MENDIP CL
Poultry Farm
UB3
The White House
LITTLE ELMS
HIGH STREET HARLINGTON
SAUNTON AVE
ACORN GR
PENDELL AVE
STRATHEARN AVE
ETON RD
LANGLEY CRES
SIPSON WAY
Hotel
DOGHURST DR
CHESTNUT CL
DOGHURST AVE
BOLTON'S LA
NEW RD
BRENDON CL
CHEVIOT CL
HALL LA
HEATH CL
DAVID CL
CAROLINE PL
NOBEL DR
WINCHESTER RD
OXFORD AVE
WINDSOR PARK RD
MALVERN RD
CRANESWATER
BLUNTS AVE
MONDIAL WAY
Hotel
Hotels
TRIUMPH CL
HARLINGTON CNR
Hotel
A4
BATH RD
NEWBURY RD
NEWPORT RD
WEST RAMP
TUNNEL RD W
TUNNEL RD E
EAST RAMP
NETTLETON RD
Visitor Ctr
NORWOOD CRES
NEWALL RD
NEPTUNE RD
NORTHOLT RD
NORTHROP RD
NORTHERN PERIMETER RD (W)
NENE RD
Hotel
Hotel
NORTHERN PERIMETER RD
NORTH HATTON RD
P
CRANFORD LA
TW5
Vehicle Subway
TUNNEL RD W
TUNNEL RD E
ENFIELD ROAD RDBT
ENFIELD RD
EASTERN PERIMETER RD
Heathrow Airport London
EASTCHURCH ROAD RDBT
EXETER WAY
EXETER RD
EASTCHURCH RD
CALSHOT WAY
CALSHOT RD
Terminal 1
CRANWELL RD
CHEDDAR RD
CATALINA RD
CROMER RD
COURTNEY RD
CHRISTCHURCH RD
CROYDON RD
CONWAY RD
CHESTER RD
CAMBERLEY RD
CAMBORNE CRES
CANBERRA RD
CAMBORNE RD
INNER RING W
INNER RING E
CONTROL TOWER RD
CLIFTON RD
Heathrow Central
TW6
Queen's Building
PO
Terminal 2
EASTLEIGH RD
ELMDON RD
HATTON CROSS RDBT
VISCOUNT WAY
Hatton Cross
LITHGOW'S RD
EASTERN PERIMETER RD
A30
DICK TURPIN WAY
STEAM FARM LA
FAGG'S RD
RADIUS PK
ST THERESA'S RD
ST ANTHONY'S WAY
Service Tunnel
Hatton
MYRTLE AVE
WELLINGTON RD
Cemy
SOUTHERN PERIMETER RD
GREAT SOUTH-WEST RD
SHEFFIELD WAY
CAIN'S LA
UNWIN AVE
HATTON RD
Terminal 4
PO
STRATFORD RD
SALISBURY RD
SWINDON RD
P
Marjory Kinnon Sch
TW14
Masts
SHOLTO RD
TUNNEL LINK RD
SEALAND RD
SNOWDON RD
SHEFFIELD RD
ORCHARD AVE
EDWARD RD
Bedfont Inf & Jun Schs
Heathrow Terminal 4
SCARBOROUGH RD
SWANSEA RD
SHREWSBURY RD
THE GARDENS
HAZELMERE CL
MARRIOTT CL
Duke of Northumberland's River
BEACON RDBT
SOUTHERN PERIMETER RD
PENINSULAR CL
REGIS CT
THACKERY LODGE
KINGSTON AVE
WELWYN AVE
WHITE BRIDGE CL
TURPIN RD
ELMCROFT CL
ENGLEHEART DR
CRANE RD
BEDFONT RD
SANCTUARY RD
BEACON RD
Longford River
SCYLLA RD
SCYLLA CRES
BEDFONT CL
HORSHAM RD
MONTROSE RD
BISHOPS DR
WEST RD
BENSINGTON CT
NORTH RD
NEW RD
TARGET CL
NORTHUMBERLAND CRES
DORCHESTER DR
RICHMOND AVE
LONGFORD AVE
STAINES RD
A315
RUSKIN AVE
BROADVIEW EST
07
A
08
B
09
C
4
77
3
76
2
75
1
74

45

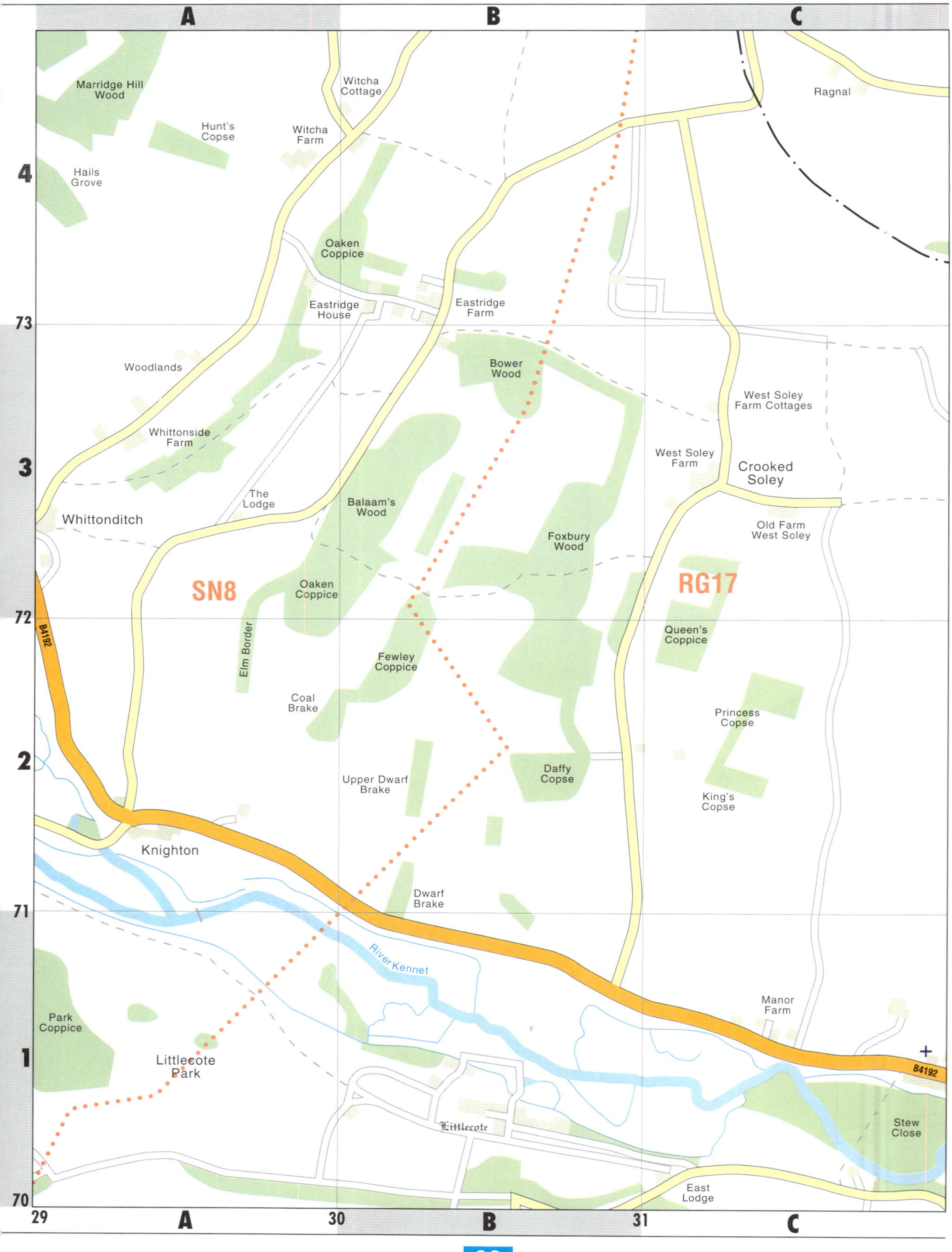
A
B
C
Marridge Hill Wood
Witcha Cottage
Ragnal
Hunt's Copse
Witcha Farm
Hails Grove
4
Oaken Coppice
Eastridge House
Eastridge Farm
73
Woodlands
Bower Wood
West Soley Farm Cottages
Whittonside Farm
West Soley Farm
Crooked Soley
3
The Lodge
Balaam's Wood
Whittonditch
Old Farm West Soley
Foxbury Wood
SN8
Oaken Coppice
RG17
72
B4192
Elm Border
Queen's Coppice
Fewley Coppice
Coal Brake
Princess Copse
2
Daffy Copse
Upper Dwarf Brake
King's Copse
Knighton
Dwarf Brake
71
River Kennet
Manor Farm
Park Coppice
1
Littlecote Park
B4192
Littlecote
Stew Close
East Lodge
70
29
30
31

99

46
74

A B C

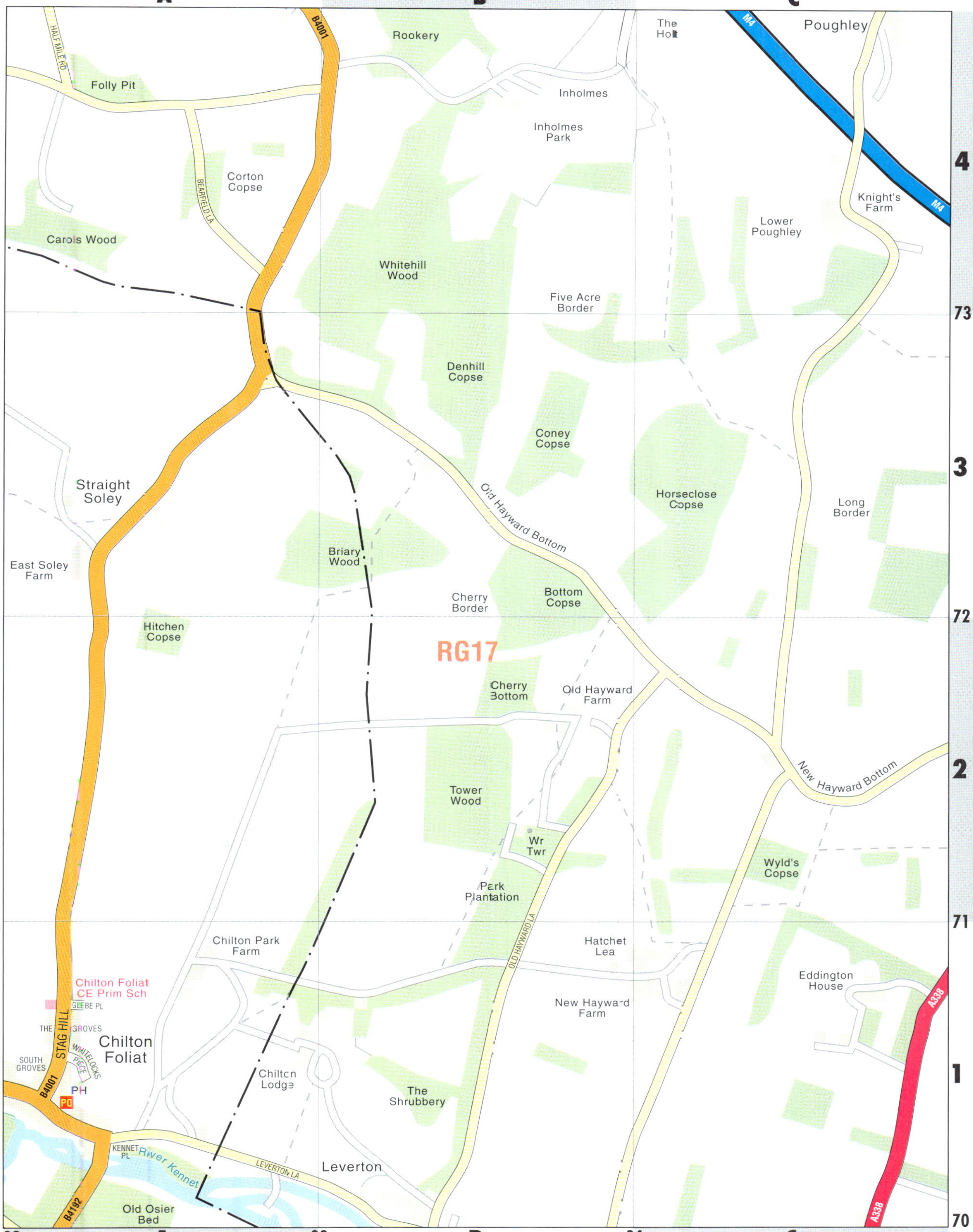

A B C

100
74

73
47

A
B
C
4
73
3
72
2
71
1
70
35
36
37
B4000
ERMIN ST
A338
Fisher's Farm
Somercourt
Tommylands Copse
The Pheasant Inn (PH)
Shefford Woodlands
Templars Farm
BARN COTTS
M4
14
Newtown Lodge Farm
Breach Copse
Lovelocks
North Hidden Farm
Norbin's Wood
North Hidden Cottages
RG17
Hungerford Newtown
Lower Farm
Jeffrey's Border
Wickfield Copse
Windingwood La
The Tally-ho (PH)
RADLEY BOTTOM
HUNGERFORD NEWTOWN
PO
Little Hidden Farm
North Denford Farm
Winding Wood
Windingwood Bottom
Dunkin's Copse
Heath Hanger La
Heath Hanger Copse
Stibbs Wood
Three Gate Copse
Radley Farm
The Hassock
Great Hidden Farm

73
101

48
76

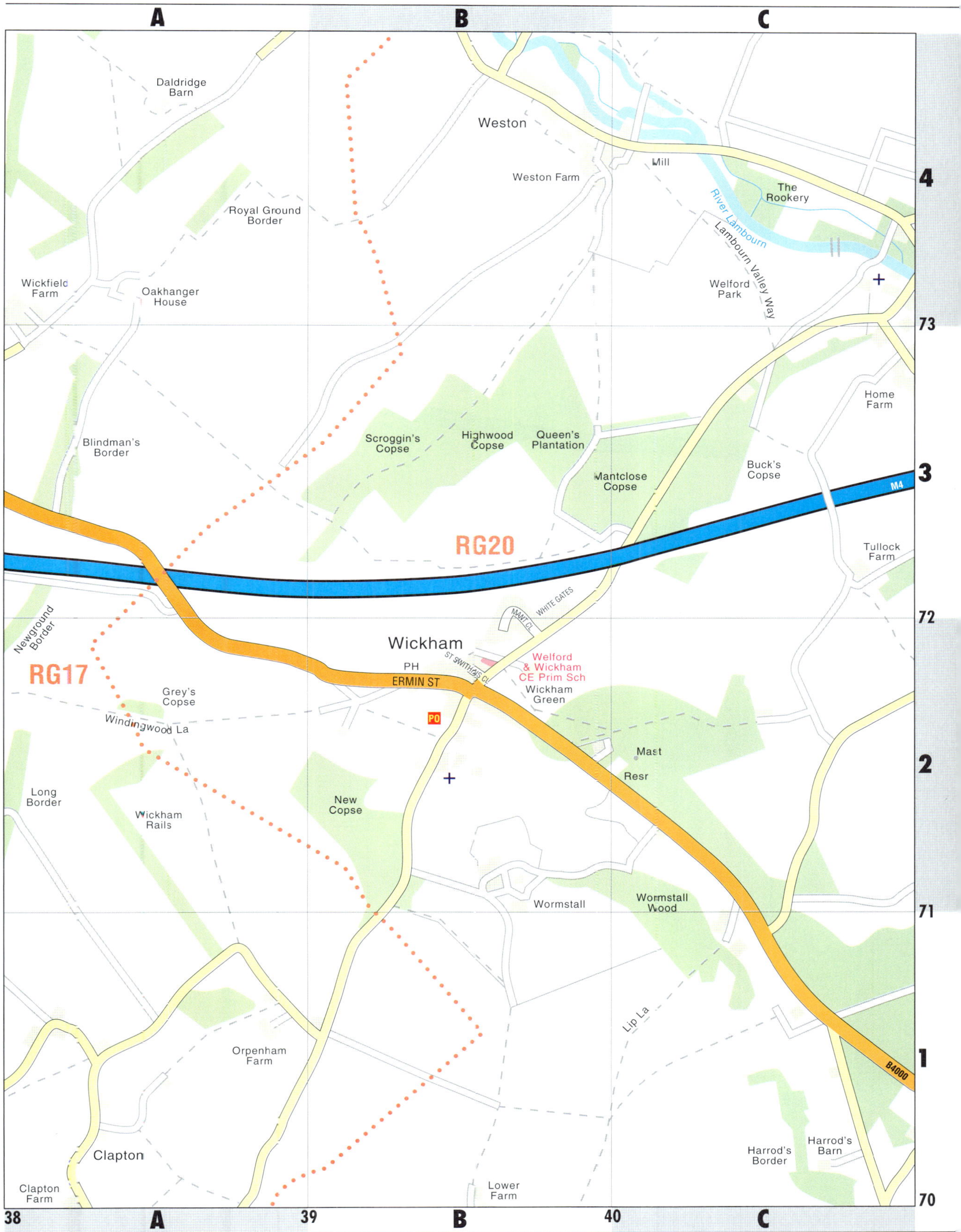
A
B
C
Daldridge Barn
Weston
Weston Farm
Mill
The Rookery
River Lambourn
Lambourn Valley Way
Royal Ground Border
Wickfield Farm
Oakhanger House
Welford Park
Home Farm
Blindman's Border
Scroggin's Copse
Highwood Copse
Queen's Plantation
Mantclose Copse
Buck's Copse
M4
RG20
Tullock Farm
Newground Border
RG17
WHITE GATES
MANT CL
Wickham
PH
ST SWITHUNS CL
ERMIN ST
Welford & Wickham CE Prim Sch
Wickham Green
Grey's Copse
Windingwood La
PO
Mast
Resr
Long Border
Wickham Rails
New Copse
Wormstall
Wormstall Wood
Lip La
Orpenham Farm
B4000
Clapton
Clapton Farm
Lower Farm
Harrod's Border
Harrod's Barn
4
73
3
72
2
71
1
70
38
39
40

102
76

75
49

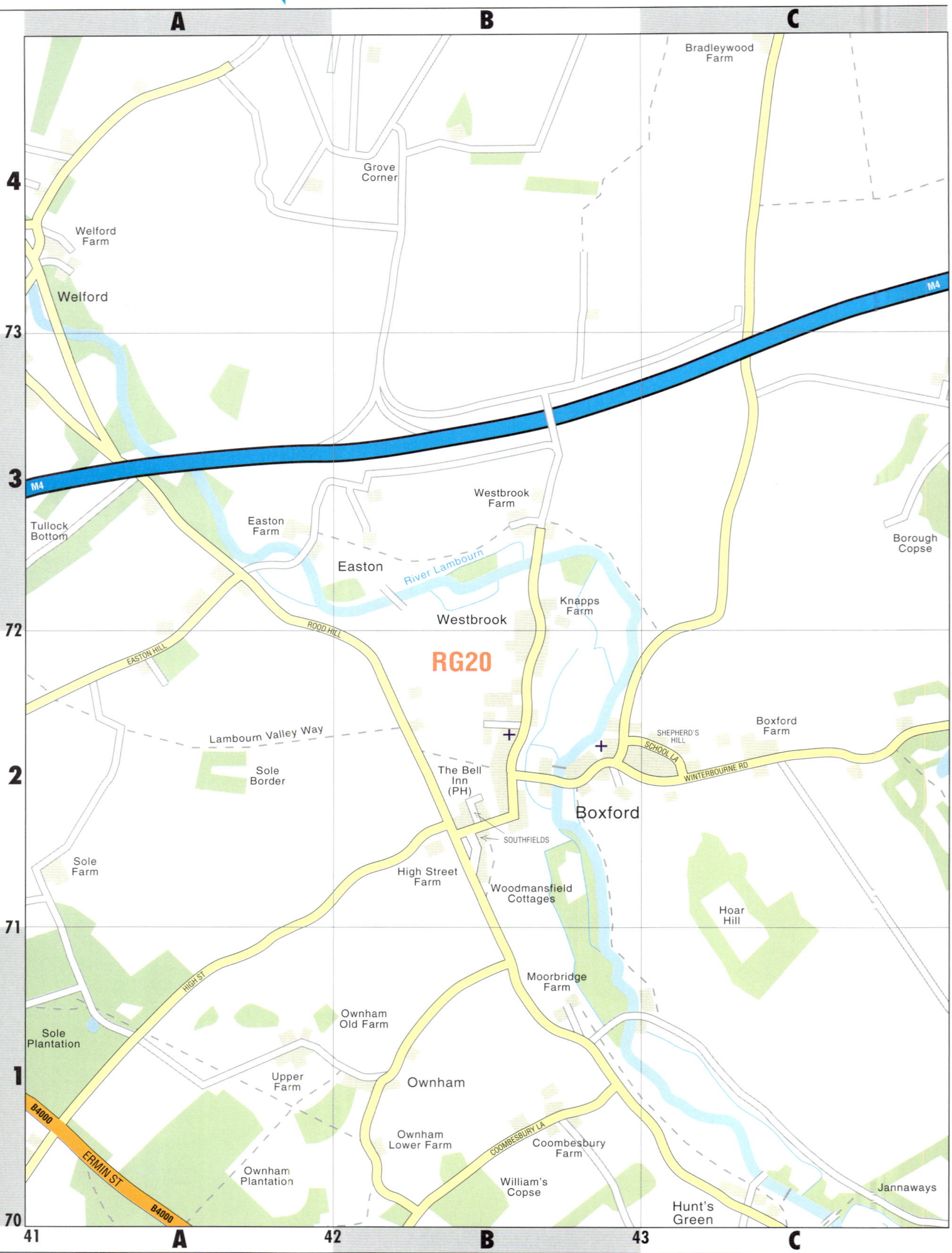
A
B
C
Bradleywood Farm
Grove Corner
Welford Farm
Welford
M4
Tullock Bottom
Easton Farm
Westbrook Farm
Easton
River Lambourn
Westbrook
Knapps Farm
Borough Copse
ROOD HILL
EASTON HILL
RG20
Lambourn Valley Way
Sole Border
The Bell Inn (PH)
SHEPHERD'S HILL
SCHOOL LA
WINTERBOURNE RD
Boxford Farm
Boxford
SOUTHFIELDS
Sole Farm
High Street Farm
Woodmansfield Cottages
Hoar Hill
Moorbridge Farm
HIGH ST
Ownham Old Farm
Sole Plantation
Upper Farm
Ownham
B4000
ERMIN ST
Ownham Lower Farm
COOMBESBURY LA
Coombesbury Farm
Ownham Plantation
William's Copse
Hunt's Green
Jannaways
4
73
3
72
2
71
1
70
41
42
43

75
103

50
78

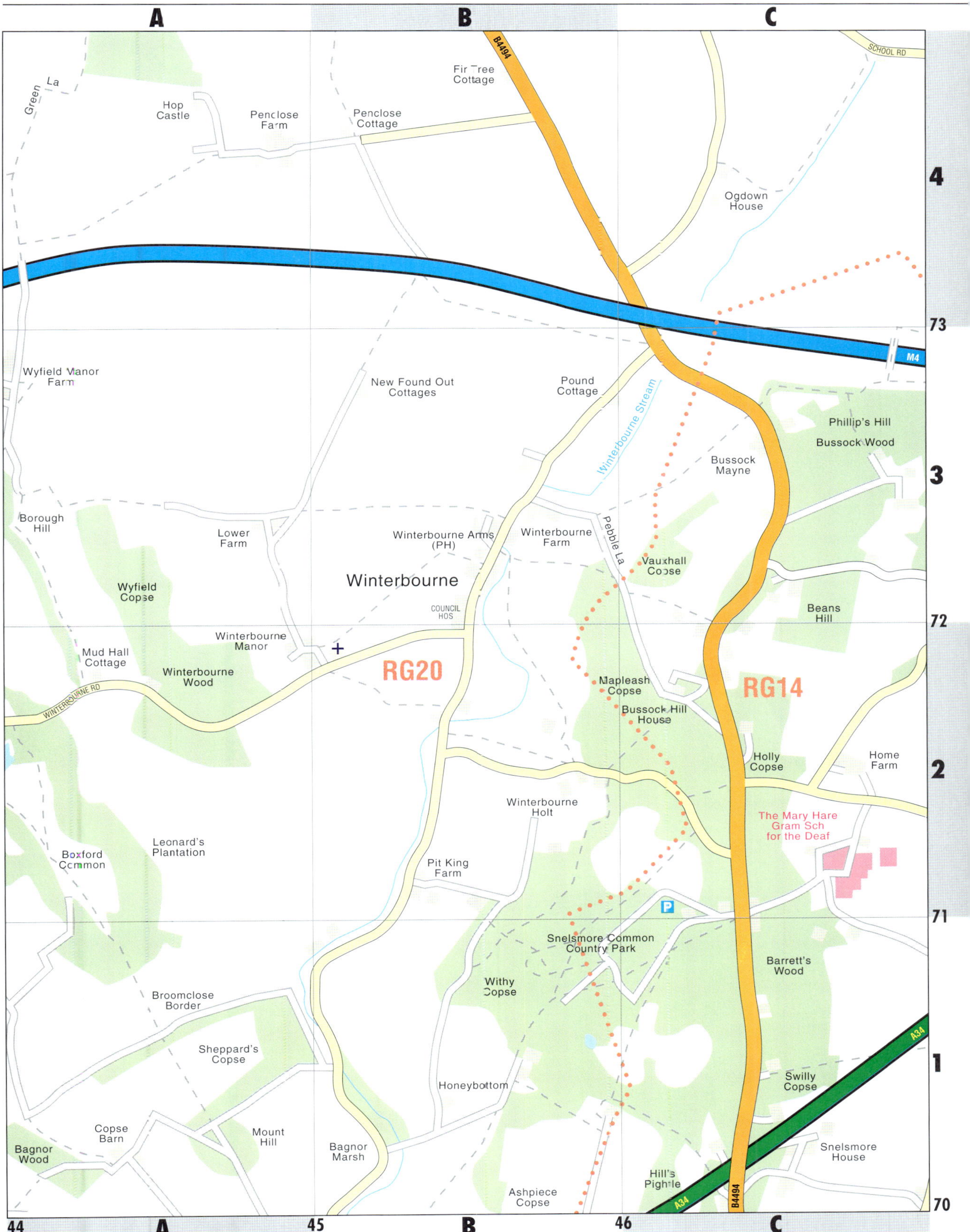
A
B
C
Green La
Hop Castle
Penclose Farm
Penclose Cottage
Fir Tree Cottage
B4494
SCHOOL RD
Ogdown House
4
M4
73
Wyfield Manor Farm
New Found Out Cottages
Pound Cottage
Winterbourne Stream
Phillip's Hill
Bussock Wood
Bussock Mayne
3
Borough Hill
Lower Farm
Winterbourne Arms (PH)
Winterbourne Farm
Pebble La
Vauxhall Copse
Winterbourne
Wyfield Copse
COUNCIL HOS
Beans Hill
72
Mud Hall Cottage
Winterbourne Manor
Winterbourne Wood
WINTERBOURNE RD
RG20
Mapleash Copse
Bussock Hill House
RG14
Holly Copse
Home Farm
2
Winterbourne Holt
The Mary Hare Gram Sch for the Deaf
Leonard's Plantation
Boxford Common
Pit King Farm
P
71
Snelsmore Common Country Park
Barrett's Wood
Withy Copse
Broomclose Border
Sheppard's Copse
A34
1
Honeybottom
Swilly Copse
Copse Barn
Mount Hill
Bagnor Wood
Bagnor Marsh
Snelsmore House
Hill's Pightle
Ashpiece Copse
B4494
A34
70
44
A
45
B
46
C

104
78

77
51

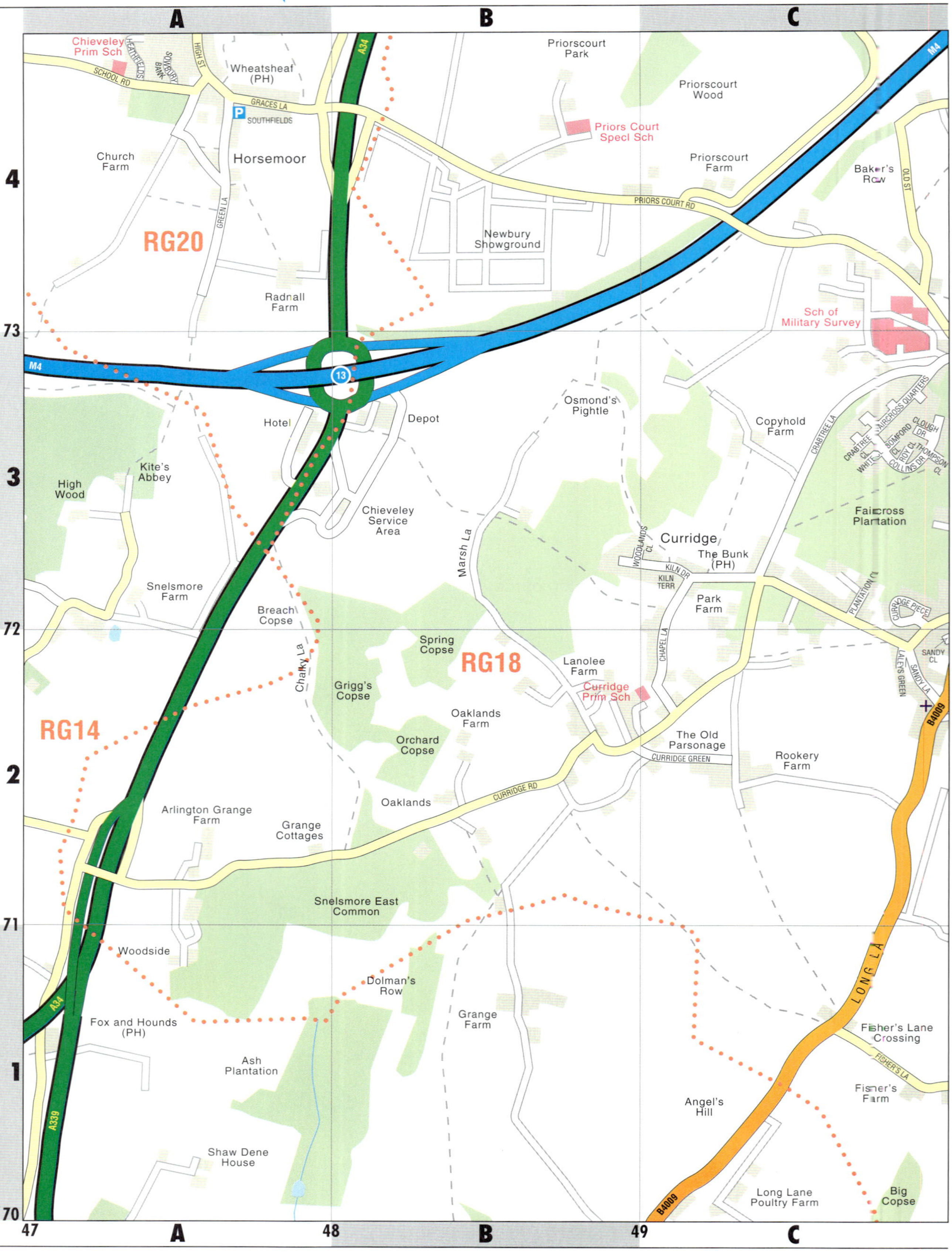
A
B
C
4
73
3
72
2
71
1
70
47
48
49
Chieveley Prim Sch
SCHOOL RD
HEATHFIELDS
SOWBURY BANK
HIGH ST
Wheatsheaf (PH)
GRACES LA
SOUTHFIELDS
A34
Priorscourt Park
Priorscourt Wood
Priors Court Specl Sch
Church Farm
Horsemoor
Priorscourt Farm
Baker's Row
OLD ST
M4
PRIORS COURT RD
GREEN LA
RG20
Newbury Showground
Radnall Farm
Sch of Military Survey
13
Osmond's Pightle
Hotel
Depot
Copyhold Farm
CRABTREE LA
High Wood
Kite's Abbey
Chieveley Service Area
Faircross Plantation
Marsh La
Curridge
WOODLANDS CL
The Bunk (PH)
KILN DR
KILN TERR
Snelsmore Farm
Breach Copse
Park Farm
PLANTATION CL
CURRIDGE PIECE
Spring Copse
RG18
Lanolee Farm
CHAPEL LA
SANDY CL
LALEYS GREEN
SANDY LA
Chalky La
Grigg's Copse
Curridge Prim Sch
RG14
Oaklands Farm
B4009
Orchard Copse
The Old Parsonage
CURRIDGE GREEN
Rookery Farm
Oaklands
CURRIDGE RD
Arlington Grange Farm
Grange Cottages
Snelsmore East Common
Woodside
LONG LA
Dolman's Row
Grange Farm
Fox and Hounds (PH)
Fisher's Lane Crossing
FISHER'S LA
Ash Plantation
Angel's Hill
Fisher's Farm
A339
Shaw Dene House
Long Lane Poultry Farm
Big Copse

77
105

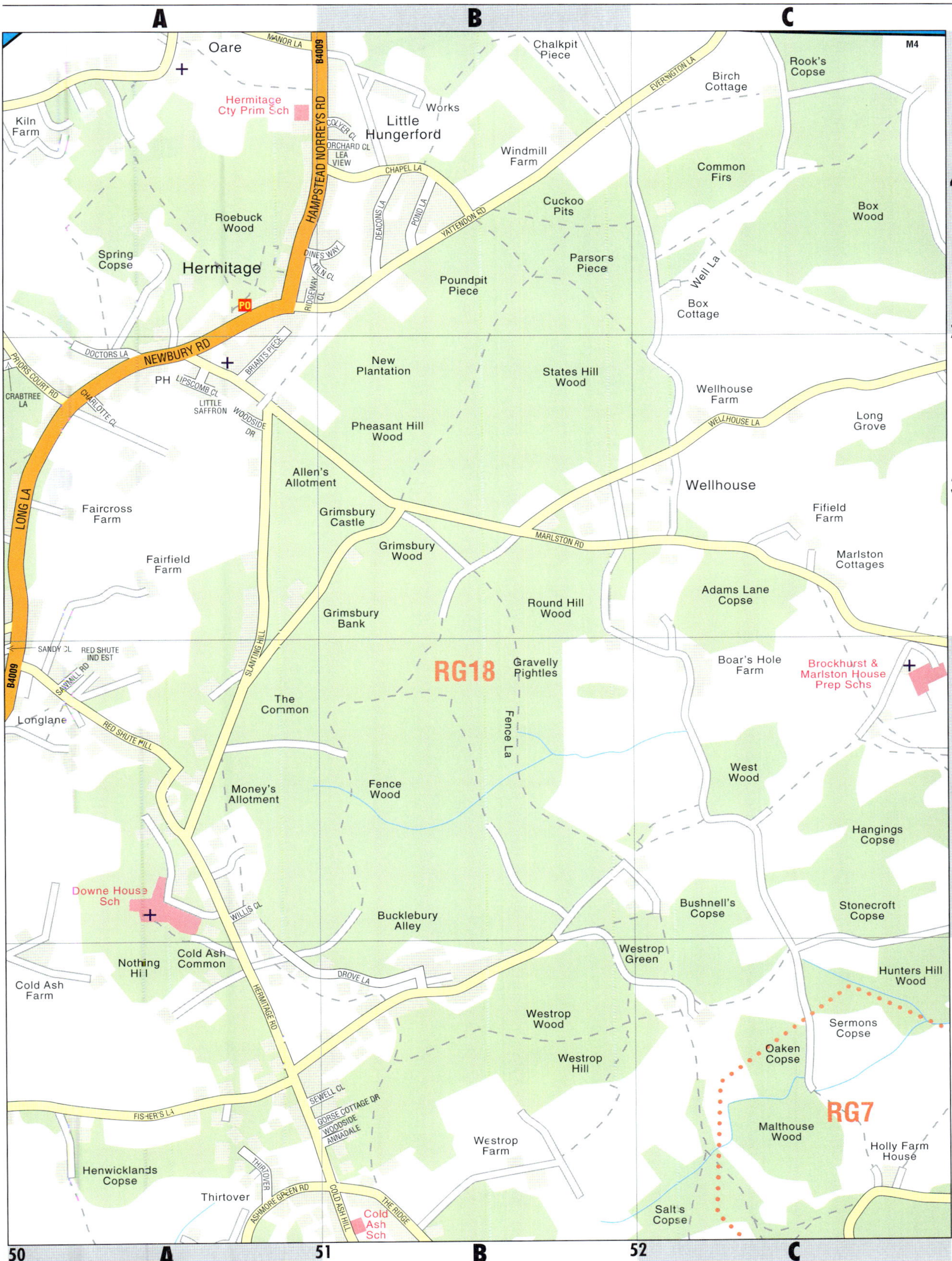
A
B
C
Oare
MANOR LA
B4009
Chalkpit Piece
EVERINGTON LA
Birch Cottage
Rook's Copse
M4
Kiln Farm
Hermitage Cty Prim Sch
HAMPSTEAD NORREYS RD
COLYER CL
ORCHARD CL
LEA VIEW
Works
Little Hungerford
Windmill Farm
Common Firs
CHAPEL LA
4
Roebuck Wood
DEACONS LA
POND LA
YATTENDON RD
Cuckoo Pits
Box Wood
Spring Copse
Hermitage
DINES WAY
KILN CL
RIDGEWAY CL
Poundpit Piece
Parsons Piece
Well La
Box Cottage
PO
DOCTORS LA
NEWBURY RD
BRIANTS PIECE
73
PRIORS COURT RD
CRABTREE LA
PH
LIPSCOMB CL
LITTLE SAFFRON
CHARLOTTE CL
WOODSIDE DR
New Plantation
States Hill Wood
Wellhouse Farm
Pheasant Hill Wood
WELLHOUSE LA
Long Grove
Allen's Allotment
Wellhouse
3
LONG LA
Faircross Farm
Grimsbury Castle
Fifield Farm
Grimsbury Wood
MARLSTON RD
Marlston Cottages
Fairfield Farm
Round Hill Wood
Adams Lane Copse
Grimsbury Bank
72
SANDY CL
RED SHUTE IND EST
SLANTING HILL
RG18
Gravelly Pightles
Boar's Hole Farm
Brockhurst & Marlston House Prep Schs
B4009
SAWMILL RD
Longlane
The Common
RED SHUTE HILL
Fence La
West Wood
2
Money's Allotment
Fence Wood
Hangings Copse
Downe House Sch
WILLIS CL
Bucklebury Alley
Bushnell's Copse
Stonecroft Copse
71
Nothing Hill
Cold Ash Common
Westrop Green
Hunters Hill Wood
Cold Ash Farm
DROVE LA
HERMITAGE RD
Westrop Wood
Sermons Copse
Oaken Copse
Westrop Hill
1
SEWELL CL
GORSE COTTAGE DR
WOODSIDE
ANNADALE
FISHER'S LA
RG7
Malthouse Wood
Westrop Farm
Holly Farm House
THIRTOVER
Henwicklands Copse
Thirtover
ASHMORE GREEN RD
COLD ASH HILL
THE RIDGE
Cold Ash Sch
Salt's Copse
70
50
51
52

79
53

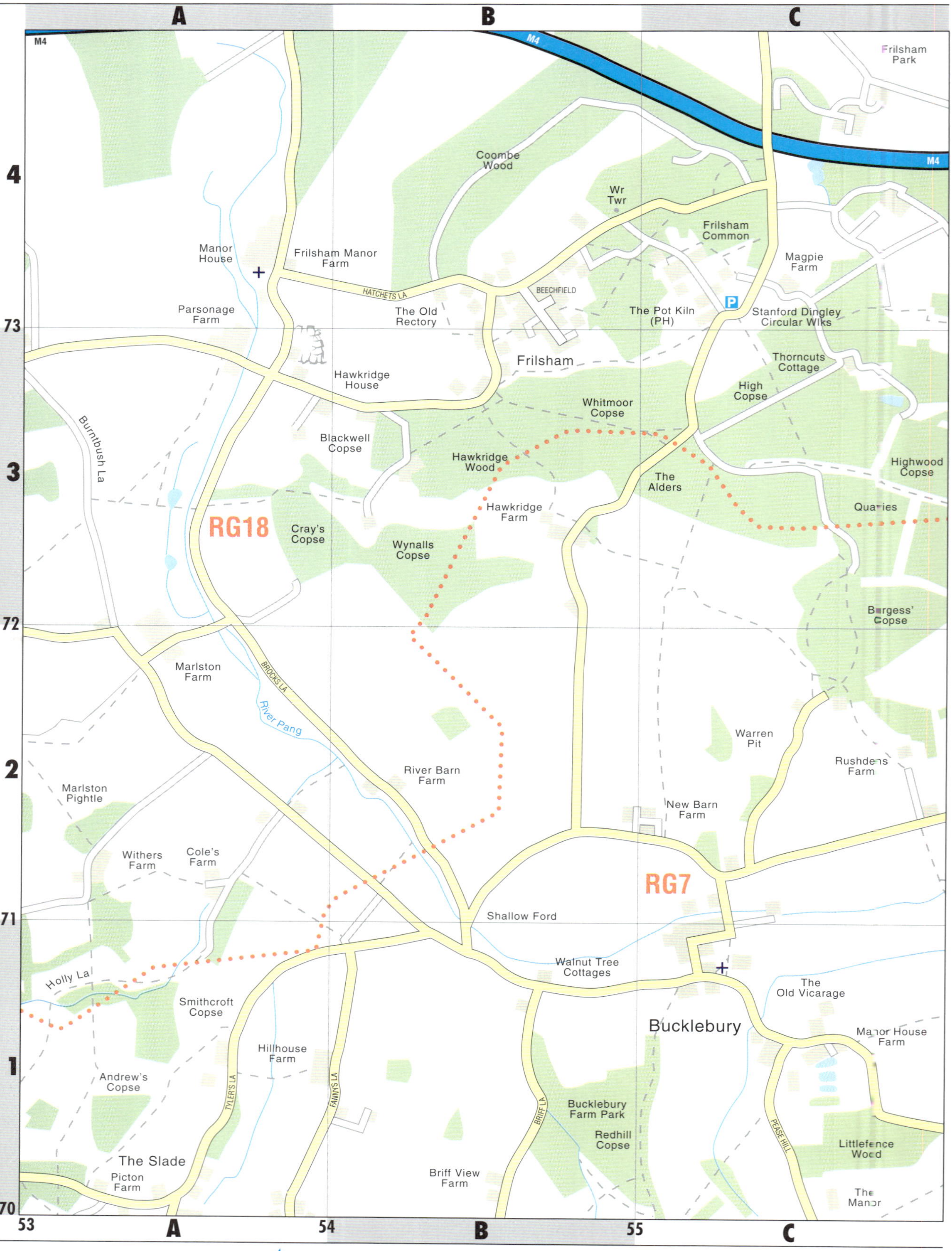
A
B
C
4
73
3
72
2
71
1
70
53
54
55
M4
Frilsham Park
Coombe Wood
Wr Twr
Frilsham Common
Magpie Farm
Manor House
Frilsham Manor Farm
HATCHETS LA
BEECHFIELD
The Pot Kiln (PH)
Stanford Dingley Circular Wlks
Parsonage Farm
The Old Rectory
Frilsham
Thorncuts Cottage
Hawkridge House
High Copse
Whitmoor Copse
Burntbush La
Blackwell Copse
Hawkridge Wood
The Alders
Highwood Copse
RG18
Hawkridge Farm
Quarries
Cray's Copse
Wynalls Copse
Burgess' Copse
Marlston Farm
BROCKS LA
River Pang
Warren Pit
Rushdens Farm
River Barn Farm
Marlston Pightle
New Barn Farm
Withers Farm
Cole's Farm
RG7
Shallow Ford
Holly La
Walnut Tree Cottages
The Old Vicarage
Smithcroft Copse
Bucklebury
Manor House Farm
Hillhouse Farm
Andrew's Copse
TYLER'S LA
FANNY'S LA
BRIFF LA
Bucklebury Farm Park
Redhill Copse
PEASE HILL
Littlefence Wood
The Slade
Picton Farm
Briff View Farm
The Manor

79
107

54
82

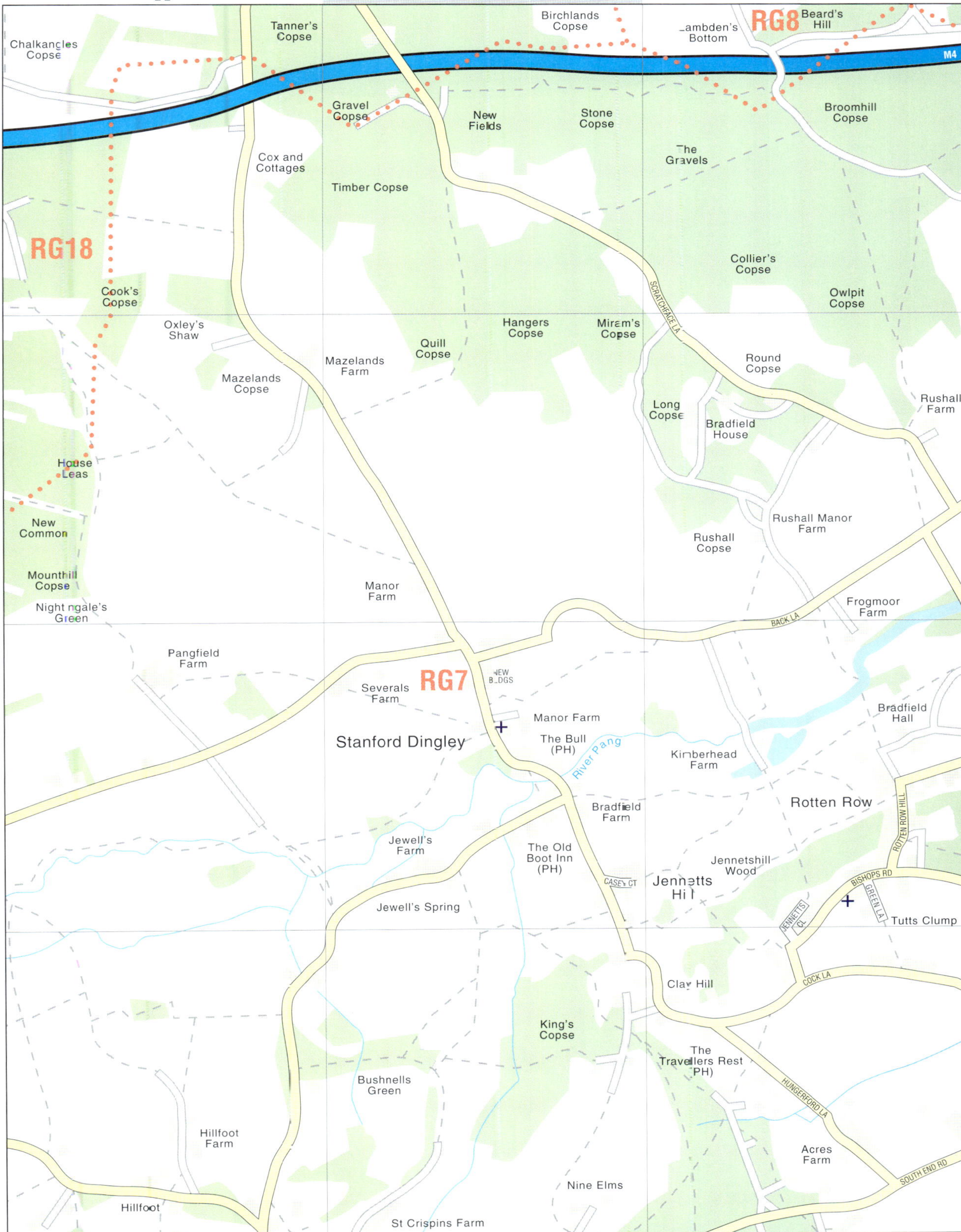
A
B
C
Chalkancles Copse
Tanner's Copse
Birchlands Copse
Lambden's Bottom
RG8
Beard's Hill
M4
Gravel Copse
New Fields
Stone Copse
Broomhill Copse
Cox and Cottages
Timber Copse
The Gravels
4
RG18
Collier's Copse
Cook's Copse
Owlpit Copse
Scratchface La
73
Oxley's Shaw
Hangers Copse
Miram's Copse
Quill Copse
Mazelands Farm
Round Copse
Mazelands Copse
Rushall Farm
Long Copse
Bradfield House
3
House Leas
New Common
Rushall Manor Farm
Rushall Copse
Mounthill Copse
Manor Farm
Frogmoor Farm
Nightingale's Green
Back La
72
Pangfield Farm
RG7
New Bldgs
Severals Farm
Bradfield Hall
Manor Farm
Stanford Dingley
The Bull (PH)
River Pang
Kimberhead Farm
2
Rotten Row
Bradfield Farm
Rotten Row Hill
Jewell's Farm
The Old Boot Inn (PH)
Jennetshill Wood
Bishops Rd
Casey Ct
Jennetts Hill
Green La
Jewell's Spring
Jennetts Cl
Tutts Clump
71
Clay Hill
Cock La
King's Copse
The Travellers Rest (PH)
1
Bushnells Green
Hungerford La
Hillfoot Farm
Acres Farm
South End Rd
Nine Elms
Hillfoot
St Crispins Farm
70
56
57
58

108
82

81
55
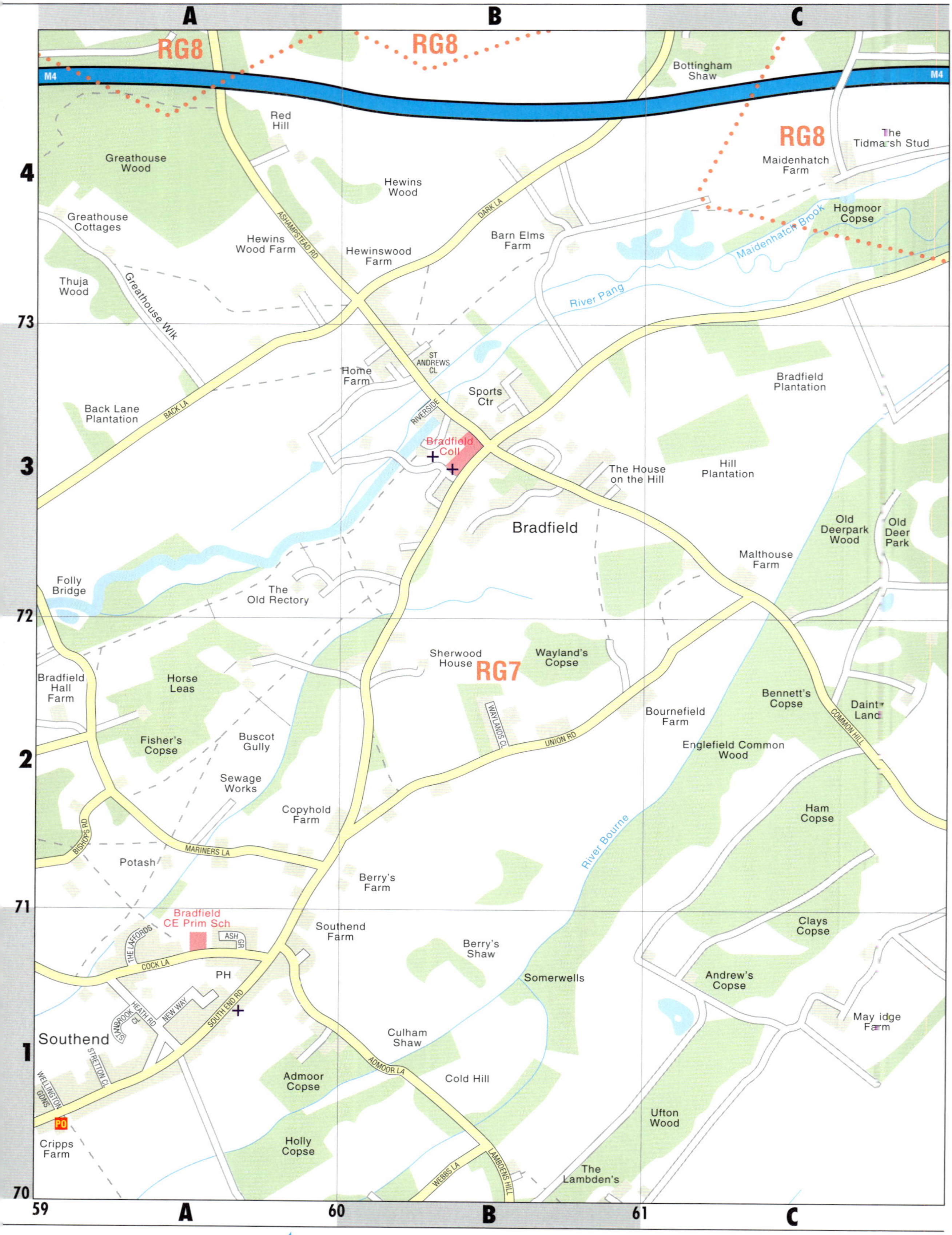
A
B
C
RG8
RG8
M4
M4
Bottingham Shaw
Red Hill
RG8
The Tidmarsh Stud
Maidenhatch Farm
Greathouse Wood
4
Hewins Wood
Greathouse Cottages
Hogmoor Copse
Maidenhatch Brook
ASHAMPSTEAD RD
DARK LA
Barn Elms Farm
Hewins Wood Farm
Hewinswood Farm
Thuja Wood
Greathouse Wlk
River Pang
73
ST ANDREWS CL
Home Farm
Bradfield Plantation
Sports Ctr
Back Lane Plantation
BACK LA
RIVERSIDE
Bradfield Coll
3
The House on the Hill
Hill Plantation
Old Deerpark Wood
Old Deer Park
Bradfield
Malthouse Farm
Folly Bridge
The Old Rectory
72
Sherwood House
Wayland's Copse
RG7
Bradfield Hall Farm
Horse Leas
Bennett's Copse
Dainty Land
Bournefield Farm
WAYLANDS CL
COMMON HILL
UNION RD
Fisher's Copse
Buscot Gully
Englefield Common Wood
2
Sewage Works
Copyhold Farm
Ham Copse
BISHOPS RD
MARINERS LA
River Bourne
Potash
Berry's Farm
71
Bradfield CE Prim Sch
Southend Farm
Clays Copse
THE LAFFORDS
ASH GR
Berry's Shaw
COCK LA
PH
Somerwells
Andrew's Copse
HEATH RD
NEW WAY
SOUTH END RD
STANBROOK CL
May idge Farm
Southend
Culham Shaw
1
STRETTON CL
ADMOOR LA
Admoor Copse
Cold Hill
WELLINGTON GDNS
PO
Ufton Wood
Cripps Farm
Holly Copse
WEBBS LA
LAMBDENS HILL
The Lambden's
70
59
A
60
B
61
C
81
109

56
84

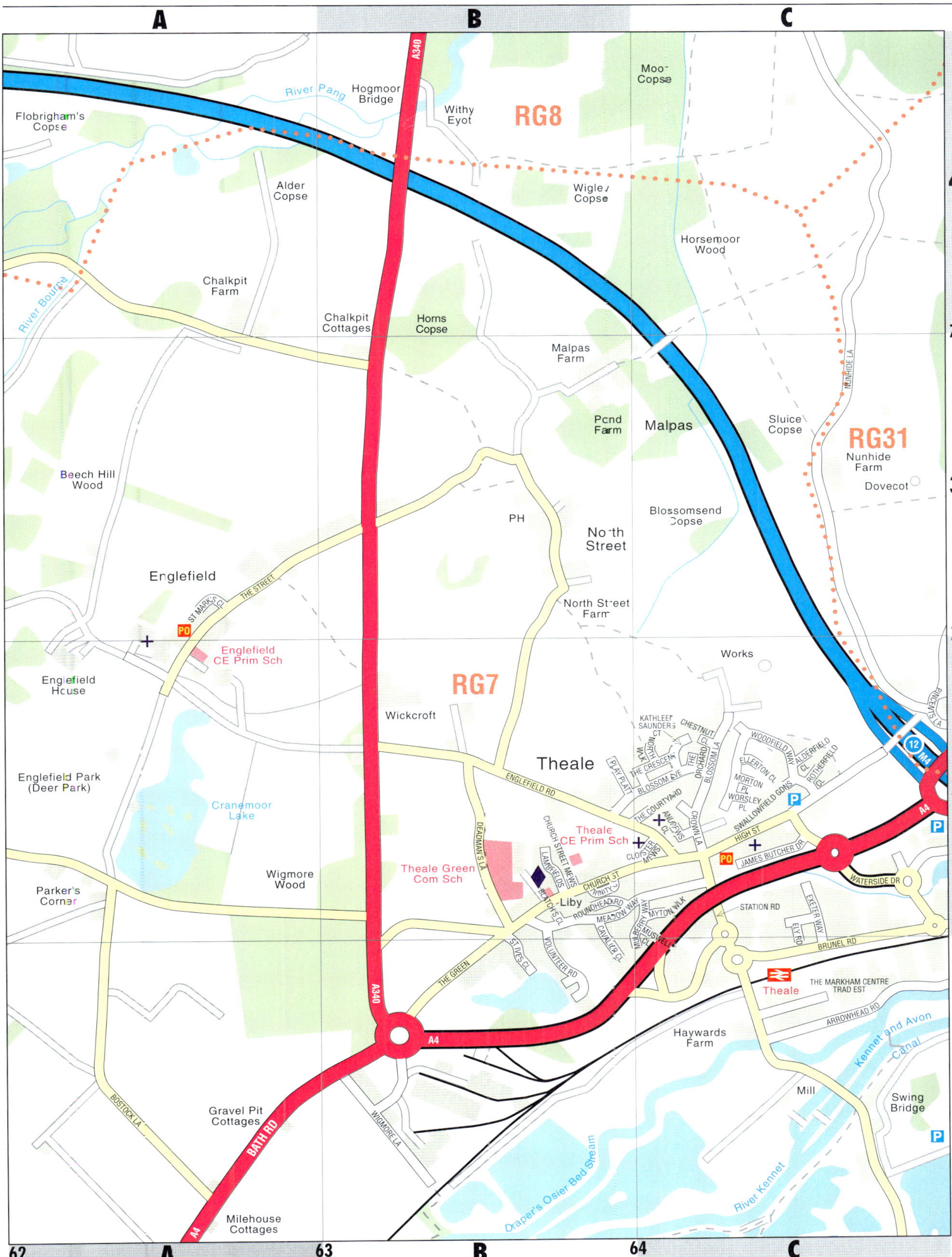
A
B
C
4
73
3
72
2
71
1
70
62
63
64
River Pang
Hogmoor Bridge
Flobrigham's Copse
Withy Eyot
RG8
Moor Copse
Alder Copse
Wigley Copse
Horsemoor Wood
Chalkpit Farm
River Bourne
Chalkpit Cottages
Horns Copse
Malpas Farm
Pond Farm
Malpas
Sluice Copse
RG31
Nunhide Farm
Dovecot
NUNHIDE LA
Beech Hill Wood
PH
North Street
Blossomsend Copse
Englefield
THE STREET
ST MARK'S CL
PO
North Street Farm
Englefield CE Prim Sch
Works
Englefield House
RG7
Wickcroft
KATHLEEN SAUNDERS CT
CHESTNUT
WOODFIELD WAY
ALDERFIELD CL
ROTHERFIELD CL
PINCENTS LA
12
M4
Theale
ENGLEFIELD RD
THE CRESCENT
NORTH WALK
PLAY PLATT
BLOSSOM AVE
THE ORCHARD
BLOSSOM LA
ELLERTON CL
MORTON PL
WORSLEY PL
SWALLOWFIELD GDNS
Englefield Park (Deer Park)
Cranemoor Lake
THE COURTYARD
CROWN LA
HIGH ST
DEADMAN'S LA
CHURCH STREET MEWS
Theale CE Prim Sch
CLOISTER MEWS
JAMES BUTCHER DR
A4
Theale Green Com Sch
LAMBFIELDS
CHURCH ST
TRINITY
WATERSIDE DR
Wigmore Wood
Parker's Corner
BEECH'S CL
Liby
ROUNDHEAD RD
MEADOW WAY
MULBERRY WAY
MYTON WLK
STATION RD
EXETER WAY
ELY RD
CAVALIER CL
MUSWELL CL
BRUNEL RD
ST IVES CL
VOLUNTEER RD
THE GREEN
A340
THE MARKHAM CENTRE TRAD EST
Theale
ARROWHEAD RD
Kennet and Avon Canal
Haywards Farm
Mill
Swing Bridge
BOSTOCK LA
Gravel Pit Cottages
BATH RD
WIGMORE LA
Draper's Osier Bed Stream
River Kennet
Milehouse Cottages

110
84

83
57

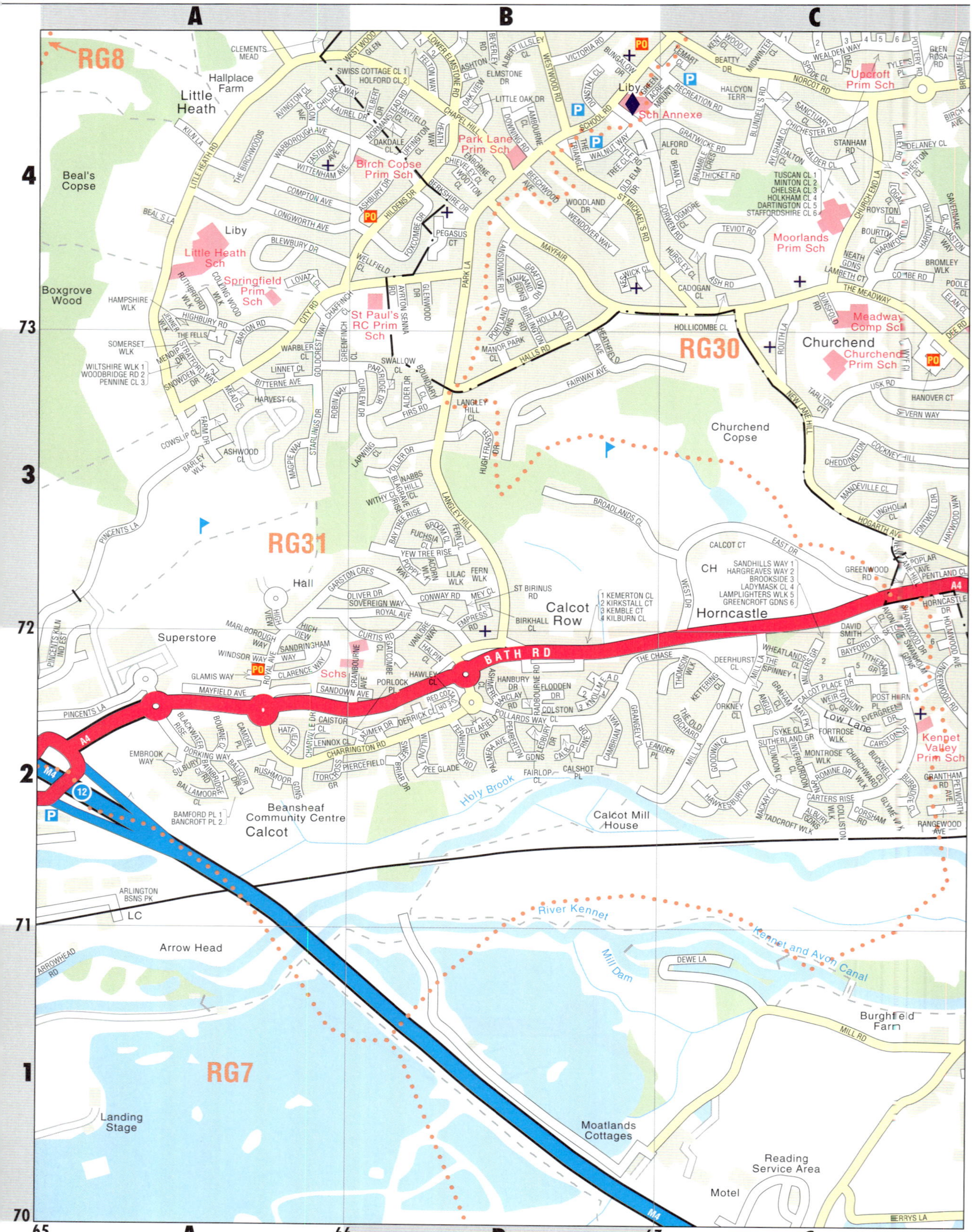
A
B
C
RG8
Little Heath
Hallplace Farm
Beal's Copse
Boxgrove Wood
Liby
Little Heath Sch
Springfield Prim Sch
St Paul's RC Prim Sch
Birch Copse Prim Sch
Park Lane Prim Sch
Sch Annexe
Upcroft Prim Sch
Moorlands Prim Sch
Meadway Comp Sch
Churchend
Churchend Prim Sch
RG30
Churchend Copse
RG31
Hall
Superstore
Calcot Row
Horncastle
BATH RD
A4
Schs
Kennet Valley Prim Sch
Low Lane
Holy Brook
Beansheaf Community Centre
Calcot
Calcot Mill House
ARLINGTON BSNS PK
LC
Arrow Head
River Kennet
Kennet and Avon Canal
Mill Dam
DEWE LA
Burghfield Farm
MILL RD
RG7
Landing Stage
Moatlands Cottages
Reading Service Area
Motel
M4
12
4
73
3
72
2
71
1
70
65
66
67

83
111

C4
1 CAMBRIDGE ST
2 LITTLE ST
3 CANNON ST
4 FOXGLOVE GDNS
5 STANLEY GR
6 MASON CT
7 CAROLINE ST
8 MALTHOUSE LA
9 STRATHEDEN PL
10 VINCENT HO
11 BURFORD CT
12 BRUNSWICK LODGE
13 TAYLOR CT

58

C4
14 TETBURY CT
15 BELLEVUE TERR
16 WINDSOR CT
17 ALLISON CT
18 CHERWELL CRES
19 BRANKSOME CT

86

C4
20 NATHAN CT
21 FRANKLIN CT
22 MULLION CT
23 NICHOLAS CT
24 ALEXANDER CT
25 CHANCERY MEWS
26 SEAFIELD CT
27 HERITAGE CT

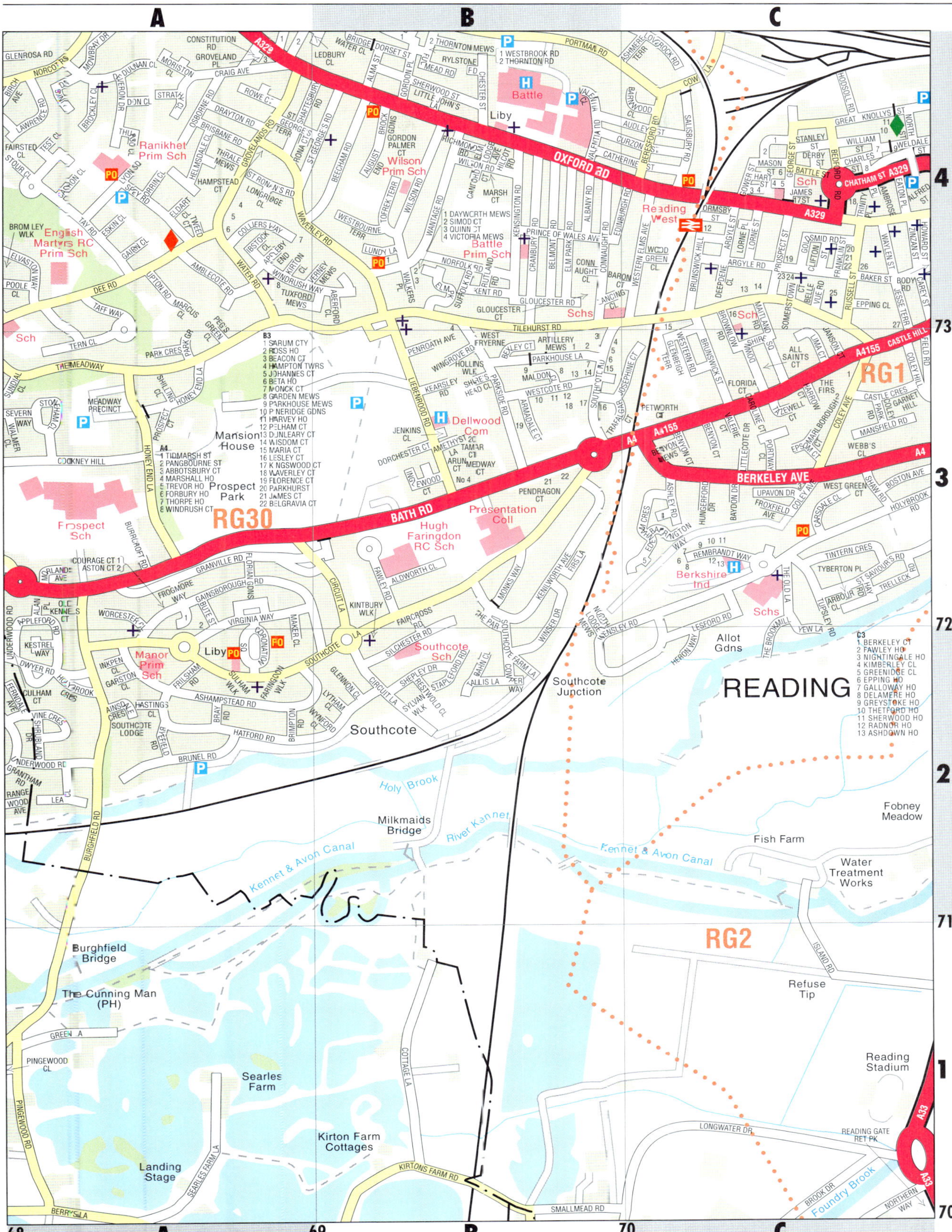

112
86

A4
1 BELLMAN CT
2 MONTROSE HO
3 FRIARS WLK
4 SHOESMITHS CT
5 HARRIS ARC
6 ANSTEY RD
7 TALBOT CT
8 MALTINGS PL
9 WATERSIDE GDNS
10 SWAN PL
11 YIELD HALL LA
12 THORN LA
13 HIGHBRIDGE WHARF

85

A4
14 CRANE WHARF
15 MARKET WAY
16 MAYFLOWER CT
17 KINGS REACH CT
18 CHAPEL CT
19 SOUTHERN CT

59

A4
20 THE CHAMBERS
21 MARIE DAVIS CT
B4
1 THE PLUMMERY
2 SELBORNE CT
3 GRANTLEY HTS
4 OSPREY CT
5 SIDMOUTH CT
6 GREYS CT
7 PADLEY CT
8 TYRREL CT
9 THE DELL
10 ROYAL CT
11 HARRY TEE CT
12 KENNET SIDE
13 WEIRSIDE CT
14 MORRISS CT
15 MANDELA CT
16 VICTORIA WAY
17 RUPERT WLK
18 ICARUS CT
19 RUPERT SQ
20 KINGSGATE PL
21 HAVEN CT
22 SAXON CT
23 CARNOUSTIE CT
24 HENRY CT
25 EDWARD PL
26 CHARLES PL
27 ALDERNEY CT
28 SHELLEY CT
29 JOHN BALLIOL CT
30 TURNBERRY CT
31 GULLANE CT
32 GLENEAGLES CT
33 TROON CT
34 APPLETON HO
35 ST ANDREWS CT
36 PRESTWICK CT
37 WEAVERS CT

A B C

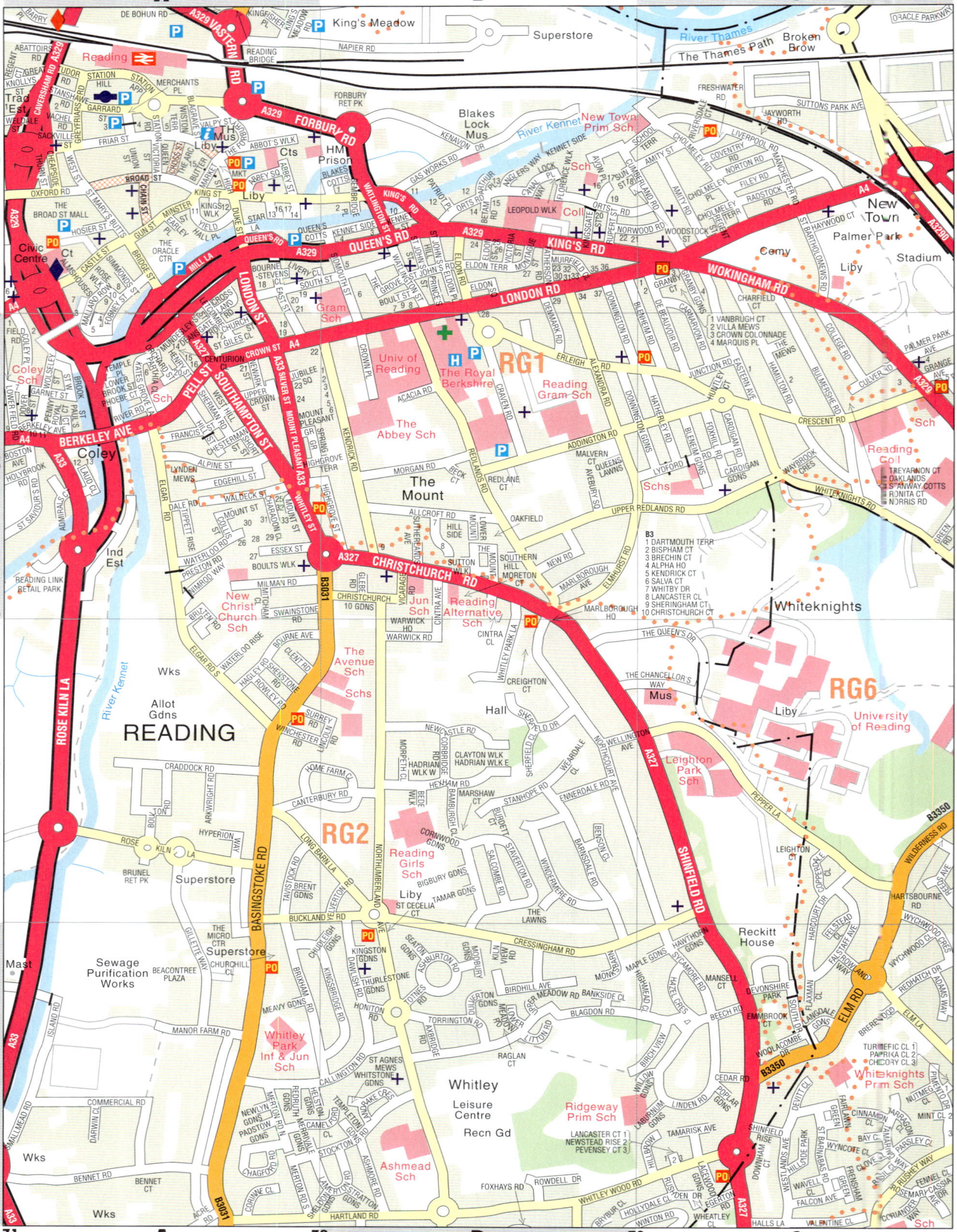

71 A 72 B 73 C

A3
1 BLENHEIM TERR
2 CHERITON CT
3 WILLOW ST
4 AVOCET CT
5 NEW BRIGHT ST
6 FOUNDRY PL
7 GARNET HILL
8 CHURCH TERR
9 ST SAVIOUR'S TERR
10 CRANFORD MEWS
11 RODNEY CT
12 BUNYAN CT
13 BELFORD CT
14 ST GILES CT
15 SOLENT CT
16 HAMBLE CT
17 LETCOMBE CT
18 ELIZABETH MEWS
19 BLENHEIM CT

85

A3
20 DOROTHY ST
21 PRIORS CT
22 NELSON TERR
23 SILVER STREET FLATS
24 WINDSOR SQ
25 JACK PRICE CT
26 AVELEY WLK
27 MELLOR WLK
28 ELIZABETH WLK

113

A3
29 SPRING TERR
30 KINVER WLK
31 BLYTH WLK
32 TAYNTON WLK
33 WESTERHAM WLK

60 88

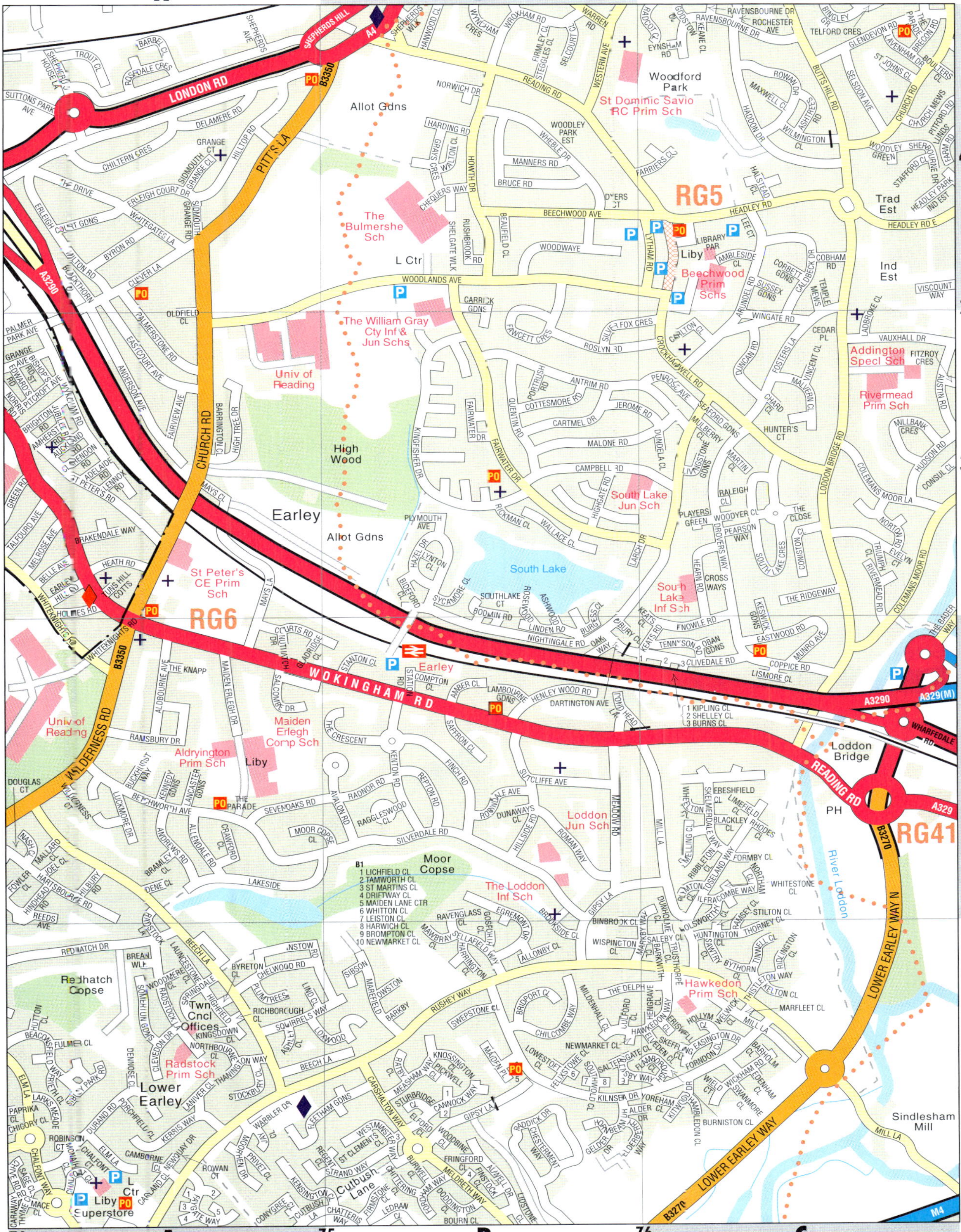

A B C
74 75 76
70 71 72 73

A1
1 WARNSHAM CL
2 SHARPETHORPE CL
3 BERSTEAD CL
4 WATERSFIELD CL
5 RUSTINGTON CL

114 88

87
61

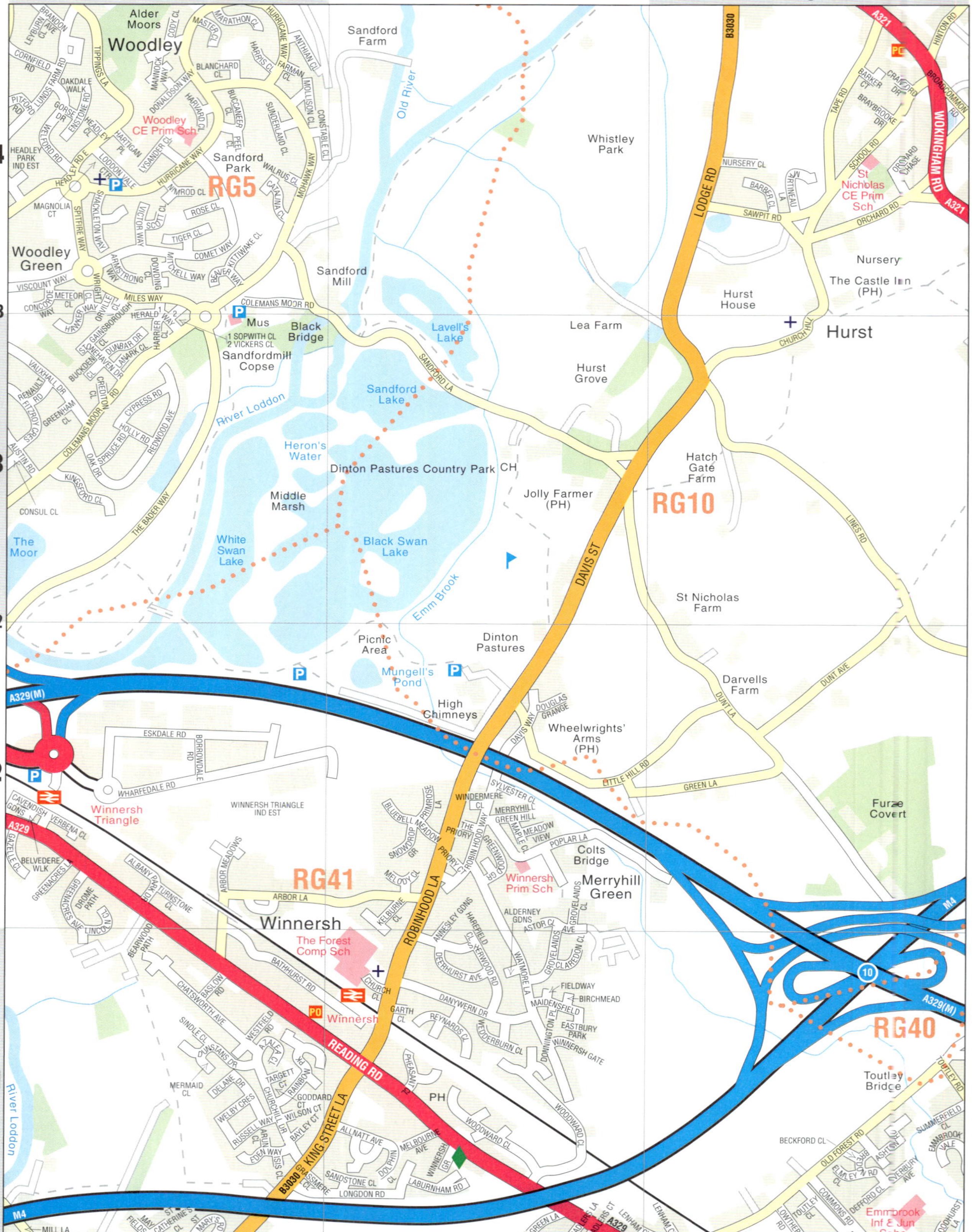
A
B
C
4
3
2
1
73
72
71
70
77
78
79
Woodley
Alder Moors
Woodley CE Prim Sch
Sandford Park
RG5
Woodley Green
Sandford Farm
Old River
Sandford Mill
Whistley Park
Lodge Rd
B3030
Hurst House
Lea Farm
Hurst
Hurst Grove
St Nicholas CE Prim Sch
Nursery
The Castle Inn (PH)
Wokingham Rd
A321
Mus
Black Bridge
Sandfordmill Copse
Lavell's Lake
Sandford Lake
River Loddon
Heron's Water
Dinton Pastures Country Park
CH
Middle Marsh
Jolly Farmer (PH)
Hatch Gate Farm
RG10
Davis St
The Moor
White Swan Lake
Black Swan Lake
Emm Brook
St Nicholas Farm
Picnic Area
Dinton Pastures
Mungell's Pond
High Chimneys
Darvells Farm
Wheelwrights' Arms (PH)
A329(M)
Winnersh Triangle
Winnersh Triangle Ind Est
RG41
Robinhood La
Colts Bridge
Merryhill Green
Winnersh Prim Sch
Furze Covert
M4
Winnersh
The Forest Comp Sch
Winnersh
Reading Rd
A329
King Street La
PH
RG40
Toutley Bridge
River Loddon
Emmbrook Inf & Jun Schs

87
115

62
90

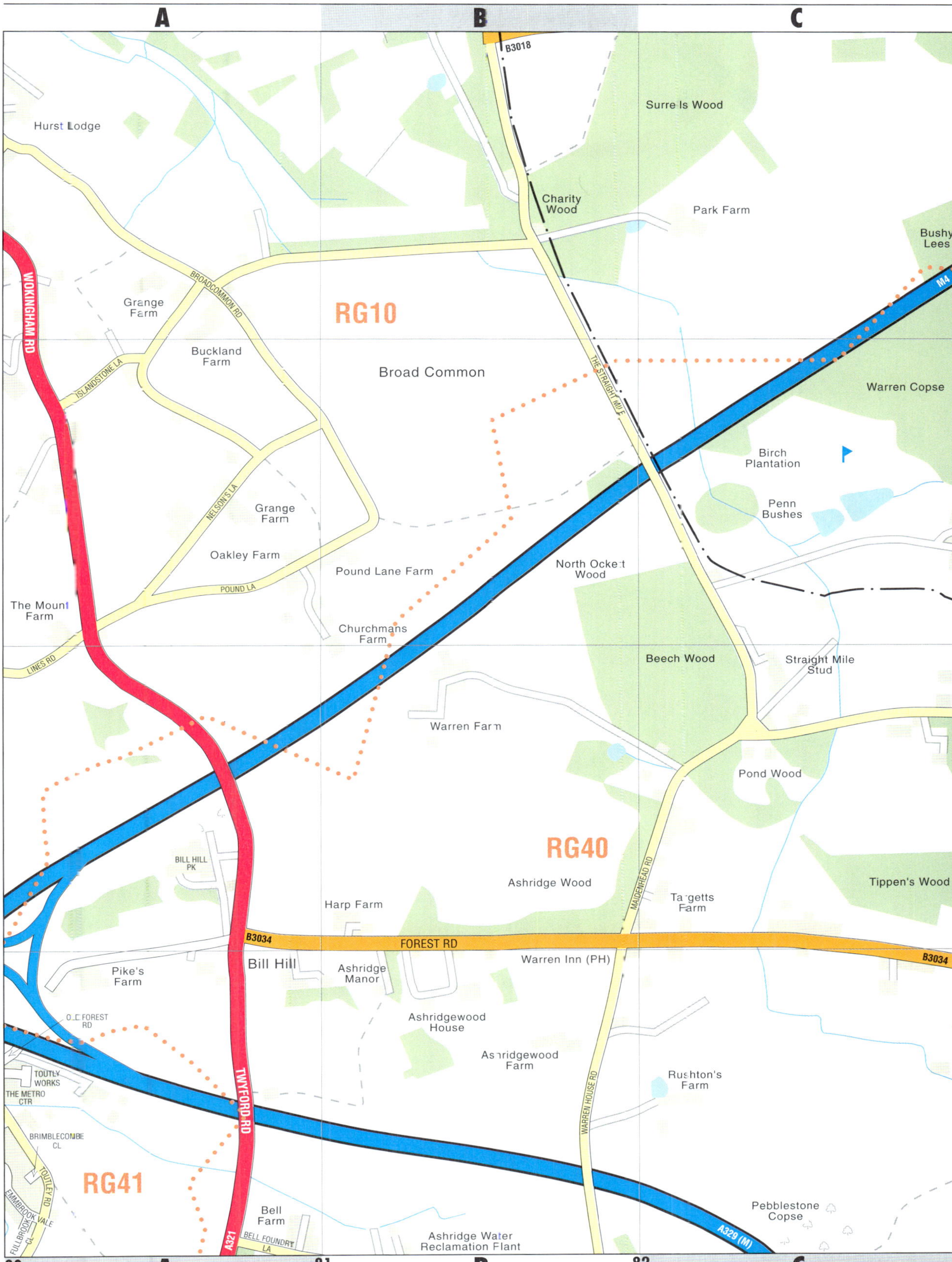
A
B
C
4
73
3
72
2
71
1
70
80
81
82
B3018
Hurst Lodge
Surrels Wood
Charity Wood
Park Farm
Bushy Lees
M4
WOKINGHAM RD
BROADCOMMON RD
Grange Farm
RG10
Buckland Farm
Broad Common
ISLANDSTONE LA
THE STRAIGHT MILE
Warren Copse
Birch Plantation
NELSON'S LA
Grange Farm
Penn Bushes
Oakley Farm
Pound Lane Farm
North Ockett Wood
POUND LA
The Mount Farm
Churchmans Farm
LINES RD
Beech Wood
Straight Mile Stud
Warren Farm
Pond Wood
RG40
BILL HILL PK
Ashridge Wood
MAIDENHEAD RD
Targetts Farm
Tippen's Wood
Harp Farm
B3034
FOREST RD
Warren Inn (PH)
Bill Hill
Pike's Farm
Ashridge Manor
OLD FOREST RD
Ashridgewood House
Ashridgewood Farm
TOUTLEY WORKS
THE METRO CTR
TWYFORD RD
WARREN HOUSE RD
Rushton's Farm
BRIMBLECOMBE CL
TOUTLEY RD
RG41
EMMBROOK VALE
FULLBROOK CL
Bell Farm
Pebblestone Copse
A329 (M)
A321
BELL FOUNDRY LA
Ashridge Water Reclamation Plant

116
90

89
63

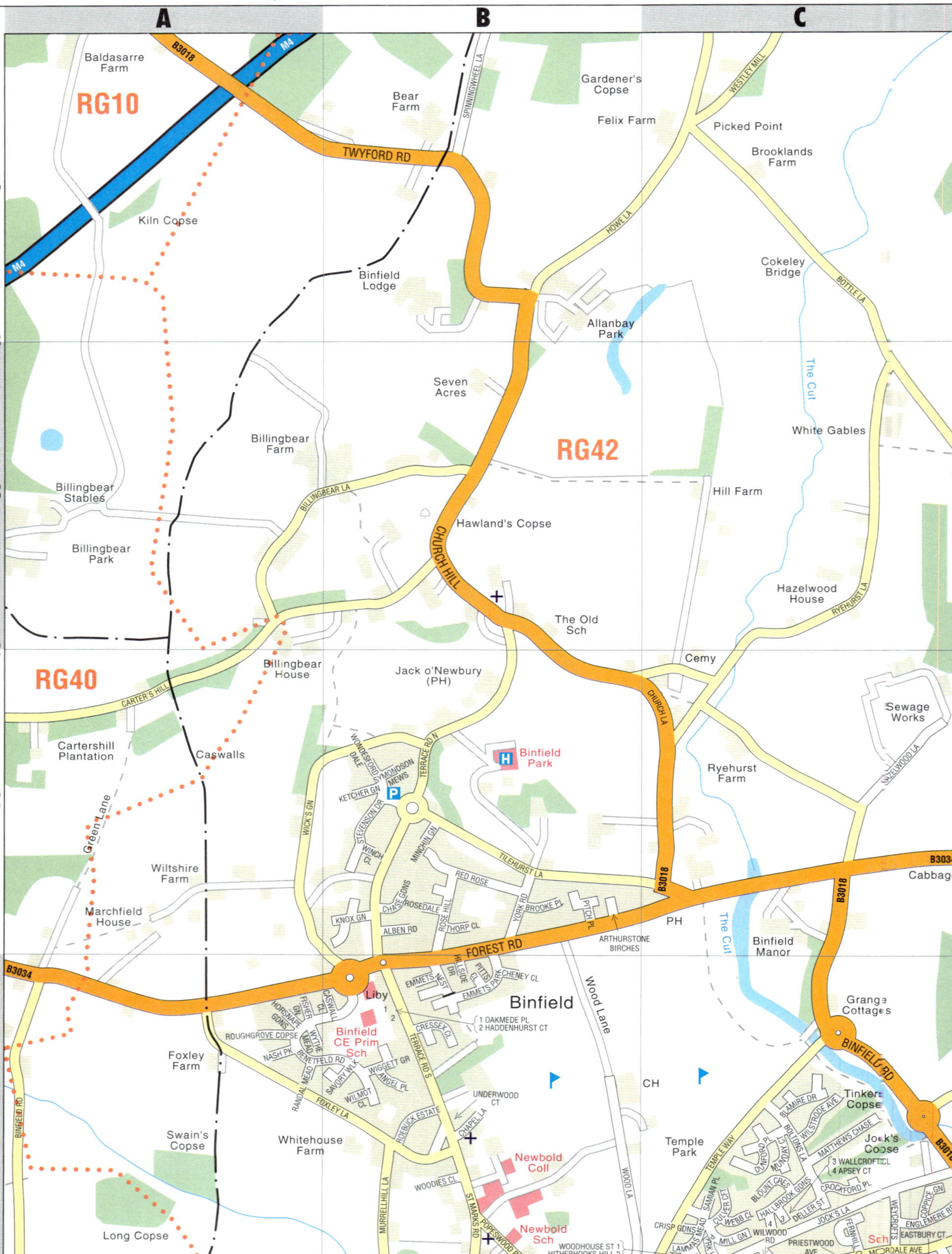
A
B
C
4
73
3
72
2
71
1
70
83
84
85
RG10
RG42
RG40
Baldasarre Farm
Bear Farm
Gardener's Copse
Felix Farm
Picked Point
Brooklands Farm
TWYFORD RD
B3018
M4
Kiln Copse
Binfield Lodge
Allanbay Park
Cokeley Bridge
Seven Acres
The Cut
White Gables
Billingbear Farm
Billingbear Stables
BILLINGBEAR LA
Hawland's Copse
Hill Farm
Billingbear Park
CHURCH HILL
Hazelwood House
The Old Sch
Billingbear House
Jack o'Newbury (PH)
Cemy
CARTER'S HILL
CHURCH LA
Sewage Works
Cartershill Plantation
Caswalls
Binfield Park
Ryehurst Farm
Green Lane
Wiltshire Farm
TILEHURST LA
B3034
Cabbage
Marchfield House
FOREST RD
PH
Binfield Manor
Liby
Binfield
Grange Cottages
Binfield CE Prim Sch
Foxley Farm
Wood Lane
CH
BINFIELD RD
Tinkers Copse
Jock's Copse
Swain's Copse
Whitehouse Farm
Newbold Coll
Temple Park
Long Copse
Newbold Sch
Sch
SPINNINGWHEEL LA
WESTLEY MILL
HOWE LA
BOTTLE LA
RYEHURST LA
HAZELWOOD LA
WONDESFORD DALE
SYMONDSON MEWS
TERRACE RD N
KETCHER GN
STEVENSON DR
WINCH CL
WICK'S GN
MINCHIN GN
RED ROSE
CHASE GDNS
ROSEDALE
ROSE HILL
THORP CL
YORK RD
BROOKE PL
PITCH PL
ARTHURSTONE BIRCHES
KNOX GN
ALBEN RD
HILLSIDE DR
PITTS CL
CHENEY CL
EMMETS NEST
EMMETS PARK
1 OAKMEDE PL
2 HADDENHURST CT
HORSNAPE GDNS
FISHER GN
CASWALL CL
ROUGHGROVE COPSE
NASH PK
WYTHE MEAD
BENETFELD RD
CRESSEX CL
TERRACE RD S
SAVORY WLK
WIGGETT GR
ANGEL PL
WILMOT CL
RANDAL MEAD
FOXLEY LA
ROEBUCK ESTATE
UNDERWOOD CT
CHAPEL LA
WOODIES CL
MURRELLHILL LA
ST MARKS RD
POPESWOOD RD
WOODHOUSE ST 1
HITHERHOOKS HILL 2
WOOD LA
BINFIELD RD
TEMPLE WAY
BLAMIRE DR
WILSTRODE AVE
MATTHEWS CHASE
3 WALLCROFT CL
4 APSEY CT
CROCKFORD PL
DUNFORD PL
MUNDAY CT
BOLTONS LA
BLOUNT CRES
HALLBROOK GDNS
DELLER ST
JOCK'S LA
CULVER CT
SAMIAN PL
WEBB CL
MILL GN
WILWOOD RD
CRISP GDNS
LAMMAS MEAD
PARK LA
PRIESTWOOD AVE
FERNHILL CL
WEYCROFTS
COPPICE GN
ENGLEMERE RD
EASTBURY CT
MORDALE AVE

89
117

64
92
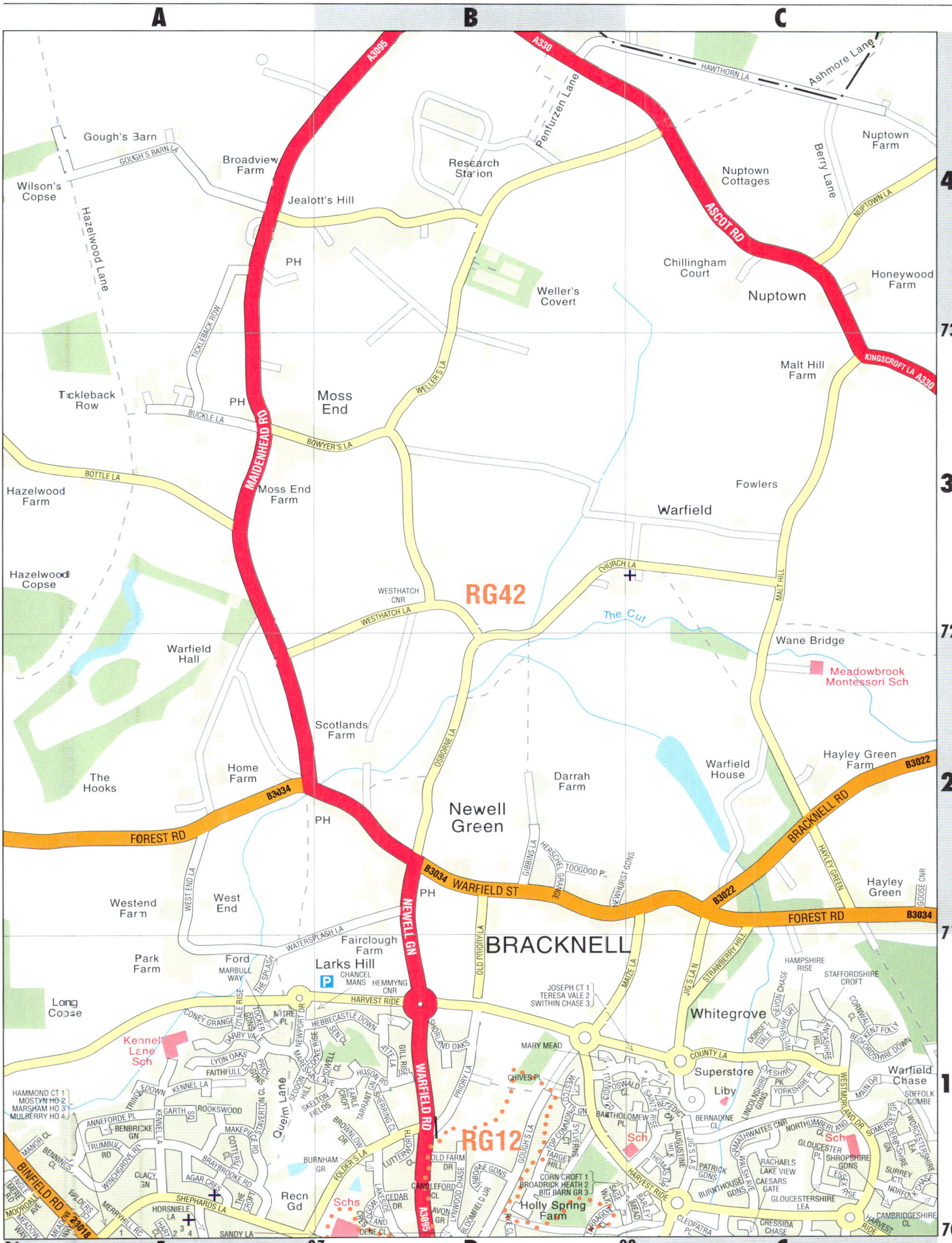
A
B
C
Gough's Barn
GOUGH'S BARN LA
Wilson's Copse
Broadview Farm
Jealott's Hill
Research Station
Penfurzen Lane
HAWTHORN LA
Ashmore Lane
Nuptown Farm
Nuptown Cottages
Berry Lane
ASCOT RD
NUPTOWN LA
Chillingham Court
Nuptown
Honeywood Farm
Hazelwood Lane
PH
Weller's Covert
TICKLEBACK ROW
Tickleback Row
Moss End
WELLER'S LA
KINGSCROFT LA A330
Malt Hill Farm
BUCKLE LA
BOWYER'S LA
MAIDENHEAD RD
BOTTLE LA
Hazelwood Farm
Moss End Farm
Fowlers
Warfield
Hazelwood Copse
CHURCH LA
MALT HILL
WESTHATCH CNR
WESTHATCH LA
RG42
The Cut
Warfield Hall
Wane Bridge
Meadowbrook Montessori Sch
Scotlands Farm
OSBORNE LA
Darrah Farm
Warfield House
Hayley Green Farm
The Hooks
Home Farm
B3022
B3034
FOREST RD
Newell Green
BRACKNELL RD
GIBBINS LA
HERSCHEL GRANGE
TOOGOOD PL
NEWHURST GDNS
HAYLEY GREEN
Hayley Green
GOOSE CNR
WARFIELD ST
WEST END LA
Westend Farm
West End
NEWELL GN
B3034
FOREST RD
Fairclough Farm
WATERSPLASH LA
OLD PRIORY LA
BRACKNELL
Park Farm
Ford
MARBULL WAY
Larks Hill
CHANCEL MANS
HEMMYNG CNR
MAIZE LA
JIG'S LA N
STRAWBERRY HILL
HAMPSHIRE RISE
STAFFORDSHIRE CROFT
JOSEPH CT
TERESA VALE
SWITHIN CHASE
Long Copse
HARVEST RIDE
CONEY GRANGE
MITRE PL
HEBBECASTLE DOWN
Whitegrove
Kennel Lane Sch
DARBY VALE
NEWPORT DR
LYON OAKS
MARY MEAD
COUNTY LA
FAITHFULL CL
PRICE GDNS
ATTE LA
GILL RISE
Superstore
Liby
Warfield Chase
KENNEL LA
Quelm Lane
HOWELL CL
SEDDON HILL
CHIVES PL
HAMMOND CT
MOSTYN HO
MARSHAM HO
MULBERRY HO
EDOWN
GARTH SQ
ROOKSWOOD
STAVERTON CL
SKELTON FIELDS
EARLE CROFT
TARRANT GN
SHERRING CL
PRIORY LA
ALL SAINTS RISE
BENEDICT GN
BERNADINE CL
LINCOLNSHIRE GDNS
YORKSHIRE PL
WESTMORLAND DR
SUFFOLK COMBE
ANNEFORDE PL
BENBRICKE GN
KENNEL LA
MAKEPIECE RD
BARTHOLOMEW PL
NORTHUMBERLAND CL
Sch
RG12
MANOR CL
TRUMBULL RD
BENNINGS CL
COTTERELL CL
BRAYBROOKE RD
BURNHAM GR
BROWNLOW DR
LUTTERWORTH CL
OLD FARM DR
TARGET HILL
AUGUSTINE WALK
SMATHWAITES CNR
GLOUCESTER PL
SHROPSHIRE GDNS
SOMERSET GR
WINCHGROVE RD
CLACY GN
AGAR CRES
THE CROFT
Recn Gd
FOLDERS LA
CANDLEFORD CL
CORN CROFT
BROADRICK HEATH
BIG BARN GR
PATRICK GDNS
RACHAELS LAKE VIEW
CAESARS GATE
ESSEX RISE
SURREY CT
NORFOLK CHASE
BINFIELD RD
MOORDALE AVE
SHEPHARDS LA
HORSNIELE LA
Schs
CEDAR DR
AVON GR
Holly Spring Farm
HARVEST RIDE
BURNTHOUSE GDNS
GLOUCESTERSHIRE LEA
CAMBRIDGESHIRE CL
MERRYHILL RD
SANDY LA
DENE CL
CLEOPATRA PL
CRESSIDA CHASE
B3018
A3095
A330
86
87
88
70
71
72
73
4
3
2
1
118
92

91
65

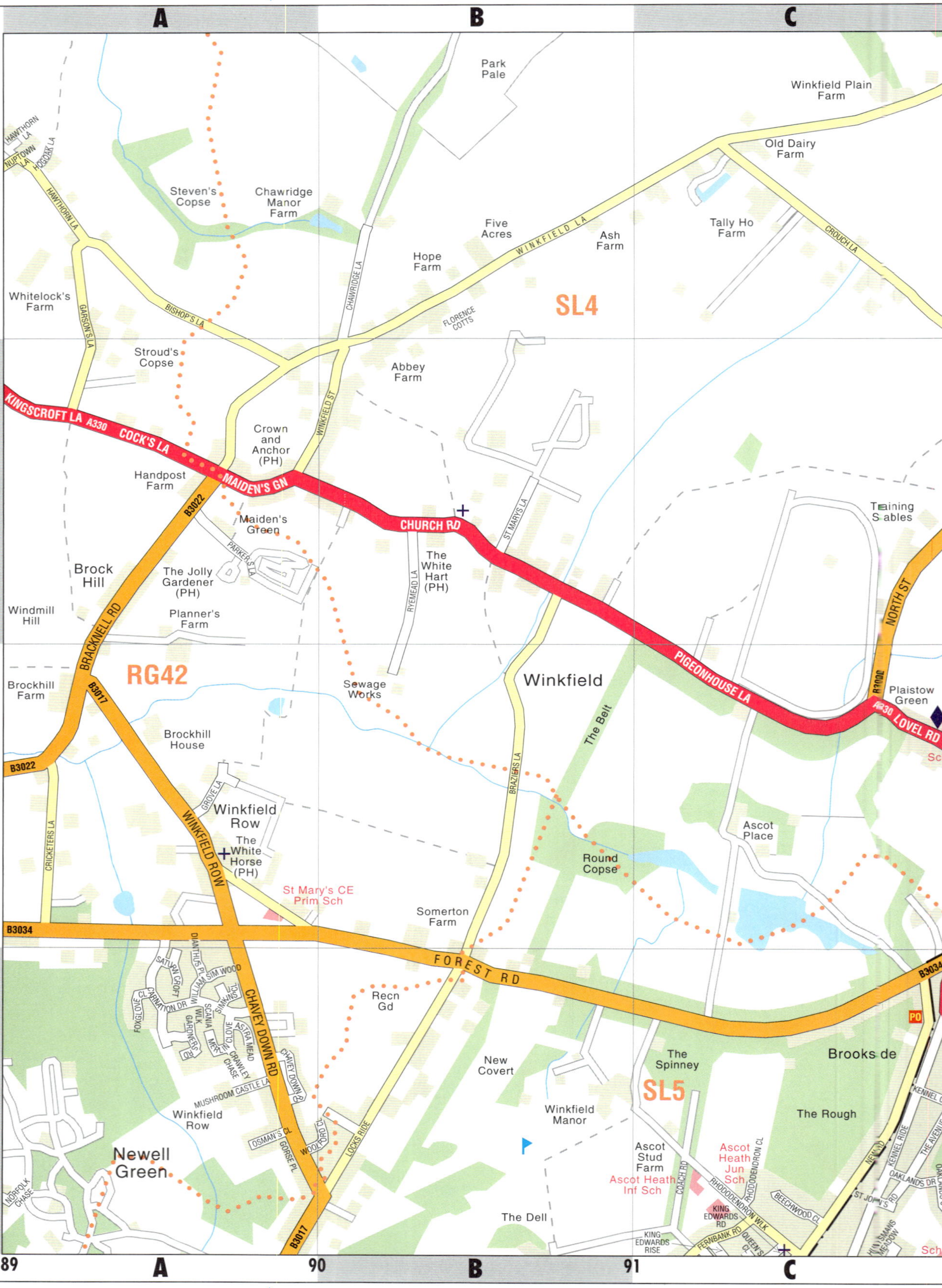
Park Pale
Winkfield Plain Farm
Old Dairy Farm
Steven's Copse
Chawridge Manor Farm
Five Acres
Ash Farm
Tally Ho Farm
Hope Farm
Whitelock's Farm
SL4
Stroud's Copse
Abbey Farm
Crown and Anchor (PH)
Handpost Farm
Maiden's Green
The White Hart (PH)
Brock Hill
The Jolly Gardener (PH)
Windmill Hill
Planner's Farm
Brockhill Farm
RG42
Sewage Works
Winkfield
Plaistow Green
Brockhill House
Winkfield Row
The White Horse (PH)
Ascot Place
Round Copse
St Mary's CE Prim Sch
Somerton Farm
Recn Gd
The Spinney
New Covert
SL5
Winkfield Row
Winkfield Manor
Newell Green
Ascot Stud Farm
Ascot Heath Jun Sch
Ascot Heath Inf Sch
The Dell
The Rough
Brooks de
Training Stables
KINGSCROFT LA A330
COCK'S LA
MAIDEN'S GN
CHURCH RD
PIGEONHOUSE LA
LOVEL RD
B3022
BRACKNELL RD
B3017
WINKFIELD ROW
B3034
FOREST RD
CHAVEY DOWN RD
WINKFIELD LA
CROUCH LA
BISHOP'S LA
CHAWRIDGE LA
WINKFIELD ST
ST MARYS LA
RYEMEAD LA
BRAZIERS LA
NORTH ST
The Belt
LOCKS RIDE
CRICKETERS LA
GARSON'S LA
HAWTHORN LA
NUPTOWN LA
HOGOAK LA
PARKER'S LA
GROVE LA
FLORENCE COTTS
MUSHROOM CASTLE LA
OSMAN'S CL
GORSE PL
WOODFORD CL
CHAVEY DOWN
NORFOLK CHASE
FOXGLOVE CL
CARNATION DR
SATURN CROFT
DIANTHUS PL
SIM WOOD
RHODODENDRON WLK
RHODODENDRON CL
BEECHWOOD CL
COACH RD
KING EDWARDS RD
KING EDWARDS RISE
FERNBANK RD
KENNEL CL
KENNEL RIDE
THE AVENUE
OAKLANDS DR
ST JOHN'S RD
HUNTSMANS MEADOW
Sch
89
90
91
A
B
C
70
71
72
73
1
2
3
4

91
119

66
94

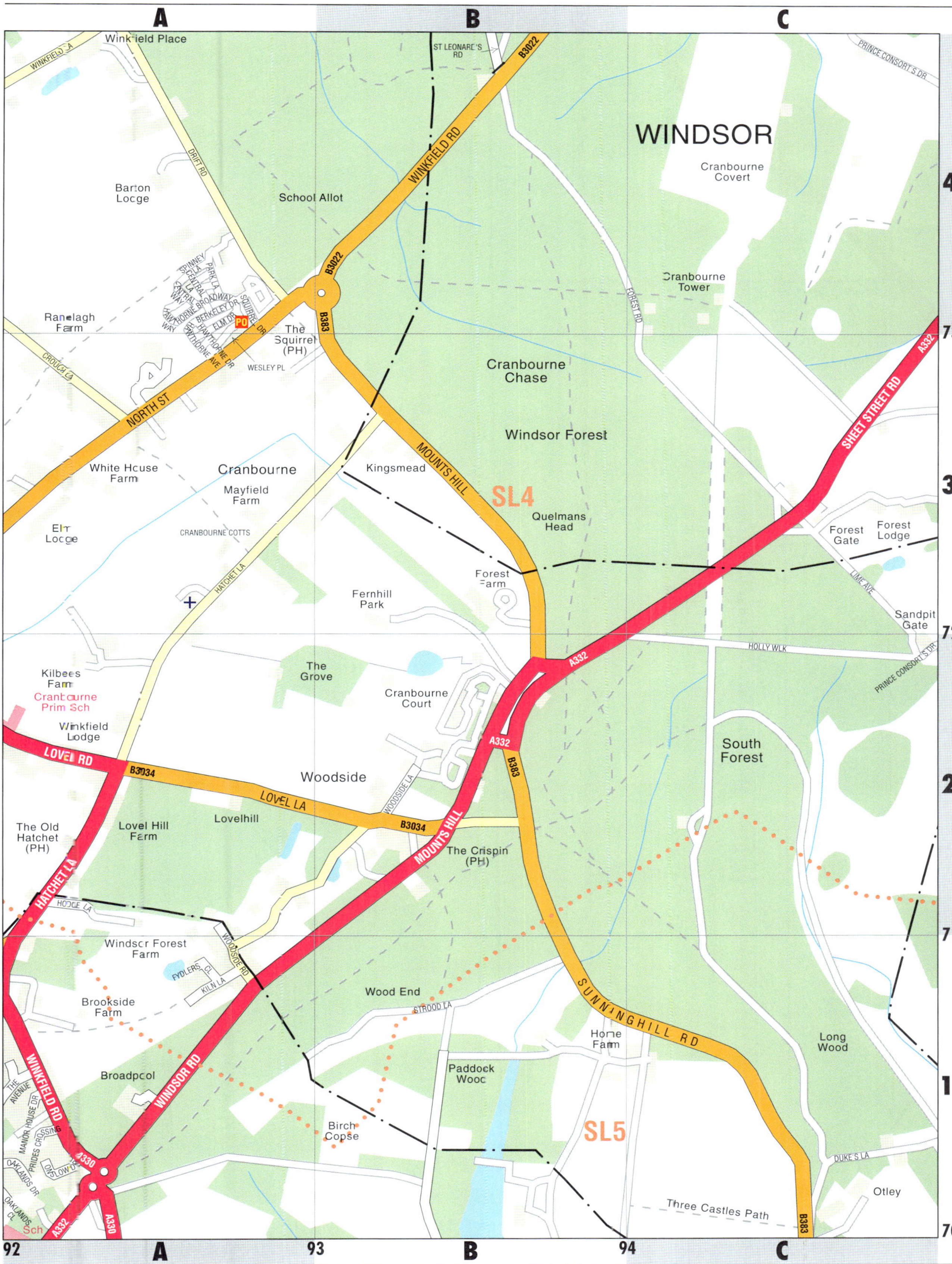

A
B
C
4
3
2
1
73
72
71
70
92
93
94
WINDSOR
Winkfield Place
WINKFIELD LA
ST LEONARD'S RD
B3022
PRINCE CONSORT'S DR
DRIFT RD
Barton Lodge
School Allot
WINKFIELD RD
Cranbourne Covert
Cranbourne Tower
Ranelagh Farm
SPINNEY LA
CENTRAL WAY
PARK LA
BROADWAY
HAWTHORNE WAY
BERKELEY DR
SQUIRREL DR
ELM DR
PO
The Squirrel (PH)
B383
WESLEY PL
CROUCH LA
FOREST RD
Cranbourne Chase
NORTH ST
Windsor Forest
White House Farm
Cranbourne
Mayfield Farm
Kingsmead
MOUNTS HILL
SL4
SHEET STREET RD
A332
Elm Lodge
CRANBOURNE COTTS
Quelmans Head
Forest Gate
Forest Lodge
HATCHET LA
Forest Farm
LIME AVE
Fernhill Park
Sandpit Gate
HOLLY WLK
Kilbees Farm
Cranbourne Prim Sch
The Grove
Cranbourne Court
South Forest
Winkfield Lodge
LOVEL RD
B3034
Woodside
WOODSIDE LA
LOVEL LA
The Old Hatchet (PH)
Lovel Hill Farm
Lovelhill
The Crispin (PH)
HODGE LA
Windsor Forest Farm
WOODSIDE RD
FYDLERS CL
KILN LA
Wood End
STROOD LA
SUNNINGHILL RD
Brookside Farm
Home Farm
Long Wood
Paddock Wood
Broadpool
WINDSOR RD
THE AVENUE
MANOR HOUSE DR
PRIDES CROSSING
Birch Copse
SL5
OAKLANDS DR
OAKLANDS CL
DUKE'S LA
A330
Otley
Three Castles Path
Sch

120
94

93
67

A
B
C
4
3
2
1
73
72
71
70
95
96
97
A332
SHEET STREET RD
Flemish Farm
Pickleherring Pond
Ranger's Lodge
Beehive Hill
PRINCE CONSORT'S DR
Russel's Pond
Fiddle Covert
Battle Bourne
The Gallop
Seymours Plantation
Prince of Wales Pond
THE LONG WLK
Rush Pond
Bear's Rails
Bear's Rails Pond
Cemy
BEARS RAILS PK
CRIMP HILL
Statue
Snow Hill
Spring Hill
Cookes Hill
SL4
Richardson's Lawn
RICHARDSON'S LAWN COTTS
THE VILLAGE
QUEEN ANNE'S CL
PO
Isle of Wight Pond
The Village
Poets Lawn
Deepstrood
Three Castles Path
Royal Lodge
BISHOPSGATE RD
The Fox & Hounds (PH)
Queen Anne's Ride
Windsor Great Park
Dark Wood
The Royal Prim Sch
Bishopsgate
Cow Pond
Chapel Wood
PARK CLOSE COTTS
MEZEL HILL COTTS
CUMBERLAND LODGE
Hilton's Covert
DUKE'S LA
Mezel Hill
RHODODENDRON RIDE
The Sun (PH)
Square Covert
Wilderness
Park Close
WICK LA
The Savill Gardens
Parkside House
Slans Hill
Great Meadow Pond
Leiper Hill
Temple Hill
TW20
P
SL5
Mill Pond
Obelisk
Norfolk Farm
Norfolk Plantation
Statue
Smith's Lawn
Rosy Bottom
Obelisk Pond
Polo Gds

93
121

68
96

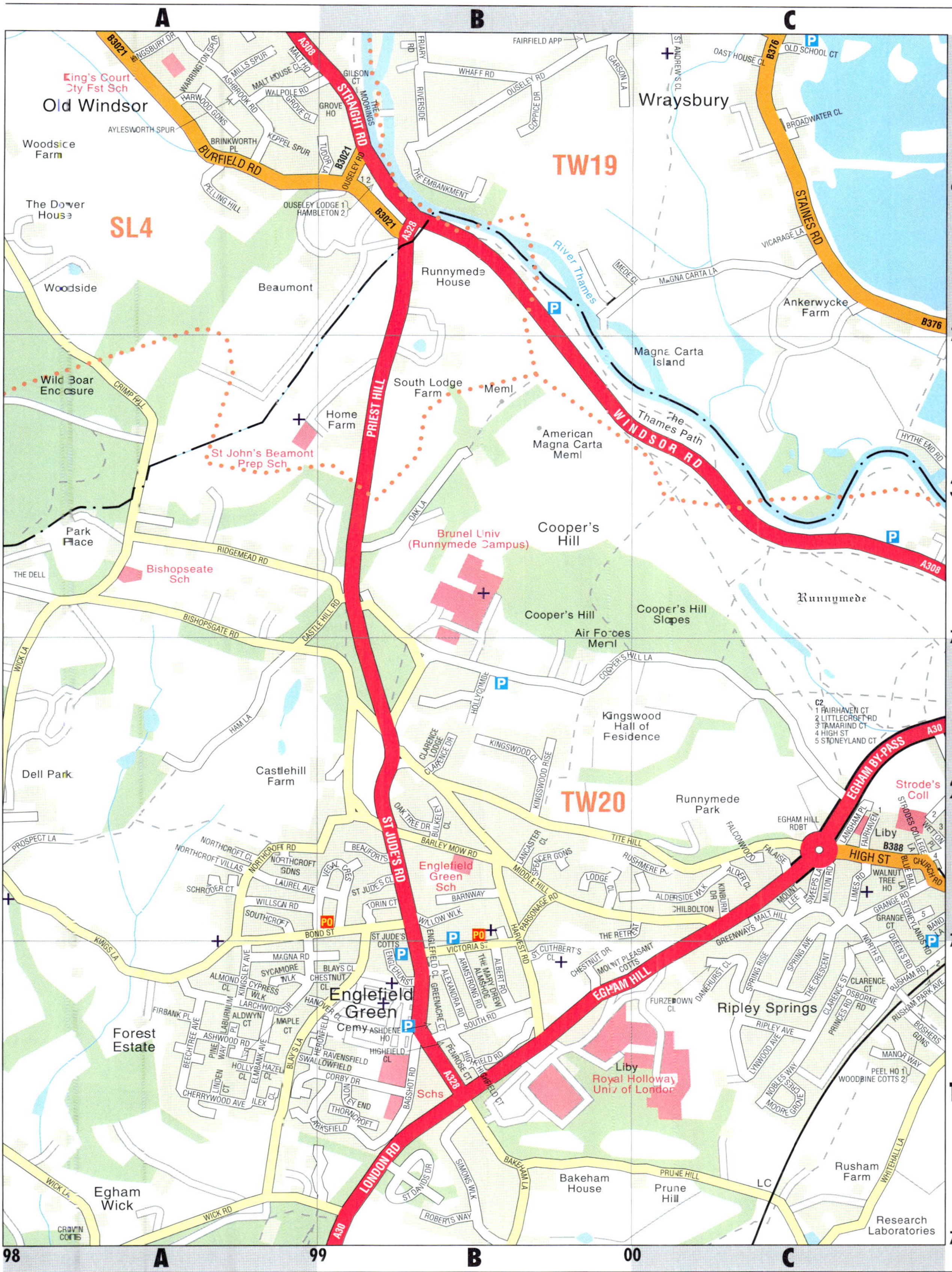
Old Windsor
Wraysbury
TW19
SL4
TW20
Englefield Green
Egham Wick
Forest Estate
Ripley Springs
Runnymede
Cooper's Hill
Magna Carta Island
River Thames
WINDSOR RD
PRIEST HILL
ST JUDE'S RD
EGHAM HILL
STAINES RD
EGHAM BY-PASS
LONDON RD

122
96

95 69

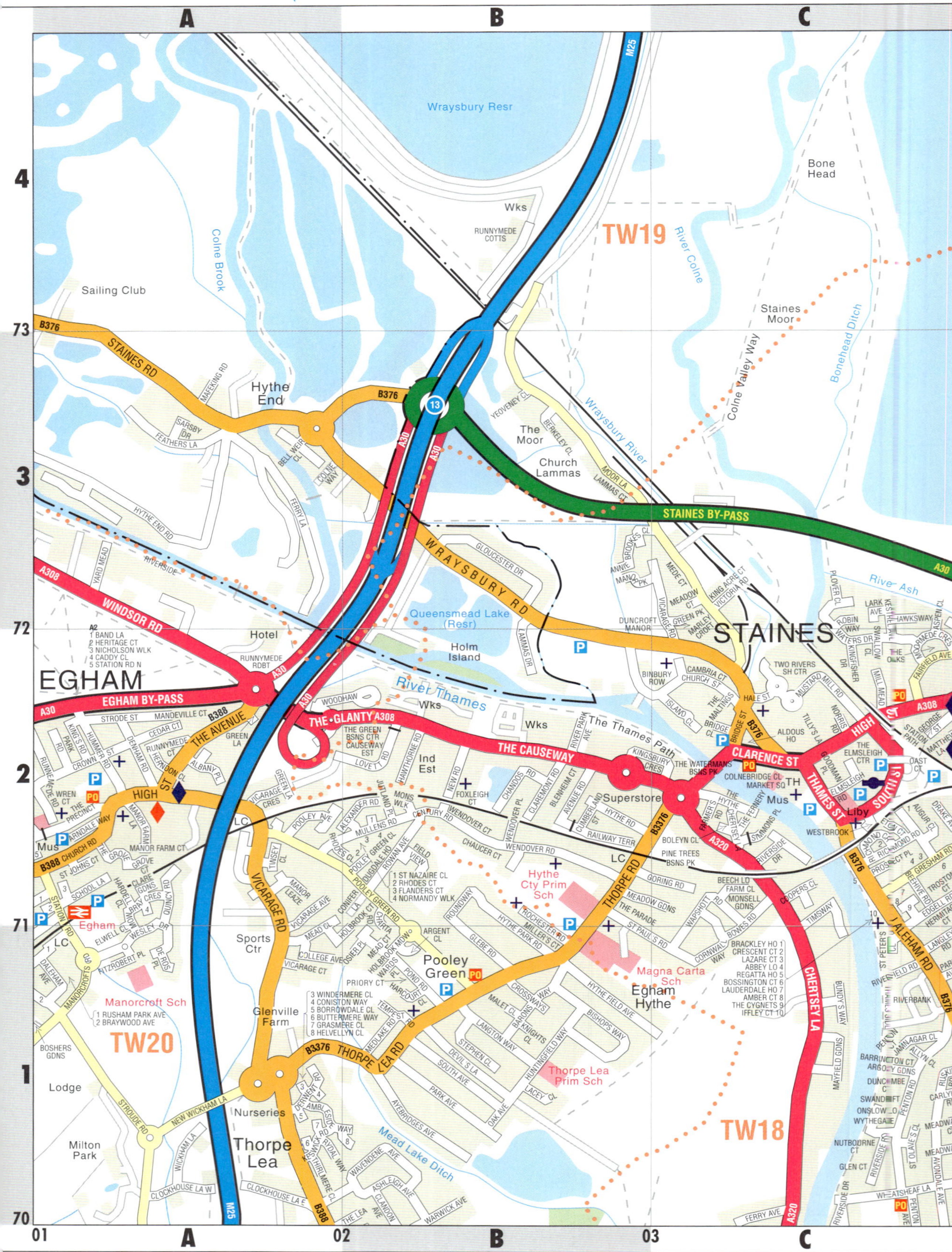

A
B
C
4
73
3
72
2
71
1
70
01
02
03
Wraysbury Resr
M25
Wks
RUNNYMEDE COTTS
TW19
River Colne
Colne Brook
Bone Head
Sailing Club
Staines Moor
Colne Valley Way
Bonehead Ditch
B376
STAINES RD
Hythe End
13
The Moor
Church Lammas
Wraysbury River
STAINES BY-PASS
A30
HYTHE END RD
RIVERSIDE
A308
WINDSOR RD
WRAYSBURY RD
Queensmead Lake (Resr)
Holm Island
Hotel
RUNNYMEDE RDBT
STAINES
River Ash
EGHAM
EGHAM BY-PASS
River Thames
THE GLANTY
The Thames Path
THE CAUSEWAY
CLARENCE ST
HIGH ST
THAMES ST
SOUTH ST
THE AVENUE
Ind Est
Superstore
Mus
Liby
TH
Wks
TWO RIVERS SH CTR
THE ELMSLEIGH CTR
STRODE ST
MANDEVILLE CT
B388
HIGH
CHURCH RD
Egham
Manorcroft Sch
TW20
VICARAGE RD
Sports Ctr
Glenville Farm
Pooley Green
Hythe Cty Prim Sch
Magna Carta Sch
Egham Hythe
THORPE RD
B3376
A320
CHERTSEY LA
THORPE LEA RD
Thorpe Lea Prim Sch
TW18
LALEHAM RD
Lodge
Milton Park
Nurseries
Thorpe Lea
NEW WICKHAM LA
STROUDE RD
CLOCKHOUSE LA W
CLOCKHOUSE LA E
Mead Lake Ditch
WHEATSHEAF LA
FERRY AVE

95 123

70
98

A
B
C
King George VI Resr
Staines Resrs
Stanwell
TW19
West Bedfont
St Mary's CE Sch
St Anne's Prim Sch
Town Farm Cty Prim Sch
Recn Gd
Cemy
Ashford
The Ashford High Sch
St David's Jun Sch
TW15
Clarendon Cty Prim Sch
Spelthorne Coll
Hengrove Farm
Shortwood Cty Inf Sch
Birch Green
Shortwood Pond
Shortwood Common
Ashford Park Cty Prim Sch
Sports Centre
HM Remand Ctr
Staines
Knowle Green
TW18
Staines Reservoirs Aqueduct
River Ash
Kingscroft Cty Jun Sch
Our Lady of the Rosary RC Sch
The Matthew Arnold Sch
Buckland Cty Jun & Inf Sch
ASHFORD
Ashford Manor
Works
Queen Mary Resr
STANWELL MOOR RD
LONDON RD
STAINES BY-PASS
KINGSTON RD
TOWN LA
STANWELL RD
CHURCH RD
FORDBRIDGE RD
ASHFORD RD
LALEHAM RD
STAINES RD
KINGSTON RD
A30
A308
A3044
B378
B377
B376
4
73
3
72
2
71
1
70
04
05
06

124
98

97
71

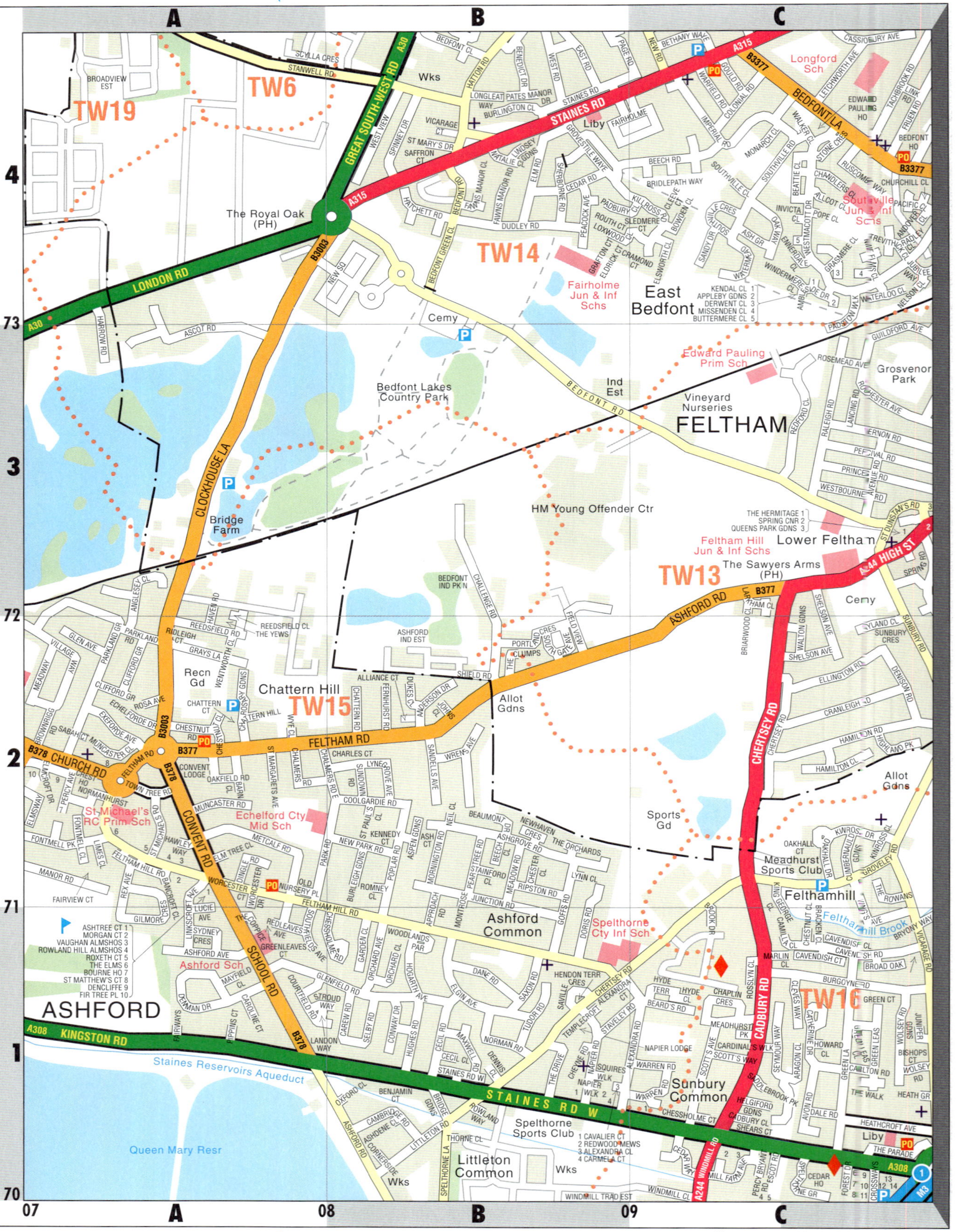

97
125

C1
1 TASMAN CT
2 WILLOW CT
3 CATLE CL
4 KILLIGREW HO
5 GRANTHAM HO
6 ASH LODGE
7 LIME LODGE
8 OAK LODGE
9 ELM CT
10 WILLOW LODGE
11 SYCAMORE LODGE
12 ISOBEL HO
13 PRISCILLA HO
14 SUNBURY CROSS CTR

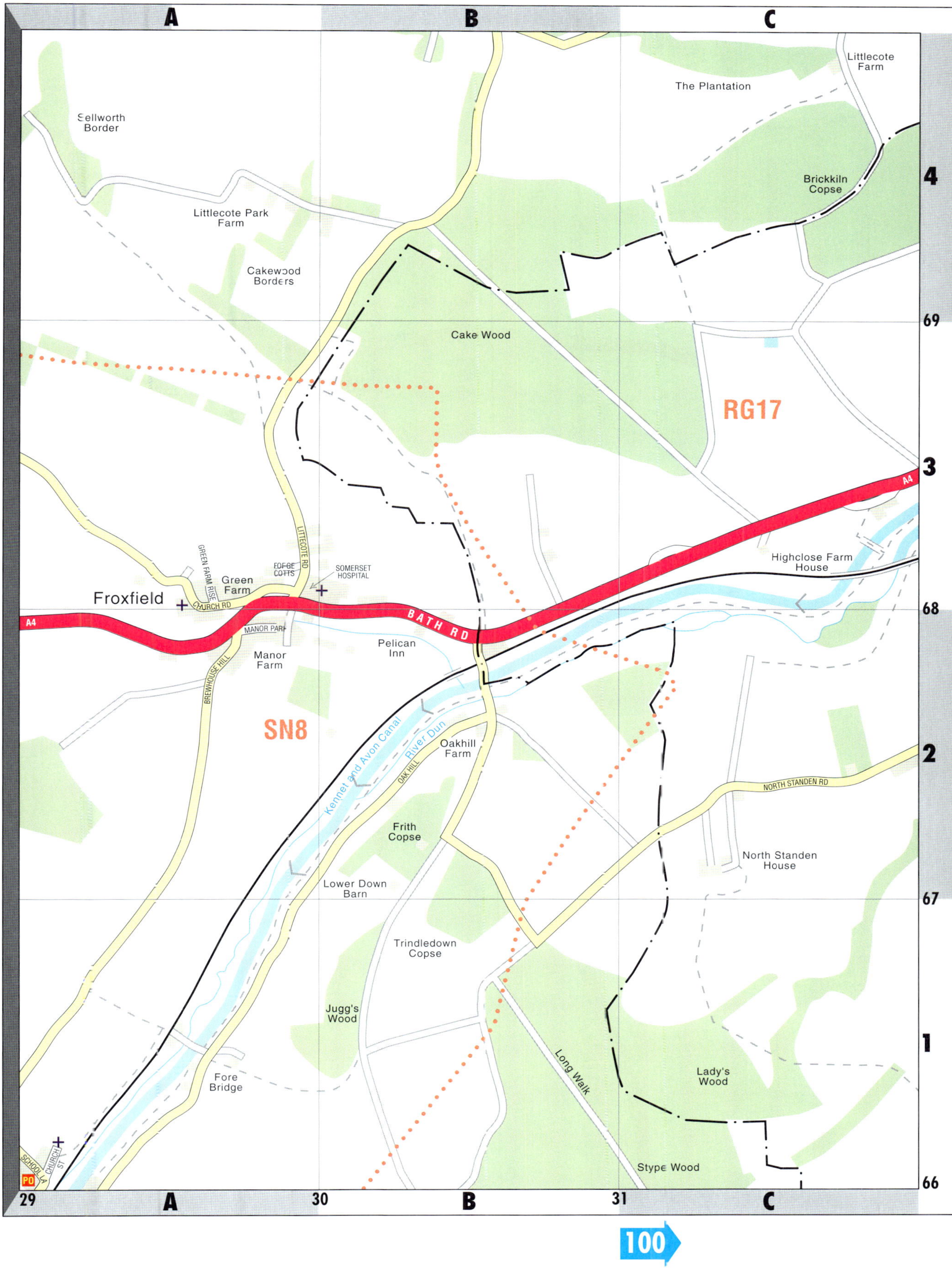
72
100
A
B
C
Littlecote Farm
The Plantation
Sellworth Border
Brickkiln Copse
4
Littlecote Park Farm
Cakewood Borders
69
Cake Wood
RG17
3
A4
LITTLECOTE RD
GREEN FARM RISE
Green Farm
FORGE COTTS
SOMERSET HOSPITAL
Highclose Farm House
Froxfield
CHURCH RD
BATH RD
68
MANOR PARK
Manor Farm
Pelican Inn
BREWHOUSE HILL
SN8
Kennet and Avon Canal
River Dun
Oakhill Farm
OAK HILL
2
NORTH STANDEN RD
Frith Copse
North Standen House
Lower Down Barn
67
Trindledown Copse
Jugg's Wood
1
Long Walk
Fore Bridge
Lady's Wood
SCHOOL LA
CHURCH ST
PO
Stype Wood
66
29
30
31
100

99
73

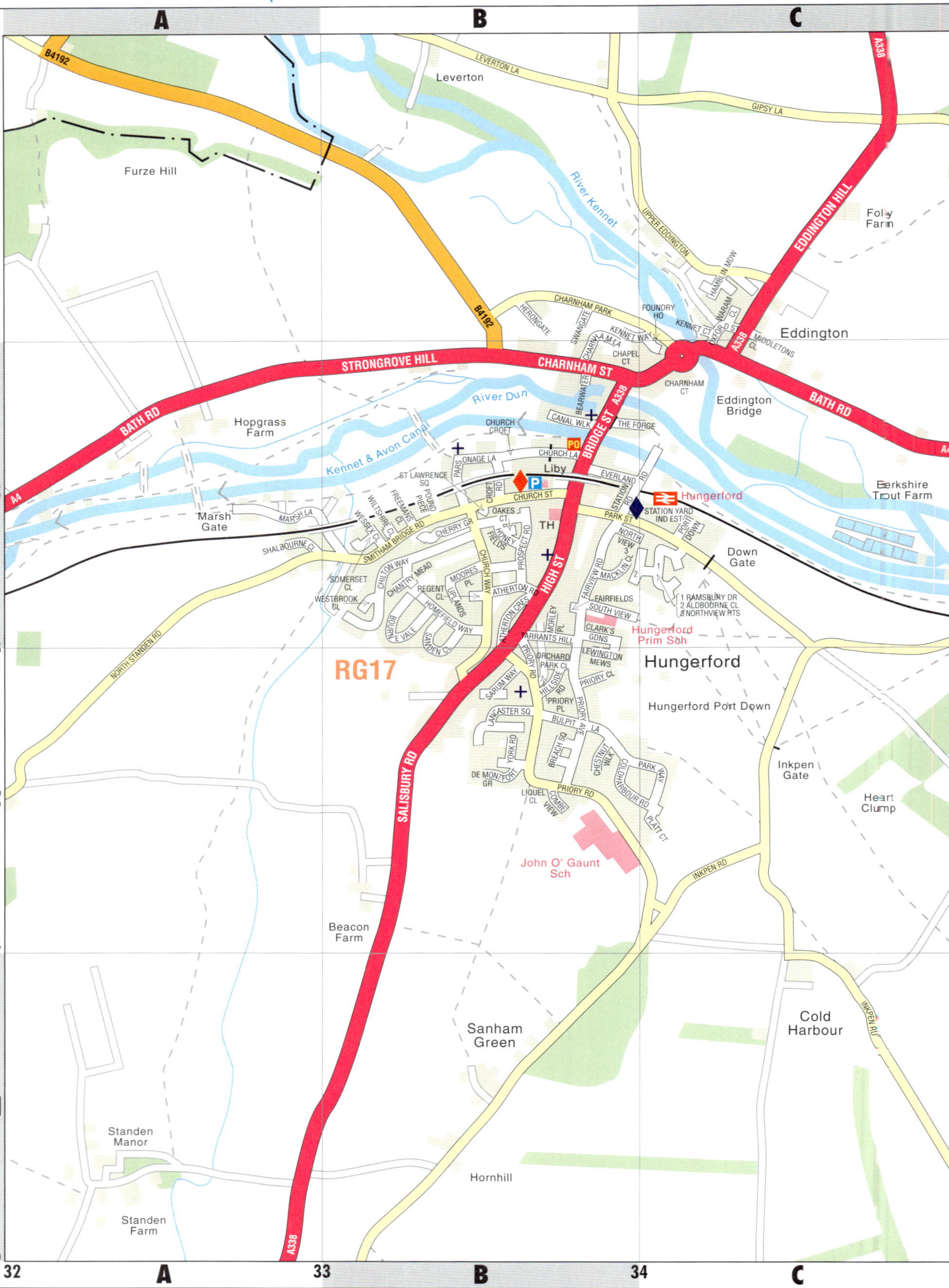
Leverton
Furze Hill
River Kennet
Foly Farm
Eddington
Hopgrass Farm
River Dun
Kennet & Avon Canal
Eddington Bridge
Berkshire Trout Farm
Marsh Gate
Hungerford
Down Gate
RG17
Hungerford Prim Sch
Hungerford Port Down
Inkpen Gate
Heart Clump
John O' Gaunt Sch
Beacon Farm
Sanham Green
Cold Harbour
Standen Manor
Standen Farm
Hornhill
STRONGROVE HILL
CHARNHAM ST
BATH RD
BRIDGE ST
HIGH ST
SALISBURY RD
EDDINGTON HILL
NORTH STANDEN RD
INKPEN RD
LEVERTON LA
GIPSY LA
UPPER EDDINGTON
CHURCH ST
PARK ST
PRIORY RD
1 RAMSBURY DR
2 ALDBOURNE CL
3 NORTHVIEW HTS

99
126

74
102

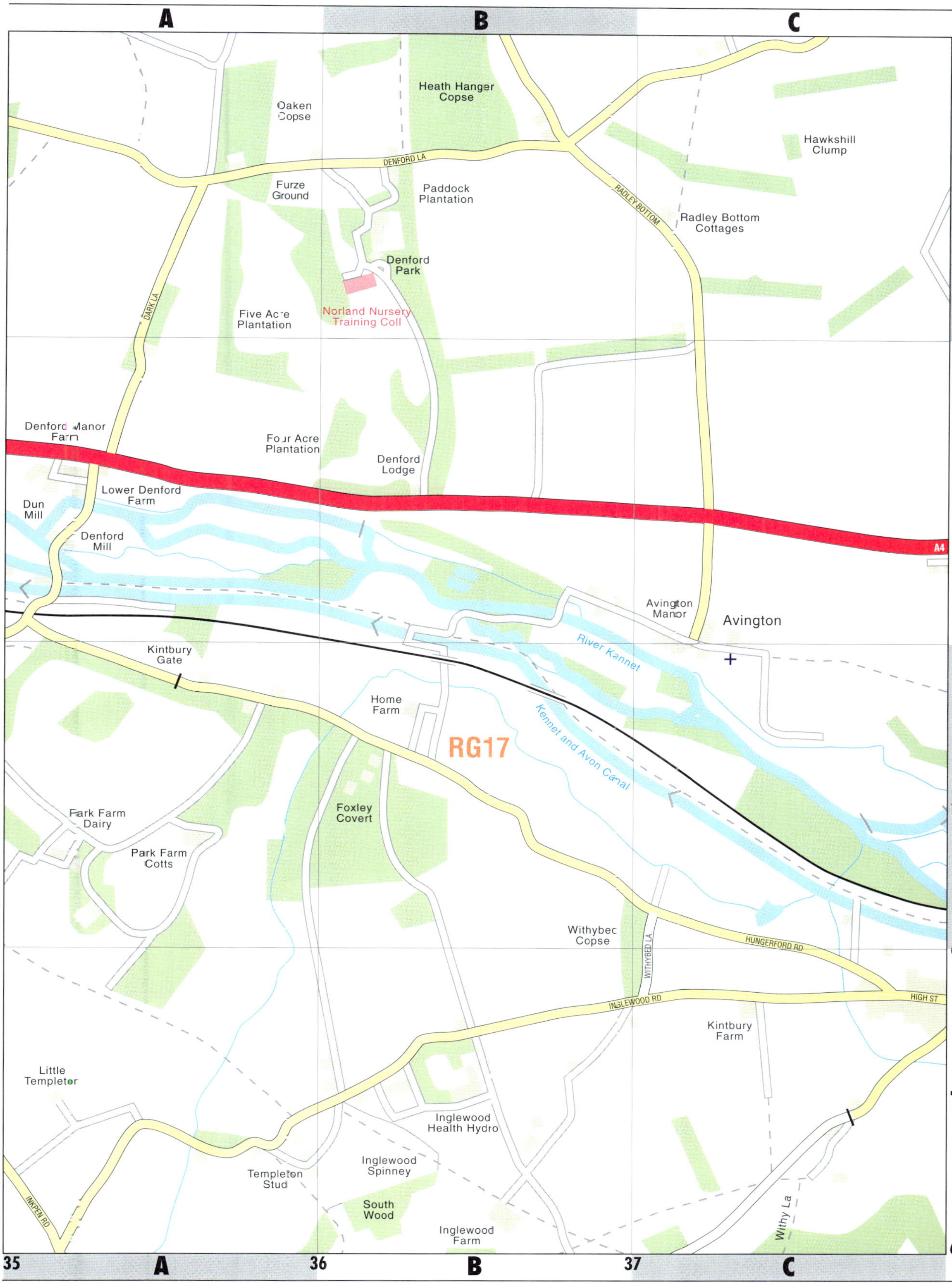

127
102

101 75

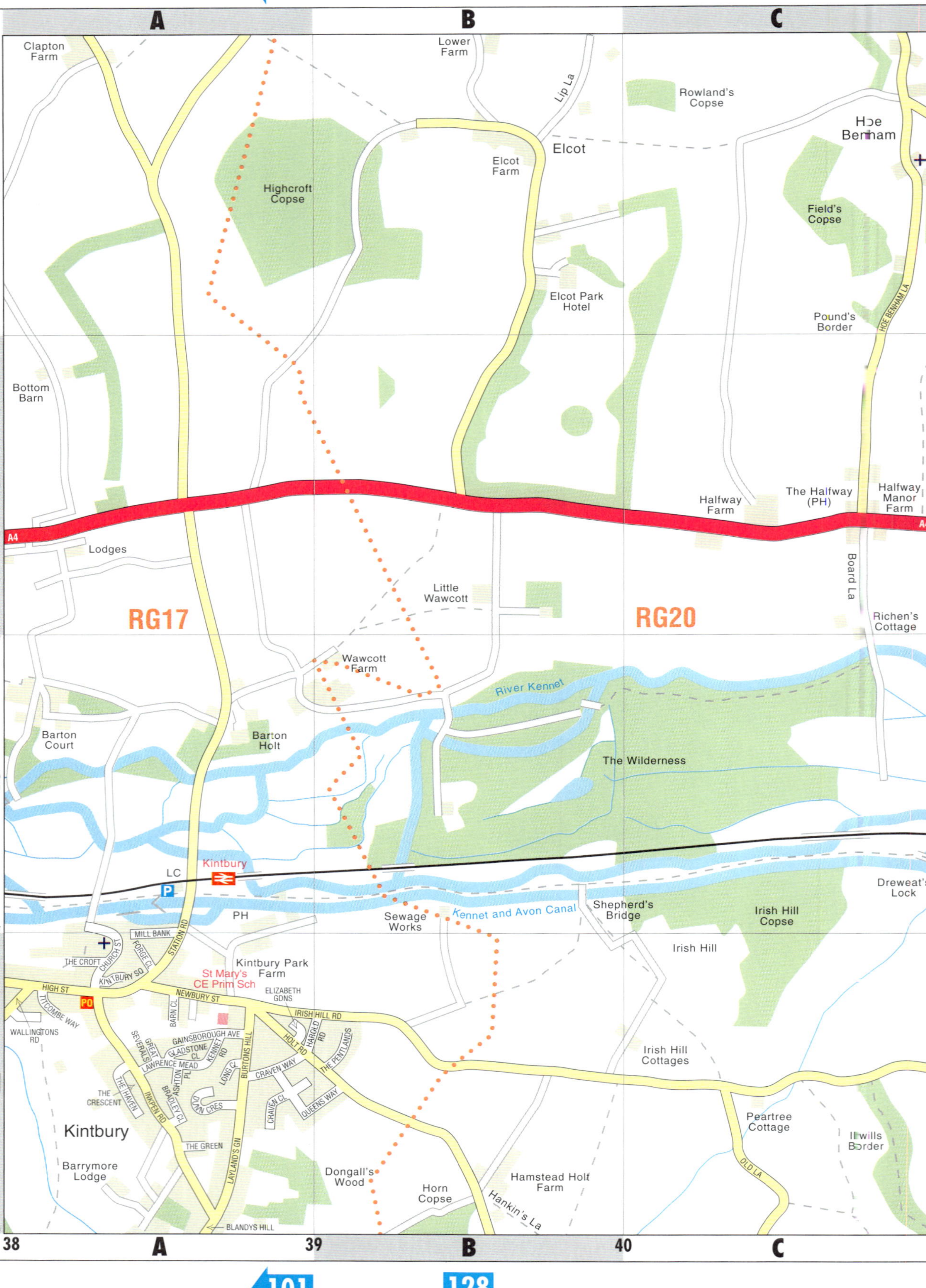

101 128

76
104

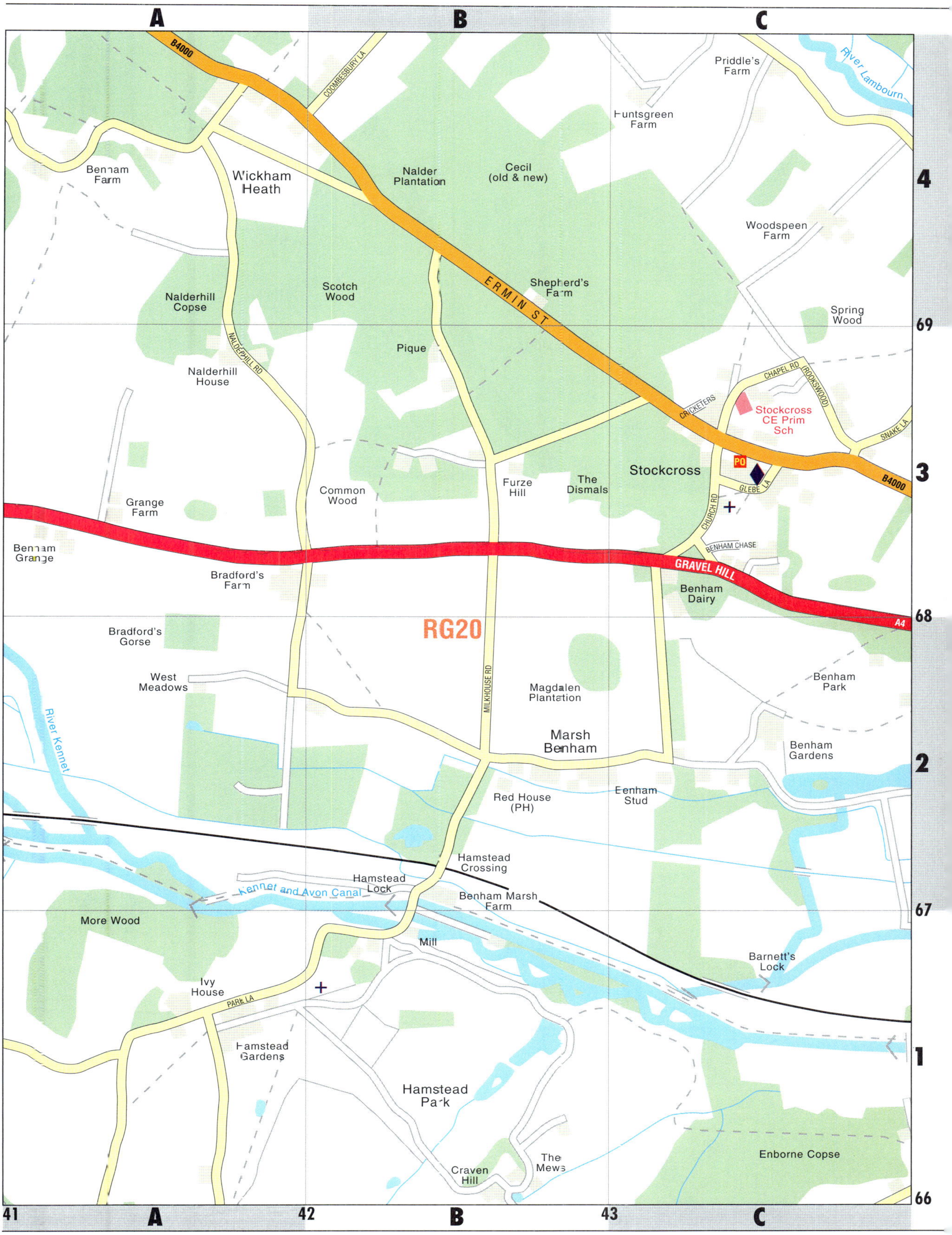

129
104

103 77

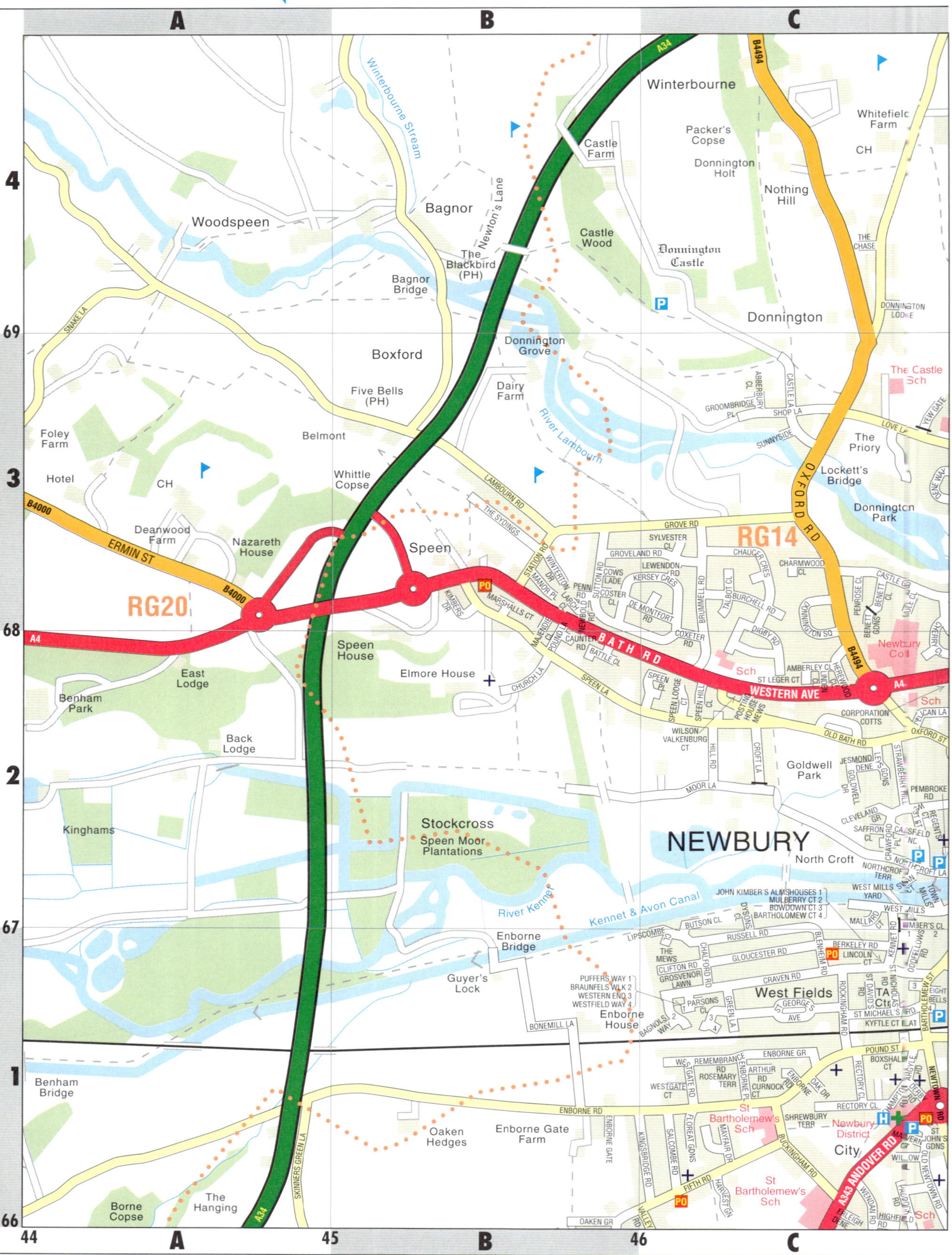

103 130

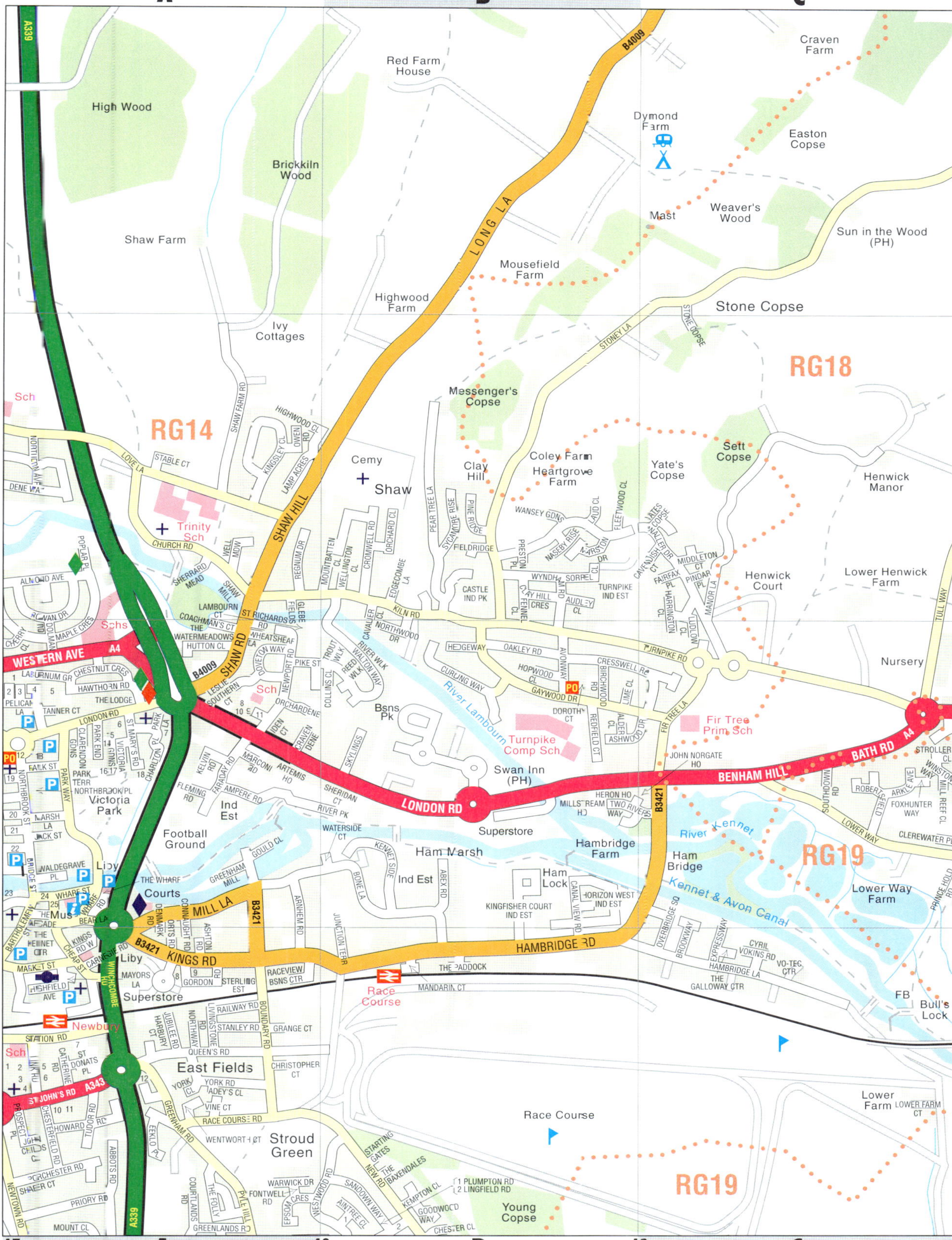

A1
1 FAIR CLOSE HO
2 LINK HO
3 MADEIRA PL
4 KENNET CT
5 SHEFFORD LODGE
6 L[illegible]HESTER CT
7 ASHRIDGE CT
8 GORDON CT
9 ROMANO CT
10 HILARY HO
11 QUEENS CT
12 WINCHESTER HO

A2
1 CORPORATION COTTS
2 ANGEL CT
3 WESTBOURNE TERR
4 LYNTON CT
5 SPEENHAMLAND CT
6 ST MARY'S CT
7 ST JOSEPH'S CT
8 NORTH VIEW GDNS
9 SOUTH VIEW GDNS
10 KENNET PL
11 NEWPORT CL
12 THE BROADWAY
13 THE PENTANGLE
14 ST MARY'S PL
15 BEECH CT
16 ASH CT
17 CHESTNUT CT
18 CONISTON CT
19 ALBERT RD
20 WEAVER'S WLK
21 CROMWELL PL
22 PEMBROKE RD
23 TOWN MILLS
24 MANSION HOUSE ST
25 MARKET PL

105
79

105
132

80
108

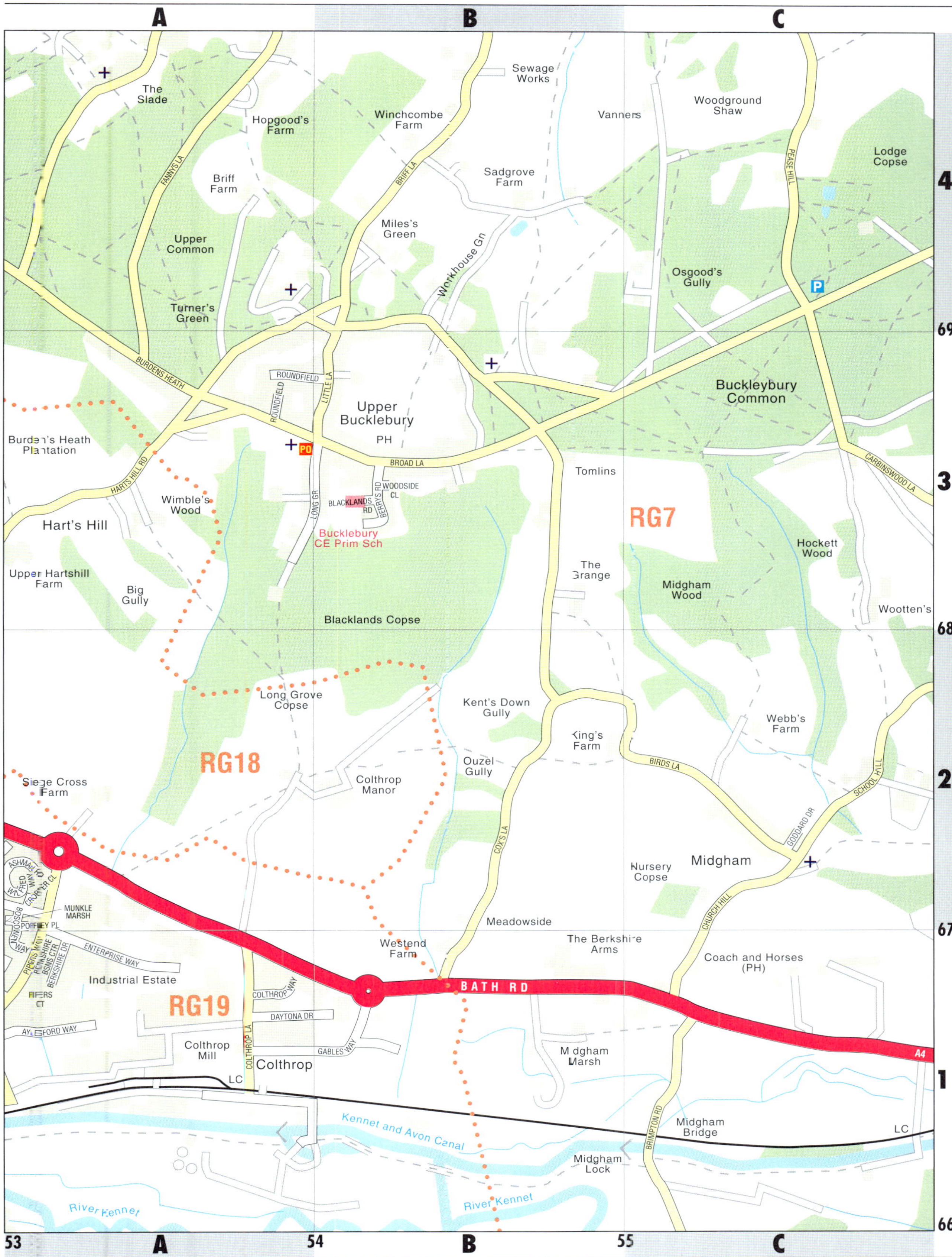

133
108

107
81

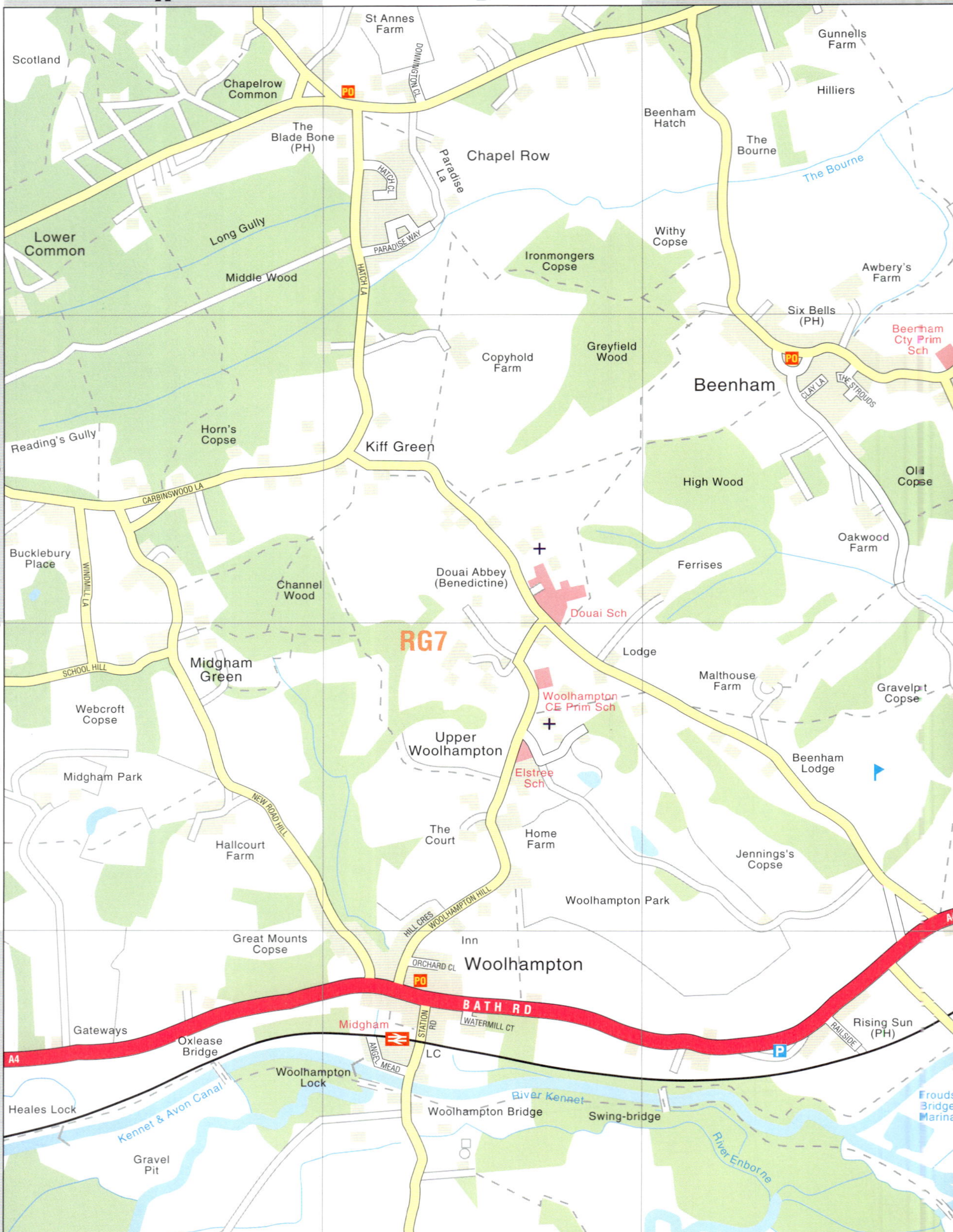

107
134

82
110

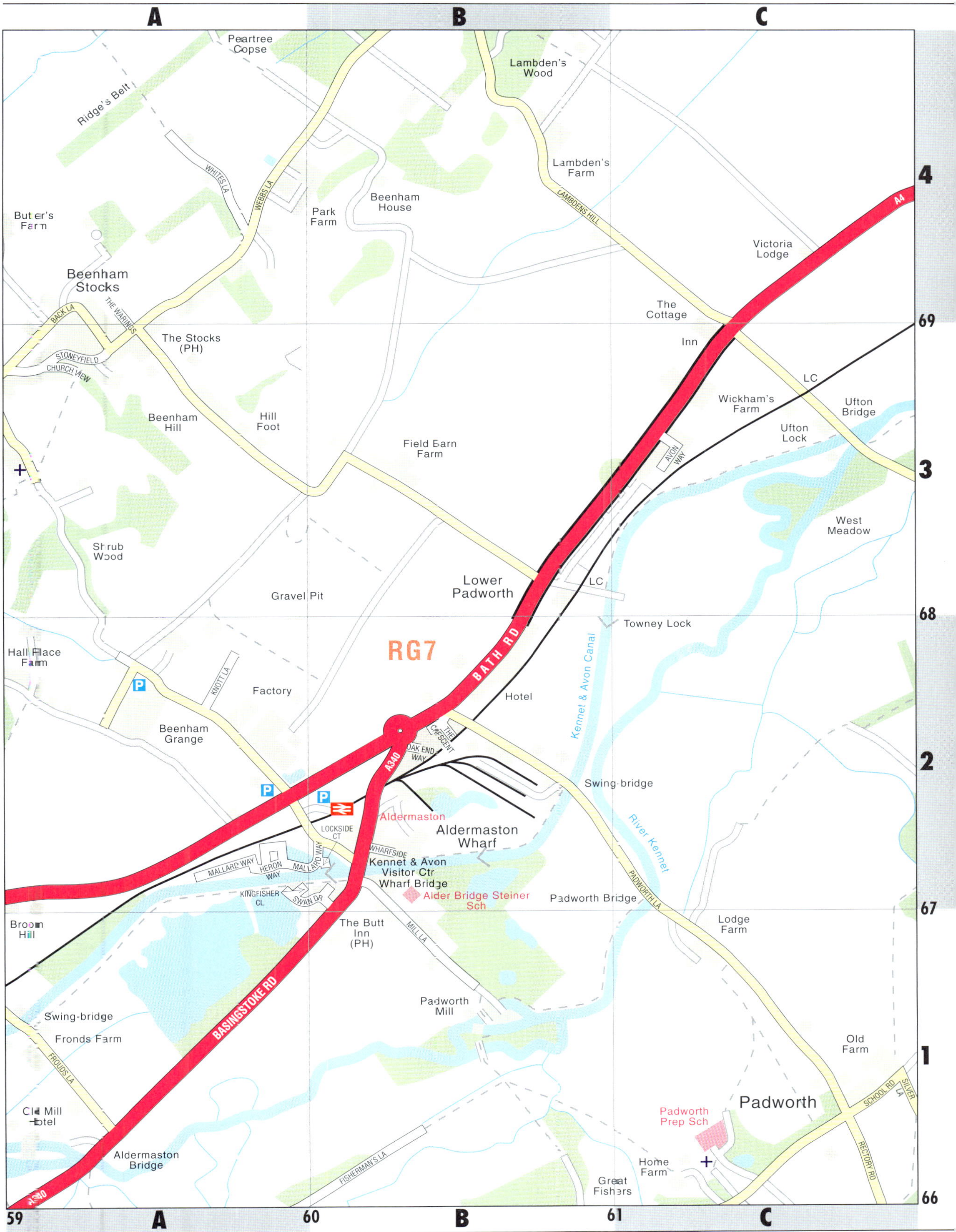

135
110

109
83

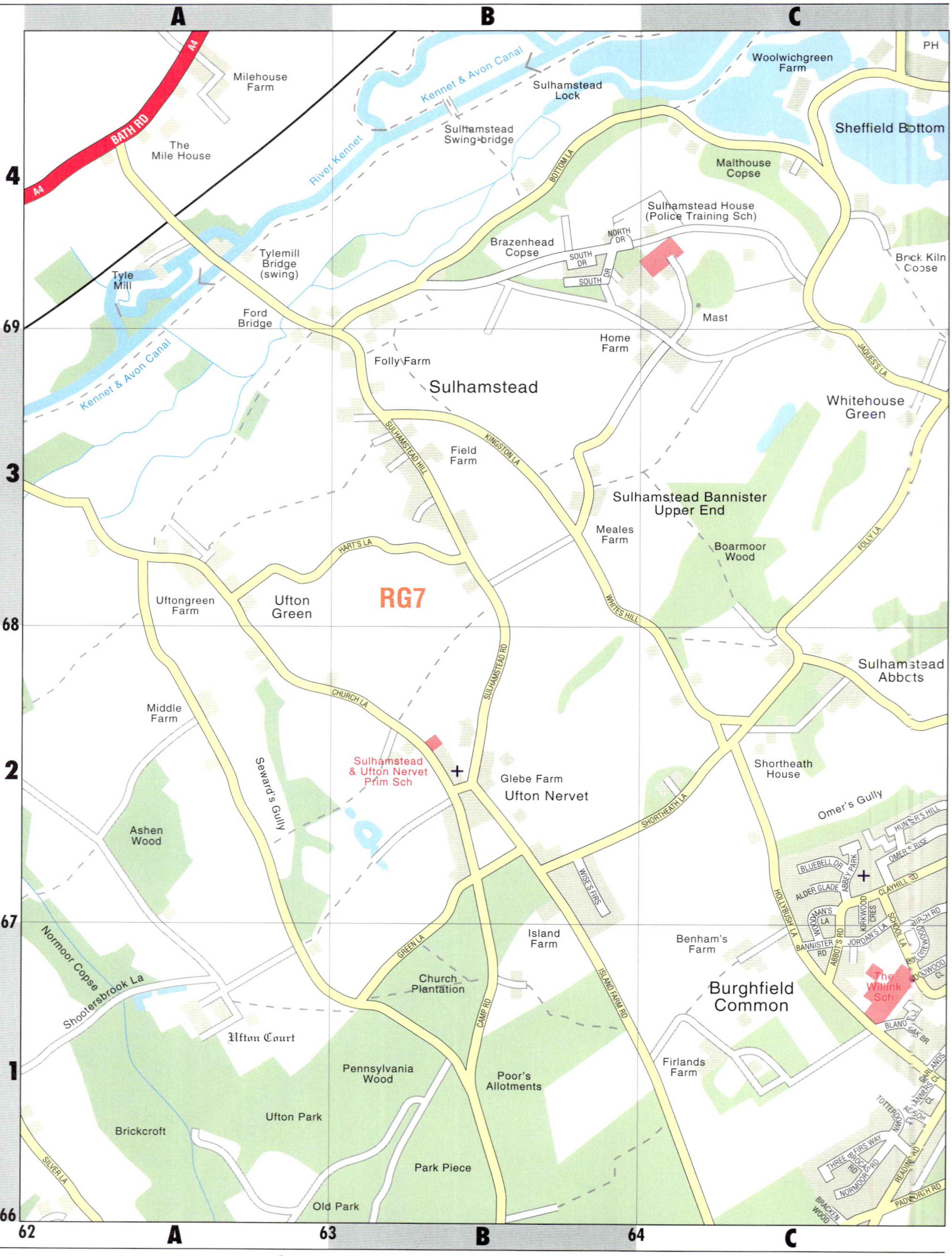

109
136

84
112

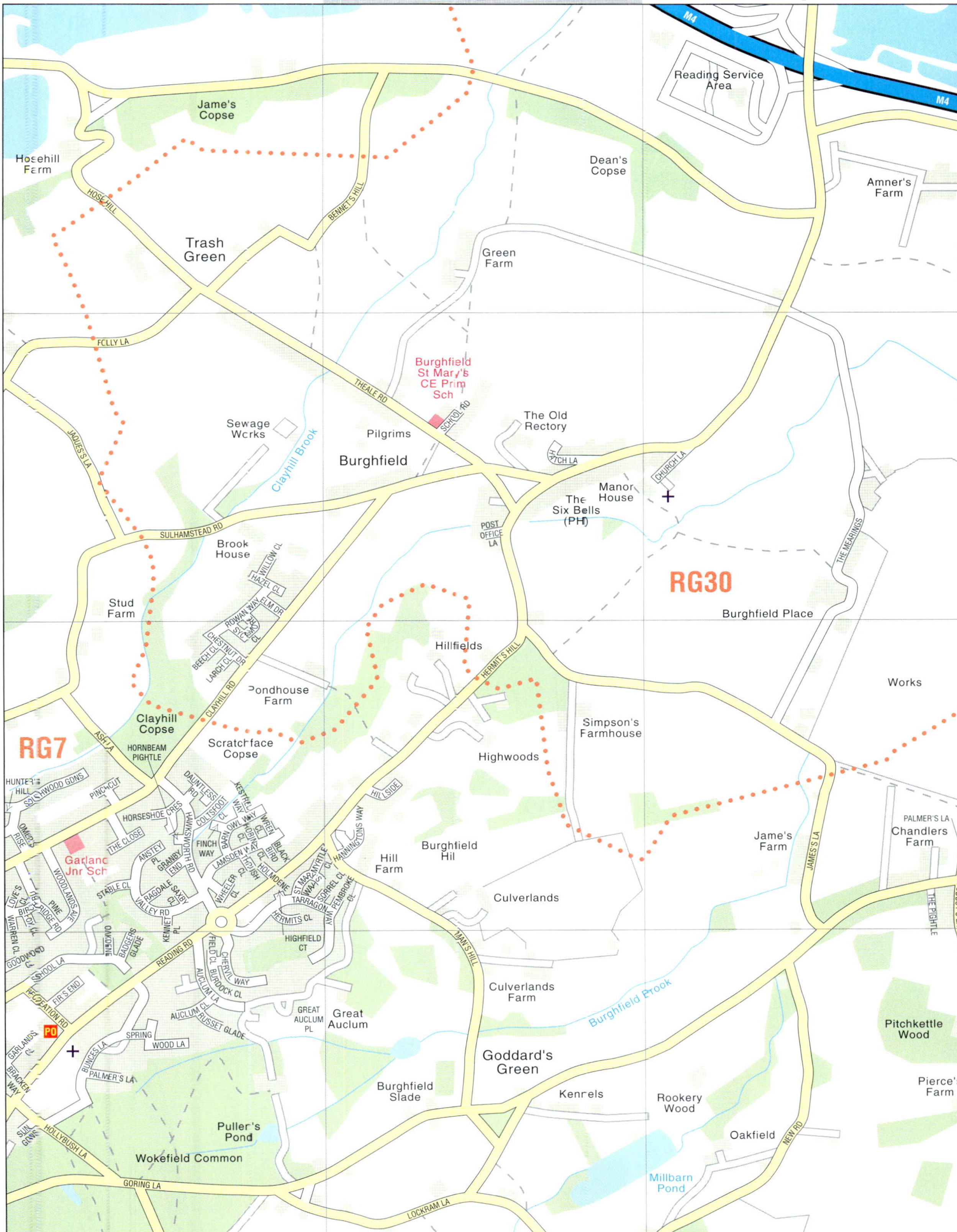

137
112

111
85

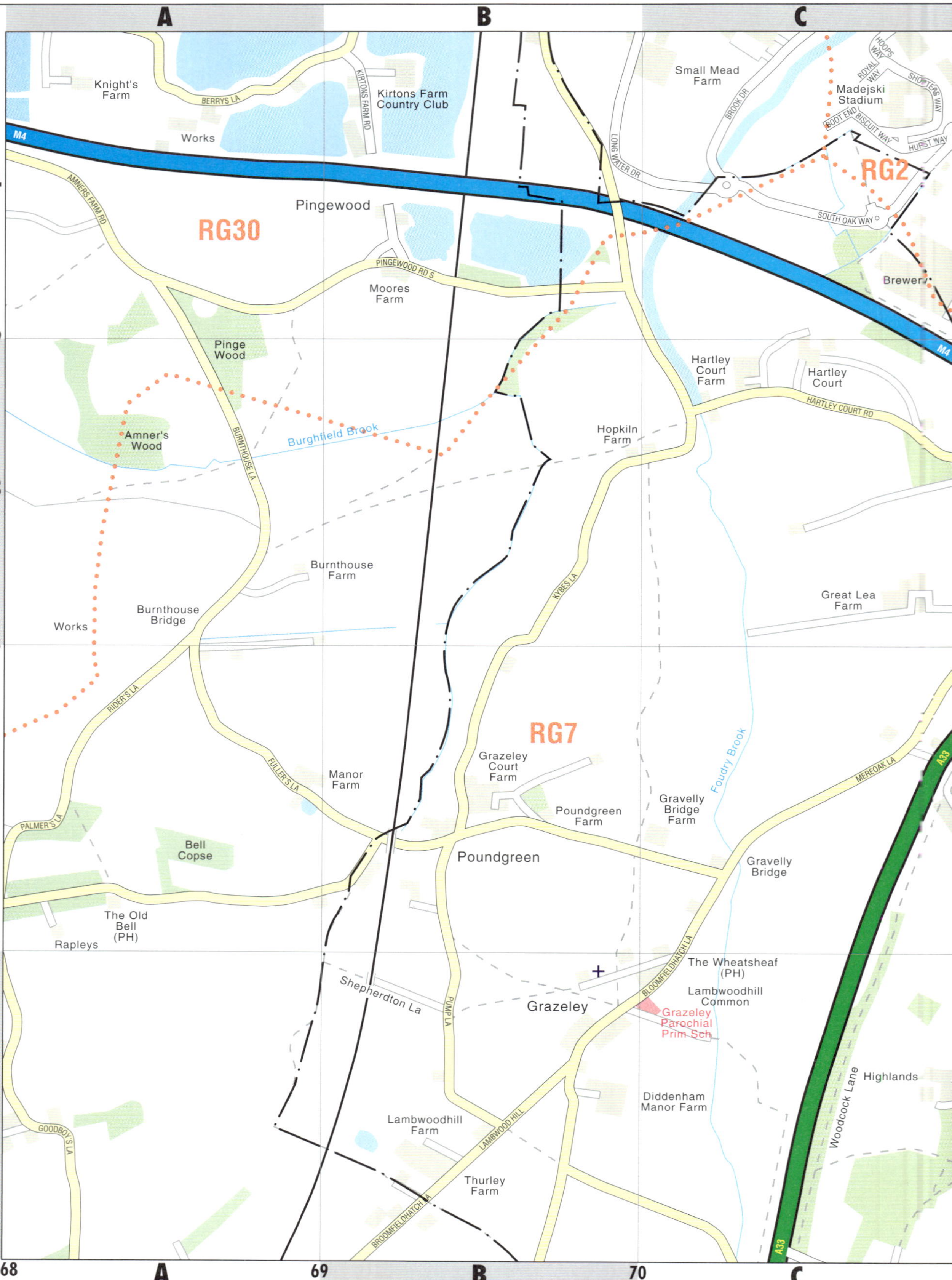

111
138

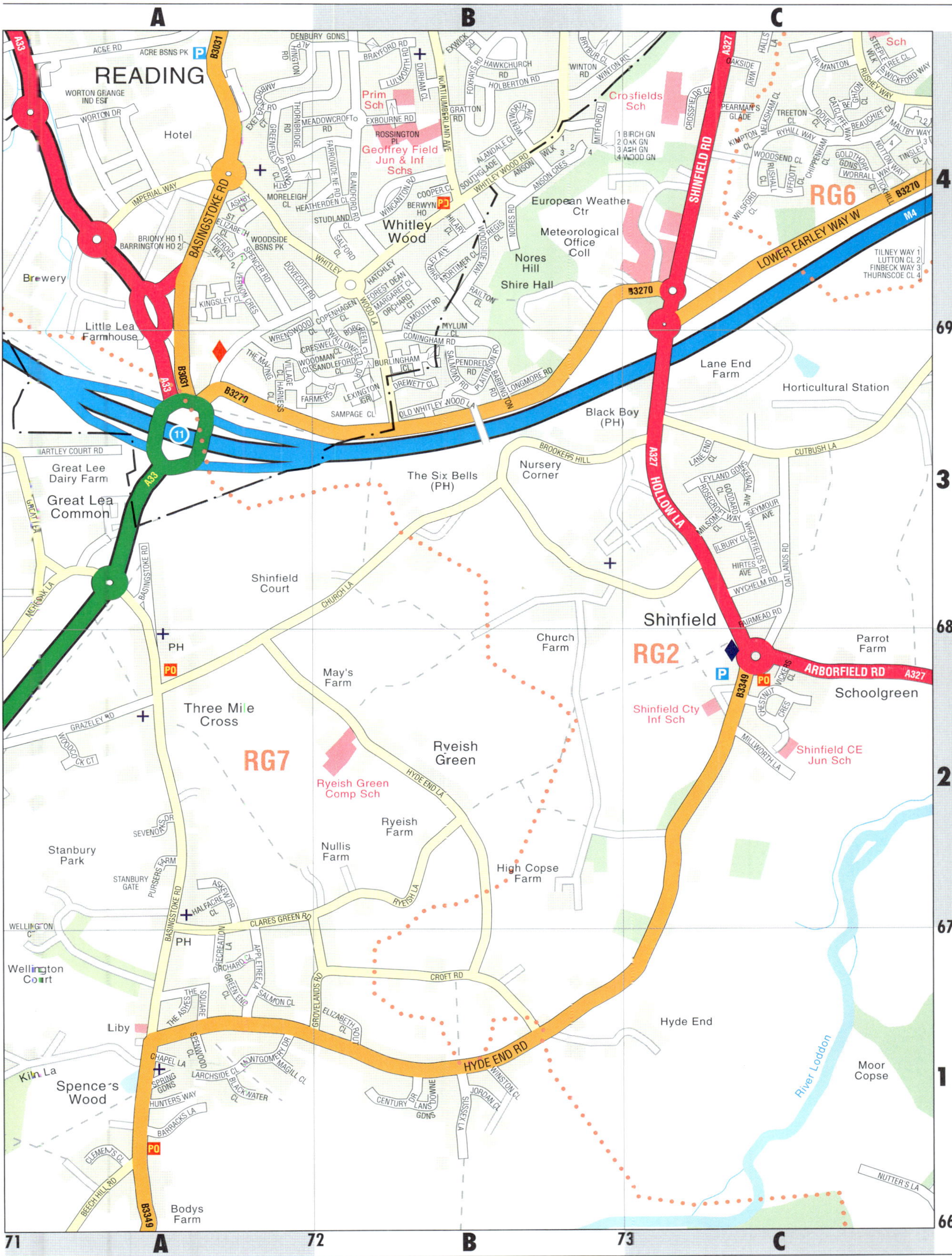
A
B
C
READING
Hotel
Brewery
Little Lea Farmhouse
Great Lee Dairy Farm
Great Lea Common
Prim Sch
Geoffrey Field Jun & Inf Schs
Crosfields Sch
Sch
Whitley Wood
European Weather Ctr
Meteorological Office Coll
Nores Hill
Shire Hall
RG6
LOWER EARLEY WAY W
M4
B3270
SHINFIELD RD
A327
A33
B3031
BASINGSTOKE RD
IMPERIAL WAY
WHITLEY WOOD RD
Lane End Farm
Horticultural Station
Black Boy (PH)
The Six Bells (PH)
Nursery Corner
BROOKERS HILL
CUTBUSH LA
HOLLOW LA
Shinfield Court
CHURCH LA
Shinfield
Church Farm
RG2
Parrot Farm
ARBORFIELD RD
Schoolgreen
Shinfield Cty Inf Sch
Shinfield CE Jun Sch
B3349
PH
PO
May's Farm
Three Mile Cross
RG7
Ryeish Green
Ryeish Green Comp Sch
HYDE END LA
Ryeish Farm
Nullis Farm
High Copse Farm
Stanbury Park
CLARES GREEN RD
CROFT RD
Wellington Court
Liby
HYDE END RD
Hyde End
Kiln La
Spencer's Wood
River Loddon
Moor Copse
Bodys Farm
BEECH HILL RD
NUTTER'S LA
4
69
3
68
2
67
1
66
71
72
73

113
87

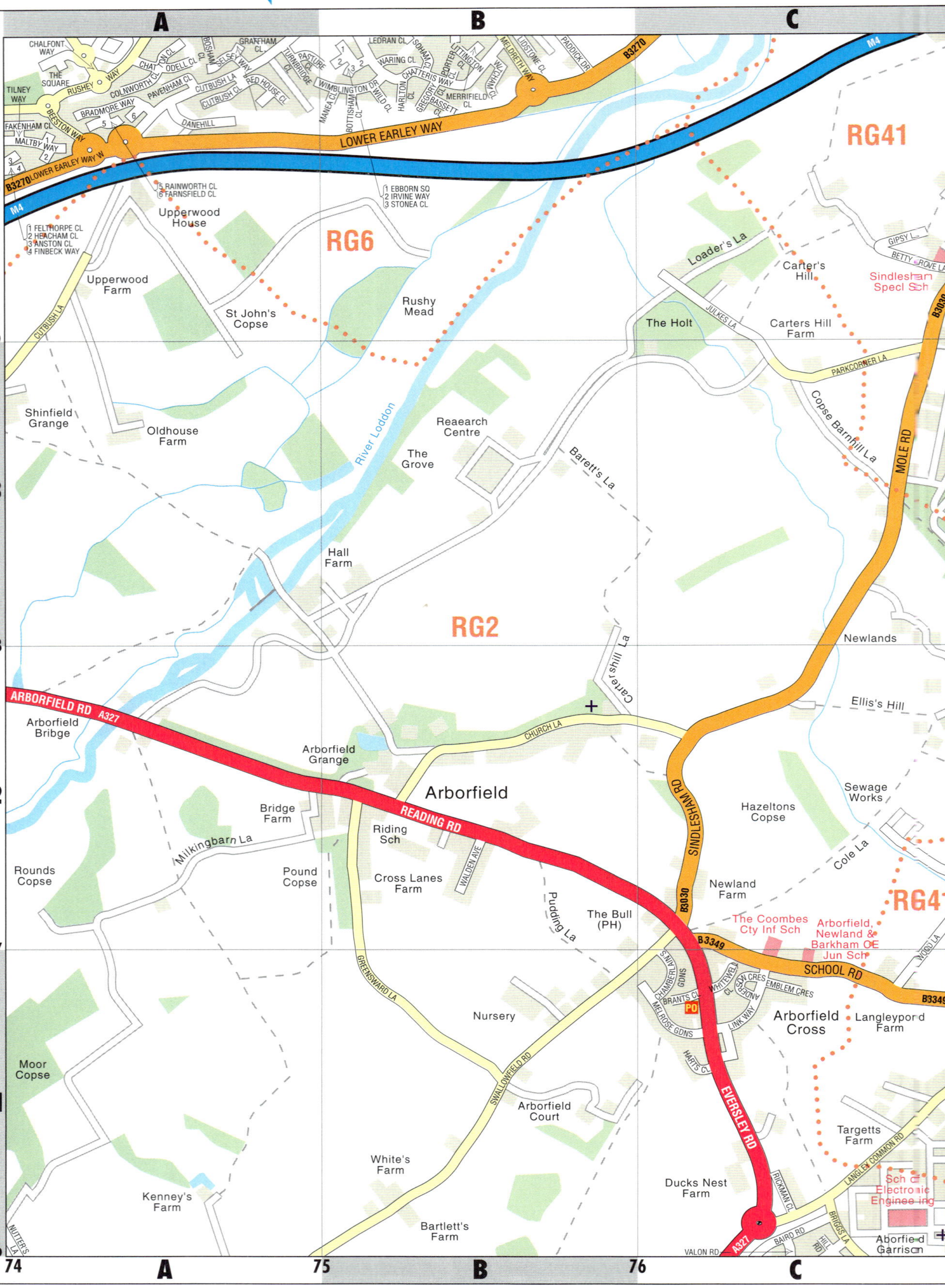

113
140

A B C

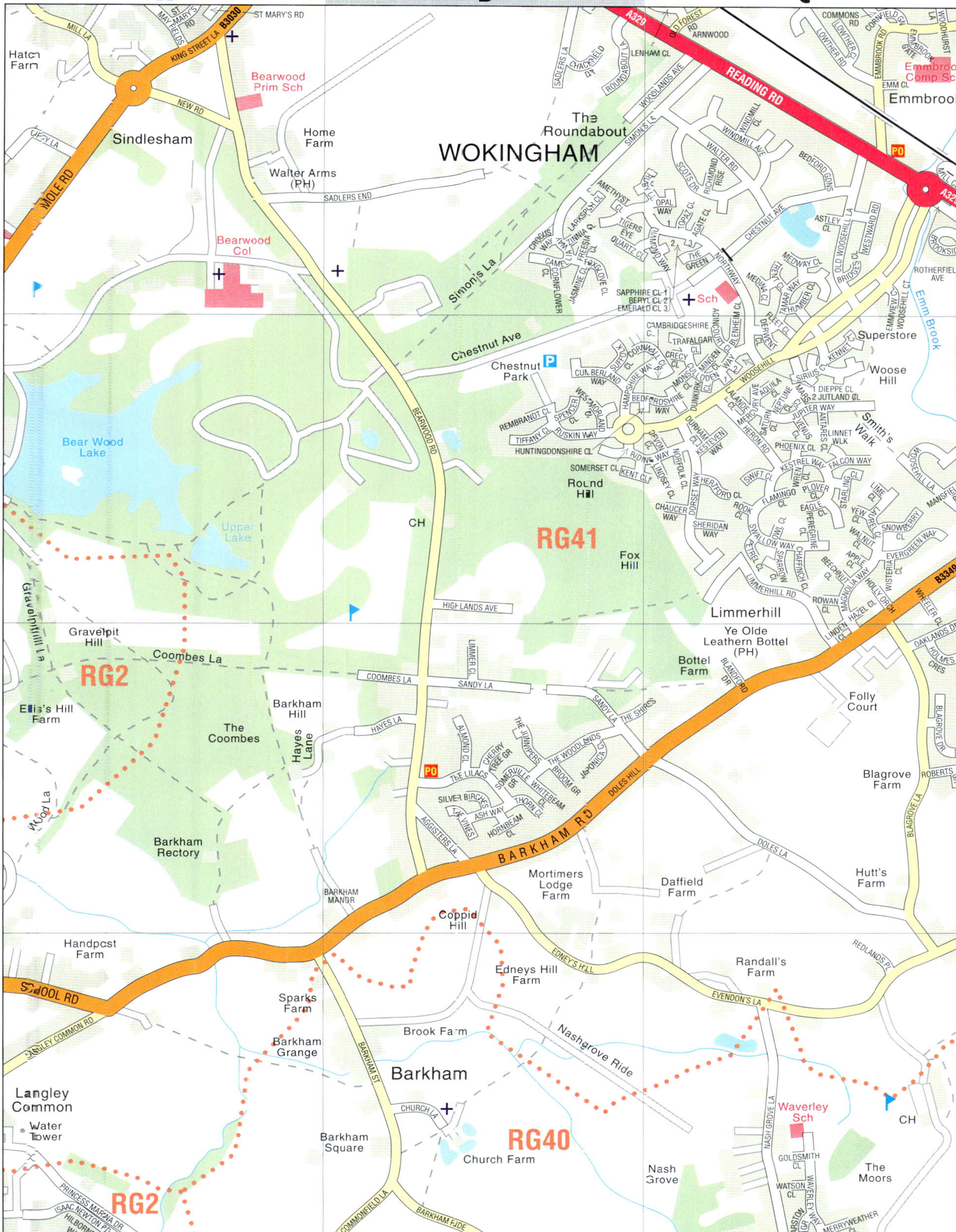

4 69 3 68 2 67 1 66

77 A 78 B 79 C

115
89

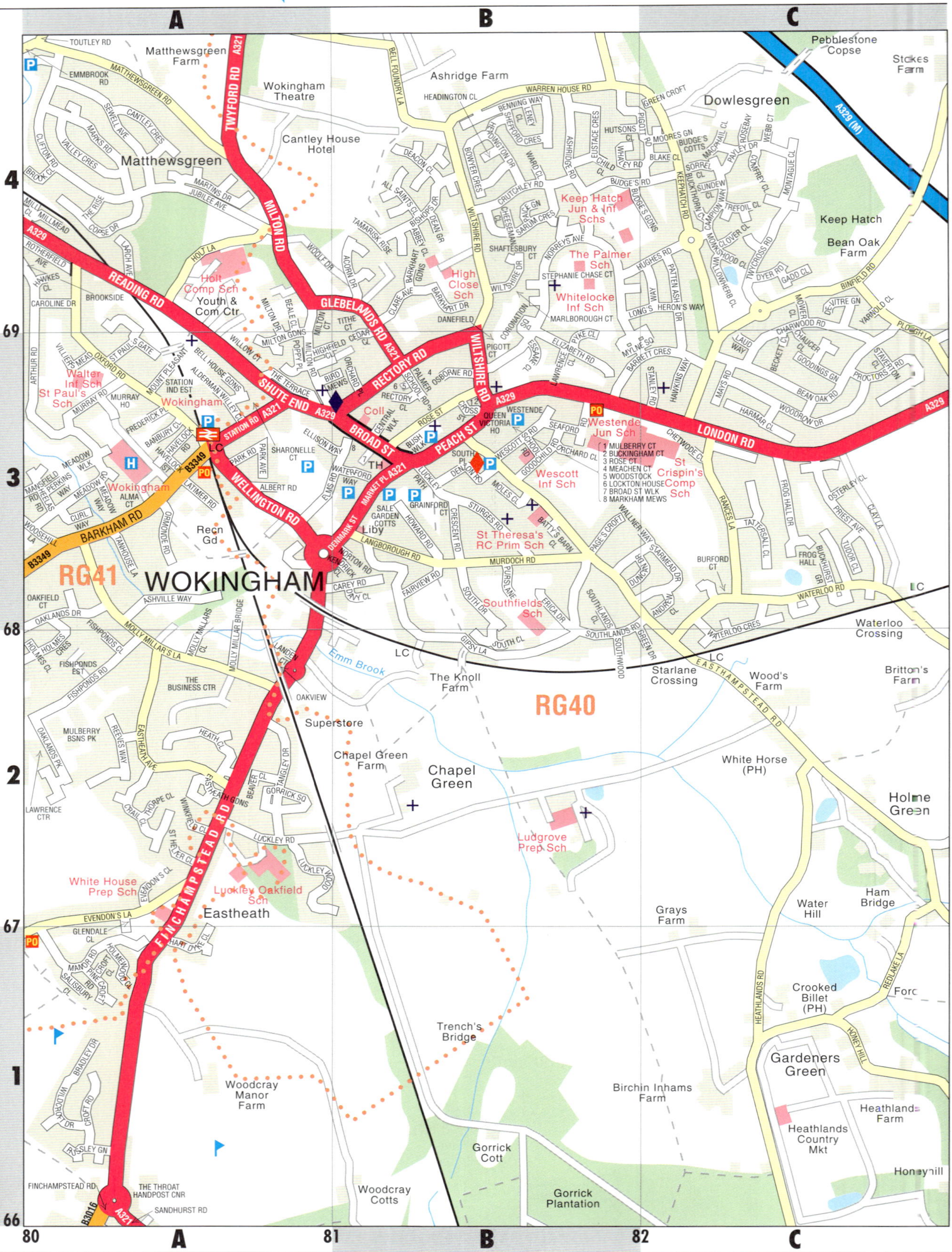

115
142

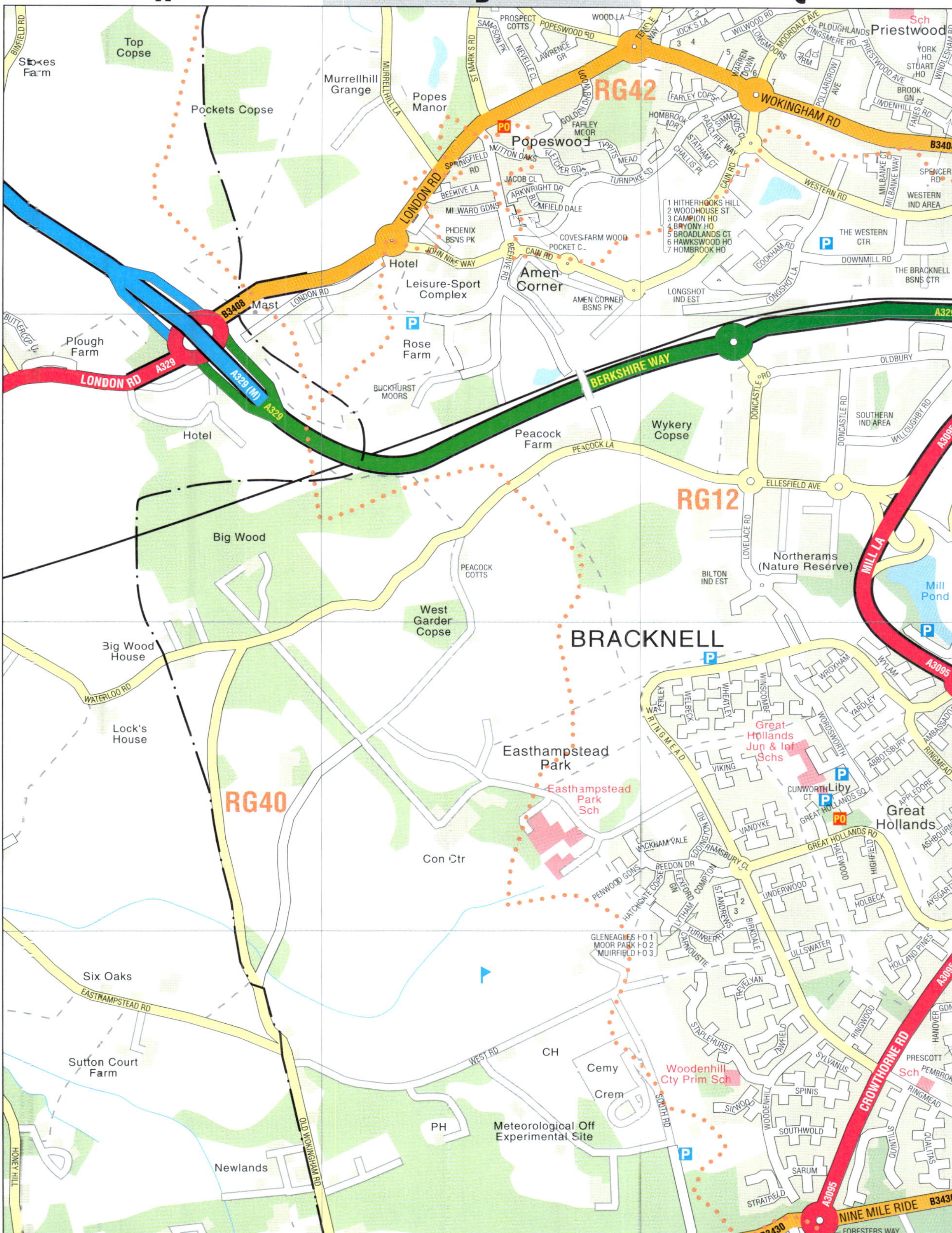
90
118
A
B
C
Top Copse
Stokes Farm
Pockets Copse
Murrellhill Grange
Popes Manor
RG42
Popeswood
Priestwood
WOKINGHAM RD
LONDON RD
Hotel
Leisure-Sport Complex
Amen Corner
Mast
Plough Farm
Rose Farm
BUCKHURST MOORS
BERKSHIRE WAY
Hotel
Peacock Farm
Wykery Copse
RG12
Big Wood
Northerams (Nature Reserve)
Mill Pond
MILL LA
West Garden Copse
BRACKNELL
Big Wood House
Lock's House
Easthampstead Park
Easthampstead Park Sch
Great Hollands Jun & Inf Schs
Great Hollands
RG40
Con Ctr
Six Oaks
Sutton Court Farm
CH
Cemy
Crem
Woodenhill Cty Prim Sch
Meteorological Off Experimental Site
PH
Newlands
CROWTHORNE RD
NINE MILE RIDE
4
3
2
1
69
68
67
66
83
84
85
143
118

A4
1 PRIESTWOOD SQ
2 SALTIRE GDNS
3 WINDLEBROOK GN
4 APPLETREE PL
5 PORTMAN CL
6 HART CL
7 BIRCHETTS CL
8 ASHRIDGE GN

117

B4
1 LYNWOOD CHASE
2 DENE CL
3 LAKESIDE
4 EDMONDS CT

91

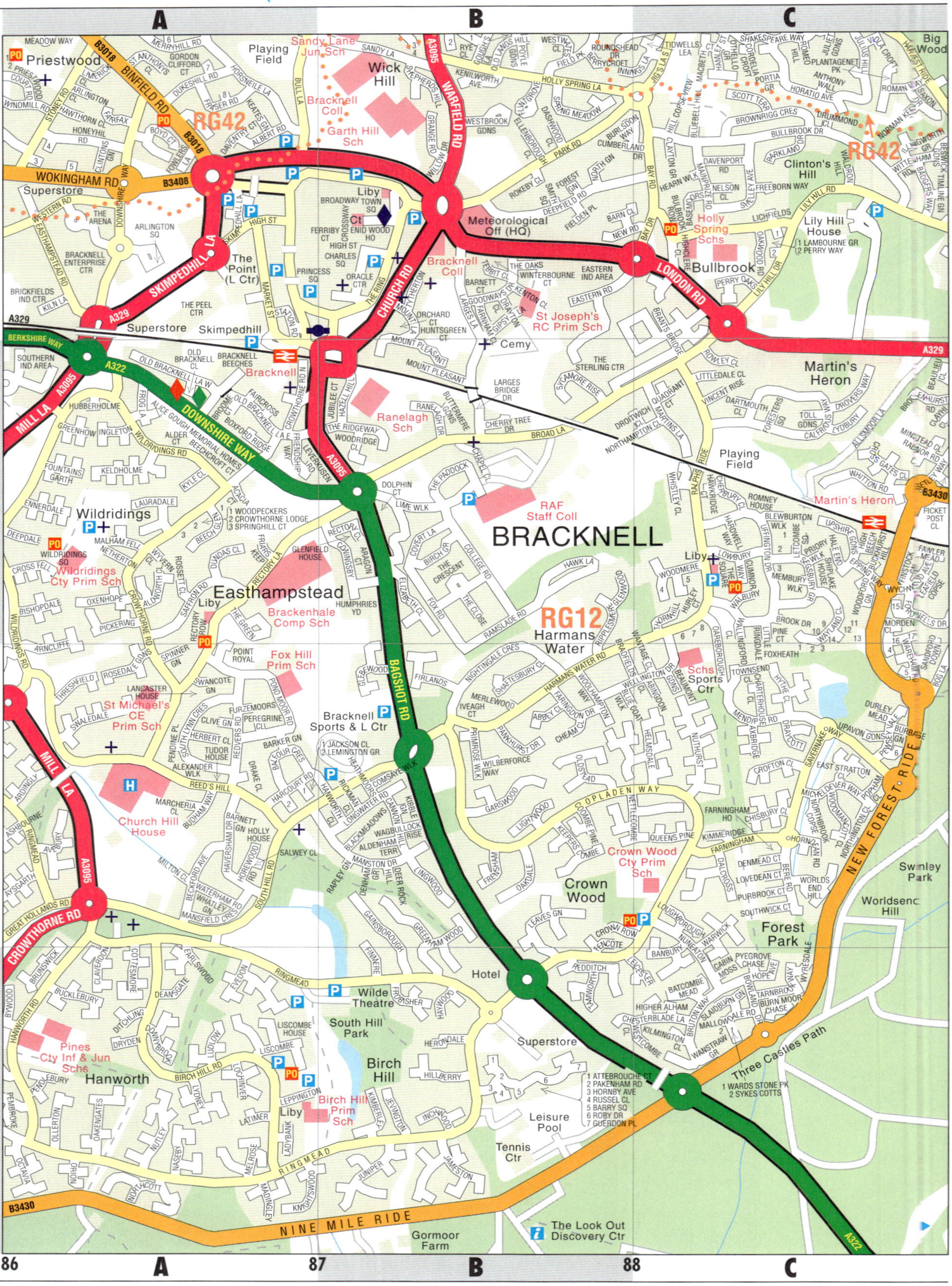

117

144

C2
1 MULBERRY CT
2 ROWAN
3 LINDEN
4 LYTCHET MINSTER CL
5 STOKEFORD CL
6 FROXFIELD DOWN

C3
1 HOWORTH CT
2 BOVENEY HO
3 BOULTERS HO
4 HEATHERMOUNT
5 HAMBLEDEN CT
6 CLEEVE HO
7 RUSHY HO
8 CULHAM HO
9 THE WILLOWS
10 CEDARS
11 MAPEL CT
12 GREENWOOD
13 LARCHWOOD
14 THE FIRS
15 CHARLBURY CL
16 HOLTON HEATH
17 BLOXWORTH CL

92 120

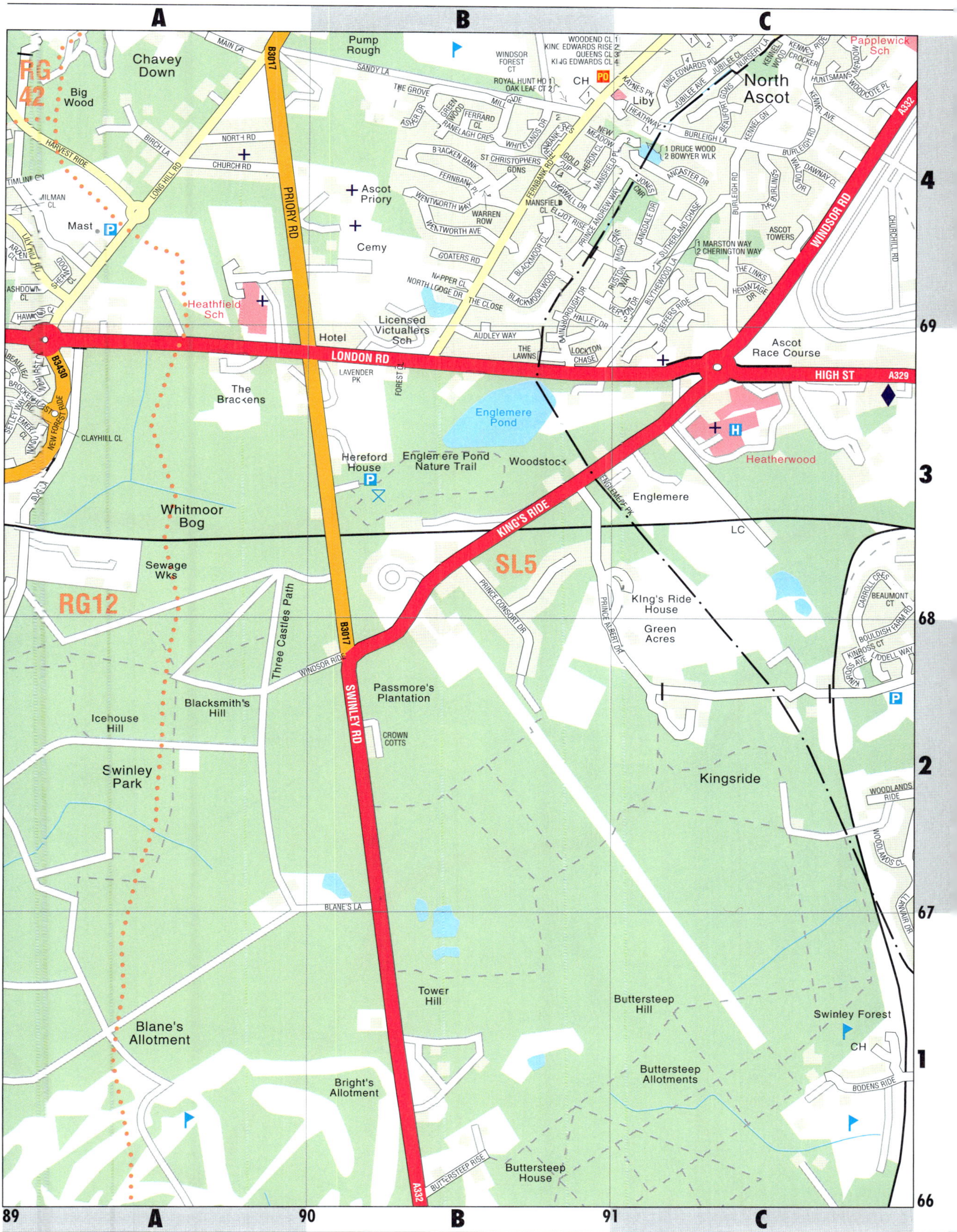

145 120

119
93

A B C

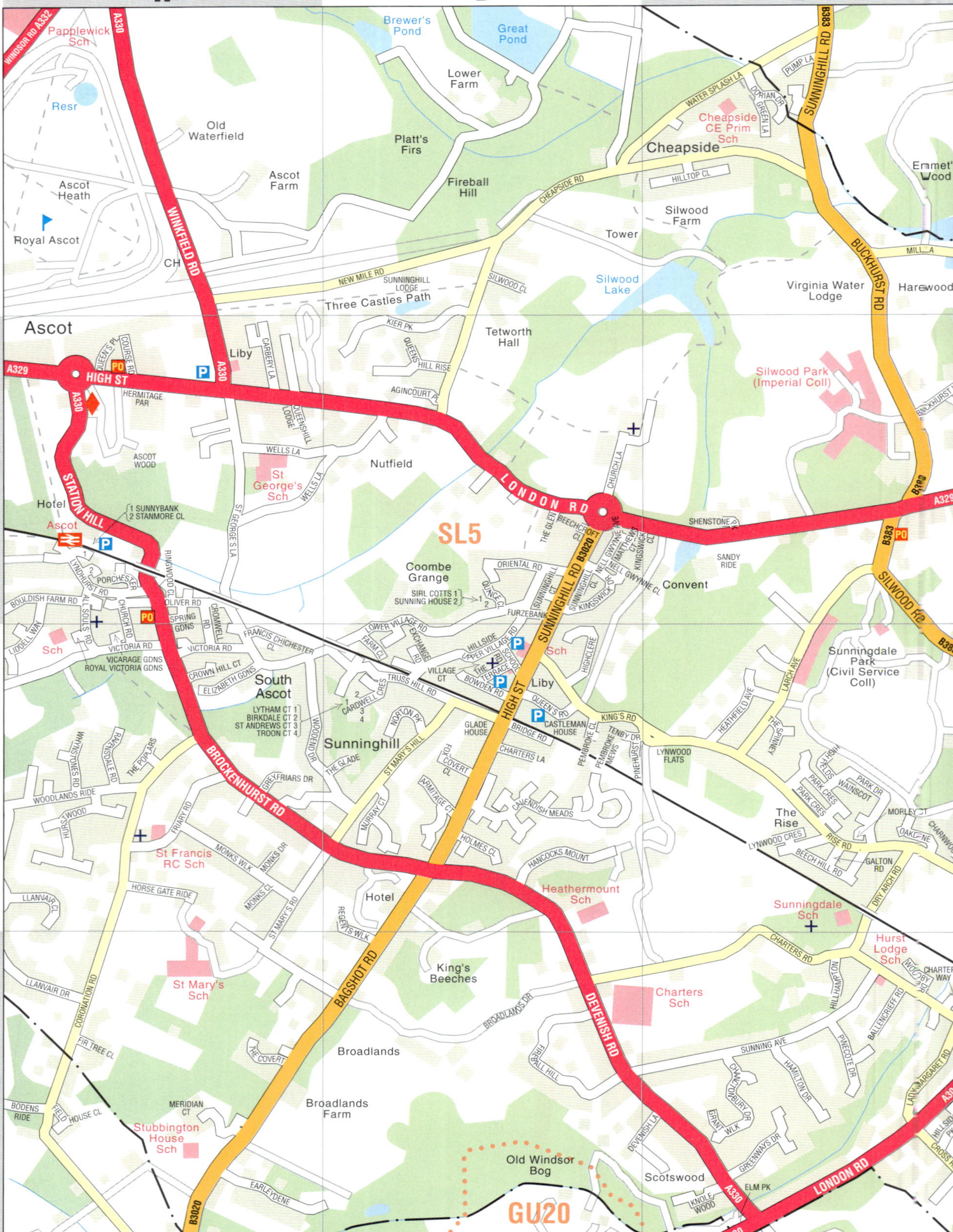

4

69

3

68

2

67

1

66

92 A 93 B 94 C

119
146

94
122

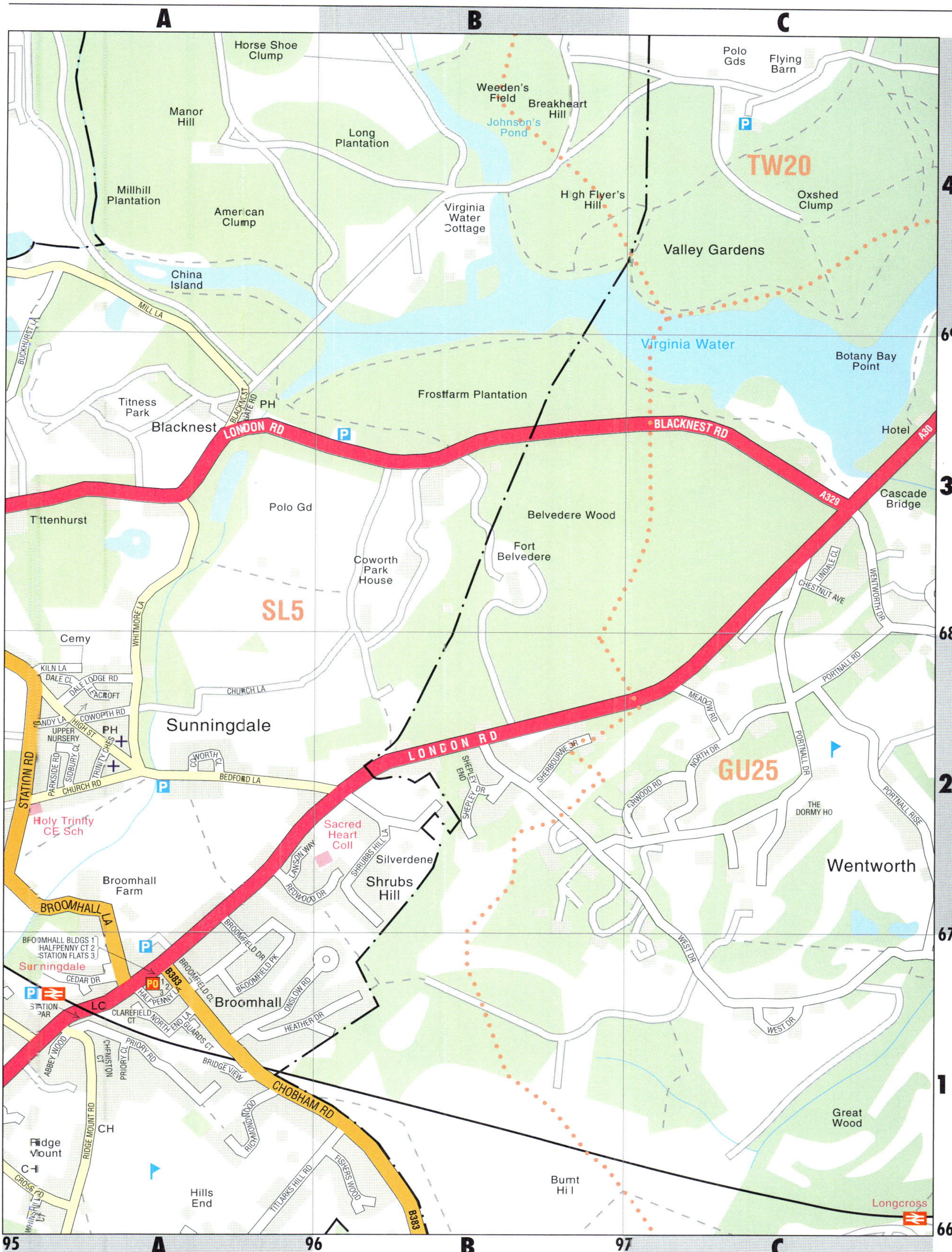
A
B
C
4
69
3
68
2
67
1
66
95
96
97
Horse Shoe Clump
Manor Hill
Long Plantation
Weeden's Field
Breakheart Hill
Johnson's Pond
Polo Gds
Flying Barn
TW20
Millhill Plantation
American Clump
Virginia Water Cottage
High Flyer's Hill
Oxshed Clump
Valley Gardens
China Island
MILL LA
BUCKHURST LA
Virginia Water
Botany Bay Point
Titness Park
Blacknest
PH
BLACKNEST GATE RD
LONDON RD
Frostfarm Plantation
BLACKNEST RD
Hotel
A30
A329
Cascade Bridge
Tittenhurst
Polo Gd
Belvedere Wood
Fort Belvedere
Coworth Park House
SL5
LINDALE CL
CHESTNUT AVE
WENTWORTH DR
Cemy
WHITMORE LA
KILN LA
DALE CL
DALE LODGE RD
LEACROFT
CHURCH LA
COWORTH RD
HIGH ST
UPPER NURSERY
Sunningdale
PH
STATION RD
PARKSIDE RD
SIDBURY CL
TRINITY CRES
CHURCH RD
COWORTH CL
BEDFORD LA
LONDON RD
MEADOW RD
PORTNALL RD
SHERBOURNE DR
SHEPLEY END
SHEPLEY DR
NORTH DR
GU25
PORTNALL DR
ASHWOOD RD
THE DORMY HO
PORTNALL RISE
Holy Trinity CE Sch
Sacred Heart Coll
LAWSON WAY
SHRUBBS HILL LA
Silverdene
Shrubs Hill
REDWOOD DR
Wentworth
Broomhall Farm
BROOMHALL LA
BROOMFIELD DR
BROOMFIELD PK
BROOMHALL BLDGS 1
HALFPENNY CT 2
STATION FLATS 3
Sunningdale
CEDAR DR
PO
B383
BROOMFIELD CL
ONSLOW RD
WEST DR
Broomhall
STATION PAR
LC
HALFPENNY LA
CLAREFIELD CT
NORTH END LA
GUARDS CT
HEATHER DR
WEST DR
ABBEY WOOD
CHRISTON CT
PRIORY CL
PRIORY RD
BRIDGE VIEW
CHOBHAM RD
Great Wood
RICHMOND WOOD
CH
Ridge Mount
RIDGE MOUNT RD
CH
CROSS RD
Hills End
TITLARKS HILL RD
FISHERS WOOD
Burnt Hill
Longcross
B383

122

121 95

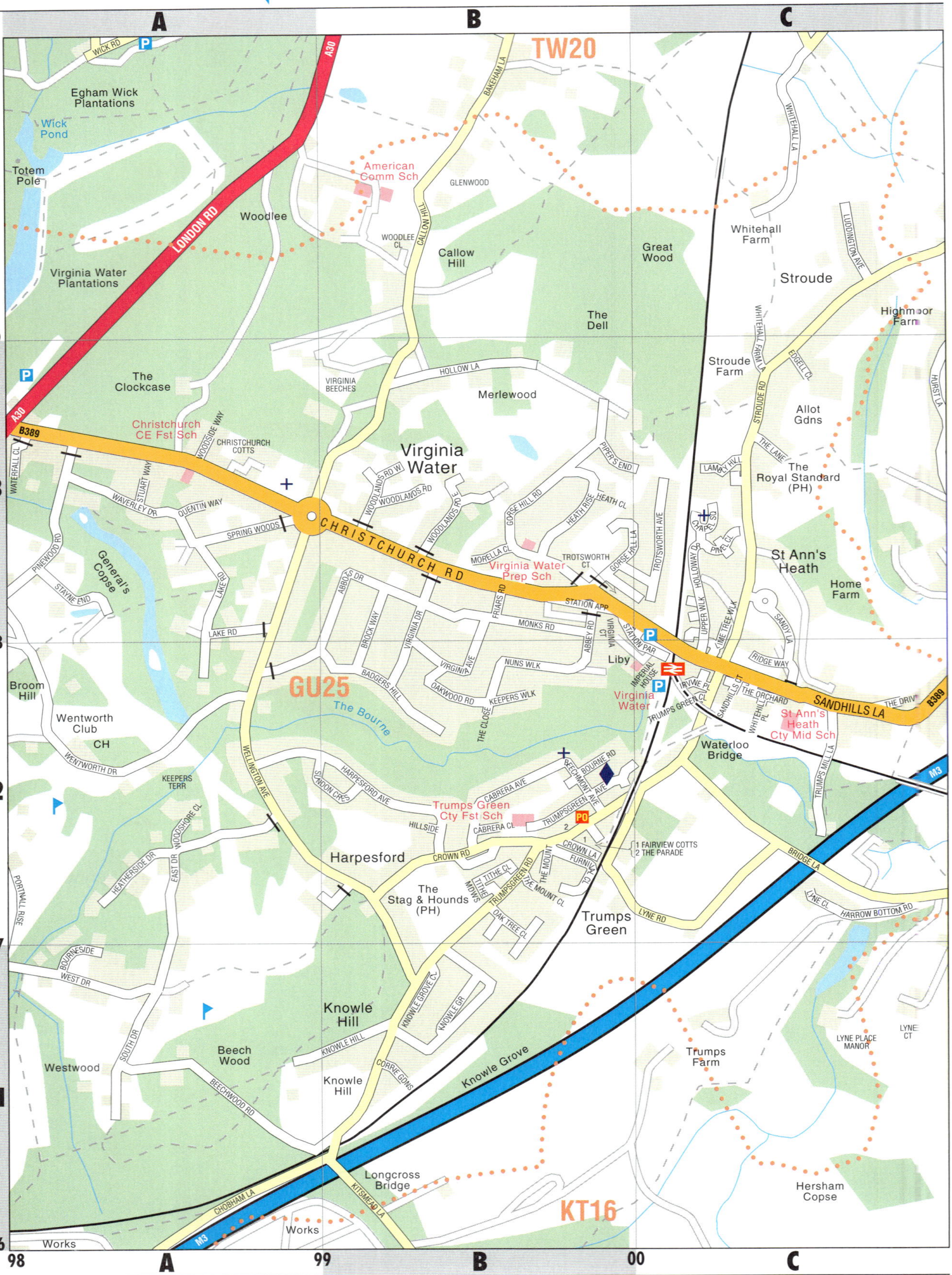
A
B
C
TW20
GU25
KT16
Egham Wick Plantations
Wick Pond
Totem Pole
Woodlee
Virginia Water Plantations
LONDON RD
American Comm Sch
Callow Hill
Great Wood
Whitehall Farm
Stroude
The Dell
Highmoor Farm
Stroude Farm
The Clockcase
Merlewood
Allot Gdns
Christchurch CE Fst Sch
Virginia Water
The Royal Standard (PH)
CHRISTCHURCH RD
St Ann's Heath
Home Farm
Virginia Water Prep Sch
General's Copse
Broom Hill
Wentworth Club
CH
Liby
The Bourne
Waterloo Bridge
St Ann's Heath Cty Mid Sch
SANDHILLS LA
Trumps Green Cty Fst Sch
Harpesford
The Stag & Hounds (PH)
Trumps Green
Knowle Hill
Beech Wood
Westwood
Knowle Grove
Trumps Farm
LYNE PLACE MANOR
Longcross Bridge
Hersham Copse
Works
M3
A30
B389
98
99
00
66
67
1
2
68
3
69
4

121

96
124

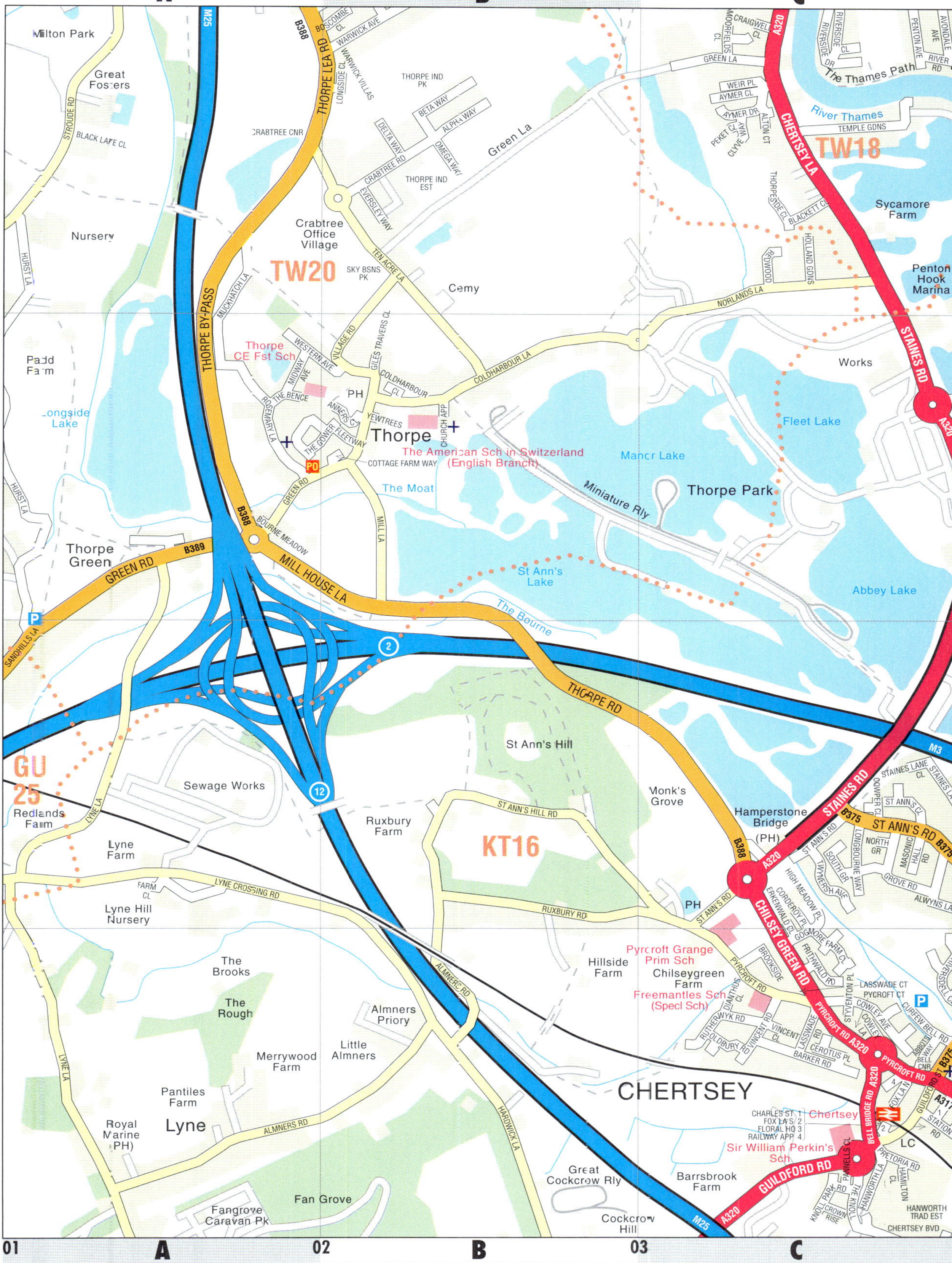
Milton Park
Great Fosters
Nursery
Padd Farm
Longside Lake
Thorpe Green
Redlands Farm
Lyne Farm
Lyne Hill Nursery
Sewage Works
Crabtree Office Village
TW20
Thorpe
Thorpe CE Fst Sch
The American Sch in Switzerland (English Branch)
The Moat
Cemy
Manor Lake
Thorpe Park
Miniature Rly
St Ann's Lake
The Bourne
Fleet Lake
Abbey Lake
Works
TW18
River Thames
The Thames Path
Sycamore Farm
Penton Hook Marina
St Ann's Hill
Monk's Grove
Ruxbury Farm
KT16
Hamperstone Bridge (PH)
GU25
The Brooks
The Rough
Almners Priory
Little Almners
Merrywood Farm
Pantiles Farm
Royal Marine (PH)
Lyne
Fan Grove
Fangrove Caravan Pk
Hillside Farm
Pyrcroft Grange Prim Sch
Chilseygreen Farm
Freemantles Sch (Specl Sch)
CHERTSEY
Chertsey
Sir William Perkin's Sch
Great Cockcrow Rly
Cockcrow Hill
Barrsbrook Farm
M25
M3
THORPE BY-PASS
THORPE LEA RD
GREEN RD
MILL HOUSE LA
THORPE RD
COLDHARBOUR LA
Green La
NORLANDS LA
CHERTSEY LA
STAINES RD
ST ANN'S RD
ST ANN'S HILL RD
RUXBURY RD
LYNE CROSSING RD
ALMNERS RD
HARDWICK LA
GUILDFORD RD
CHILSEY GREEN RD
PYRCROFT RD
LYNE LA
STROUDE RD
SANDHILLS LA
HANWORTH TRAD EST
CHERTSEY BVD

123
97

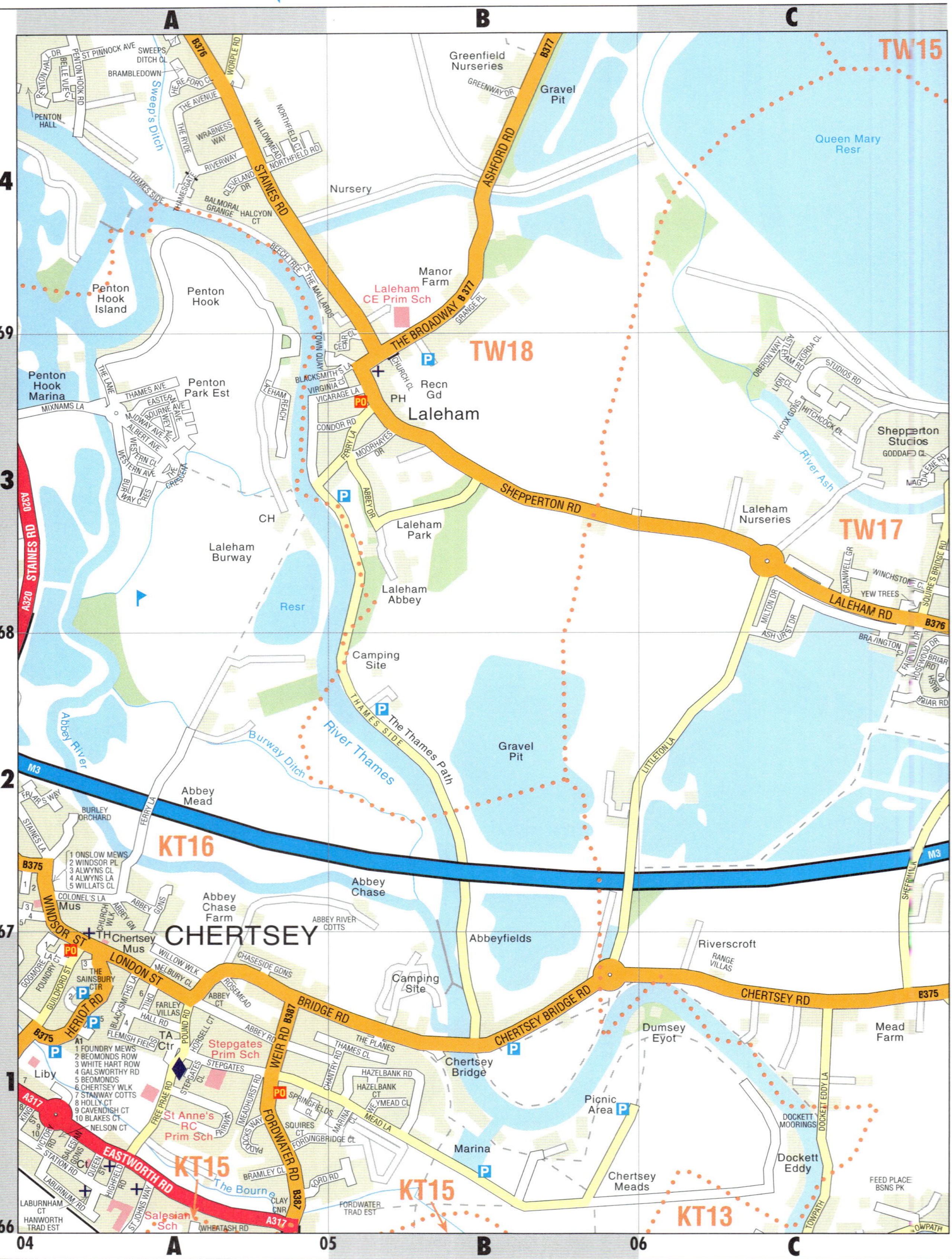
TW18
TW17
TW15
KT16
KT15
KT13
Laleham
CHERTSEY
Queen Mary Resr
Laleham Burway
Penton Hook
Penton Hook Island
Penton Hook Marina
Penton Park Est
Laleham Abbey
Laleham Park
Laleham Nurseries
Shepperton Studios
Abbey Mead
Abbey Chase
Abbey Chase Farm
Abbeyfields
Riverscroft
Dumsey Eyot
Chertsey Bridge
Chertsey Meads
Dockett Eddy
Mead Farm
Gravel Pit
River Thames
SHEPPERTON RD
CHERTSEY BRIDGE RD
CHERTSEY RD
STAINES RD
THE BROADWAY
ASHFORD RD
LALEHAM RD
LONDON ST
BRIDGE RD
EASTWORTH RD
WINDSOR ST
LITTLETON LA

123

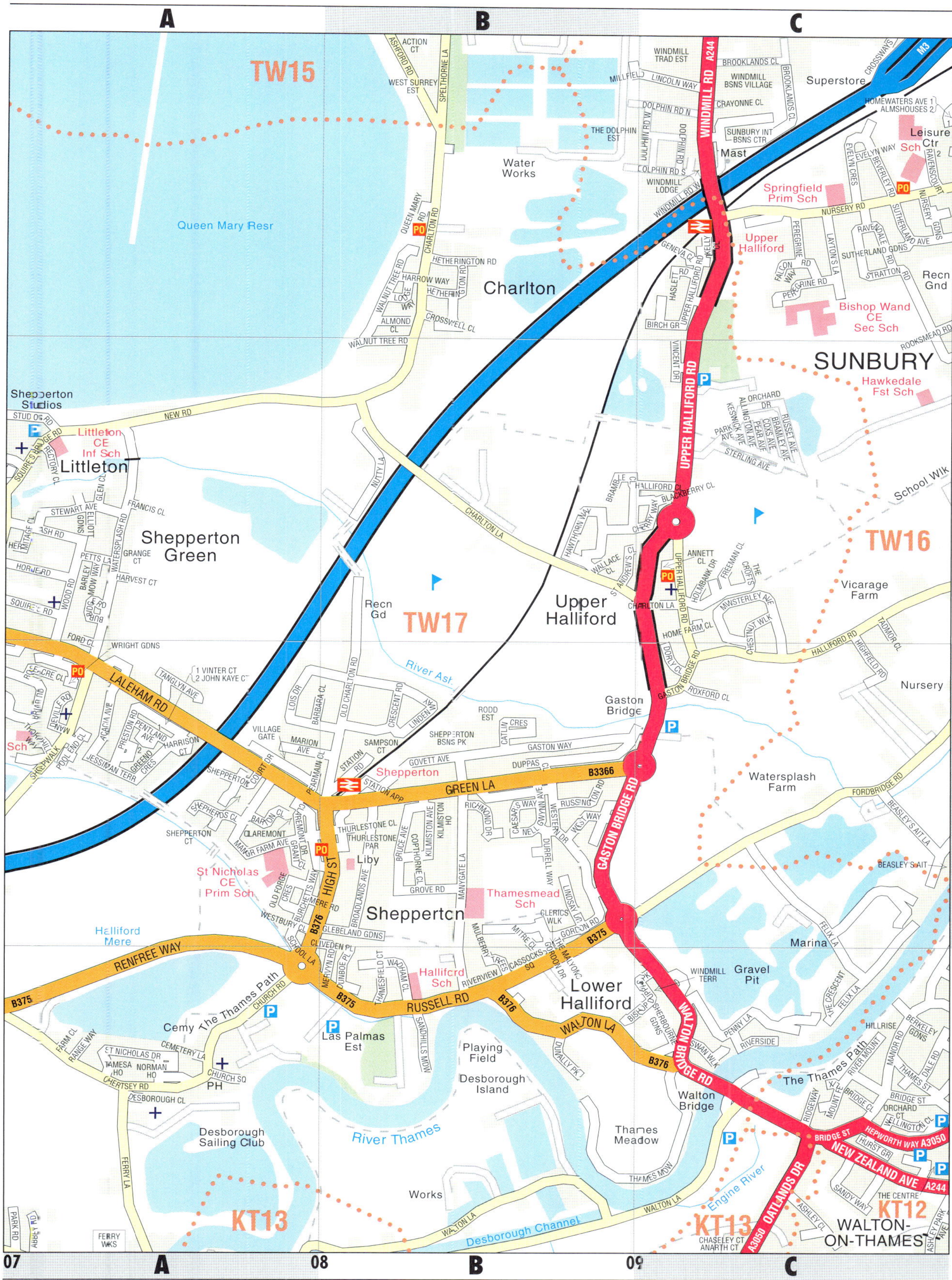
A
B
C
TW15
Queen Mary Resr
Water Works
Charlton
Superstore
Leisure Ctr
Springfield Prim Sch
Upper Halliford
SUNBURY
Hawkedale Fst Sch
Bishop Wand CE Sec Sch
Recn Gnd
Shepperton Studios
Littleton CE Inf Sch
Littleton
Shepperton Green
Recn Gd
TW17
Upper Halliford
TW16
Vicarage Farm
School Wlk
River Ash
Gaston Bridge
Nursery
Watersplash Farm
Shepperton
St Nicholas CE Prim Sch
Liby
Thamesmead Sch
Sheppertcn
Halliford Mere
Halliford Sch
Lower Halliford
Marina
Gravel Pit
Cemy
The Thames Path
Las Palmas Est
Playing Field
Desborough Island
Walton Bridge
Desborough Sailing Club
River Thames
Thames Meadow
Works
KT13
Desborough Channel
Engine River
KT12
WALTON-ON-THAMES
WINDMILL RD
UPPER HALLIFORD RD
GASTON BRIDGE RD
WALTON BRIDGE RD
LALEHAM RD
GREEN LA
RENFREE WAY
RUSSELL RD
WALTON LA
HIGH ST
NEW RD
CHARLTON LA
NURSERY RD
HALLIFORD RD
FORDBRIDGE RD
NEW ZEALAND AVE
OATLANDS DR
HEPWORTH WAY
BRIDGE ST
A244
B3366
B375
B376
A3050
M3
07
08
09
66
67
68
69
1
2
3
4

100

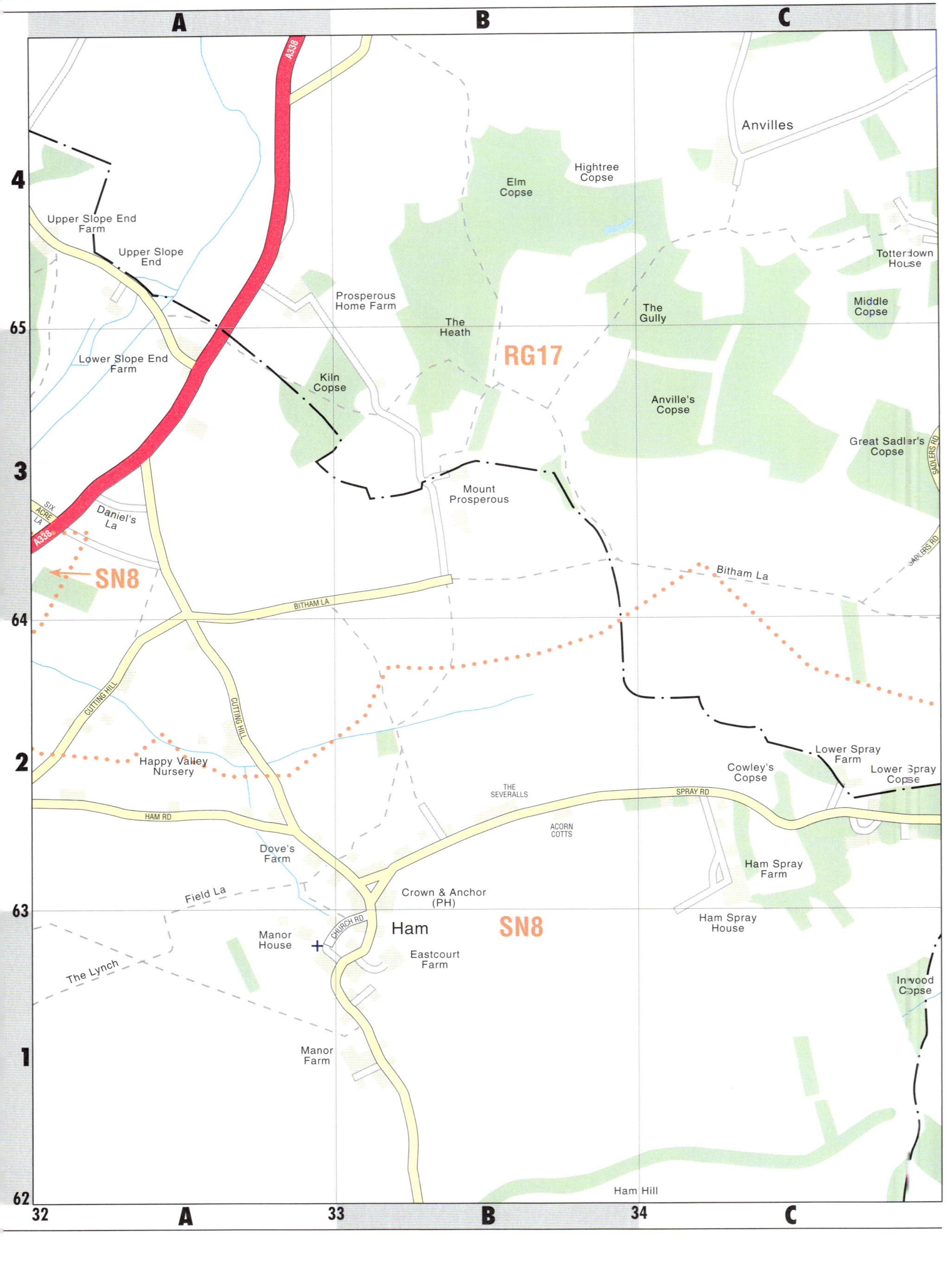
A
B
C
4
65
3
64
2
63
1
62
32
33
34
A338
Anvilles
Hightree Copse
Elm Copse
Upper Slope End Farm
Upper Slope End
Totterdown House
Prosperous Home Farm
Middle Copse
The Gully
The Heath
RG17
Lower Slope End Farm
Kiln Copse
Anville's Copse
Great Sadler's Copse
SADLERS RD
Mount Prosperous
SIX ACRE LA
Daniel's La
SN8
Bitham La
BITHAM LA
CUTTING HILL
Happy Valley Nursery
Lower Spray Farm
Cowley's Copse
Lower Spray Copse
THE SEVERALLS
SPRAY RD
HAM RD
ACORN COTTS
Dove's Farm
Ham Spray Farm
Field La
Crown & Anchor (PH)
Manor House
CHURCH RD
Ham
SN8
Ham Spray House
Eastcourt Farm
The Lynch
Inwood Copse
Manor Farm
Ham Hill

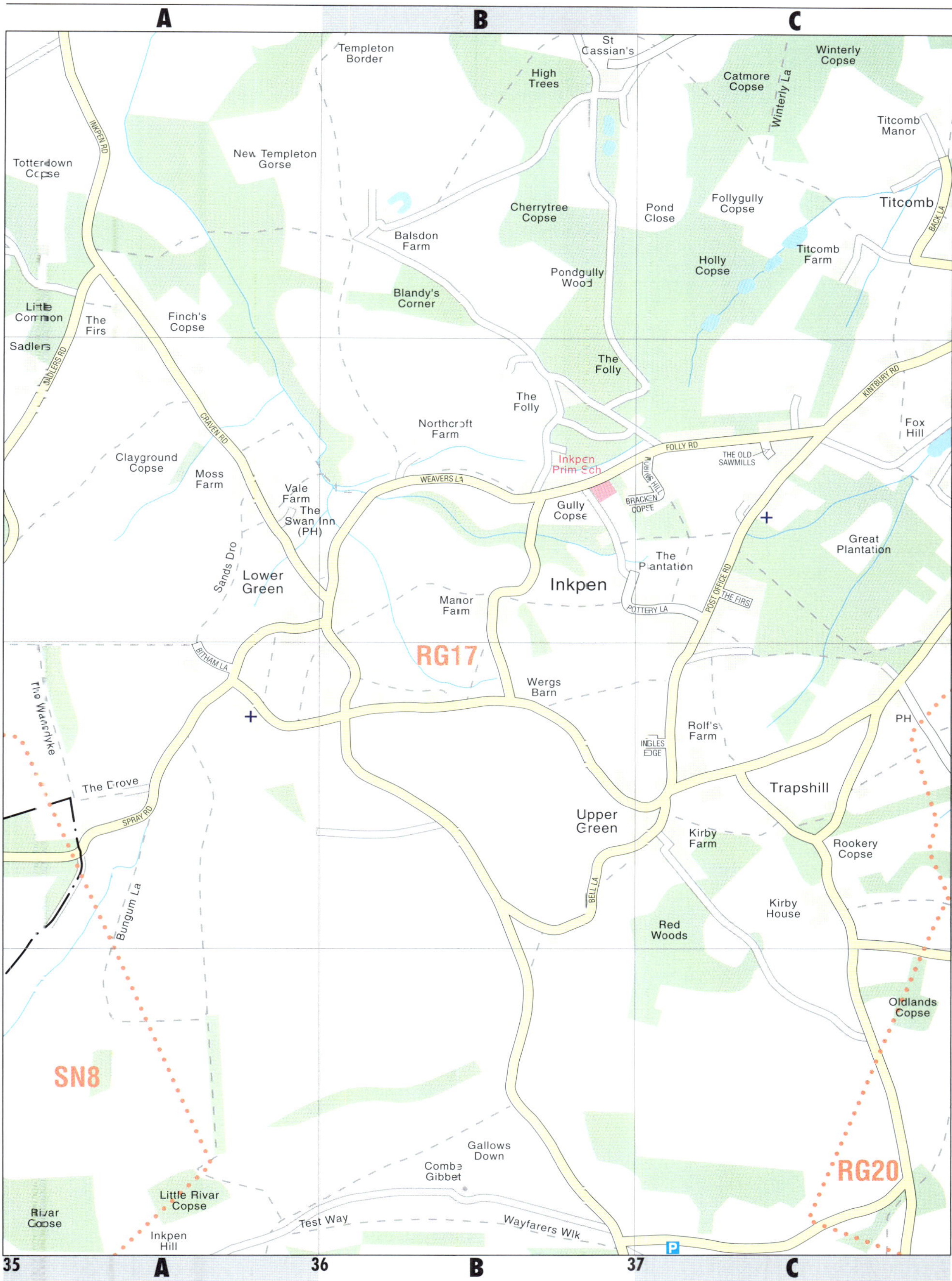
A
B
C
Templeton Border
St Cassian's
High Trees
Catmore Copse
Winterly La
Winterly Copse
Titcomb Manor
INKPEN RD
Totterdown Copse
New Templeton Gorse
Cherrytree Copse
Pond Close
Follygully Copse
Titcomb
BACK LA
Balsdon Farm
Titcomb Farm
Holly Copse
Pondgully Wood
Blandy's Corner
Little Common
The Firs
Finch's Copse
Sadlers
SADLERS RD
The Folly
The Folly
KINTBURY RD
CRAVEN RD
Northcroft Farm
Fox Hill
FOLLY RD
THE OLD SAWMILLS
Clayground Copse
Moss Farm
Inkpen Prim Sch
WEAVERS LA
Vale Farm
The Swan Inn (PH)
Gully Copse
BRACKEN COPSE
Great Plantation
Sands Dro
Lower Green
The Plantation
Inkpen
POST OFFICE RD
THE FIRS
Manor Farm
POTTERY LA
RG17
BITHAM LA
Wergs Barn
The Wansdyke
Rolf's Farm
INGLES EDGE
PH
The Drove
Trapshill
SPRAY RD
Upper Green
Kirby Farm
Rookery Copse
BELL LA
Bungum La
Kirby House
Red Woods
Oldlands Copse
SN8
Gallows Down
Combe Gibbet
RG20
Little Rivar Copse
Rivar Copse
Test Way
Wayfarers Wlk
Inkpen Hill
P
4
65
3
64
2
63
1
62
35
36
37

127 102

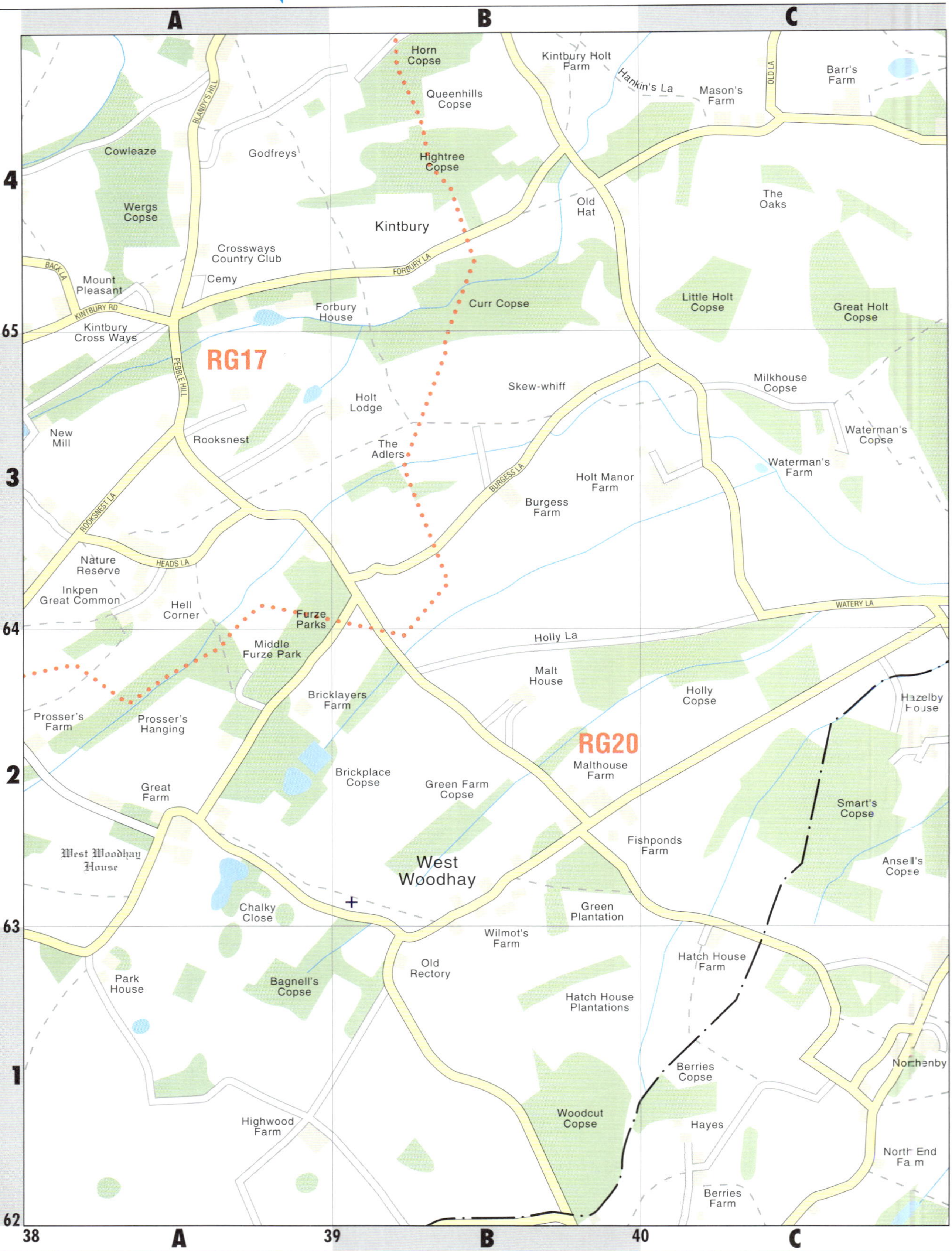

127 148

103
130

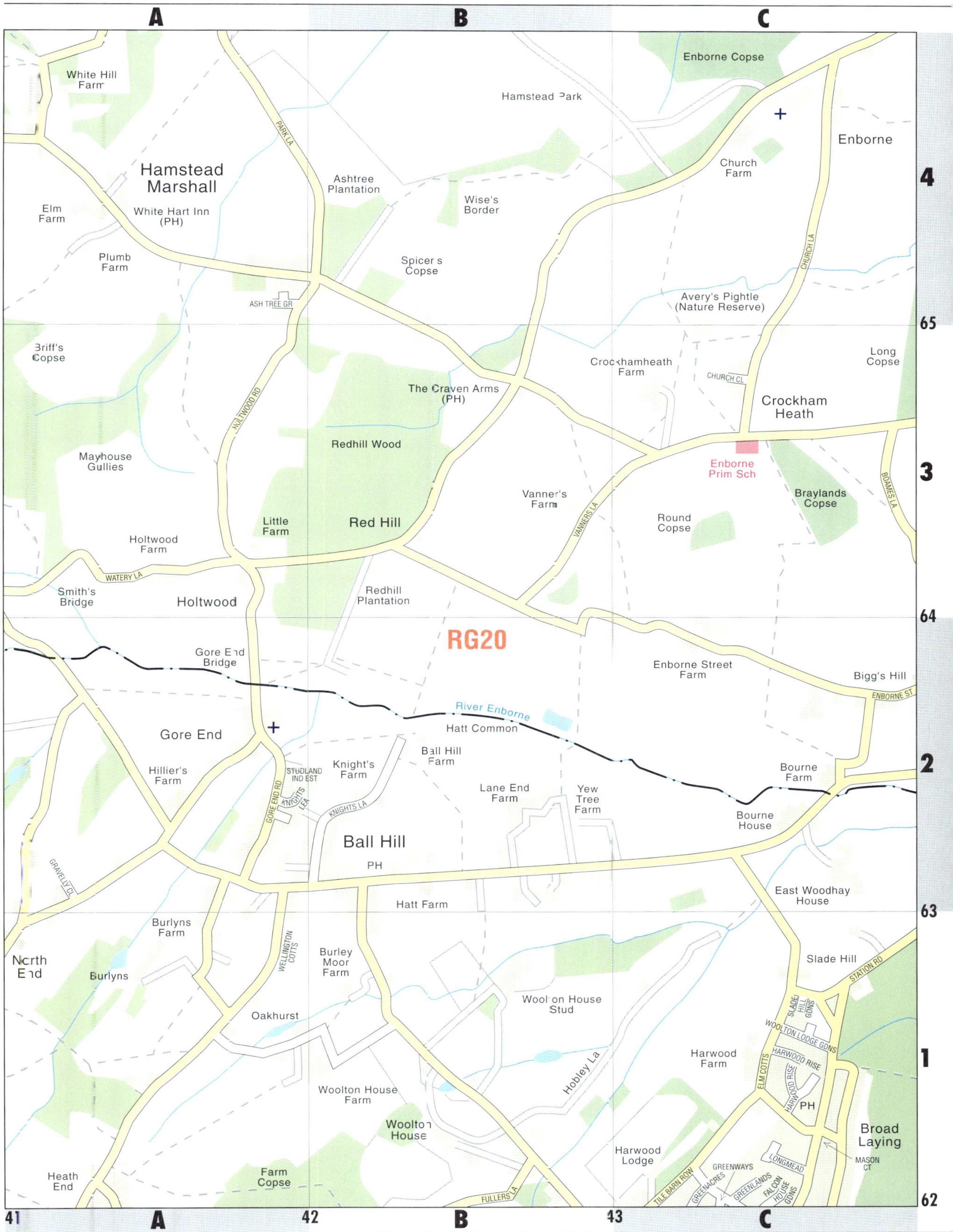
A
B
C
White Hill Farm
Hamstead Park
Enborne Copse
Enborne
Hamstead Marshall
Ashtree Plantation
Church Farm
PARK LA
Elm Farm
White Hart Inn (PH)
Wise's Border
Plumb Farm
Spicer's Copse
CHURCH LA
ASH TREE GR
Avery's Pightle (Nature Reserve)
Briff's Copse
Crockhamheath Farm
Long Copse
CHURCH CL
The Craven Arms (PH)
Crockham Heath
HOLTWOOD RD
Redhill Wood
Mayhouse Gullies
Enborne Prim Sch
Braylands Copse
BOAMES LA
Vanner's Farm
VANNERS LA
Round Copse
Little Farm
Red Hill
Holtwood Farm
WATERY LA
Redhill Plantation
Smith's Bridge
Holtwood
RG20
Gore End Bridge
Enborne Street Farm
Bigg's Hill
ENBORNE ST
River Enborne
Hatt Common
Gore End
Ball Hill Farm
Knight's Farm
Hillier's Farm
STUDLAND IND EST
Bourne Farm
Lane End Farm
Yew Tree Farm
GORE END RD
KNIGHTS LEA
KNIGHTS LA
Bourne House
Ball Hill
GRAVELLY CL
PH
East Woodhay House
Hatt Farm
Burlyns Farm
WELLINGTON COTTS
Burley Moor Farm
Slade Hill
STATION RD
North End
Burlyns
SLADE HILL GDNS
Woolton House Stud
Oakhurst
WOOLTON LODGE GDNS
HARWOOD RISE
Harwood Farm
Hobley La
ELM COTTS
HARWOOD RISE
PH
Woolton House Farm
Woolton House
Broad Laying
Harwood Lodge
GREENWAYS
LONGMEAD
MASON CT
Heath End
Farm Copse
TILE BARN ROW
GREENACRES
GREENLANDS
FALCON HOUSE GDNS
FULLERS LA
4
65
3
64
2
63
1
62
41
42
43

130

129
104

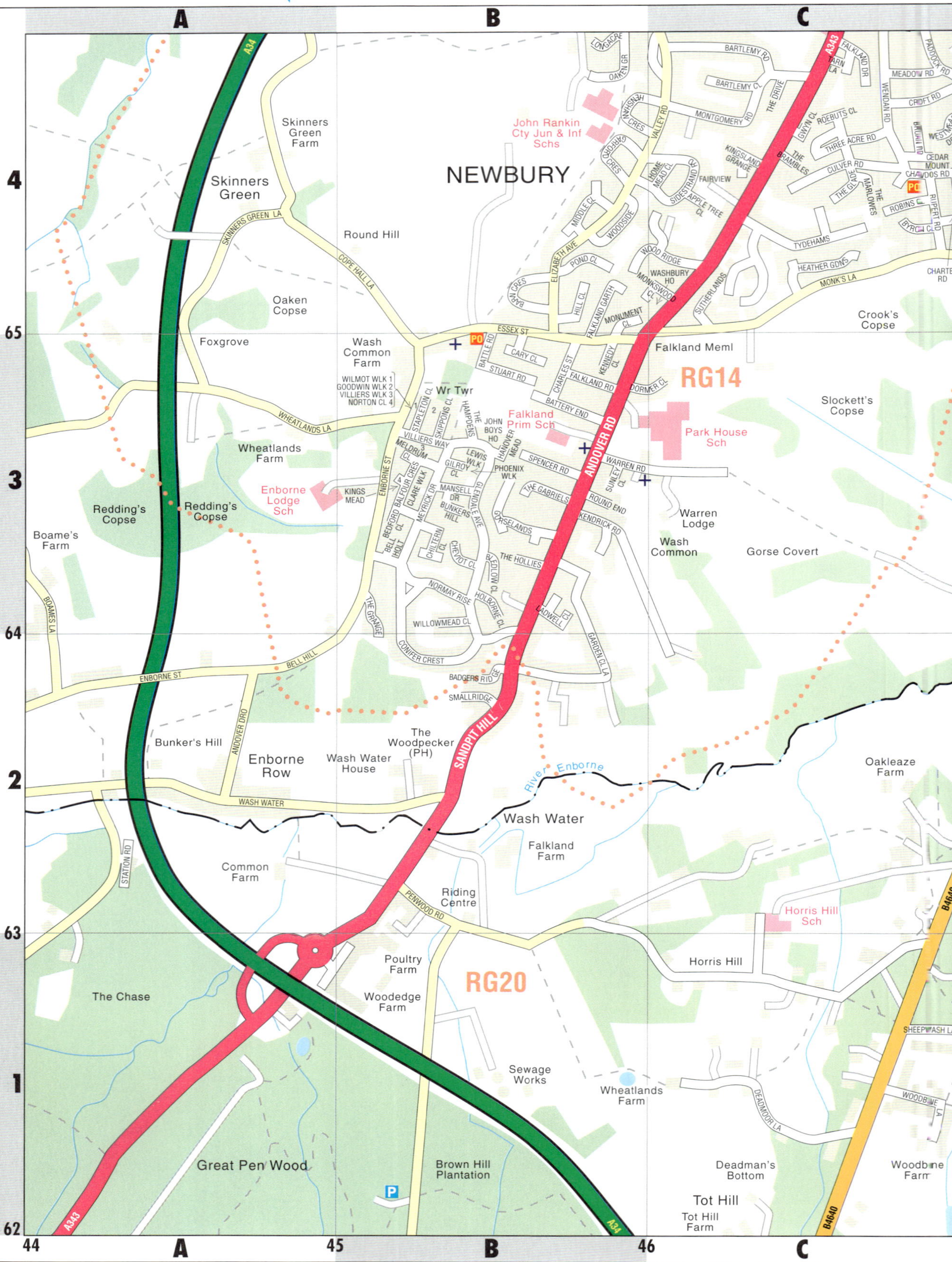
A
B
C
4
65
3
64
2
63
1
62
44
45
46
NEWBURY
RG14
RG20
Skinners Green Farm
Skinners Green
SKINNERS GREEN LA
Round Hill
COPE HALL LA
Oaken Copse
Foxgrove
Wash Common Farm
WILMOT WLK 1
GOODWIN WLK 2
VILLIERS WLK 3
NORTON CL 4
Wr Twr
WHEATLANDS LA
Wheatlands Farm
Redding's Copse
Redding's Copse
Boame's Farm
BOAMES LA
Enborne Lodge Sch
KINGS MEAD
ENBORNE ST
BELL HILL
THE GRANGE
John Rankin Cty Jun & Inf Schs
Falkland Prim Sch
Park House Sch
Falkland Meml
ESSEX ST
ANDOVER RD
STUART RD
CARY CL
BATTLE RD
CHARLES ST
FALKLAND RD
KENNEDY CL
DORMER CL
BATTERY END
SPENCER RD
WARREN RD
SUNLEY CL
ROUND END
KENDRICK RD
THE GABRIELS
GORSELANDS
THE HOLLIES
LADWELL CL
GARDEN CL LA
HOLBORNE CL
NORMAY RISE
WILLOWMEAD CL
CONIFER CREST
BADGERS RIDGE
SMALLRIDGE
SANDPIT HILL
BEDFORD
BELL HOLT
CHILTERN CL
CHEVIOT CL
BEDLOW CL
GLENDALE AVE
BUNKERS HILL
MANSELL DR
MEYRICK DR
CLARE WLK
BALFOUR CRES
MELDRUM CL
VILLIERS WAY
STAPLETON CL
SKIPPONS CL
HAMPDENS
JOHN BOYS HO
HANOVER MEAD
LEWIS WLK
GILROY CL
PHOENIX WLK
Warren Lodge
Wash Common
Gorse Covert
Slockett's Copse
Crook's Copse
MONK'S LA
CHARTER RD
TYDEHAMS
HEATHER GDNS
SUTHERLANDS
MONKSWOOD CL
WASHBURY HO
WOOD RIDGE
MONUMENT CL
FALKLAND GARTH
HILL CL
POND CL
BARN CRES
ELIZABETH AVE
WOODSIDE
MIDDLE CL
GARFORD CRES
HOME MEAD CL
SIDESTRAND RD
APPLE TREE CL
FAIRVIEW
KINGSLAND GRANGE
THE BRAMBLES
VALLEY RD
KENSINGTON CRES
MONTGOMERY RD
OAKEN GR
LONGACRE
BARTLEMY RD
BARTLEMY CL
THE DRIVE
A343
TARN LA
FALKLAND DR
PADDOCK RD
MEADOW RD
WENDAN RD
CROFT RD
ROEBUTS CL
GWYN CL
THREE ACRE RD
CULVER RD
THE GLADE
MARLOWES
THE RIDINGS
CEDAR MOUNT
CHANDOS RD
ROBINS CL
RIPPERT RD
BYRCH CL
WESTMEAD DR
Bunker's Hill
ANDOVER DRO
Enborne Row
Wash Water House
The Woodpecker (PH)
WASH WATER
Wash Water
River Enborne
Oakleaze Farm
STATION RD
Common Farm
Falkland Farm
Riding Centre
PENWOOD RD
Horris Hill Sch
Horris Hill
Poultry Farm
Woodedge Farm
The Chase
Sewage Works
Wheatlands Farm
DEADMOOR LA
SHEEPWASH LA
WOODBINE LA
B4640
Woodbine Farm
Deadman's Bottom
Tot Hill
Tot Hill Farm
Great Pen Wood
Brown Hill Plantation
A34
A343

129

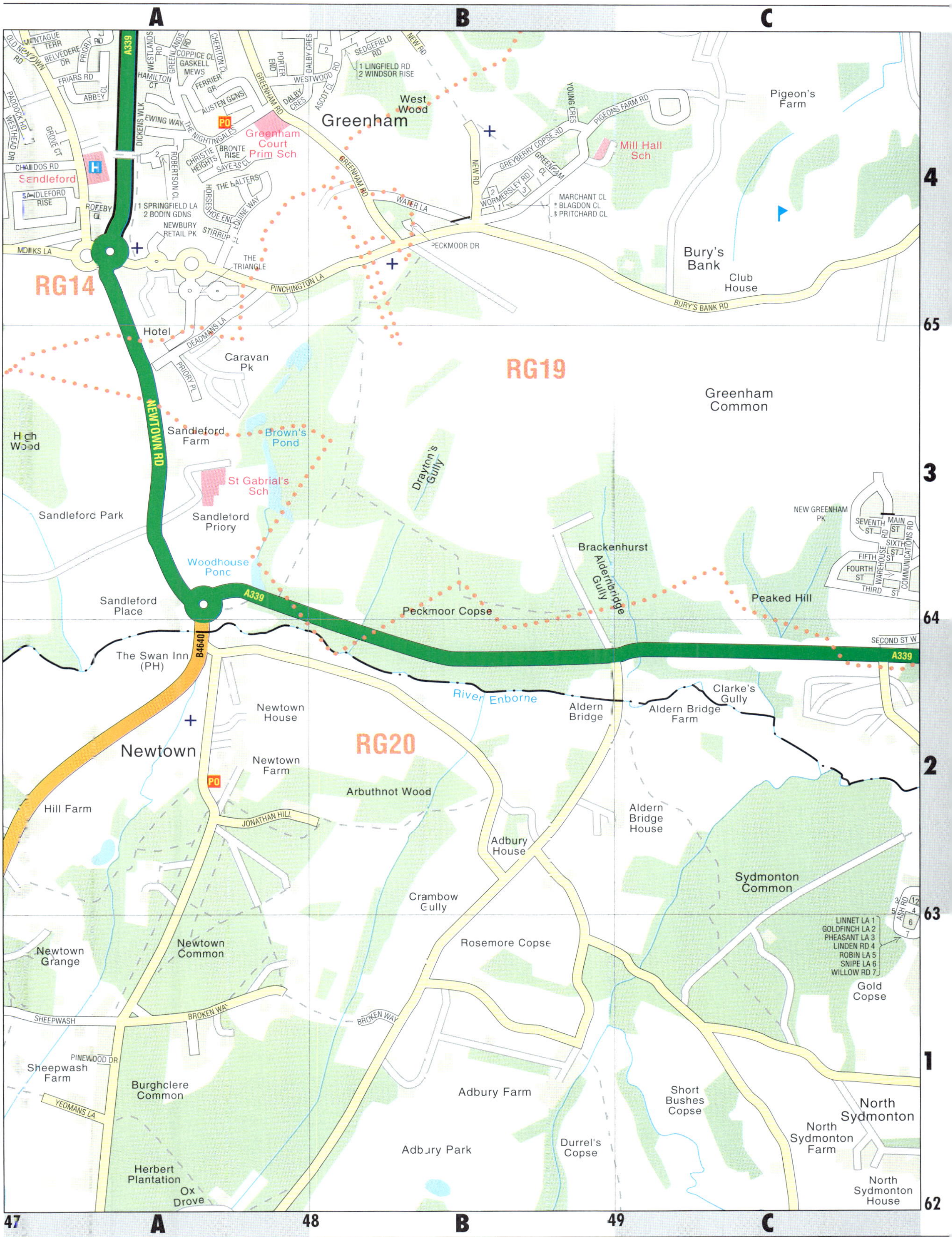
A
B
C
Greenham
West Wood
Greenham Court Prim Sch
Mill Hall Sch
Pigeon's Farm
Sandleford
RG14
RG19
RG20
Bury's Bank
Club House
BURY'S BANK RD
PINCHINGTON LA
PECKMOOR DR
WATER LA
GREENHAM RD
NEW RD
PIGEONS FARM RD
YOUNG CRES
GREYBERRY COPSE RD
WORMERSLEY RD
MARCHANT CL
BLAGDON CL
PRITCHARD CL
1 LINGFIELD RD
2 WINDSOR RISE
SEDGEFIELD RD
WESTWOOD RD
ASCOT CL
DALBY CRES
PORTER END
MONTAGUE TERR
BELVEDERE DR
PRIORY RD
FRIARS RD
ABBEY CL
OLD NEWTOWN RD
PADDOCK RD
WESTHEAD DR
GROVE CT
CHANDOS RD
SANDLEFORD RISE
ROKEBY CL
MONKS LA
A339
WESTLANDS RD
GREENLANDS RD
COPPICE CL
GASKELL MEWS
CHERITON CL
HAMILTON CT
FERRIER GR
AUSTEN GDNS
DICKENS WLK
EWING WAY
THE NIGHTINGALES
CHRISTIE HEIGHTS
BRONTE RISE
SAYERS CL
ROBERTSON CL
HORSESHOE END
THE HALTERS
EQUINE WAY
STIRRUP CL
1 SPRINGFIELD LA
2 BODIN GDNS
NEWBURY RETAIL PK
THE TRIANGLE
DEADMANS LA
Hotel
Caravan Pk
PRIORY PL
High Wood
Sandleford Farm
Brown's Pond
NEWTOWN RD
St Gabrial's Sch
Drayton's Gully
Greenham Common
Sandleford Park
Sandleford Priory
Woodhouse Pond
Brackenhurst
Alderbridge Gully
NEW GREENHAM PK
SEVENTH ST
MAIN ST
SIXTH ST
FIFTH ST
FOURTH ST
THIRD ST
WAREHOUSE RD
COMMUNICATIONS RD
Peaked Hill
Sandleford Place
Peckmoor Copse
SECOND ST W
The Swan Inn (PH)
B4640
River Enborne
Aldern Bridge
Aldern Bridge Farm
Clarke's Gully
Newtown House
Newtown
Newtown Farm
Hill Farm
Arbuthnot Wood
JONATHAN HILL
Aldern Bridge House
Adbury House
Sydmonton Common
Crambow Gully
Rosemore Copse
Newtown Grange
Newtown Common
LINNET LA 1
GOLDFINCH LA 2
PHEASANT LA 3
LINDEN RD 4
ROBIN LA 5
SNIPE LA 6
WILLOW RD 7
ASH RD
Gold Copse
SHEEPWASH
BROKEN WAY
PINEWOOD DR
Sheepwash Farm
YEOMANS LA
Burghclere Common
Adbury Farm
Short Bushes Copse
North Sydmonton
North Sydmonton Farm
Adbury Park
Durrel's Copse
Herbert Plantation
Ox Drove
North Sydmonton House
4
65
3
64
2
63
1
62
47
48
49

131
106

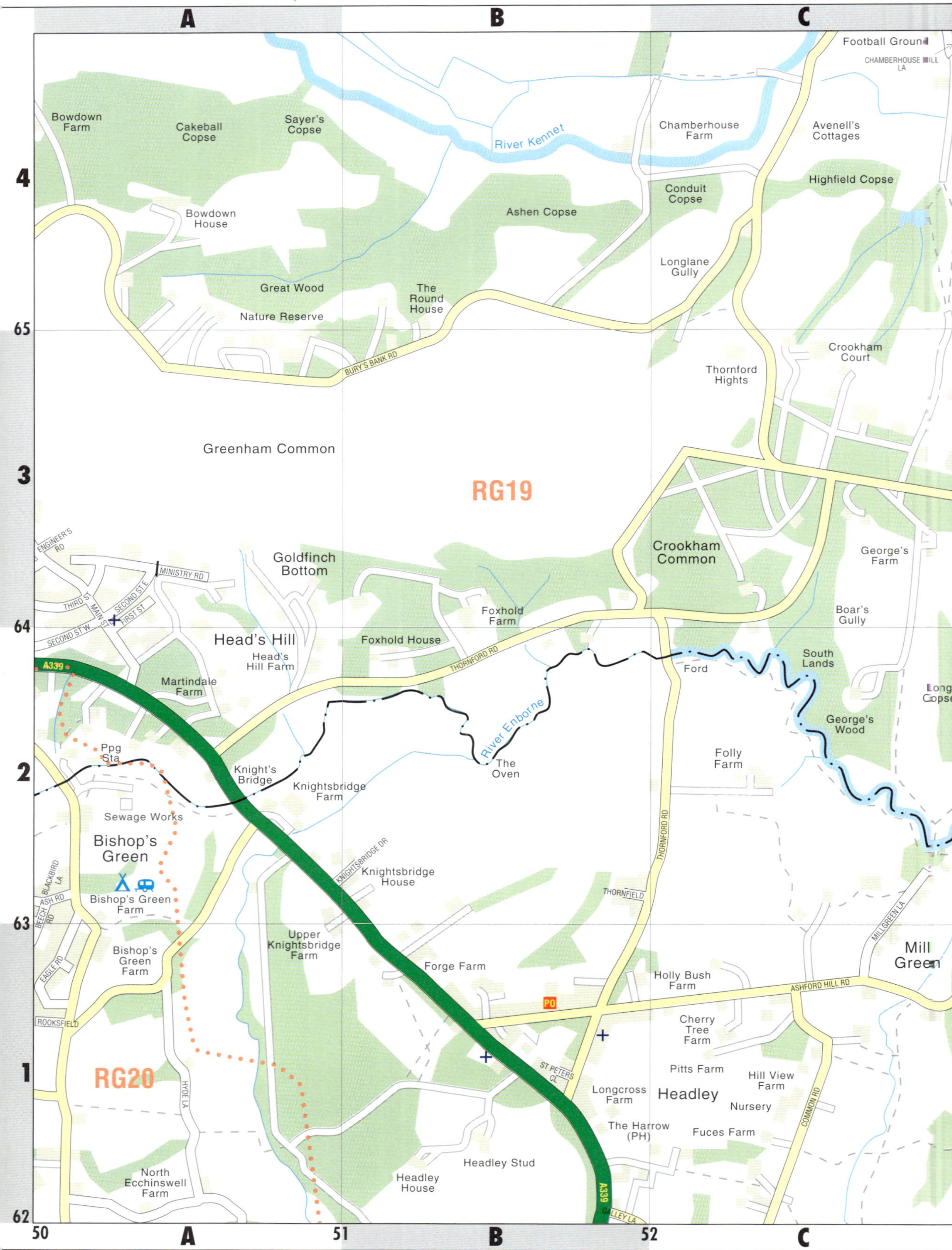
A
B
C
4
3
2
1
65
64
63
62
50
51
52
Football Ground
CHAMBERHOUSE MILL LA
Bowdown Farm
Cakeball Copse
Sayer's Copse
River Kennet
Chamberhouse Farm
Avenell's Cottages
Highfield Copse
Conduit Copse
Ashen Copse
Bowdown House
Longlane Gully
Great Wood
Nature Reserve
The Round House
BURY'S BANK RD
Crookham Court
Thornford Hights
Greenham Common
RG19
ENGINEER'S RD
MINISTRY RD
Goldfinch Bottom
Crookham Common
George's Farm
THIRD ST
MAIN ST
SECOND ST E
FIRST ST
SECOND ST W
Foxhold Farm
Boar's Gully
Head's Hill
Foxhold House
Head's Hill Farm
THORNFORD RD
Ford
South Lands
Long Copse
A339
Martindale Farm
River Enborne
George's Wood
Ppg Sta
Folly Farm
The Oven
Knight's Bridge
Knightsbridge Farm
Sewage Works
Bishop's Green
KNIGHTSBRIDGE DR
Knightsbridge House
BLACKBIRD LA
ASH RD
BEECH RD
Bishop's Green Farm
THORNFORD RD
THORNFIELD
MILLGREEN LA
Upper Knightsbridge Farm
Mill Green
Bishop's Green Farm
EAGLE RD
Forge Farm
Holly Bush Farm
ASHFORD HILL RD
PO
ROOKSFIELD
Cherry Tree Farm
RG20
ST PETERS CL
Pitts Farm
Hill View Farm
HYDE LA
Longcross Farm
Headley
Nursery
COMMON RD
The Harrow (PH)
Fuces Farm
North Ecchinswell Farm
Headley Stud
Headley House
GALLEY LA

131

107
134

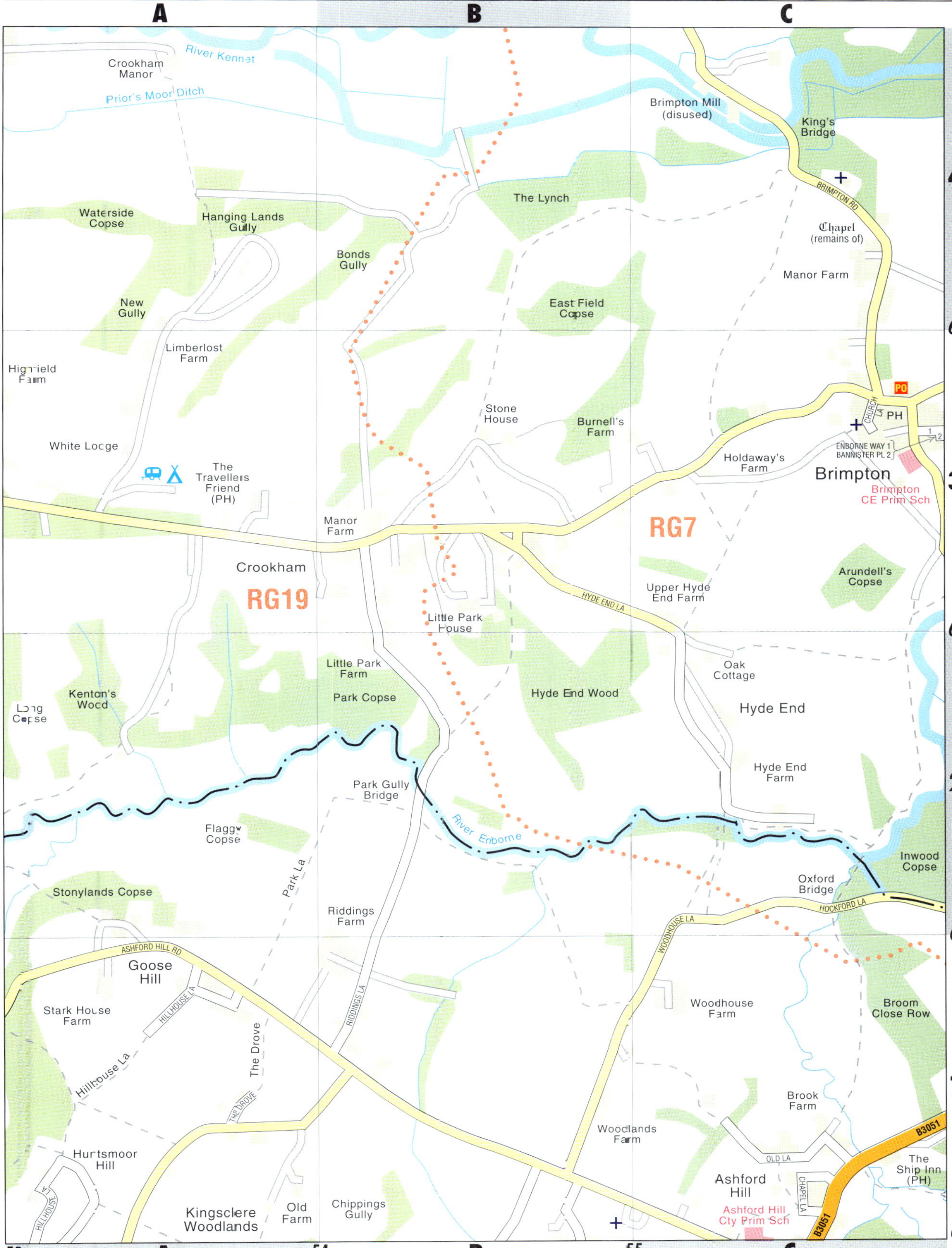
River Kennet
Crookham Manor
Prior's Moor Ditch
Brimpton Mill (disused)
King's Bridge
Brimpton Rd
Chapel (remains of)
Manor Farm
The Lynch
Waterside Copse
Hanging Lands Gully
Bonds Gully
New Gully
East Field Copse
Limberlost Farm
Highfield Farm
Stone House
Burnell's Farm
PO
PH
Church La
Enborne Way 1
Bannister Pl 2
Holdaway's Farm
Brimpton
Brimpton CE Prim Sch
White Lodge
The Travellers Friend (PH)
Manor Farm
RG7
Crookham
RG19
Upper Hyde End Farm
Hyde End La
Arundell's Copse
Little Park House
Oak Cottage
Little Park Farm
Kenton's Wood
Long Copse
Park Copse
Hyde End Wood
Hyde End
Hyde End Farm
Park Gully Bridge
River Enborne
Flaggy Copse
Inwood Copse
Oxford Bridge
Hockford La
Stonylands Copse
Park La
Riddings Farm
Woodhouse La
Ashford Hill Rd
Goose Hill
Hillhouse La
Stark House Farm
Riddings La
Woodhouse Farm
Broom Close Row
The Drove
Brook Farm
Hurtsmoor Hill
Woodlands Farm
Old La
B3051
The Ship Inn (PH)
Ashford Hill
Chapel La
Ashford Hill Cty Prim Sch
Kingsclere Woodlands
Old Farm
Chippings Gully
Hillhouse
A
B
C
53
54
55
62
63
64
65
1
2
3
4

134

133
108

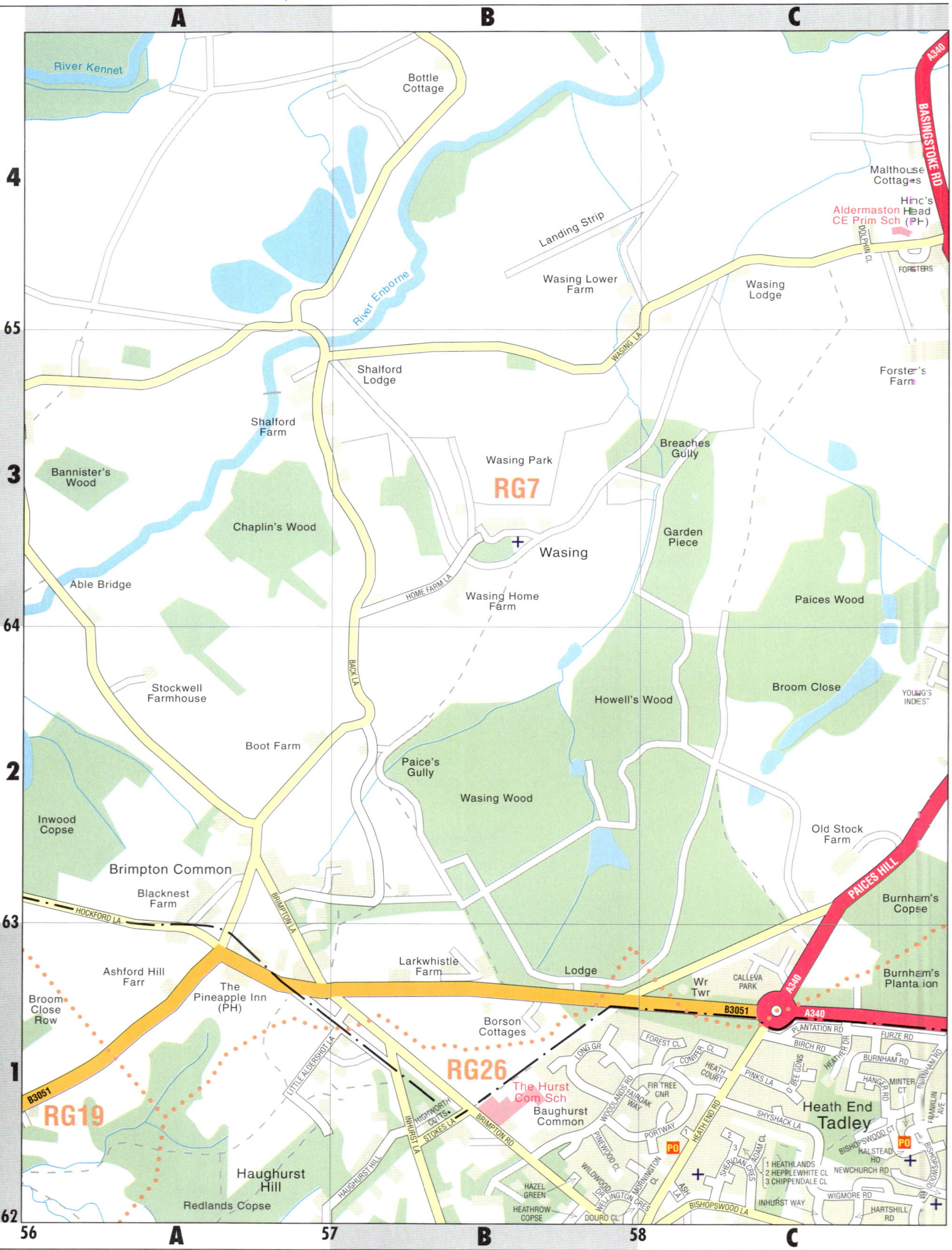
A
B
C
4
65
3
64
2
63
1
62
56
57
58
River Kennet
Bottle Cottage
River Enborne
Landing Strip
Wasing Lower Farm
Wasing Lodge
Malthouse Cottages
Hinc's Head (PH)
Aldermaston CE Prim Sch
DOLPHIN CL
FORSTERS
BASINGSTOKE RD
A340
Shalford Lodge
WASING LA
Forster's Farm
Shalford Farm
Breaches Gully
Wasing Park
RG7
Bannister's Wood
Chaplin's Wood
Garden Piece
Wasing
Able Bridge
HOME FARM LA
Wasing Home Farm
Paices Wood
BACK LA
Stockwell Farmhouse
Howell's Wood
Broom Close
YOUNG'S INDEST
Boot Farm
Paice's Gully
Wasing Wood
Inwood Copse
Old Stock Farm
Brimpton Common
PAICES HILL
Blacknest Farm
BRIMPTON LA
Burnham's Copse
HOCKFORD LA
Larkwhistle Farm
Lodge
Ashford Hill Farm
The Pineapple Inn (PH)
Broom Close Row
Wr Twr
CALLEVA PARK
Burnham's Plantation
B3051
Borson Cottages
PLANTATION RD
FURZE RD
LITTLE ALDERSHOT LA
LONG GR
FOREST CL
CONIFER CL
BIRCH RD
HEATHER DR
BURNHAM RD
RG26
HEATH COURT
PINKS LA
BEE GDNS
FIR TREE CNR
FAIROAK WAY
HANGER RD
MINTER CT
The Hurst Com Sch
WOODLANDS RD
HEATH END RD
Heath End
Tadley
FRANKLIN AVE
RG19
HIGHWORTH COTTS
STOKES LA
BRIMPTON RD
Baughurst Common
PORTWAY
SHYSHACK LA
BISHOPSWOOD CT
INHURST LA
PINEWOOD CL
ADAM CL
HALSTEAD RD
PO
SHERIDAN CRES
1 HEATHLANDS
2 HEPPLEWHITE CL
3 CHIPPENDALE CL
NEWCHURCH RD
Haughurst Hill
HAUGHURST HILL
WILDWOOD DR
MORNINGTON CL
ASH LA
WIGMORE RD
HAZEL GREEN
WELLINGTON CRES
HEATHROW COPSE
DOURO CL
BISHOPSWOOD LA
INHURST WAY
HARTSHILL RD
Redlands Copse

133

109
136

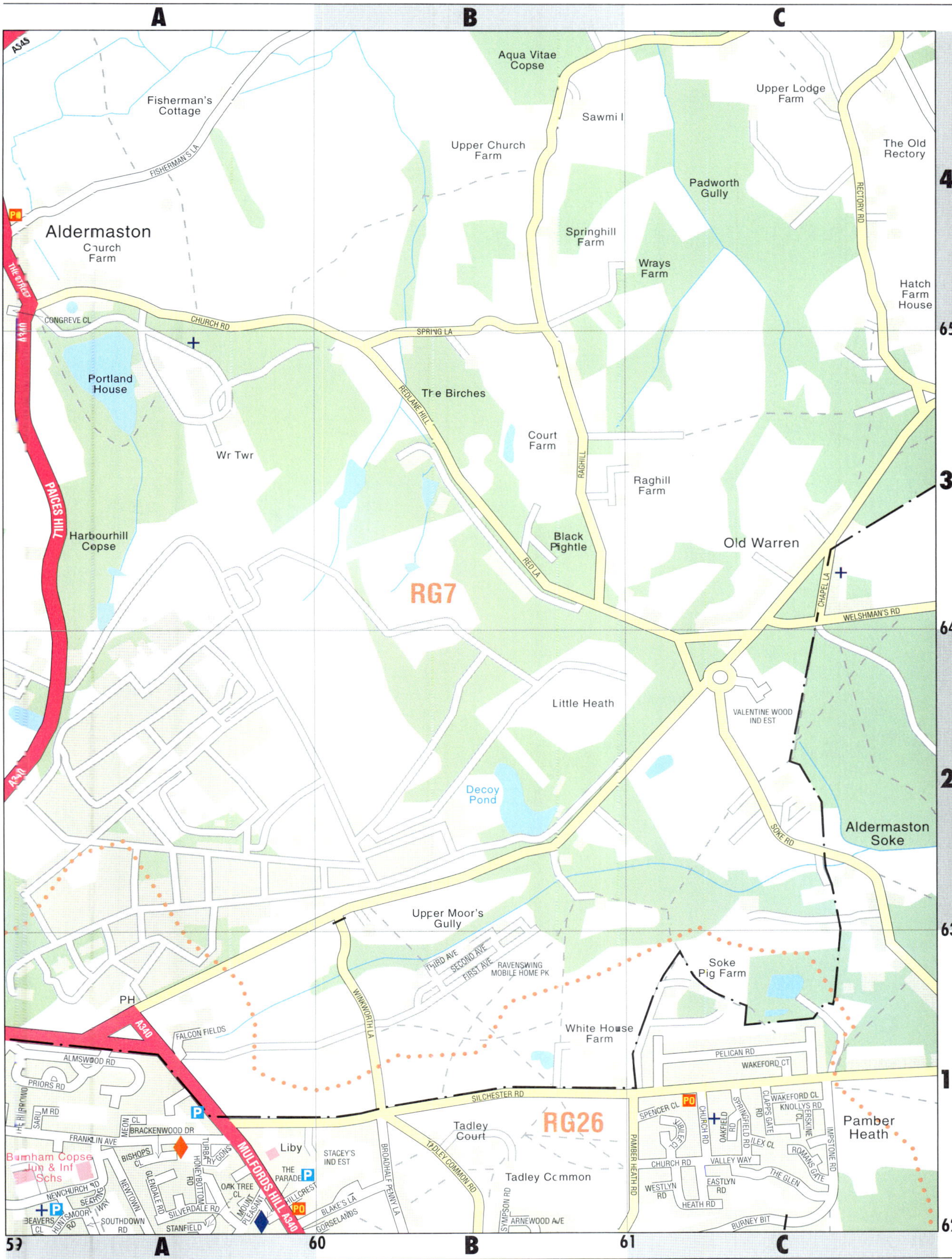
A
B
C
4
3
2
1
65
64
63
62
59
60
61
A4S
Fisherman's Cottage
FISHERMAN'S LA
Aqua Vitae Copse
Sawmi l
Upper Church Farm
Upper Lodge Farm
The Old Rectory
RECTORY RD
Padworth Gully
Springhill Farm
Wrays Farm
Hatch Farm House
Aldermaston
Church Farm
THE STREET
CONGREVE CL
CHURCH RD
SPRING LA
Portland House
The Birches
REDLANE HILL
Court Farm
RAGHILL
Raghill Farm
Wr Twr
PAICES HILL
Harbourhill Copse
Black Pightle
RED LA
Old Warren
CHAPEL LA
WELSHMAN'S RD
RG7
Little Heath
VALENTINE WOOD IND EST
A340
Decoy Pond
SOKE RD
Aldermaston Soke
Upper Moor's Gully
THIRD AVE
SECOND AVE
FIRST AVE
RAVENSWING MOBILE HOME PK
Soke Pig Farm
PH
WINKWORTH LA
FALCON FIELDS
White House Farm
PELICAN RD
WAKEFORD CT
ALMSWOOD RD
PRIORS RD
SILCHESTER RD
WAKEFORD CL
KNOLLYS RD
SPENCER CL
PO
CHURCH RD
SPRINGFIELD RD
OAKFIELD RD
CLAPPS GATE RD
ERSKINE CL
Pamber Heath
RG26
Tadley Court
JUBILEE CL
ILEX CL
IMPSTONE RD
ROMANS GATE
MEON CL
BRACKENWOOD DR
FRANKLIN AVE
BISHOPS CL
TURBARY GDNS
HONEYBOTTOM RD
MULFORDS HILL A340
Liby
STACEY'S IND EST
BROADHALF PENNY LA
TADLEY COMMON RD
PAMBER HEATH RD
CHURCH RD
VALLEY WAY
THE GLEN
Burnham Copse Jun & Inf Schs
NEWCHURCH RD
SEAWING WAY
NEWTOWN
GLENDALE RD
OAK TREE CL
THE PARADE
HILLCREST
Tadley Common
WESTLYN RD
EASTLYN RD
HEATH RD
BEAVERS CL
HUNTSMOOR RD
SOUTHDOWN RD
SILVERDALE RD
STANFIELD
MOUNT PLEASANT
BLAKE'S LA
GORSELANDS
SYMPSON RD
ARNEWOOD AVE
BURNEY BIT

136

135
110

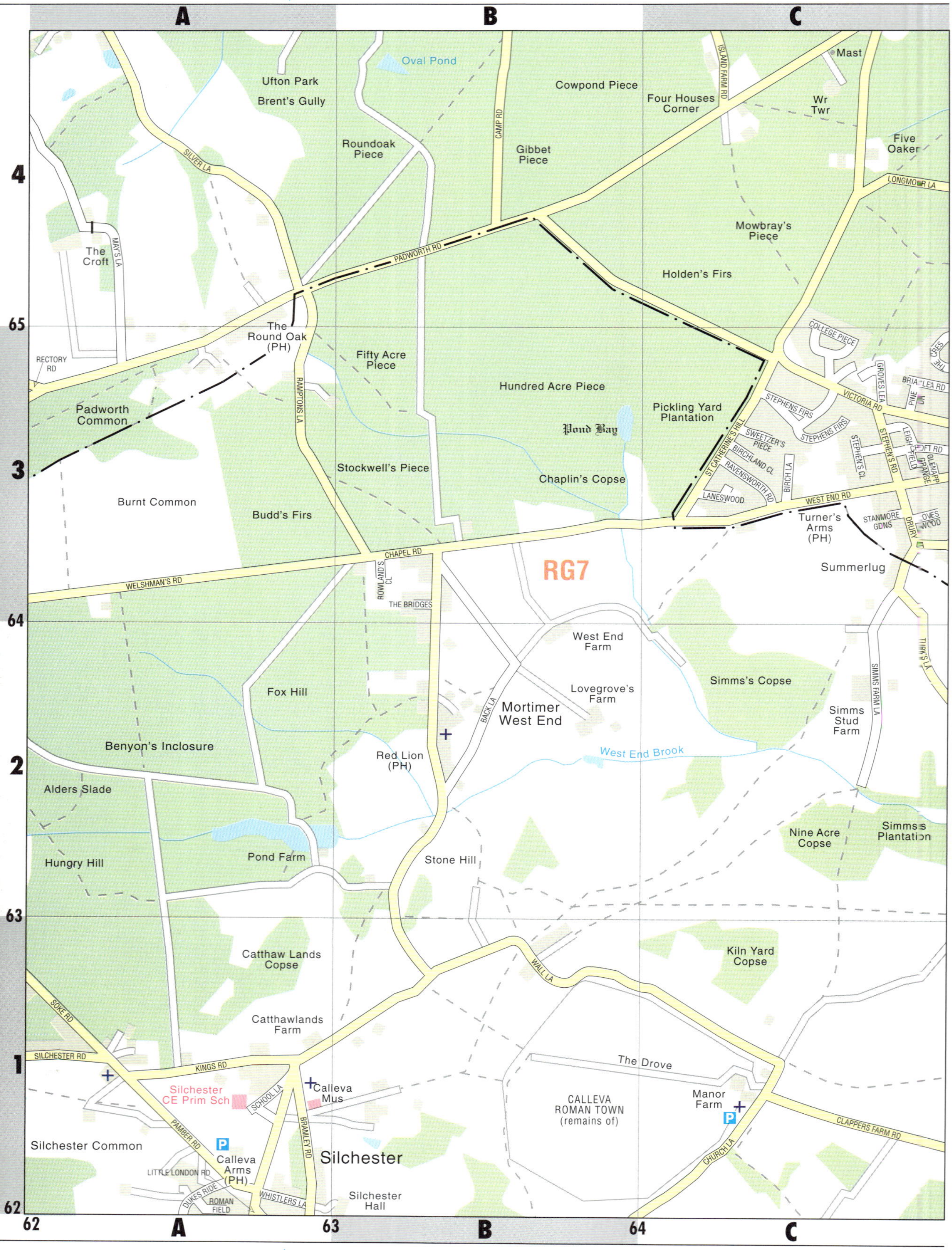
A
B
C
4
65
3
64
2
63
1
62
62
63
64
Oval Pond
Ufton Park
Brent's Gully
Roundoak Piece
Cowpond Piece
Four Houses Corner
Mast
Wr Twr
Five Oaker
ISLAND FARM RD
CAMP RD
Gibbet Piece
SILVER LA
LONGMOOR LA
Mowbray's Piece
The Croft
MAY'S LA
PADWORTH RD
Holden's Firs
RECTORY RD
The Round Oak (PH)
Fifty Acre Piece
COLLEGE PIECE
Padworth Common
RAMPTONS LA
Hundred Acre Piece
Pickling Yard Plantation
GROVES LEA
BRIA LEA RD
VICTORIA RD
STEPHENS FIRS
Pond Bay
SWEETZER'S PIECE
BIRCHLAND CL
STEPHEN'S CL
STEPHENS RD
ST CATHERINE'S HILL
RAVENSWORTH RD
Stockwell's Piece
Chaplin's Copse
BIRCH LA
LANESWOOD
WEST END RD
Burnt Common
Budd's Firs
Turner's Arms (PH)
STANMORE GDNS
DRURY
CHAPEL RD
RG7
Summerlug
WELSHMAN'S RD
ROWLAND'S CL
THE BRIDGES
West End Farm
TIBBY'S LA
Simms's Copse
Fox Hill
Lovegrove's Farm
Mortimer West End
BACK LA
Simms Stud Farm
SIMMS FARM LA
Benyon's Inclosure
Red Lion (PH)
West End Brook
Alders Slade
Nine Acre Copse
Simms's Plantation
Hungry Hill
Pond Farm
Stone Hill
Kiln Yard Copse
Catthaw Lands Copse
WALL LA
SOKE RD
Catthawlands Farm
SILCHESTER RD
KINGS RD
The Drove
Silchester CE Prim Sch
SCHOOL LA
Calleva Mus
CALLEVA ROMAN TOWN (remains of)
Manor Farm
CLAPPERS FARM RD
PAMBER RD
BRAMLEY RD
Silchester Common
Silchester
Calleva Arms (PH)
CHURCH LA
LITTLE LONDON RD
DUKES RIDE
ROMAN FIELD
WHISTLERS LA
Silchester Hall

135

111
138

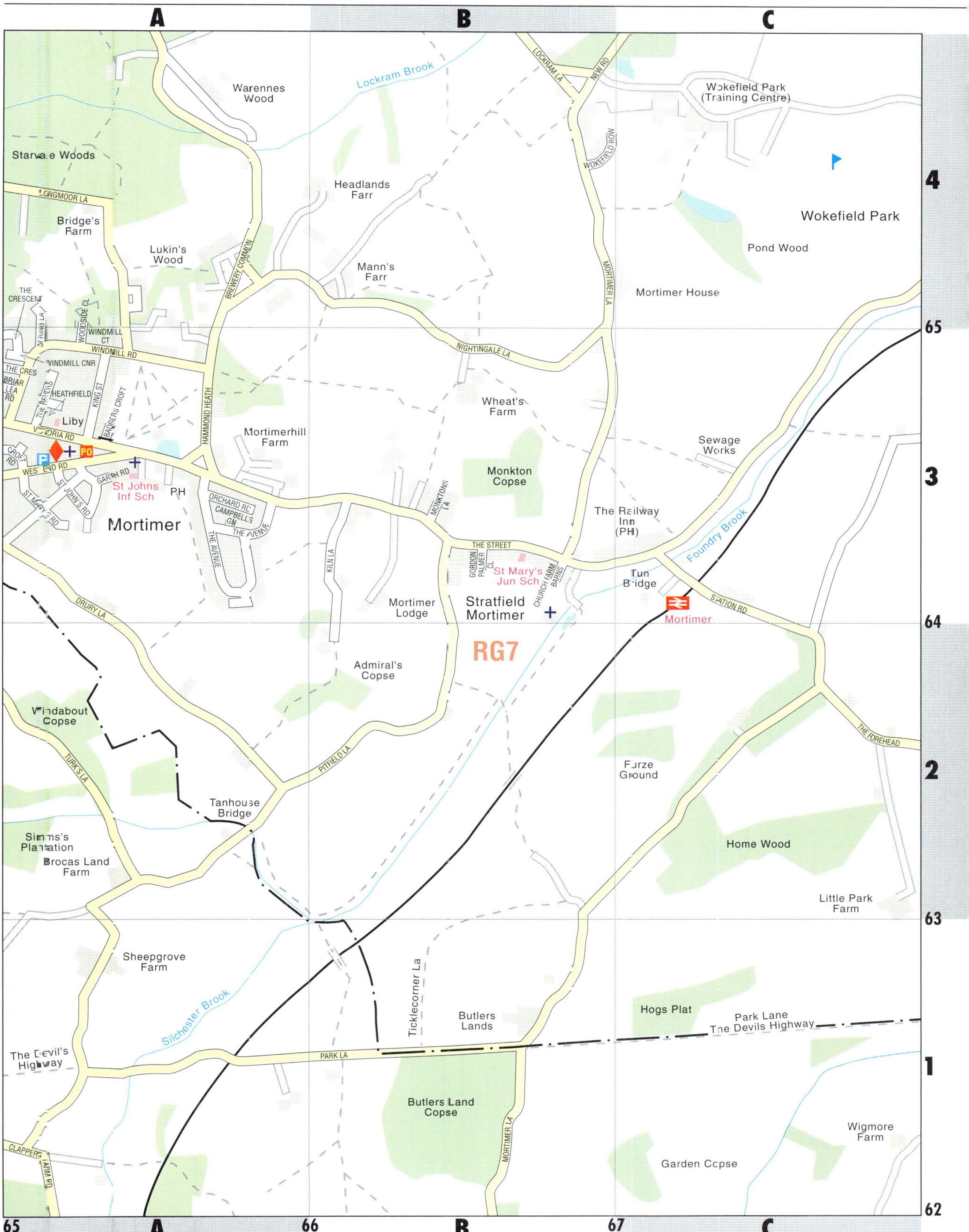
A
B
C
Warennes Wood
Lockram Brook
Lockram La
New Rd
Wokefield Park (Training Centre)
Starvale Woods
Headlands Farr
Longmoor La
Bridge's Farm
Lukin's Wood
Brewery Common
Mann's Farr
Wokefield Row
Wokefield Park
Pond Wood
Mortimer La
Mortimer House
The Crescent
Woodside Cl
Windmill Ct
Windmill Rd
Windmill Cnr
The Cres
Briar Lea Rd
Heathfield
The Rounds
King St
Badgers Croft
Hammond Heath
Nightingale La
Liby
Victoria Rd
Mortimerhill Farm
Wheat's Farm
PO
P
West End Rd
Garth Rd
St Johns Inf Sch
PH
St John's Rd
St Mary's Rd
Orchard Rd
Campbell's Gn
The Avenue
Mortimer
Monkton Copse
Monktons La
Sewage Works
The Railway Inn (PH)
Kiln La
The Street
Gordon Palmer Cl
St Mary's Jun Sch
Church Farm Barns
Tun Bridge
Foundry Brook
Drury La
Mortimer Lodge
Stratfield Mortimer
Station Rd
Mortimer
RG7
Admiral's Copse
Windabout Copse
Turk's La
Pitfield La
The Forehead
Furze Ground
Tanhouse Bridge
Simms's Plantation
Brocas Land Farm
Home Wood
Little Park Farm
Sheepgrove Farm
Ticklecorner La
Silchester Brook
Butlers Lands
Hogs Plat
Park Lane
The Devils Highway
The Devil's Highway
Park La
Butlers Land Copse
Mortimer La
Wigmore Farm
Clappers Farm Rd
Garden Copse
4
65
3
64
2
63
1
62
66
67

138

137
112

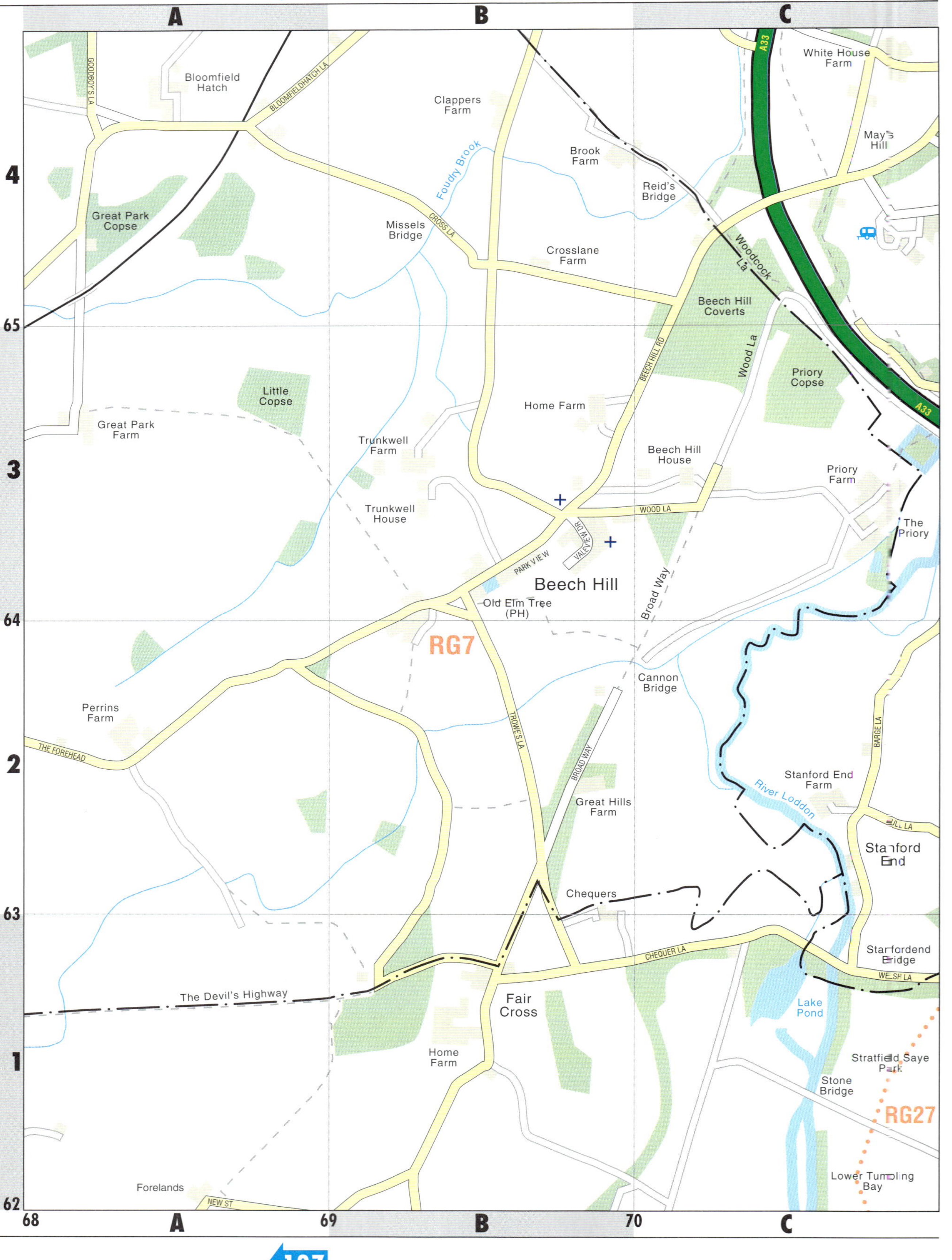
A
B
C
4
3
2
1
65
64
63
62
68
69
70
Bloomfield Hatch
GOODBOY'S LA
BLOOMFIELDHATCH LA
Clappers Farm
Brook Farm
Foudry Brook
Reid's Bridge
White House Farm
May's Hill
A33
Great Park Copse
Missels Bridge
CROSS LA
Crosslane Farm
Woodcock La
Beech Hill Coverts
Wood La
Priory Copse
BEECH HILL RD
Little Copse
Home Farm
Great Park Farm
Trunkwell Farm
Beech Hill House
Priory Farm
Trunkwell House
WOOD LA
The Priory
VALEVIEW DR
PARK VIEW
Beech Hill
Broad Way
Old Elm Tree (PH)
RG7
Cannon Bridge
Perrins Farm
THE FOREHEAD
TROWE'S LA
BROAD WAY
BARGE LA
Stanford End Farm
River Loddon
Great Hills Farm
Stanford End
Chequers
CHEQUER LA
Stanfordend Bridge
WELSH LA
The Devil's Highway
Fair Cross
Lake Pond
Home Farm
Stratfield Saye Park
Stone Bridge
RG27
Forelands
NEW ST
Lower Tumbling Bay

137

113
140

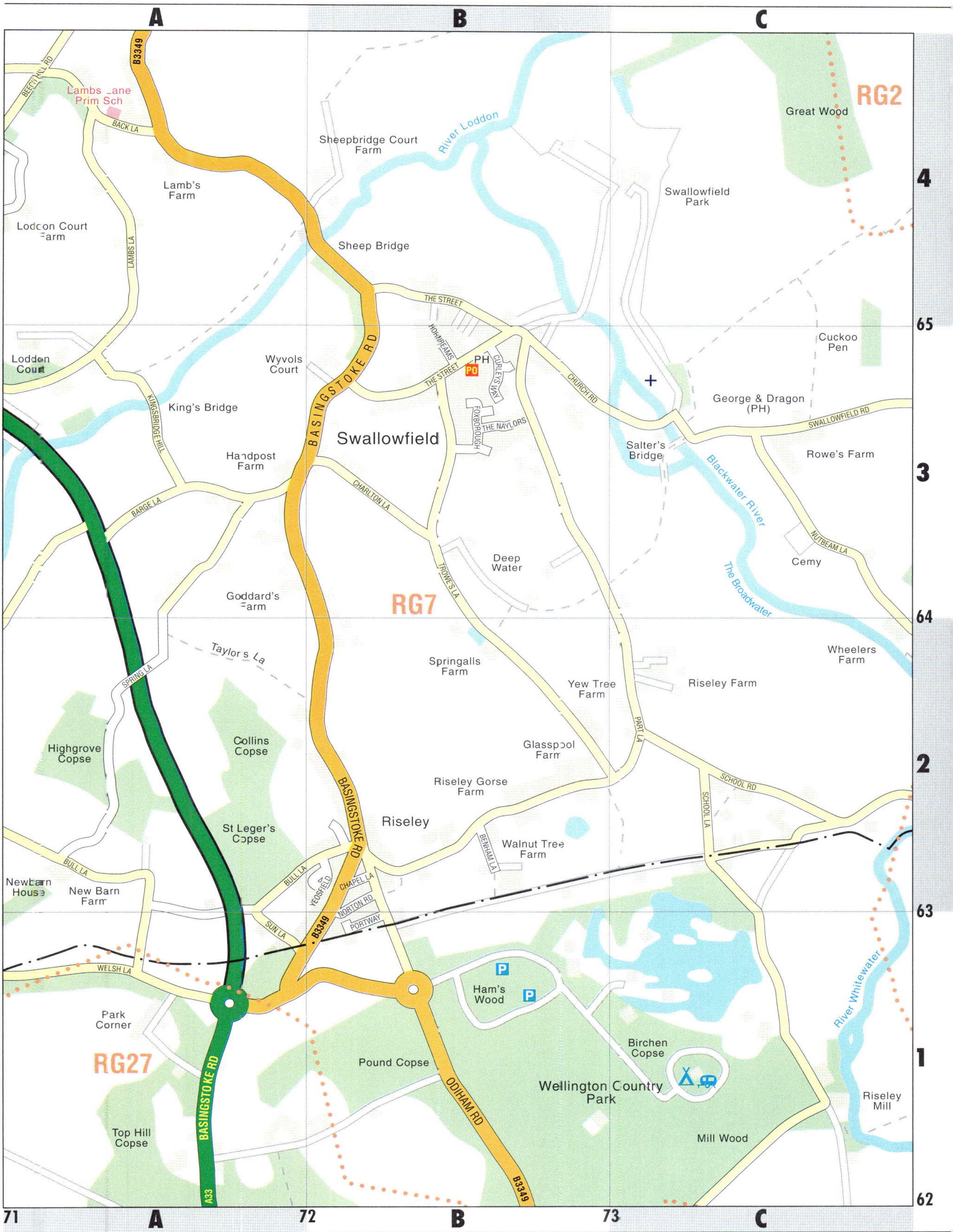
A
B
C
4
65
3
64
2
63
1
62
71
72
73
B3349
Lambs Lane Prim Sch
BACK LA
Lamb's Farm
Loddon Court Farm
LAMBS LA
Loddon Court
Sheepbridge Court Farm
River Loddon
Sheep Bridge
Swallowfield Park
Great Wood
RG2
THE STREET
Wyvols Court
King's Bridge
KINGSBRIDGE HILL
BASINGSTOKE RD
PH
PO
CURLEYS WAY
FOXBOROUGH
THE NAYLORS
CHURCH RD
Cuckoo Pen
George & Dragon (PH)
SWALLOWFIELD RD
Salter's Bridge
Rowe's Farm
Swallowfield
Handpost Farm
BARGE LA
CHARLTON LA
Blackwater River
NUTBEAM LA
Cemy
Deep Water
The Broadwater
TROWE'S LA
Goddard's Farm
RG7
Taylor's La
SPRING LA
Springalls Farm
Yew Tree Farm
Riseley Farm
Wheelers Farm
Highgrove Copse
Collins Copse
Glasspool Farm
PART LA
SCHOOL RD
SCHOOL LA
Riseley Gorse Farm
Riseley
St Leger's Copse
Walnut Tree Farm
BENHAM LA
BULL LA
Newbarn House
New Barn Farm
YEOSFIELD
CHAPEL LA
NORTON RD
PORTWAY
SUN LA
WELSH LA
P
Ham's Wood
Park Corner
RG27
Birchen Copse
River Whitewater
Pound Copse
ODIHAM RD
Wellington Country Park
Riseley Mill
Mill Wood
Top Hill Copse
A33

140

139
114

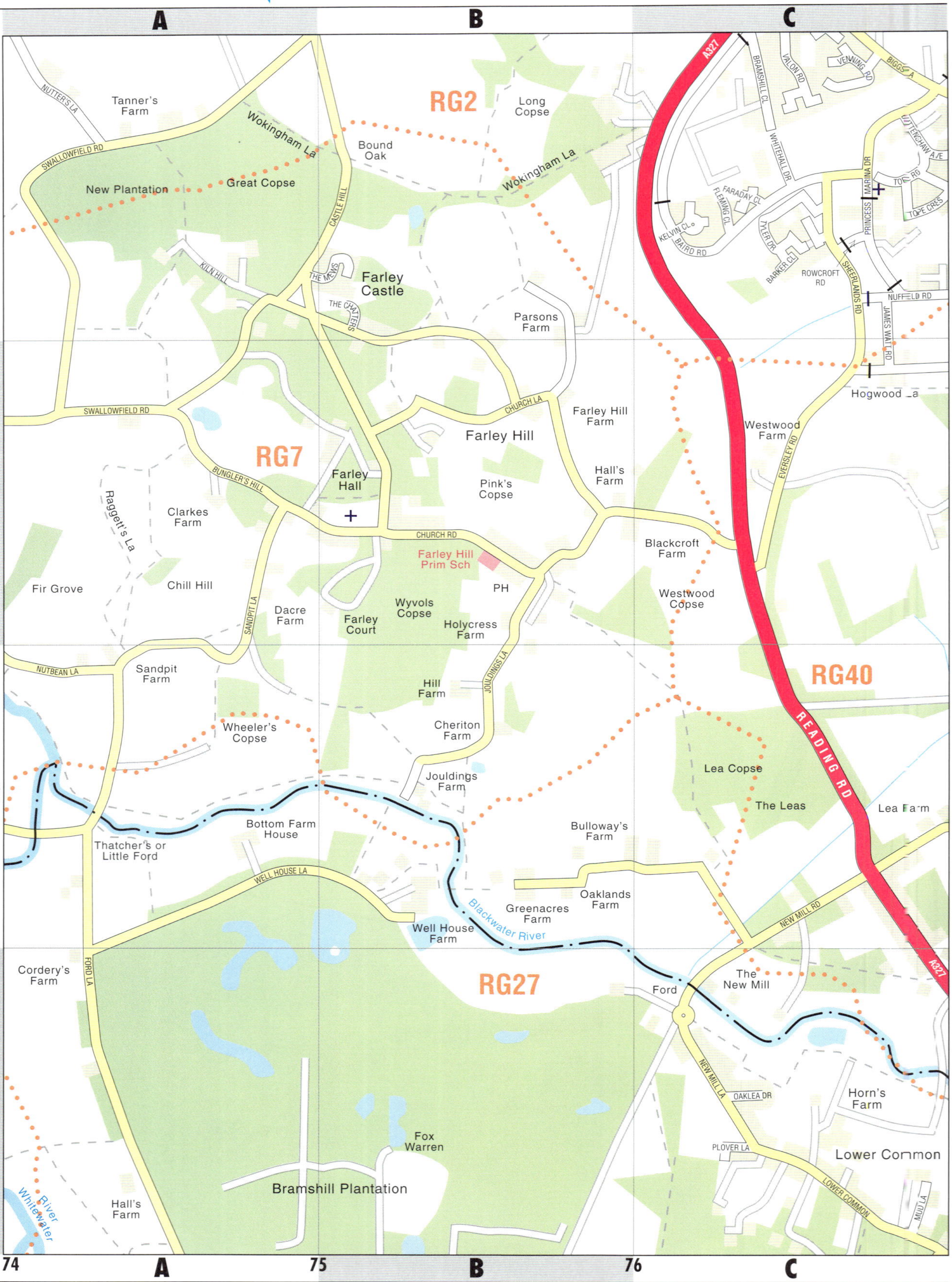
A
B
C
4
65
3
64
2
63
1
62
74
75
76
RG2
RG7
RG40
RG27
Tanner's Farm
NUTTER'S LA
SWALLOWFIELD RD
Wokingham La
Bound Oak
Long Copse
New Plantation
Great Copse
CASTLE HILL
KILN HILL
THE MEWS
Farley Castle
THE CHATTERS
Parsons Farm
SWALLOWFIELD RD
CHURCH LA
Farley Hill Farm
Farley Hill
RG7
BUNGLER'S HILL
Farley Hall
Pink's Copse
Hall's Farm
Raggett's La
Clarkes Farm
CHURCH RD
Farley Hill Prim Sch
Blackcroft Farm
Fir Grove
Chill Hill
PH
Westwood Copse
Dacre Farm
Farley Court
Wyvols Copse
Holycress Farm
SANDPIT LA
NUTBEAN LA
Sandpit Farm
Hill Farm
JOULDINGS LA
Wheeler's Copse
Cheriton Farm
Jouldings Farm
Lea Copse
The Leas
Lea Farm
Bottom Farm House
Thatcher's or Little Ford
Bulloway's Farm
WELL HOUSE LA
Oaklands Farm
Greenacres Farm
Well House Farm
Blackwater River
NEW MILL RD
Cordery's Farm
FORD LA
Ford
The New Mill
NEW MILL LA
OAKLEA DR
Horn's Farm
Fox Warren
PLOVER LA
Lower Common
Bramshill Plantation
LOWER COMMON
MUD LA
Hall's Farm
River Whitewater
A327
READING RD
BRAMSHILL CL
VALON RD
VENNING RD
BIGGS LA
WHITEHALL DR
MARINA DR
TOE RD
TOPE CRES
PRINCESS
FARADAY CL
FLEMING CL
KELVIN CL
BAIRD RD
TYLER DR
BARKER CL
ROWCROFT RD
SHEERLANDS RD
NUFFIELD RD
JAMES WATT RD
Hogwood La
Westwood Farm
EVERSLEY RD

139

115
142

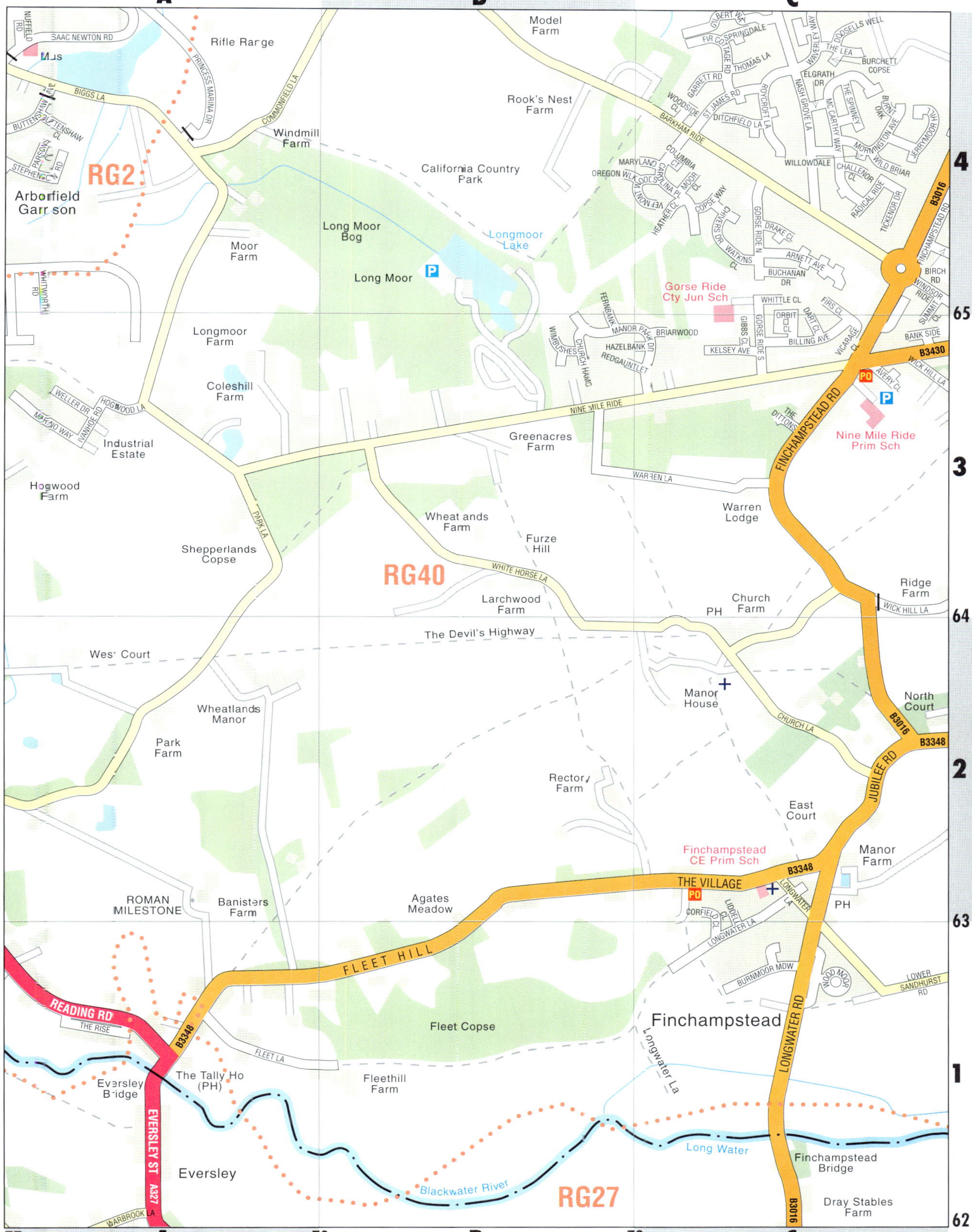
A
B
C
4
65
3
64
2
63
1
62
77
78
79
Rifle Range
Mus
BIGGS LA
COMMONFIELD LA
PRINCESS MARINA DR
ISAAC NEWTON RD
NUFFIELD RD
RG2
Arborfield Garrison
Windmill Farm
Model Farm
Rook's Nest Farm
California Country Park
Long Moor Bog
Longmoor Lake
Long Moor
Moor Farm
Longmoor Farm
Coleshill Farm
WHITWORTH RD
WELLER DR
HOGWOOD LA
IVANHOE RD
MORANO WAY
Industrial Estate
Hogwood Farm
NINE MILE RIDE
Greenacres Farm
BARKHAM RIDE
Gorse Ride Cty Jun Sch
Nine Mile Ride Prim Sch
FINCHAMPSTEAD RD
B3016
B3430
WICK HILL LA
Warren Lodge
WARREN LA
THE DITTONS
Shepperlands Copse
PARK LA
Wheat ands Farm
Furze Hill
RG40
WHITE HORSE LA
Larchwood Farm
Church Farm
PH
Ridge Farm
The Devil's Highway
West Court
Wheatlands Manor
Manor House
North Court
CHURCH LA
B3348
JUBILEE RD
Park Farm
Rectory Farm
East Court
Finchampstead CE Prim Sch
Manor Farm
THE VILLAGE
ROMAN MILESTONE
Banisters Farm
Agates Meadow
FLEET HILL
LONGWATER LA
BURNMOOR MDW
WOOD MOOR
LOWER SANDHURST RD
READING RD
THE RISE
Fleet Copse
Finchampstead
Longwater La
LONGWATER RD
FLEET LA
The Tally Ho (PH)
Eversley Bridge
Fleethill Farm
EVERSLEY ST
A327
Eversley
Blackwater River
Long Water
RG27
Finchampstead Bridge
Dray Stables Farm
WARBROOK LA

142

141
116

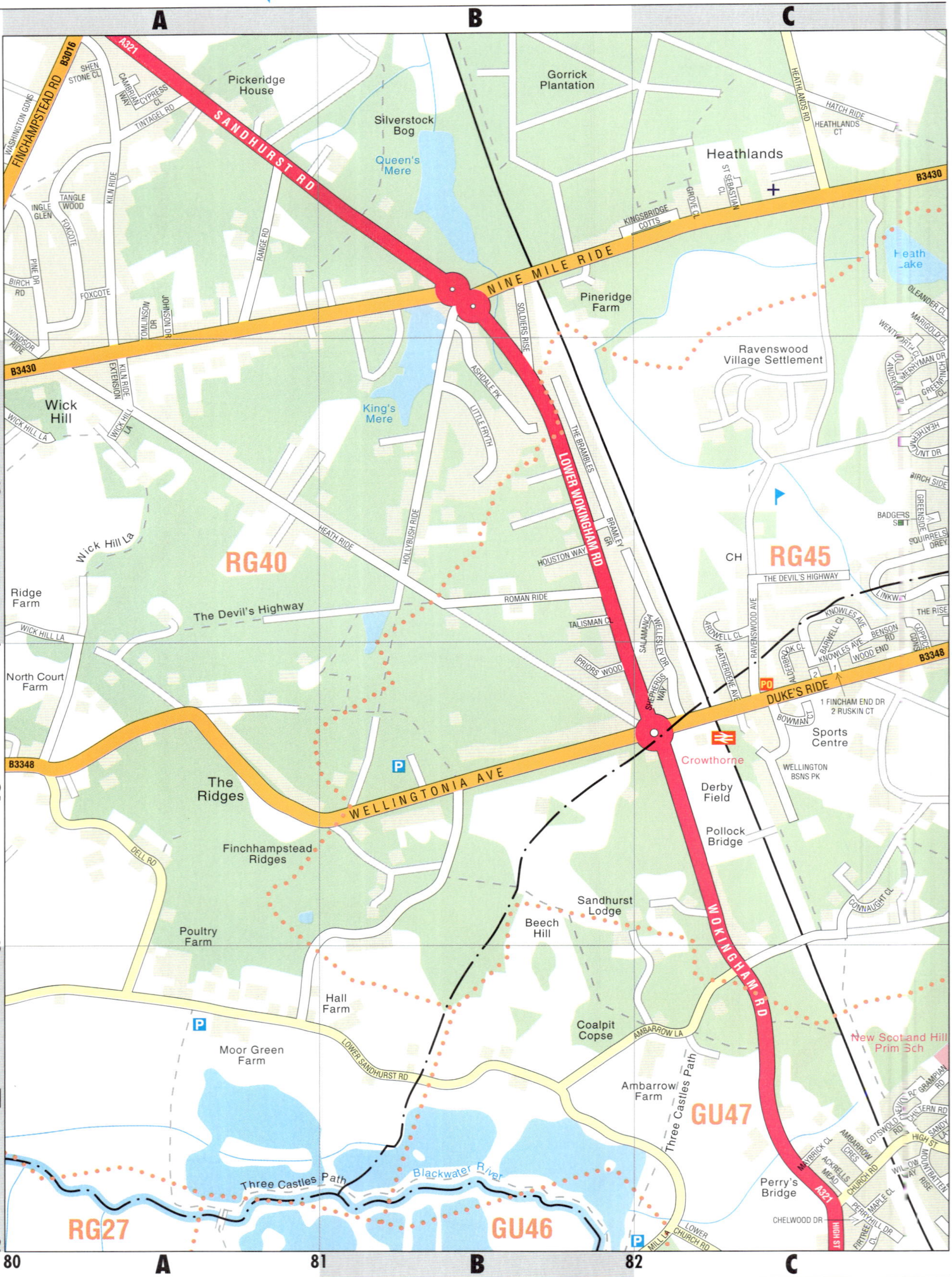

141
149

117
144

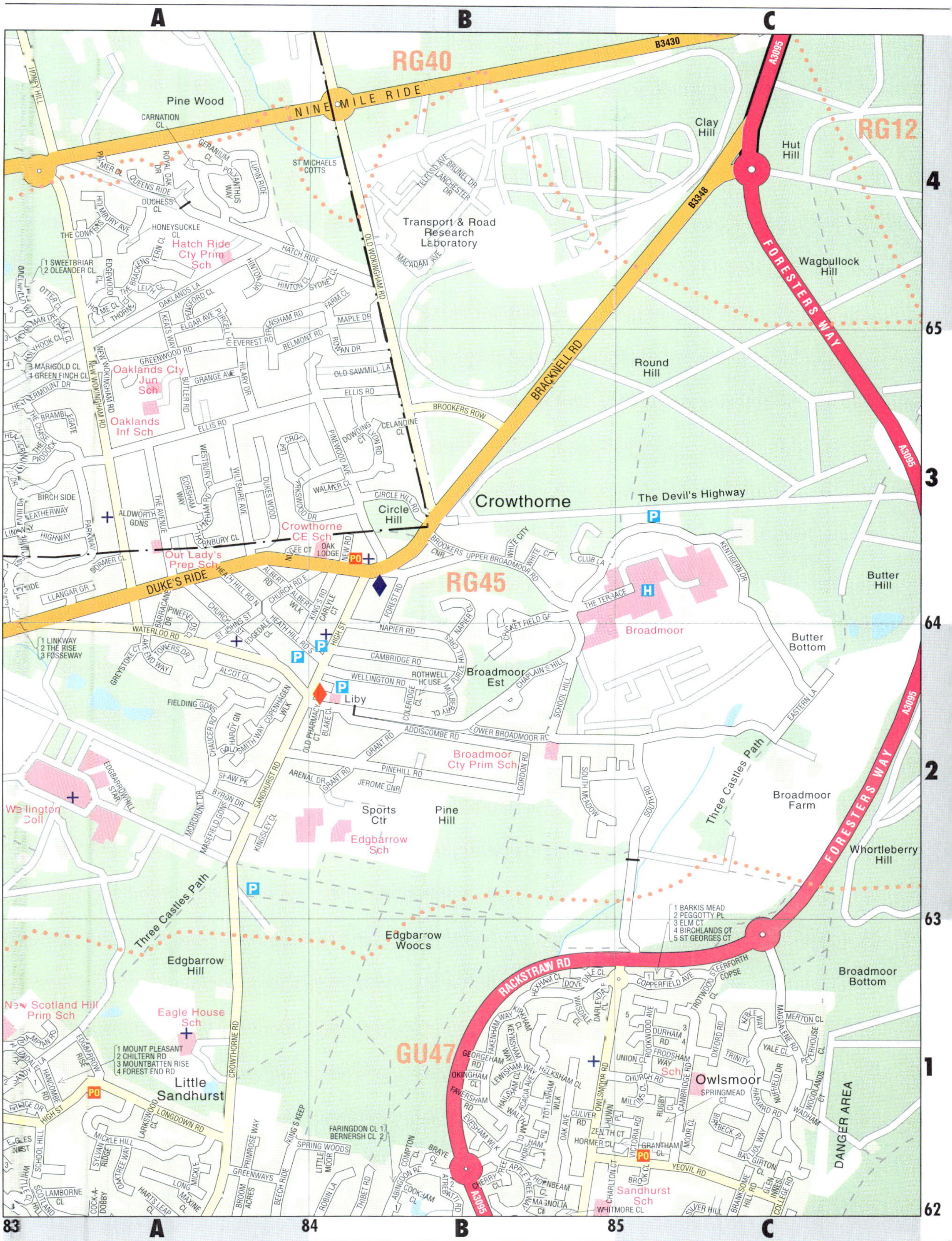

150
144

143
118

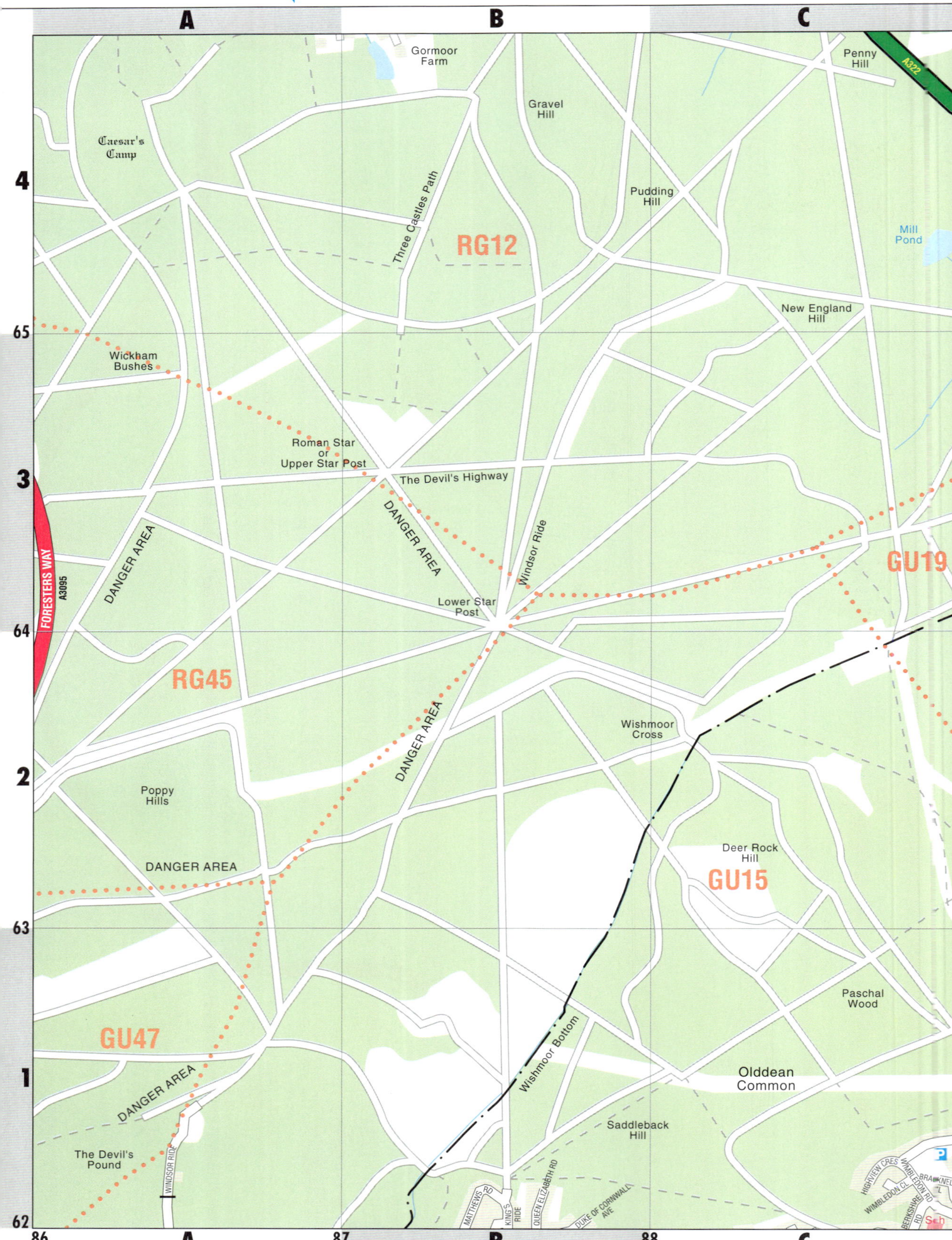

143
151

119
146

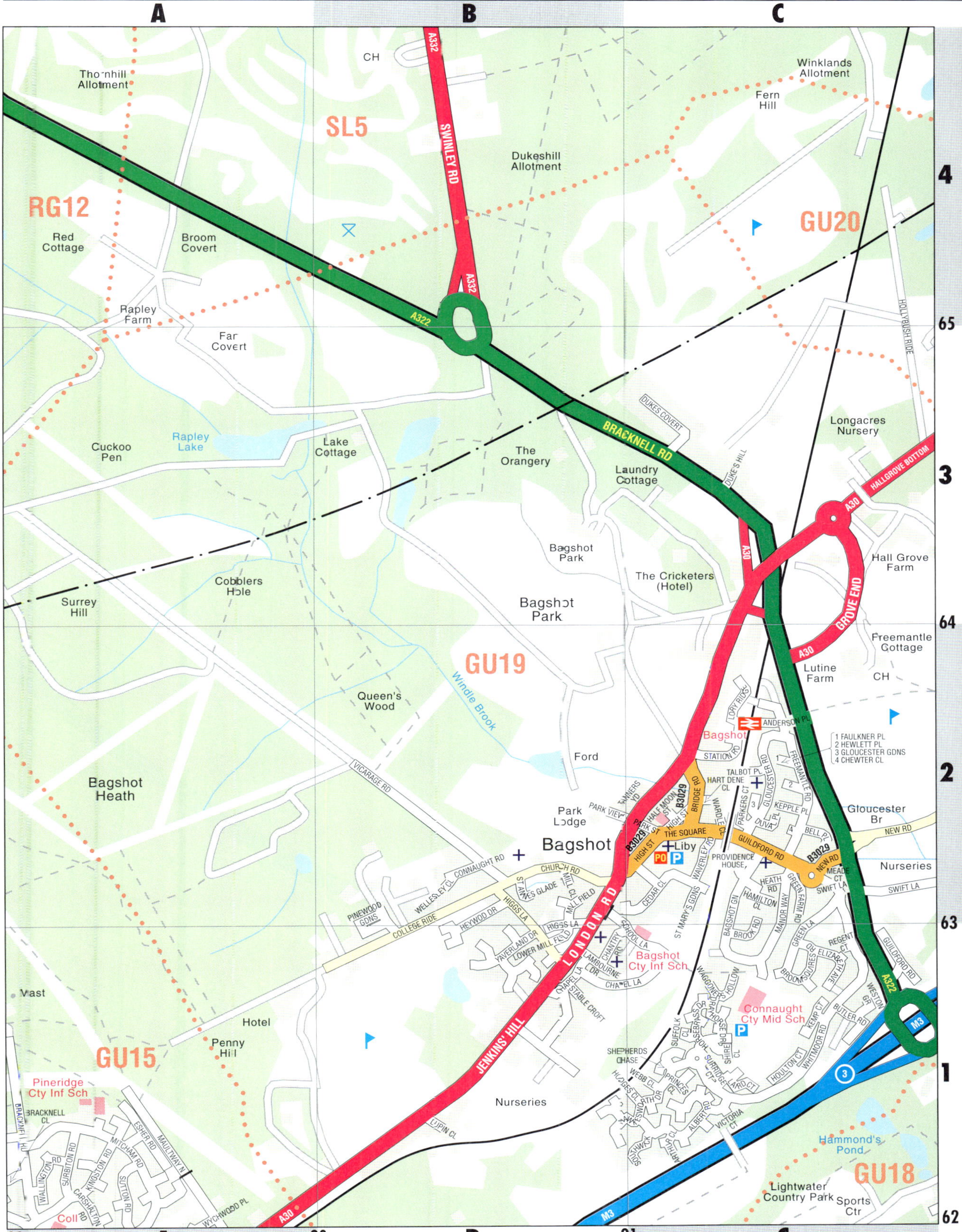

152
146

145
120

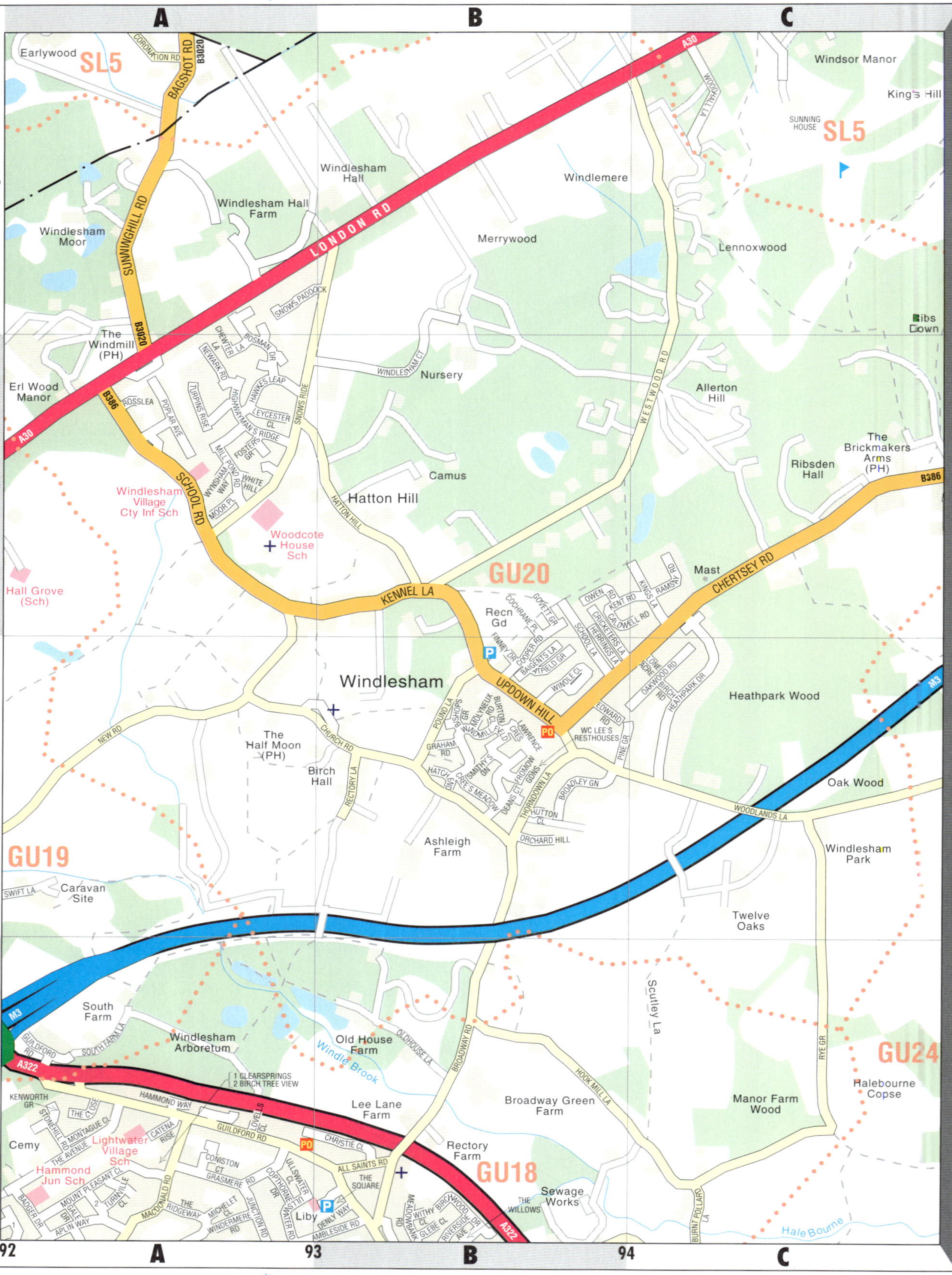

145
153

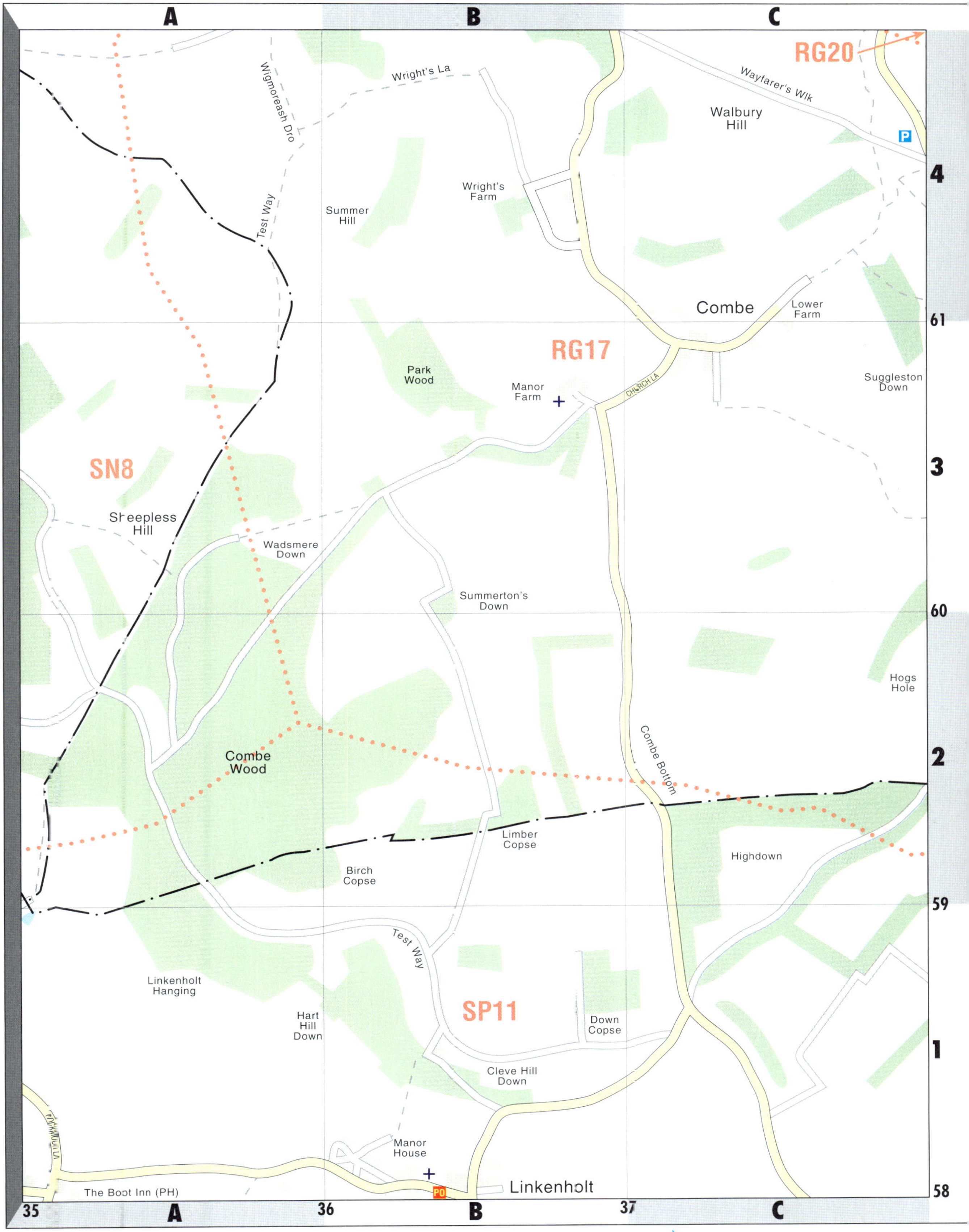
A
B
C
RG20
Wayfarer's Wlk
Walbury Hill
Wright's La
Wigmoreash Dro
Test Way
Summer Hill
Wright's Farm
Combe
Lower Farm
RG17
Park Wood
Manor Farm
CHURCH LA
Suggleston Down
SN8
Sheepless Hill
Wadsmere Down
Summerton's Down
Hogs Hole
Combe Bottom
Combe Wood
Limber Copse
Highdown
Birch Copse
Test Way
Linkenholt Hanging
Hart Hill Down
SP11
Down Copse
Cleve Hill Down
Manor House
Linkenholt
The Boot Inn (PH)
PO
4
61
3
60
2
59
1
58
35
36
37

147
128

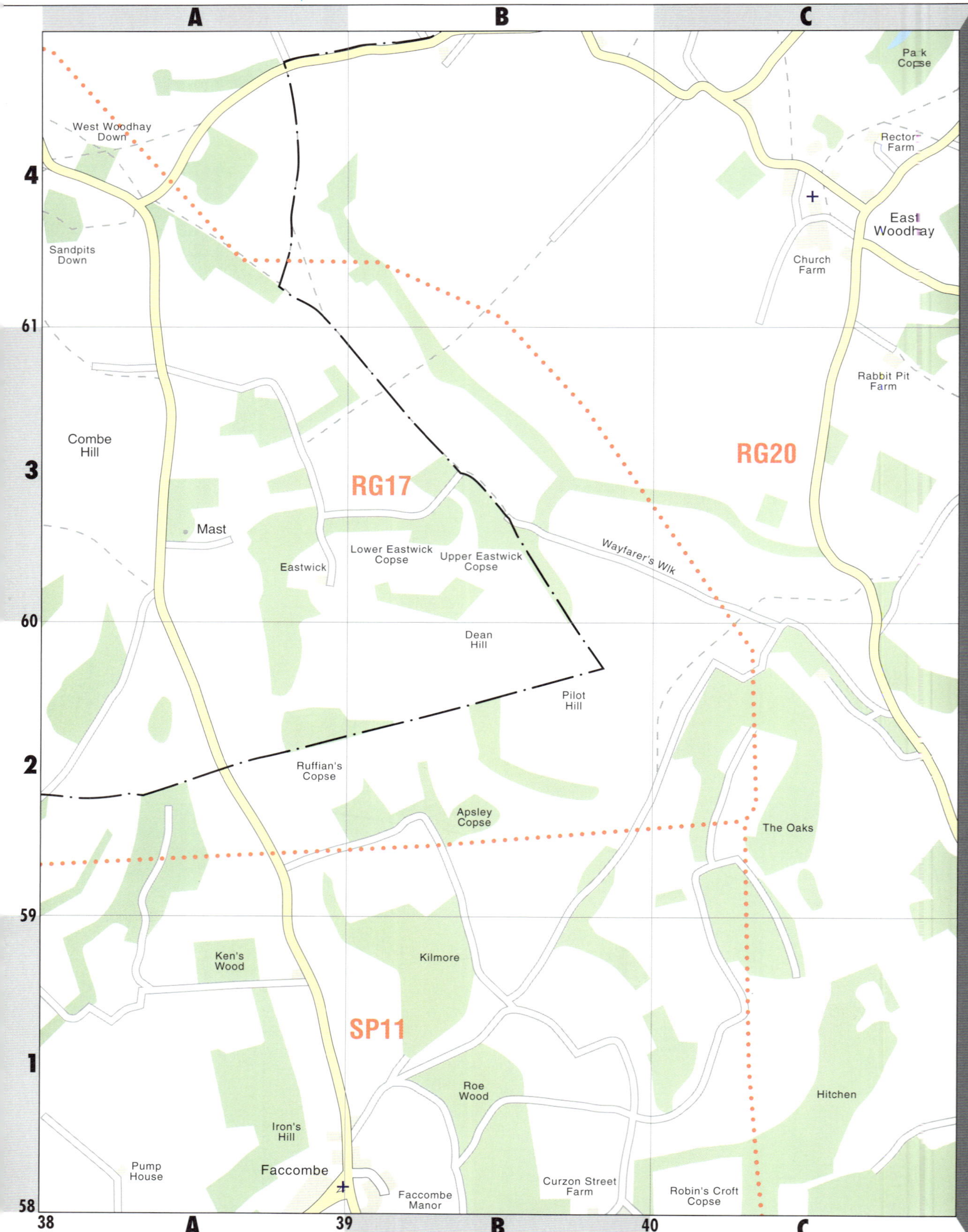
A
B
C
4
61
3
60
2
59
1
58
38
39
40
West Woodhay Down
Sandpits Down
Combe Hill
Mast
Eastwick
Lower Eastwick Copse
Upper Eastwick Copse
RG17
RG20
SP11
Dean Hill
Pilot Hill
Wayfarer's Wlk
Ruffian's Copse
Apsley Copse
The Oaks
Ken's Wood
Kilmore
Roe Wood
Iron's Hill
Pump House
Faccombe
Faccombe Manor
Curzon Street Farm
Robin's Croft Copse
Hitchen
Church Farm
Rabbit Pit Farm
Rector Farm
East Woodhay
Park Copse

147

142
150

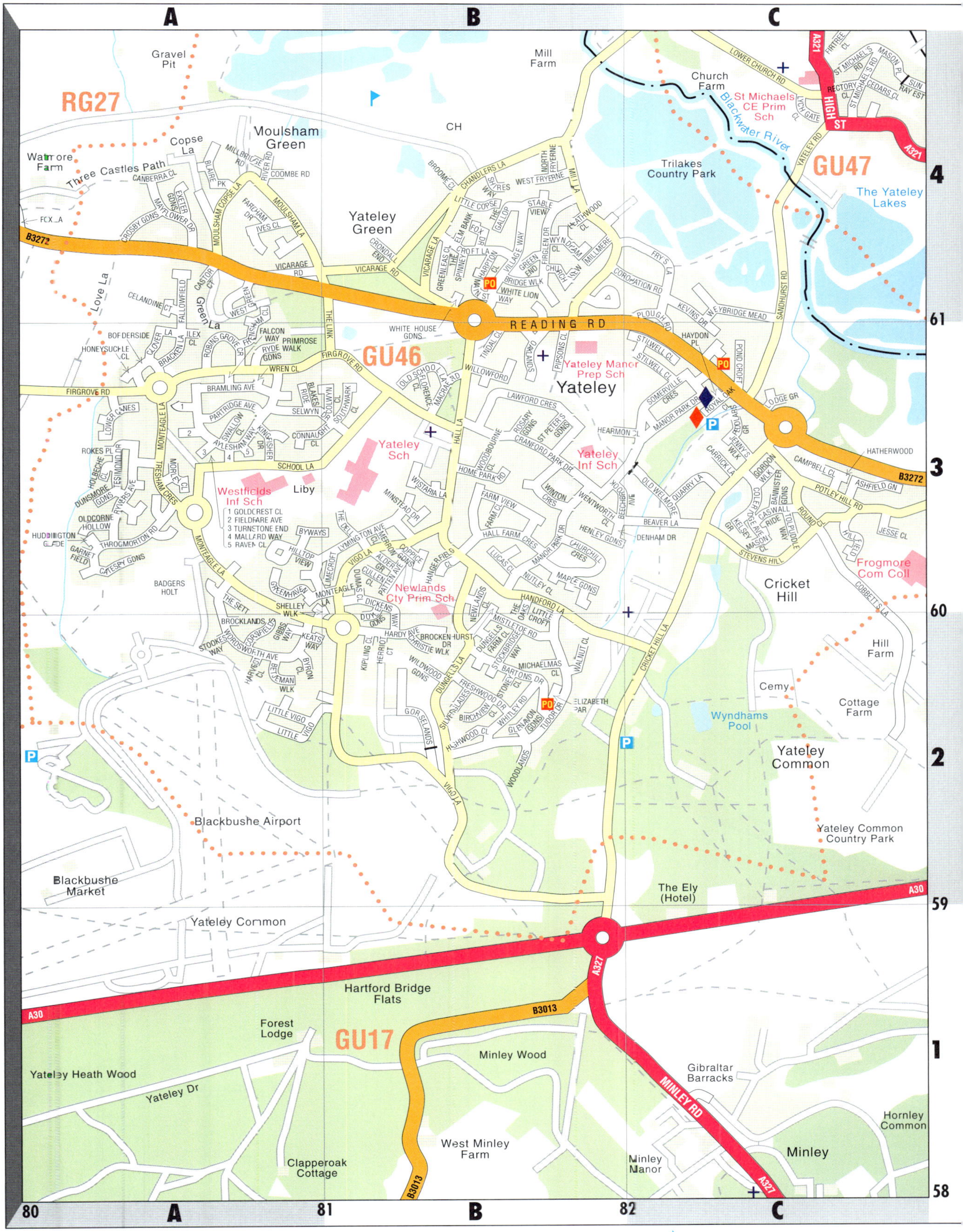
A
B
C
RG27
GU46
GU47
GU17
Gravel Pit
Mill Farm
Church Farm
St Michaels CE Prim Sch
Blackwater River
Moulsham Green
Copse La
Three Castles Path
Yateley Green
Trilakes Country Park
The Yateley Lakes
B3272
READING RD
Yateley
Yateley Manor Prep Sch
Yateley Sch
Yateley Inf Sch
Westfields Inf Sch
Liby
Newlands Cty Prim Sch
Cricket Hill
Frogmore Com Coll
Hill Farm
Cemy
Cottage Farm
Wyndhams Pool
Yateley Common
Yateley Common Country Park
Badgers Holt
Blackbushe Airport
Blackbushe Market
Yateley Common
The Ely (Hotel)
A30
A327
B3013
Hartford Bridge Flats
Forest Lodge
Yateley Heath Wood
Yateley Dr
Minley Wood
West Minley Farm
Clapperoak Cottage
Gibraltar Barracks
MINLEY RD
Minley Manor
Minley
Hornley Common
A321
HIGH ST
FIRGROVE RD
80
81
82
58
59
60
61
1
2
3
4

150

149
143

B4
1 MULBERRY CL
2 MAY CL
3 SHRIVENHAM CL
4 CENTURION CL
5 CHAFFINCH CL
6 TARBAT CT
7 ROCKFIELD WAY
8 BALINTORE CT

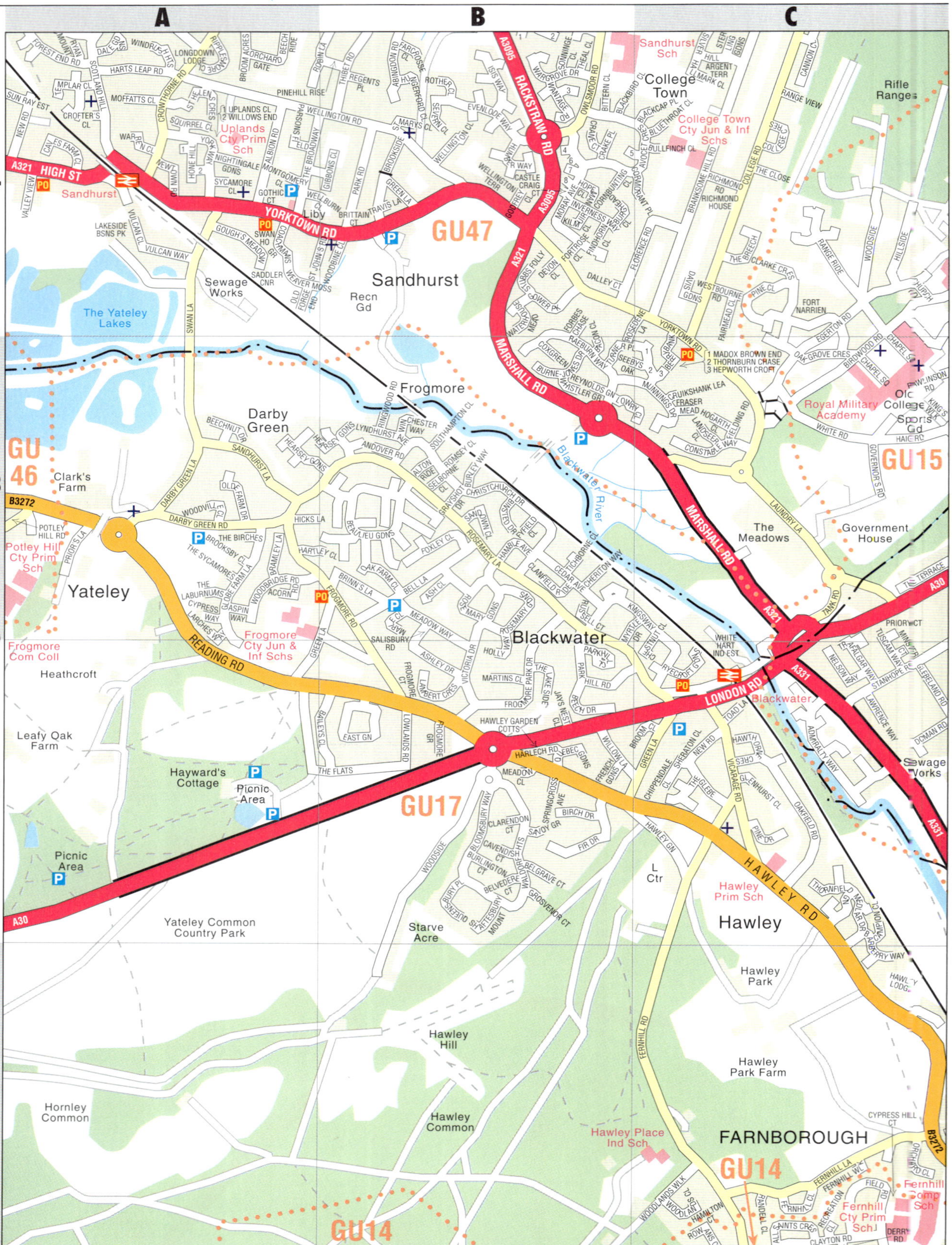

149

144
152

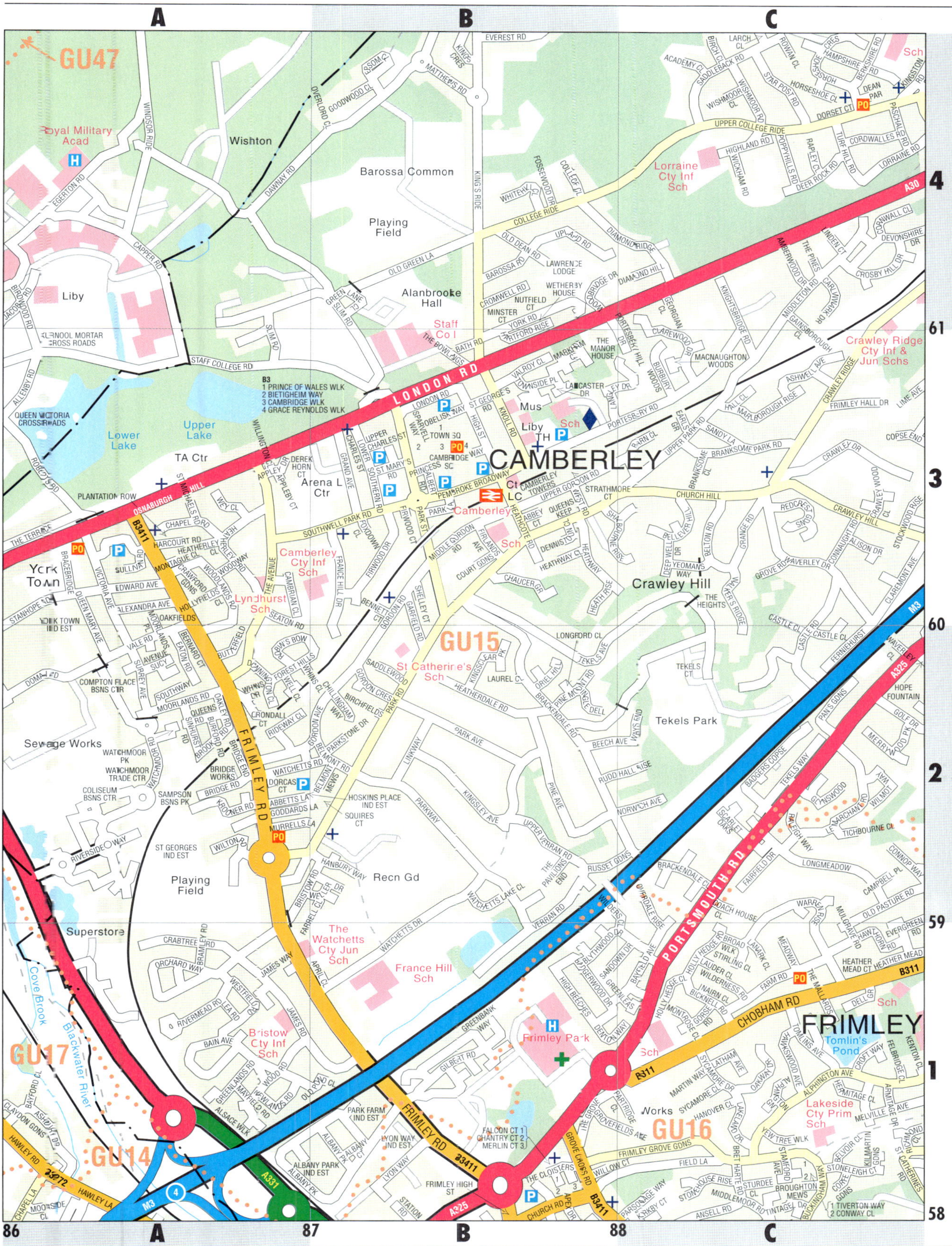
A
B
C
4
3
2
1
61
60
59
58
86
87
88
GU47
GU15
GU16
GU17
GU14
Royal Military Acad
Wishton
Barossa Common
Playing Field
Alanbrooke Hall
Staff Col
Liby
Lower Lake
Upper Lake
TA Ctr
Arena L Ctr
York Town
Camberley Cty Inf Sch
Lyndhurst Sch
CAMBERLEY
Camberley
Mus
Liby
TH
Sch
Crawley Hill
Crawley Ridge Cty Inf & Jun Schs
Lorraine Cty Inf Sch
St Catherine's Sch
Tekels Park
Sewage Works
Playing Field
Recn Gd
Superstore
The Watchetts Cty Jun Sch
France Hill Sch
Bristow Cty Inf Sch
Frimley Park
FRIMLEY
Tomlin's Pond
Lakeside Cty Prim Sch
Works
Blackwater River
Cove Brook
LONDON RD
FRIMLEY RD
PORTSMOUTH RD
CHOBHAM RD
OSNABURGH HILL
COLLEGE RIDE
UPPER COLLEGE RIDE
CHURCH HILL
STAFF COLLEGE RD
A30
A325
A331
M3
B3411
B311
B3272
PO
H
P

152

151
145

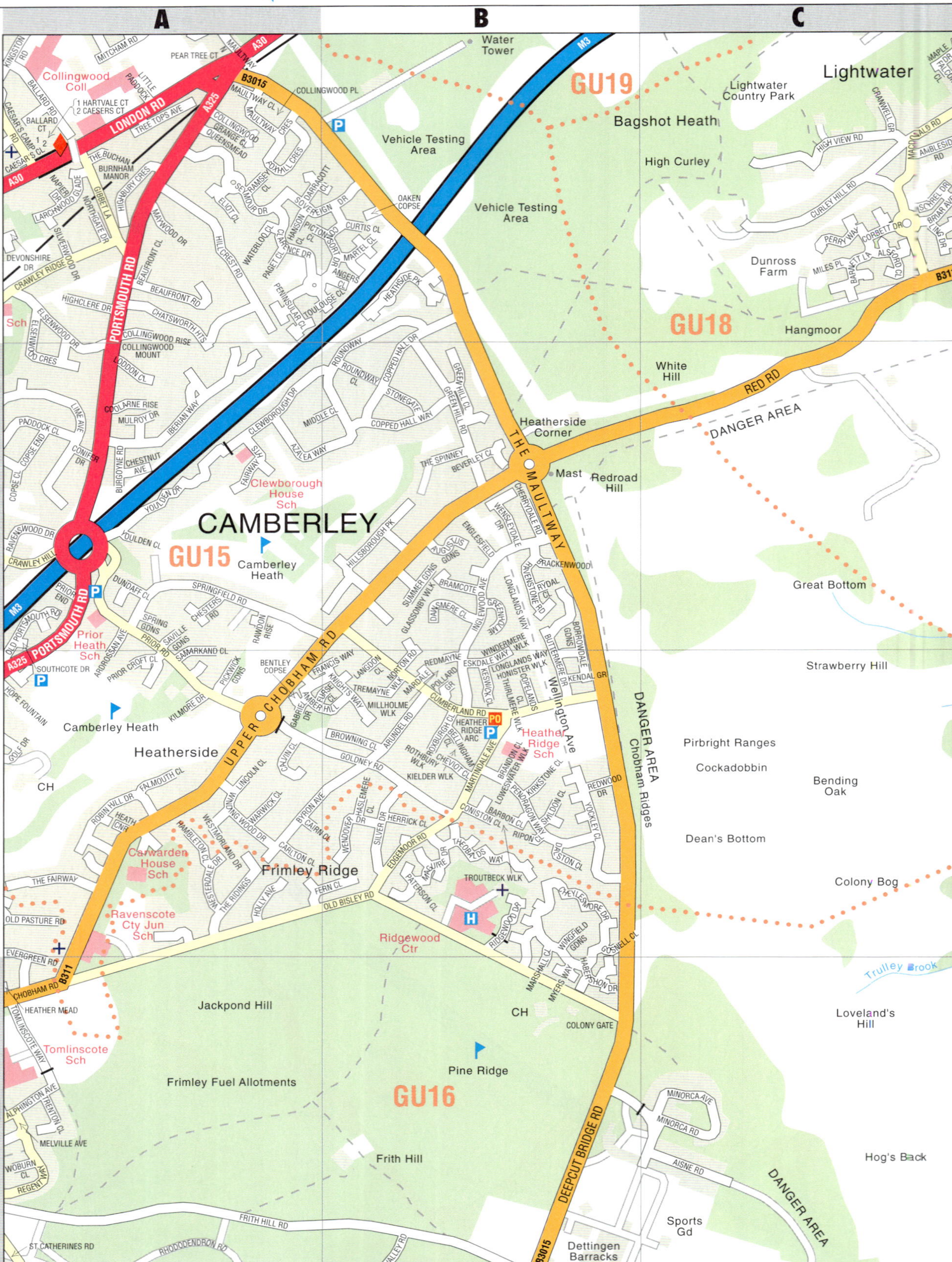
A
B
C
4
3
2
1
61
60
59
58
89
90
91
Lightwater
Lightwater Country Park
Bagshot Heath
High Curley
GU19
GU18
GU15
GU16
Water Tower
Vehicle Testing Area
Vehicle Testing Area
Dunross Farm
Hangmoor
White Hill
RED RD
DANGER AREA
Heatherside Corner
Mast
Redroad Hill
THE MAULTWAY
CAMBERLEY
Camberley Heath
Clewborough House Sch
Collingwood Coll
LONDON RD
PORTSMOUTH RD
A30
A325
M3
B3015
B311
Great Bottom
Strawberry Hill
Pirbright Ranges
Cockadobbin
Bending Oak
Dean's Bottom
Colony Bog
Trulley Brook
Loveland's Hill
Hog's Back
DANGER AREA Chobham Ridges
Wellington Ave
UPPER CHOBHAM RD
Heatherside
Camberley Heath
Prior Heath Sch
Heather Ridge Sch
Frimley Ridge
Carwarden House Sch
Ravenscote Cty Jun Sch
Ridgewood Ctr
Jackpond Hill
Tomlinscote Sch
Frimley Fuel Allotments
Pine Ridge
Frith Hill
DEEPCUT BRIDGE RD
Sports Gd
Dettingen Barracks
FRITH HILL RD
ST CATHERINES RD
RHODODENDRON RD
CHOBHAM RD
OLD BISLEY RD
COLONY GATE
MINORCA AVE
MINORCA RD
AISNE RD
CH
CH

151

146

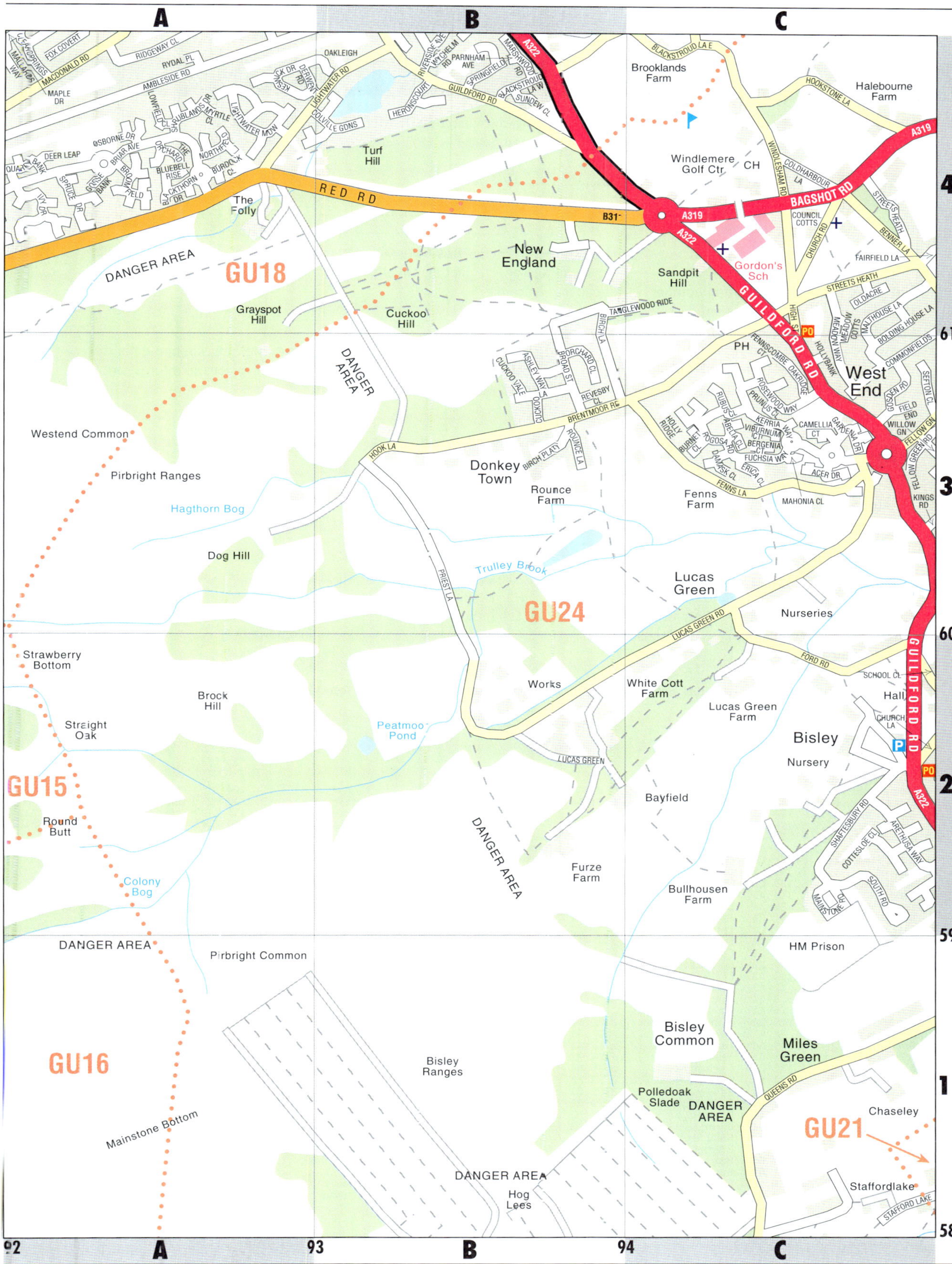
A
B
C
4
61
3
60
2
59
1
58
92
93
94
Brooklands Farm
Halebourne Farm
Windlemere Golf Ctr
CH
Turf Hill
The Folly
RED RD
B31
A322
A319
BAGSHOT RD
GUILDFORD RD
New England
Sandpit Hill
Gordon's Sch
GU18
DANGER AREA
Grayspot Hill
Cuckoo Hill
West End
PH
PO
Westend Common
Pirbright Ranges
Hagthorn Bog
Donkey Town
Rounce Farm
Fenns Farm
Dog Hill
Trulley Brook
Lucas Green
GU24
Nurseries
Strawberry Bottom
Brock Hill
Works
White Cott Farm
Lucas Green Farm
Straight Oak
Peatmoor Pond
Bisley
Nursery
GU15
Round Butt
Bayfield
Furze Farm
Bullhousen Farm
Colony Bog
HM Prison
Pirbright Common
GU16
Bisley Ranges
Bisley Common
Miles Green
Polledoak Slade
Chaseley
GU21
Mainstone Bottom
Hog Lees
Staffordlake
HOOK LA
BRENTMOOR RD
PRIEST LA
LUCAS GREEN RD
FORD RD
QUEENS RD
STAFFORD LAKE
HOOKSTONE LA
WINDLESHAM RD
STREETS HEATH
CHURCH RD
HIGH ST
FENNS LA
MAHONIA CL
SCHOOL CL
SHAFTESBURY RD
SOUTH RD
MAINSTONE RD

Index

Street names are listed alphabetically and show the locality, the Postcode District, the page number and a reference to the square in which the name falls on the map page

Garden Mews **8** Reading RG30..............**85** B3

Full street name This may have been abbreviated on the map

Location number If present, this indicates the street's position on a congested area of the map instead of the name

Town, village or locality in which the street falls.

Postcode District for the street name

Page number of the map on which the street name appears

Grid square in which the centre of the street falls

Schools, hospitals,sports centres, railway stations, shopping centres, industrial estates, public amenities and otherplaces of interest are also listed. These are highlighted in magenta

Abbreviations used in the index

Abbr	Meaning	Abbr	Meaning	Abbr	Meaning	Abbr	Meaning	Abbr	Meaning
App	**Approach**	Cl	**Close**	Espl	**Esplanade**	N	**North**	S	**South**
Arc	**Arcade**	Comm	**Common**	Est	**Estate**	Orch	**Orchard**	Sq	**Square**
Ave	**Avenue**	Cnr	**Corner**	Gdns	**Gardens**	Par	**Parade**	Strs	**Stairs**
Bvd	**Boulevard**	Cotts	**Cottages**	Gn	**Green**	Pk	**Park**	Stps	**Steps**
Bldgs	**Buildings**	Ct	**Court**	Gr	**Grove**	Pas	**Passage**	St	**Street, Saint**
Bsns Pk	**Business Park**	Ctyd	**Courtyard**	Hts	**Heights**	Pl	**Place**	Terr	**Terrace**
Bsns Ctr	**Business Centre**	Cres	**Crescent**	Ind Est	**Industrial Estate**	Prec	**Precinct**	Trad	**Trading Est**
Bglws	**Bungalows**	Dr	**Drive**	Intc	**Interchange**	Prom	**Promenade**	Wlk	**Walk**
Cswy	**Causeway**	Dro	**Drove**	Junc	**Junction**	Ret Pk	**Retail Park**	W	**West**
Ctr	**Centre**	E	**East**	La	**Lane**	Rd	**Road**	Yd	**Yard**
Cir	**Circus**	Emb	**Embankment**			Rdbt	**Roundabout**		

Town and village index

Aldermaston.........135 A3
Aldworth.............32 A2
Arborfield...........114 B1
Ascot 120 A1
Ashampstead 54 A3
Ashford..............97 A3
Aston Tirrold.........12 C4
Bagshot 145 B1
Ball Hill.............129 C1
Barkham.............115 A1
Beech Hill...........138 A1
Beedon...............51 B4
Beenham 108 C3
Binfield..............90 A1
Bisham 18 A1
Bisley 153 C2
Blackwater 150 A2
Blewbury 12 A3
Bourne End............3 A1
Boxford...............76 A1
Bracknell 118 B2
Bradfield.............82 A1
Brands Hill 69 A4
Brightwalton..........28 B1
Brimpton 133 C3
Bucklebury 80 A1
Burchett's Green 38 A3
Burghfield Common ...110 B1
Burnham..............21 A1
Camberley 151 A1
Caversham 59 A1
Chaddleworth.........49 A2
Charlton 125 B4
Charvil 61 A1
Chertsey 124 A1
Chieveley 51 A1
Chilton 10 B4
Chilton Foliat 73 A4
Cholsey...............14 A4
Cold Ash............106 A4
Colnbrook............69 A3
Combe 147 C3
Compton..............31 B2
Cookham 20 A3
Crowthorne 143 A4
Datchet...............68 A3
Dorney 41 A2
Earley 87 A1
East Bedfont..........98 A3
East Garston..........47 A2
East Isley 30 A3
Egham 96 A1
Englefield Green.......95 A1
Eton 67 B4
Farnborough (Berks) ...28 A4
Farnborough (Hants) ..150 C1
Farnham Common 22 A1
Fawley (Berks) 27 B2
Fawley (Bucks)........15 A3
Feltham 98 B2
Finchampstead.......141 A1
Flackwell Heath 3 A3
Frimley 151 B1
Froxfield 99 A1
Fulmer 23 A3
Goring 34 A3
Great Shefford 48 A1
Greenham...........131 B4
Ham 126 A2
Hambleden 16 A4
Hampstead Norreys 52 C3
Hamstead Marshall....129 A4
Harlington 71 A1
Harmondsworth 70 A2
Hatton 71 B1
Headley 132 C1
Henley-on-T..........15 A2
Hermitage 79 A1
Holyport 65 A4
Horton 69 A1
Hungerford..........100 A2
Hungerford Newtown...74 A2
Hurley...............17 A1
Hurst 88 B2
Inkpen 127 B2
Iver..................44 A3
Iver Heath............23 B1
Kintbury 102 A1
Knowl Hill............37 A3
Laleham 124 A4
Lambourn............25 A1
Leckhampstead 49 C3
Letcombe Bassett.......6 B4
Lightwater 152 C4
Linkenholt 147 A1
Little Marlow 2 A2
Littleton 125 A2
Littlewick Green 38 A2
Lower Basildon........34 A1
Lower Halliford.......125 B4
Lyne 123 A1
Maidenhead 39 A1
Mapledurham..........57 C3
Marlow 1 A1
Marlow Bottom..........1 A3
Medmenham 17 A2
Mortimer 137 A3
Moulsford............13 B2
Newbury............104 B1
Newell Green 92 A3
Newtown 131 C1
North Ascot 119 C4
Oakley Green 66 A1
Old Windsor 95 A3
Padworth 109 B2
Pangbourne 56 A1
Peasemore 50 A4
Poyle 69 B3
Purley on T...........57 A1
Reading 86 A2
Remenham Hill........16 A1
Sandhurst...........150 A4
Shefford Woodlands....74 B4
Shepperton..........125 A1
Shinfield............113 A1
Shiplake 35 A1
Silchester...........136 A1
Slough 42 A3
Sonning 60 C1
South Stoke 14 A2
Staines 96 B3
Stanford Dingley.......81 B2
Stanwell 97 A3
Stockcross 104 A4
Stoke Poges 22 C1
Streatley.............34 A3
Sulham...............56 C3
Sulhamstead.........110 B1
Sunbury 125 C3
Sunningdale.........121 A1
Swallowfield.........139 A1
Tadley..............134 A1
Taplow 20 C1
Thatcham...........106 A1
Theale 83 A1
Thorpe 123 A3
Thorpe Lea...........96 A1
Tidmarsh 56 A1
Twyford...............61 A3
Upper Basildon........55 A3
Upper Halliford.......125 B3
Virginia Water 122 A2
Waltham St Lawrence...62 A4
Walton-on-T 125 C1
Wargrave 36 B1
Wentworth 121 A1
West End 153 C3
West Ilsley 10 A1
West Woodhay 128 A3
Whitchurch-on-T......56 B4
White Waltham........63 A3
Wickham 75 B2
Windlesham 146 A2
Windsor 67 A2
Winkfield 92 A1
Winnersh 88 A1
Winterbourne.........77 B3
Wokingham 116 A1
Wooburn Green 3 B2
Wooburn Moor 3 C4
Woodley 88 A3
Woolhampton........108 B1
Wraysbury 68 B1
Yateley 149 A2
Yattendon.............53 A1

3

3 Acre Mobile Home Pk SL0 .44 A4

A

Abattoirs Rd RG1 .86 A4
Abberbury Cl RG14 .104 C3
Abbetts La GU15 .151 A2
Abbey Cl Bracknell RG12 .118 B2
Newbury RG14 .131 A4
Slough SL1 .41 C3
Wokingham RG40 .116 B4
Abbey Cotts SL7 .17 A2
Abbey Ct Camberley GU15 .151 B3
Chertsey KT16 .124 A1
Abbey Dr TW18 .124 B3
Abbey Gdns KT16 .124 A2
Abbey Gn KT16 .124 A2
Abbey Jun Sch RG1 .86 B3
Abbey Lodge TW18 .96 C2
Abbey Pk RG7 .110 C2
Abbey Rd Bourne End SL8 .2 C3
Chertsey KT16 .124 A1
Lower Halliford TW17 .125 A1
Virginia Water GU25 .122 B3
Abbey River Cotts KT16 .124 B2
Abbey Sq RG1 .86 A4
Abbey St RG1 .86 A4
Abbey Way SL7 .18 B3
Abbey Wood SL5 .121 A1
Abbot Cl TW18 .97 B1
Abbot's Wlk SL4 .66 C3
Abbots Dr GU25 .122 B3
Abbots Rd
Burghfield Common RG7 .110 C1
Newbury RG14 .105 A1
Abbots Way KT16 .123 C1
Abbots Wlk RG1 .86 A4
Abbotsbury RG12 .117 C2
Abbotsbury Ct 3 RG30 .85 A4
Abbotsmead Pl RG4 .59 A1
Abbotts Way SL1 .41 B3
Abelia Cl GU24 .153 C3
Abell Gdns SL6 .19 A1
Aberaman RG4 .58 C3
Aberdeen Ave SL1 .42 A3
Aberford Cl RG30 .85 B4
Abex Rd RG14 .105 B2
Abingdon Cl RG12 .118 C2
Abingdon Dr RG4 .59 B3
Abingdon Rd
East Isley RG20 .30 C4
Sandhurst GU47 .143 B1
Abingdon Wlk SL6 .19 C2
Abington SL3 .69 B4
Abney Court Dr SL8 .3 A1
Abotts Mead OX10 .14 A4
Abrahams Rd RG9 .15 B2
Acacia RG9 .15 B1
Acacia Ave Littleton TW17 .125 A2
Sandhurst GU47 .143 B1
Wraysbury TW19 .68 C2
Acacia Ct RG12 .118 A3
Acacia Mews UB7 .70 B4
Acacia Rd Reading RG1 .86 B3
Staines TW18 .97 A2
Academy Cl GU15 .151 C4
Accommodation La UB7 .70 B4
Acer Dr GU24 .153 C3
Ackrells Mead GU47 .142 C1
Acorn Cotts SN8 .126 B2
Acorn Dr Thatcham RG18 .106 B3
Wokingham RG40 .116 B4
Acorn Gr UB3 .71 C4
Acorn Rd GU17 .150 A3
Acorn Wlk RG31 .84 B3
Acre Bsns Pk RG2 .113 A4
Acre Pas SL4 .67 B3
Acre Rd RG2 .113 A4
Acre The SL7 .1 C1
Action Ct TW15 .125 B4
Adam Cl Slough SL1 .42 A3
Tadley RG26 .134 C1
Adam Ct RG9 .15 C1
Adams Way RG6 .86 C1
Addington Cl SL4 .67 A2
Addington Rd RG1 .86 B3
Addington Spec Sch RG5 .87 C3
Addiscombe Chase RG31 .57 A2
Addiscombe Rd RG45 .143 B2
Addison Cl SL0 .44 C3
Addison Ct SL6 .20 A1
Addison Rd RG1 .59 A1
Adelaide Cl SL1 .42 A2
Adelaide Rd Ashford TW15 .97 B2
Reading RG6 .87 A3
Adelaide Sq SL4 .67 B3
Adelphi Gdns SL1 .42 C2
Adey's Cl RG14 .105 A1
Adkins Rd RG10 .62 C4
Admirals Ct RG2 .86 A3
Admiralty Way GU15 .150 C2
Admoor La RG7 .82 B1
Adwell Dr RG6 .87 B1
Adwell Sq RG9 .15 B1
Adwood Ct RG19 .106 C2
Aeriel Bsns Pk RG17 .45 C2
Agar Cres RG42 .91 A1
Agars Pl SL3 .68 A4
Agate Cl RG41 .115 C4
Aggisters La RG41 .115 B2
Agincourt Cl RG41 .115 C3
Agincourt Pl SL5 .120 B3
Agricola Way RG19 .106 C1
Ainsdale Cres RG30 .85 A2
Aintree RG17 .25 A1
Aintree Cl Newbury RG14 .105 B1
Poyle SL3 .69 C3
Air Forces Meml TW20 .95 B2
Airport Way TW19 .70 A2
Aisne Rd GU16 .152 C1
Ajax Ave SL1 .42 A3
Alan Pl RG30 .85 A3
Alan Way SL3 .43 C4
Alandale Cl RG2 .113 B4
Albain Cres TW15 .97 C3
Albany Ct GU16 .151 B1
Albany Park Dr RG41 .88 A2
Albany Park Ind Est GU15 .151 B1
Albany Pk Frimley GU15 .151 B1
Poyle SL3 .69 B4
Albany Pl TW20 .96 A2
Albany Rd Old Windsor SL4 .68 A1
Reading RG30 .85 B4
Windsor SL4 .67 B3
Alben Rd RG42 .90 B2
Albert Ave KT16 .124 A3
Albert Cl 28 SL1 .42 C2
Albert Illsley Cl RG31 .84 B4
Albert Pl SL4 .42 A1
Albert Rd Ashford TW15 .97 C2
Bagshot GU19 .145 C1
Bracknell RG42 .118 A4
Camberley GU15 .151 B3
Caversham RG4 .58 C2
Crowthorne RG45 .143 A3
Englefield Green TW20 .95 B1
Henley-on-T RG9 .15 C1
19 Newbury RG14 .105 A2
Windsor SL4 .67 C2
Wokingham RG40 .116 A3
Albert St Maidenhead SL6 .39 C4
Slough SL1 .42 C2
Windsor SL4 .67 A3
Albert Wlk RG45 .143 A3
Albion SL3 .44 A1
Albion Cl SL2 .43 A3
Albion Cotts SL6 .19 B4
Albion Pl 2 SL4 .67 A3
Albion Rd GU47 .150 A4
Albion Terr RG1 .86 B4
Albury Cl RG30 .58 B1
Albury Gdns RG31 .84 C2
Alcot Cl RG45 .143 A2
Aldborough Spur SL1 .42 C4
Aldbourne Ave RG6 .87 A2
Aldbourne Cl RG17 .100 B3
Aldbourne Rd SL1 .41 A4
Aldeburgh Cl RG4 .59 B4
Aldebury Rd SL6 .19 C1
Alden View SL4 .66 B3
Aldenham Cl RG4 .59 B3
Aldenham Terr RG12 .118 B2
Alder Bridge Steiner Sch RG7 .109 B2
Alder Cl
Englefield Green TW20 .95 C2
Newbury RG14 .105 B2
Slough SL1 .41 C3
Alder Ct RG12 .118 A3
Alder Dr Earley RG6 .87 B1
Reading RG31 .84 B3
Alder Glade RG7 .110 C2
Alder Gr GU46 .149 B3
Alderbourne La SL3 .23 C4
Alderbrook Cl RG45 .142 C2
Alderbury Rd SL3 .43 C2
Alderbury Rd W SL3 .43 C2
Alderfield Cl RG7 .83 C2
Alderley Cl RG5 .60 C1
Alderman Willey Cl RG41 .116 A3
Aldermaston CE Prim Sch RG7 .134 C4
Aldermaston Sta RG7 .109 B2
Alderney Ct 27 RG1 .86 B4
Alderney Gdns RG41 .88 B1
Alders The RG18 .106 B2
Alderside Wlk TW20 .95 C2
Aldin Ave N SL1 .43 A2
Aldin Ave S SL1 .43 A2
Aldous Ho TW18 .96 C2
Aldridge Rd SL2 .22 A1
Aldryington Prim Sch RG6 .87 A2
Aldwick Dr SL6 .39 B3
Aldworth Cl
Bracknell RG12 .118 A3
Reading RG30 .85 B3
Aldworth Gdns RG45 .143 A3
Aldworth Rd
Compton RG20 .31 C2
Upper Basildon RG8 .55 A3
Aldwyn Ct TW20 .95 A1
Alexander Ct 24 RG1 .85 C4
Alexander Fst Sch SL4 .66 B2
Alexander Rd Egham TW20 .96 B2
Thatcham RG19 .106 C1
Alexander Wlk RG12 .118 A2
Alexandra Ave GU15 .151 A3
Alexandra Cl Ashford TW15 .98 B1
Staines TW18 .97 B1
Alexandra Ct TW15 .98 B1
Alexandra Rd
Ashford TW15 .98 C1
Englefield Green TW20 .95 B1
Maidenhead SL6 .39 B4
Reading RG1 .86 B3
Slough SL1 .42 B2
Windsor SL4 .67 B3
Alford Cl RG30 .84 B4
Alfred Davis Ct SL7 .1 B2
Alfred St RG1 .85 C4
Alfred Sutton Prim Sch RG1 .86 C3
Alice Gough Memorial Homes RG12 .118 A3
Alice La SL1 .21 A1
Alison Cl RG7 .110 C1
Alison Dr GU15 .151 C3
All Hallows Rd RG4 .59 B2
All Saints' Ave SL6 .39 B4
All Saints CE Inf Sch RG1 .85 C4
All Saints CE Jun Sch SL6 .39 B3
All Saints Cl RG40 .116 B4
All Saints Cres GU14 .150 C1
All Saints Ct RG30 .85 C3
All Saints Rd GU18 .146 B1
All Saints Rise RG42 .91 C1
All Souls Cotts SL3 .43 C4
All Souls' Rd SL5 .120 A3
Allanson Rd SL7 .1 C2
Allcot Cl TW14 .98 C4
Allcroft Rd RG1 .86 B3
Allenby Rd Maidenhead SL6 .39 A4
Sandhurst GU15 .151 A3
Allendale Cl GU47 .143 A1
Allendale Rd RG6 .87 A2
Allerds Rd SL2 .22 A2
Alleyns La SL6 .19 B4
Allhusen Gdns SL3 .23 C4
Alliance Ct TW15 .98 B2
Allington Ave TW17 .125 C3
Allington Ct SL2 .42 C3
Allison Ct 17 RG1 .85 C4
Allison Gdns RG8 .57 B3
Allkins Ct SL4 .67 B3
Allnatt Ave RG41 .88 B1
Allonby Cl RG6 .87 B1
Allsmoor La RG12 .118 C3
Allyn Cl TW18 .96 C1
Alma Ct Burnham SL1 .21 B1
Eton SL4 .41 C1
Wokingham RG41 .116 A3
Alma Rd Eton SL4 .41 C1
Windsor SL4 .67 B3
Alma St RG30 .85 B4
Almners Rd KT16 .123 A1
Almond Ave RG14 .105 A3
Almond Cl Charlton TW17 .125 B4
Englefield Green TW20 .95 A1
Windsor SL4 .67 A3
Wokingham RG41 .115 B2
Almond Dr Caversham RG4 .59 C2
Thatcham RG18 .106 B2
Almond Rd SL1 .21 B1
Almons Way SL2 .43 A4
Almshouses Eton SL4 .67 B4
Reading RG1 .86 A4
Sunbury TW16 .125 C4
Almswood Rd RG26 .135 A1
Alpha Ho 4 RG1 .86 B3
Alpha St N SL1 .43 A2
Alpha St S SL1 .42 C2
Alpha Way TW20 .123 B4
Alphington Ave GU16 .151 C1
Alphington Gn GU16 .151 C1
Alphington Rd RG2 .113 A4
Alpine St RG1 .86 A3
Alsace Wlk GU15 .151 A1
Alsford Cl GU18 .152 C4
Alston Gdns SL6 .39 C4
Alston Mews RG19 .106 B1
Alston Wlk RG4 .59 B1
Altmore SL6 .38 C2
Alton Ct TW18 .123 C4
Alton Ride GU17 .150 B3
Altona Way SL1 .42 A4
Altwood Bailey SL6 .39 A3
Altwood CE Comp Sch SL6 .39 A3
Altwood Cl
Maidenhead SL6 .39 A3
Slough SL1 .41 C4
Altwood Dr SL6 .39 A3
Altwood Rd SL6 .39 A3
Alvista Ave SL6 .41 A4
Alwyn Inf Sch SL6 .39 A4
Alwyn Rd SL6 .39 A4
Alwyns Cl KT16 .124 A2
Alwyns La KT16 .124 A2
Alyson Ct 2 SL6 .19 C1
Amanda Ct Ashford TW15 .97 C3
Slough SL3 .43 B2
Ambarrow Cres GU47 .142 C1
Ambarrow La GU47 .142 C1
Ambassador RG12 .117 C2
Amber Cl RG6 .87 B2
Amber Ct TW18 .96 C2
Amber Hill GU15 .152 A2
Amberley Cl RG14 .104 C2
Amberley Ct SL6 .20 B2
Amberley Dr RG10 .61 B3
Amberley Pl 20 SL4 .67 B3
Amberley Rd SL2 .41 C4
Amberwood Dr GU15 .151 C4
Amblecote Rd RG30 .85 A4
Ambleside Cl RG5 .87 C4
Ambleside Dr TW14 .98 C4
Ambleside Rd GU18 .153 A4
Ambleside Way TW20 .96 A1
Ambrook Rd RG2 .113 A4
Ambrose Pl RG1 .85 C4
Ambury Rd RG8 .32 C2
Amen Corner Bsns Pk RG12 .117 B4
Amerden Cl SL6 .40 B4
Amerden La SL6 .40 B4
Amerden Way SL1 .42 A2
American Comm Sch GU25 .122 B4
American Magna Carta Meml TW20 .95 B3
American Sch in Switzerland (English Branch) The TW20 .123 B3
Amersham Rd RG4 .59 B1
Amethyst Cl RG41 .115 B4
Amethyst La RG30 .85 B3
Amherst Rd RG6 .87 A3
Amity Rd RG1 .86 C4
Amity St RG1 .86 C4
Ammanford RG4 .58 C3
Amners Farm Rd RG30 .112 A4
Ampere Rd RG14 .105 A2
Anarth Ct KT13 .125 C1
Ancaster Dr SL5 .119 C4
Ancastle Gr RG9 .15 B1
Andermans SL4 .66 B3
Anderson Ave RG6 .87 A3
Anderson Cres RG2 .114 C1
Anderson Dr TW15 .98 B2
Anderson Pl GU19 .145 C2
Andover Cl
East Bedfont TW14 .98 C4
Reading RG31 .57 B1
Andover Ct TW19 .97 B4
Andover Dro RG20 .130 A2
Andover Rd
Blackwater GU17 .150 B3
Newbury RG14 .130 B3
Andrew Cl RG40 .116 C3
Andrews Cl RG7 .83 C2
Andrews Rd RG6 .87 A2
Andrews Reach SL8 .3 A1
Andrews Way SL7 .1 B4
Angel Ct 2 RG14 .105 A2
Angel Mead RG7 .108 B1
Angel Pl RG42 .90 B1
Angers Cl GU15 .152 B4
Angle Field Rd RG4 .59 B2
Anglers Way RG1 .86 B4
Anglesey Cl TW15 .98 A3
Angus Cl RG31 .84 C2
Annadale RG18 .79 B1
Anne Cl SL6 .19 C1
Anneforde Pl RG42 .91 A1
Anners Cl TW20 .123 B3
Annesley Gdns RG41 .88 B2
Annett Cl TW17 .125 C3
Annie Brookes Cl TW18 .96 B3
Ansculf Rd SL2 .22 A1
Ansell Rd GU16 .151 C1
Anslow Pl SL1 .41 B4
Anson Cres RG2 .113 B4
Anson Ct TW15 .97 C4
Anson Wlk RG2 .113 B4
Anstey Pl RG7 .111 A2
Anstey Rd 6 RG1 .86 A4
Anston Cl RG6 .114 A4
Antares Cl RG41 .115 C3
Anthian Cl RG5 .88 A4
Anthony Wall RG42 .118 C4
Anthony Way SL1 .41 B3
Antrim Rd RG5 .87 B3
Anvil Ct Slough SL3 .44 A1
Thatcham RG18 .106 B2
Apex Dr GU16 .151 B1
Aplin Way GU18 .146 A1
Apple Cl Purley on T RG31 .57 A2
Wokingham RG41 .115 C3
Apple Tree Cl RG14 .130 C4
Apple Tree Way GU47 .143 B1
Appleby Ct GU15 .151 A3
Appleby End RG30 .85 A4
Appleby Gdns TW14 .98 C4
Applecroft SL6 .39 B2
Appledore RG12 .117 C2
Appleford Cl RG19 .106 B1
Appleford Rd RG30 .85 A3
Appleton Ho 34 RG1 .86 B4
Appletree La
Shinfield RG7 .113 A1
Slough SL3 .43 B2
Appletree Pl 4 RG42 .118 A4
Appley Dr GU15 .151 A3
Approach Rd
Ashford TW15 .98 B1
Taplow SL6 .40 C4
April Cl GU15 .151 B1
Apsey Ct RG42 .90 C1
Apsley Cotts SL6 .19 C4
Apsley Ho SL1 .43 A2
Aquila Cl RG41 .115 C3
Aragon Cl TW16 .98 C1
Aragon Ct RG12 .118 B3
Arbor La RG41 .88 A2
Arbor Mdws RG41 .88 A2
Arborfield Cl SL1 .42 C2
Arborfield, Newland & Barkham CE Jun Sch RG2 .114 C1
Arborfield Rd RG2 .113 C2
Arbour Cl RG1 .85 C3
Arbour Vale Sch SL2 .42 C4
Arc The RG1 .86 A4
Arcade The Goring RG8 .34 B3
Newbury RG14 .105 A2
Archangel Way RG18 .106 C2
Archer Cl SL6 .39 B4
Archway Rd RG4 .59 A1
Arden Cl RG12 .119 A4
Ardingly RG12 .118 A2
Ardler Rd RG4 .59 B1
Ardrossan Ave GU15 .152 A3
Ardrossan Cl SL2 .22 B1
Ardwell Cl RG45 .142 C3
Arena L Ctr GU15 .151 B3
Arena The RG12 .118 A4
Arenal Dr RG45 .143 B2
Arethusa Way GU24 .153 C2
Argent Cl TW20 .96 B1
Argent Terr GU47 .150 C4
Argosy Gdns TW18 .96 C1
Argosy La TW19 .97 B4
Argyle Rd Newbury RG14 .104 C1
Reading RG1 .85 C4
Argyle St RG1 .85 C4
Argyll Ave SL1 .42 A3
Aries Ho HP10 .3 A4
Arkle Ave RG19 .105 C2
Arkley Ct SL6 .40 B1
Arkwright Dr RG42 .117 B4
Arkwright Rd Poyle SL3 .69 C3
Reading RG2 .86 A2
Arlington Bsns Pk RG7 .84 A2
Arlington Cl
Bracknell RG42 .118 A4
Maidenhead SL6 .39 A4
Arlington Rd TW15 .97 C2
Arlington Sq RG12 .118 A4
Armadale Ct RG30 .85 B3
Armitage Ct SL5 .120 B2
Armitage Dr GU16 .151 C1
Armour Hill RG31 .57 B1
Armour Rd RG31 .57 B1
Armour Wlk RG31 .57 B1
Armstrong Rd TW20 .95 B1
Armstrong Way RG5 .88 A4
Arncliffe RG12 .118 A2
Arndale Way TW20 .96 A2
Arnett Ave RG40 .141 C4
Arnewood Ave RG26 .135 B1
Arnhem Rd RG14 .105 A2
Arnold Rd TW18 .97 B1
Arnside Cl RG10 .61 B4
Arnwood RG41 .115 C4
Arrowhead Rd RG7 .83 C1
Arrowsmith Way RG19 .106 C1
Artemis Ho RG14 .105 A2
Arthur Cl GU19 .145 C1
Arthur Pl RG1 .86 B4
Arthur Rd Newbury RG14 .104 C1
Slough SL1 .42 B2
Windsor SL4 .67 B3
Wokingham RG41 .116 A3
Arthurstone Birches RG42 .90 B2
Artillery Mews RG30 .85 B3
Arun Cl RG41 .88 A1
Arun Ct RG30 .85 B3
Arundel Cl SL6 .39 A4
Arundel Ct SL3 .43 B1
Arundel Rd Frimley GU15 .152 B2
Woodley RG5 .87 C4
Ascot Heath Inf Sch SL5 .92 C1
Ascot Heath Jun Sch SL5 .92 C1
Ascot Race Course SL5 .119 C3
Ascot Rd
East Bedfont TW14 .98 A3
Holyport SL6 .65 A4
Newell Green RG42 .91 C4
Ascot Sta SL5 .120 A3
Ascot Twrs SL5 .119 C4
Ascot Wood SL5 .120 A3
Ash Cl Blackwater GU17 .150 B3
Brightwalton RG20 .28 B2
Slough SL3 .44 A2
Ash Copse RG4 .59 C4
Ash Ct Ashford TW15 .98 B2
Caversham RG4 .59 A2
16 Newbury RG14 .105 A2
Ash Gate RG18 .106 C2
Ash Gn RG2 .113 B4
Ash Gr Bradfield RG7 .82 A1
East Bedfont TW14 .98 C4
Staines TW18 .97 B1
Stoke Poges SL2 .22 C3
Ash La
Burghfield Common RG7 .111 A2
Tadley RG26 .134 C1
Windsor SL4 .66 B3
Ash Lodge 6 TW16 .98 C1
Ash Rd Littleton TW17 .125 A3
Newtown RG20 .131 C1
Reading RG30 .84 C4
Ash Terr RG18 .106 A4
Ash Tree Gr RG20 .129 A4
Ash Way RG41 .115 B2
Ashampstead Rd
Bradfield RG7 .82 A4
Reading RG30 .85 A2
Upper Basildon RG8 .55 A3
Ashbourne RG12 .117 C2
Ashbourne Gr SL6 .39 B2
Ashbourne Ho 5 SL1 .42 C2
Ashbourne Way RG19 .106 A2
Ashbrook Rd SL4 .95 A4
Ashburton Rd RG2 .86 B1
Ashbury Dr
Farnborough (Hants) GU17 .151 A1
Reading RG31 .84 B4
Ashby Ct RG2 .113 A4
Ashby Way UB7 .71 A4
Ashcroft Cl RG4 .58 C3
Ashcroft Ct SL1 .21 A2
Ashcroft Rd SL6 .39 B4
Ashdale Cl TW19 .97 C3
Ashdale Pk RG40 .142 B3
Ashdene Cl TW15 .98 B1
Ashdene Ho TW20 .95 B1
Ashdown SL6 .20 A2
Ashdown Cl RG12 .119 A4

Ashdown Ho 13 RG30 85 C3
Ashen Cross SL3 44 A4
Ashenden Wlk SL2 22 B4
Asher Dr SL5 119 B4
Ashes The RG7 113 A1
Ashfield Gn GU46 149 C3
Ashford Ave TW15 98 A1
Ashford CE Prim Sch TW15 98 A1
Ashford Cl TW15 97 C2
Ashford Cres TW15 97 C3
Ashford High Sch The TW15 97 C3
Ashford Hill Cty Prim Sch RG19 133 C1
Ashford Hill Rd RG19 132 C1
Ashford Hospl TW15 97 C3
Ashford Ind Est TW15 98 B2
Ashford La SL4 41 A2
Ashford Manor Golf Club TW15 97 C1
Ashford Park Cty Prim Sch TW15 97 B2
Ashford Rd
Feltham TW13, TW15 98 C3
Littleton TW15 98 B1
Staines TW18 124 B4
Ashford Sta TW15 97 C3
Ashgrove Rd TW15 98 B2
Ashlea Ho TW15 97 C2
Ashleigh Ave TW20 96 B1
Ashley HP10 3 C4
Ashley Cl Earley RG6 87 A1
Walton-on-T KT12, KT13 125 C1
Ashley Ct SL6 40 A4
Ashley Dr GU17 150 B2
Ashley Hill Pl RG10 36 C4
Ashley Park Ave KT12 125 C1
Ashley Pk SL6 20 A1
Ashley Rd RG1 85 C3
Ashley Way GU24 153 B3
Ashman Rd RG19 107 A2
Ashmead Sch RG2 86 B1
Ashmere Cl RG31 84 B2
Ashmere Terr RG30 85 C4
Ashmore Green Rd RG18 106 A4
Ashmore Rd RG2 86 B1
Ashridge Ct 7 RG14 105 A1
Ashridge Gn 3 RG42 118 A4
Ashridge Rd RG40 116 B4
Ashton Cl RG31 84 B4
Ashton Pl Kintbury RG17 102 A1
Maidenhead SL6 39 A3
Ashton Rd Newbury RG14 105 A1
Wokingham RG41 88 C1
Ashtree Ct TW15 98 A2
Ashtrees Rd RG5 87 C4
Ashurst Dr TW17 124 C3
Ashview Cl TW15 97 C2
Ashview Gdns TW15 97 C2
Ashville Way RG41 116 A3
Ashwell Ave GU15 151 C3
Ashwell Ct TW15 97 C3
Ashwood RG5 87 B2
Ashwood Cl RG31 84 A3
Ashwood Dr RG14 105 B2
Ashwood Rd TW20 95 A1
Ashworth Dr RG19 106 B1
Askew Dr RG7 113 A2
Aspect Park Golf Ctr RG9 16 B1
Aspen Cl Slough SL2 42 A4
Staines TW18 96 C3
Aspen Gdns TW15 98 B2
Aspin Way GU17 150 A3
Astleham Rd TW17 124 C3
Astley Cl RG41 115 C4
Aston Ave RG31 84 A4
Aston Cl RG8 56 B3
Aston Ct RG30 85 A3
Aston Ferry La RG9 16 B3
Aston La RG9 16 B2
Aston Mead SL4 66 C3
Aston St OX11 12 C4
Aston Villas SL2 22 B4
Astor Cl Maidenhead SL6 40 A3
Winnersh RG41 88 B2
Astra Mead RG42 92 A1
Atfield Gr GU20 146 B2
Atherton Cl Reading RG30 84 C4
Stanwell TW19 70 B1
Atherton Cres RG17 100 B3
Atherton Ct SL4 67 B4
Atherton Pl RG17 25 A2
Atherton Rd RG17 100 B3
Athlone Cl SL6 19 C1
Atrebatti Rd GU47 143 B1
Atte La RG42 91 B1
Attebrouche Ct RG12 118 B1
Auburn Ct RG4 59 A1
Auckland Cl SL6 40 A4
Auckland Rd RG6 87 A3
Auclum Cl RG7 111 A1
Auclum La RG7 111 A1
Audley Cl RG14 105 B3
Audley Dr SL6 39 A3
Audley St RG30 85 C4
Audley Way SL5 119 B3
Augur Cl TW18 96 C2
August End Reading RG30 85 B4
Slough SL3 43 C4
Augustine Cl SL3 69 C2
Augustine Wlk RG42 91 C1
Augustus Gdns GU15 152 B3
Austen Gdns RG14 131 A4
Austin Rd RG5 87 C3
Austins Gate SL6 38 C4
Australia Ave SL6 39 C4
Australia Rd SL1 43 A2
Auton Pl RG9 35 B4
Autumn Cl Caversham RG4 59 B4
Slough SL1 41 C3
Autumn Wlk
Maidenhead SL6 39 A3
Wargrave RG10 36 B1
Avalon Rd Bourne End SL8 3 A3
Earley RG6 87 B2
Avebury Bracknell RG12 118 A2
Slough SL1 42 A3
Avebury Sq RG1 86 B3
Aveley Wlk 26 RG1 86 A3
Avenue Rd Egham TW18 96 B2
Feltham TW13 98 C3
Maidenhead SL6 40 A3
Avenue Sch The RG2 86 B2
Avenue Sucy GU15 151 A2
Avenue The Bourne End SL8 3 A2
Camberley GU15 151 A3
Crowthorne RG45 143 A3
Datchet SL3 68 A3
Egham TW20 96 A2
Farnham Common SL2 22 A4
Lightwater GU18 146 A1
Maidenhead SL6 20 B2
Mortimer RG7 137 A3
North Ascot SL5 92 C1
Old Windsor SL4 68 A1
Staines TW18 124 A4
Wraysbury TW19 68 B2
Averil Ct SL6 41 B4
Avery Cl RG40 141 C3
Avington Cl RG31 84 A4
Avocet Cres GU47 150 C4
Avocet Ct 4 RG1 86 A3
Avon Cl Reading RG31 84 C3
Slough SL1 41 C3
Avon Gr RG12 91 B1
Avon Pl RG1 86 B4
Avon Rd TW16 98 C1
Avon Way RG7 109 C3
Avondale SL6 19 B1
Avondale Ave TW18 96 C1
Avondale Rd TW15, TW19 97 B3
Avonway RG14 105 B2
Axbridge RG12 118 C2
Axbridge Rd RG2 86 B1
Ayebridges Ave TW20 96 B1
Aylesbury Cres SL1 42 B4
Aylesford Way RG19 107 A1
Aylesham Way GU46 149 A3
Aylesworth Ave SL2 22 A1
Aylesworth Spur SL4 95 A4
Aylsham Cl RG30 84 C4
Aymer Cl TW18 123 C4
Aymer Dr TW18 123 C4
Ayrton Senna Rd RG31 84 B4
Aysgarth RG12 118 A2
Aysgarth Pk SL6 40 A1
Azalea Cl RG41 88 A1
Azalea Way Frimley GU15 152 A3
Slough SL3 43 C4

B

Babbington Rd RG2 113 B3
Bachelors Acre SL4 67 B3
Back La Beenham RG7 109 A4
Brimpton RG7 134 B2
Kintbury RG17 127 C4
Shinfield RG7 139 A4
Silchester RG7 136 B2
Stanford Dingley RG7 81 C2
Back St RG17 47 B3
Backsideans RG10 36 B1
Bacon Cl GU47 150 B3
Bad Godesberg Way SL6 39 C4
Baden Cl TW18 97 A1
Bader Gdns SL1 42 A2
Bader Way The RG5 88 A3
Badgebury Rise SL7 1 B4
Badgemoor La RG9 15 B2
Badgemore Cty Prim Sch RG9 15 B1
Badger Cl SL6 39 B2
Badger Dr
Lightwater GU18 146 A1
Twyford RG10 61 B4
Badgers Cl TW15 97 C2
Badgers Copse GU15 151 C2
Badgers Croft RG7 137 A3
Badgers Glade RG7 111 A1
Badgers Hill GU25 122 B2
Badgers Holt GU46 149 A3
Badgers Ridge RG20 130 B2
Badgers Rise RG4 59 A3
Badgers Sett RG45 142 C3
Badgers Way
Bracknell RG12 118 C4
Marlow Bottom SL7 1 B4
Badgers Wlk RG9 36 A2
Badgers Wood SL2 22 B4
Badgerwood Dr GU16 151 B1
Badminton Rd SL6 39 A3
Bagnols Way RG14 104 C1
Bagshot Cty Inf Sch GU19 145 C1
Bagshot Gn GU19 145 C2
Bagshot Rd Ascot SL5 120 B1
Bracknell RG12 118 B2
Englefield Green TW20 95 B1
West End GU24 153 C4
Bagshot Sta GU19 145 C2
Baigents La GU20 146 B2
Bailey Cl Maidenhead SL6 39 C4
Windsor SL4 67 A3
Bailey Ho 7 SL8 3 A2
Bailey's La RG10 62 C2
Baileys Cl GU17 150 B2
Baily Ave RG18 106 A2
Bain Ave GU15 151 A1
Bainbridge Rd RG31 84 A2
Bainhurst Cotts SL6 38 A3
Baird Cl SL1 42 A2
Baird Rd RG2 140 C4
Bakeham La TW20 95 B1
Baker St Aston Tirrold OX11 12 C4
Reading RG1 85 C4
Baker's Orch HP10 3 C3
Bakers Ct TW19 70 B1
Bakers La SL6 38 C4
Baldwin Rd SL1 21 B1
Baldwin's Shore SL4 67 B4
Balfour Cres
Bracknell RG12 118 A2
Newbury RG14 130 B3
Balfour Dr RG31 84 A2
Balfour Pl SL7 1 B2
Balintore Ct 8 GU47 150 B4
Ball Pit Rd RG20 30 A3
Ballamoor Cl RG31 84 A2
Ballard Ct GU15 152 A4
Ballard Gn SL4 66 C4
Ballard Rd GU15 152 A4
Ballencrieff Rd SL5 120 C1
Balliol Rd RG4 58 B2
Balliol Way GU47 143 C1
Balme Cl RG10 61 A2
Balmoral SL6 19 A1
Balmoral Cl SL1 41 C4
Balmoral Gdns SL4 67 B2
Balmoral Grange TW18 124 A4
Balmore Dr RG4 59 A2
Balmore Ho RG4 59 A2
Balmore Pk RG4 59 A2
Bamburgh Cl RG2 86 B2
Bamford Pl RG31 84 A2
Banbury RG12 118 C1
Banbury Ave SL1 41 C4
Banbury Cl RG41 116 A3
Banbury Gdns RG4 59 B2
Bancroft Cl TW15 98 A2
Bancroft Pl RG31 84 A2
Band La 1 TW20 96 A2
Bangors Cl SL0 44 C4
Bangors Rd S SL0 44 C4
Bank Side RG40 141 C3
Banks Spur SL1 42 A2
Bankside Cl RG2 86 B1
Bannard Rd SL6 39 A3
Bannister Cl SL3 43 C2
Bannister Gdns GU46 149 C3
Bannister Pl RG7 133 C3
Bannister Rd RG7 110 C1
Barbara Cl TW17 125 A2
Barbaras Mdw RG31 57 A1
Barbel Cl RG6 87 A4
Barber Cl RG10 88 C4
Barberry Way GU17 150 C1
Barbon Cl GU15 152 B2
Barbrook Cl RG31 57 B2
Barchester Rd SL3 43 C2
Barclay Rd RG31 84 B2
Barclose Ave RG4 59 B2
Bardney Cl SL6 39 B2
Bardolphs Cl RG4 58 B4
Bardown RG20 51 A1
Barefoot Cl RG31 57 A1
Barfield Rd RG18 106 A2
Barge La RG7 139 A3
Bargeman Rd SL6 39 C3
Barholm Cl RG6 87 C1
Barkby RG6 87 B1
Barker Cl RG2 140 C4
Barker Ct RG10 88 C4
Barker Gn RG12 118 A2
Barker Rd KT16 123 C1
Barkham Manor RG41 115 B2
Barkham Rd
Barkham RG41 115 B2
Wokingham RG41 116 A3
Barkham Ride
Barkham RG40 115 B1
Wokingham RG40 141 C4
Barkham St RG40 115 B1
Barkhart Dr RG40 116 B4
Barkhart Gdns RG40 116 B4
Barkis Mead GU47 143 C1
Barkwith Cl RG6 87 C1
Barley Cl RG19 106 C1
Barley Fields HP10 3 C4
Barley Mead RG42 91 C1
Barley Mow Rd TW20 95 B2
Barley Mow Way TW17 125 A3
Barley Way 6 SL7 1 B1
Barley Wlk RG31 84 A3
Barn Cl Ashford TW15 98 A2
Bracknell RG12 118 B4
Camberley GU15 151 C3
Farnham Common SL2 22 A4
Kintbury RG17 102 A1
Maidenhead SL6 19 C1
Reading RG30 85 B2
Barn Cotts RG17 74 B4
Barn Cres RG14 130 B4
Barn Dr SL6 39 A2
Barn La RG9 15 B2
Barn Owl Way RG7 111 A2
Barnard Cl RG4 59 B3
Barnards Hill SL7 1 B1
Barnes Way SL0 44 C3
Barnett Ct RG12 118 B4
Barnett Gn RG12 118 A2
Barnett La GU18 152 C4
Barnfield Iver SL0 44 C4
Slough SL1 41 B3
Barnfield Cl SL6 19 C3
Barnhill Cl SL7 1 B2
Barnhill Gdns SL7 1 B2
Barnhill Rd SL7 1 B2
Barnsdale Rd RG2 86 B2
Barnway TW20 95 B2
Barnwood Cl RG30 85 C4
Baroma Way RG9 15 C1
Baron Ct RG30 85 C4
Barons Mead RG9 15 B1
Barons Way TW20 96 B1
Barossa Rd GU15 151 B4
Barr's Rd SL6 41 A4
Barracane Dr RG45 143 A3
Barrack La SL4 67 B3
Barracks La RG7 113 A1
Barrett Cres RG40 116 C3
Barrington Cl RG6 87 A3
Barrington Ct TW18 96 C1
Barrington Ho RG2 113 A4
Barrington Way RG30 85 C3
Barry Ave SL4 67 B4
Barry Pl RG1 86 A4
Barry Sq RG12 118 B1
Barry Terr TW15 97 C3
Barry View SL4 66 B3
Bartelotts Rd SL2 21 C1
Bartholemew Pl RG42 91 C1
Bartholomew Ct RG14 104 C1
Bartholomew St RG14 104 C1
Bartlemy Cl RG14 130 C4
Bartlemy Rd RG14 130 C4
Bartletts La SL6 65 A4
Barton Cl TW17 125 A2
Barton Rd Reading RG31 84 A4
Slough SL3 43 C2
Bartons Dr GU46 149 B2
Barwell Cl RG45 142 C2
Basemoors RG12 118 C4
Basford Way SL4 66 B2
Basil Cl RG6 86 C1
Basildon CE Prim Sch RG8 55 A3
Basingstoke Rd
Aldermaston RG7 109 A1
Reading RG2 86 A2
Swallowfield RG7 139 B3
Baskerville La RG9 36 A2
Baslow Rd RG41 88 A1
Basmore La RG9 36 A2
Bass Mead SL6 19 C3
Bassett Cl RG6 114 B4
Bassett Rd OX12 6 C4
Bassett Way SL2 21 C1
Batcombe Mead RG12 118 C1
Bates Cl SL3 43 C4
Bath Ct SL6 39 B3
Bath Rd Camberley GU15 151 B3
Froxfield SN8,RG17 99 B2
Harlington TW6, UB7 71 B3
Harmondsworth TW6, UB7 70 C3
Hungerford RG17 100 C4
Knowl Hill RG10 37 B2
Littlewick Green SL6 38 B3
Maidenhead SL6 39 B3
Newbury RG14 104 B2
Poyle SL3, UB7 69 C3
Reading RG30, RG31 85 B3
Slough SL1,SL6 41 B3
Sonning RG4 60 C1
Thatcham RG7,RG19 107 B1
Woolhampton RG7 108 B1
Bathurst Cl SL0 44 C2
Bathurst Rd RG41 88 A1
Bathurst Wlk SL0 44 C2
Battery End RG14 130 B3
Battle Cl RG14 104 B2
Battle Hospl RG30 85 B4
Battle Prim Sch RG30 85 B4
Battle Rd Goring RG8 34 C4
Newbury RG14 130 B3
Battle St RG1 85 C4
Battlemead Cl SL6 20 B2
Batty's Barn Cl RG40 116 B3
Baxendales The RG14 105 B1
Baxter Cl SL1 42 C2
Bay Cl RG6 86 C1
Bay Dr RG12 118 C4
Bay Rd RG12 118 C4
Bay Tree Ct SL1 21 B1
Bay Tree Rise RG31 84 B3
Baydon Dr RG1 85 C3
Baydon Rd RG17 24 C1
Bayfield Ave GU16 151 C1
Bayford Cl GU17 151 A1
Bayford Dr RG31 84 C2
Bayley Cres SL1 41 A4
Bayley Ct RG41 88 A1
Baylis Court Sch SL1,SL2 42 B4
Baylis Par SL1 42 C4
Baylis Rd SL1 42 C3
Bayliss Rd RG10 36 B1
Baysfarm Ct TW6, UB7 70 B3
Beach's Ho TW18 97 A2
Beacon Ct Colnbrook SW3 69 B4
3 Reading RG30 85 B3
Beacon Rd TW19, TW6 71 A1
Beacon Rdbt TW6 71 A1
Beaconsfield Cotts SL8 3 A1
Beaconsfield Rd SL2 22 B3
Beaconsfield Way RG6 87 A1
Beacontree Plaza RG2 86 A1
Beal's La RG31 84 A4
Beale Cl RG40 116 A4
Beale Park Wildlife Pk RG8 55 C4
Beales Farm Rd RG17 25 A1
Bean Oak Rd RG40 116 C3
Beancroft Rd RG19 106 B1
Bear La Newbury RG14 105 A2
Wargrave RG10 37 A2
Beard's Rd TW15 98 C1
Bearfield La RG17 73 A4
Bears Rails Pk SL4 94 C4
Bearwater RG17 100 B3
Bearwood Coll RG41 115 A4
Bearwood Path RG41 88 A1
Bearwood Prim Sch RG41 115 A4
Bearwood Rd RG41 115 B3
Beasley's Ait TW16,TW17 125 C2
Beasley's Ait La TW16, TW17 125 C2
Beattie Cl TW14 98 C4
Beatty Dr RG30 84 C4
Beauchief Cl RG6 113 C4
Beaufield Cl RG5 87 B4
Beaufort Cl SL7 1 C1
Beaufort Gdns Marlow SL7 1 C1
North Ascot SL5 119 C4
Beaufort Pl SL6 40 B2
Beauforts TW20 95 B2
Beaufront Cl GU15 152 A4
Beaufront Rd GU15 152 A4
Beaulieu Cl
Bracknell RG12 119 A3
Datchet SL3 68 A3
Beaulieu Gdns GU17 150 B3
Beaumaris Ct SL1 42 B4
Beaumont Cl SL6 39 A2
Beaumont Cotts 1 SL4 67 B3
Beaumont Ct Ascot SL5 119 C3
Slough SL3 43 B4
Beaumont Dr TW15 98 B2
Beaumont Gdns RG12 118 C2
Beaumont Rd Slough SL2 42 B4
Windsor SL4 67 B3
Beaumont Rise SL7 1 C1
Beaver Cl RG41 116 A2
Beaver La GU46 149 C3
Beaver Way RG5 88 A4
Beavers Cl RG26 135 A1
Beck Ct RG1 86 B3
Beckett Cl RG40 116 C3
Beckford Ave RG12 118 A2
Beckford Cl RG41 88 C1
Beckford Ct RG19 106 B2
Beckfords RG8 55 A3
Beckins Way HP10 3 B4
Bede Wlk RG2 86 B2
Bedfont Cl TW14 71 B1
Bedfont Court Est TW19 70 A2
Bedfont Ct TW19 70 A2
Bedfont Green Cl TW14 98 B4
Bedfont Ho TW14 98 C4
Bedfont Ind Pk N TW15 98 B3
Bedfont Inf Sch TW14 71 C1
Bedfont Jun Sch TW14 71 C1
Bedfont La TW14, TW13 98 C4
Bedfont Lakes Ctry Pk TW14 98 B3
Bedfont Rd
Feltham TW13, TW14 98 B3
Stanwell TW19 70 C1
Bedford Ave SL1 42 A4
Bedford Cl Maidenhead SL6 39 A2
Newbury RG14 130 B3
Bedford Dr SL2 22 A3
Bedford Gdns RG41 115 C4
Bedford La SL5 121 A2
Bedford Rd RG1 85 C4
Bedfordshire Down RG42 91 C1
Bedfordshire Way RG41 115 C3
Bedwins La SL6 19 A3
Beech RG9 15 B1
Beech Ave GU15 151 B2
Beech Cl Ashford TW15 98 B2
Burghfield Common RG30 111 A2
Hampstead Norreys RG18 53 A3
Maidenhead SL6 39 A4
Stanwell TW19 97 B4
Beech Ct Caversham RG4 59 A2
1 Marlow SL7 1 C1
15 Newbury RG14 105 A2
Beech Dr GU17 150 B2
Beech Glen RG12 118 A3
Beech Hill Rd
Beech Hill RG7 138 C3
Sunningdale SL5 120 C2
Beech La RG6 87 A1
Beech Lodge TW18 96 C2
Beech Rd
East Bedfont TW14 98 C4
Mapledurham RG4 58 B4
Newtown RG20 132 A2
Purley on T RG8 57 A3
Reading RG2 86 C1
Slough SL3 43 C2
Beech Ride GU47 143 A1
Beech Tree La TW18 124 A4
Beech Wlk RG19 106 C1
Beecham Rd RG30 85 B4
Beechbrook Ave GU46 149 B3
Beechcroft RG18 53 A3
Beechcroft Cl SL5 120 B3
Beechcroft Ct RG12 118 A3
Beeches Dr SL2 22 A4
Beeches Rd SL2 22 A4
Beeches The Goring RG8 34 A3
Reading RG31 57 B2
Staines TW18 97 A2

Beechfield RG13 80 B4
Beechingstoke 4 SL7 1 C2
Beechmont Ave GU25 122 B2
Beechnut Cl RG41 115 C3
Beechnut Dr GU17 150 A3
Beechtree Ave
Englefield Green TW20 95 A1
Marlow Bottom SL7 1 B3
Beechwood Ave
Reading RG31 84 B4
Staines TW18 97 A1
Woodley RG5 87 B4
Beechwood Cl SL5 92 C1
Beechwood Dr
Maidenhead SL6 39 A3
Marlow SL7 18 A4
Beechwood Gdns SL1 42 C2
Beechwood Prim Schs
RG5 87 C4
Beechwood Rd Slough SL2 42 B4
Wentworth GU25 122 A1
Beechwood Sec Sch SL2 22 A1
Beedon CE Prim Sch
RG20 51 B4
Beedon Dr RG12 117 C2
Beehive La RG12 117 B4
Beehive Rd
Bracknell RG12, RG42 117 B4
Staines TW18 96 C2
Beenham Cty Prim Sch
RG7 108 C3
Beeston Way RG6 114 A4
Beggars Hill Rd RG10 61 A1
Beighton Cl RG6 113 C4
Belfast Ave SL1 42 B4
Belford Ct 13 RG1 86 A3
Belgrave Ct GU17 150 B2
Belgrave Par SL1 42 C3
Belgrave Rd SL1 42 C3
Belgravia Ct 22 RG30 85 B3
Bell Bridge Rd KT16 123 C1
Bell Bsns Ctr SL6 39 C3
Bell Cl SL2 43 A4
Bell Cnr KT16 123 C1
Bell Ct SL6 17 C2
Bell Foundry La RG40 116 B4
Bell Hill RG14 130 A2
Bell Holt RG14 130 B3
Bell House Gdns RG41 116 A3
Bell La Aldworth RG8 32 C2
Blackwater GU17 150 B3
Eton SL4 41 C1
Henley-on-T RG9 15 C2
Inkpen RG17 127 B2
Bell Pl GU19 145 C2
Bell St Henley-on-T RG9 15 C1
Maidenhead SL6 39 C3
Bell View SL4 66 C3
Bell View Cl SL4 66 C3
Bell Weir Cl TW19 96 A3
Belle Ave RG6 87 A3
Belle Vue Cl TW18 124 A4
Belle Vue Rd
Henley-on-T RG9 35 B4
Reading RG1 85 C4
Belleisle RG8 57 A3
Bellever Hill GU15 151 C3
Bellevue Terr 15 RG1 85 C4
Bellingham Cl GU15 152 B2
Bellingham Wlk RG4 59 A3
Bellman Ct 1 RG1 86 A4
Bells Hill SL2 23 A2
Bells Hill Gn SL2 23 A3
Bells La SL3 69 A2
Bellsfield Ct SL4 41 C1
Bellswood La SL0 44 A4
Belmont SL2 42 A4
Belmont Cotts SL3 69 B4
Belmont Cres SL6 39 B4
Belmont Dr SL6 39 B4
Belmont Mews GU15 151 B2
Belmont Park Ave SL6 39 B4
Belmont Park Rd SL6 39 B4
Belmont Rd
Camberley GU15 151 B2
Crowthorne RG45 143 A3
Maidenhead SL6 39 B4
Reading RG30 85 B4
Belmont Vale SL6 39 B4
Belton Rd GU15 151 C3
Belvedere Ct GU17 150 B2
Belvedere Dr RG14 131 A4
Belvedere Mans SL1 42 B2
Belvedere Wlk RG41 88 A2
Belvoir Cl GU16 151 C1
Bembridge Ct 20 SL1 42 C2
Bembridge Pl RG1 86 B4
Benbricke Gn RG42 91 A1
Bence The TW20 123 A3
Bencombe Rd SL7 1 C3
Benedict Dr TW14 98 B4
Benedict Gn RG42 91 C1
Benen-Stock Rd TW19 70 A1
Benetfeld Rd RG42 90 A1
Benett Cl RG14 104 C3
Benett Gdns RG14 104 C3
Benham Chase RG20 103 C3
Benham Hill
Newbury RG18 105 C2
Thatcham RG18 106 A2
Benham La RG7 139 B2
Benhams La RG9 15 C4
Benjamin Ct TW15 98 B1
Benner La GU24 153 C4
Bennet Ct RG2 86 A1
Bennet Rd RG2 86 A1
Bennett Ct GU15 151 B3
Bennetts Cl SL1 42 A3
Bennetts Hill RG7,RG30 111 B4
Benning Cl SL4 66 B2
Bennings Cl RG42 91 A1
Bensington Ct TW14 71 B1
Benson Cl Reading RG2 86 B2
Slough SL2 43 A3
Benson Rd RG45 142 C3
Bentley Copse GU15 152 A2
Bentley Pk SL2 21 B2
Bentley Rd SL1 42 A3
Benyon Ct RG1 85 C3
Benyon Mews RG1 85 C3
Beomonds 5 KT16 124 A1
Beomonds Row 2 KT16 124 A1
Bere Court Rd RG8 56 A2
Bere Rd RG12 118 C2
Beresford Ave SL2 43 B3
Beresford Rd RG30 85 C4
Bergenia Ct GU24 153 C3
Berkeley Ave RG1 85 C3
Berkeley Cl TW19 96 B3
Berkeley Ct 1 RG1 85 C3
Berkeley Dr SL4 93 A4
Berkeley Gdns KT12 125 C1
Berkeley Mews SL7 1 C1
Berkeley Rd RG14 104 C1
Berkley Cl SL6 39 A4
Berkshire Ave SL1 42 A4
Berkshire Bsns Ctr RG19 107 A1
Berkshire Coll
of Agriculture SL6 18 A1
Berkshire Coll
of Agriculture
(Hall Place) SL6 38 A4
Berkshire Dr Reading RG31 84 B4
Thatcham RG19 107 A1
Berkshire Ind Hospl RG1 85 C3
Berkshire Lodge 1 SL6 39 C3
Berkshire Rd
Camberley GU15 151 C4
Henley-on-T RG9 35 B4
Berkshire Way RG12 117 B3
Bernadine Cl RG42 91 C1
Bernard Ct GU15 151 A2
Berners Cl SL1 41 C3
Bernersh Cl GU47 143 B1
Berries Rd SL6 20 A4
Berry Field SL2 43 B4
Berry Hill SL6 40 B4
Berry Hill Ct SL6 40 B4
Berrybank GU47 150 C3
Berrycroft RG12 118 B4
Berrylands Rd RG4 59 A2
Berrys La RG30 85 A1
Berrys Rd RG7 107 B3
Berryscroft Ct TW18 97 B1
Berryscroft Rd TW18 97 B1
Berstead Cl 3 RG6 87 A1
Berwick Ave SL1 42 A3
Berwick Cl SL7 1 B2
Berwick La SL7 1 B2
Berwick Rd SL7 1 B2
Berwyn Ho RG2 113 B4
Beryl Cl RG41 115 C4
Bessels Way OX11 12 A4
Bestobell Rd SL1 42 B4
Beswick Gdns RG12 118 C4
Beta Ho 6 RG30 85 B3
Beta Way TW20 123 B4
Betam Rd RG1 86 B4
Betchworth Ave RG6 87 A2
Bethany Waye TW14 98 C4
Bethesda Cl RG8 55 A3
Bethesda St RG8 55 A4
Betjeman Wlk GU46 149 A2
Betteridge Rd RG19 106 C1
Betty Grove La RG41 114 C4
Beverley Cl Frimley GU15 152 B3
Marlow SL7 1 A1
Thatcham RG18 106 B2
Beverley Ct SL1 43 A2
Beverley Gdns
Maidenhead SL6 19 A1
Wargrave RG10 36 C1
Beverley Rd Reading RG31 57 B1
Sunbury TW16 125 C4
Bevers The RG7 137 A3
Bexley Ct RG30 85 B3
Bexley St SL4 67 B3
Bibury Cl RG5 87 B2
Bicknell Rd GU16 151 C1
Biddles Cl 6 SL1 41 C3
Bideford Cl RG5 87 B3
Bideford Spur SL2 22 A1
Bier Path The RG8 14 A2
Bietigheim Way 2 GU15 151 B3
Big Barn Gr RG42 91 B1
Big La RG17 25 A2
Bigbury Gdns RG2 86 B2
Bigfrith La SL6 19 A3
Biggs La RG2,RG40 141 A4
Bill Hill Pk RG41 89 A2
Billet La SL0, SL3 44 A4
Billet Rd TW18, TW19 97 A3
Billing Ave RG40 141 C3
Billingbear La RG42 90 A3
Billington Way RG18 106 B3
Bilton Ind Est RG12 117 C3
Binbrook Cl RG6 87 B1
Binbury Row TW18 96 C2
Binfield CE Prim Sch
RG42 90 B1
Binfield Park Hospl RG42 90 B2
Binfield Rd
Bracknell, Priestwood RG42 91 A1
Wokingham RG40 116 C4
Bingham Dr TW18 97 B1
Bingham Rd SL1 41 A4
Binghams The SL6 40 A2
Bingley Gr RG5 60 C1
Binsted Dr GU17 150 B3
Birch Ave RG30 85 A4
Birch Cl GU15 151 C4
Birch Copse Prim Sch
RG31 84 B4
Birch Dr GU17 150 B2
Birch Gn Reading RG2 113 B4
Staines TW18 97 A2
Birch Gr Bracknell RG12 118 B3
Slough SL2 42 A4
Upper Halliford TW17 125 C4
Windsor SL4 66 B3
Birch Hill Prim Sch
RG12 118 A1
Birch Hill Rd RG12 118 A1
Birch La Mortimer RG7 136 C3
West End GU24 153 B4
Winkfield RG12, SL5 119 A4
Birch Platt GU24 153 B3
Birch Rd
Burghfield Common RG7 111 A2
Tadley RG26 134 C1
Windlesham GU20 146 C2
Wokingham RG40 142 A4
Birch Side RG45 143 A3
Birch Tree View GU18 146 A1
Birch View RG2 86 C1
Birches The
Blackwater GU17 150 A3
Goring RG8 34 A3
Birchetts Cl 2 RG42 118 A4
Birchfields GU15 151 B2
Birchington Rd SL4 67 A3
Birchland Cl RG7 136 C3
Birchlands Ct GU47 143 C1
Birchmead RG41 88 B1
Birchview Cl GU46 149 B2
Birchwood Cl RG4 59 B3
Birchwood Dr GU18 146 B1
Birchwood Rd RG14 105 B2
Birchwoods The RG31 84 A4
Bird Mews RG40 116 A3
Bird Mount Cotts SL4 67 B4
Birdhill Ave RG2 86 B1
Birds La RG7 107 C2
Birdwood Rd
Maidenhead SL6 39 A4
Sandhurst GU15 150 C3
Birkbeck Pl GU47 143 C1
Birkdale RG12 117 C1
Birkdale Ct SL5 120 B2
Birkhall Cl RG31 84 B3
Birley Rd SL1 42 B4
Biscuit Way RG2 112 C4
Bisham Abbey National
Sports Ctr SL7 18 B4
Bisham CE Prim Sch SL7 18 B4
Bisham Ct Bisham SL7 18 C3
10 Slough SL1 42 C2
Bisham Gn SL7 18 C3
Bishop Ct SL6 39 B3
Bishop Ctr The SL6 40 C4
Bishop Duppas Pk TW17 125 C1
Bishop Wand CE Sec Sch
TW16 125 C4
Bishop's La SL4 92 A4
Bishopdale RG12 118 A3
Bishops Cl RG26 135 A1
Bishops Ct TW16 98 C1
Bishops Dr
East Bedfont TW14 71 B1
Wokingham RG40 116 B4
Bishops Farm Cl SL4 66 A3
Bishops Gr GU20 146 B2
Bishops Orch SL2 22 A1
Bishops Rd Bradfield RG7 81 C2
Reading RG6 87 A3
Bishops Way TW20 96 B1
Bishops Wlk HP10 3 C3
Bishopsgate Sch TW20 95 A3
Bishopsgate Rd TW20 95 A3
Bishopswood Ct RG26 134 C1
Bishopswood La RG26 134 C1
Bishopswood Rd RG26 134 C1
Bispham Ct 2 RG1 86 B3
Bissley Dr SL6 39 A2
Bitham La Ham RG17 126 A3
Inkpen RG17 127 A2
Bitham Rd OX12 8 B4
Bittern Cl GU47 150 B4
Bitterne Ave RG31 84 A3
Bix Hill RG9 15 A3
Bix La SL5 38 C4
Black Boy La SL6 17 B2
Black Butts Cotts SL6 20 A4
Black Horse Cl SL4 66 B3
Black Lake Cl TW20 123 A4
Black Park Ctry Pk SL3 23 C2
Black Park Rd SL3 23 C2
Blackberry Cl TW17 125 C3
Blackbird Cl
Burghfield Common RG7 111 A2
Sandhurst GU47 150 B4
Blackbird La RG20 132 A2
Blackburn Trad Est TW19 70 C1
Blackcap Pl GU47 150 C4
Blackdown Way RG19 106 B1
Blackett Cl TW18 123 C4
Blacklands Rd RG7 107 B3
Blackley Cl RG6 87 C2
Blackmeadows RG12 118 B2
Blackmoor Cl SL5 119 B4
Blackmoor Wood SL5 119 B4
Blacknest Gate Rd SL5 121 A3
Blacknest Rd GU25, SL5 121 C3
Blackpond La SL2 22 A2
Blacksmith Row SL3 44 A1
Blacksmith's La TW18 124 B3
Blacksmiths La KT16 124 A1
Blackstroud La E
GU18, GU24 153 C4
Blackstroud La W GU18 153 B4
Blackthorn Cl Earley RG6 87 A4
Purley on T RG31 57 A1
Blackthorn Dell SL3 43 B2
Blackthorn Dr
Lightwater GU18 153 A4
Thatcham RG18 106 B3
Blackthorne Cres SL3 69 C3
Blackthorne Rd SL3 69 C2
Blackwater Cl
Caversham RG4 59 C2
Shinfield RG7 113 A1
Blackwater Rise RG31 84 A2
Blackwater Sta GU17 150 C2
Blaenant RG4 58 C3
Blaenavon RG4 58 C3
Blagdon Cl RG19 131 B4
Blagdon Rd RG2 86 B1
Blagrave La RG4 58 B2
Blagrave Rise RG31 84 B3
Blagrave St RG1 86 A4
Blagrove Dr RG41 115 C2
Blagrove La RG41 115 C2
Blair Rd SL1 42 C3
Blaire Pk GU46 149 A4
Blake Cl Crowthorne RG45 143 B2
Wokingham RG40 116 C4
Blakeney Ct SL6 19 C1
Blakeney Fields RG17 48 A2
Blakes Cotts Reading RG1 86 B4
Wargrave RG10 37 A1
Blakes Ct 10 KT16 124 A1
Blakes La Tadley RG26 135 B1
Wargrave RG10 37 A1
Blakes Lock Mus RG1 86 B4
Blakes Rd RG10 36 C2
Blakes Ride GU46 149 A3
Blamire Dr RG42 90 C1
Blanchard Cl RG5 88 A4
Blandford Cl SL3 43 B2
Blandford Dr RG41 115 C2
Blandford Rd RG2 113 B4
Blandford Rd N SL3 43 B2
Blandford Rd S SL3 43 B2
Blands Cl RG7 110 C1
Blandy Rd RG9 35 B4
Blandys Hill RG17 128 A4
Blandys La RG8 55 A3
Blane's La SL5 119 B2
Blatchs Cl RG7 83 B2
Blay's La TW20 95 A1
Blays Cl TW20 95 B1
Bledlow Cl RG14 130 B3
Blenheim Cl Slough SL3 43 C3
Wokingham RG41 115 C3
Blenheim Cotts RG18 106 A4
Blenheim Ct Egham TW18 96 B2
19 Reading RG1 86 A3
Blenheim Gdns RG1 86 C3
Blenheim Rd
Caversham RG4 59 A2
Maidenhead SL6 39 A4
Newbury RG14 104 C1
Reading RG1 86 C3
Slough SL3 43 B1
Blenheim Terr 1 RG1 86 A3
Bletchmore Cl UB3 71 B4
Blewburton Wlk RG12 118 C3
Blewbury Dr RG31 84 A4
Blewbury Hill OX11 12 A4
Blinco La SL3 43 C4
Blind La
Bourne End HP10, SL8 3 A3
Lambourn RG17 25 A1
Blomfield Dale RG42 117 B4
Blondell Cl UB7 70 B4
Bloomfield Dr RG12 91 B1
Bloomfield Rd SL6 39 A3
Bloomfieldhatch La
Beech Hill RG7 138 A4
Shinfield RG7 112 C1
Bloomsbury Way GU17 150 B2
Blossom Ave RG7 83 C2
Blossom La RG7 83 C2
Blount Cres RG42 90 C1
Bloxworth Cl 17 RG12 118 C3
Blue Ball La TW20 95 C2
Blue Coat Wlk RG12 118 B2
Bluebell Dr RG7 110 C2
Bluebell Hill RG12 118 C4
Bluebell Mdw RG41 88 B2
Bluebell Rise GU18 153 A4
Bluebell Way RG18 106 B3
Bluecoats RG18 106 B2
Bluethroat Cl GU47 150 C4
Blumfield Cres SL1 41 C4
Blumfield Ct SL1 21 B1
Blundells Rd RG30 84 C4
Blunden Dr SL3 44 B1
Blunts Ave UB7 71 A4
Blyth Ave RG19 106 C1
Blyth Wlk 31 RG1 86 A3
Blythe Cl SL0 44 C4
Blythewood La SL5 119 C4
Blythwood Dr GU16 151 B1
Boames La RG20 129 C3
Boarlands Cl SL1 41 C3
Boathouse Reach RG9 15 C1
Bobgreen Ct RG2 113 B3
Bobmore La SL7 1 C2
Bockhampton Rd RG17 25 B1
Bockmer La SL7 17 A4
Bodens Ride SL5 119 C1
Bodin Gdns RG14 131 A4
Bodmin Ave SL2 42 A4
Bodmin Cl RG19 106 B1
Bodmin Rd RG5 87 B3
Body Rd RG1 85 C4
Bog La RG12 119 A3
Bohams Rd OX11 11 B3
Bold's Ct SL2 23 A3
Bolding House La GU24 153 C4
Boldrewood RG7 110 C1
Boleyn Cl TW18 96 C2
Bolingbroke Way RG19 106 C2
Bolney Rd RG9 36 A3
Bolney Trevor Dr RG9 36 A2
Bolton Ave SL4 67 B2
Bolton Cres SL4 67 B2
Bolton Rd SL4 67 B2
Bolton Row RG20 50 B4
Bolton's La UB3 71 B4
Boltons La RG42 90 C1
Bolwell Cl RG10 61 C2
Bomer Cl UB7 71 A4
Bomford Cl RG18 78 C3
Bond St TW20 95 B2
Bone La RG14 105 B2
Bonemill La RG20 104 B1
Bones La RG9 35 A2
Boot End RG2 112 C4
Booth Dr TW18 97 B1
Borderside Slough SL2 43 A4
Yateley GU46 149 A3
Borrowdale Cl TW20 96 A1
Borrowdale Gdns GU15 152 B2
Borrowdale Rd RG41 88 A2
Boscombe Cl TW20 123 B4
Boscowen Way RG19 107 A1
Bosham Cl RG6 114 A4
Boshers Gdns TW20 95 C1
Bosman Dr GU20 146 A3
Bossington Ct TW18 96 C2
Bostock La RG7 83 A1
Boston Ave RG1 85 C3
Boston Dr SL8 3 A2
Boston Gr SL1 42 B4
Boston Rd RG9 35 C4
Bosworth Gdns RG5 87 C2
Botany Cl RG19 106 C2
Botham Dr SL1 42 C2
Bothy The RG10 36 B1
Botmoor Way RG20 48 C4
Bottisham Cl RG6 114 B4
Bottle La Knowl Hill SL6 38 A1
Newell Green RG42 91 A3
Bottom La RG7 110 B4
Bottom Waltons
Caravan Site SL2 21 C2
Bouldish Farm Rd SL5 120 A3
Boult St RG1 86 B4
Boulters Cl
Maidenhead SL6 20 B1
Slough SL1 42 A2
Woodley RG5 87 C4
Boulters Ct SL6 20 B1
Boulters Gdns SL6 20 B1
Boulters Ho 3 RG12 118 C3
Boulters La SL6 20 B1
Boulton Rd RG2 86 A2
Boults Wlk RG2 86 A3
Boundary Cl RG31 84 B3
Boundary La RG4 58 C2
Boundary Pl HP10 3 B4
Boundary Rd
Newbury RG14 105 A1
Staines TW15 97 B2
Taplow SL6 40 C4
Wooburn Green HP10 3 B4
Bourn Cl RG6 87 B1
Bourne Arch RG18 106 A2
Bourne Ave
Chertsey KT16 124 A3
Reading RG2 86 A2
Windsor SL4 67 B2
Bourne Cl Bourne End SL8 3 A3
Reading RG31 84 A2
Bourne End Bsns Ctr 8
SL8 3 A2
Bourne End Rd SL6,SL8 20 C4
Bourne End Sta SL8 3 A2
Bourne Ho TW15 98 A2
Bourne Mdw TW20 123 A3
Bourne Rd Pangbourne RG8 56 C3
Slough SL1 42 B2
Thatcham RG19 106 A2
Wentworth GU25 122 B2
Bourne-Stevens Cl RG1 86 A4
Bourne Vale RG17 100 B3
Bourneside GU25 122 A1
Bourton Cl RG30 84 C4
Bouverie Way SL3 43 C1
Boveney Cl SL1 42 A2
Boveney Ho 2 RG12 118 C3
Boveney New Rd SL4 41 C1
Boveney Rd SL4 41 B1
Bovingdon Hts SL7 1 A1
Bowden Cl TW14 98 C4
Bowden Rd SL5 120 B2
Bowdown Ct RG14 104 C1
Bower Ct 3 SL1 41 C3
Bower Way SL1 41 C3
Bowes Rd Egham TW18 96 C1
Thatcham RG19 106 B1
Bowes-Lyon Cl 7 SL4 67 B3
Bowfell Cl RG31 57 B1
Bowland Dr RG12 118 C1
Bowling Ct RG9 15 B2

Bowling Green La RG8 57 A3
Bowling Green Rd RG18 106 A3
Bowlings The GU15 151 B3
Bowman Ct RG45 142 C2
Bowmans Cl SL1 21 A2
Bowry Dr TW19 68 C1
Bowyer Cres RG40 116 B4
Bowyer Dr SL1 41 C3
Bowyer Wlk SL5 119 C4
Bowyers La RG42 91 B3
Boxford Ridge RG12 118 A3
Boxshall Ct RG14 104 C1
Boyd Ct RG42 118 A4
Boyn Hill Ave SL6 39 B3
Boyn Hill Cl SL6 39 B3
Boyn Hill Rd SL6 39 B3
Boyn Valley Rd SL6 39 B3
Boyndon Rd SL6 39 B4
Boyne Hill CE Inf Sch SL6 39 B3
Bracebridge GU15 151 A3
Bracken Bank SL5 119 B4
Bracken Cl Ashford TW16 98 C1
Farnham Common SL2 22 B4
Purley on T RG31 57 B1
Bracken Copse RG17 127 C3
Bracken La GU46 149 A3
Bracken Rd SL6 39 B2
Bracken Way
Burghfield Common RG7 111 A1
Flackwell Heath HP10 3 A4
Brackendale Cl GU15 151 C2
Brackendale Rd GU15 151 B2
Brackenforde SL3 43 B2
Brackenhale Comp Sch RG12 118 A3
Brackens The RG45 143 A4
Brackenwood
Burghfield Common RG7 110 C1
Frimley GU15 152 B3
Brackenwood Dr RG26 135 A1
Brackley Ho TW18 96 C2
Bracknell Beeches RG12 118 A3
Bracknell Bsns Ctr The RG12 117 C4
Bracknell Cl GU15 144 C1
Bracknell Coll
Bracknell RG12 118 B4
Bracknell, Wick Hill RG12 118 B4
Bracknell Enterprise Ctr RG12 118 A4
Bracknell Rd
Bagshot GU19 145 C3
Camberley GU15 145 A1
Crowthorne RG45 143 B3
Winkfield RG42 92 A3
Bracknell Sports & L Ctr RG12 118 B2
Bracknell Sta RG12 118 A3
Brackstone Cl RG4 59 B1
Bradbury Gdns SL3 23 B4
Bradcutts La SL6 19 C4
Bradenham La SL7 18 B3
Bradfield CE Prim Sch RG7 82 A1
Bradfield Coll RG7 82 B3
Bradfields RG12 118 B2
Bradford Rd SL1 42 A4
Brading Way RG8 57 B3
Bradley Cl RG17 102 A1
Bradley Dr RG40 116 A1
Bradley Rd SL1 42 C3
Bradley-Moore Sq RG18 106 C3
Bradmore Way RG6 114 A4
Bradshaw Cl SL4 66 C3
Bradwell Rd RG31 57 B2
Braemar SL6 63 B4
Braemar Ct 1 SL7 1 B1
Braemar Gdns SL1 42 A2
Braemore Cl RG19 106 B1
Brakendale Way RG6 87 A3
Bramber Ct SL1 42 A3
Bramber Mews RG4 59 C2
Bramble Cl TW17 125 B3
Bramble Cres RG30 84 C4
Bramble Dr SL6 39 A2
Brambledown TW18 124 A4
Bramblegate RG45 143 A3
Brambles The
Crowthorne RG45 142 B3
Newbury RG14 130 C4
Bramblings RG4 58 C3
Bramcote GU15 152 B3
Bramley Ave TW17 125 C3
Bramley Chase SL6 39 B2
Bramley Cl Chertsey KT16 124 A1
Earley RG6 87 A2
Maidenhead SL6 39 B2
Staines TW18 97 B1
Bramley Gr RG45 142 B3
Bramley La GU17 150 A3
Bramley Rd
Camberley GU15 151 A1
Silchester RG7 136 A1
Brambling Ave GU46 149 A3
Brammas Cl SL1 42 B2
Brampton Chase RG9 36 A2
Brampton Ct SL6 40 A4
Bramshaw Rd RG30 58 A1
Bramshill Cl RG2 140 C4
Bramwell Cl RG19 106 C1
Bran Cl RG30 84 C4
Brandon Ave RG5 88 A4
Brandon Cl GU15 152 B2
Brands Rd SL3 69 A4
Branksome Cl GU15 151 C3
Branksome Ct 10 RG1 85 C4
Branksome Hill Rd GU47 150 C4
Branksome Park Rd GU15 151 C3
Brants Bridge RG12 118 C4
Brants Cl RG2 114 C1
Braunfels Wlk RG14 104 C1
Bravington Cl TW17 124 C2
Bray Cl SL6 40 B2
Bray Ct SL6 40 B1
Bray Rd Maidenhead SL6 40 A3
Reading RG30 85 A2
Braybank SL6 40 B2
Braybrooke Dr RG10 88 C4
Braybrooke Gdns RG10 36 B1
Braybrooke Rd
Bracknell RG42 91 A1
Wargrave RG10 36 B1
Braye Cl GU47 143 B1
Brayfield Rd SL6 40 B2
Brayford Rd RG2 113 B4
Braywick Park & Nature Ctr SL6 40 A2
Braywick Rd SL6 40 A2
Braywood Ave TW20 96 A1
Braywood CE Fst Sch SL4 65 C3
Braywood Cotts SL4 66 A3
Braziers La SL4, SL5 92 B2
Breach Sq RG17 100 B2
Breadcroft La SL6 38 C2
Breadcroft Rd SL6 38 C2
Bream Cl SL7 18 B4
Brean Wlk RG6 87 A1
Brechin Ct 3 RG1 86 B3
Brecon Ct SL1 42 B2
Brecon Rd RG5 87 C4
Bredon Rd RG41 88 C1
Bredward Cl SL1 21 A1
Breech The GU47 150 C4
Breedons Hill RG8 56 B3
Bremer Rd TW18, TW19 97 A3
Brendon Cl Harlington UB3 71 B4
Reading RG30 57 C1
Brent Cl RG19 106 B1
Brent Gdns RG2 86 A2
Brent Rd SL8 3 A2
Brentmoor Rd GU24 153 B3
Brerewood RG5 86 C1
Bret Harte Rd GU16 151 C1
Brew Tower SL7 1 B1
Brewery Comm RG7 137 A4
Brewhouse Hill SN8 99 A2
Briants Ave RG4 59 B1
Briants Piece RG18 79 A3
Briar Ave GU18 153 A4
Briar Cl Burnham SL6 41 A4
Caversham RG4 59 A3
Briar Dene SL6 19 B1
Briar Glen SL6 19 C3
Briar Rd TW17 125 A2
Briar Way SL2 42 A4
Briarlea Rd RG7 136 C3
Briars Cl RG8 56 C3
Briars The Slough SL3 43 C1
Stanwell TW19 70 A1
Briarwood RG40 141 C3
Briarwood Cl TW13 98 C3
Brickfield La Burnham SL1 21 A2
Harlington UB3 71 B4
Brickfields Ind Ctr RG12 118 A4
Bridge Ave Cookham SL6 19 C3
Maidenhead SL6 40 A4
Bridge Cl Slough SL1 41 C3
Staines TW18 96 C2
Walton-on-T KT12 125 C1
Bridge Ct SL6 40 B4
Bridge End GU15 151 A2
Bridge Gdns TW15 98 B1
Bridge La GU25, KT16 122 C2
Bridge Rd Ascot SL5 120 B2
Bagshot GU19 145 C2
Camberley GU15 151 A2
Chertsey KT16 124 A1
Maidenhead SL6 40 A4
Bridge St Caversham RG4 59 A1
Colnbrook SL3 69 B4
Hungerford RG17 100 B3
Maidenhead SL6 40 A4
Newbury RG14 105 A2
Reading RG1 86 A4
Staines TW18 96 C2
Walton-on-T KT12 125 C1
Bridge View SL5 121 A1
Bridge Walk GU46 149 B4
Bridge Works GU15 151 A2
Bridgeman Ct 5 SL4 67 A3
Bridgeman Dr SL4 67 A3
Bridges Cl RG41 115 C4
Bridges The RG7 136 B3
Bridgestone Dr SL8 3 B2
Bridgewater Cl RG30 58 B1
Bridgewater Ct SL3 44 A1
Bridgewater Terr SL4 67 B3
Bridgewater Way SL4 67 B3
Bridle Cl SL6 19 C1
Bridle Rd SL6 19 C1
Bridlepath Way TW14 98 C4
Bridlington Spur SL1 42 A2
Bridport Cl RG6 87 B1
Bridport Way SL2 22 A1
Brierley Pl RG31 57 B2
Briff La RG7 107 B4
Brigham Rd RG1 59 A1
Brighton Rd RG6 87 A3
Brighton Spur SL2 22 A1
Brightside Ave TW18 97 B1
Brightwalton CE Prim Sch RG20 28 B2
Brigidine Sch The SL4 67 B2
Brill Cl Caversham RG4 59 A2
Maidenhead SL6 39 B2
Marlow SL7 1 B1
Brimblecombe Cl RG41 89 A1
Brimpton CE Prim Sch RG7 133 C3
Brimpton La RG7 134 A2
Brimpton Rd
Brimpton RG7 133 C4
Reading RG30 85 A2
Tadley RG26 134 B1
Brinkworth Pl SL4 95 A4
Brinn's La GU17 150 B3
Briony Ho RG2 113 A4
Brisbane Rd RG30 85 A4
Bristol Cl TW19 70 C1
Bristol Ct 10 TW19 70 C1
Bristol Way SL1 42 C3
Bristow Ct Caversham RG4 59 A1
Marlow SL7 2 A2
Bristow Cty Inf Sch GU15 151 A1
Bristow Rd GU15 151 A2
Britannia Ind Est SL3 69 C3
Britannia Way TW19 97 B4
Brittain Ct GU47 150 B4
Britten Rd RG2 86 A3
Britwell Rd SL1 21 B1
Brixham Rd RG2 86 A1
Broad Hinton RG10 61 C2
Broad La Bracknell RG12 118 B3
Bucklebury RG7 107 B3
Wooburn Green HP10 3 C3
Broad Ley's SL4 66 C4
Broad Oak Ashford TW16 98 C1
Slough SL2 22 B1
Broad Oak Ct SL2 22 B1
Broad Platts SL3 43 B2
Broad St East Isley RG20 30 C4
Reading RG1 86 A4
West End GU24 153 B3
Wokingham RG40 116 B3
Broad St Wlk RG40 116 B3
Broad Street Mall The RG1 86 A4
Broad Way RG7 138 B2
Broad Wlk GU16 151 C1
Broadacre TW18 97 A2
Broadcommon Rd RG10 89 A4
Broadhalfpenny La RG26 135 B1
Broadlands Ave TW17 125 B2
Broadlands Cl RG31 84 B3
Broadlands Ct RG42 117 C4
Broadlands Dr SL5 120 B1
Broadley Gn GU20 146 B2
Broadmark Rd SL2 43 A3
Broadmeadow End RG18 106 C2
Broadmoor Cty Prim Sch RG45 143 B2
Broadmoor Hospl RG45 143 C3
Broadmoor La RG10, SL6 63 A3
Broadrick Heath RG42 91 C1
Broadview Est TW19 98 A4
Broadwater Cl TW19 95 C4
Broadwater La RG10 61 C1
Broadwater Pk SL6 40 C1
Broadwater Rd RG10 61 C2
Broadway Bracknell RG12 118 B4
Maidenhead SL6 39 C4
Staines TW18 97 A1
Thatcham RG19 106 B2
Winkfield SL4 93 A4
Broadway Ctyd RG19 106 B2
Broadway Mall 6 SL6 39 C4
Broadway Rd GU18,GU20 146 B1
Broadway The
Laleham TW18 124 B4
Lambourn RG17 25 A2
12 Newbury RG14 105 A2
Sandhurst GU47 150 A4
Brocas Rd RG7 110 C1
Brocas St SL4 67 B4
Brocas Terr SL4 67 B4
Brock Gdns RG30 85 B4
Brock La SL6 39 C4
Brock La Mall 7 SL6 39 C4
Brock Way GU25 122 B3
Brockenhurst Dr GU46 149 B3
Brockenhurst Rd
Ascot SL5 120 A2
Bracknell RG12 119 A3
Brockhurst & Marlston House Prep Schs RG18 79 C2
Brocklands GU46 149 A2
Brockley Cl RG30 85 A4
Brocks La RG7 & RG18 80 A2
Brocks Way RG9 36 A2
Brockway SL3 44 A1
Broken Furlong SL4 42 A1
Broken Way RG20 131 A1
Bromley Wlk RG30 84 C4
Brompton Cl 9 RG6 87 B1
Brompton Dr SL6 19 B1
Bromycroft Rd SL2 22 A1
Bronte Rise RG14 131 A4
Brook Cl Sandhurst GU47 143 C1
Stanwell TW19 97 C4
Wokingham RG41 116 A4
Brook Cres SL1 41 C4
Brook Dr Ashford TW16 98 C1
Bracknell RG12 118 C3
Reading RG30 112 C4
Brook Gn RG42 117 C4
Brook Ho SL1 42 B2
Brook La RG10 62 C2
Brook Path SL1 41 C3
Brook Rd Bagshot GU19 145 C1
Camberley GU15 151 A2
Brook St Twyford RG10 61 B2
Windsor SL4 67 B3
Brook St W RG1 86 A3
Brookbank HP10 3 B2
Brookdene Cl SL6 19 C1
Brooke Furmston Pl SL7 1 C2
Brooke Pl RG42 90 B2
Brookers Cnr RG45 143 B3
Brookers Hill RG2 113 B3
Brookers Row RG45 143 B3
Brookfield Ho SL3 68 B3
Brookfield Rd HP10 3 B2
Brookfields Specl Sch RG31 57 B2
Brookhouse Dr HP10 3 B2
Brooklands Cl TW16 125 C4
Brooklyn Dr RG4 59 A3
Brookmill The RG1 85 C3
Brooks Rd RG18 106 C2
Brooksby Cl GU17 150 A3
Brooksby Rd RG31 57 B1
Brookside Chertsey KT16 123 C1
Colnbrook SL3 69 B4
Reading RG31 84 C2
Sandhurst GU47 150 B4
Slough SL3 43 C4
Wokingham RG41 115 C4
Brookside Ave
Staines TW15 97 B2
Wraysbury TW19 68 C2
Brookside Cl RG6 87 B1
Brookway RG14 105 C1
Broom Acres GU47 143 A1
Broom Cl
Blackwater GU17 150 C2
Reading RG31 84 B3
Broom Field GU18 153 A4
Broom Gr RG41 115 B2
Broom Hill Cookham SL6 19 C3
Stoke Poges SL2 23 A3
Broom Ho SL3 43 C1
Broome Cl GU46 149 B4
Broome Ct RG12 118 A3
Broome Lodge TW18 97 A2
Broomfield TW18 97 A1
Broomfield Cl SL5 121 A1
Broomfield Dr SL5 121 A2
Broomfield Pk SL5 121 A1
Broomfield Rd RG30 84 C4
Broomhall Bldgs SL5 121 A1
Broomhall La SL5 121 A2
Broomsquires Rd GU19 145 C1
Broughton Cl RG30 58 B1
Broughton Mews GU16 151 C1
Brownfield Gdns SL6 39 C3
Browngraves Rd UB3 71 B4
Browning Cl
Frimley GU15 152 B2
Thatcham RG18 106 B2
Brownlow Dr RG42 91 B1
Brownlow Rd RG1 85 C4
Brownrigg Cres RG12 118 C4
Brownrigg Rd TW15 98 A2
Browns Ct SL1 41 C3
Brownsfield Rd RG18 106 B2
Bruan Rd RG14 130 C4
Bruce Ave TW17 125 B2
Bruce Cl SL1 42 A3
Bruce Rd RG5 87 B4
Bruce Wlk SL4 66 B3
Brucewood Par SL7 1 C3
Brudenell SL4 66 C2
Brummell Rd RG14 104 C3
Brunel Cl SL6 39 C3
Brunel Ctr SL6 39 B3
Brunel Dr
Crowthorne RG45 143 B4
Woodley RG5 60 C1
Brunel Rd Maidenhead SL6 39 B3
Reading RG30 85 A2
Theale RG7 83 C1
Brunel Ret Pk RG2 86 A2
Brunel Univ (Runnymede Campus) TW20 95 B3
Brunel Way SL1 42 C3
Brunswick RG12 118 A1
Brunswick Hill RG1 85 C4
Brunswick Lodge 12 RG1 85 C4
Brunswick St RG1 85 C3
Bruton Way RG12 118 C1
Bryant Ave SL2 42 C4
Bryants La RG18 53 C1
Bryants Pl RG8 57 A3
Brybur Cl RG2 113 B4
Bryer Pl SL4 66 B2
Bryony Ho RG42 117 C4
Bryony Way TW16 98 C1
Bsns Village The SL2 43 A3
Buccaneer Cl RG5 88 A4
Buccleuch Rd SL3 68 A4
Buchan The GU15 152 A4
Buchanan Dr RG40 141 C4
Buchanan Sq RG19 106 C1
Buck Side RG4 59 A1
Buckden Cl RG5 88 A3
Buckfield Ct SL0 44 C2
Buckham Hill
RG17 & RG20 48 B3
Buckhurst Gr RG40 116 C3
Buckhurst Hill RG12 118 C3
Buckhurst La SL5 121 A3
Buckhurst Moors RG12 117 B3
Buckhurst Rd SL5 120 C4
Buckhurst Way RG6 87 A2
Buckingham Ave SL1 42 A4
Buckingham Ave E SL1 42 B4
Buckingham Ct
Staines TW18 97 A2
Wokingham RG40 116 B3
Buckingham Dr RG4 59 A3
Buckingham Gate SL7 17 B4
Buckingham Gdns 12 SL1 42 C2
Buckingham Ho 4 SL6 39 C3
Buckingham Rd RG14 104 C1
Buckingham Way GU16 151 C1
Buckland Ave SL2 43 A2
Buckland Cres SL4 66 C3
Buckland Cty Jun & Inf Sch TW18 97 B1
Buckland Gate SL3 23 A1
Buckland Rd RG2 86 A2
Buckle La RG42 91 A3
Bucklebury RG12 118 A1
Bucklebury CE Prim Sch RG7 107 B3
Bucklebury Cl SL6 40 B1
Bucklebury Farm Pk RG7 80 B1
Bucknell Ave RG8 56 C3
Bucknell Cl RG31 84 C2
Buckthorn Cl RG40 116 C4
Budebury Rd TW18 97 A2
Budge's Cotts RG40 116 C4
Budge's Gdns RG40 116 C4
Budge's Rd RG40 116 B4
Budham Way RG12 118 A2
Buffins SL6 20 C1
Bulbrook Row RG12 118 C4
Bulkeley Ave SL4 67 A2
Bulkeley Cl TW20 95 B2
Bull La Bracknell RG42 118 A4
Swallowfield RG7 139 A2
Bull Meadow The RG8 33 C3
Bullbrook Dr RG12 118 C4
Bullfinch Cl GU47 150 C4
Bulmershe Rd RG1 86 C3
Bulpit La RG17 100 B2
Bulstrode Pl SL1 42 C2
Bunby Rd SL2 22 C3
Bunces Cl SL4 42 A1
Bunces La RG7 111 A1
Bundy's Way TW18 96 C1
Bungalow Dr RG31 84 B4
Bunglers Hill RG7 140 A3
Bunkers Hill RG14 130 B3
Bunten Meade SL1 42 A3
Bunyan Ct 12 RG1 86 A3
Burbage Gn RG12 118 C2
Burbidge Cl RG31 84 C2
Burbidge Rd TW17 125 A3
Burbury Woods GU15 151 C3
Burchell Rd RG14 104 C3
Burchett Copse RG40 141 C4
Burchett's Green CE Inf Sch SL6 38 A4
Burchett's Green Rd SL6 18 B1
Burchetts Green La SL6 38 B3
Burchetts Green Rd SL6 38 A4
Burchetts Way TW17 125 A2
Burcombe Way RG4 59 A2
Burcot Gdns SL6 19 C2
Burdens Heath RG7 107 A3
Burdett Ct RG2 86 B2
Burdock Cl
Burghfield Common RG7 111 A1
Lightwater GU18 153 A4
Burfield Rd SL4, TW19 95 A4
Burford Cl SL7 1 B3
Burford Ct 11 Reading RG1 85 C4
Wokingham RG40 116 C3
Burford Cty Comb Sch SL7 1 B3
Burford Gdns SL1 41 B4
Burford Rd GU15 151 A2
Burfords RG17 47 B3
Burges Way TW18 97 A2
Burgess Cl RG5 87 B2
Burgess La RG17,RG20 128 B3
Burgett Rd SL1 42 A2
Burghead Cl GU47 150 B4
Burghfield Rd RG30 85 A2
Burghfield St Mary's CE Prim Sch RG30 111 B3
Burgoyne Rd
Ashford TW16 98 C1
Camberley GU15 152 A3
Burleigh Gdns TW15 98 B2
Burleigh La SL5 119 C4
Burleigh Mews RG4 59 B3
Burleigh Rd SL5 119 C4
Burley Orch KT16 124 A2
Burley Way GU17 150 B3
Burlingham Cl RG2 113 B3
Burlings The SL5 119 C4
Burlington Ave SL1 42 C2
Burlington Cl TW14 98 B4
Burlington Ct
Blackwater GU17 150 B2
1 Slough SL1 42 C2
Burlington Rd
Burnham SL1 21 A1
Reading RG30 84 B4
2 Slough SL1 42 C2
Burlsdon Way RG12 118 C4
Burn Moor Chase RG12 118 C1
Burn Wlk SL1 21 A1
Burne-Jones Dr GU47 150 B3
Burnet Cl GU24 153 C3
Burnetts Rd SL4 66 C3
Burney Bit RG26 135 C1
Burnham Beeches (Nature Reserve) SL2 22 A4
Burnham Cl Bourne End SL8 3 A2
Windsor SL4 66 B3
Burnham Copse Jun & Inf Schs RG26 135 A1

Burnham Gr RG42 91 B1
Burnham Gram Sch SL1 21 B1
Burnham La SL1 41 C4
Burnham Manor GU15 152 A4
Burnham Rd RG26 134 C1
Burnham Rise RG4 59 B4
Burnham Sta SL1 41 B4
Burnham Upper Sch SL1 41 A4
Burniston Cl RG6 87 C1
Burnmoor Mdw RG27 141 C1
Burns Cl RG5 87 C2
Burns Wlk RG18 106 B2
Burnt Oak Cookham SL6 19 C4
Wokingham RG40 141 C4
Burnt Pollard La GU18 146 C1
Burnthouse Gdns RG42 91 C1
Burnthouse La RG7,RG30 112 A3
Burrcroft Rd RG30 85 A3
Burrell Rd RG20 31 C2
Burroughs Cres SL8 3 A2
Burroway Rd SL3 44 A2
Burrows Hill Cl
TW19, TW6 70 B2
Burrows The RG26 135 A1
Burton Cl Twyford RG10 61 C1
Windlesham GU20 146 B2
Burton Way SL4 66 C2
Burtons Hill RG17 102 A1
Burway Cres KT16 124 A3
Burwell Cl RG6 87 B1
Burys Bank Rd RG19 132 B3
Bush Rd TW17 124 C2
Bush Wlk RG40 116 B3
Business Ctr The RG41 116 A2
Butchers La SL6 63 B4
Bute St RG30 85 A3
Butler Ct 5 SL7 1 C2
Butler Rd Bagshot GU19 145 C1
Crowthorne RG45 143 A3
Butlers Cl SL4 66 B3
Butson Cl RG14 104 C2
Buttenshaw Ave RG2 141 A4
Buttenshaw Cl RG2 141 A4
Butter Market RG1 86 A4
Buttercup Cl RG40 117 A3
Buttercup Pl RG18 106 B2
Buttercup Sq TW19 97 B4
Butterfield
Camberley GU15 151 A2
Wooburn Green HP10 3 B2
Buttermere Ave SL1 41 B4
Buttermere Cl TW14 98 C4
Buttermere Dr GU15 152 B2
Buttermere Gdns RG12 118 B3
Buttermere Way TW20 96 A1
Buttersteep Rise
GU20, SL5 119 B1
Butts Furlong RG20 28 B2
Butts Hill Rd RG5 87 C4
Buxton Ave RG4 58 C2
Buxton Rd TW15 97 B2
Bybend Cl SL2 22 A2
Byefield Rd RG30 85 A2
Byeways Cl RG10 37 C2
Byland Dr SL6 40 A1
Byreton Cl RG6 87 A1
Byron SL3 44 A1
Byron Ave GU15 152 A2
Byron Cl 6 Marlow SL7 1 C2
Newbury RG14 130 C4
Twyford RG10 61 C2
Yateley GU46 149 A2
Byron Dr RG45 143 A2
Byron Rd Earley RG6 87 A4
Twyford RG10 61 C2
Bythorn Cl RG6 87 C1
Byways Burnham SL1 41 A4
Yateley GU46 149 A3
Bywood RG12 118 A1
Byworth Cl RG2 113 A4

C

Cabin Moss RG12 118 C1
Cabrera Ave GU25 122 B2
Cabrera Cl GU25 122 B2
Cadbury Cl TW16 98 C1
Cadbury Rd TW16 98 C1
Caddy Cl 4 TW20 96 A2
Cadogan Cl Holyport SL6 65 A4
Reading RG30 84 C4
Cadwell Dr SL6 39 B2
Caesar's Camp Rd GU15 152 A4
Caesar's Cl GU15 152 A4
Caesar's Way TW17 125 B2
Caesars Gate RG42 91 C1
Caesers Ct GU15 152 A4
Cages Wood Dr SL2 22 A4
Cain Rd RG12, RG42 117 C4
Cain's La TW14 71 C1
Cairn Cl GU15 152 A2
Cairngorm Pl SL2 22 B1
Cairngorm Rd RG19 106 B1
Caistor Cl RG31 84 A2
Calard Dr RG18 106 A3
Calbourne Dr RG31 84 B2
Calbroke Rd SL2 21 C1
Calcot Ct RG31 84 C3
Calcot Place Dr RG31 84 C2
Caldbeck Dr RG5 87 C4
Calder Cl Maidenhead SL6 19 C1
Reading RG30 84 C4
Calder Ct Maidenhead SL6 19 B1
Slough SL3 43 C1
Calder Way SL3 69 C2
Caldicott Prep Sch SL2 22 A3
Caldwell Rd GU20 146 B3
Caledonia Rd TW19 97 C4
Caleta Cl RG4 59 B1
Calfridus Way RG12 118 C3
California Ctry Pk RG2 141 B4
Calleva Mus RG7 136 A1
Calleva Pk RG7 134 C1
Calleva Roman Town
RG7 136 B1
Callington Rd RG2 86 B1
Callins La RG10 63 A2
Callis Farm Cl TW19 70 C1
Callow Hill GU25, TW20 122 B4
Calshot Pl RG31 84 B2
Calshot Rd TW6 71 A3
Calshot Way TW6 71 A3
Calvin Cl GU15 152 A2
Camberley Cty Inf Sch
GU15 151 B3
Camberley Heath
Golf Course GU15 152 A3
Camberley Rd TW6 71 A2
Camberley Sta GU15 151 B3
Camberley Towers GU15 151 B3
Camborne Cl Earley RG6 87 A1
Harmondsworth TW6 71 A2
Camborne Cres TW6 71 A2
Camborne Rd TW6 71 A2
Camborne Way TW6 71 A2
Cambria Ct Slough SL3 43 B2
Staines TW18 96 C2
Cambria Gdns TW19 97 C4
Cambrian Cl GU15 151 A3
Cambrian Way
Reading RG31 84 B2
Wokingham RG40 142 A4
Cambridge Ave
Burnham SL1 21 A2
Slough SL1 42 A4
Cambridge Cl UB7 70 B4
Cambridge Ho 2 SL4 67 B3
Cambridge Rd
Crowthorne RG45 143 B2
Littleton TW15 98 B1
Marlow SL7 1 B1
Sandhurst GU47 143 C1
Cambridge Sq GU15 151 B3
Cambridge St 1 RG1 85 C4
Cambridge Wlk 3 GU15 151 B3
Cambridgeshire Cl
Bracknell RG42 91 C1
Wokingham RG41 115 C3
Camden Pl Bourne End SL8 3 A2
Reading RG31 84 A2
Camden Rd SL6 19 B1
Cameford Cl RG2 86 A1
Camelia Ct GU24 153 C3
Camellia Way RG41 115 B4
Camgate Est TW19 97 C4
Camilla Cl TW16 98 C1
Camley Gdns SL6 39 A4
Camley Park Dr SL6 38 C4
Camm Ave SL4 66 C2
Camp Rd RG7 110 B1
Campbell Cl GU46 149 C3
Campbell Pl GU16 151 C2
Campbell Rd RG5 87 B3
Campbells Gn RG7 137 A3
Camperdown SL6 20 A1
Camperdown Ho 36 SL4 67 B3
Campion Cl GU17 150 C2
Campion Ho RG42 117 C4
Campion Way RG40 116 C4
Canada Rd SL1 43 A2
Canal View Rd RG14 105 B2
Canal Walk RG17 100 B3
Canal Way RG1 86 B4
Canal Wharf SL3 44 A2
Canberra Cl GU46 149 A4
Canberra Rd TW6 71 A2
Candleford Cl RG12 91 B1
Candover Cl UB7 70 B4
Canford Ct RG30 85 B4
Cannock Cl SL6 40 A3
Cannock Way RG6 87 B1
Cannon Cl GU47 150 C4
Cannon Court Rd SL6 19 B2
Cannon Hill RG12 118 B2
Cannon Hill Cl SL6 40 B1
Cannon La SL6 38 C2
Cannon St 3 RG1 85 C4
Cannondown Rd SL6 19 C3
Canon Hill Dr SL6 40 A2
Canon Hill Way SL6 40 A1
Canon's Cloisters SL4 67 B4
Canopus Way TW19 97 C4
Cansfield End RG14 104 C2
Canterbury Ave SL2 22 B1
Canterbury Ct TW15 97 C2
Canterbury Rd RG2 86 B2
Cantley Cres RG41 116 A4
Cantley House Hotel
RG40 116 A4
Cape Villas SL0 44 C4
Capper Rd GU15 151 A4
Capricorn Ho HP10 3 A4
Captains Gorse RG8 54 C3
Caraway Rd RG6 87 A1
Carbery La SL5 120 A3
Carbinswood La RG7 108 A3
Cardiff Rd RG1 58 C1
Cardigan Cl SL1 41 C3
Cardigan Gdns RG1 86 C3
Cardigan Rd RG1 86 C3
Cardinal Cl RG4 59 A1
Cardinal's Wlk TW16 98 C1
Cardinals Wlk SL6 41 B4
Cardwell Cres SL5 120 B2
Carew Rd TW15 98 B1
Carey Cl SL4 67 A2
Carey Rd RG40 116 B3
Carey St RG1 85 C4
Cariad Ct RG8 34 A4
Carisbrooke Cl
Caversham RG4 59 B3
Maidenhead SL6 39 B3
Carisbrooke Ct SL1 42 C3
Carland Cl RG6 87 A1
Carlesgill Pl RG9 35 C4
Carlile Gdns RG10 61 B3
Carlinwark Dr GU15 151 C4
Carlisle Rd Reading RG31 57 C2
Slough SL1 42 B3
Carlton Cl Frimley GU15 152 A2
Woodley RG5 87 C3
Carlton Ct TW18 97 A2
Carlton Ho TW19 70 B1
Carlton Rd Ashford TW16 98 C1
Caversham RG4 58 C3
Slough SL2 43 A3
Carlyle Ct RG45 143 B3
Carlyle Rd TW18 97 A1
Carmarthen Rd SL1 42 C3
Carmela Ct TW15 98 B1
Carnarvon Rd RG1 86 C3
Carnation Cl RG45 143 A4
Carnation Dr RG42 92 A1
Carnegie Rd RG14 105 A1
Carnoustie RG12 117 C1
Carnoustie Ct 28 RG1 86 B4
Carolina Pl RG40 141 C4
Caroline Ct Ashford TW15 98 A1
Marlow SL7 1 C2
Caroline Dr RG41 116 A4
Caroline Pl UB3 71 C4
Caroline St 7 RG1 85 C4
Carrick Gdns RG5 87 B4
Carrick La GU46 149 C3
Carrington Ave HP10 3 A4
Carrington Cty Mid Sch The
HP10 3 A4
Carrington Rd SL1 42 C3
Carroll Cres SL5 119 C3
Carron Cl RG30 85 A4
Carsdale Cl RG1 85 C3
Carshalton Rd GU15 145 A1
Carshalton Way RG6 87 B1
Carston Gr RG31 84 C2
Carter Cl SL4 67 A3
Carters Hill RG40 & RG42 90 A2
Carters Rise RG31 84 C2
Cartmel Dr RG5 87 B3
Carwarden House Sch
GU15 152 A2
Cary Cl RG14 130 B3
Casey Ct RG7 81 B2
Cassia Dr RG6 86 C1
Cassiobury Ave TW14 98 C4
Cassocks Sq TW17 125 B1
Castle Ave SL3 68 A4
Castle Cl 3 Charlton TW16 98 C1
Frimley GU15 151 C2
Castle Cres RG1 85 C3
Castle Ct SL6 39 B4
Castle Dr SL6 39 B4
Castle End Rd RG10 62 A4
Castle Farm Caravan Site
SL4 66 B3
Castle Gr RG14 104 C3
Castle Hill Maidenhead SL6 39 C4
Reading RG1 85 C3
Swallowfield RG7 140 B4
Windsor SL4 67 C3
Castle Hill Rd TW20 95 B3
Castle Hill Terr SL6 39 C4
Castle Ind Pk RG14 105 B3
Castle La RG14 104 C3
Castle Lodge SL6 39 C4
Castle Mews SL6 39 C4
Castle Rd GU15 151 C2
Castle St Reading RG1 86 A4
Slough SL1 42 C2
Castlecraig Ct GU47 150 B4
Castleman Ho SL5 120 B2
Castleton Ct SL7 1 C1
Castleview Comb Sch
SL3 43 B1
Castleview Ho 11 SL4 67 B3
Castleview Rd SL3 43 B1
Castor Ct GU46 149 A4
Caswall Cl RG42 90 B1
Caswall Ride GU46 149 C3
Catalina Cl RG5 88 A4
Catalina Rd TW6 71 A2
Catcliffe Way RG6 113 C4
Catena Rise GU18 146 A1
Catesby Gdns GU46 149 A3
Catherine Dr TW16 98 C1
Catherine Rd RG14 105 A1
Catherine St RG30 85 C4
Catlin Cres TW17 125 B2
Catmore Rd RG20 29 B4
Caunter Rd RG14 104 B2
Causeway Est TW20 96 B2
Causeway The
Caversham RG4 59 B1
Egham TW18, TW20 96 B2
Maidenhead SL6 40 B2
Marlow SL7 1 C1
Causmans Way RG31 57 B1
Cavalier Cl Newbury RG14 105 B3
Theale RG7 83 B1
Cavalier Ct TW15 98 B1
Cavalry Cres SL4 67 B1
Cavendish Cl
Ashford TW16 98 C1
Burnham SL6 41 A4
Cavendish Ct
Ashford TW16 98 C1
Blackwater GU17 150 B2
9 Chertsey KT16 124 A1
Newbury RG14 105 C3
Poyle SL3 69 C3
Cavendish Gdns RG41 88 A2
Cavendish Meads SL5 120 B2
Cavendish Rd
Ashford TW16 98 C1
Caversham RG4 59 B3
Caversham Hill RG4 59 A2
Caversham Park Dr RG4 59 B3
Caversham Park Prim Sch
RG4 59 B3
Caversham Park Rd RG4 59 C3
Caversham Prim Sch
RG4 59 A2
Caversham Rd RG1 59 A1
Caversham Wharf RG1 59 A1
Caves Farm Cl GU47 150 A4
Cawcott Dr SL4 66 C3
Cawsam Gdns RG4 59 B2
Caxton Cl RG30 58 B1
Caxton Ct RG9 15 C1
Cecil Aldin Dr RG31 57 B2
Cecil Cl TW15 98 B1
Cecil Rd Ashford TW15 98 B1
Iver SL0 44 C4
Cecil Way SL2 21 C1
Cedar RG9 15 B1
Cedar Ave GU17 150 B3
Cedar Chase SL6 20 B1
Cedar Cl Bagshot GU19 145 C2
Laleham TW18 124 B3
Wokingham RG40 116 B3
Cedar Ct Egham TW20 96 A2
Maidenhead SL6 39 B4
Marlow SL7 1 C1
6 Windsor SL4 67 A3
Cedar Dr Bracknell RG42 91 B1
Cookham SL6 19 C4
Marlow Bottom SL7 1 B4
Pangbourne RG8 56 B2
Sunningdale SL5 121 A1
Cedar Gr RG19 106 B2
Cedar Ho TW16 98 C1
Cedar Mount RG14 130 C4
Cedar Pl RG5 87 C3
Cedar Rd
East Bedfont TW14 98 B4
Reading RG2 86 C1
Cedar Way Charlton TW16 98 C1
Slough SL3 43 C1
Cedar Wood Cres RG4 59 A2
Cedars 10 RG12 118 C3
Cedars Cl GU47 149 C4
Cedars Rd SL6 40 A4
Cedars The RG31 57 B1
Celandine Cl RG45 143 B3
Celandine Ct GU46 149 A4
Celandine Gr RG18 106 C2
Celia Cres TW15 97 B1
Cell Farm SL4 68 A1
Cell Farm Ave SL4 68 A1
Celsea Pl OX10 14 A4
Cemetery La TW17 125 A1
Centenary Bsns Pk RG9 15 C1
Central Dr SL1 41 C3
Central Est SL6 39 C4
Central La SL4 93 A4
Central Way SL4 93 A4
Central Wlk RG40 116 B3
Centre The
Farnham Common SL2 22 B3
Walton-on-T KT12 125 C1
Centurion Cl Reading RG1 86 A3
4 Sandhurst GU47 150 B4
Century Dr RG7 113 B1
Century Rd TW20 96 B2
Cerotus Pl KT16 123 C1
Chackfield Dr RG41 115 B4
Chaddleworth St Andrews
CE Prim Sch
RG20 49 A4
Chaffinch Cl Reading RG31 84 A4
5 Sandhurst GU47 150 B4
Wokingham RG41 115 C3
Chagford Rd RG2 86 A1
Chain St RG1 86 A4
Chainhill Rd OX12 8 A4
Chalcott SL1 42 C2
Chalcraft Cl RG9 35 B4
Chalfont Cl RG6 87 A1
Chalfont Ct RG6 87 A1
Chalfont Way RG6 87 A1
Chalford HP10 3 C3
Chalford Rd RG14 104 C1
Chalgrove Cl SL6 40 A3
Chalgrove Way RG4 59 A3
Chalk Hill
Aston Tirrold OX11 12 C4
Shiplake RG9 35 B3
Chalk Pit La SL1 21 A2
Chalklands SL8 3 A2
Chalkpit La SL7 1 A2
Challenge Rd TW15 98 B3
Challenor Cl RG40 141 C4
Challis Pl RG42 117 C4
Challow Ct SL6 19 B1
Chalmers Rd TW15 98 A2
Chalmers Rd E TW15 98 B2
Chalvey Cty Fst Sch SL1 42 B2
Chalvey Gdns SL1 42 C2
Chalvey Gr SL1 42 A2
Chalvey Pk SL1 42 C2
Chalvey Rd E SL1 42 C2
Chalvey Rd W SL1 42 B2
Chamberhouse Mill Rd
RG19 106 C1
Chamberlains Gdns RG2 114 C1
Chambers The 20 RG1 86 A4
Champion Rd RG4 59 B1
Chancel Mans RG42 91 B1
Chancellors Way The
RG6 86 C2
Chancery Mews 25 RG1 85 C4
Chancery Pl SL4 67 B4
Chanctonbury Dr SL5 120 C1
Chandlers Cl TW14 98 C4
Chandlers La GU46 149 B4
Chandos Mall 13 SL1 42 C2
Chandos Rd Egham TW18 96 B2
Newbury RG14 131 A4
Chantry Cl SL4 67 A3
Chantry Ct GU16 151 B1
Chantry Mead RG17 100 B3
Chantry Rd Bagshot GU19 145 B1
Chertsey KT16 124 B1
Chapel Arches SL6 40 A4
Chapel Cl Bracknell RG12 118 B3
South Stoke RG8 14 B2
Chapel Ct
Hungerford RG17 100 B3
Maidenhead SL6 39 B2
18 Reading RG1 86 A4
Thatcham RG18 106 C2
Chapel Hill Reading RG31 84 B4
Windsor SL4 67 B3
Chapel La
Ashampstead RG8 54 A4
Bagshot GU19 145 B1
Binfield RG42 90 B1
Blewbury OX11 12 A4
Farnborough (Hants) GU14 151 A1
Headley RG19 133 C1
Hermitage RG18 79 B4
Hermitage, Curridge RG18 78 C2
Lambourn RG17 25 A2
Shinfield RG7 113 A1
Silchester RG7 135 C3
Stoke Poges SL2 23 A3
Swallowfield RG7 139 B2
Yattendon RG18 53 C1
Chapel Rd
Camberley GU15 151 A3
Flackwell Heath HP10 3 A4
Silchester RG7 136 B3
Stockcross RG20 103 C3
Chapel Row RG10 61 B2
Chapel Sq
Sandhurst GU15 150 C3
Virginia Water GU25 122 C3
Chapel St Marlow SL7 1 C1
Slough SL1 42 C2
Thatcham RG18 106 B2
Chapels Cl SL1 41 C3
Chaplain's Hill RG45 143 B2
Chaplin Cres TW16 98 C1
Chapman La HP10, SL8 3 A3
Chapman Wlk RG18 106 A2
Chapter Mews SL4 67 B4
Charadon Cl RG2 86 A3
Chard Cl RG5 87 C3
Charfield Ct RG1 86 C4
Charlbury Cl 15 RG12 118 C3
Charlecombe Ct TW18 97 A2
Charles Ct TW15 98 B2
Charles Evans Way RG4 59 B1
Charles Gdns SL2 43 A4
Charles Ho 9 SL4 67 B3
Charles Pl 26 RG1 86 B4
Charles Rd Cholsey OX10 14 A4
Staines TW18 97 B1
Charles Sq RG12 118 B4
Charles St Chertsey KT16 123 C1
Newbury RG14 130 B3
Reading RG1 85 C4
Windsor SL4 67 B3
Charlock Cl RG18 106 C3
Charlotte Cl RG18 79 A3
Charlton SL4 66 B3
Charlton Cl SL1 42 A2
Charlton Ct GU47 143 B1
Charlton La
Swallowfield RG7 139 B3
Upper Halliford TW17 125 B3
Charlton Pl
Newbury RG14 105 A2
2 Windsor SL4 66 B3
Charlton Rd TW17 125 B4
Charlton Row 5 SL4 66 B3
Charlton Sq 4 SL4 66 B3
Charlton Way SL4 66 B3
Charlton Wlk 3 SL4 66 B3
Charlville Dr RG31 84 A2
Charmwood Cl RG14 104 C3
Charnham Ct RG17 100 C3
Charnham La RG17 100 B3
Charnham Pk RG17 100 B4
Charnham St RG17 100 B3
Charnwood SL5 120 C2
Charrington Rd RG31 84 B2
Charta Rd TW20 96 B2
Charter Cl SL1 42 C2
Charter Rd Newbury RG14 130 C4
Slough SL1 41 C3
Charterhouse Cl RG12 118 C2
Charters La SL5 120 B2
Charters Rd SL5 120 C1
Charters Sch SL5 120 B1
Charters Way SL5 120 C1
Charvil House Rd RG10 61 A3

Charvil La RG4 60 C2
Charvil Meadow Rd RG10 61 A3
Charwood Rd RG40 116 C4
Chase Gdns RG42 90 B2
Chase The
Crowthorne RG45 143 A3
Maidenhead SL6 19 B2
Marlow SL7 2 A2
Newbury RG14 104 C4
Reading RG31 84 B2
Chaseley Ct KT13 125 C1
Chaseside Ave RG10 61 B4
Chaseside Gdns KT16 124 A1
Chatfield SL2 42 A4
Chatham Ct 3 SL1 43 A2
Chatham St RG1 85 C4
Chatsworth Ave RG41 88 A1
Chatsworth Cl
Caversham RG4 59 B3
Maidenhead SL6 39 B3
Chatsworth Hts GU15 152 A4
Chatteris Way RG6 114 B4
Chattern Ct TW15 98 A2
Chattern Hill TW15 98 A2
Chattern Rd TW15 98 B2
Chatters The RG7 140 B4
Chatton Cl RG6 114 A4
Chaucer Cl Caversham RG4 59 A3
Windsor SL4 67 B2
Wokingham RG40 116 C3
Chaucer Cres RG14 104 C3
Chaucer Ct TW18 96 B2
Chaucer Gr GU15 151 B3
Chaucer Rd Ashford TW15 97 C2
Crowthorne RG45 143 A2
Chaucer Way RG41 115 C3
Chauntry Cl SL6 40 B3
Chauntry Rd SL6 40 A3
Chavey Down Rd RG42 92 A1
Chawridge La SL4 92 B4
Chazey Cl RG4 58 B4
Chazey Rd RG4 58 B2
Cheam Cl RG12 118 B2
Cheap St Compton RG20 31 C3
Newbury RG14 105 A1
Cheapside RG1 86 A4
Cheapside CE Prim Sch
SL5 120 C4
Cheapside Rd SL5 120 B4
Cheddar Rd TW6 71 A3
Cheddington Cl RG30 84 C3
Cheeseman Cl RG40 116 B4
Chelford Way RG4 58 C2
Chelmsford Ct 35 SL4 67 B3
Chelsea Cl RG30 84 C4
Chelwood Dr GU47 142 C1
Chelwood Rd RG6 87 A1
Cheney Cl RG42 90 B1
Cheniston Ct SL5 121 A1
Cheniston Gr SL6 38 C4
Chepstow Rd RG31 57 B1
Chequer La RG7 138 C1
Chequers Orch SL0 44 C4
Chequers Way RG5 87 B4
Cherbury Cl RG12 118 C3
Cherington Gate SL6 19 A1
Cherington Way SL5 119 C4
Cheriton Ave RG10 61 B3
Cheriton Cl RG14 131 A4
Cheriton Ct 2 RG1 86 A3
Cheriton Way GU17 150 B3
Cherries The SL2 43 A4
Cherry Ave SL3 43 B2
Cherry Cl Caversham RG4 59 B4
Flackwell Heath HP10 3 A4
Newbury RG14 104 C2
Cherry Cnr HP10 3 A4
Cherry Garden La SL6 38 C2
Cherry Gr RG17 100 B3
Cherry Orch
Great Shefford RG17 48 A2
Staines TW18 97 A2
Stoke Poges SL2 23 A3
Cherry Rise HP10 3 A4
Cherry Tree Ave TW18 97 A1
Cherry Tree Cl GU47 143 B1
Cherry Tree Dr RG12 118 B3
Cherry Tree Gr RG41 115 B2
Cherry Tree La SL3 23 C3
Cherry Tree Rd SL2 22 B3
Cherry Way Horton SL3 69 B2
Upper Halliford TW17 125 C3
Cherrydale Rd GU15 152 B3
Cherrygarden La SL6 63 C4
Cherrywood Ave TW20 95 A1
Cherrywood Gdns HP10 3 A4
Chertsey Bridge Rd
KT16, TW18 124 B1
Chertsey Bvd KT16 123 C1
Chertsey La TW18 96 C1
Chertsey Mus KT16 124 A1
Chertsey Rd
Ashford TW15 &TW16 98 B1
Feltham TW13 &TW16 98 C2
Lower Halliford TW17 125 A1
Shepperton TW17 124 C1
Windlesham GU20 146 C3
Chertsey Sta KT16 123 C1
Chertsey Wlk 6 KT16 124 A1
Chervil Way RG7 111 A1
Cherwell Cl Brands Hill SL3 69 A4
Maidenhead SL6 40 A4
Cherwell Cres 18 RG1 85 C4
Cherwell Rd Bourne End SL8 3 A2
Caversham RG4 59 A3
Cheseridge Rd RG20 31 B2
Cheshire Ct SL1 43 A2
Cheshire Pk RG42 91 C1
Chessholme Ct TW16 98 C1
Chessholme Rd TW15 98 B1
Chester Cl Ashford TW15 98 B2
Newbury RG14 105 B1
Chester Rd Harlington TW6 71 A2
Slough SL1 42 B4
Chester St Caversham RG4 59 A1
Reading RG30 85 B4
Chesterblade La RG12 118 C1
Chesterfield Mews TW15 97 C2
Chesterfield Rd
Ashford TW15 97 C2
Newbury RG14 105 A1
Chesterman St RG1 86 A3
Chesterment Way RG6 87 B1
Chesters Rd GU15 152 A3
Chesterton Dr TW19 97 C4
Chesterton Rd RG18 106 B3
Chestnut Ave
Camberley GU15 152 A3
Caversham RG4 59 C2
Slough SL3 43 C2
Wentworth GU25 121 C3
Wokingham RG41 115 C4
Chestnut Cl
Ashford, Chattern Hill TW15 98 A2
Ashford, Felthamhill TW16 98 C1
Blackwater GU17 150 C2
Englefield Green TW20 95 B1
Harlington UB7 71 A4
Maidenhead SL6 20 A1
Medmenham SL7 17 B4
Theale RG7 83 C2
Chestnut Cres
Newbury RG14 105 A2
Shinfield RG2 113 C2
Chestnut Ct 17 RG14 105 A2
Chestnut Dr
Burghfield Common RG30 111 A2
Englefield Green TW20 95 B1
Windsor SL4 66 C2
Chestnut Gr
Purley on T RG8 57 B3
Staines TW18 97 B1
Chestnut La RG17 25 C2
Chestnut Manor Cl TW18 97 A2
Chestnut Pk SL4 40 C2
Chestnut Rd TW15 98 A2
Chestnut Wlk
Hungerford RG17 100 B2
Upper Halliford TW17 125 C3
Chestnuts The RG9 36 A2
Chetwode Cl RG40 116 C3
Cheveley Gdns SL1 21 B2
Cheviot Cl Frimley GU15 152 B2
Harlington UB3 71 B4
Maidenhead SL6 40 A3
Newbury RG14 130 B3
Cheviot Dr RG10 61 A2
Cheviot Rd
Sandhurst GU47 142 C1
Slough SL3 44 A1
Chewter Cl GU19 145 C2
Chewter La GU20 146 A3
Cheylesmore Dr GU16 152 B2
Cheyne Rd TW15 98 B1
Chichester Ct Slough SL1 43 A2
Stanwell TW19 97 C4
Chichester Rd RG30 84 C4
Chicory Cl RG6 86 C1
Chieveley Cl RG31 84 B4
Chieveley Prim Sch RG20 78 A4
Chilbolton TW20 95 C2
Chilcombe Way RG6 87 B1
Child Cl RG40 116 B4
Child St RG17 25 A2
Childrey Way RG31 84 A4
Chillingham Way GU15 151 B2
Chilsey Green Rd KT16 123 C1
Chiltern Cl
Henley-on-T RG9 35 A4
Newbury RG14 130 B3
Staines TW18 97 A2
Chiltern Coll The RG4 59 A2
Chiltern Cres RG6 87 A4
Chiltern Ct Caversham RG4 59 A3
Windsor SL4 67 A3
Chiltern Ct Mews SL4 67 A3
Chiltern Dr RG10 61 A2
Chiltern End Cl RG9 35 B4
Chiltern Gn HP10 3 A4
Chiltern Rd Burnham SL1 41 A4
Caversham RG4 59 B2
Maidenhead SL6 40 A3
Marlow SL7 1 B1
Sandhurst GU47 142 C1
Chiltern View RG8 57 B3
Chiltern Wlk RG8 56 C3
Chilterns Cl HP10 3 A4
Chilterns Pk SL8 3 A3
Chilton Ct SL6 41 B4
Chilton Cty Prim Sch
OX11 10 B4
Chilton Foliat CE Prim Sch
RG17 73 A1
Chilton Way RG17 100 B3
Chilwick Rd SL2 21 C1
Chippendale Cl
Blackwater GU17 150 C2
Tadley RG26 134 C1
Chippenham Cl RG6 113 C4
Chisbury Cl RG12 118 C2
Chiswick Lodge 2 SL7 1 B1
Chitterfield Gate UB7 71 A4
Chittering Cl RG6 87 B1
Chive Rd RG6 87 A1
Chivers Dr RG40 141 C4
Chives Pl RG42 91 B1
Chobham La GU25 122 A1
Chobham Rd
Frimley GU16 151 C1
Sunningdale SL5 121 A1
Choke La SL6 19 A2
Cholmeley Pl RG1 86 C4
Cholmeley Rd RG1 86 C4
Cholmeley Terr RG1 86 C4
Cholsey Rd RG19 106 C2
Choseley Cl RG10 37 C2
Choseley Rd RG10 37 C2
Chrislaine Cl TW19 70 B1
Christ the King
RC Prim Sch RG2 113 B4
Christ the King RC Sch
TW19 70 C1
Christchurch CE Fst Sch
GU25 122 A3
Christchurch Cotts
GU25 122 A3
Christchurch Ct 10 RG1 86 B3
Christchurch Dr GU17 150 B3
Christchurch Gdns RG2 86 B3
Christchurch Rd
Harlington TW6 71 A2
Reading RG2 86 B3
Virginia Water GU25 122 B3
Christian Sq SL4 67 B3
Christie Cl GU18 146 B1
Christie Hts RG14 131 A4
Christie Wlk GU46 149 B2
Christmas La 2 SL2 22 B4
Christopher Ct
Ashford TW15 97 C2
Newbury RG14 105 A1
Christopher Ho 6 SL2 22 B4
Chudleigh Gdns RG2 86 B1
Church App TW20 123 B3
Church Ave RG9 15 C1
Church Cl Eton SL4 67 B4
Hamstead Marshall RG20 129 C3
Laleham TW18 124 B3
Lambourn RG17 25 A1
Maidenhead SL6 39 B3
Winnersh RG41 88 B1
Church Cotts SL6 20 C1
Church Croft RG17 100 B3
Church Dr SL6 40 B2
Church End La RG30 84 C4
Church Farm Barns RG7 137 B3
Church Gate RG19 106 B2
Church Gr SL3 43 B4
Church Hams RG40 141 B3
Church Hill Binfield RG42 90 B3
Camberley GU15 151 C3
Chilton OX11 10 B4
Hurst RG10 88 C3
Woolhampton RG7 107 C2
Church Hill House Hospl
RG12 118 A2
Church La Arborfield RG2 114 B2
Ascot SL5 120 B3
Ashampstead RG8 54 A3
Barkham RG40 115 B1
Binfield RG42 90 B2
Bisley GU24 153 C2
Brimpton RG7 133 C3
Burghfield Common RG30 111 C3
Caversham RG4 59 C4
Chieveley RG20 51 A1
Combe RG17 147 C3
Finchampstead RG40 141 C2
Hamstead Marshall RG20 129 C4
Hungerford RG17 100 B3
Maidenhead SL6 40 B2
Newbury RG14 104 B2
Newell Green RG42 91 B3
Padworth RG7 110 B2
Reading RG2 113 B3
Shiplake RG9 35 C1
Silchester RG7 136 C1
Slough SL2, SL3 43 B4
Stoke Poges SL2 22 C1
Sunningdale SL5 121 A2
Swallowfield RG7 140 B3
Thatcham RG19 106 B2
Twyford RG10 61 C3
17 Windsor SL4 67 B3
Yattendon RG18 53 C1
Church Mews
Purley on T RG8 57 B3
Woodley RG5 87 C4
Church Pk TW15 97 C2
Church Path SL6 40 B2
Church Rd
Aldermaston RG7 135 A4
Arborfield RG7 140 B3
Ascot SL5 120 A3
Ashford TW15 97 C2
Bagshot GU19 145 B2
Blewbury OX11 12 A4
Bracknell RG12 118 B4
Caversham RG4 59 A1
Cookham SL6 19 A3
Earley RG6 87 A3
Egham TW20 96 A2
Farnham Common SL2 22 B1
Frimley GU16 151 B1
Froxfield SN8 99 A3
Ham SN8 126 B1
Little Marlow SL7 2 B3
Lower Halliford TW17 125 A1
Maidenhead SL6 40 A3
Newbury RG14 105 A3
Old Windsor SL4 68 A1
Church Rd *continued*
Pangbourne RG8 56 B3
Sandhurst GU15 150 C4
Sandhurst,
Owlsmoor GU47 143 C1
Silchester RG26 135 C1
Stockcross RG20 103 C3
Sunningdale SL5 121 A2
Swallowfield RG7 139 B3
West End GU24 153 C4
Windlesham GU20 146 B2
Winkfield SL4 92 B3
Winkfield, Chavey Down SL5 119 A4
Woodley RG5 87 C4
Church Rd E RG45 143 A3
Church Row SL3 23 B4
Church Side RG20 30 C3
Church Sq TW17 125 A1
Church St
Burnham SL1 21 B1
Caversham RG4 59 A1
Crowthorne RG45 143 A2
Froxfield SN8 99 A1
Great Shefford RG17 48 A2
Hampstead Norreys RG18 52 C3
Henley-on-T RG9 15 B1
Hungerford RG17 100 B3
Kintbury RG17 102 A1
Reading RG1 86 A3
Slough SL1 42 B2
Slough, Upton Park SL1 42 C2
Staines TW18 96 C2
Theale RG7 83 B2
Twyford RG10 61 B2
Wargrave RG10 36 B1
15 Windsor SL4 67 B3
Church Street Mews RG7 83 B2
Church Terr
8 Reading RG1 86 A3
Windsor SL4 66 C3
Church View
Beenham RG7 109 A3
8 Slough SL1 43 A2
White Waltham SL6 63 C4
Yateley GU46 149 B4
Church Views SL6 39 C4
Church Way RG17 100 B3
Church Wlk KT16 124 A2
Churchend Prim Sch
RG30 84 C3
Churchfield Mews SL2 43 A4
Churchill Cl
East Bedfont TW14 98 C4
Flackwell Heath HP10 3 A4
Reading RG2 86 A1
Churchill Cres GU46 149 B3
Churchill Ct TW18 97 B1
Churchill Dr Marlow SL7 1 C2
Winnersh RG41 88 A1
Churchill Rd
North Ascot SL5 119 C4
Slough SL3 43 C1
Churchmead Sch SL3 68 A4
Churchward Wlk RG31 84 C2
Churchway RG20 10 A1
Churn Rd RG20 31 B3
Cinnamon Cl RG6 86 C1
Cintra Ave RG2 86 B3
Cintra Cl RG1 86 B3
Cippenham Inf Sch SL1 41 B3
Cippenham La SL1 42 A3
Cippenham Mid Sch SL1 41 C3
Circle Hill Rd RG45 143 B3
Circuit La RG30 85 B3
City Rd RG31 84 A4
Clacy Gn RG42 91 A1
Claires Court Sch SL6 20 A1
Clandon Ave TW20 96 B1
Clanfield Cres RG31 57 B1
Clanfield Ride GU17 150 B3
Clappers Farm Rd RG7 136 C1
Clappers Mdw SL6 20 B1
Clapps Gate Rd RG26 135 C1
Clapton App HP10 3 B4
Clare Ave RG40 116 B4
Clare Dr SL2 22 A4
Clare Gdns TW20 96 A2
Clare Rd Maidenhead SL6 39 B3
Slough SL6 41 B4
Stanwell TW19 97 C4
Clare Wlk RG14 130 B3
Claredon Cl RG41 88 B1
Clarefield Cl SL6 19 A1
Clarefield Ct SL5 121 A1
Clarefield Dr SL6 19 A1
Claremont Poyle SL3 69 B3
Shepperton TW17 125 A2
Claremont Ave GU15 151 C3
Claremont Dr TW17 125 A2
Claremont Gdns SL7 1 C1
Claremont Rd
Egham TW18 96 B2
Marlow SL7 1 C1
Windsor SL4 67 B3
Clarence Cres SL4 67 B3
Clarence Ct Egham TW20 95 C1
Maidenhead SL6 39 C4
Windsor SL4 67 A3
Clarence Dr
Camberley GU15 152 A4
Englefield Green TW20 95 B2
Clarence Lodge TW20 95 B2
Clarence Rd
Henley-on-T RG9 15 B1
Windsor SL4 67 A3
Clarence St Egham TW20 95 C1
Staines TW18 96 C2
Clarence Way RG31 84 A2
Clarendon Ct
Blackwater GU17 150 B2
Slough SL2 43 A3
Clarendon Cty Prim Sch
TW15 97 C2
Clarendon Gdns RG14 105 A2
Clarendon Rd
Ashford TW15 97 C2
Reading RG6 87 A3
Clares Green Rd RG7 113 A2
Clarewood Dr GU15 151 C3
Clarke Cres GU15 150 C4
Clarks Gdns RG17 100 B3
Classics The RG17 25 A1
Claverdon RG12 118 A1
Clay Cl Flackwell Heath HP10 3 A4
Purley on T RG31 57 A1
Clay Cnr KT16 124 A1
Clay Hill Cres RG14 105 B3
Clay La Beenham RG7 108 C3
Wokingham RG40 116 C3
Claycots Inf Sch SL2 22 A1
Claycots Jun Sch SL2 22 A1
Claydon Ct
2 Caversham RG4 59 A1
Staines TW18 97 A2
Claydon Gdns GU17 151 A1
Clayhall La SL4 67 C1
Clayhill Cl RG12 119 A3
Clayhill Rd RG7,RG30 111 A2
Clayton Ct SL3 44 A2
Clayton Gr RG12 118 C4
Clayton Rd GU14 150 C1
Clayton Wlk RG2 86 B2
Claytons Cty Comb Sch
SL8 3 A3
Claytons Mdw SL8 3 A2
Cleares Pasture SL1 21 A1
Clearsprings GU18 153 A4
Cleeve Ct TW14 98 C4
Cleeve Down RG8 34 B4
Cleeve Ho 6 RG12 118 C3
Cleeve Rd RG8 34 A4
Clements Cl Shinfield RG7 113 A1
Slough SL1 43 A2
Clements Mead RG31 57 A1
Clements Rd RG9 15 B2
Clent Rd RG2 86 A2
Cleopatra Pl RG42 91 C1
Clerewater Pl RG19 105 C2
Clerics Wlk TW17 125 B2
Cleve Ct RG8 34 A4
Clevedon Dr RG6 87 A1
Clevedon Rd RG31 57 C2
Clevehurst Cl SL2 23 A3
Cleveland RG10 61 A2
Cleveland Cl
Maidenhead SL6 40 A3
Wooburn Green HP10 3 C4
Cleveland Dr TW18 124 A4
Cleveland Gr RG14 104 C2
Cleveland Pk TW19 70 C1
Clevemede RG8 34 B4
Cleves Ct SL4 66 C2
Cleves Way TW16 98 C1
Clewborough Dr GU15 152 A3
Clewborough House Sch
GU15 152 A3
Clewer Ave SL4 67 A3
Clewer Ct Rd SL4 67 A4
Clewer Fields SL4 67 B3
Clewer Green CE Fst Sch
SL4 67 A2
Clewer Hill Rd SL4 66 C2
Clewer New Town SL4 67 A3
Clewer Pk SL4 67 A4
Clifford Gr TW15 98 A2
Clifford Way SL8 3 A3
Clifton Cl SL6 40 A2
Clifton Ct 8 TW19 70 C1
Clifton Lodge Eton SL4 42 A1
10 Slough SL1 43 A2
Clifton Park Rd RG4 59 A1
Clifton Rd Harlington TW6 71 A2
Newbury RG14 104 C1
Slough SL1 43 A2
Wokingham RG41 116 A4
Clifton Rise
Wargrave RG10 36 C1
Windsor SL4 66 B3
Clifton St RG1 85 C4
Clintons Gn RG42 118 A4
Clive Ct SL1 42 B2
Clive Gn RG12 118 A2
Clivedale Rd RG5 87 C2
Cliveden SL6 20 C4
Cliveden Mead SL6 20 B1
Cliveden Pl TW17 125 B2
Cliveden Rd SL6 20 C2
Clivemont Rd SL6 39 C4
Clockhouse La
TW14, TW15 98 A3
Clockhouse La E TW20 96 A1
Clockhouse La W TW20 96 A1
Cloister Mews RG7 83 C2
Cloisters The
Caversham RG4 59 A2
Frimley GU16 151 B1
Clonmel Cl RG4 59 B1
Clonmel Way SL1 21 A1
Close End RG17 25 A1
Close The
Aston Tirrold OX11 12 C4
Bourne End SL8 3 A3
Bracknell RG12 118 B3
Burghfield Common RG7 111 A2
Burnham SL1 41 B3
Great Shefford RG17 48 A2

Close The *continued*
Hampstead Norreys RG18 ..52 C3
Henley-on-T RG9 ..35 B4
Lightwater GU18 ..146 A1
North Ascot SL5 ..119 B4
Sandhurst GU47 ..150 C4
Thatcham RG18 ..106 A2
Virginia Water GU25 ..122 B2
Woodley RG5 ..87 C3
Clough Dr RG18 ..78 C3
Clove Cl RG6 ..86 C1
Clover Cl RG40 ..116 C4
Clover La GU46 ..149 A3
Club La RG45 ..143 B3
Clumps The TW13,TW15 ..98 B2
Clyde Rd TW19 ..97 C4
Clyve Way TW18 ..123 C4
Coach Ho The HP10 ..3 C3
Coach House Cl GU16 ..151 C2
Coach Rd SL5 ..92 C1
Coach Ride SL7 ..1 B2
Coachman's Lodge 28 SL4 ..67 B3
Coachmans Ct RG14 ..105 A2
Coachmans Gr GU47 ..150 A4
Coalmans Way SL1,SL6 ..41 A4
Coalport Way RG30 ..57 C1
Cobb Cl SL3 ..68 B3
Cobbetts La GU46,GU17 ..149 C3
Cobblers Cl SL2 ..22 A2
Cobham Cl SL1 ..41 C3
Cobham Rd RG5 ..87 C4
Cochrane Cl RG19 ..106 C2
Cochrane Pl GU20 ..146 B3
Cock La RG7 ..82 A1
Cock's La RG42 SL4 ..92 A3
Cock-A-Dobby GU47 ..143 A1
Cockett Rd SL3 ..43 C2
Cockney Hill RG30 ..84 C3
Cody Cl RG5 ..88 A4
Coe Spur SL1 ..42 A2
Coftards SL2 ..43 B4
Cokers Ct 2 SL8 ..3 A2
Cold Ash Hill RG18 ..106 B4
Cold Ash St Mark's CE Prim Sch RG18 ..79 B1
Cold Grove Cotts SL6 ..20 C1
Coldharbour Cl
Henley-on-T RG9 ..35 B4
Thorpe TW20 ..123 B3
Coldharbour La
Thorpe TW20 ..123 B3
West End GU24 ..153 C4
Coldharbour Rd RG17 ..100 B2
Coldicutt St RG4 ..59 B1
Coldmoorholme La SL8 ..2 C2
Colemans Moor La RG5 ..87 C3
Colemans Moor Rd RG5 ..88 A3
Colenorton Cres SL4 ..41 C1
Coleridge Ave GU46 ..149 C3
Coleridge Cl
Crowthorne RG45 ..143 B2
Twyford RG10 ..61 C2
Coleridge Cres SL3 ..69 C3
Coleridge Rd TW15 ..97 C2
Coley Ave RG1 ..85 C3
Coley Hill RG1 ..85 C3
Coley Park Prim Sch RG1 ..85 C3
Coley Park Rd RG1 ..85 C3
Coley Pl RG1 ..86 A3
Coley Prim Sch RG1 ..86 A3
Colin Way SL1 ..42 A2
Coliseum Bsns Ctr GU15 ..151 A2
Collaroy Glen RG18 ..106 B4
Collaroy Rd RG18 ..106 B4
College Ave Egham TW20 ..96 A1
Maidenhead SL6 ..39 C4
Slough SL1 ..42 C2
College Cl GU15 ..151 B4
College Cres
Sandhurst GU47 ..150 C4
Windsor SL4 ..67 B3
College Glen SL6 ..39 B4
College Piece RG7 ..136 C3
College Rd
Bracknell RG12 ..118 B3
Maidenhead SL6 ..39 C4
Reading RG6 ..86 C3
Sandhurst GU47 ..150 C4
Slough SL1 ..41 C3
College Ride
Bagshot GU19 ..145 B1
Camberley GU15 ..151 B4
College Rise SL6 ..39 B4
College Town Cty Inf Sch GU47 ..150 C4
College Town Cty Jun Sch GU47 ..150 C4
College Way Ashford TW15 ..97 C2
East Garston RG17 ..47 B3
Colleton Cty Prim Sch The RG10 ..61 C2
Colleton Dr RG10 ..61 C2
Collier Cl SL6 ..19 C1
Colliers Way RG30 ..85 A4
Collingwood Coll GU15 ..152 A4
Collingwood Grange Cl GU15 ..152 A4
Collingwood Mount GU15 ..152 A3
Collingwood Pl GU15 ..152 A4
Collingwood Rise GU15 ..152 A4
Collingwood Wlk RG31 ..84 A4
Collins Cl RG14 ..105 B2
Collins Dr RG18 ..78 C3
Collinswood Rd 1 SL2 ..22 B4
Collis St RG2 ..86 A3
Colliston Wlk RG31 ..84 C2
Collum Green Rd SL2 ..23 A4
Coln Cl SL6 ..39 C4
Coln Trad Est SL3 ..69 C3
Colnbrook By-Pass
Colnbrook SL3, UB7 ..69 B4
Harmondsworth UB7 ..70 B4
Colnbrook CE Prim Sch SL3 ..69 B4
Colnbrook Ct SL3 ..69 C3
Colndale Rd SL3 ..69 C3
Colne Bank SL3, TW19 ..69 B2
Colne Orch SL0 ..44 C3
Colne Reach TW19 ..69 C1
Colne Way TW19 ..96 A3
Colnebridge Cl TW18 ..96 C2
Colnworth Cl RG6 ..114 A4
Colonel's La KT16 ..124 A2
Colonial Rd
East Bedfont TW14 ..98 C4
Slough SL1 ..43 A2
Colonnade SL6 ..40 A4
Colony Gate GU16 ..152 B1
Colston Cl RG31 ..84 B2
Colthrop La RG19 ..107 A1
Colthrop Way RG19 ..107 A1
Coltsfoot Cl RG7 ..111 A2
Columbia Ct RG40 ..141 C4
Colville Gdns GU18 ..153 B4
Colwyn Cl GU46 ..149 B3
Colyer Cl RG18 ..79 B4
Colyton Way RG8 ..57 B3
Combe Rd RG30 ..84 C4
Combe View RG17 ..100 B2
Combermere Cl SL4 ..67 A3
Comet Rd TW19 ..97 B4
Comet Way RG5 ..88 A4
Comfrey Cl RG40 ..116 C4
Commercial Rd
Reading RG2 ..86 A1
Staines TW18 ..97 A1
Common Hill RG7 ..82 C2
Common La
Brightwalton RG20 ..28 B3
Eton SL4 ..42 B1
Common Rd Dorney SL4 ..41 B1
Eton SL4 ..42 A1
Flackwell Heath HP10 ..3 A4
Headley RG19 ..132 C1
Slough SL3 ..44 A1
Common The HP10 ..3 A4
Common Wood SL2 ..22 B4
Commonfield La RG40 ..141 A4
Commonfields GU24 ..153 C3
Commons Rd RG41 ..88 C1
Communications Rd RG19 ..131 C3
Compton Ave RG31 ..84 A4
Compton CE Prim Sch RG20 ..31 C2
Compton Cl
Bracknell RG12 ..117 C2
Earley RG6 ..87 B2
Sandhurst GU47 ..143 B1
Compton Ct SL1 ..41 C4
Compton Dr SL6 ..39 A4
Compton Manor RG20 ..31 B2
Compton Place Bsns Ctr GU15 ..151 A2
Comsaye Wlk RG12 ..118 B2
Concorde Rd SL6 ..39 B2
Concorde Way Slough SL1 ..42 B2
Woodley RG5 ..88 A4
Condor Cl RG31 ..57 B2
Condor Rd TW18 ..124 B3
Conegar Ct SL1 ..42 C3
Coney Grange RG42 ..91 A1
Coneygree Cl RG6 ..87 A1
Congreve Cl RG7 ..135 A4
Conifer Cl RG26 ..134 C1
Conifer Crest RG14 ..130 B2
Conifer Dr
Camberley GU15 ..152 A3
Purley on T RG31 ..57 A1
Conifer La TW20 ..96 B2
Conifers The
Crowthorne RG45 ..143 A4
Maidenhead SL6 ..39 A4
Coningham Rd RG2 ..113 B3
Coningsby RG12 ..118 B3
Coningsby Cl SL6 ..39 B2
Coningsby La SL6 ..65 B3
Conisboro Ave RG4 ..58 C3
Conisboro Way RG4 ..58 C3
Coniston Cl Frimley GU15 ..152 B2
Thatcham RG19 ..106 A2
Woodley RG5 ..87 C3
Coniston Cres SL1 ..41 B4
Coniston Ct
Lightwater GU18 ..146 A1
18 Newbury RG14 ..105 A2
Coniston Dr RG30 ..57 C1
Coniston Way TW20 ..96 A1
Conkers SL6 ..40 A4
Connaught Ave TW15 ..97 C2
Connaught Cl
Crowthorne RG45 ..142 C2
Maidenhead SL6 ..19 C1
Reading RG30 ..85 B4
Yateley GU46 ..149 A3
Connaught Cty Mid Sch GU19 ..145 C1
Connaught Rd
Bagshot GU19 ..145 B2
Camberley GU15 ..151 C3
Newbury RG14 ..105 A2
Reading RG30 ..85 B4
Slough SL1 ..43 A2
Conniston Cl SL7 ..1 A1
Connop Way GU16 ..151 C2
Consort Dr GU15 ..152 B4
Constable Cl RG5 ..88 A4
Constable Way GU47 ..150 C3
Constitution Rd RG30 ..85 A4
Consul Cl RG5 ..88 A3
Control Tower Rd TW6 ..71 A2
Convent Lodge TW15 ..98 A2
Convent Rd Ashford TW15 ..98 A2
Windsor SL4 ..67 A3
Conway Cl GU16 ..151 C1
Conway Dr Ashford TW15 ..98 B1
Thatcham RG18 ..106 A3
Conway Rd Burnham SL6 ..41 A4
Harlington TW6 ..71 A2
Reading RG31 ..84 B3
Cooke Rise RG42 ..91 A1
Cookham Cl GU47 ..143 B1
Cookham Dean Bottom La SL6 ..19 B4
Cookham Dean CE Prim Sch SL6 ..19 A4
Cookham Lodge 15 SL6 ..39 C3
Cookham Rd
Bracknell RG12 ..117 C4
Maidenhead SL6 ..19 C2
Cookham Rise Cty Prim Sch SL6 ..19 C3
Cookham Sta SL6 ..19 C4
Coolarne Rise GU15 ..152 A3
Coolgardie Rd TW15 ..98 B2
Coombe Ct RG19 ..106 C2
Coombe Hill OX12 ..28 A4
Coombe Pine RG12 ..118 B2
Coombe Rd Compton RG20 ..31 C1
Yateley GU46 ..149 A4
Coombe Sq RG19 ..106 C2
Coombe The RG8 ..33 C3
Coombes Cty Inf Sch The RG2 ..114 C2
Coombes La RG41 ..115 B2
Coombesbury La RG20 ..76 B1
Cooper Cl RG2 ..113 B4
Cooper Rd Henley-on-T RG9 ..15 B2
Windlesham GU20 ..146 B2
Cooper Way SL1 ..42 A2
Cooper's Hill La TW20 ..95 B2
Coopers Cl TW18 ..96 C2
Coopers Cres RG18 ..106 B2
Cope Ct SL6 ..39 B4
Cope Hall La RG14 ..130 B4
Copelands Cl GU15 ..152 B2
Copenhagen Cl RG2 ..113 B4
Copenhagen Wlk RG45 ..143 A2
Copped Hall Dr GU15 ..152 B3
Copped Hall Way GU15 ..152 B3
Copper Beech Cl SL4 ..66 B3
Copperage Rd OX12 ..9 A1
Copperdale Cl RG6 ..86 C2
Copperfield Ave GU47 ..143 C1
Copperfields
Ashford TW16 ..98 C1
Reading RG4 ..58 C2
Coppermill Rd TW19 ..69 A1
Coppice Cl RG14 ..131 A4
Coppice Dr TW19 ..95 B4
Coppice Gdns
Crowthorne RG45 ..142 C3
Yateley GU46 ..149 B3
Coppice Gn RG42 ..90 C1
Coppice Rd RG5 ..87 C2
Coppice The TW15 ..98 A1
Coppins La SL0 ..44 C4
Copse Ave RG4 ..59 C2
Copse Cl Camberley GU15 ..152 A3
Marlow SL7 ..1 B1
Purley on T RG31 ..57 B2
Slough SL1 ..41 C3
Copse Dr RG41 ..116 A4
Copse End GU15 ..152 A3
Copse Mead RG5 ..60 C1
Copse The RG10 ..36 C2
Copse Way RG40 ..141 C4
Copthall Ho SL6 ..40 A4
Copthorn Cl SL6 ..39 A2
Copthorne Chase TW15 ..97 C2
Copthorne Cl TW17 ..125 B2
Copthorne Dr GU18 ..146 A1
Corbett Dr GU18 ..152 C4
Corbett Gdns RG5 ..87 C4
Corbridge Rd RG2 ..86 B2
Corby Cl RG5 ..61 A1
Corby Dr TW20 ..95 B1
Cordelia Croft RG42 ..118 C4
Cordelia Gdns TW19 ..97 C4
Cordelia Rd TW19 ..97 C4
Corderoy Cl RG19 ..106 C1
Corderoy Pl KT16 ..123 C2
Cordwalles Cty Jun Sch GU15 ..151 C4
Cordwalles Rd GU15 ..151 C4
Cordwallis Est SL6 ..39 C4
Cordwallis Pk SL6 ..39 C4
Cordwallis Rd SL6 ..39 C4
Cordwallis St SL6 ..39 C4
Cores End Rd SL8 ..3 A2
Corfe Gdns Frimley GU16 ..151 C1
Slough SL1 ..42 A3
Corfe Mews RG4 ..59 C2
Corfe Pl SL6 ..39 B4
Corfield Cl RG40 ..141 C2
Coriander Way RG6 ..86 C1
Corinne Cl RG2 ..86 A1
Cormorant Pl GU47 ..150 C4
Corn Croft RG42 ..91 C1
Cornbunting Cl GU47 ..150 B4
Cornel Ho 1 SL4 ..67 B2
Cornerside TW15 ..98 B1
Cornfield Gn RG41 ..115 C4
Cornfield Rd RG5 ..88 A4
Cornfields GU46 ..149 A2
Cornflower Cl RG41 ..115 B4
Cornwall Ave SL2 ..22 B1
Cornwall Cl Bracknell RG42 ..91 C1
Camberley GU15 ..151 C4
Eton SL4 ..41 C1
Maidenhead SL6 ..19 C1
Purley on T RG31 ..57 A2
Wokingham RG41 ..115 B3
Cornwall Lodge 11 SL6 ..39 C3
Cornwall Way TW18 ..96 C1
Cornwell Rd SL4 ..68 A1
Cornwood Gdns RG2 ..86 B2
Coronation Ave SL3 ..43 C4
Coronation Rd Ascot SL5 ..120 A1
Littlewick Green SL6 ..38 A3
Yateley GU46 ..149 C4
Coronation Sq
Reading RG30 ..85 A2
Wokingham RG40 ..116 B4
Corporation Cotts 1 RG14 ..105 A2
Corrie Gdns GU25 ..122 B1
Corsair Cl TW19 ..97 C4
Corsair Rd TW19 ..97 C4
Corsham Rd RG31 ..84 C2
Corsham Way RG45 ..143 A3
Corwen Rd RG30 ..84 C4
Coster Cl RG14 ..104 B3
Costers Cotts SL8 ..3 A1
Cotswold Cl
Maidenhead SL6 ..40 A3
Slough SL1 ..42 A2
Staines TW18 ..97 A2
Cotswold Rd GU47 ..142 C1
Cotswold Way RG31 ..57 B1
Cottage Farm Way TW20 ..123 B3
Cottage La RG30 ..85 B1
Cotterell Cl RG42 ..91 A1
Cotterell Gdns RG10 ..61 C2
Cottesbrooke Cl SL3 ..69 B3
Cottesloe Cl GU24 ..153 C2
Cottesmore RG12 ..118 A1
Cottesmore Rd RG5 ..87 B3
Coulson Way SL1 ..41 A4
Council Cotts GU24 ..153 C4
Council Hos RG18 ..77 B3
Country Life Ho SL3 ..68 A4
County La RG42 ..91 C1
Courage Ct RG30 ..85 A3
Courage Shire Horse Ctr SL6 ..38 B3
Course Rd SL5 ..120 A3
Court Cl SL6 ..40 B1
Court Cres SL1 ..42 B4
Court Dr SL6 ..20 B2
Court Farm Ho SL1 ..42 A3
Court Farm Ind Est TW19 ..70 C1
Court Garden L Complex SL7 ..1 B1
Court Gdns GU15 ..151 B3
Court Hill Rd OX12 ..7 B4
Court La Burnham SL1 ..21 B1
Dorney SL4 ..41 A2
Iver SL0 ..44 C3
Court Rd SL6 ..20 B2
Court The RG18 ..106 B2
Courtenay Dr RG4 ..59 A4
Courtfield Dr SL6 ..39 B3
Courtfield Rd TW15 ..98 A1
Courthouse Cty Jun Sch SL6 ..39 A4
Courthouse Rd SL6 ..39 B4
Courtlands 14 SL6 ..39 C3
Courtlands Ave SL3 ..43 B1
Courtlands Hill RG8 ..56 B2
Courtlands Rd RG14 ..105 A1
Courtney Rd TW6 ..71 A2
Courts Rd RG6 ..87 A2
Courtyard The
17 Bourne End SL8 ..3 A2
Theale RG7 ..83 C2
Coventry Rd RG1 ..86 C4
Coverdale Way SL2 ..21 C1
Covert La RG12 ..118 B3
Covert The SL5 ..120 A1
Coves Farm Wood RG42 ..117 B4
Cow La East Isley RG20 ..30 C4
Moulsford OX10 ..13 C2
Reading RG1 ..58 C1
Cowley Ave KT16 ..123 C1
Cowley La KT16 ..123 C1
Coworth Cl SL5 ..121 A2
Coworth Rd SL5 ..121 A2
Cowper Cl KT16 ..123 C2
Cowper Rd SL2 ..22 A1
Cowper Way RG30 ..85 B2
Cowslade RG14 ..104 B3
Cowslip Cl RG31 ..84 A3
Cowslip Cres RG18 ..106 C3
Cox Green Comp Sch SL6 ..39 A2
Cox Green La SL6 ..39 B2
Cox Green Rd SL6 ..39 B2
Coxborrow Cl SL6 ..19 C4
Coxeter Rd RG14 ..104 C2
Coxgreen GU47 ..150 B3
Coxs Ave TW17 ..125 C3
Coxs La RG7 ..107 B2
Crabtree Cl RG18 ..78 C3
Crabtree Cnr TW20 ..123 A4
Crabtree La RG18 ..78 C3
Crabtree Office Village TW20 ..123 B4
Crabtree Rd
Camberley GU15 ..151 A1
Thorpe TW20 ..123 B4
Craddock Rd RG2 ..86 A2
Crafnant Ct TW15 ..97 C2
Crafts End OX11 ..10 C4
Craig Ave RG30 ..85 A4
Craigwell Cl TW18 ..123 C4
Crail Cl RG41 ..116 A2
Crake Pl GU47 ..150 B4
Cramond Ct TW14 ..98 C4
Cranbourne Ave
Reading RG31 ..84 B2
Windsor SL4 ..66 C3
Cranbourne Cl SL1 ..42 B3
Cranbourne Cotts SL4 ..93 A3
Cranbourne Gdns RG30 ..58 A1
Cranbourne Prim Sch SL5 ..93 A2
Cranbourne Rd SL1 ..42 B3
Cranbrook Dr SL6 ..19 B1
Cranbury Rd RG30 ..85 B4
Crane Ct GU47 ..150 B4
Crane Rd TW19 ..71 A1
Crane Wharf 14 RG1 ..86 A4
Craneswater UB3 ..71 C4
Cranford Ave TW19 ..97 C4
Cranford Cl Hurst RG10 ..88 C4
Stanwell TW19 ..97 C4
Cranford House Sch OX10 ..13 C3
Cranford La
Harlington TW6 ..71 C3
Harlington UB3 ..71 C4
Hatton TW6 ..71 C2
Cranford Mews 10 RG1 ..86 A3
Cranford Park Dr GU46 ..149 B3
Cranleigh Rd TW13 ..98 C2
Cranmer Cl RG31 ..57 A2
Cranwell Gr
Lightwater GU18 ..152 C4
Littleton TW17 ..124 C3
Cranwell Rd TW6 ..71 A3
Craufurd Ct SL6 ..39 C4
Craufurd Rise SL6 ..39 C4
Craven Cl RG17 ..102 A1
Craven Dene RG14 ..105 A2
Craven Rd Inkpen RG17 ..127 A3
Newbury RG14 ..104 C1
Reading RG1 ..86 B3
Craven Way RG17 ..102 A1
Crawford Cl RG6 ..87 A2
Crawford Gdns GU15 ..151 A3
Crawford Pl RG14 ..104 C2
Crawley Chase RG42 ..92 A1
Crawley Dr GU15 ..151 C3
Crawley Hill GU15 ..151 C3
Crawley Ridge GU15 ..151 C3
Crawley Ridge Cty Inf Sch GU15 ..151 C3
Crawley Ridge Cty Jun Sch GU15 ..151 C4
Crawley Wood Cl GU15 ..151 C3
Crawshay Dr RG4 ..59 A4
Crayle St SL2 ..22 A1
Crayonne Cl TW16 ..125 C4
Crazies Hill CE Prim Sch RG10 ..36 C3
Crecy Cl RG41 ..115 C3
Crediton Cl RG5 ..88 A3
Cree's Mdw GU20 ..146 B2
Creighton Ct RG2 ..86 B2
Cremyll Rd RG1 ..58 C1
Crendon Ct RG4 ..59 A1
Crescent Ct TW18 ..96 C2
Crescent Dale SL6 ..39 C3
Crescent Dr SL6 ..39 C4
Crescent Rd
Reading, Tilehurst RG31 ..57 B1
Reading, Whiteknights RG1 ..86 C3
Shepperton TW17 ..125 B2
Wokingham RG40 ..116 B3
Crescent The
Ashford TW15 ..97 C2
Bracknell RG12 ..118 B3
Chertsey KT16 ..124 A3
Earley RG6 ..87 B2
Egham TW20 ..95 C1
Harlington UB3 ..71 B4
Kintbury RG17 ..102 A1
Lower Halliford TW17 ..125 C1
Maidenhead SL6 ..39 C4
Mortimer RG7 ..137 A3
Padworth RG7 ..109 B2
Shiplake RG9 ..36 A2
Slough SL1 ..42 C2
Theale RG7 ..83 C2
Crescent Villas 5 SL4 ..67 B3
Cress Rd SL1 ..42 A2
Cressex Cl RG42 ..90 B1
Cressida Chase RG42 ..91 C1
Cressingham Rd RG2 ..86 B1
Cressington Pl SL8 ..3 A2
Cresswell Rd RG14 ..105 B2
Cresswell Row SL7 ..1 B1
Cresswells Mead SL6 ..40 B1
Crest Cl RG10 ..61 C3
Crest Ho TW15 ..98 A2
Crest The RG4 ..59 B3
Creswell Cl RG2 ..113 B3
Cricket Field Gr RG45 ..143 B2
Cricket Hill La GU17,GU46 ..149 C2
Cricketers RG20 ..103 C3
Cricketers La
Windlesham GU20 ..146 B2
Winkfield RG42 ..92 A2
Crimp Hill SL4,TW20 ..95 A3
Crisp Gdns RG42 ..90 C1

Crisp Rd RG9 15 B2
Crispin Cl RG4 58 B3
Crispin Way SL2 22 B4
Crocker Cl SL5 119 C4
Crockford Pl RG42 90 C1
Crockhamwell Rd RG5 87 C3
Crocus Mead RG18 106 C2
Crocus Way RG41 115 B4
Croft Cl Harlington UB3 71 B4
Wokingham RG41 116 A1
Croft Cnr SL4 68 A1
Croft La Newbury RG14 104 C2
Yateley GU46 149 B4
Croft Rd Goring RG8 34 B3
Hungerford RG17 100 B3
Mortimer RG7 136 C3
Newbury RG14 130 C4
Shinfield RG7 113 B1
Wokingham RG40 116 A1
Croft The Bracknell RG42 91 A1
Kintbury RG17 102 A1
Maidenhead SL6 39 B3
Marlow SL7 2 A2
Croft Way GU16 151 C1
Crofter's Cl GU47 150 A4
Crofters SL4 68 A1
Crofthill Rd SL2 22 A1
Crofton Cl RG12 118 C2
Crofts The TW17 125 C3
Cromer Cl RG31 57 B1
Cromer Ct SL1 42 C4
Cromer Rd TW6 71 A3
Cromwell Cl RG9 35 C4
Cromwell Dr SL1 42 C4
Cromwell Gdns SL7 1 C1
Cromwell Pl 21 RG14 105 A2
Cromwell Rd Ascot SL5 120 A2
Camberley GU15 151 B4
Caversham RG4 59 A1
Henley-on-T RG9 35 C4
Maidenhead SL6 39 B4
Marlow SL7 1 C1
Newbury RG14 105 B3
Crondall Ct GU15 151 A2
Crondall End GU46 149 B4
Cropper Cl RG19 107 A2
Crosby Gdns GU46 149 A4
Crosby Hill Dr GU15 151 C4
Crosfields Sch RG2 113 C4
Cross Fell RG12 118 A3
Cross Gates Cl RG12 118 C3
Cross Keys Rd RG8 14 B2
Cross La RG7 138 B4
Cross Oak SL4 67 A3
Cross Rd SL5 121 A1
Cross St Reading RG1 86 A4
Wokingham RG40 116 B3
Crossfields Cl RG2 113 C4
Crossland Rd RG1 86 A4
Crossway RG12 118 B4
Crossways Charlton TW16 98 C1
Egham TW20 96 B1
Woodley RG5 87 C3
Crossways Ct 31 SL4 67 B3
Crosswell Cl TW17 125 B4
Crosthwaite Way SL1 41 B4
Crouch La SL4 92 C4
Crow Piece La SL2 21 C2
Crowfield Dr RG19 106 A2
Crowle Rd RG17 25 A1
Crown Acre Cl RG19 106 B2
Crown Cl SW3 69 B4
Crown Colonnade RG1 86 C4
Crown Cotts
Bracknell SL5 119 B2
Englefield Green TW20 95 A1
Windsor SL4 67 B2
Crown Ct RG19 106 B2
Crown Hill Ct SL5 120 A2
Crown La Burnham SL2 22 A2
Maidenhead SL6 40 A4
Marlow SL7 1 B1
Theale RG7 83 C2
Wentworth GU25 122 B2
Crown Mdw SL3 69 A4
Crown Mead RG19 106 B2
Crown Pl Reading RG1 86 B3
Sandhurst GU47 143 C1
Crown Rd Marlow SL7 1 B1
Wentworth GU25 122 B2
Crown Rise KT16 123 C1
Crown Row RG12 118 B2
Crown St Egham TW20 96 A2
Reading RG1 86 A3
Crown Wood Cty Prim Sch RG12 118 C2
Crowsley Rd RG9 36 A2
Crowthorne CE Sch RG45 143 B3
Crowthorne Lodge RG12 118 A3
Crowthorne Rd
Bracknell RG40, RG12 117 C1
Bracknell, Easthampstead RG12 118 A3
Sandhurst GU47 143 A1
Crowthorne Rd N RG12 118 A3
Crowthorne Sta RG45 142 C2
Croxley Rise SL6 39 B3
Croydon Rd TW6 71 A2
Cruikshank Lea GU47 150 C3
Crummock Cl SL1 41 B4
Crutchley Rd RG40 116 B4
Cuba Cotts SL6 20 A2
Cuckoo La GU24 153 B3
Cuckoo Vale GU24 153 B3
Culford Cl RG6 87 B1
Culham Ct RG30 85 A2
Culham Dr SL6 19 C1
Culham Ho 8 RG12 118 C3
Cullen Cl GU46 149 B3
Cullern's Pass SL6 39 C3
Culley Way SL6 39 A2
Culloden Way RG41 115 C3
Culver Croft RG42 90 C1
Culver La RG6 87 A4
Culver Rd Newbury RG14 130 C4
Reading RG6 86 C3
Sandhurst GU47 143 B1
Cumberland Ave SL2 22 A2
Cumberland Dr RG12 118 C4
Cumberland Lodge SL4 94 B2
Cumberland Rd
Ashford TW15 97 B3
Frimley GU15 152 B2
Reading RG1 86 C4
Cumberland St TW18 96 B2
Cumberland Way RG41 115 B3
Cumbernauld Gdns TW16 98 C2
Cumbrae Cl SL2 43 A3
Cumbria Cl SL6 39 B2
Cumnor Way RG12 118 C3
Cunworth Ct RG12 117 C2
Curfew Bell Rd KT16 123 C1
Curl Way RG41 116 A3
Curlew Cl RG19 106 B2
Curlew Dr RG31 84 B3
Curley Hill Rd GU18 152 C4
Curleys Way RG7 139 B3
Curling Way RG14 105 B2
Curls La SL6 39 C2
Curls Rd SL6 39 B2
Curnock Ct RG14 104 C1
Curridge Gn RG18 78 C2
Curridge Piece RG18 78 C3
Curridge Prim Sch RG18 78 B2
Curridge Rd RG18 78 B2
Curriers La SL1 21 B4
Curtis Cl GU15 152 B4
Curtis Rd RG31 84 B2
Curzon Mall 15 SL1 42 C2
Curzon St RG30 85 C4
Cutbush Cl RG6 114 A4
Cutbush La RG2 & RG6 114 A4
Cutting Hill SN8,RG17 126 A2
Cuttings The RG18 52 C3
Cwmcarn RG4 58 C3
Cygnet Cl RG19 106 A2
Cygnets The TW18 96 C2
Cypress Cl RG40 142 A4
Cypress Hill Ct GU14 150 C1
Cypress Ho SL3 44 A1
Cypress Rd RG5 88 A3
Cypress Way GU17 150 A3
Cypress Wlk TW20 95 A1

D

Dacre Ave RG4 59 C2
Dagmar Rd SL4 67 B3
Dair House Sch SL2 22 B2
Dairy Ct SL6 65 A4
Dairy La RG9 16 A4
Dalby Cres RG14 131 A4
Dalcross RG12 118 C2
Dale Cl SL5 121 A2
Dale Ct SL1 42 B2
Dale Gdns GU47 150 A4
Dale Lodge Rd SL5 121 A2
Dale Rd Ashford TW16 98 C1
Reading RG2 86 A3
Walton-on-T KT12 125 C1
Daleham Ave TW20 96 A1
Dalley Ct GU47 150 B4
Dalston Cl GU15 152 B2
Dalton Cl RG30 84 C4
Damask Cl GU24 153 C3
Damer Gdns RG9 35 C4
Damson Gr SL1 42 B2
Dandridge Cl SL3 43 B1
Dandridge Dr SL8 3 B2
Dane Rd TW15 98 B1
Danefield RG40 116 B3
Danehill RG6 114 A4
Danehurst Cl TW20 95 C1
Danes Ct SL6 39 B4
Danes Gdns SL6 19 C3
Danesfield Sch SL7 17 C4
Danvers Cl RG19 106 B1
Danywern Dr RG41 88 B1
Darby Green La GU17 150 A3
Darby Green Rd GU17 150 A3
Darby La RG8 55 A3
Darby Vale RG42 91 A1
Darell Rd RG4 58 C2
Dark La Bradfield RG7 82 B4
Purley on T RG31 57 A1
Wargrave RG10 36 B1
Wickham RG17 101 A4
Darleydale Cl GU47 143 B1
Darling's La SL6 18 C1
Darracott Cl GU15 152 A4
Darrell Cl SL3 43 C1
Dart Cl Brands Hill SL3 69 A4
Thatcham RG18 106 A3
Wokingham RG40 141 C3
Dartington Ave RG5 87 B2
Dartington Cl RG30 84 C4
Dartmouth Cl RG12 118 C3
Dartmouth Ct 27 SL1 42 C2
Dartmouth Terr 1 RG1 86 B3
Darvill's La SL1 42 B2
Darvills La RG10 62 C1
Darwall Dr SL5 119 B4
Darwin Cl RG2 86 A1
Darwin Rd SL3 43 C2
Dashwood Cl
Bracknell RG12 118 B4
Slough SL3 43 B1
Datchet Pl SL3 68 A3
Datchet Rd Horton SL3 68 C2
Old Windsor SL4 68 A2
Slough SL3 42 C1
Windsor SL4 67 B4
Datchet Sta SL3 68 A3
Dauntless Rd RG7 111 A2
Davenport Rd RG12 118 C4
Daventry Cl SL3 69 C3
Daventry Ct RG42 118 A4
David Cl UB3 71 C4
David Ct TW18 97 A2
David Rd SL3 69 C3
David Smith Ct RG31 84 C3
Davis Cl SL7 1 C1
Davis Gdns GU47 150 C4
Davis St RG10 88 B3
Davis Way RG10 88 B2
Davy Cl RG40 116 B3
Dawes East Rd SL1 21 B1
Dawes Moor Cl SL2 43 B4
Dawley Ride SL3 69 C3
Dawlish Rd RG2 86 B1
Dawn Redwood Cl SL3 69 A2
Dawnay Cl SL5 119 C4
Dawnay Rd GU15 151 A4
Daws Ct SL0 44 C4
Dawsmere Cl GU15 152 B3
Dawson Cl SL4 67 A3
Daytona Dr RG19 107 A1
Dayworth Mews RG30 85 B4
De Beauvoir Rd RG1 86 C3
De Bohun Rd RG1 86 A4
De Havilland Way TW19 70 C1
De Montfort Gr RG17 100 B2
De Montfort Rd
Newbury RG14 104 C3
Reading RG1 59 A1
De Ros Pl TW20 96 A1
De-Vitre Gn RG40 116 C4
Deacon Cl RG40 116 B4
Deacon Ct SL4 66 B3
Deacon Way RG30 58 A1
Deaconfield RG8 14 B2
Deacons La RG18 79 B4
Deadman's La RG7 83 B2
Deadmans La RG14, RG19 131 A3
Deadmoor La RG20 130 C1
Deal Ave SL1 41 C4
Dean Cl SL4 66 B2
Dean Gr RG40 116 B4
Dean La SL6 19 B4
Dean Par GU15 151 C4
Dean St SL7 1 B1
Dean's Cloisters SL4 67 B4
Deanfield Ave RG9 15 B1
Deanfield Cl SL7 1 B2
Deanfield Rd RG9 15 B1
Deans Cl SL2 23 A2
Deans Ct GU20 146 B2
Deans Farm RG4 59 B1
Deansfield Cl SL6 19 B1
Deansgate RG12 118 A1
Deansgate Rd RG1 86 A3
Decies Way SL2 23 A2
Dedmere Ct SL7 1 C1
Dedmere Rd SL7 1 C1
Dedmere Rise SL7 1 C1
Dedworth Dr SL4 66 C3
Dedworth Green Fst Sch SL4 66 C3
Dedworth Manor SL4 66 C3
Dedworth Mid Sch SL4 66 C3
Dedworth Rd SL4 66 B3
Dee Rd RG30 85 A4
Deena Cl SL1 41 C3
Deep Field SL3 68 A4
Deep Well Dr GU15 151 C3
Deepcut Bridge Rd GU16 152 B1
Deepdale RG12 118 A3
Deepdene Cl RG1 85 C4
Deepfield Rd RG12 118 B4
Deer Leap GU18 153 A4
Deer Rock Hill RG12 118 B2
Deer Rock Rd GU15 151 C4
Deerhurst Ave RG41 88 B1
Deerhurst Cl RG31 84 C2
Deerswood SL6 20 A1
Defford Cl RG41 88 C1
Delafield Dr RG31 84 B2
Delaford Cl SL0 44 C4
Delamere Ho 8 RG1 85 C3
Delamere Rd RG6 87 A4
Delane Dr RG41 88 A1
Delaney Cl RG30 84 C4
Delft Cl RG30 84 C4
Dell Cl SL2 22 B4
Dell Gr GU16 151 C1
Dell Rd
Finchampstead RG40 142 A2
Purley on T RG31 57 B1
Dell The
Englefield Green TW20 95 A3
Maidenhead SL6 38 C1
9 Reading RG1 86 B4
Yateley GU46 149 B3
Deller St RG42 90 C1
Dellwood Com Hospl RG30 85 B3
Delph The RG6 87 B1
Delta Way TW20 123 B4
Delwood Pk RG4 58 C2
Denbeigh Pl RG1 58 C1
Denborough Cres SL6 39 B3
Denbury Gdns RG2 113 B4
Denby Way RG30 57 C1
Dencliffe TW15 98 A2
Dene Cl 2 Bracknell RG12 118 B4
Earley RG6 87 A2
Dene Hollow OX11 10 C4
Dene Way RG14 105 A3
Denefield Sch RG31 57 A2
Denford La RG17 101 B4
Denham Cl SL6 39 B3
Denham Dr GU46 149 B3
Denham Gr RG12 118 B2
Denham Rd TW20 96 A2
Denison Rd TW13 98 C2
Denly Way GU18 146 B1
Denman Dr TW15 98 A1
Denmark Ave RG5 61 A1
Denmark Rd
Newbury RG14 105 A2
Reading RG1 86 B3
Denmark St
Maidenhead SL6 39 C4
Wokingham RG40 116 B3
Denmead Ct RG12 118 C2
Dennis Cl TW15 98 B1
Dennis Way SL1 41 B3
Dennistoun Cl GU15 151 B3
Dennose Cl RG6 87 A1
Denny Rd SL3 43 C1
Denton Cl RG19 106 B1
Denton Ct SL7 1 C2
Denton Rd RG40 116 B3
Denton Way GU16 151 B1
Depot Rd SL6 40 A3
Derby Cl RG17 25 A1
Derby Rd Caversham RG4 59 A2
Newbury RG14 104 C1
Derby St RG1 85 C4
Derbyshire Gn RG42 91 C1
Derek Horn Ct GU15 151 A3
Derek Rd SL6 40 B4
Deri Dene Cl 2 TW19 70 C1
Derrick Cl RG31 84 B2
Derry Rd GU14 150 C1
Derwent Ave RG30 57 C1
Derwent Cl
East Bedfont TW14 98 C4
Wokingham RG41 115 C3
Derwent Dr Burnham SL1 41 B4
Maidenhead SL6 39 B4
Derwent Rd
Lightwater GU18 153 A4
Thatcham RG19 106 A2
Thorpe Lea TW20 96 A1
Desborough Cl TW17 125 A1
Desborough Sch SL6 39 C3
Deseronto Wharf Ind Est SL3 43 C2
Desford Way TW15 97 C3
Devenish La SL5 120 B1
Devenish Rd SL5 120 B1
Devereux Rd SL4 67 B3
Deverills Way SL3 44 B1
Deveron Dr RG30 85 A4
Devil's La TW20 96 B1
Devils Highway The RG45 142 C3
Devitt Cl RG2 86 C1
Devon Ave SL1 42 B4
Devon Chase RG42 91 C1
Devon Cl Sandhurst GU47 150 B4
Wokingham RG41 115 C3
Devon Dr RG4 59 C2
Devonshire Cl SL2 22 A2
Devonshire Dr GU15 151 C4
Devonshire Gdns RG31 57 A2
Devonshire Gn SL2 22 A2
Devonshire Lodge 10 SL6 39 C3
Devonshire Pk RG2 86 C1
Dewberry Down RG18 106 C2
Dewe La RG30 84 C1
Dhoon Rise SL6 39 C3
Diamedes Ave TW19 97 B4
Diamond Cotts RG10 37 B3
Diamond Hill GU15 151 C4
Diamond Rd SL1 43 A2
Diamond Ridge GU15 151 C4
Diamond Way RG41 115 C4
Diana Cl SL3 43 C4
Dianthus Cl KT16 123 C1
Dianthus Pl RG42 92 A1
Dick Turpin Way TW14 71 C2
Dickens Cl RG4 59 B1
Dickens Way GU46 149 B3
Dickens Wlk RG14 131 A4
Dido Rd OX11 9 C4
Dieppe Cl RG41 115 C3
Digby Rd RG14 104 C2
Dines Way RG18 79 B4
Dingle Rd TW15 98 A2
Dinton Pastures Ctry Pk RG10 88 B3
Disraeli Ct SL3 69 A4
Ditchfield La RG40 141 C4
Ditchling RG12 118 A1
Ditton Park Rd SL3 68 C4
Ditton Rd Datchet SL3 68 B4
Slough SL3 68 C4
Dittons The RG40 141 C3
Divine Mercy Coll RG9 15 C3
Dobson's La RG9 15 B4
Dockett Eddy La TW17 124 C1
Dockett Moorings KT16 124 C1
Doctors La RG18 79 A3
Doddington Cl RG6 87 B1
Dodsells Well RG40 141 C4
Dodsfield Rd SL2 22 A1
Dog La RG8 54 A3
Doghurst Ave UB3 71 A4
Doghurst Dr UB7 71 A4
Dogkennel La OX12 27 B2
Doles Hill RG41 115 B2
Doles La RG41 115 C2
Dolman Rd RG14 105 A2
Dolphin Cl Brimpton RG7 134 C4
Winnersh RG41 88 B1
Dolphin Ct Bracknell RG12 118 B3
Slough SL1 43 A2
Stanwell TW19 97 A3
Dolphin Ct N TW19 97 A3
Dolphin Est The TW16 125 B4
Dolphin Rd
Charlton TW16 125 C4
Slough SL1 43 A2
Dolphin Rd N TW16 125 C4
Dolphin Rd S TW16 125 C4
Dolphin Rd W TW16 125 C4
Doman Rd GU15 151 A2
Domoney Cl RG19 106 C2
Don Cl RG30 85 A4
Donaldson Way RG5 88 A4
Doncastle Rd RG12 117 C3
Donegal Cl RG4 59 B2
Donkey Dr SL8 3 A2
Donkey La SL8 3 A2
Donkin Hill RG4 59 B2
Donnington Castle RG14 104 C4
Donnington Cl
Bucklebury RG7 108 B4
Camberley GU15 151 A2
Donnington Gdns
Maidenhead SL6 19 C1
Reading RG1 86 C3
Donnington Lodge RG14 104 C4
Donnington Pl RG41 88 B1
Donnington Rd RG1 86 B3
Donnington Sq RG14 104 C3
Donnybrook RG12 118 A1
Dorcas Ct GU15 151 A2
Dorchester Cl SL6 19 A1
Dorchester Ct
Reading RG30 85 B3
Staines TW18 97 A2
Dorchester Dr TW14 71 C1
Dorian Dr SL5 120 C4
Doris Rd TW15 98 B1
Dorking Way RG31 84 A2
Dorly Cl TW17 125 C2
Dormer Cl
Crowthorne RG45 143 A3
Newbury RG14 130 C3
Dormy Ho The GU25 121 C2
Dornels SL2 43 B4
Dorney Ct SL4 41 A2
Dorney Cty Comb Sch SL4 40 C2
Dorney Lake Rowing Ctr SL4 66 A4
Dorney Reach Rd SL4 40 C2
Dorney Wood Rd SL1 21 B3
Dorothy Ct RG14 105 B2
Dorothy St 20 RG1 86 A3
Dorset Ct GU15 151 C4
Dorset Lodge 9 SL6 39 C3
Dorset Rd Ashford TW15 97 B3
Windsor SL4 67 B3
Dorset St RG30 85 B4
Dorset Vale RG42 91 C1
Dorset Way RG41 115 C3
Douai Sch RG7 108 C3
Doublet Cl RG19 106 A2
Douglas Ct Earley RG6 87 A2
Marlow SL7 2 A2
Douglas Grange RG10 88 C2
Douglas La TW19 68 C1
Douglas Rd
Caversham RG4 59 B1
Slough SL2 42 B4
Stanwell TW19 70 B1
Doultons The TW18 97 A1
Douro Cl RG26 134 B1
Dove Cl RG6 113 C4
Dove Ct TW19 97 C4
Dove House Cres SL2 21 C1
Dovecote Rd RG2 113 A4
Dovedale Cl
Caversham RG4 58 C2
Sandhurst GU47 143 B1
Dover Rd SL1 41 C4
Dover St RG1 86 A3
Doveton Way RG14 105 A2
Dowding Cl RG5 88 A4
Dowding Ct RG45 143 B3
Dower Pk SL4 66 C2
Down Pl SL4 66 A4
Downe House Sch RG18 79 A2
Downend La RG20 51 A1
Downfield La SL6 63 B3
Downfield Rd RG10 63 A2
Downham Ct RG2 86 C1
Downing Path SL2 21 C1
Downing Rd RG31 84 B4
Downlands RG17 47 B3
Downmill Rd RG12 117 C4
Downs Cl RG17 46 C4
Downs Rd Aldworth RG20 32 A2
Slough SL3 43 B2
Downs Sch The RG20 31 B2
Downs View OX11 12 C4
Downs Way Chilton OX11 9 C4
Purley on T RG31 57 C1
Downshire Cl RG17 48 A2
Downshire Sq RG1 85 C3

Downshire Way
Bracknell, Priestwood RG12 118 A3
Bracknell, Skimpedhill RG12, RG42 118 A4
Downside OX11 10 B4
Downsway Sch RG31 57 B2
Doyle Gdns GU46 149 B2
Drain Hill RG17 25 A2
Drake Ave Slough SL3 43 B1
Staines TW18 96 C2
Drake Cl Bracknell RG12 118 A2
Wokingham RG40 141 C4
Draper Cl RG19 106 B1
Draycott RG12 118 C2
Drayhorse Dr GU19 145 C1
Drayton Cl RG12 118 B4
Drayton Rd RG30 85 A4
Dresden Way RG30 57 C1
Drew Mdw SL2 22 B4
Drewett Cl RG2 113 B3
Drift Rd Holyport SL4,SL6 65 B2
Oakley Green SL4 66 A1
Drift Way SL3 69 B4
Driftway Cl 4 RG6 87 B1
Drill Hall Rd KT16 124 A1
Drive The Ashford TW15 98 B1
Bourne End SL8 2 C2
Datchet SL3 68 A3
Earley RG6 87 A4
Newbury RG14 130 C4
Slough SL3 43 C2
Virginia Water GU25 122 C2
Wraysbury TW19 68 B1
Droitwich Cl RG12 118 C3
Dromepath RG41 88 A2
Dropmore Rd SL1 21 B3
Drove La RG18 79 B1
Drove The RG19 133 A1
Drovers Way
Bracknell RG12 118 C3
Woodley RG5 87 C3
Druce Way RG19 106 B2
Druce Wood SL5 119 C4
Drummond Cl RG12 118 C4
Drummond Ho 4 SL4 67 B2
Drury La RG7 137 A3
Dry Arch Rd SL5 120 C2
Dryden RG12 118 A1
Dryden Cl RG18 106 B3
Du Pre Wlk HP10 3 B2
Duchess Cl RG45 143 A4
Duchess St SL1 41 C3
Dudley Cl RG31 57 C1
Dudley Ct SL1 43 A2
Dudley Mews RG31 57 C1
Dudley Rd Ashford TW15 97 C2
East Bedfont TW14 98 B4
Duffield La SL2 22 C3
Duffield Pk SL2 23 A1
Duffield Rd RG5 60 C1
Dugdale Ho TW20 96 B2
Duke Of Cornwall Ave GU15 144 B1
Duke St Eton SL4 67 B4
Henley-on-T RG9 15 C1
Reading RG1 86 A4
Duke's Hill GU19 145 C3
Duke's La
Old Windsor SL4, SL5 94 A2
Winkfield SL5 93 C1
Duke's Ride RG45 143 A3
Dukes Cl TW15 98 B2
Dukes Covert GU19 145 C3
Dukes Pl SL7 1 B1
Dukes Ride RG7 136 A1
Dukes Wood RG45 143 A3
Dukeshill Rd RG42 118 A4
Dulnan Cl RG30 85 A4
Dulverton Gdns RG2 86 B1
Dumas Cl GU46 149 B3
Dumbarton Way RG4 59 C3
Dunally Pk TW17 125 B1
Dunaways Cl RG6 87 B2
Dunbar Cl SL2 43 A3
Dunbar Dr RG5 88 A3
Dunboe Pl TW17 125 B1
Duncan Dr RG40 116 C3
Duncan Gdns
Purley on T RG8 57 B2
Staines TW18 97 A1
Duncan Rd RG5 87 C3
Duncannon Cres SL4 66 B2
Duncombe Ct TW18 96 C1
Duncroft SL4 66 C2
Duncroft Manor TW18 96 C3
Dundaff Cl GU15 152 A3
Dundas Cl RG12 118 A3
Dundee Rd SL1 42 A4
Dundela Cl RG5 87 C3
Dunford Pl RG42 90 C1
Dungells Farm Cl GU46 149 B2
Dungells La GU46 149 B2
Dungrovehill La SL6 18 B2
Dunholme Cl RG6 87 C1
Dunholme End SL6 39 B2
Dunkirk Cl RG41 115 C3
Dunleary Ct 13 RG30 85 B3
Dunluce Gdns RG8 56 C3
Dunn Cres RG17 102 A1
Dunnock Way RG10 36 C2
Dunoon Cl RG31 84 C2
Dunsfold Rd RG30 84 C4
Dunsmore Gdns GU46 149 A3
Dunstable Ho 11 SL7 1 C1
Dunstall Cl RG31 84 B4
Dunstan Ct TW18 97 A2
Dunstan Park Inf Sch RG18 106 B2
Dunstan Rd RG18 106 C2
Dunstans Dr RG41 88 A1
Dunster Cl RG4 59 B3
Dunster Gdns SL1 42 A3
Dunt Ave RG10 88 C2
Dunt La RG10 88 C2
Dunwood Ct SL6 39 B3
Duppas Cl TW17 125 B2
Dupre Cl SL1 41 C2
Durand Rd RG6 87 A1
Durant Way RG31 57 B2
Durham Ave SL1 42 A4
Durham Cl Reading RG2 113 B4
Wokingham RG41 115 C3
Durham Rd GU47 143 C1
Durley Mead RG12 118 C2
Durrell Way TW17 125 B2
Dutch Barn Cl TW19 70 B1
Dutton Way SL0 44 C4
Duval Pl GU19 145 C2
Dwyer Rd RG30 85 A2
Dyer Straits OX12 9 C4
Dyers Ct RG5 87 B4
Dyson Cl SL4 67 A2
Dysons Cl RG14 104 C2
Dysonswood La RG4 58 C4

E

Eagle Cl Crowthorne RG45 143 A4
Wokingham RG41 115 C3
Eagle House Sch GU47 143 A1
Eagle Rd RG20 132 A1
Eagles Nest GU47 143 A1
Earle Croft RG42 91 B1
Earley Hill Rd RG6 87 A3
Earley Pl RG1 86 A4
Earley Sta RG6 87 B2
Earleydene SL5 120 A1
Earls Gr GU15 151 C3
Earls La SL1 41 C3
Earlsfield SL6 40 B1
Earlsfield Cl RG4 59 C2
Earlswood RG12 118 A1
Easby La RG6 87 B1
Easington Dr RG6 87 C1
East Berkshire Coll
Maidenhead SL6 39 B3
Slough SL3 44 A2
Windsor SL4 67 B3
East Burnham Cotts SL2 22 A2
East Burnham La SL2 22 A2
East Cres SL4 66 C3
East Dr Reading RG31 84 C3
Stoke Poges SL2 22 C1
Wentworth GU25 122 A2
East Gn GU17 150 B2
East La RG20 51 A1
East Paddock SL6 18 C3
East Park Farm Dr RG10 61 A2
East Ramp TW6 71 A3
East Rd East Bedfont TW14 98 B4
Maidenhead SL6 39 C4
East Ridge SL8 3 A2
East St RG1 86 A4
East Stratton Cl RG12 118 C2
East View Cl RG10 36 C1
East View Rd RG10 36 C1
Eastbourne Rd SL1 42 A4
Eastbridge SL2 43 A3
Eastbury Ave RG31 84 A4
Eastbury Ct RG42 90 C1
Eastbury Pk RG41 88 B1
Eastbury Shute RG17 46 C1
Eastchurch Rd TW6 71 C2
Eastchurch Road Rdbt TW6 71 C3
Eastcourt Ave RG6 87 A3
Eastcroft SL2 22 A1
Eastern Ave
Chertsey KT16 124 A3
Reading RG1 86 C3
Eastern Dr SL8 3 B2
Eastern Ind Area RG12 118 B4
Eastern La RG45 143 C2
Eastern Perimeter Rd
Hatton TW14 71 C2
Hatton TW6 71 C3
Eastern Rd RG12 118 B4
Eastfield OX11 12 A4
Eastfield Cl 4 SL1 43 A2
Eastfield La RG8 56 B4
Eastfield Rd SL1 41 A4
Easthampstead Park Sch RG12 117 B2
Easthampstead Rd
Bracknell RG12 118 A4
Wokingham RG40 116 C2
Eastheath Ave RG41 116 A2
Eastheath Gdns RG41 116 A2
Eastleigh Rd TW6 71 C2
Eastlyn Rd RG26 135 C1
Easton Hill RG20 76 A2
Eastwood Ct 1 SL7 1 C2
Eastwood Rd RG5 87 C2
Eastworth Rd KT15, KT16 124 A1
Eaton Pl RG1 85 C4
Eaton Rd GU15 151 A3
Ebborn Sq RG6 114 B4
Ebsworth Cl SL6 20 B2
Eccles Cl RG4 59 B1
Echelford Cty Mid Sch TW15 98 A2
Echelforde Dr TW15 98 A2
Eddington Hill RG17 100 C4
Eddington Rd RG12 117 C2
Eddystone Wlk TW19 97 C4
Eden Cl SL3 44 A1
Eden Way RG41 88 A1
Edenhall Cl RG31 57 B2
Edenham Cl RG6 87 C1
Edenham Cres RG1 85 C3
Edgar Milward Cl RG30 58 A1
Edgar Wallace Pl SL8 3 A3
Edgbarrow Rise GU47 143 A1
Edgbarrow Sch RG45 143 B2
Edgbarrowhill Star RG45 143 A2
Edgcumbe Park Dr RG45 143 A3
Edgecombe La RG14 105 B3
Edgedale Cl RG45 143 A3
Edgehill St RG1 86 A3
Edgell Cl GU25 122 C3
Edgell Rd TW18 96 C2
Edgemoor Rd GU16 152 B2
Edgewood Cl RG45 143 A4
Edinburgh Ave SL1 42 A4
Edinburgh Dr TW18 97 B1
Edinburgh Rd
Maidenhead SL6 19 C1
Marlow SL7 1 C2
Reading RG30 85 C4
Edith Rd SL6 39 A4
Edmonds Ct 4 RG12 118 B4
Edmunds Way SL2 43 A4
Edneys Hill RG41 115 B1
Edward Ave GU15 151 A3
Edward Ct TW18 97 B1
Edward Pauling Ho TW14 98 C4
Edward Pauling Prim Sch TW13 98 C3
Edward Pl 25 RG1 86 B4
Edward Rd Hatton TW14 71 C1
Twyford RG10 61 A3
Windlesham GU20 146 B2
Edward Way TW15 97 C3
Edwards Ct SL1 42 C2
Edwards Hill RG17 25 A1
Edwin Cl RG19 106 C2
Eeklo Pl RG14 105 A1
Egerton Rd Reading RG2 86 C1
Sandhurst GU15 150 C4
Slough SL2 21 C1
Egham By-Pass TW20 96 A2
Egham Hill TW20 95 B1
Egham Hill Rdbt TW20 95 C2
Egham Mus TW20 96 A2
Egham Sta TW20 96 A2
Eghams Ct 9 SL8 3 A2
Egremont Dr RG6 87 B2
Egremont Gdns SL1 42 A3
Egypt La SL2 22 A4
Eight Acres SL1 21 A1
Eight Bells RG14 104 C1
Eisenhower Ave RG20 49 A2
Elan Cl RG30 84 C4
Elbow Mdw SL3 69 C3
Eldart Cl RG30 85 A4
Elder Cl RG31 57 B1
Elderberry Way RG6 87 B1
Elderfield Cres OX11 10 B4
Elderfield Rd SL2 22 C3
Eldon Pl RG1 86 B4
Eldon Rd RG1 86 B4
Eldon Sq RG1 86 B4
Eldon St RG1 86 B4
Eldon Terr RG1 86 B4
Eldrick Ct TW14 98 B4
Elford Cl RG6 87 B1
Elgar Ave RG45 143 A4
Elgar Rd RG2 86 A3
Elgar Rd S RG2 86 A2
Elgarth Dr RG40 141 C4
Elgin Ave TW15 98 B1
Elgin Cres TW6 71 C3
Elgin Ho SL3 69 C3
Eliot Cl Camberley GU15 152 A4
Caversham RG4 59 A2
Thatcham RG18 106 B3
Elizabeth Ave
Bagshot GU19 145 C1
Newbury RG14 130 B4
Staines TW18 97 B1
Elizabeth Cl
Bracknell RG12 118 B3
Cookham SL6 19 C4
Henley-on-T RG9 35 A4
Elizabeth Ct 9 Slough SL1 43 A2
Wargrave RG10 36 C1
Elizabeth Gdns Ascot SL5 120 A2
Kintbury RG17 102 A1
Elizabeth Ho TW15 97 C2
Elizabeth Mews 18 RG1 86 A3
Elizabeth Par GU46 149 B2
Elizabeth Rd
Henley-on-T RG9 35 A4
Marlow SL7 1 C2
Wokingham RG40 116 B3
Elizabeth Rout Cl RG7 113 B1
Elizabeth Way SL2 22 C2
Elizabeth Wlk 23 RG1 86 A3
Elizabethan Cl TW19 97 B4
Elizabethan Way TW19 97 B4
Ellenborough Cl RG12 118 B3
Ellerton Cl RG7 83 C2
Ellesfield Ave RG12 117 C3
Ellesmere Cl RG4 59 C3
Ellies Mews TW15 97 C3
Elliman Ave SL2 42 C3
Ellington Ct SL6 40 B4
Ellington Gdns SL6 40 B4
Ellington Pk SL6 19 C1
Ellington Prim Sch SL6 19 C1
Ellington Rd Feltham TW13 98 C2
Ellington Rd *continued*
Taplow SL6 40 B4
Elliot Dr SL7 1 C2
Elliot Rise SL5 119 B4
Elliots Way RG4 59 A1
Elliott Gdns TW17 125 A3
Ellis Ave SL1 42 C2
Ellis Rd RG45 143 A3
Ellison Cl SL4 66 C2
Ellison Ho 23 SL4 67 B3
Ellison Way RG40 116 A3
Elm Bank GU46 149 B4
Elm Cl
Farnham Common SL2 22 B3
Stanwell TW19 97 B4
Elm Cotts RG20 129 C1
Elm Croft SL3 68 B3
Elm Ct 5 Charlton TW16 98 C1
Sandhurst GU47 143 C1
Elm Dr
Burghfield Common RG30 111 A3
Winkfield SL4 93 A4
Elm Gr Maidenhead SL6 39 C4
Thatcham RG18 106 A3
Elm La Bourne End SL8 2 C3
Earley RG6 86 C1
Elm Lodge Ave RG30 85 B4
Elm Park Rd RG30 85 B4
Elm Pk Reading RG30 85 B4
Sunningdale SL5 120 C1
Elm Rd Earley RG2 & RG6 86 C1
East Bedfont TW14 98 B4
Mapledurham RG4 58 B4
Windsor SL4 67 A2
Elm Tree Cl TW15 98 A2
Elmar Gn SL2 22 A1
Elmbank Ave TW20 95 A1
Elmcroft RG8 34 B3
Elmcroft Cl TW14 71 C1
Elmcroft Dr TW15 98 A2
Elmdon Rd TW6 71 C2
Elmhurst Ballet Sch GU15 151 B3
Elmhurst Ct SL3 44 A2
Elmhurst Rd Goring RG8 34 B4
Reading RG1 86 B3
Slough SL3 44 A2
Thatcham RG18 106 A3
Elmleigh Ct RG4 59 B2
Elmley Cl RG41 88 C1
Elms Ave RG19 106 C2
Elms Dr SL8 3 B2
Elms Rd RG40 116 A3
Elms The TW15 98 A2
Elmshott La SL1 41 C3
Elmsleigh Ctr The TW18 96 C2
Elmsleigh Rd TW18 96 C2
Elmslie Ct SL6 39 C4
Elmstone Dr RG31 57 B1
Elmsway TW15 98 A2
Elmwood SL6 20 A2
Elmwood Rd SL2 43 A3
Elsenwood Cres GU15 152 A3
Elsenwood Dr GU15 152 A4
Elsinore Ave TW19 97 C4
Elsley Rd RG31 57 C2
Elstow Ave RG4 59 B3
Elstree Cl RG31 57 B1
Elstree Sch RG7 108 B2
Elsworth Cl TW14 98 C4
Eltham Ave Caversham RG4 59 C3
Slough SL1 41 C2
Elton Dr SL6 39 B4
Elvaston Way RG30 85 A4
Elveden Cl RG6 87 C1
Elvendon Rd RG8 34 B4
Elwell Cl TW20 96 A1
Ely Ave SL1 42 B4
Ely Rd Hatton TW6 71 C3
Theale RG7 83 C2
Embankment The TW19 95 B4
Ember Rd SL3 44 A2
Emblem Cres RG2 114 C1
Embrook Way RG31 84 A2
Emerald Cl RG41 115 C4
Emerald Ct SL1 42 C2
Emerson Ct HP10 3 C3
Emery Acres RG8 55 A3
Emery Down Cl RG12 119 A3
Emlyns Bldgs SL4 67 B4
Emm Cl RG41 115 C4
Emma La RG10 36 C1
Emmbrook Comp Sch RG41 115 C4
Emmbrook Ct RG2 86 C1
Emmbrook Gate RG41 115 C4
Emmbrook Inf Sch RG41 88 C1
Emmbrook Jun Sch RG41 88 C1
Emmbrook Rd RG41 115 C4
Emmbrook Vale RG41 89 A1
Emmer Green Ct RG4 59 B3
Emmer Green Prim Sch RG4 59 A3
Emmets Nest RG42 90 B1
Emmets Pk RG42 90 B1
Emmview Cl RG41 115 C4
Empress Rd RG31 84 B3
Enborne Cl RG31 84 B4
Enborne Gate RG14 104 B1
Enborne Gdns RG12 91 B1
Enborne Gr RG14 104 C1
Enborne Lodge Sch RG14 130 A3
Enborne Pl RG14 104 C1
Enborne Prim Sch RG20 129 C3
Enborne Rd RG14 104 B1
Enborne St
Hamstead Marshall RG20 130 A2
Enborne St *continued*
Newbury RG14 130 B3
Enborne Way RG7 133 C3
Enfield Rd TW6 71 C3
Enfield Road Rdbt TW6 71 C3
Engineers Rd RG19 132 A3
Englefield CE Prim Sch RG7 83 A2
Englefield Cl TW20 95 B1
Englefield Green Sch TW20 95 B2
Englefield Rd RG7 83 B2
Engleheart Dr TW14 71 C1
Englehurst TW20 95 B1
Englemere Pk SL5 119 B3
Englemere Pond Nature Trail SL5 119 B3
Englemere Rd RG42 90 C1
Englesfield GU15 152 B3
English Gdns TW19 68 B1
English Martyrs RC Prim Sch RG30 85 A4
Enid Wood Ho RG12 118 B4
Ennerdale RG12 118 A3
Ennerdale Cl TW14 98 C4
Ennerdale Cres SL1 41 B4
Ennerdale Rd RG2 86 B2
Ennerdale Way RG19 106 A2
Ensign Cl TW19 97 B4
Ensign Way TW19 97 B4
Enstone Rd RG5 88 A4
Enterprise Way RG19 107 A1
EP Collier Prim Sch RG1 59 A1
Epping Cl RG1 85 C4
Epping Ho 6 RG1 85 C3
Epping Way RG12 118 C3
Epsom Cl GU15 151 B4
Epsom Cres RG14 105 A1
Epsom Ct RG1 85 C3
Epsom Sq TW6 71 C3
Equine Way RG14 131 A4
Eric Ave RG4 59 A3
Erica Cl Slough SL1 41 C3
West End GU24 153 C3
Erica Dr RG40 116 B3
Eriswell Cl RG6 87 C1
Erkenwald Cl KT16 123 C2
Erleigh Court Dr RG6 87 A4
Erleigh Court Gdns RG6 87 A4
Erleigh Dene RG14 104 C1
Erleigh Rd RG1 86 B3
Ermin St Lambourn RG17 46 B1
Stockcross RG20 103 B4
Wickham RG20 75 B2
Ermin Wlk RG19 106 A2
Errington Dr SL4 67 A3
Erskine Cl RG26 135 C1
Escot Rd TW16 98 C1
Esher Cres TW6 71 C3
Esher Rd GU15 145 A1
Eskdale Gdns SL6 40 A1
Eskdale Rd RG41 88 A2
Eskdale Way GU15 152 B2
Eskin Cl RG30 85 A4
Essame Cl RG40 116 B3
Essex Ave SL2 42 B4
Essex Pl RG17 25 A2
Essex Rise RG42 91 C1
Essex St Newbury RG14 130 B4
Reading RG2 86 A3
Ethel Rd TW15 97 C2
Eton Cl SL3 68 A4
Eton Coll SL4 67 B4
Eton Ct Eton SL4 67 B4
Staines TW18 96 C2
Eton End PNEU Sch SL3 68 A4
Eton Pl SL7 1 B1
Eton Porny CE Comb Sch SL4 67 B4
Eton Rd Datchet SL3 68 A4
Harlington UB3 71 C4
Eton Sq SL4 67 B4
Eton Wick CE Fst Sch SL4 42 A1
Eton Wick Rd SL4 42 A1
Eton Wlk 22 SL1 42 C2
European Weather Ctr RG2 113 B4
Eustace Cres RG40 116 B4
Evedon RG12 118 A1
Evelyn Cres TW16 125 C4
Evelyn Ct RG5 87 C3
Evelyn Way TW16 125 C4
Evendon's Cl RG41 116 A2
Evendon's La
Barkham RG41 115 C1
Wokingham RG41 116 A2
Evenlode SL6 39 C4
Evenlode Rd SL8 3 A2
Evenlode Way GU47 150 B4
Everard Ave SL1 42 C2
Everest Rd
Camberley GU15 151 B4
Crowthorne RG45 143 A3
Stanwell TW19 97 C4
Evergreen Ct TW19 97 B4
Evergreen Dr RG31 84 C2
Evergreen Rd GU16 152 A2
Evergreen Way
Stanwell TW19 97 B4
Wokingham RG41 115 C3
Everington La RG18 53 A1
Everland Rd RG17 100 B3
Eversley Rd
Arborfield RG2 114 C1
Barkham RG40 140 C3

Eversley St RG27 141 A1
Eversley Way TW20 123 B4
Evesham Rd RG4 59 A3
Evesham Wlk GU47 143 B1
Evreham Rd SL0 44 C4
Evreux Cl RG19 106 C1
Ewing Way RG14 131 A4
Exbourne Rd RG2 113 B4
Exchange Rd SL5 120 B2
Exeforde Ave TW15 98 A2
Exeter Ct RG2 113 A4
Exeter Gdns GU46 149 A4
Exeter Rd TW6 71 C2
Exeter Way Hatton TW6 71 C3
Theale RG7 83 C2
Exmoor Rd RG19 106 B2
Explorer Ave TW19 97 C4
Expressway RG14 105 C1
Exwick Sq RG2 113 B4
Eylham RG8 57 A3
Eynsford Cl RG4 59 C3
Eynsham Rd RG5 87 C4
Eyre Gn SL2 22 A1

F

Fagg's Rd TW14 71 C2
Fair Close Ho 1 RG14 105 A1
Fair Lawn Gn RG2 86 C1
Fair Mile RG9 15 B2
Fair Mile Hospl OX10 14 A4
Fair View Cotts SL6 19 C4
Fairacre SL6 39 B3
Fairacres Ind Est SL4 66 B3
Faircroft SL2 22 A1
Faircross RG12 118 A3
Faircross Quarters RG18 78 C3
Faircross Rd RG30 85 B3
Fairfax RG42 118 A4
Fairfax Cl RG4 59 A2
Fairfax Pl RG14 105 C3
Fairfield RG20 31 B2
Fairfield App TW19 68 B1
Fairfield Ave Datchet SL3 68 B4
Farnham Common SL2 22 A2
Staines TW18 96 C2
Fairfield Cl SL3 68 B4
Fairfield Dr GU16 151 C2
Fairfield La GU24 153 C4
Fairfield Rd Burnham SL1 21 B1
Goring RG8 34 B4
Wraysbury TW19 68 B1
Fairfields RG17 100 B3
Fairford Rd
Maidenhead SL6 39 C4
Purley on T RG31 57 B1
Fairhaven TW20 95 C2
Fairhaven Ct 1 TW20 95 C2
Fairholme TW14 98 C4
Fairholme Jun & Inf Schs
TW14 98 B4
Fairholme Rd TW15 97 C2
Fairlawn Pk SL4 66 C2
Fairlawns Cl TW18 97 A1
Fairlea SL6 39 A2
Fairlie Rd SL1 42 A4
Fairlight Ave SL4 67 B3
Fairlop Cl RG31 84 B2
Fairmead Cl GU47 150 C4
Fairmead Rd RG2 113 C3
Fairmile Ct RG9 15 B2
Fairoak Way RG26 134 B1
Fairsted Cl RG30 85 A4
Fairview RG14 130 C4
Fairview Ave RG6 87 A3
Fairview Cotts GU25 122 B2
Fairview Ct TW15 98 A2
Fairview Dr TW17 124 C2
Fairview Est RG9 35 C4
Fairview Rd Burnham SL6 41 A4
Hungerford RG17 100 B3
Slough SL2 21 C1
Wokingham RG40 116 B3
Fairwater Dr RG5 87 B3
Fairway KT16 124 A1
Fairway Ave RG30 84 B3
Fairway Dr RG10 61 A3
Fairway Hts GU15 152 A3
Fairway The Burnham SL1 21 B2
Flackwell Heath HP10 3 B4
Frimley GU15 152 A2
Maidenhead SL6 39 A2
Fairways TW15 98 A1
Faithfull Cl RG42 91 A1
Fakenham Cl RG6 114 A4
Fakenham Way GU47 143 B1
Falaise TW20 95 C2
Falcon Ave RG2 86 C1
Falcon Cl GU18 152 C4
Falcon Ct GU16 151 B1
Falcon Dr TW19 70 C1
Falcon Fields RG26 135 A1
Falcon House Gdns
RG20 129 C1
Falcon Way
Sunbury TW16 125 C4
Wokingham RG41 115 C3
Yateley GU46 149 A3
Falcons Croft HP10 3 C4
Falconwood TW20 95 C2
Falkland Dr RG14 130 C4
Falkland Garth RG14 130 B4
Falkland Ho SL6 39 C4
Falkland Prim Sch RG14 130 B3
Falkland Rd
Caversham RG4 59 A1
Newbury RG14 130 B3
Fallowfield GU46 149 A4
Fallowfield Cl RG4 59 A2
Falmouth Cl GU15 152 A2
Falmouth Rd
Reading RG2 113 B4
Slough SL1 42 A4
Falmouth Way RG19 106 C2
Falstaff Ave RG6 86 C1
Fane Way SL6 39 B3
Fanes Cl RG42 117 C4
Fannys La RG7 80 B1
Faraday Cl Arborfield RG2 140 C4
Slough SL2 42 A4
Faraday Rd
Newbury RG14 105 A2
Slough SL2 42 A4
Farcrosse Cl GU47 150 B4
Fareham Dr GU46 149 A4
Faringdon Cl GU47 143 B1
Faringdon Dr RG12 118 B2
Faringdon Wlk RG30 85 A2
Farleigh Mews RG4 59 C3
Farley Copse RG42 117 C4
Farley Hill Prim Sch
RG7 140 B3
Farley Moor RG42 117 B4
Farley Villas KT16 124 A1
Farm Cl Ascot SL5 120 B2
Bracknell RG42 117 C4
Crowthorne RG45 143 B4
Egham TW18 96 C2
Lower Halliford TW17 125 A1
Lyne KT16 123 A2
Maidenhead SL6 40 B1
Maidenhead, Highway SL6 39 A4
Purley on T RG8 57 B3
Yateley GU46 149 B3
Farm Cres SL2 43 B4
Farm Dr Old Windsor SL4 68 A1
Reading RG31 84 A3
Farm Lea HP10 3 C4
Farm Rd Bourne End SL8 2 C2
Burnham SL6 41 A3
Frimley GU16 151 C1
Goring RG8 34 B3
Henley-on-T RG9 35 C4
Maidenhead SL6 39 A4
Staines TW18 97 A1
Farm View GU46 149 B3
Farm Way TW19 69 C1
Farm Yd SL4 67 B4
Farman Cl RG5 88 A4
Farmer's Rd TW18 96 C2
Farmers Cl Maidenhead SL6 39 A2
Reading RG2 113 B3
Farmers End RG10 61 A2
Farmers Gate RG18 106 B3
Farmers Way SL6 39 A2
Farmiloe Cl RG8 57 B2
Farnburn Ave SL1 42 A4
Farnell Rd TW18 97 A3
Farnham Cl RG12 118 B4
Farnham Common
Cty Inf Sch SL2 22 A4
Farnham Common
Cty Jun Sch SL2 22 B4
Farnham Common Ho 3
SL2 22 B4
Farnham Dr RG4 59 C2
Farnham La SL2 22 A2
Farnham Park La SL2 22 B2
Farnham Rd SL1, SL2 42 B4
Farningham RG12 118 C2
Farningham Ho RG12 118 C2
Farnsfield Cl RG6 114 A4
Farrell Cl GU15 151 B2
Farrer Theatre SL4 42 B1
Farrier Ct 11 SL8 3 A2
Farriers Cl RG5 87 C4
Farriers La RG20 30 C4
Farrowdene Rd RG2 113 B4
Farthing Green La SL2 23 A2
Farthingales The SL6 40 A4
Fatherson Rd RG1 86 B4
Faulkner Pl GU19 145 C2
Faversham Rd GU47 143 B1
Fawcett Cres RG5 87 B3
Fawcett Rd SL4 67 A3
Fawler Mead RG12 118 C3
Fawley Bottom Rd RG9 15 A4
Fawley Cl SL6 19 B1
Fawley Ct RG9 15 C3
Fawley Mews 2 RG1 85 C3
Fawley Rd RG30 85 B3
Fawns Manor Cl TW14 98 B4
Fawns Manor Rd TW14 98 B4
Fawsley Cl SL3 69 C4
Faygate Way RG6 87 A1
Feathers La TW19 96 A3
Felbridge Cl GU16 151 C1
Felbridge Ct UB3 71 B4
Felix La TW17 125 C2
Felixstowe Cl RG6 87 B1
Fellow Gn GU24 153 C3
Fellow Green Rd GU24 153 C3
Fellowes Ct UB3 71 B4
Fells The RG31 84 A3
Felstead Cl RG6 86 C2
Feltham Hill
Jun & Inf Schs TW13 98 C3
Feltham Hill Rd TW15 98 B1
Feltham Rd TW15 98 B2
Felthorpe Cl RG6 114 A4
Felton Way RG31 84 B4
Fencote RG12 118 B2
Fennel Cl Earley RG6 86 C1
Newbury RG14 105 B3
Fenns La GU24 153 C3
Fennscombe Ct GU24 153 C3
Fenton Ave TW18 97 B2
Fern Cl Crowthorne RG45 143 A4
Frimley GU16 152 B2
Reading RG31 84 B3
Fern Dr SL6 41 A4
Fern Glen RG31 57 B1
Fern Wlk Ashford TW15 97 B2
Reading RG31 84 B3
Fernbank RG40 141 B4
Fernbank Cres SL5 119 B4
Fernbank Pl SL5 119 B4
Fernbank Rd SL5 119 B4
Fernbrook Rd RG4 58 C3
Ferndale Ave RG30 85 A2
Ferndale Cl RG31 57 C2
Ferndale Ct RG19 106 B2
Ferndale Pk SL6 65 C4
Ferndale Rd TW15 97 C2
Ferne Cl RG8 34 B4
Fernery The TW18 96 C2
Fernhill Cl Bracknell RG42 90 C1
Farnborough (Hants) GU17 150 C1
Fernhill Comp Sch
GU14 150 C1
Fernhill Cty Prim Sch
GU14 150 C1
Fernhill La GU17 150 C1
Fernhill Rd GU14,GU17 150 C1
Fernhill Wlk GU17 150 C1
Fernhurst Rd
Ashford TW15 98 B2
Reading RG31 84 B2
Ferniehurst GU15 151 C2
Fernley Ct SL6 19 B1
Ferrard Cl SL5 119 B4
Ferrers Cl SL1 41 C3
Ferriby Ct RG12 118 B4
Ferrier Gr RG14 131 A4
Ferry Ave TW18 96 C1
Ferry End SL6 40 B2
Ferry La Bourne End SL8 3 A1
Chertsey KT16 124 A2
Cookham SL6 20 A4
Goring RG8 34 A3
Hambleden RG9 16 B3
Laleham TW18 124 B3
Lower Halliford TW16,TW17 125 A1
Medmenham SL7 17 A3
South Stoke RG8 14 A2
Wargrave RG10 36 B1
Wraysbury TW19 96 A3
Ferry Rd Maidenhead SL6 40 B2
South Stoke RG8 14 B2
Ferry Wks TW17 125 A1
Festival Cotts SL3 69 B4
Fettiplace RG17 48 A2
Fidlers La RG20 30 C4
Fidlers Wlk RG10 36 C1
Field Cl
Burghfield Common RG7 111 A1
Harlington UB3 71 B4
Field End GU24 153 C3
Field House Cl SL5 120 A1
Field Hurst SL3 43 C1
Field La GU16 151 C1
Field Pk RG12 118 B4
Field Rd
Farnborough (Hants) GU14 150 C1
Peasemore RG20 29 B1
Reading RG1 86 A3
Field View Caversham RG4 59 A2
Egham TW20 96 B2
Feltham TW13 98 B3
Fielden Pl RG12 118 B4
Fieldfare Ave GU46 149 A3
Fieldhead Gdns SL8 3 A2
Fieldhouse Ind Est SL7 1 C1
Fieldhouse La SL7 1 C1
Fieldhouse Way SL7 1 C1
Fielding Gdns
Crowthorne RG45 143 A2
Slough SL3 43 B2
Fielding Rd
Maidenhead SL6 39 A4
Sandhurst GU47 150 C3
Fieldings The SL6 65 A4
Fieldridge RG14 105 B3
Fields The SL1 42 B2
Fieldview Ct TW18 97 A1
Fieldway RG41 88 B1
Fifehead Cl TW15 97 C1
Fifield Cotts SL6 65 B3
Fifield La SL4,SL6 65 B2
Fifield Rd SL6 65 B4
Fifth Rd RG14 104 C1
Fifth St RG19 131 C3
Filbert Dr RG31 84 B4
Filey Rd RG1 86 C4
Filey Spur SL1 42 A2
Filmer Rd SL4 66 B3
Finbeck Way RG6 113 C4
Finch Ct SL6 39 B3
Finch Rd RG6 87 B2
Finch Way RG7 111 A2
Fincham End Dr RG45 142 C2
Finchampstead
CE Prim Sch RG40 141 C2
Finchampstead Rd
Finchampstead RG40 141 C3
Finchampstead RG40 142 A4
Wokingham RG41, RG40 116 A2
Findhorn Cl GU47 150 B4
Fineleigh Ct SL1 42 C3
Finmere RG12 118 B1
Finney Dr GU20 146 B2
Finstock Cl RG6 87 B1
Finstock Gn RG12 118 C3
Fir Cottage Rd RG40 141 C4
Fir Dr GU17 150 B2
Fir Tree Ave SL2 22 C1
Fir Tree Cl SL5 120 A1
Fir Tree Cnr RG26 134 C1
Fir Tree Cotts RG20 10 A1
Fir Tree La RG14 105 C2
Fir Tree Paddock RG20 10 A1
Fir Tree Pl TW15 98 A2
Fir Tree Prim Sch RG14 105 C2
Firbank Pl TW20 95 A1
Fircroft Cl Reading RG31 57 B1
Stoke Poges SL2 23 A3
Fireball Hill SL5 120 B1
Firglen Dr GU46 149 B4
Firgrove Rd RG27,GU46 149 B3
Firlands RG12 118 B2
Firlands Ave GU15 151 B3
Firmstone Cl RG6 87 B1
Firs Ave SL4 66 C2
Firs Cl RG40 141 C4
Firs Dr SL3 43 C3
Firs End RG7 111 A1
Firs La Maidenhead SL6 38 C2
Reading RG30 85 B3
Firs Rd RG31 84 B3
Firs The 14 Bracknell RG12 118 C3
Inkpen RG17 127 C3
Maidenhead SL6 39 C4
Reading RG30 85 C3
Thatcham RG18 106 A2
First Ave Marlow SL7 2 A1
Tadley RG7 135 B1
First Cres SL1 42 B4
First St RG19 132 A3
Firtree Cl GU47 142 C1
Firview Cl SL7 1 C1
Firwood Ct GU15 151 B3
Firwood Dr GU15 151 B3
Firwood Rd GU25 121 C2
Fisher Gn RG42 90 A1
Fisherman's Way SL8 3 A2
Fishermans La RG7 135 A4
Fishermans Retreat SL7 1 C1
Fishers Cotts RG4 59 B3
Fishers Ct RG4 59 B3
Fishers La RG18 79 A1
Fishers Wood SL5 121 B1
Fishery Rd SL6 40 B3
Fishguard Spur SL1 43 A2
Fishponds Cl RG41 116 A2
Fishponds Est RG41 116 A2
Fishponds Rd RG41 116 A2
Fitzrobert Pl TW20 96 A1
Fitzroy Cres RG5 88 A3
Five Acre RG31 57 A1
Five Acres HP10 3 C4
Flag Staff Sq RG19 106 C1
Flambards RG4 59 B1
Flamborough Cl RG6 87 C1
Flamborough Spur SL1 42 A2
Flamingo Cl RG41 115 C3
Flanders Ct TW20 96 B2
Flats The GU17 150 B2
Flaxman Cl RG6 86 C1
Flecker Cl RG18 106 B3
Fleet Cl RG41 115 C3
Fleet Hill RG40 141 B1
Fleet La RG40 141 A1
Fleetbrook Ho SL3 68 B3
Fleetham Gdns RG6 87 B1
Fleetway TW20 123 B3
Fleetwood Cl RG14 105 B3
Fleetwood Ct 7 TW19 70 C1
Fleetwood Rd SL2 42 C3
Fleming Cl RG2 140 C4
Fleming Rd RG14 105 A2
Flemish Fields KT16 124 A1
Fletcher Gdns RG42 117 B4
Flexford Gn RG12 117 C2
Flintgrove RG12 118 B4
Flintjack Pl RG17 25 A1
Flintlock Cl TW19 70 A2
Flodden Dr RG31 84 B2
Floral Ho KT16 123 C1
Floral Way RG18 106 C3
Floreat Gdns RG14 104 C1
Florence Ave SL6 40 A4
Florence Cl GU46 149 B3
Florence Cotts SL4 92 B4
Florence Ct 19 RG30 85 B3
Florence Gdns TW18 97 A1
Florence Rd GU47 150 C4
Florence Wlk RG1 86 B4
Florian Gdns RG30 85 A3
Florida Ct Reading RG30 85 C3
Staines TW18 97 A2
Flowers Hill RG8 56 B2
Flowers Piece RG8 54 A3
Fobney St RG1 86 A4
Fokerham Rd RG19 106 C1
Folder's La RG42 91 B1
Foliejohn Way SL6 38 C1
Folkestone Ct SL3 44 A1
Follet Cl SL4 68 A1
Folly La RG7,RG30 110 C3
Folly Rd Inkpen RG17 127 C3
Lambourn RG17 25 A2
Folly The RG14 105 A1
Fontmell Cl TW15 98 A2
Fontmell Pk TW15 98 A2
Fontwell Cl SL6 39 A4
Fontwell Dr RG30 84 C3
Fontwell Rd RG14 105 A1
Forbes Chase GU47 150 B4
Forbury Ho 6 RG30 85 A4
Forbury La RG17,RG20 128 B4
Forbury Rd RG1 86 B4
Forbury Ret Pk RG1 86 B4
Forbury The RG1 86 A4
Ford Cl Ashford TW15 97 C1
Littleton TW17 125 A2
Ford La RG7 140 A1
Ford Rd Ashford TW15 97 C2
Bisley GU24 153 C2
Chertsey KT16 124 A1
Fordbridge Ct TW15 97 C1
Fordbridge Rd
Ashford TW15 97 C2
Upper Halliford
TW16, TW17 125 C2
Fordham Way RG6 87 B1
Fordingbridge Cl KT16 124 A1
Fordwater Rd KT15, KT16 124 A1
Fordwater Trad Est
KT16 124 B1
Fordwells Dr RG12 118 C3
Forehead The RG7 137 C2
Forest Cl Bracknell SL5 119 B3
Tadley RG26 134 C1
Forest Comp Sch The
RG41 88 B1
Forest Dean RG2 113 B4
Forest Dr TW16 98 C1
Forest End Rd GU47 150 A4
Forest Gn RG12 118 B4
Forest Green Rd SL6 65 B3
Forest Hill RG30 57 C1
Forest Hills GU15 151 A2
Forest Rd Binfield RG42 90 B2
Crowthorne RG45 143 B3
Windsor SL4 93 C4
Windsor, Dedworth SL4 66 C3
Winkfield RG42, SL5 92 B1
Forest View Cotts SL6 65 B3
Foresters Sq RG12 118 C3
Foresters Way RG45 143 C4
Forge Cl Caversham RG4 59 B1
Kintbury RG17 102 A1
Forge Cotts SN8 99 A3
Forge Dr SL2 22 B3
Forge Hill RG18 53 A3
Forge The Harlington UB3 71 B4
Hungerford RG17 100 B4
Forlease Cl SL6 40 A3
Forlease Dr SL6 40 A3
Forlease Rd SL6 40 A3
Formby Cl Earley RG6 87 C2
Slough SL3 44 B1
Forndon Cl RG6 87 C1
Forsters RG7 134 C4
Fort Narrien GU15 150 C4
Fortrose Cl GU47 150 B4
Fortrose Wlk RG31 84 C2
Forty Green Dr SL7 1 A1
Fosseway RG45 143 A3
Fosswood Dr GU15 151 B4
Foster Ave SL4 66 C2
Fosters Gr GU20 146 A3
Fosters La RG5 87 C3
Fosters Path SL2 21 C1
Fotherby Ct SL6 40 A3
Fotheringay Gdns SL1 42 A3
Foundation Pk SL6 38 C2
Foundry Ct KT16 124 A1
Foundry Ho RG17 100 C3
Foundry La SL3 69 A2
Foundry Mews 1 KT16 124 A1
Foundry Pl 6 RG1 86 A3
Fountain Gdns SL4 67 B2
Fountains Garth RG12 118 A3
Fourth Ave SL7 2 A1
Fourth St RG19 131 C3
Fowler Cl RG6 87 A1
Fowlers La RG42 118 A4
Fox Cl RG7 111 A1
Fox Covert GU18 153 A4
Fox Covert Cl SL5 120 B1
Fox Dr GU46 149 B4
Fox Hill Prim Sch RG12 118 A1
Fox La RG27 149 A4
Fox La N KT16 123 C1
Fox La S KT16 123 C1
Fox Rd Bracknell RG12 118 B1
Slough SL3 43 B1
Foxborough RG7 139 B3
Foxborough Cl SL3 44 A1
Foxborough Ct SL6 39 C2
Foxborough Prim Sch
SL3 44 A1
Foxbury RG17 25 A1
Foxcombe Dr RG31 84 B4
Foxcote RG40 142 A4
Foxdown Cl GU15 151 B3
Foxes Piece SL7 1 C2
Foxes Piece Comb Sch SL7 1 C2
Foxes Wlk RG10 61 A2
Foxglove Cl Stanwell TW19 97 B4
Winkfield RG42 92 A1
Wokingham RG41 115 B4
Foxglove Gdns 4 RG1 85 C4
Foxglove Way
Thatcham RG18 106 B3
Thatcham RG18 106 C3
Foxhays Rd RG2 113 B4
Foxheath RG12 118 C2
Foxherne SL3 43 B2
Foxhill Cl RG4 60 A3
Foxhill Cres GU15 152 A4
Foxhill La RG4 59 C3
Foxhill Rd RG1 86 C3
Foxhollow Dr SL2 22 B4
Foxhunt Gr RG31 84 C2

Foxhunter Way RG19 105 C2
Foxleigh Ct TW18 96 B2
Foxley Cl GU17 150 B3
Foxley La RG42 90 B1
Foxley PNEU Sch RG10 63 A1
Framewood Manor SL2 23 B3
Framewood Rd SL2, SL3 23 B3
Framlingham Dr RG4 59 C3
Frampton Cl RG5 60 C1
France Hill Dr GU15 151 B3
France Hill Sch GU15 151 B1
Frances Ave SL5 20 B1
Frances Rd SL4 67 B3
Frances The RG18 106 B2
Francis Baily Prim Sch RG19 106 C2
Francis Chichester Cl SL5 120 A2
Francis Cl TW17 125 A3
Francis Gdns RG42 91 B1
Francis St RG1 86 A3
Francis Way Burnham SL1 41 B3
Frimley GU15 152 B2
Francomes Field RG17 25 B1
Frank Lunnon Cl SL8 3 B2
Frank Sutton Way SL1 42 B3
Franklin Ave Slough SL2 42 A4
Tadley RG26 135 A1
Franklin Ct 21 RG1 85 C4
Franklin St RG1 85 C4
Franklyn Cres SL4 66 B2
Frascati Way SL6 39 C4
Fraser Ave RG4 59 B3
Fraser Mead GU47 150 C3
Fraser Rd RG42 118 A4
Frederick Ho TW15 97 C2
Frederick Pl RG41 116 A3
Free Prae Rd KT16 124 A1
Freeborn Way RG12 118 C4
Freeman Cl TW17 125 C3
Freemans Cl
Hungerford RG17 100 B3
Stoke Poges SL2 23 A3
Freemantle Rd GU19 145 C2
Freemantles Sch (Specl Sch) KT16 123 C1
Freesia Cl RG41 115 B4
French Gdns GU17 150 B2
Frenchum Gdns SL1 41 C3
Frensham RG12 118 B2
Frensham Cl GU46 149 A3
Frensham Gn RG2 86 C1
Frensham Rd RG45 143 A4
Frensham Wlk SL2 22 B3
Freshfield Cl RG6 87 C2
Freshfields La RG20 51 A1
Freshwater Rd RG1 86 C4
Freshwood Dr GU46 149 B2
Friar St RG1 86 A4
Friars Keep RG12 118 A3
Friars Rd Newbury RG14 131 A4
Virginia Water GU25 122 B3
Friars Way KT16 124 A2
Friars Wlk 3 RG1 86 A4
Friary Dr TW19 68 B1
Friary Rd Ascot SL5 120 A2
Wraysbury TW19 95 B4
Friary The SL4 68 B1
Friday St RG9 15 C1
Friendship Way RG12 118 A3
Frieth Cl RG6 87 A1
Frilsham Rd RG30 85 A2
Frimley Cl RG5 87 B4
Frimley Grove Gdns GU16 151 C1
Frimley Hall Dr GU15 151 C3
Frimley High St GU16 151 B1
Frimley Park Hospl GU16 151 B1
Frimley Rd
Camberley GU15 151 A2
Frimley GU15, GU16 151 B1
Fringford Cl RG6 87 B1
Frith Hill Rd GU16 152 A1
Frithe The SL2 43 A4
Frithwald Rd KT16 123 C1
Frobisher RG12 118 B1
Frobisher Cres TW19 97 C4
Frobisher Gdns TW19 97 C4
Frodsham Way GU47 143 C1
Frog Hall RG40 116 C3
Frog Hall Dr RG40 116 C3
Frog La RG12 118 A3
Frogmill SL6 17 B2
Frogmill Ct SL6 17 B2
Frogmore Cl SL1 42 A2
Frogmore Com Coll GU46 149 C3
Frogmore Ct GU17 150 B2
Frogmore Cty Inf Sch GU17 150 A3
Frogmore Cty Jun Sch GU17 150 A3
Frogmore Gr GU17 150 B2
Frogmore Park Dr GU17 150 B2
Frogmore Rd GU17 150 B3
Frogmore Way RG30 85 A3
Fromer Rd HP10 3 B2
Fromont Dr RG19 106 B2
Fromow Gdns GU20 146 B2
Front St RG17 47 B3
Frouds Bridge Marina RG7 108 C1
Frouds La RG7 109 A1
Froxfield Ave RG1 85 C3
Froxfield Down 6 RG12 118 C2
Fruen Rd TW14 98 C4
Fry Ct RG4 59 A2
Frymley Hill SL4 66 B3
Frys La GU46 149 C4
Fuchsia Cl RG31 84 B3
Fuchsia Way GU24 153 C3
Fullbrook Cl
Maidenhead SL6 40 A4
Wokingham RG41 89 A1
Fullbrook Cres RG31 57 B2
Fuller Cl RG19 106 C1
Fullers La Ball Hill RG20 129 B1
Burghfield Common RG7 112 A2
Fullers Yd SL6 20 A1
Fulmead Rd RG30 85 B4
Fulmer Chase SL3 23 B4
Fulmer Cl RG6 87 A1
Fulmer Common Rd SL3 23 C3
Fulmer Cty Fst Sch SL3 23 C4
Fulmer Rd SL3 23 C4
Furlong Cl SL8 3 A2
Furlong Rd SL8 3 A2
Furness SL4 66 B3
Furness Pl 8 SL4 66 B3
Furness Row 9 SL4 66 B3
Furness Sq 6 SL4 66 B3
Furness Way SL4 66 B3
Furness Wlk 7 SL4 66 B3
Furnival Ave SL2 42 A4
Furnival Cl GU25 122 B2
Furrow Way SL6 39 A2
Furse Cl GU15 152 B2
Furze Hill Cres RG45 143 B2
Furze Platt Cty Inf Sch SL6 19 B1
Furze Platt Cty Jun Sch SL6 19 B1
Furze Platt Halt SL6 19 C1
Furze Platt Rd SL6 19 A1
Furze Platt Sch SL6 19 B1
Furze Rd Maidenhead SL6 19 B1
Tadley RG26 134 C1
Furzebank SL5 120 B3
Furzedown Cl TW20 95 C1
Furzemoors RG12 118 A2
Furzen Cl SL2 22 A1
Fuzzens Wlk SL4 66 C3
Fydlers Cl SL5 93 A1
Fyfield Cl GU17 150 B3
Fyfield Rd RG19 106 B1
Fylingdales RG19 106 B1

G

Gables Ave TW15 97 C2
Gables Cl Datchet SL3 68 A4
Maidenhead SL6 40 A4
Gables Way RG19 107 B1
Gabriel Dr GU15 152 A2
Gabriels The RG14 130 B3
Gage Cl SL6 39 C2
Gainsborough
Bracknell RG12 118 B2
Cookham SL6 19 C3
Gainsborough Ave RG17 102 A1
Gainsborough Cl
Camberley GU15 151 C4
Woodley RG5 88 A3
Gainsborough Cres RG9 35 B4
Gainsborough Dr
Maidenhead SL6 39 B2
North Ascot SL5 119 B4
Gainsborough Hill RG9 35 B4
Gainsborough Rd
Henley-on-T RG9 35 B4
Reading RG30 85 A3
Gairn Cl RG30 85 A4
Galahad Cl SL1 42 A2
Gale Dr GU18 146 A1
Galley La RG19 132 B1
Galleymead Rd SL3 69 C3
Gallop The GU46 149 B4
Gallops The RG20 30 C3
Galloway Chase SL2 43 A3
Galloway Ctr The RG14 105 C1
Galloway Ho 7 RG1 85 C3
Gallys Rd SL4 66 B3
Galsworthy Dr RG4 59 C3
Galsworthy Rd 4 KT16 124 A1
Galton Rd SL5 120 C2
Galvin Rd SL1 42 B3
Garde Rd RG4 60 C2
Garden Cl Ashford TW15 98 B1
Maidenhead SL6 39 A3
Garden Close La RG14 130 B2
Garden Cotts SL3 69 B4
Garden Mews
8 Reading RG30 85 B3
Slough SL1 42 C3
Gardeners La RG8 55 B2
Gardenia Dr GU24 153 C3
Gardens The Hatton TW14 71 B1
South Stoke RG8 14 B2
Gardner Ho SL6 19 C1
Gardner Rd SL6 19 C1
Gardners Rd RG42 92 A1
Garfield Pl 26 SL4 67 B3
Garfield Rd GU15 151 B3
Garford Cres RG14 130 B4
Garland Jnr Sch RG7 111 A2
Garlands Cl RG7 111 A1
Garnet Cl SL1 42 A2
Garnet Ct SL7 1 B1
Garnet Field GU46 149 A3
Garnet Hill 7 RG1 86 A3
Garnet St RG1 86 A3
Garrard Rd SL2 21 C1
Garrard St RG1 86 A4
Garrett Rd RG40 141 C4
Garrick Cl TW18 97 A1
Garson La TW19 95 B4
Garson's La SL4 92 A4
Garston Cl RG30 85 A2
Garston Cres RG31 84 A3
Garston Gr RG40 115 C1
Garswood RG12 118 B2
Garth Cl RG41 88 B1
Garth Hill Sch RG12 118 B4
Garth Rd RG7 137 A3
Garth Sq RG42 91 A1
Gas La SL6 40 A2
Gas Works Rd RG1 86 B4
Gascon's Gr SL2 22 A1
Gaskell Mews RG14 131 A4
Gaskells End RG4 58 B4
Gaston Bridge Rd
Shepperton TW17 125 B2
Upper Halliford TW17 125 C2
Gaston Way TW17 125 B2
Gatcombe Cl RG31 84 B2
Gatehampton Rd RG8 34 B3
Gatewick Cl SL1 42 C3
Gatward Ave SL6 39 A2
Gaveston Rd SL2 21 C1
Gayhurst Cl RG4 59 B3
Gays La SL6 65 A4
Gaywood Dr RG14 105 B2
Gazelle Cl RG41 88 A2
Geffers Ride SL5 119 C4
Gelder Dr RG6 87 B1
Genesis Cl TW19 97 C4
Geneva Cl TW17 125 C4
Geoffrey Field Jun & Inf Schs RG2 113 B4
Geoffreyson Rd RG4 58 C3
George Cl SL7 1 C2
George Green Rd SL3 43 C4
George Palmer Inf Sch RG2 86 B2
George Palmer Jun Sch RG2 86 B2
George St Caversham RG4 59 A1
Reading RG1 85 C4
Staines TW18 96 C2
George V Pl SL4 67 B4
Georgeham Rd GU47 143 B1
Georges Dr HP10 3 B4
Georgian Cl
Camberley GU15 151 C4
Staines TW18 97 A2
Geranium Cl RG45 143 A4
Gerrards Cross Rd SL2 23 A4
Gervaise Cl SL1 41 C3
Gibbet La GU15 152 A4
Gibbins La RG42 91 B2
Gibbons Cl GU47 150 B4
Gibbs Cl RG40 141 C3
Gibbs Way GU46 149 A2
Gibraltar La SL6 2 B1
Gibson Ct SL3 43 C1
Gibson Pl TW19 70 B1
Gifford Cl RG4 59 C3
Gifford Ho 2 RG4 59 B1
Gilbert Ct RG18 106 B2
Gilbert Rd GU15 151 B1
Gilbert Way RG40 141 C4
Gilbey Wlk HP10 3 B2
Gilchrist Way SL6 38 A3
Giles Travers Cl TW20 123 B3
Gill Rise RG42 91 B1
Gillette Way RG2 86 A1
Gilliat Rd SL1 42 C3
Gilliatt Cl SL0 44 C4
Gillotts Cl RG9 35 A4
Gillotts La RG9 35 A4
Gillotts Sch RG9 35 A4
Gilman Cres SL4 66 B2
Gilmore Cl SL3 43 B2
Gilmore Cres TW15 98 A1
Gilpin Way UB3 71 B4
Gilroy Cl RG14 130 B3
Gilson Ct SL4 95 B4
Gingells Farm Rd RG10 61 C3
Gipsy La Arborfield RG41 114 C4
Bracknell RG12 118 B4
Earley RG6 87 B2
Hungerford RG17 100 C4
Reading RG30 57 C1
Wokingham RG40 116 B2
Wokingham, Sindlesham RG41 115 A4
Girton Cl GU47 143 C1
Glade Ho Ascot SL5 120 B2
3 Marlow SL7 1 C1
Glade Rd SL7 1 C1
Glade The Ascot SL5 120 B2
Newbury RG14 130 C4
Purley on T RG8 57 B2
Staines TW18 97 A1
Gladridge Cl RG6 87 B2
Gladstone Cl RG17 102 A1
Gladstone Ind Est SL6 39 C4
Gladstone La RG18 106 B4
Gladstone Way SL1 42 A3
Glaisdale RG19 106 B1
Glamis Way RG31 84 A2
Glanmor Rd SL2 43 A3
Glanty The TW20 96 A2
Glasgow Rd SL1 42 A4
Glassonby Wlk GU15 152 B3
Glebe Cl Dorney SL6 40 C2
Lightwater GU18 146 B1
Moulsford OX10 13 C3
Glebe Cotts RG8 14 B2
Glebe Field RG20 49 A4
Glebe Gdns RG4 60 C2
Glebe La Sonning RG4 60 C2
Glebe La *continued*
Stockcross RG20 103 C3
Glebe Pl RG17 73 A1
Glebe Rd Egham TW20 96 B1
Maidenhead SL6 40 A3
Old Windsor SL4 68 A1
Purley on T RG8 57 A3
Reading RG2 86 B3
Staines TW18 97 A2
Glebe Ride RG8 34 A3
Glebe The Aldworth RG8 32 C2
Blackwater GU17 150 C2
Glebefields RG14 105 A3
Glebeland Gdns TW17 125 B2
Glebeland Rd GU15 150 C2
Glebelands RG19 106 B2
Glebelands Rd RG40 116 B4
Glebewood RG12 118 B2
Glen Ave TW15 98 A2
Glen Cl TW17 125 A3
Glen Ct TW18 96 C1
Glen Innes GU47 143 C1
Glen The Ascot SL5 120 B3
Silchester RG26 135 C1
Slough SL3 43 B1
Glenalmond Ho TW15 97 C3
Glenapp Grange RG7 136 C3
Glenavon Gdns Slough SL3 43 B2
Yateley GU46 149 B2
Glenbeigh Terr RG1 85 C3
Glendale Ave RG14 130 B3
Glendale Cl RG41 116 A2
Glendale Rd RG26 135 A1
Glendevon Rd RG5 87 C4
Gleneagles Cl TW19 70 B1
Gleneagles Ct 32 RG1 86 B4
Gleneagles Ho RG12 117 C2
Glenfield Ho RG12 118 B3
Glenfield Rd TW15 98 B1
Glenhaven Dr TW19 70 A1
Glenhurst Cl GU17 150 C2
Glenmore Cl RG19 106 B1
Glenn Miller Cl RG20 49 A3
Glennon Cl RG30 85 B2
Glenrhondda RG4 58 C3
Glenrosa Rd RG30 85 A4
Glentworth Pl SL1 42 B3
Glenwood Bracknell RG12 118 B3
Virginia Water GU25 122 B4
Glenwood Dr RG31 84 B4
Globe Farm La GU17 150 A3
Glory Cl HP10 3 C4
Glory Hill La HP9 3 C4
Glory Mill La HP10 3 C4
Gloucester Ave SL1 42 B4
Gloucester Cres TW18 97 B1
Gloucester Ct RG30 85 B4
Gloucester Dr TW18, TW19 96 B3
Gloucester Gdns GU19 145 C2
Gloucester Pl
Bracknell RG42 91 C1
Windsor SL4 67 B3
Gloucester Rd
Bagshot GU19 145 C2
Maidenhead SL6 19 C1
Newbury RG14 104 C1
Reading RG30 85 B4
Gloucestershire Lea RG42 91 C1
Glyme Wlk RG31 84 C2
Glyncastle RG4 58 C3
Glynswood GU15 151 C2
Glynwood Ho SL6 40 A4
Goaters Rd SL5 119 B4
Goddard Cl
Littleton TW17 124 C3
Shinfield RG2 113 C3
Goddard Ct RG41 88 A1
Goddard Dr RG7 107 C2
Goddards La GU15 151 A2
Goddington Rd SL8 3 A3
Godfrey Cl GU47 150 B4
Godolphin Inf Sch SL1 42 B4
Godolphin Jun Sch SL1 42 B4
Godolphin Rd SL1 42 B3
Godstow Cl RG5 87 C4
Goffs Rd TW15 98 B1
Gogmore Farm Cl KT16 123 C1
Gogmore La KT16 124 A1
Gold Cup La SL5 119 B4
Goldcrest Cl GU46 149 A3
Goldcrest Way RG31 84 A3
Golden Ball La SL6 19 A2
Golden Oak SL2 22 B3
Golden Orb Wood RG42 117 B4
Goldfinch La RG20 131 C2
Golding Cl RG19 106 C2
Goldney Rd GU15 152 B2
Goldsmid Rd RG1 85 C4
Goldsmith Cl
Thatcham RG18 106 B3
Wokingham RG40 115 C1
Goldsmith Way RG45 143 A2
Goldsworthy Way SL1 41 B4
Goldthorpe Gdns RG6 113 C4
Goldwell Dr RG14 104 C2
Golf Dr GU15 151 C2
Gooch Cl RG10 61 C3
Goodboys La RG7 112 A1
Goodchild Rd RG40 116 B3
Goodings Gn RG40 116 C3
Goodings La RG17 47 A2
Goodliffe Gdns RG31 57 B2
Goodman Pk SL2 43 B3
Goodman Pl TW18 96 C2
Goodrich Cl RG4 59 C3
Goodways Dr RG12 118 B4
Goodwin Cl RG31 84 C2
Goodwin Mdws HP10 3 C3
Goodwin Rd SL2 21 C1
Goodwin Wlk RG14 130 B3
Goodwood Cl
Burghfield Common RG7 111 A1
Camberley GU15 151 B4
Goodwood Rise SL7 1 B4
Goodwood Way RG14 105 B1
Goose Cnr RG42 91 C2
Goose Gn
Farnham Common SL2 22 A2
Lambourn RG17 25 A2
Goose Green Way RG19 106 B2
Goose La RG20 49 C3
Gordon Ave GU15 151 B2
Gordon Cl TW18 97 A1
Gordon Clifford Ct RG42 118 A4
Gordon Cres
Camberley GU15 151 B2
Compton RG20 31 B2
Gordon Ct 8 RG14 105 A1
Gordon Dr TW17 125 B1
Gordon Palmer Cl RG7 137 B3
Gordon Palmer Ct RG30 85 B4
Gordon Pl RG30 85 B4
Gordon Rd Ashford TW15 97 C3
Camberley GU15 151 B3
Crowthorne RG45 143 B2
Maidenhead SL6 39 B4
Newbury RG14 105 A1
Shepperton TW17 125 B2
Thatcham RG18 106 A3
Windsor SL4 66 C3
Gordon Wlk GU46 149 C3
Gordon's Sch GU24 153 C4
Gore End Rd RG20 129 A2
Gore Rd SL1 21 A1
Gore The SL1 21 A1
Goring CE Prim Sch RG8 34 B4
Goring La RG7 111 A1
Goring Rd TW18 96 C2
Goring & Streatley Sta RG8 34 B3
Gorrick Sq RG41 116 A2
Gorse Bank GU18 153 A4
Gorse Cottage Dr RG18 79 B1
Gorse Dr RG5 88 A4
Gorse Hill La GU25 122 B3
Gorse Hill Rd GU25 122 B3
Gorse Meade SL1 42 A3
Gorse Pl RG42 92 A1
Gorse Rd Cookham SL6 19 C3
Frimley GU16 151 C1
Gorse Ride Cty Jun Sch RG40 141 C4
Gorse Ride N RG40 141 C4
Gorse Ride S RG40 141 C3
Gorselands
Caversham RG4 59 A3
Newbury RG14 130 B3
Tadley RG26 135 B1
Yateley GU46 149 B2
Gosbrook Ho 1 RG4 59 B1
Gosbrook Rd RG4 59 A1
Gosden Rd GU24 153 C3
Gosforth Cl RG6 87 B1
Goslar Way SL4 67 A3
Gosling Gn SL3 43 C2
Gosling Rd SL3 43 C2
Gosnell Cl GU16 152 B2
Gossmore Cl SL7 1 C1
Gossmore La SL7 1 C1
Gossmore Wlk SL7 1 C1
Goswell Hill SL4 67 B3
Goswell Rd SL4 67 B3
Gothic Ct Harlington UB3 71 B4
Sandhurst GU47 150 A4
Gough's La
Bracknell RG12 118 B4
Newell Green RG12 91 B1
Gough's Mdw GU47 150 A4
Goughs Barn La RG42 91 A4
Gould Cl RG14 105 A2
Gould Rd TW14 98 C4
Goulders Cotts RG10 36 C4
Governor's Rd GU15 150 C3
Govett Ave TW17 125 B2
Govett Gr GU20 146 B3
Gower Pk GU47 150 B4
Gower St RG1 85 C4
Gower The TW20 123 B3
Gowings Gn SL1 41 C2
Grace Ct SL1 42 B3
Grace Reynolds Wlk 4 GU15 151 B3
Graces La RG20 78 A4
Graffham Cl RG6 114 A4
Grafton Cl Maidenhead SL6 19 C1
Slough SL3 43 C4
Grafton Ct TW14 98 B4
Grafton Rd RG30 84 B4
Graham Cl Blewbury OX11 12 A4
Maidenhead SL6 39 B3
Reading RG31 84 C2
Graham Rd Cookham SL6 19 C3
Windlesham GU20 146 B2
Grahame Ave RG8 56 B3
Grainford Ct RG40 116 B3
Grampian Cl UB3 71 B4
Grampian Rd GU47 143 A1
Grampian Way SL3 44 A1
Gramps Hill OX12 6 C3
Granby Ct RG1 86 C4
Granby End RG7 111 A2
Granby Gdns RG1 86 C4
Grand Ave GU15 151 B3

Grange Ave
Crowthorne RG45 ....143 A3
Reading RG6 ....87 A3
Grange Cl Goring RG8 .....34 A3
Wraysbury TW19 ....68 C1
Grange Ct Earley RG6 ......87 A4
Egham TW20 ....95 C2
Littleton TW17 ....125 A3
Newbury RG14 ....105 A1
Staines TW18 ....97 A2
Grange Dr HP10 ....3 B2
Grange Gdns SL2 ....22 B4
Grange La SL6 ....19 C4
Grange Pl TW18 ....124 B4
Grange Rd Bracknell RG12 .118 B4
Camberley GU15 ....151 C3
Cookham SL6 ....19 C4
Egham TW20 ....95 C2
Henley-on-T RG9 ....15 C1
Grange The Burnham SL1 ...21 B1
Caversham RG4 ....58 B3
Newbury RG14 ....130 B3
Old Windsor SL4 ....68 A1
Grange Way SL0 ....44 C4
Grangely Cl RG31 ....84 B2
Grangewood SL3 ....43 B4
Grant Ave SL1 ....42 C4
Grant Cl TW17 ....125 A2
Grant Ho 5 SL8 ....3 A2
Grant Rd RG45 ....143 B2
Grant Wlk SL5 ....120 C1
Grantham Cl GU47 ......143 C1
Grantham Ho 5 TW16 .....98 C1
Grantham Rd RG30 ....84 C2
Granthams The RG17 ......25 A2
Grantley Hts 3 RG1 ....86 B4
Granville Ave SL2 ....42 B4
Granville Rd RG30 ....85 A3
Grasholm Way SL3 ....44 B1
Grasmere SL4 ....66 C4
Grasmere Ave
Reading RG30 ....57 C1
Slough SL2 ....43 A3
Grasmere Cl
East Bedfont TW14 ....98 C4
Thorpe Lea TW20 ....96 A1
Grasmere Par SL2 ....43 A3
Grasmere Rd GU18 ....146 A1
Grass Hill RG4 ....58 C2
Grassington Pl RG19 .....106 B2
Grassmead RG19 ....106 C1
Grassmere Cl RG41 ....88 A1
Grassy La SL6 ....39 C4
Grattan Ct SL7 ....2 A2
Gratton Dr SL4 ....66 C2
Gratton Rd RG2 ....113 B4
Gratwicke Rd RG30 ....84 C4
Gravel Hill Caversham RG4 .59 A3
Henley-on-T RG9 ....15 B1
Stockcross RG20 ....103 C3
Gravel Rd RG9 ....35 A1
Gravelly Cl RG20 ....129 A2
Graveney Dr RG4 ....58 C2
Gravett Cl RG9 ....35 B4
Gray Ct SL4 ....66 B3
Gray's Mon SL2 ....22 C1
Gray's Pl SL2 ....42 C3
Gray's Rd SL1 ....42 C3
Grayling Cl SL7 ....18 B4
Grayling Ct 4 RG1 ....59 A1
Grays Cres RG5 ....87 B4
Grays La TW15 ....98 A2
Grays Park Rd SL2 ....23 A1
Grayshot Dr GU17 ....150 B3
Grazeley Parochial Prim Sch RG7 ....112 C1
Grazeley Rd RG7 ....113 A2
Great Auclum Pl RG7 ....111 A1
Great Barn Ct RG19 ....106 B2
Great Hill Cres SL6 ....39 B3
Great Hollands Jun & Inf Sch RG12 ....117 C2
Great Hollands Rd RG12 .117 C2
Great Hollands Sq RG12 .117 C2
Great Knollys St RG1 .....85 C4
Great Lea RG7 ....113 A3
Great Marlow Sch SL7 .....1 C2
Great Severals RG17 .....102 A1
Great South-West Rd
East Bedfont TW14 ....98 B4
Hatton TW6, TW14 ....71 B1
Grebe Ct TW18 ....97 A2
Green Acre Mount RG30 ...84 B4
Green Bsns Ctr The TW20 .96 B2
Green Cl Burnham SL6 .....41 A4
Maidenhead SL6 ....19 C1
Green Cres HP10 ....3 B4
Green Croft RG40 ....116 C4
Green Ct TW16 ....98 C1
Green Dr RG40 ....116 C2
Green Dragon La HP10 ......3 A4
Green End GU46 ....149 B4
Green End Cl RG7 ....113 A1
Green Farm Rd GU19 ....145 C2
Green Farm Rise SN8 .....99 A3
Green Finch Cl RG45 .....142 C3
Green Hill Cl GU15 ....152 B3
Green Hill Rd GU15 ....152 B3
Green La Ascot SL5 ....120 C4
Ashford TW16 ....98 C1
Bagshot GU19 ....145 C1
Blackwater GU17 ....150 A2
Blackwater, Hawley GU17 .150 C2
Bradfield RG7 ....81 C2
Burghfield Common RG30 ...85 A1
Green La *continued*
Burnham SL1 ....21 B2
Caversham RG9 ....35 A1
Chieveley RG20 ....78 A4
Datchet SL3 ....68 A3
Egham TW20 ....96 A2
Farnham Common SL2 .....22 A3
Henley-on-T RG9 ....35 B4
Holyport SL6 ....64 A3
Hurst RG10 ....88 C2
Littlewick Green SL6 ....38 A3
Maidenhead SL6 ....40 A3
Newbury RG14 ....104 C1
Padworth RG7 ....110 B1
Pangbourne RG8 ....56 B3
Sandhurst GU47 ....150 B4
Shepperton TW17 ....125 B2
Thatcham RG19 ....106 B2
Thorpe TW18 ....123 C4
Windsor SL4 ....67 A3
Wokingham RG41 ....88 B1
Green Lane Cl GU15 .....151 B4
Green Lane Ct SL1 ....21 B1
Green Leas TW16 ....98 C1
Green Leas Cl TW16 ....98 C1
Green Leys SL6 ....19 C1
Green Pk TW18 ....96 C3
Green Rd Reading RG6 .....87 A3
Thorpe TW20 ....123 A3
Green The
Bracknell RG12 ....118 A3
Burnham SL1 ....21 A1
Chilton OX11 ....10 C4
Datchet SL3 ....68 A4
Kintbury RG17 ....102 A1
Slough SL1 ....42 B2
Staines TW18 ....97 B2
Theale RG7 ....83 B1
Wokingham RG41 ....115 C4
Wooburn Green HP10 ....3 C3
Wraysbury TW19 ....68 C1
Green Verges SL7 ....1 C2
Green Wood SL5 ....119 B4
Greenacre SL4 ....66 C3
Greenacre Ct TW20 ....95 B1
Greenacres RG20 ....129 C1
Greenacres Ave RG41 .....88 A2
Greenacres La RG41 ....88 A2
Greenaway Terr TW19 .....97 C4
Greenbank Way GU15 ....151 B1
Greencroft Gdns RG30 ....84 C2
Greendale Mews SL2 ......43 A3
Greene Fielde End TW18 ..97 B1
Greenfern Ave SL1 ....41 B4
Greenfield Way RG45 ....143 A4
Greenfields SL6 ....40 A3
Greenfields Rd RG2 ......113 A4
Greenfinch Cl RG31 ....84 A3
Greenham Cl
Greenham RG19 ....131 B4
Woodley RG5 ....88 A3
Greenham Court Prim Sch RG14 ....131 A4
Greenham Mill RG14 ......105 A2
Greenham Rd RG14 ....105 A1
Greenham Wood RG12 ....118 B2
Greenhaven GU46 ....149 A3
Greenholme GU15 ....152 B3
Greenhow RG12 ....118 A3
Greenidge Cl 5 RG1 ....85 C3
Greenlake Terr TW18 ......97 A1
Greenlands Ball Hill RG20 .129 C1
Flackwell Heath HP10 ....3 A4
Greenlands Ct
Maidenhead SL6 ....39 A4
Staines TW18 ....97 A2
Greenlands Rd
Camberley GU15 ....151 A1
Newbury RG14 ....105 A1
Staines TW18 ....97 A2
Greenleaf Ct SL3 ....68 A4
Greenleas GU16 ....151 C1
Greenleas Ave RG4 ....59 A4
Greenleas Cl GU46 ....149 B4
Greenleaves Ct TW15 .....98 A1
Greeno Cres TW17 ....125 A2
Greenock Rd SL1 ....42 A4
Greenside Bourne End SL8 ...3 A3
Crowthorne RG45 ....142 C3
Slough SL2 ....42 A4
Greensward La RG2 ......114 B1
Greenview Ct TW15 ....97 C2
Greenway Dr TW18 ....124 B4
Greenway The
Fawley OX12 ....27 B4
Slough SL1 ....41 B3
Greenways Ball Hill RG20 ..129 C1
Egham TW20 ....95 C2
Lambourn RG17 ....25 A1
Sandhurst GU47 ....143 A1
Greenways Dr
Maidenhead SL6 ....39 A4
Sunningdale SL5 ....120 C1
Greenwood 12 RG12 .....118 C3
Greenwood Gr RG41 ......88 B2
Greenwood Rd
Crowthorne RG45 ....143 A3
Reading RG30 ....84 C3
Gregory Cl RG6 ....114 B4
Gregory Dr SL4 ....68 A1
Grenfell Ave SL6 ....39 C3
Grenfell Pl SL6 ....39 C3
Grenfell Rd SL6 ....39 C3
Grenville Cl SL1 ....21 A2
Gresham Ct TW18 ....97 A2
Gresham Rd Slough SL1 ....42 A4
Staines TW18 ....97 A2
Gresham Way RG30 ....58 A1
Greyberry Copse Rd
RG19 ....131 B4
Greyfriars Dr SL5 ....120 A2
Greyfriars Rd RG1 ....86 A4
Greys Ct 6 RG1 ....86 B4
Greys Hill RG9 ....15 B1
Greys Rd RG9 ....15 B1
Greystoke Ct RG45 ....143 A2
Greystoke Ho 9 RG1 ......85 C3
Greystoke Rd
Caversham RG4 ....59 B2
Slough SL2 ....41 C4
Griffin Cl Maidenhead SL6 .39 C3
Slough SL1 ....42 B2
Griffiths Cl RG19 ....106 C1
Grindle Cl RG18 ....106 B3
Gringer Hill SL6 ....39 C4
Groombridge Pl RG14 ...104 C3
Grosvenor Ct
Blackwater GU17 ....150 B2
Slough SL1 ....42 C4
Grosvenor Dr SL6 ....40 B4
Grosvenor Lawn RG14 ...104 C1
Grosvenor Rd
Caversham RG4 ....59 B2
Staines TW18 ....97 A1
Grove Cl Old Windsor SL4 ...95 A4
2 Slough SL1 ....43 A2
Wokingham RG40 ....142 C4
Grove Cotts RG4 ....59 A3
Grove Cross Rd GU16 ....151 B1
Grove Ct Egham TW20 .....96 A2
Maidenhead SL6 ....39 B4
Newbury RG14 ....131 A4
Grove Cty Prim Sch The GU16 ....151 C1
Grove End GU19 ....145 C3
Grove Hill RG4 ....59 A2
Grove Ho Ashford TW15 ....97 C2
Old Windsor SL4 ....95 B4
Grove La RG42 ....92 A2
Grove Pk SL6 ....63 C4
Grove Rd Burnham SL1 .....21 C2
Camberley GU15 ....151 C3
Caversham RG4 ....59 A3
Chertsey KT16 ....123 C2
Henley-on-T RG9 ....15 C1
Maidenhead SL6 ....39 C4
Newbury RG14 ....104 C3
Shepperton TW17 ....125 B2
Windsor SL4 ....67 B3
Grove The Egham TW20 ....96 A2
Frimley GU16 ....151 B1
Medmenham SL7 ....17 C3
North Ascot SL5 ....119 B4
Reading RG1 ....86 B4
Slough SL1 ....43 A2
Thatcham RG18 ....106 B2
Twyford RG10 ....61 B3
Grovebarns TW18 ....97 A1
Grovefields Ave GU16 ....151 B1
Groveland Pl RG30 ....85 A4
Groveland Rd RG14 ......104 C3
Grovelands Ave RG41 .....88 B1
Grovelands Cl RG41 ....88 B2
Grovelands Rd
Reading RG30 ....85 A4
Shinfield RG7 ....113 B1
Groveley Rd TW13, TW16 ...98 C2
Groves Cl SL8 ....3 B2
Groves Lea RG7 ....136 C3
Groves The RG17 ....73 A1
Groves Way SL6 ....19 C3
Grovestile Waye TW14 .....98 B4
Grubwood La SL6 ....19 A4
Guards Club Rd SL6 ....40 B4
Guards Ct SL5 ....121 A1
Guards Rd SL4 ....66 B3
Guards Wlk 1 SL4 ....66 B3
Guerdon Pl RG12 ....118 B1
Guildford Ave TW13 ....98 C3
Guildford Rd
Bagshot GU19 ....145 C1
Bagshot GU19 ....145 C2
Bisley GU24 ....153 C2
Chertsey KT16 ....123 C1
Lightwater GU18 ....146 A1
West End GU24 ....153 C4
Guildford St
Chertsey KT16 ....124 A1
Staines TW18 ....97 A1
Gullane Ct 31 RG1 ....86 B4
Gun St RG1 ....86 A4
Gunthorpe Rd SL7 ....2 A2
Gurney Cl RG4 ....58 B3
Gurney Dr RG4 ....58 B3
Gwendale SL6 ....19 B1
Gwendoline Ct TW15 ......97 C2
Gweneth Ct SL7 ....1 B2
Gwent Cl SL6 ....39 A2
Gwyn Cl RG14 ....130 C4
Gwynne Cl
Purley on T RG31 ....57 B2
Windsor SL4 ....66 C3
Gwyns Piece RG17 ....25 A2
Gypsy La Marlow SL7 ....1 C2
Stoke Poges SL2 ....22 C4

H

Habershon Dr GU16 .....152 B1
Haddenhurst Ct RG42 .....90 B1
Haddon Dr RG5 ....87 C4
Haddon Rd SL6 ....39 B3
Hadfield Rd TW19 ....70 B1
Hadleigh Rise RG4 ....59 C3
Hadley Ct SL3 ....69 C3
Hadlow Ct SL1 ....42 B3
Hadrian Cl TW19 ....97 C4
Hadrian Way TW19 ....97 B4
Hadrian Wlk E RG2 ....86 B2
Hadrian Wlk W RG2 ....86 B2
Hafod RG4 ....58 C3
Hag Hill La SL6 ....41 A4
Hag Hill Rise SL6 ....41 A4
Hagley Rd RG2 ....86 A2
Haig Dr SL1 ....42 A2
Haig Rd GU15 ....150 C3
Hailey La RG20 ....29 C1
Haileybury Ct SL4 ....67 A2
Hailsham Cl GU47 ....143 B1
Halcyon Ct TW18 ....124 A4
Halcyon Terr RG30 ....84 C4
Haldane Rd RG4 ....58 C3
Hale SL4 ....66 C3
Hale End RG12 ....118 C3
Hale St TW18 ....96 C2
Halewood RG12 ....117 C2
Half Mile Rd RG17 ....46 A1
Half Moon St GU19 ....145 C2
Halfacre Cl RG7 ....113 A2
Halfpenny Ct SL5 ....121 A1
Halfpenny La Cholsey OX10 .13 B3
Sunningdale SL5 ....121 A1
Halfway Hos SL6 ....19 C2
Halifax Cl SL6 ....39 A4
Halifax Pl RG18 ....106 B2
Halifax Rd SL6 ....39 A4
Halifax Way SL6 ....39 A4
Halkingcroft SL3 ....43 B2
Hall Cl GU15 ....151 C3
Hall Ct SL3 ....68 A4
Hall Farm Cres GU46 .....149 B3
Hall Grove (Sch) GU19 ...146 A3
Hall La Harlington UB3 .....71 B4
Yateley GU46 ....149 B3
Hall Mdw SL1 ....21 A2
Hall Place La SL6 ....38 A4
Hallbrook Gdns RG42 ......90 C1
Halldore Hill SL6 ....19 C4
Halley Dr SL5 ....119 B4
Hallgrove Bottom GU19 ..145 C3
Halliford Cl TW17 ....125 C3
Halliford Rd TW16, TW17 .125 C3
Halliford Sch TW17 ....125 B1
Hallmark Cl GU47 ....150 C4
Halls La Earley RG2 ....86 C1
Waltham St Lawrence RG10 .63 A4
Halls Rd RG30 ....84 B3
Hallsmead Ct 3 RG1 ....59 A1
Halpin Cl RG31 ....84 B2
Halstead Cl RG5 ....87 C4
Halstead Ho RG26 ....134 C1
Halters The RG14 ....131 A4
Ham Island SL4 ....68 B2
Ham La
Englefield Green TW20 .....95 A2
Old Windsor SL4 ....68 B2
Ham Rd SN8 ....126 A2
Hamble Ave GU17 ....150 B3
Hamble Ct 16 RG1 ....86 A3
Hambleden Ct RG12 ......118 C3
Hambleden Mill RG9 ....16 B4
Hambleden Pl RG9 ....16 B3
Hambleden Rise RG9 ......16 B4
Hambleden Wlk SL6 ....19 C1
Hambledon Cl RG6 ....87 C1
Hambleton TW19 ....95 B4
Hambleton Cl GU16 ......152 A2
Hamblin Mdw RG17 ......100 C4
Hambridge Rd RG14 ......105 B1
Hamfield Cotts SL6 ....19 C4
Hamilton Ave RG9 ....15 C1
Hamilton Cl TW13 ....98 C2
Hamilton Cl GU19 ....145 C2
Hamilton Cl KT16 ....123 C1
Hamilton Ct
Farnborough (Hants) GU17 .150 C1
Newbury RG14 ....131 A4
Hamilton Dr SL5 ....120 C1
Hamilton Gdns SL1 ....21 A1
Hamilton Pk SL6 ....39 A3
Hamilton Rd Feltham TW13 .98 C2
Reading RG1 ....86 C3
Slough SL1 ....42 A4
Wargrave RG10 ....36 C1
Hamlet St RG42 ....118 C4
Hammond Cl RG19 ....106 C1
Hammond Ct RG42 ....91 A1
Hammond End SL2 ....22 A4
Hammond Jun Sch GU18 ....146 A1
Hammond Way GU18 .....146 A1
Hammonds Heath RG7 ....137 A3
Hampden Cl SL2 ....23 A1
Hampden Rd
Caversham RG4 ....59 A1
Maidenhead SL6 ....39 A4
Slough SL3 ....43 C2
Hampdens The RG14 .....130 B3
Hampshire Ave SL1 ....42 B4
Hampshire Lodge 8 SL6 ...39 C3
Hampshire Rd GU15 ......151 C4
Hampshire Rise RG42 ......91 C1
Hampshire Way RG41 .....115 B3
Hampshire Wlk RG31 ......84 A4
Hampstead Ct RG30 ....85 A4
Hampstead Hill RG9 ....60 B4
Hampstead Norreys CE Prim Sch RG18 ....52 C3
Hampstead Norreys Rd
RG18 ....79 A4
Hampton Ho SL3 ....69 B4
Hampton Rd RG14 ....104 C1
Hampton Twrs 4 RG30 ....85 B3
Hanbury Cl SL1 ....41 A4
Hanbury Dr RG31 ....84 B2
Hanbury Way GU15 ....151 B2
Hanbury Wlk RG19 ....106 B1
Hancocks Mount SL5 ......120 B2
Hancombe Rd GU47 ....143 A1
Handford La GU46 ....149 B3
Hanger Rd RG26 ....134 C1
Hangerfield Cl GU46 ......149 B3
Hangmans Stone La RG20 .49 A3
Hanley Cl SL4 ....66 B3
Hannibal Rd TW19 ....97 C4
Hanningtons Way RG7 ...111 B2
Hanover Cl
Englefield Green TW20 .....95 B1
Frimley GU16 ....151 C1
Slough SL1 ....43 A2
Windsor SL4 ....66 C3
Hanover Ct Caversham RG4 .59 B3
Reading RG30 ....84 C3
Hanover Gdns RG12 ......117 C1
Hanover Mead
Maidenhead SL6 ....40 B2
Newbury RG14 ....130 B3
Hanover Way SL4 ....66 C3
Hanson Cl GU15 ....152 A4
Hanwood Cl RG5 ....87 B4
Hanworth Cl RG12 ....118 B2
Hanworth La KT16 ....123 C1
Hanworth Rd RG12 ....118 A1
Hanworth Trad Est KT16 .123 C1
Harborough Cl SL1 ....41 B3
Harbury Ct RG14 ....105 A1
Harcourt TW19 ....68 C1
Harcourt Cl Dorney SL4 ....40 C2
Egham TW20 ....96 B1
Henley-on-T RG9 ....15 B1
Harcourt Dr RG6 ....86 C2
Harcourt Rd
Bracknell RG12 ....118 A2
Camberley GU15 ....151 A3
Dorney SL4 ....40 C2
Windsor SL4 ....66 C3
Hardell Cl TW20 ....96 A2
Harding Rd RG5 ....87 B4
Hardwell Way RG12 ......118 C3
Hardwick Cl SL6 ....39 A4
Hardwick La KT16 ....123 B1
Hardwick Rd Reading RG30 .84 C4
Whitchurch-on-T RG8 .....56 B4
Hardy Ave GU46 ....149 B2
Hardy Cl Caversham RG4 ...59 B1
Slough SL1 ....42 A3
Thatcham RG18 ....106 B3
Hardy Gn RG45 ....143 A2
Hare Shoots SL6 ....39 C3
Harebell Dr RG18 ....106 C3
Harefield Cl RG41 ....88 B1
Harefield Rd SL6 ....39 A4
Harewood Dr RG18 ....106 B4
Harewood Pl SL1 ....43 A2
Hargrave Rd SL6 ....39 B4
Hargreaves Way RG31 .....84 C2
Harkness Rd SL1 ....41 A4
Harlech Ave RG4 ....59 B3
Harlech Rd GU17 ....150 B2
Harley Rd RG4 ....59 A2
Harlington Cl UB3 ....71 B4
Harlington Cnr UB3 ....71 B3
Harlton Cl RG6 ....114 B4
Harmans Water Cty Inf Sch RG12 ....118 C2
Harmans Water Cty Jun Sch RG12 ....118 C2
Harmans Water Rd RG12 .118 B2
Harmar Cl RG40 ....116 C3
Harmondsworth La UB7 ....70 C4
Harmondsworth Prim Sch UB7 ....70 B4
Harness Cl RG2 ....113 A3
Harold Rd RG17 ....102 A1
Harpesford Ave GU25 ....122 B2
Harpsden Rd RG9 ....35 C4
Harpsden Way RG9 ....35 C4
Harpton Cl GU46 ....149 B4
Harrier Cl RG5 ....88 A3
Harrington Cl Earley RG6 ...87 B1
Newbury RG14 ....105 C3
Windsor SL4 ....66 C2
Harris Arc 5 RG1 ....86 A4
Harris Cl Lambourn RG17 ...25 A2
Woodley RG5 ....88 A4
Harrison Cl RG10 ....61 C2
Harrison Ct TW17 ....125 A2
Harrison Way SL1 ....41 B3
Harrogate Ct SL3 ....44 A1
Harrogate Rd RG4 ....58 C2
Harrow Bottom Rd GU25 .122 C2
Harrow Cl SL6 ....19 C1
Harrow Ct RG1 ....85 C3
Harrow La SL6 ....19 C1
Harrow Mkt The SL3 ....44 A2
Harrow Rd
Ashford TW14,TW15 ....98 A3
Slough SL3 ....43 C2
Harrow Way TW17 ....125 B4
Harry Tee Ct 11 RG1 ....86 B4
Hart Cl 6 RG42 ....118 A4
Hart Dene Cl GU19 ....145 C2
Hart Dyke Cl RG41 ....116 A1
Hart St Henley-on-T RG9 ....15 C1
Reading RG1 ....85 C4
Hartford Rise GU15 ....151 B3
Hartigan Pl RG5 ....88 A4
Hartland Cl SL1 ....42 B3
Hartland Rd RG2 ....86 B1
Hartley Cl
Blackwater GU17 ....150 A3

Hartley Cl *continued*
Stoke Poges SL3 23 B2
Hartley Copse SL4 68 A1
Hartley Court Rd RG7 112 C3
Hartley Way RG18 106 C2
Hartmead Rd RG19 106 C2
Harts Cl RG2 114 C1
Harts Hill Rd RG18 106 C2
Harts La RG7 110 B3
Harts Leap Cl GU47 143 A1
Harts Leap Rd GU47 150 A4
Hartsbourne Rd RG6 87 A2
Hartshill Rd RG26 134 C1
Hartslock Ct RG8 56 A3
Hartslock View RG8 34 C1
Hartslock Way RG31 57 B1
Hartvale Ct GU15 152 A4
Harvard Cl RG5 88 A4
Harvard Rd GU47 143 C1
Harvest Cl Reading RG31 84 A3
Yateley GU46 149 A2
Harvest Ct TW17 125 A3
Harvest Gn RG14 104 C1
Harvest Hill SL8 3 B1
Harvest Hill Rd SL6 39 C2
Harvest Rd TW20 95 B1
Harvest Ride
Bracknell RG42 91 B1
Winkfield RG12, RG42, SL5 119 A4
Harvey Ho 11 RG30 85 B3
Harvey Rd SL3 44 A2
Harwell Int Bsns Ctr OX11 9 C4
Harwich Cl 8 RG6 87 B1
Harwich Rd SL1 42 A4
Harwood Gdns SL4 95 A4
Harwood Rd SL7 1 B1
Harwood Rise RG20 129 C1
Haslemere Cl GU16 152 B2
Haslemere Rd SL4 67 A3
Haslett Rd TW17 125 C4
Hasting Cl SL6 40 B1
Hastings Mdw SL2 23 A2
Hatch Cl RG7 108 B4
Hatch End GU20 146 B2
Hatch Gate La RG10 37 A3
Hatch La Bucklebury RG7 108 B4
Burghfield Common RG30 111 B3
Harmondsworth TW6, UB7 70 B4
Windsor SL4 67 A3
Hatch Ride
Crowthorne RG45 143 A4
Wokingham RG40 142 C4
Hatch Ride Cty Prim Sch
RG45 143 A4
Hatch The SL4 66 B4
Hatchet La SL4, SL5 93 A3
Hatchets La RG18 80 B4
Hatchett Rd TW14 98 B4
Hatchgate Cl RG18 106 B4
Hatchgate Copse RG12 117 C2
Hatchgate Gdns SL1 21 B1
Hatchley RG2 113 B4
Hatfield Cl SL6 39 B3
Hatfield Ct RG31 84 A2
Hatfield Rd SL1 43 A2
Hatford Rd RG30 85 A2
Hatherley Rd RG1 86 C3
Hatherwood GU46 149 C3
Hatt Cl RG20 50 B4
Hatton Ave SL2 22 B1
Hatton Cross Rdbt TW6 71 C2
Hatton Cross Sta TW6 71 C2
Hatton Ct SL4 67 B3
Hatton Hill
Ashampstead RG8 54 A4
Windlesham GU20 146 B3
Hatton Rd
East Bedfont TW14 98 B4
Hatton TW14, TW6 71 C1
Haughurst Hill RG26 134 B1
Havelock Cres SL6 39 A4
Havelock Rd
Maidenhead SL6 39 A4
Wokingham RG41 116 A3
Havelock St RG41 116 A3
Haven Ct 21 RG1 86 B4
Haven Of Rest SL6 40 A4
Haven Rd TW15 98 A3
Haven The RG17 102 A1
Haversham Dr RG12 118 A2
Haw La Aldworth RG8 32 C1
Ashampstead RG8,RG18 53 C4
Hawk La RG12 118 B3
Hawkchurch Rd RG2 113 B4
Hawkedale Fst Sch
TW16 125 C3
Hawkedon Prim Sch RG6 87 C1
Hawkedon Way RG6 87 C1
Hawker Ct SL3 44 A2
Hawker Way RG5 88 A4
Hawkes Cl RG41 116 A4
Hawkes Leap GU20 146 A3
Hawkesbury Dr RG31 84 C2
Hawkesworth Dr GU19 145 C1
Hawkins Cl RG12 119 A4
Hawkins Way RG40 116 C3
Hawkridge Ct RG12 118 C3
Hawks Hill SL8 3 B1
Hawkshill Rd SL2 22 A1
Hawksway TW18 96 C3
Hawkswood Ave GU16 151 C1
Hawkswood Ho RG42 117 C4
Hawkswood La SL9 23 C4
Hawksworth Rd RG7 111 A2
Hawley Cl RG31 84 B2
Hawley Garden Cotts
GU17 150 B2
Hawley Gn GU17 150 C2
Hawley La GU14,GU17 151 A1
Hawley Lodge GU17 150 C1
Hawley Place Ind Sch
GU17 150 C1
Hawley Prim Sch GU17 150 C2
Hawley Rd GU17 150 C2
Hawley Way TW15 98 A2
Hawthorn Cl
Bracknell RG42 118 A4
Marlow SL7 1 C2
Hawthorn Gdns RG2 86 C1
Hawthorn La Burnham SL2 22 A3
Newell Green, Hawthorn Hill
RG42 91 C4
Newell Green,
Nuptown RG42 92 A4
Hawthorn Rd
Frimley GU16 151 C1
Newbury RG14 105 A2
Hawthorn Way
Sonning RG4 60 C2
Upper Halliford TW17 125 B3
Hawthorne Ave SL4 93 A3
Hawthorne Cres
Blackwater GU17 150 C2
Slough SL1 42 C4
Hawthorne Ct TW19 97 B4
Hawthorne Dr SL4 93 A4
Hawthorne Rd
Caversham RG4 59 C2
Egham TW20 96 B2
Hawthorne Way
Great Shefford RG17 48 A2
Stanwell TW19 97 B4
Winkfield SL4 93 A4
Hawthornes RG31 57 A2
Hawthorns Prim Sch The
RG41 115 C4
Hawthorns The
Charvil RG10 61 A2
Flackwell Heath HP10 3 A4
Poyle SL3 69 C3
Wooburn Green HP10 3 C3
Hawtrey Cl SL1 43 A2
Hawtrey Rd SL4 67 B3
Hay La SL3 23 B4
Hay Rd RG1 85 C3
Haydon Ct SL6 39 C3
Haydon Pl GU46 149 C3
Hayes La RG41 115 B2
Hayes Pl SL7 1 B1
Hayfield Cl RG31 84 B4
Hayfield Ct RG17 46 C3
Hayley Gn RG42 91 C2
Haymill Rd SL1,SL2 21 B1
Haynes Cl SL3 43 C1
Hayse Hill SL4 66 B3
Hayward Pl SL8 3 B1
Haywards Cl RG9 15 B1
Haywards Mead SL4 41 C1
Haywards The RG18 106 B2
Haywood RG12 118 B1
Haywood Ct RG1 86 C4
Haywood Way RG30 84 C3
Hazel Cl
Burghfield Common RG30 111 A3
Englefield Green TW20 95 A1
Marlow Bottom SL7 1 B3
Wokingham RG41 115 C3
Hazel Cres RG2 86 C1
Hazel Dr RG5 87 B3
Hazel Gn RG26 134 B1
Hazel Gr Staines TW18 97 B1
Thatcham RG18 106 B3
Hazel Rd RG8 57 B2
Hazelbank RG40 141 C3
Hazelbank Ct KT16 124 B1
Hazelbank Rd KT16 124 B1
Hazeldene RG20 51 A1
Hazelhurst Rd SL1 21 B2
Hazell Cl SL6 39 C4
Hazell Hill RG12 118 B3
Hazell Way SL2 22 C3
Hazelmere Cl TW14 71 C1
Hazelmere Rd SL2 43 A3
Hazels Paddock RG18 106 B4
Hazelwood Cl RG31 57 B1
Hazelwood La RG42 90 C2
Heacham Cl RG6 114 A4
Headington Cl
Maidenhead SL6 39 A4
Wokingham RG40 116 B4
Headington Dr RG40 116 B4
Headington Rd SL6 39 A4
Headley Cl RG5 88 A4
Headley Park Ind Est RG5 87 C4
Headley Rd RG5 87 C4
Headley Rd E RG5 88 A4
Heads La RG17 128 A3
Heardman Cl RG19 106 C1
Hearmon Cl GU46 149 C3
Hearn Rd RG5 87 C3
Hearn Wlk RG12 118 C4
Hearne Dr SL6 40 A1
Hearsey Gdns GU17 150 B3
Heath Cl Harlington UB3 71 B4
Stanwell TW19 70 B1
Virginia Water GU25 122 B3
Wokingham RG41 116 A2
Heath Cnr GU15 152 A2
Heath Ct RG26 134 C1
Heath Dr RG9 35 A1
Heath End Rd RG26 134 C1
Heath Gr TW16 98 C1
Heath Hill Rd N RG45 143 A3
Heath Hill Rd S RG45 143 A2
Heath La RG18 106 B3
Heath Rd Bagshot GU19 145 C2
Heath Rd *continued*
Bradfield RG7 82 A1
Reading RG6 87 A3
Silchester RG26 135 C1
Wooburn Moor HP9 3 C4
Heath Ride RG40,RG45 142 B3
Heath Rise
Camberley GU15 151 B3
Virginia Water GU25 122 B3
Heathacre SL3 69 C3
Heathcote SL6 40 A1
Heathcote Ct 2 SL4 67 B2
Heathcote Rd GU15 151 B3
Heathcroft Ave TW16 98 C1
Heather Cl RG40 141 C4
Heather Dr
Sunningdale SL5 121 A1
Tadley RG26 134 C1
Thatcham RG18 106 B3
Heather Gdns RG14 130 C4
Heather Mead GU16 151 C1
Heather Mead Ct GU16 151 C1
Heather Ridge Arc GU15 152 B2
Heather Ridge
Cty Inf Sch GU15 152 B2
Heatherdale Rd GU15 151 B2
Heatherden Cl RG2 113 B4
Heatherdene Ave RG45 142 C2
Heatherley Cl GU15 151 A3
Heatherley Rd GU15 151 A3
Heathermount 4 RG12 118 C3
Heathermount Dr RG45 143 A3
Heathermount Sch SL5 120 B2
Heathers The TW19 97 C4
Heatherside Dr GU25 122 A2
Heatherway RG45 143 A3
Heatherwood Hospl SL5 119 C3
Heathfield RG7 137 A3
Heathfield Ave Ascot SL5 120 C2
Reading RG30 84 B3
Shiplake RG9 35 A1
Heathfield Cl RG9 35 A1
Heathfield Ct TW15 97 C3
Heathfield Rd SL1 3 C1
Heathfield Sch SL5 119 A4
Heathfields RG20 78 A4
Heathlands RG26 134 C1
Heathlands Country Mkt
RG40 116 C1
Heathlands Ct RG40 142 C4
Heathlands Dr SL6 39 A3
Heathlands Rd RG40 116 C1
Heathmoors RG12 118 B2
Heathpark Dr GU20 146 C2
Heathrow Airport London
TW6 71 A3
Heathrow Airport Visitor Ctr
TW6 71 B3
Heathrow Bvd UB7 70 C4
Heathrow Central Sta
TW6 71 A2
Heathrow Cl TW6 70 A3
Heathrow Copse RG26 134 B1
Heathrow Sch UB7 70 C4
Heathrow Terminal 4 Sta
TW6 71 B1
Heathside Pk GU15 152 B4
Heathway
Camberley GU15 151 B3
North Ascot SL5 119 C4
Reading RG31 84 B4
Heathway Cl GU15 151 B3
Heathwood Cl GU46 149 B4
Heavens Lea SL8 3 B1
Hebbecastle Down RG42 91 B1
Hebden Cl RG19 106 B1
Hedge Lea HP10 3 B4
Hedgeway RG14 105 B2
Hedingham Mews SL6 39 B4
Hedley Rd HP10 3 A4
Hedsor Hill SL8 3 B1
Hedsor La HP10,SL1 3 C1
Hedsor Rd SL8 3 A1
Hedsor View Cotts SL6 19 C4
Heelas Rd RG41 115 A3
Heights The
Camberley GU15 151 C3
Marlow SL7 18 A4
Helen Cotts SL4 66 B3
Helena Rd SL4 67 B3
Helgiford Gdns TW16 98 C1
Helksham Cl GU47 143 B1
Hellyer Way SL8 3 B2
Helmsdale RG12 118 C2
Helmsdale Cl RG30 85 A4
Helston Gdns RG2 86 A1
Helston La SL4 67 A3
Helvellyn Cl TW20 96 A1
Hemdean Hill RG4 59 A2
Hemdean House Sch RG4 59 A2
Hemdean Rd RG4 59 A2
Hemdean Rise RG4 59 A2
Hemming Way SL2 22 A1
Hemmyng Cnr RG42 91 B1
Hempson Ave SL3 43 B2
Hemsdale SL6 19 A1
Hemwood Rd SL4 66 B2
Hencroft St N SL1 42 C2
Hencroft St S SL1 42 C2
Hendon Terr TW15 98 B1
Hendon Way TW19 70 B1
Hendons Way SL6 40 A1
Hengrave Cl RG6 87 C1
Hengrove Cres TW15 97 B3
Henley Coll The
(Deanfield Bldgs) RG9 15 B1
Henley Coll The
(Rotherfield Bldgs) RG9 15 B1
Henley Coll The
(Southfield Bldgs) RG9 15 B1
Henley Gdns GU46 149 B3
Henley Lodge 12 SL6 39 C3
Henley Rd Bisham SL6 18 A1
Caversham RG9 59 B2
Hurley SL6 17 B2
Marlow SL7 18 A4
Shiplake RG9 60 B4
Slough SL1 41 C4
Henley Trinity Prim Sch
RG9 15 B1
Henley Wood Rd RG6 87 B2
Henley-on-Thames Sta
RG9 15 C1
Henry Ct 24 RG1 86 B4
Henry Rd SL1 42 B2
Henry St RG1 86 A3
Henrys The RG18 106 B2
Henshaw Cres RG14 130 B4
Hensworth Rd TW15 97 B2
Henwick Cl RG18 106 A3
Henwick La RG18 106 A2
Henwood Copse RG8 55 A3
Hepplewhite Cl RG26 134 C1
Hepworth Croft GU47 150 C3
Hepworth Way KT12 125 C1
Herald Way RG5 88 A3
Herbert Cl RG12 118 A2
Hereford Cl TW18 124 A4
Herewood Cl RG14 104 C2
Heriot Rd KT16 124 A1
Heritage Ct 2
Egham TW20 96 A2
27 Reading RG1 85 C4
Hermitage Cl
Frimley GU16 151 C1
Littleton TW17 125 A3
Slough SL3 43 B2
Hermitage Ct TW18 96 C2
Hermitage Cty Prim Sch
RG18 79 A4
Hermitage Dr
North Ascot SL5 119 C4
Twyford RG10 61 B3
Hermitage La SL4 67 A2
Hermitage Par SL5 120 A3
Hermitage Rd RG18 79 A1
Hermitage The
Feltham TW13 98 C3
Lambourn RG17 46 C4
Hermits Cl RG7 111 A2
Hermits Hill RG7,RG30 111 B2
Herndon Cl TW20 96 A2
Heroes Wlk RG2 113 A4
Heron Cl SL5 119 B4
Heron Ct Staines TW18 97 A2
Stanwell TW19 97 C4
Heron Dr Slough SL3 44 A1
Twyford RG10 61 C3
Heron Ho RG14 105 B2
Heron Island RG4 59 B1
Heron Rd RG41 115 C3
Heron Shaw RG8 34 B4
Heron Way
Burghfield Common RG1 85 C2
Padworth RG7 109 A2
Thatcham RG19 106 A2
Heron's Way RG40 116 C4
Herondale RG12 118 B1
Heronfield TW20 95 B1
Herongate RG17 100 B4
Herons Pl SL7 1 C2
Heronscourt GU18 153 B4
Herrick Cl GU16 152 B2
Herrings La GU20 146 B2
Herriot Ct GU46 149 B2
Herschel Gram Sch SL1 42 B4
Herschel Grange RG42 91 B2
Herschel Park Dr SL1 42 C2
Herschel St SL1 42 C2
Hertford Cl Caversham RG4 59 B3
Wokingham RG41 115 C3
Hetherington Cl SL2 21 C1
Hetherington Rd TW17 125 B4
Hever Cl SL6 39 B3
Hewett Ave RG4 58 B2
Hewett Cl RG4 58 B2
Hewgate Ct RG9 15 C1
Hewlett Pl GU19 145 C2
Hexham Cl GU47 143 B1
Hexham Rd RG2 86 B2
Heynes Gn SL6 39 A2
Heywood Dr GU19 145 B2
Heywood Ave SL6 39 A1
Heywood Court Cl SL6 39 A1
Heywood Gdns SL6 39 A1
Hibbert Rd SL6 40 A2
Hibbert's Alley 25 SL4 67 B3
Hickox Ct HP10 3 C4
Hicks La GU17 150 A3
Higgs La GU19 145 B2
High Beech RG12 118 C3
High Beeches GU16 151 B1
High Close Sch RG40 116 B4
High Fields SL5 120 C2
High Heavens Wood SL7 1 B4
High Mdw RG4 58 B2
High Meadow Pl KT16 123 C2
High Rd SL6 19 C3
High St Ascot SL5 120 A3
Ascot, Sunninghill SL5 120 B2
Bagshot GU19 145 C2
Boxford RG20 76 A1
Bracknell RG12 118 A4
Burnham SL1 21 B1
Camberley GU15 151 B3
Chieveley RG20 51 A1
High St *continued*
Colnbrook SL3 69 B4
Compton RG20 31 B2
Cookham SL6 20 A4
Crowthorne RG45 143 B2
Datchet SL3 68 A3
East Isley RG20 30 C4
4 Egham TW20 95 C2
Eton SL4 67 B4
Feltham TW13 98 C3
Goring RG8 34 B3
Harlington UB3 71 B4
Harmondsworth UB7 70 B4
Hungerford RG17 100 B3
Iver SL0 44 C4
Kintbury RG17 102 A1
Lambourn RG17 25 A1
Lambourn, Upper
Lambourn RG17 24 C3
Maidenhead SL6 40 B2
Marlow SL7 1 C1
Pangbourne RG8 56 B3
Reading RG1 86 A4
Sandhurst GU47 149 C4
Sandhurst,
Little Sandhurst GU47 143 A1
Shepperton TW17 125 B2
Slough, Langley SL3 44 A1
Slough, Upton SL1 42 C2
Sonning RG4 60 B2
Staines TW18 96 C2
Stanwell TW19 70 B1
Streatley RG8 34 A3
Sunningdale SL5 121 A2
Taplow SL6 20 C1
Thatcham RG19 106 B2
Theale RG7 83 C2
Twyford RG10 61 B2
Wargrave RG10 36 B1
West End GU24 153 C4
Whitchurch-on-T RG8 56 B4
Windsor SL4 67 B3
Wraysbury TW19 68 C1
High St Mall 1 SL6 39 C4
High Street Harlington
UB3 71 B4
High Town Rd SL6 39 C4
High Tree Dr RG6 87 A3
High View Cl SL7 1 B4
High View Rd GU18 152 C4
Highbeeches Cl SL7 1 B4
Highbridge Cl RG4 59 C3
Highbridge Wharf 13 RG1 86 A4
Highbury Cres GU15 152 A4
Highbury Rd RG31 84 A4
Highclere SL5 120 B2
Highclere Cl RG12 118 C4
Highclere Dr GU15 152 A4
Highcliffe Cl RG5 60 C1
Highdown Ave RG4 59 A3
Highdown Hill Rd RG4 59 A3
Highdown Sixth Form
Comp Sch RG4 59 A3
Higher Alham RG12 118 C1
Highfield Bracknell RG12 117 C2
Earley RG6 87 A1
Highfield Ave RG14 105 A1
Highfield Cl
Englefield Green TW20 95 B1
Wokingham RG40 116 A3
Highfield Ct
Burghfield Common RG7 111 A2
Burnham SL2 22 A2
Englefield Green TW20 95 B1
Highfield La SL6 39 A2
Highfield Pk Marlow SL7 1 A1
Wargrave RG10 36 C2
Highfield Rd Bourne End SL8 3 A2
Chertsey KT16 124 A1
Englefield Green TW20 95 B1
Flackwell Heath HP10 3 A4
Maidenhead SL6 39 A4
Newbury RG14 104 C1
Purley on T RG31 57 B2
Upper Halliford TW16 125 C2
Windsor SL4 66 C2
Highgate Rd RG5 87 B3
Highgrove Pk SL6 39 C4
Highgrove Pl RG10 61 C3
Highgrove St RG1 86 B3
Highgrove Terr RG1 86 A3
Highland Pk TW13 98 C2
Highland Rd GU15 151 C4
Highlands HP10 3 A4
Highlands Ave RG41 115 B3
Highlands La RG9 35 A4
Highlands Sch The RG31 57 B1
Highlands The SL2 22 B4
Highlea Ave HP10 3 A4
Highmead Cl RG2 86 C1
Highmoor Rd RG4 58 C2
Highview GU21 84 A3
Highview Cres GU15 144 C1
Highway RG45 143 A3
Highway Ave SL6 39 A3
Highway Rd SL6 39 A3
Highwayman's Ridge
GU20 146 A3
Highwood Cl
Newbury RG14 105 A3
Yateley GU46 149 B2
Highwoods Cl SL7 1 B4
Highwoods Dr SL7 1 B4
Highworth Cotts RG26 134 B1
Highworth Way RG31 57 A1

Hilary Cl RG2 113 B4
Hilary Dr RG45 143 A3
Hilary Ho 10 RG14 105 A1
Hilborne Way RG2 115 A1
Hilbury Rd RG6 87 A2
Hilcot Rd RG30 85 B4
Hildens Dr RG31 84 B4
Hill Cl Newbury RG14 130 B4
Wooburn Green HP10 3 C4
Hill Copse View RG12 118 C4
Hill Cres RG7 108 B2
Hill Farm App HP10 3 C4
Hill Farm Rd
Marlow Bottom SL7 1 C3
Taplow SL6 20 C1
Hill Gdns RG8 34 A3
Hill Lands RG10 36 B1
Hill Piece OX11 10 C4
Hill Pl SL2 22 A3
Hill Prim Sch The RG4 59 B3
Hill Rd Arborfield RG2 114 C1
Newbury RG14 104 C2
Hill Side RG1 86 B3
Hill St RG1 86 A3
Hill Top Dr SL7 1 A1
Hill View Rd TW19 68 B1
Hillary Ct TW19 97 C4
Hillary Rd SL3 43 C2
Hillberry RG12 118 B1
Hillbrow RG2 86 C1
Hillcrest
Hampstead Norreys RG18 52 C3
Tadley RG26 135 A1
Hillcrest Ave SL6 19 C3
Hillcrest Rd GU15 152 A4
Hilldrop La RG17 46 A2
Hillersdon SL2 43 A4
Hillfield GU46 149 C3
Hillgreen La RG20 50 B4
Hillhampton SL5 120 C1
Hillhouse La RG19 133 A1
Hillingdon Ave TW19 97 C4
Hillmead Ct SL6 40 C4
Hillrise Brands Hill SL3 69 A4
Walton-on-T KT12 125 C1
Hills La SL6 19 B4
Hillsborough Pk GU15 152 B3
Hillside Ascot SL5 120 B2
Burghfield Common RG7 111 B2
East Garston RG17 47 B3
Maidenhead SL6 39 B3
Sandhurst GU15 150 C4
Slough SL1 42 C2
Wentworth GU25 122 B2
Whitchurch-on-T RG8 56 B4
Hillside Dr RG42 90 B1
Hillside Pk Earley RG2 86 C1
Sunningdale SL5 120 C1
Hillside Rd Earley RG6 87 B2
Hungerford RG17 100 B2
Marlow SL7 1 C2
Hilltop Cl SL5 120 C4
Hilltop Fst Sch SL4 66 C2
Hilltop Rd Caversham RG4 58 B3
Earley RG6 87 A4
Twyford RG10 61 C4
Hilltop View GU46 149 A3
Hillview Cl RG31 57 A1
Hilmanton RG6 113 C4
Hilperton Rd 3 SL1 42 C2
Hindhead Rd RG6 87 A2
Hinksey Cl SL3 44 A2
Hinton Cl RG45 143 A4
Hinton Dr RG45 143 A4
Hinton Pk RG10 61 C1
Hinton Rd Hurst RG10 62 A1
Slough SL1 41 C3
Hintonhatch Cnr RG10 62 A1
Hirstwood RG30 57 C1
Hirtes Ave RG2 113 C3
Hitcham Ho SL1 21 A1
Hitcham La Burnham SL1 21 A1
Taplow SL1,SL6 20 C1
Hitcham Rd SL1,SL6 41 A4
Hitchcock Cl TW17 124 C3
Hitherhooks Hill RG42 90 C1
Hithermoor Rd TW19 70 A1
Hobart Ct SL7 2 A2
Hobbis Dr SL6 39 A3
Hockett La SL6 19 A3
Hockford La RG7 134 A2
Hockham Rd RG20 31 C3
Hockley La SL2 23 A3
Hodge La SL5 93 A2
Hodgedale La RG10 37 B3
Hodges Cl GU19 145 C1
Hodsoll Rd RG1 85 C4
Hoe Benham La RG20 102 C4
Hogarth Ave Ashford TW15 98 B1
Reading RG30 84 C3
Hogarth Cl
Sandhurst GU47 150 C3
Slough SL1 41 C3
Hogfair La SL1 21 B1
Hogmoor La RG10 61 C1
Hogoak La SL4 92 A4
Hogwood La RG40 141 A3
Holbeche Cl GU46 149 A3
Holbeck RG12 117 C2
Holberton Rd RG2 113 B4
Holborn Hill OX12 6 B4
Holborne Cl RG14 130 B3
Holbrook Ct TW20 96 B2
Holbrook Mdw TW20 96 B1
Holford Cl RG31 84 B4
Holkam Cl RG30 84 C4
Holkham Cl RG30 57 C1
Holland Ct TW15 97 C1
Holland Gdns TW20 123 C4
Holland Pines RG12 117 C1
Holland Rd Marlow SL7 1 C2
Reading RG30 84 B4
Hollands The RG19 106 C2
Hollicombe Cl RG30 84 C4
Hollies The RG14 130 B3
Hollington Pl RG19 106 B2
Hollins Wlk RG30 85 B3
Hollow Hill La SL0 44 B3
Hollow La Shinfield RG2 113 C3
Virginia Water GU25 122 B3
Holloway Dr GU25 122 C3
Holloway La UB7 70 C4
Holly Ave GU16 152 A2
Holly Cl
Englefield Green TW20 95 A1
Farnham Common SL2 22 B4
Holly Cres SL4 66 B3
Holly Ct 8 KT16 124 A1
Holly Dr Maidenhead SL6 39 C4
Windsor SL4 67 C1
Holly Hedge Cl GU16 151 C1
Holly Hedge Rd GU16 151 C1
Holly Ho RG12 118 A2
Holly La RG8 54 A3
Holly Orch RG41 115 C3
Holly Rd RG5 88 A3
Holly Ridge GU24 153 C3
Holly Spring Cty Inf Sch RG12 118 C4
Holly Spring Cty Jun Sch RG12 118 C4
Holly Spring La RG12 118 B4
Holly Way GU17 150 B2
Holly Wlk SL4 93 C2
Hollybank GU24 153 C3
Hollybush Hill SL2 23 A3
Hollybush La Cookham SL6 19 A3
Iver SL0 44 A4
Sulhamstead RG7 110 C2
Hollybush Ride
Windlesham GU19,GU20 145 C3
Wokingham RG40,RG45 142 B3
Hollycombe TW20 95 B2
Hollycroft Cl UB7 71 A4
Hollycroft Gdns UB7 71 A4
Hollydale Cl RG2 86 C1
Hollyfields Cl GU15 151 A3
Hollym Cl RG6 87 C1
Holmanleaze SL6 40 A4
Holmbank Dr TW17 125 C3
Holmbury Ave RG45 143 A4
Holmdale SL2 43 B3
Holmdene RG7 111 A2
Holme Cl RG45 143 A4
Holme Park Farm La RG4 60 B1
Holmemoor Dr RG4 60 C1
Holmes Cl Ascot SL5 120 B2
Wokingham RG41 116 A2
Holmes Cres RG41 116 A2
Holmes Rd RG6 87 A3
Holmewood Cl RG41 116 A1
Holmlea Rd Datchet SL3 68 B3
Goring RG8 34 B3
Holmlea Wlk SL3 68 B3
Holmsdale Cl SL0 44 C4
Holmwood Ave RG30 84 C2
Holmwood Cl SL6 39 A3
Holsworthy Cl RG6 87 C2
Holt Comp Sch RG41 116 A4
Holt La Brightwalton RG20 49 C4
Wokingham RG41 116 A4
Holt Rd RG17 102 A1
Holt The RG8 57 B2
Holton Heath 16 RG12 118 C3
Holtspur Ave HP10 3 C4
Holtspur La HP10 3 C3
Holtwood Rd RG20 129 A3
Holy Family RC Sch SL3 43 C1
Holy Trinity CE Mid Sch SL7 1 B2
Holy Trinity CE Sch SL5 121 A2
Holy Trinity Prim Sch SL6 20 A4
Holybrook Cres RG30 85 A2
Holybrook Rd RG1 85 C3
Holyhook Cl RG45 143 A3
Holyport CE Prim Sch SL6 65 A4
Holyport Manor Sch SL6 64 C3
Holyport Rd SL6 40 A1
Holyport St SL6 65 A4
Holyrood Cl RG4 59 B3
Holywell Cl TW19 97 C4
Holywell Ct RG19 106 B2
Holywell Way TW19 97 C4
Hombrook Dr RG42 117 C4
Hombrook Ho RG42 117 C4
Home Croft RG31 57 A1
Home Farm Cl
Reading RG2 86 B2
Upper Halliford TW17 125 C3
Home Farm La RG7 134 B3
Home Farm Way SL3 23 B2
Home Mdw SL2 22 B2
Home Mead Cl RG14 130 C4
Home Meadow Dr HP10 3 A4
Home Park Rd GU46 149 B3
Home Wood SL7 17 C3
Homefield Way RG17 100 B3
Homelands Way RG9 15 B1
Homer Fst Sch SL4 66 B3
Homers Rd SL4 66 B3
Homeside Cl SL6 19 C1
Homestead Rd
Maidenhead SL6 39 B2
Staines TW18 97 A1
Homewaters Ave TW16 125 C4
Homewood SL3 43 B4
Hone Hill GU47 150 A4
Honesty Bottom RG20 28 B1
Honey End La RG30 85 A3
Honey Hill
Lambourn RG17 25 A2
Wokingham RG40 117 A1
Honey La SL6 17 C1
Honey Meadow Cl RG4 59 C1
Honeybottom Rd RG26 135 A1
Honeyfields RG17 100 B3
Honeyhill Rd RG42 118 A4
Honeysuckle Cl
Crowthorne RG45 143 A4
Iver SL0 44 B4
Yateley GU46 149 A3
Honister Wlk GU15 152 B2
Honiton Rd RG2 86 B1
Honnor Rd TW18 97 B1
Hook End La RG8 34 A1
Hook La GU24 153 B3
Hook Mill La GU18 146 B1
Hookstone La GU24 153 C4
Hoops Way RG2 112 C4
Hop Gdns RG9 15 B1
Hope Ave RG12 118 C1
Hope Fountain GU15 152 A2
Hopeman Cl GU47 150 B4
Hopwood Cl RG14 105 B2
Horatio Ave RG42 118 C4
Horewood Rd RG12 118 A2
Horizon West Ind Est RG14 105 B2
Hormer Cl GU47 143 B1
Horn St RG20 31 C3
Hornbeam Cl
Purley on T RG8 57 B3
Sandhurst GU47 143 B1
Wokingham RG41 115 B2
Hornbeam Dr RG6 87 B1
Hornbeam Gdns 7 SL1 43 A2
Hornbeam Pightle RG7 111 A2
Hornbeams RG7 139 B3
Hornby Ave RG12 118 B1
Horncastle Dr RG30 84 C3
Horndean Rd RG12 118 C2
Horne Rd Littleton TW17 125 A3
Thatcham RG19 106 C1
Hornsea Cl RG30 57 C1
Horris Hill Sch RG20 130 C2
Horse Cl The RG4 59 B2
Horse Gate Ride SL5 120 A2
Horsebrass Dr GU19 145 C1
Horseguards Dr SL6 40 A4
Horsell Ct KT16 124 A1
Horsemoor Cl SL3 44 A1
Horseshoe Cl GU15 151 C4
Horseshoe Cloisters 12 SL4 67 B3
Horseshoe Cres
Burghfield Common RG7 111 A2
Camberley GU15 151 C4
Horseshoe End RG14 131 A4
Horseshoe Hill SL1 21 B4
Horseshoe Pk RG8 56 B3
Horseshoe Rd RG8 56 B3
Horsham Rd
East Bedfont TW14 71 B1
Sandhurst GU47 143 B1
Horsnape Gdns RG42 90 A1
Horsneile La RG42 118 A4
Horton Cl SL6 20 B1
Horton Gdns SL3 68 C2
Horton Grange SL6 20 B1
Horton Rd Datchet SL3 68 B3
Horton SL3 69 A3
Poyle SL3, TW19 69 C2
Stanwell TW19 70 A1
Horton Trad Est SL3 69 A2
Hose Hill RG7,RG30 111 A4
Hosier St RG1 86 A4
Hoskins Place Ind Est GU15 151 A2
Houlton Ct GU19 145 C1
Houston Ct 33 SL4 67 B3
Houston Way RG45 142 B3
Howard Ave SL2 42 C4
Howard Cl TW16 98 C1
Howard Ct SL8 3 A2
Howard Rd
Newbury RG14 105 A1
Wokingham RG40 116 B3
Howard St RG1 85 C4
Howarth Rd SL6 40 A3
Howe La RG42 63 C1
Howell Cl RG42 91 B1
Howgate Dr RG8 34 B4
Howorth Ct 1 RG12 118 C3
Howth Dr RG5 87 B4
Hoylake Cl SL1 41 C2
Hrmondsworth Moor Ctry Pk UB7 70 A4
Hubbard Cl RG10 61 C1
Hubberholme RG12 118 A3
Hubert Rd SL3 43 B2
Huckleberry Cl RG8 57 B2
Huddington Glade GU46 149 A3
Hudson Rd Harlington UB3 71 B4
Woodley RG5 87 C3
Hugh Faringdon RC Sch (Specl Resource Aspergers Syndrome) RG30 85 B3
Hugh Fraser Dr RG31 84 B3
Hughenden Rd SL1 42 B4
Hughendon Cl SL6 39 B3
Hughes Rd Ashford TW15 98 B1
Wokingham RG40 116 C4
Hull Cl SL1 42 B2
Humber Cl
Thatcham RG18 106 A3
Wokingham RG41 115 C4
Humber Way
Sandhurst GU47 150 B4
Slough SL3 44 A1
Hummer Rd TW20 96 A2
Humphreys La RG17 47 B3
Humphries Yd RG12 118 B3
Hungerford Ave SL2 42 C4
Hungerford Cl GU47 150 B4
Hungerford Dr
Maidenhead SL6 19 C2
Reading RG1 85 C3
Hungerford Hill
East Garston RG17 47 C1
Lambourn RG17 25 A1
Hungerford La
Bradfield RG7 81 C1
Waltham St Lawrence RG10 62 C1
Hungerford Newtown RG17 74 A2
Hungerford Prim Sch RG17 100 B3
Hungerford Rd RG17 101 C2
Hungerford Sta RG17 100 C3
Hunstanton Cl SW3 69 B4
Hunt's La SL6 20 C2
Hunter Ct SL1 41 B4
Hunter's Ct RG5 87 C3
Huntercombe Cl SL6 41 B4
Huntercombe La N SL6 41 B4
Huntercombe La S SL6 41 B3
Hunters Chase RG4 58 C3
Hunters Hill RG7 110 C2
Hunters Mdw RG17 48 A2
Hunters Mews SL4 67 B3
Hunters Way
Shinfield RG7 113 A1
Slough SL1 41 C2
Huntingdonshire Cl RG41 115 B3
Huntingfield Way TW20 96 B1
Huntington Cl RG6 87 C1
Huntley Ct RG1 86 C3
Huntsgreen Ct RG12 118 B4
Huntsmans Mdw SL5 119 C4
Huntsmoor Rd RG26 135 A1
Huntswood La SL1,SL6 20 C2
Hurford Dr RG19 106 C2
Hurley Ct RG12 118 C3
Hurley High St SL6 17 C2
Hurley La SL6 18 A2
Hurricane Way Slough SL3 44 B1
Woodley RG5 88 A4
Hursley Cl RG30 84 C4
Hurst Com Sch The RG26 134 B1
Hurst Gr KT12 125 C1
Hurst La TW20 123 A3
Hurst Lodge Sch SL5 120 C1
Hurst Park Rd RG10 61 C1
Hurst Rd Slough SL1 41 B4
Twyford RG10 61 C2
Hurst Way RG2 112 C4
Hurstdene Ave TW18 97 A1
Hurstfield Dr SL6 41 A4
Hurstwood SL5 120 A2
Huscarle Way RG31 57 B2
Huson Rd RG42 91 B1
Hutsons Cl RG40 116 B4
Hutton Cl Earley RG6 87 A1
Newbury RG14 105 A2
Windlesham GU20 146 B2
Hyde Cl TW15 98 C1
Hyde End La
Brimpton RG7 133 B3
Shinfield RG7 113 B2
Hyde End Rd RG7 113 B1
Hyde Gn SL7 1 C1
Hyde La RG20 132 A1
Hyde Terr TW15 98 C1
Hydes The RG31 57 B2
Hyland Ho 10 SL8 3 A2
Hylle Cl SL4 66 C3
Hyperion Way RG2 86 A2
Hythe Cl RG12 118 C2
Hythe Cty Prim Sch TW18 96 B2
Hythe End Rd TW19 96 A3
Hythe Field Ave TW20 96 B1
Hythe Park Rd TW20 96 B1
Hythe Rd TW18 96 B2
Hythe The TW18 96 C2

I

Ian Mikardo Way RG4 59 B1
Iberian Way GU15 152 A3
Ibotson Ct SL3 69 C3
Ibstock Cl RG30 85 A4
Ibstone Ave RG4 59 C3
Icarus Ct 18 RG1 86 B4
Icknield Pl RG8 34 B4
Icknield Rd RG8 34 B4
Iden Ct RG14 105 A2
Iffley Ct TW18 96 C2
Ilbury Cl RG2 113 C3
Ilchester Cl SL6 39 B3
Ilchester Ct 6 RG14 105 A1
Ilchester Mews RG4 59 C3
Ilex Cl
Englefield Green TW20 95 A1
Silchester RG26 135 C1
Ilex Cl *continued*
Yateley GU46 149 A3
Ilfracombe Way RG6 87 C2
Ilkley Rd RG4 58 C2
Ilkley Way RG19 106 B1
Illingworth SL4 66 C2
Illingworth Ave RG4 59 C3
Illingworth Gr RG12 118 C4
Ilsley Prim Sch The RG20 30 C3
Ilsley Rd RG20 31 B2
Imperial Ct
Henley-on-T RG9 15 C1
Windsor SL4 67 A2
Imperial Ho GU25 122 C2
Imperial Rd
East Bedfont TW14 98 C4
Windsor SL4 67 A3
Imperial Way RG2 113 A4
Impstone Rd RG26 135 C1
In The Ray SL6 40 A4
Inchwood RG12 118 B1
India Rd SL1 43 A2
Ingle Dell GU15 151 B2
Ingle Glen RG40 142 A4
Ingleglen SL2 22 A4
Ingleside SL3 69 C3
Ingleton RG12 118 A3
Inglewood Ave GU15 152 B3
Inglewood Ct RG30 85 B3
Inglewood Rd RG17 101 C
Inhurst La RG26 134 B
Inhurst Way RG26 134 C
Inkerman Rd SL4 41 C
Inkpen Cl RG30 85 A
Inkpen Prim Sch RG17 127 B
Inkpen Rd
Hungerford RG17 100 C2
Inkpen RG17 127 A4
Kintbury RG17 102 A1
Inner Ring E TW6 71 A2
Inner Ring W TW6 71 A2
Innings La
White Waltham SL6 63 B4
Winkfield RG12 118 C4
Inniscrown Ho SL3 68 A4
Institute Rd Marlow SL7 1 C1
Taplow SL6 40 C4
Instow Rd RG6 87 A1
Invergordon Cl RG31 84 C2
Inverness Way GU47 150 B4
Invicta Cl TW14 98 C4
Inwood Cl SL6 19 A3
Iona Cres SL1 41 C4
Ipswich Rd SL1 42 A4
Irish Hill Rd RG17 102 A1
Irvine Ho SL4 66 C3
Irvine Pl GU25 122 C2
Irvine Way RG6 114 B4
Isaac Newton Rd RG2 115 A1
Isis Cl RG41 88 A1
Isis Ct RG1 59 A1
Isis Way Bourne End SL8 3 A2
Sandhurst GU47 150 B4
Island Cl TW18 96 C2
Island Farm Rd RG7 110 B1
Island Rd RG2 85 C1
Islandstone La RG10 89 A3
Islet Park Dr SL6 20 B2
Islet Park Ho SL6 20 B2
Islet Pk SL6 20 B2
Islet Rd SL6 20 B2
Isobel Ho 12 TW16 98 C1
Ivanhoe Rd RG40 141 A3
Iveagh Ct RG12 118 B2
Iver Cty Fst Sch SL0 44 C4
Iver Cty Mid Sch SL0 44 C4
Iver Lodge SL0 44 C4
Iver Sta SL0 44 C2
Iverdale Cl SL0 44 B3
Iverna Gdns TW14 71 B1
Ives Cl GU46 149 A4
Ives Rd SL3 44 A2
Ivy Cl SL6 65 A4
Ivy Cres SL1 41 C3
Ivy Dr GU18 153 A4
Ivybank RG31 57 B1
Ivydene Rd RG30 58 B1

J

Jack Price Ct 25 RG1 86 A3
Jack St RG14 105 A2
Jackson Cl RG12 118 A2
Jackson Ind Est SL8 3 A1
Jacob Cl Bracknell RG42 117 B4
Windsor SL4 66 C3
Jacob Rd GU15 151 A4
Jakes Ho SL6 40 A4
James Butcher Dr RG7 83 C2
James Cl SL7 1 C2
James Ct 21 RG30 85 B3
James Elliman Cty Inf Sch SL2 42 C4
James Elliman Cty Mid Sch SL2 42 C4
James Rd GU15 151 A1
James St Reading RG1 85 C4
Windsor SL4 67 B3
James Watt Rd RG2 140 C4
James Way GU15 151 A1
James's La RG7,RG30 111 C2
Jameston RG12 118 B1
Jamnagar Cl TW18 96 C1
Janson Ct RG1 85 C3
Japonica Cl RG41 115 B2
Jaques's La RG7 110 C3
Jardine Cotts SL2 23 A4

Jarratt Ho SL4 67 A2
Jarry Ct SL7 1 C2
Jarvis Dr RG10 61 B3
Jasmine Cl RG41 115 B4
Jay Cl RG6 87 A1
Jays Nest Cl GU17 150 B2
Jayworth Ho RG1 86 C4
Jedburgh Cl RG19 106 C2
Jefferson Cl
Caversham RG4 59 B4
Slough SL3 44 A1
Jeffries Ct SL8 3 A1
Jellicoe Cl SL1 42 A2
Jenkins Cl RG30 85 B3
Jenkins' Hill London Rd
GU19 145 B1
Jenner Wlk RG31 84 A4
Jennery La SL1 21 B1
Jennetts Cl RG7 81 C2
Jennings Field HP10 3 B4
Jennings Wharf SL4 67 B4
Jennys Wlk GU46 149 C3
Jerome Cl SL7 1 C2
Jerome Cnr GU47 143 B2
Jerome Rd RG5 87 C3
Jerrymoor Hill RG40 141 C4
Jesmond Dene RG14 104 C2
Jesse Cl GU46 149 C3
Jesse Terr RG1 85 C4
Jessiman Terr TW17 125 A2
Jevington RG12 118 B1
Jig's La N RG42 91 C1
Jig's La S Bracknell RG42 91 C1
Winkfield RG42 118 C4
Joo's La SL6 19 A4
Jock's La Binfield RG42 90 C1
Bracknell RG42 117 C4
Joel Cl RG6 87 A2
Johannes Ct 5 RG30 85 B3
John Balliol Ct 29 RG1 86 B4
John Boys Ho RG14 130 B3
John Childs Cl RG14 105 A1
John Hunt Cl RG19 106 C1
John Kaye Ct TW17 125 A2
John Kimber's
Almshouses RG14 104 C2
John Nike Way RG12 117 B4
John Norgate Ho RG18 105 C2
John O'Gaunt Sch RG17 100 B2
John Rankin Cty Inf Sch
RG14 130 B4
John Rankin Cty Jun Sch
RG14 130 B4
John Taylor Ct SL1 42 B3
Johnson Dr RG40 142 A4
Johnsons La RG18 106 B4
Jonathan Ct SL6 39 C4
Jonathan Hill RG20 131 A2
Jonathan Miller Sch The
SL1 41 C4
Jones Cnr SL5 119 C4
Jordan Cl Caversham RG4 59 C3
Shinfield RG7 113 B1
Jordans Cl TW19 97 B4
Jordans La RG7 110 C1
Joseph Ct RG42 91 C1
Josephine Ct RG1 85 C3
Jouldings La RG7 140 B2
Jourdelay's Pas SL4 67 B4
Journeys End SL2 42 C4
Jubilee Ave
North Ascot SL5 119 C4
Wokingham RG41 116 A4
Jubilee Cl
North Ascot SL5 119 C4
Silchester RG25 135 C1
Stanwell TW19 97 B4
Jubilee Ct Bracknell RG12 118 B3
Staines TW18 97 A2
Thatcham RG19 106 A2
Jubilee Rd
Finchampstead RG40 141 C2
Littlewick Green SL6 38 A3
Newbury RG14 105 A1
Reading RG6 87 A3
Jubilee Sq RG1 86 A3
Jubilee Way TW14 98 C4
Judy's Pas SL4 42 B1
Juliet Gdns RG42 118 C4
Julius Hill RG42 118 C4
Julkes La RG2 114 C4
Junction Rd Ashford TW15 98 B2
Lightwater GU18 146 A1
Reading RG1 86 C3
Junction Terr RG14 105 B1
Juniper RG12 118 B1
Juniper Ct SL1 43 A2
Juniper Dr SL6 40 A4
Juniper Gdns TW16 98 C1
Juniper Hill Cty Comb Sch
HP10 3 A4
Juniper La HP10 3 B4
Juniper Rd SL7 1 B3
Juniper Way RG31 57 B1
Junnipers The RG41 115 B2
Jupiter Way RG41 115 C3
Justice Cl RG19 106 C1
Jutland Cl RG41 115 C3
Jutland Ho SL4 66 C3
Jutland Pl TW20 96 B2

K

Katesgrove La RG1 86 A3
Katesgrove Prim Sch RG1 86 A3
Kathleen Saunders Ct
RG7 83 C2
Kaynes Pk SL5 119 C4
Kaywood Cl SL3 43 B2
Keane Cl RG5 87 C4
Kearsley Rd RG30 85 B3
Keates Gn RG42 118 A4
Keats Cl RG5 87 C2
Keats La SL4 67 B4
Keats Rd RG5 87 C2
Keats Way
Crowthorne RG45 143 A3
Yateley GU46 149 A2
Keble Rd SL6 39 C4
Keble Way GU47 143 C1
Keel Dr SL1 42 B2
Keeler Cl SL4 66 C2
Keep Hatch Inf Sch
RG40 116 B4
Keep Hatch Jun Sch
RG40 116 B4
Keepers Combe RG12 118 B2
Keepers Farm Cl SL4 66 C3
Keepers Terr GU25 122 A2
Keepers Wlk GU25 122 B2
Keephatch Rd RG40 116 C4
Keighley Cl RG19 106 B1
Kelburne Cl RG41 88 B2
Keldholme RG12 118 A3
Kelly Cl TW17 125 C4
Kelmscott Cl RG4 58 C2
Kelpatrick Rd SL1 41 B4
Kelsey Ave RG40 141 C3
Kelsey Cl SL6 39 B2
Kelsey Gr GU46 149 C3
Kelso Mews RG4 59 C3
Kelton Cl RG6 87 C1
Kelvedon Way RG4 58 C3
Kelvin Cl RG2 140 C4
Kelvin Rd RG14 105 A2
Kemble Ct RG31 84 B2
Kemerton Cl RG31 84 B2
Kemp Ct GU19 145 C1
Kempe Cl SL3 44 B1
Kempton Cl RG14 105 B1
Kemsley Chase SL2 22 B2
Kenavon Dr RG1 86 B4
Kendal Ave Caversham RG4 59 C3
Shinfield RG2 113 C3
Kendal Cl
East Bedfont TW14 98 C4
Slough SL2 43 A3
Thatcham RG18 106 B2
Kendal Dr SL2 43 A3
Kendal Gr GU15 152 B2
Kendrick Cl RG40 116 B3
Kendrick Ct 5 RG1 86 B3
Kendrick Girls' Gram Sch
RG1 86 B4
Kendrick Rd
Newbury RG14 130 B3
Reading RG1 86 B3
Slough SL3 43 A2
Kenilworth Ave
Bracknell RG12 118 B4
Reading RG30 85 B3
Kenilworth Ct SL1 42 C2
Kenilworth Gdns TW18 97 B2
Kenilworth Rd
TW15, TW19 97 B3
Kenneally SL4 66 B3
Kenneally Cl 11 SL4 66 B3
Kenneally Pl 12 SL4 66 B3
Kenneally Row 13 SL4 66 B3
Kenneally Wlk 10 SL4 66 B3
Kennedy Cl
Farnham Common SL2 22 B3
Maidenhead SL6 39 B3
Marlow SL7 1 C2
Newbury RG14 130 B3
Kennedy Ct TW15 98 B2
Kennedy Dr RG8 56 C3
Kennedy Gdns RG6 87 A2
Kennedy Ho SL1 41 B3
Kennel Ave SL5 119 C4
Kennel Cl SL5 92 C1
Kennel Gn SL5 119 C4
Kennel La Bracknell RG42 91 A1
Cookham SL6 19 B4
Windlesham GU20 146 B3
Kennel Lane Sch RG42 91 A1
Kennel Ride SL5 92 C1
Kennel Wood SL5 119 C4
Kennet & Avon Canal
Visitor Ctr RG7 109 B2
Kennet Cl RG19 106 C2
Kennet Ct
Hungerford RG17 100 C4
4 Newbury RG14 105 A1
Wokingham RG41 115 C3
Kennet Ctr The RG14 105 A1
Kennet Pl
Burghfield Common RG7 111 A2
Chilton Foliat RG17 73 A1
10 Newbury RG14 105 A2
Kennet Rd Kintbury RG17 102 A1
Maidenhead SL6 39 C4
Newbury RG14 104 C1
Kennet Sch RG19 106 C2
Kennet Side
Newbury RG14 105 B2
12 Reading RG1 86 B4
Kennet St RG1 86 B4
Kennet Valley Prim Sch
RG31 84 C2
Kennet Way RG17 100 C4
Kennett Rd Bourne End SL8 3 A2
Slough SL3 44 A2
Kensington Cl RG6 87 A1
Kensington Rd RG30 85 B4
Kent Ave SL1 42 B4
Kent Cl Staines TW18 97 B1
Wokingham RG41 115 B3
Kent Folly RG42 91 C1
Kent Lodge 6 SL6 39 C3
Kent Rd Reading RG30 85 B4
Windlesham GU20 146 B3
Kent Way SL6 19 C1
Kentigern Dr RG45 143 C3
Kenton Cl Bracknell RG12 118 B4
Frimley GU16 151 C1
Marlow SL7 1 C1
Kenton Rd RG6 87 B2
Kenton's La SL4 66 C3
Kentons La RG10 36 B4
Kentwood Cl RG30 57 C1
Kentwood Hill RG31 57 C1
Kenwood Cl
Harmondsworth UB7 71 A4
Maidenhead SL6 39 A4
Kenworth Gr GU18 146 A1
Keppel Spur SL4 95 A4
Keppel St SL4 67 B3
Kepple Pl GU19 145 C2
Kernham Dr RG31 57 B2
Kerria Way GU24 153 C3
Kerris Way RG6 87 A1
Kersey Cres RG14 104 C3
Kesteven Way RG41 115 C3
Keston Cl RG4 59 B1
Kestrel Ave TW18 96 C3
Kestrel Cl RG19 106 A2
Kestrel Path SL2 21 C1
Kestrel Way
Burghfield Common RG7 111 A2
Reading RG30 85 A2
Wokingham RG41 115 C3
Keswick Ave TW17 125 C3
Keswick Cl Frimley GU15 152 B2
Reading RG30 84 B4
Keswick Ct SL2 42 C3
Keswick Dr GU18 153 A4
Keswick Gdns RG5 87 C3
Keswick Rd TW20 96 A1
Ketcher Gn RG42 90 B2
Kettering Cl RG31 84 C2
Kevins Dr GU46 149 C4
Keynsham Way GU47 143 B1
Keys La SL6 39 C3
Kibble Gn RG12 118 B2
Kibblewhite Cres RG10 61 B3
Kidderminster Rd SL2 22 A1
Kidmore End Rd RG4 59 A4
Kidmore Rd RG4 58 C3
Kidwells Cl SL6 39 C4
Kidwells Park Dr SL6 39 C4
Kielder Wlk GU15 152 B2
Kier Pk SL5 120 B3
Kilburn Cl RG31 84 B2
Kildare Gdns RG4 59 B2
Killarney Dr SL6 39 C4
Killigrew Ho 4 TW16 98 C1
Killross Rd TW14 98 B4
Kilmartin Gdns GU16 151 C1
Kilmington Cl RG12 118 C1
Kilmiston Ave TW17 125 B2
Kilmiston Ho TW17 125 B2
Kilmore Dr GU15 152 A2
Kilmuir Cl GU47 150 B4
Kiln Cl Harlington UB3 71 B4
Hermitage RG18 79 B4
Kiln Croft Cl SL7 2 A2
Kiln Dr RG18 78 C3
Kiln Hill RG7 140 A4
Kiln La Bourne End SL8,HP10 3 B2
Bracknell RG12 118 A4
Mortimer RG7 137 B3
Reading RG31 84 A4
Shiplake RG9 35 B1
Sunningdale SL5 121 A2
Winkfield SL5 93 A1
Kiln Pl SL6 19 A2
Kiln Rd Caversham RG4 59 B4
Newbury RG14 105 B3
Kiln Ride
Upper Basildon RG8 54 C3
Wokingham RG40 142 A4
Kiln Ride Extension
RG40 142 A3
Kiln Terr RG18 78 C3
Kiln View Rd RG2 86 B1
Kilnsea Dr RG6 87 B1
Kilowna Cl RG10 61 A2
Kilross Rd TW14 98 C4
Kimber Cl SL4 67 A2
Kimber's Cl RG14 104 C2
Kimber's La SL6 39 C2
Kimberley RG12 118 B1
Kimberley Cl
4 Reading RG1 85 C3
Slough SL3 43 C1
Kimbers Dr Burnham SL1 21 B1
Newbury RG14 104 B3
Kimmeridge RG12 118 C2
Kimpton Cl RG6 113 C4
Kinburn Dr TW20 95 C2
King Acre Ct TW18 96 C3
King Edward Ct 14 SL4 67 B3
King Edward St SL1 42 B2
King Edward VII Ave
SL4, SL3 67 C4
King Edward VII Hospl
SL4 67 B2
King Edwards Cl SL5 119 C4
King Edwards Rd SL5 119 C4
King Edwards Rise SL5 119 C4
King George Cl TW16 98 C2
King James Way RG9 35 B4
King John's Cl TW19 68 B1
King John's Palace SL3 69 B3
King St Chertsey KT16 124 A1
Maidenhead SL6 39 C3
Mortimer RG7 137 A3
Reading RG1 86 A4
King Stable St SL4 67 B4
King Street La RG41 88 B1
King's Ave TW16 98 C1
King's Cl TW18 97 B1
King's Court Cty Fst Sch
SL4 95 A4
King's Gr SL6 39 C3
King's Keep GU47 143 A1
King's Rd Ascot SL5 120 B2
Crowthorne RG45 143 B3
Egham TW20 96 A2
Henley-on-T RG9 15 B1
Slough SL1 42 C2
Windsor SL4 67 B2
Windsor SL4 67 B3
King's Ride Bracknell SL5 119 B3
Camberley GU15 151 B4
King's Road Ho 27 SL4 67 B3
King's Wlk GU15 150 C3
Kingfisher Cl RG7 109 A2
Kingfisher Court Ind Est
RG14 105 B2
Kingfisher Ct Slough SL2 22 A1
Twyford RG10 61 C2
Kingfisher Dr
Staines TW18 96 C2
Woodley RG5 87 B3
Yateley GU46 149 A3
Kingfisher Pl RG1 86 A4
Kinghorn La SL6 19 B2
Kinghorn Pk SL6 19 B2
Kings Cl RG9 15 B1
Kings Cres GU15 151 B4
Kings La Cookham SL6 19 A4
Englefield Green TW20 95 A1
Windlesham GU20 146 C3
Kings Mead RG14 130 B3
Kings Meadow Rd RG1 86 A4
Kings Rd Caversham RG4 59 B1
Newbury RG14 105 A1
Reading RG1 86 B4
Silchester RG7 136 A1
West End GU24 153 C3
Kings Rd W RG14 105 A1
Kings Reach Ct 17 RG1 86 A4
Kings Terr SL3 69 A4
Kings Wlk 4
Maidenhead SL6 39 C4
Reading RG1 86 A4
Kings Wood SL7 17 B4
Kingsbridge Cotts RG40 142 C4
Kingsbridge Hill RG7 139 A3
Kingsbridge Rd
Newbury RG14 104 C1
Reading RG2 86 B1
Kingsbury Cres TW18 96 B2
Kingsbury Dr SL4 95 A4
Kingsclear Pk GU15 151 B2
Kingscroft Cty Inf Sch
TW18 97 A2
Kingscroft Cty Jun Sch
TW18 97 A1
Kingscroft La RG42 92 A3
Kingsdown Cl RG6 87 A1
Kingsfield SL4 66 B3
Kingsford Cl RG5 88 A3
Kingsgate Pl 20 RG1 86 B4
Kingsgate St RG1 86 B4
Kingsland Grange RG14 130 C4
Kingsley Ave
Camberley GU15 151 B2
Englefield Green TW20 95 A1
Kingsley Cl Charvil RG10 61 A3
Crowthorne RG45 143 A2
Newbury RG14 105 A3
Reading RG2 113 A4
Kingsley Dr SL7 1 B3
Kingsley Path SL2 21 B1
Kingsmere Rd RG42 117 C4
Kingston Ave TW14 71 C1
Kingston Cres TW15 97 B1
Kingston Gdns RG2 86 B1
Kingston La RG7 110 B3
Kingston Rd
Ashford TW15, TW17 97 C1
Camberley GU15 145 A1
Staines TW15, TW18 97 A1
Kingsway
Blackwater GU17 150 C3
Caversham RG4 59 C3
Farnham Common SL2 22 B3
Iver SL0 44 C4
Stanwell TW19 97 C4
Thatcham RG19 106 C1
Kingswick Cl SL5 120 B3
Kingswick Dr SL5 120 B3
Kingswood Cl TW20 95 B2
Kingswood Creek TW19 68 B1
Kingswood Ct
Maidenhead SL6 39 C3
17 Reading RG30 85 B3
Kingswood Hall of
Residence TW20 95 B2
Kingswood Ho SL1 42 B4
Kingswood Par SL7 1 B3
Kingswood Rise TW20 95 B2
Kinnaird Cl SL1 41 B4
Kinross Ave SL5 119 C2
Kinross Cl TW16 98 C2
Kinross Ct SL5 119 C2
Kinross Dr TW16 98 C2
Kinson Rd RG30 58 A1
Kintbury Rd RG17 127 C3
Kintbury Sq RG17 102 A1
Kintbury Sta RG17 102 A2
Kinver Wlk 30 RG1 86 A3
Kipling Cl Thatcham RG18 106 B3
Woodley RG5 87 C2
Yateley GU46 149 B2
Kipling Ct SL4 67 A3
Kirkby Ct GU16 151 C1
Kirkfell Cl RG31 57 B1
Kirkham Cl Caversham RG4 59 C3
Sandhurst GU47 143 B1
Kirkstall Ct RG31 84 B2
Kirkstone Cl GU15 152 B2
Kirkwall Spur SL1 42 C4
Kirkwood Cres RG7 110 C2
Kirton Cl RG30 85 A4
Kirtons Farm Rd
RG2 & RG30 85 B1
Kitsmead La GU25 122 B1
Kittiwake Cl RG5 88 A4
Kitwood Dr RG6 87 C1
Klondyke SL7 1 B1
Knapp Rd TW15 97 C2
Knapp The RG6 87 A2
Knappe Cl RG9 35 B4
Knighton Cl RG4 59 A2
Knights Cl Egham TW20 96 B1
Windsor SL4 66 B3
Knights La RG20 129 B2
Knights Lea RG20 129 A2
Knights Pl 32 SL4 67 B3
Knights Way
Caversham RG4 59 A3
Frimley GU15 152 B2
Knightsbridge Cres TW18 97 A1
Knightsbridge Dr RG19 132 A2
Knightsbridge Rd GU15 151 C4
Knightswood RG12 118 A1
Knole Wood SL5 120 C1
Knoll Cl OX12 6 C4
Knoll Park Rd KT16 123 C1
Knoll Rd GU15 151 B3
Knoll The Chertsey KT16 123 C1
Purley on T RG31 57 A1
Knollmead RG31 84 B2
Knollys Rd RG26 135 C1
Knolton Way SL2 43 B4
Knossington Cl RG6 87 B1
Knott La RG7 109 A2
Knowl Hill CE Prim Sch
RG10 37 C2
Knowl Hill Terr RG10 37 C2
Knowle Cl RG4 58 B2
Knowle Gn TW18 97 A2
Knowle Gr GU25 122 B1
Knowle Grove Cl GU25 122 B1
Knowle Hill GU25 122 B1
Knowle Park Ave TW18 97 A2
Knowle Rd RG5 87 C2
Knowles Ave RG45 142 C3
Knowsley Cl SL6 19 A1
Knowsley Rd RG31 57 B2
Knox Gn RG42 90 B2
Kola Ho SL2 43 A3
Korda Cl TW17 124 C3
Krooner Rd GU15 151 A2
Kurnool Mortar
Cross Roads GU15 151 A3
Kybes La RG7,RG30 112 B3
Kyftle Court Flat RG14 104 C1
Kyle Cl RG12 118 A3

L

La Roche Cl SL3 43 B2
Laburnham Ct KT16 124 A1
Laburnham Rd
Maidenhead SL6 39 C3
Winnersh RG41 88 B1
Laburnum Cl SL7 1 C2
Laburnum Gdns RG2 86 C1
Laburnum Gr
Brands Hill SL3 69 A4
Newbury RG14 105 A2
Laburnum Pl TW20 95 A1
Laburnum Rd KT16 124 A1
Laburnum Way TW19 97 C4
Laburnums The GU17 150 A3
Lacewood Gdns RG2 86 C1
Lacey Cl TW20 96 B1
Ladbroke Cl RG5 87 C3
Ladbrooke Rd SL1 42 B2
Ladwell Cl RG14 130 B3
Lady Jane Ct RG4 59 B2
Lady Margaret Rd SL5 120 C1
Ladybank RG12 118 A1
Ladyday Pl SL1 42 B3
Ladymask Cl RG31 84 C2
Laffords The RG7 82 A1
Laggan Rd SL6 19 C1
Laggan Sq SL6 19 C1
Laird Ct GU19 145 C1
Lake Ave SL1 42 B3
Lake End Ct SL6 41 A4
Lake End Rd SL4,SL6 41 A3
Lake End Way RG45 143 A2
Lake Rd GU25 122 A3
Lake Side The GU17 150 B2
Lake View SL6 20 A1
Lakeland Dr GU16 151 C1
Lakes The SL7 18 A3
Lakeside
3 Bracknell RG42 118 B4

Long Grove RG7 107 B3
Long Half Acre SL6 38 A2
Long Hedge RG17 25 B1
Long Hill Rd RG12, SL5 119 A4
Long La Brightwalton RG20 28 C2
Cookham SL6 19 B3
Hermitage RG14, RG18 78 C1
Holyport, Braywoodside SL6 64 B2
Holyport, Touchen-end SL6 64 C3
Newbury RG18 105 B4
Purley on T RG31 57 A2
Stanwell TW15, TW19 97 C4
Long Lane Prim Sch RG31 57 A2
Long Mickle GU47 143 A1
Long Readings La SL2 22 A1
Long Water Dr RG30 112 B4
Long Wlk The SL4 94 B4
Long's Way RG40 116 C4
Longacre RG14 130 B4
Longbourne Way KT16 123 C2
Longbridge Rd RG19 106 C1
Longcroft Rd RG19 106 C1
Longcross Sta GU25 121 C1
Longdon Rd RG41 88 B1
Longdown Lodge GU47 150 A4
Longdown Rd GU47 143 A1
Longfield Rd RG10 61 B3
Longford Ave
Feltham TW14 71 C1
Stanwell TW19 97 C4
Longford Cl GU15 151 B2
Longford Rdbt TW6, UB7 70 A3
Longford Sch TW14 98 C4
Longford Way TW19 97 C4
Longhurst Cl RG4 59 B2
Longlands Way GU15 152 B3
Longleat Dr RG31 57 A2
Longleat Gdns SL6 39 B3
Longleat Way TW14 98 B4
Longmead Ball Hill RG20 129 C1
Windsor SL4 66 C3
Longmead La SL1 21 B3
Longmeadow GU15, GU16 151 C2
Longmoor La RG7 137 A4
Longmoors RG42 117 C4
Longmore Rd RG2 113 B3
Longridge Cl RG30 85 A4
Longridge Scout Boating Activity Ctr SL7 18 C4
Longshot Ind Est RG12 117 C4
Longshot La RG12 117 C4
Longside Cl TW20 123 B4
Longview HP9 3 C4
Longwater Dr RG30 85 C1
Longwater La RG27,RG40 141 C2
Longwater Rd
Bracknell RG12 118 B2
Finchampstead RG40 141 C1
Longworth Ave RG31 84 A4
Longworth Dr SL6 20 B1
Lonsdale Cl SL6 20 A1
Lonsdale Way SL6 40 B1
Look Out Discovery Ctr The RG12 118 B1
Loosen Dr SL6 39 A2
Lord Knyvett Cl TW19 70 B1
Loring Rd SL4 66 C3
Lorne Cl SL1 42 A2
Lorne Pl RG1 85 C4
Lorne St RG1 85 C4
Lorraine Cty Inf Sch GU15 151 C4
Lorraine Rd GU15 151 C4
Lory Ridge GU19 145 C2
Losfield Rd SL4 66 C3
Loughborough RG12 118 C2
Loundyes Cl RG18 106 A2
Lovatt Cl RG31 84 A4
Love Green La SL0 44 C4
Love Hill La SL3 44 A3
Love La Iver SL0 44 B4
Newbury RG14 105 A3
Lovedean Ct RG12 118 C2
Lovegrove Dr SL2 21 C1
Lovejoy La SL4 66 B3
Lovel La SL5 93 A2
Lovel Rd SL5 93 A2
Lovelace Cl SL6 17 C2
Lovelace Rd RG12 117 C3
Lovell Cl RG9 35 B4
Lovells Cl GU18 146 A1
Lovelock Rd RG30 58 B1
Lovers Cl RG7 111 A2
Lovers Wood RG7 136 C3
Lovett Gdns SL6 20 B2
Lovett Rd TW20 96 B2
Lowbrook Dr SL6 39 A2
Lowbrook Prim Sch SL6 39 A2
Lowbury RG12 118 C3
Lower Armour Rd RG31 57 B1
Lower Bglws RG8 34 B4
Lower Boyndon Rd SL6 39 C3
Lower Britwell Rd SL2 21 B1
Lower Broadmoor Rd RG45 143 B2
Lower Brook St RG1 86 A3
Lower Canes GU46 149 A3
Lower Charles St GU15 151 B3
Lower Church Rd GU47 149 C4
Lower Cippenham La SL1 41 C3
Lower Common RG27 140 C1
Lower Cookham Rd SL6 20 B1
Lower Earley Way RG6 114 B4
Lower Earley Way (N) RG6 87 C1
Lower Earley Way (W) RG6 113 C4
Lower Elmstone Dr RG31 57 B1
Lower Farm Ct RG19 105 C1
Lower Field Rd RG1 86 A3
Lower Henley Rd RG4 59 B2
Lower Lees Rd SL2 22 A1
Lower Meadow Rd RG2 86 B1
Lower Mill Field GU19 145 B1
Lower Mount RG1 86 B3
Lower Pound La SL7 1 B1
Lower Rd Chilton OX11 10 B4
Cookham SL6 19 C4
Lower Ridge SL8 3 A2
Lower Sandhurst Rd RG40,GU47 142 B1
Lower Ventnor Cotts SL6 19 B4
Lower Village Rd SL5 120 B2
Lower Way RG19 106 A2
Lower Wokingham Rd RG40, RG45 142 B3
Lowes Cl RG9 36 A2
Lowestoft Cl RG6 87 B1
Lowestoft Dr SL1 41 B4
Loweswater Wlk GU15 152 B2
Lowfield Cl GU18 153 A4
Lowfield Ct RG4 59 B3
Lowfield Gn RG4 59 C2
Lowfield Rd RG4 59 B3
Lowlands Rd
Blackwater GU17 150 B2
Stanwell TW19 70 B1
Lowry Cl GU47 150 B3
Lowther Cl RG41 115 C4
Lowther Rd RG41 115 C4
Loxwood RG6 87 B1
Loxwood Cl TW14 98 C4
Lucan Dr TW18 97 B1
Lucas Cl GU46 149 B3
Lucas Gn GU24 153 B2
Lucas Green Rd GU24 153 C3
Lucey Cl RG31 57 A2
Lucie Ave TW15 98 A1
Luckley Oakfield Sch RG40 116 A2
Luckley Path RG40 116 B3
Luckley Rd RG41 116 A2
Luckley Wood RG41 116 A2
Luckmore Dr RG6 87 A2
Lud Lodge TW15 97 C3
Luddington Ave GU25, TW20 122 C4
Ludgrove Prep Sch RG40 116 B2
Ludlow RG12 118 A1
Ludlow Cl RG14 105 C3
Ludlow Ho SL6 39 C3
Ludlow Rd SL6 39 C3
Luff Cl SL4 66 C2
Luker Ave RG9 15 B2
Lulworth Rd RG2 113 B4
Lunds Farm Rd RG5 88 A4
Lundy Ct SL1 41 C3
Lundy La RG30 85 B4
Lupin Cl GU19 145 B1
Lupin Ride RG45 143 A4
Luscombe Cl RG4 59 B2
Lutman La SL6 19 C1
Lutmans Haven RG10 37 C3
Lutterworth Cl RG42 91 B1
Lutton Cl RG6 113 C4
Lych Gate Cl GU47 149 C4
Lycroft Cl RG8 34 B4
Lydbury RG12 118 C3
Lydford Ave SL2 42 B4
Lydford Rd RG1 86 C3
Lydney RG12 118 A1
Lydsey Cl SL2 22 A1
Lyefield Ct RG4 59 A3
Lyell Place E SL4 66 B2
Lyell Place W SL4 66 B2
Lyell Rd SL4 66 B2
Lyell Walk E SL4 66 B2
Lyell Walk W SL4 66 B2
Lyme Gr RG31 57 B1
Lymington Ave GU46 149 B3
Lymington Gate RG4 58 C3
Lynch Hill La SL2 21 C1
Lynch Hill Sch SL2 21 C1
Lynch La RG17 25 A2
Lynchets View RG17 24 C3
Lynden Mews RG2 86 A3
Lyndhurst Ave
Blackwater GU17 150 B3
Cookham SL6 19 C3
Lyndhurst Cl RG12 119 A3
Lyndhurst Rd Ascot SL5 120 A3
Goring RG8 34 B3
Reading RG30 58 A1
Lyndhurst Sch GU15 151 A3
Lyndwood Dr SL4 68 A1
Lyndwood Par SL4 68 A1
Lyne Cl GU25 122 C2
Lyne Crossing Rd KT16, GU25 123 A2
Lyne Ct GU25 122 C1
Lyne La KT16,TW20,GU25 123 A2
Lyne Place Manor GU25 122 C1
Lyne Rd GU25 122 C2
Lynegrove Ave TW15 98 B2
Lyneham Gdns SL6 19 A1
Lyneham Rd RG45 143 A3
Lynmouth Ct RG1 59 A1
Lynmouth Rd RG1 59 A1
Lynn Cl TW15 98 B2
Lynton Cl RG5 87 B3
Lynton Ct 4 RG14 105 A2
Lynton Gn SL6 39 C4
Lynwood Ave Egham TW20 95 C1
Slough SL3 43 B2
Lynwood Chase 1 RG12 118 B4
Lynwood Cres SL5 120 C2
Lynwood Ct TW15 97 C2
Lynwood Flats SL5 120 C2
Lyon Cl RG19 106 C1
Lyon Oaks RG42 91 A1
Lyon Rd RG45 143 B3
Lyon Sq RG30 85 A4
Lyon Way GU16 151 B1
Lyon Way Ind Est GU16 151 B1
Lysander Cl RG5 88 A4
Lysander Mead SL6 40 B4
Lytchet Minster Cl 4 RG12 118 C2
Lytham RG12 117 C2
Lytham Cl RG30 85 B2
Lytham Ct SL5 120 B2
Lytham End RG31 57 A2
Lytham Rd RG5 87 C4

M

Macadam Ave RG45 143 B4
Macbeth Ct RG42 118 C4
Macdonald Rd GU18 153 A4
Mace Cl RG6 87 A1
Mackay Cl RG31 84 C2
Mackenzie Mall 10 SL1 42 C2
Mackenzie St 9 SL1 42 C2
Macklin Cl RG17 100 B3
Macnaughton Woods GU15 151 C3
Macphail Cl RG40 116 C4
Macrae Rd GU46 149 B3
Maddle Rd RG17 24 B4
Madeira Pl 3 RG14 105 A1
Madejski Stad RG2 112 C4
Madingley RG12 118 A1
Madox Brown End GU47 150 C3
Mafeking Rd TW19 96 A3
Magdalene Rd
Littleton TW17 124 C3
Sandhurst GU47 143 C1
Magill Cl RG7 113 A1
Magna Carta La TW19 95 C4
Magna Carta Sch TW18 96 B1
Magna Rd TW20 95 A1
Magnolia Cl GU47 143 B1
Magnolia Ct RG5 88 A4
Magnolia Gdns SL3 43 B2
Magnolia Way RG41 115 C3
Magpie Cl RG19 106 A2
Magpie Way Reading RG31 84 A3
Slough SL2 21 C1
Maguire Dr GU16 152 B2
Mahonia Cl GU24 153 C3
Maiden Erlegh Comp Sch RG6 87 A2
Maiden Erlegh Dr RG6 87 A2
Maiden Lane Ctr 5 RG6 87 B1
Maiden Pl RG6 87 B1
Maiden's Gn SL4 92 A3
Maidenhead Coll Claires Court Girls SL6 39 C4
Maidenhead Court Pk SL6 20 A2
Maidenhead Office Pk SL6 38 C1
Maidenhead Rd
Binfield RG40 89 B2
Cookham SL6 19 C3
Newell Green RG42 91 A3
Windsor SL4 66 C4
Maidenhead Sta SL6 39 C3
Maidensfield RG41 88 B1
Main Dr Bracknell RG42 91 C1
Iver SL0 44 C2
Winkfield RG12, SL5 119 A4
Main St Chilton OX11 10 B4
Greenham RG19 131 C3
Newtown RG19 132 A3
Yateley GU46 149 B4
Mainprize Rd RG12 118 C4
Mainstone Rd GU24 153 C2
Maise Webster Cl TW19 97 B4
Maitland Rd RG1 85 C4
Maiwand Gdns RG31 84 B4
Maize La RG42 91 C1
Majendie Cl RG14 104 B3
Major's Farm Rd
Brands Hill SL3 69 A4
Datchet SL3 68 B4
Makepiece Rd RG42 91 A1
Maker Cl RG30 85 A2
Makins Rd RG9 35 A4
Malders La SL6 19 B2
Maldon Cl RG30 85 B3
Malet Cl TW20 96 B1
Malham Fell RG12 118 A3
Malham Rd RG19 106 B2
Mallard Cl Earley RG6 87 A2
Twyford RG10 61 C2
Mallard Ct RG14 104 C2
Mallard Dr SL1 41 C3
Mallard Row RG1 86 A4
Mallard Way
Padworth RG7 109 A2
Yateley GU46 149 A3
Mallards The
Frimley GU16 151 C1
Great Shefford RG17 48 A2
Laleham TW18 124 A4
Mallards Way GU18 153 A4
Mallory Ave RG4 59 B3
Mallow Pk SL6 19 B1
Mallowdale Rd RG12 118 C1
Malone Rd RG5 87 B3
Malpas Rd SL2 43 A3
Malt Hill Egham TW20 95 C2
Newell Green RG42 91 C3
Malt Ho SL4 95 A4
Malt House Cl SL4 95 A4
Malt Shovel La RG17 24 C2
Maltby Way RG6 114 A4
Malthouse Cl RG19 106 C1
Malthouse La 8
Reading RG1 85 C4
West End GU24 153 C4
Malthouse Way 7 SL7 1 B1
Maltings Pl 8 RG1 86 A4
Maltings The Staines TW18 96 C2
Thatcham RG19 106 C1
West Ilsley RG20 10 A1
Malton Ave SL1 42 A3
Malvern Cl RG5 87 C3
Malvern Ct Brands Hill SL3 69 A4
Newbury RG14 104 C1
Reading RG1 86 B3
Malvern Rd Harlington UB3 71 C4
Maidenhead SL6 19 B1
Malvern Way RG10 61 B4
Malyons The TW17 125 B2
Man's Hill RG7 111 B1
Managua Cl RG4 59 C1
Manchester Rd RG1 86 C4
Mandarin Ct RG14 105 B1
Mandela Ct 5 RG1 86 B4
Mandeville Cl RG30 84 C3
Mandeville Ct TW20 96 A2
Mandeville Rd TW17 125 A2
Manea Cl RG6 114 B4
Manfield Cl SL2 22 A1
Manners Rd RG5 87 B4
Mannock Way RG5 88 A4
Manor Bglws RG20 31 B2
Manor Cl RG42 91 A1
Manor Cres RG20 31 B2
Manor Ct Marlow SL7 1 B2
Slough, Cippenham SL1 41 C3
23 Slough, Upton Park SL1 42 C2
Manor Farm Ave TW17 125 A2
Manor Farm Cl SL4 66 C2
Manor Farm Cotts SL4 68 A1
Manor Farm Ct TW20 96 A2
Manor Farm Ho SL4 66 C2
Manor Farm La
Egham TW20 96 A2
Tidmarsh RG8 56 B1
Manor Farm Rd RG2 86 A1
Manor Gdns HP10 3 C3
Manor Gr SL6 65 B3
Manor House Dr SL5 93 A1
Manor House La SL3 68 A3
Manor House The GU15 151 B3
Manor La Chieveley RG20 51 A1
Harlington UB3 71 B4
Hermitage RG18 79 A4
Leckhampstead RG20 49 C2
Maidenhead SL6 39 C2
Newbury RG14 105 C3
Manor Leaze TW20 96 A2
Manor Park Cl RG30 84 B3
Manor Park Dr
Wokingham RG40 141 C3
Yateley GU46 149 B3
Manor Pk Froxfield SN8 99 A2
Staines TW18 96 B3
Manor Pl Newbury RG14 104 B3
Staines TW18 97 A2
Manor Prim Sch RG30 85 A2
Manor Rd Ashford TW15 98 A2
Goring RG8 34 A3
Henley-on-T RG9 35 B4
Letcombe Bassett OX12 7 B3
Maidenhead SL6 39 C2
Walton-on-T KT12 125 C1
Whitchurch-on-T RG8 56 B4
Windsor SL4 66 C3
Wokingham RG41 116 A1
Manor Way Bagshot GU19 145 C2
Egham TW20 95 C1
Holyport SL6 65 A4
Manor Wood Gate RG9 36 A2
Manorcroft Sch TW20 96 A1
Manorcrofts Rd TW20 96 A1
Manse Cl UB3 71 B4
Mansel Cl SL2 43 A4
Mansell Cl SL4 66 C3
Mansell Ct RG2 86 C1
Mansell Dr RG14 130 B3
Mansfield Cl SL5 119 B4
Mansfield Cres RG12 118 A2
Mansfield Pl SL5 119 B4
Mansfield Rd
Reading RG1 85 C3
Wokingham RG41 116 A3
Mansion House St 24 RG14 105 A2
Mansion La SL0 44 B3
Manston Dr RG12 118 B2
Mant Cl RG20 75 B3
Manygate La TW17 125 B2
Mapel Ct 11 RG12 118 C3
Maple Cl Blackwater GU17 150 B3
Maidenhead SL6 39 B3
Sandhurst GU47 142 C1
Winnersh RG41 88 B2
Maple Cres
Newbury RG14 105 A2
Slough SL2 43 A3
Maple Ct
Englefield Green TW20 95 A1
Goring RG8 34 A3
Marlow SL7 1 C2
Windsor SL4 67 B2
Maple Dr
Crowthorne RG45 143 B4
Lightwater GU18 152 C4
Maple Gdns Reading RG2 86 C1
Stanwell TW19 97 C3
Yateley GU46 149 B3
Maple La RG8 55 A3
Maple Rise SL7 1 C2
Mapledene RG4 58 C2
Mapledurham Dr RG8 57 B3
Mapledurham Ho RG31 57 C3
Mapledurham View RG31 57 B1
Mapledurham Watermill RG31 57 C3
Mapledurham Wlk SL6 19 C2
Maples The 15 SL8 3 A2
Maplin Pk SL3 44 A2
Marathon Cl RG5 88 A4
Marbeck Cl SL4 66 B3
Marbull Way RG42 91 A1
Marchant Cl RG19 131 B4
Marchant Ct SL7 2 A2
Marcheria Cl RG12 118 A2
Marchwood Ave RG4 59 B4
Marcia Ct SL1 41 C3
Marconi Rd RG14 105 A2
Marcus Cl RG30 85 A4
Mardale GU15 152 B2
Mardy RG4 58 C3
Mare La RG10 63 C2
Marefield RG6 87 B1
Marefield Rd SL7 1 B1
Marescroft Rd SL2 21 C1
Mareshall Ave RG42 91 A1
Marfleet Cl RG6 87 C1
Margaret Cl Reading RG2 113 B4
Staines TW18 97 B1
Maria Ct 13 RG30 85 B3
Marie Davis Ct 21 RG1 86 A4
Marigold Cl RG45 142 C3
Marina Cl KT16 124 B1
Marina Way SL1 41 B3
Mariners La RG7 82 A2
Marino Way RG40 141 A3
Marion Ave TW17 125 A2
Marish Ct SL3 44 A2
Marish Cty Fst Sch SL3 44 A2
Marish Jun Sch SL3 44 A2
Marish Wharf Ind Est SL3 43 C2
Marjory Kinnon Sch TW14 71 C1
Markby Way RG6 87 C1
Market La SL3 44 B2
Market Pl Colnbrook SL3 69 B4
Henley-on-T RG9 15 B1
25 Newbury RG14 105 A2
Reading RG1 86 A4
Wokingham RG40 116 B3
Market Sq Marlow SL7 1 B1
Staines TW18 96 C2
Market St Bracknell RG12 118 A4
Maidenhead SL6 39 C4
Newbury RG14 105 A1
18 Windsor SL4 67 B3
Market Way 15 RG1 86 A4
Markham Centre Trad Est The RG7 83 C1
Markham Ct GU15 151 B3
Markham Mews RG40 116 B3
Marks Rd RG41 116 A4
Marlborough Ave RG1 86 B3
Marlborough Cl SL6 39 A3
Marlborough Ct
Reading RG1 85 C3
Slough SL1 41 C4
Wokingham RG40 116 B4
Marlborough Ho
5 Maidenhead SL6 39 C3
Reading RG1 86 B3
Marlborough Rd
Ashford TW15 97 C2
Maidenhead SL6 39 A3
Slough SL3 43 C1
Marlborough Rise GU15 151 C3
Marlborough Way RG31 84 A2
Marley Croft TW18 96 C3
Marlin Cl TW16 98 C1
Marlin Ct SL7 1 B1
Marling Cl RG31 57 B1
Marlow Bottom SL7 1 B3
Marlow Bridge La SL7 18 C4
Marlow CE Inf Sch SL7 1 B2
Marlow Com Hospl SL7 1 C1
Marlow Lodge 13 SL6 39 C3
Marlow Mill SL7 1 C1
Marlow Rd Bisham SL7 18 B4
Bisham SL6 18 C2
Henley-on-T RG9 15 C2
Little Marlow SL7,SL8 2 B3
Maidenhead SL6 39 C4
Marlow Bottom SL7 1 A4
Marlow Sta SL7 1 C1
Marlowes The RG14 130 C4
Marlston Rd RG18 79 B3
Marmion Rd RG9 35 C4
Marquis Pl RG1 86 C4
Marriott Cl TW14 71 B1
Mars Cl RG41 115 C3
Marsack St RG4 59 B1
Marsh Ct RG30 85 B4
Marsh La
Hungerford RG17 100 A3
Newbury RG14 105 A2
Taplow SL6 40 C3
Marsh Rd RG18 106 C2

Marshall Cl Frimley GU16 152 B1
Purley on T RG8 57 B2
Marshall Ho 4 RG30 85 A4
Marshall Rd GU47 150 B3
Marshalls Ct RG14 104 B3
Marsham Ho RG42 91 A1
Marshaw Ct RG2 86 B2
Marshfield SL3 68 B3
Marshgate Trad Est SL6 41 A4
Marshland Sq RG4 59 A3
Marshwood Rd GU18 153 B4
Marston Dr RG14 105 B3
Marston Way SL5 119 C4
Martel Cl GU15 152 B4
Marten Pl RG31 57 A2
Martin Cl Windsor SL4 66 B3
Woodley RG5 87 C3
Martin Rd Maidenhead SL6 39 C4
Slough SL1 42 C2
Martin Way GU16 151 C1
Martin's Heron Sta RG12 118 C3
Martin's Plain SL2 22 C2
Martindale Ave GU15 152 B2
Martineau La RG10 88 C4
Martins Cl GU17 150 B2
Martins Dr RG41 116 A4
Martins La RG12 118 C3
Martins The RG19 106 C1
Marunden Gn SL2 21 C1
Mary Drew Almshouse The TW20 95 B1
Mary Hare Gram Sch for the Deaf The RG18 77 C2
Mary Mead RG42 91 B1
Mary Morgan Ct SL2 42 B4
Maryland RG40 141 C4
Maryside SL3 43 C2
Mascoll Path SL2 21 C1
Masefield Gdns RG45 143 A2
Masefield Rd RG18 106 B2
Masefield Way TW19 97 C4
Mason Cl GU46 149 C3
Mason Ct Ball Hill RG20 129 C1
6 Reading RG1 85 C4
Mason Pl GU47 149 C4
Mason St RG1 85 C4
Mason's Ct SL1 41 C3
Masonic Hall Rd KT16 123 C2
Masons Rd SL1 41 C3
Master Cl RG5 88 A4
Mathisen Way SL3 69 C3
Matlock Rd RG4 58 C2
Matson Dr RG9 15 C1
Matthew Arnold Cl TW18 97 B1
Matthew Arnold Sch The TW18 97 B1
Matthews Chase RG42 90 C1
Matthews Cl RG19 106 A2
Matthews Ct SL5 120 B3
Matthews La TW18 96 C2
Matthews Rd GU15 151 B4
Matthewsgreen Rd RG41 116 A4
Maudsley Ho SL6 40 A4
Maultway Cl GU15 152 A4
Maultway Cres GU15 152 A4
Maultway N GU15 145 A1
Maultway The GU15, GU16 152 B3
Mawbray Cl RG6 87 B1
Maxine Cl GU47 143 A1
Maxwell Cl RG5 87 C4
Maxwell Rd TW15 98 B1
May Cl 2 GU47 150 B4
May Fields RG41 115 A4
May Pk RG31 84 C2
May Tree Cl SL7 1 B3
May's La RG7 136 A4
Maybrick Cl GU47 142 C1
Maybury Cl SL1 41 B4
Mayfair RG30 84 B4
Mayfair Dr RG14 104 C1
Mayfield Ave RG31 84 A2
Mayfield Cl TW15 98 A1
Mayfield Cotts RG20 31 B2
Mayfield Dr RG4 59 B2
Mayfield Gdns TW18 96 C1
Mayfield Rd
Camberley GU15 151 A1
Wooburn Green HP10 3 C3
Mayflower Ct 16 RG1 86 A4
Mayflower Dr GU46 149 A4
Mayflower Way SL2 22 B4
Maynard Cl RG18 106 B3
Maynard Ct Staines TW18 97 A2
Windsor SL4 67 A3
Mayors La RG14 105 A1
Mayow Cl RG19 106 C1
Maypole Rd SL6 41 A4
Mays Cl RG6 87 A3
Mays La RG6 87 A3
Mays Rd RG40 116 C3
Maywood Dr GU15 152 A4
McCarthy Way RG40 141 C4
McCraes Wlk RG10 36 B1
Mckay Trad Est SL3 69 C3
McNair Cl RG6 87 A1
Meachen Ct RG40 116 B3
Mead Ave SL3 44 A2
Mead Cl Egham TW20 96 A1
7 Marlow SL7 1 C2
Peasemore RG20 50 B4
Reading RG31 84 A3
Slough SL3 44 A2
Mead Ct TW20 96 B1
Mead Haze SL6 20 B1
Mead La Chertsey KT16 124 B1
Lower Basildon RG8 34 C1
Upper Basildon RG8 55 B3
Mead The RG17 48 A2
Mead Way SL1 41 B4
Mead Wlk SL3 44 A2
Meade Ct GU19 145 C2
Meadfield Ave SL3 44 A2
Meadfield Rd SL3 44 A2
Meadhurst Pk TW16 98 C1
Meadhurst Rd KT16 124 A1
Meadhurst Sports Club TW16 98 C2
Meadow Bank 16 SL8 3 A2
Meadow Cl
Blackwater GU17 150 B2
Compton RG20 31 C3
Goring RG8 34 B3
Marlow SL7 1 C1
Moulsford OX10 13 C2
Old Windsor SL4 68 A1
Thatcham RG19 106 B2
Meadow Cotts GU24 153 C4
Meadow Ct TW18 96 C3
Meadow Gdns TW18 96 B2
Meadow La SL4 67 B4
Meadow Rd Ashford TW15 98 B2
Earley RG6 87 B2
Henley-on-T RG9 15 C1
Newbury RG14 130 C4
Reading RG1 58 C1
Slough SL3 43 C2
Wentworth GU25 121 C2
Wokingham RG41 116 A3
Meadow Vale Prim Sch
Binfield RG42 90 C1
Bracknell RG42 117 C4
Meadow View
Marlow Bottom SL7 1 C3
Winnersh RG41 88 B2
Meadow View La SL6 64 C4
Meadow Way
Blackwater GU17 150 B3
Bracknell RG42 91 A1
Dorney SL4 40 C2
Holyport SL6 65 B3
Old Windsor SL4 68 A1
Theale RG7 83 B2
West End GU24 153 C3
Wokingham RG41 116 A3
Meadow Wlk RG41 116 A3
Meadowbank Rd GU18 146 B1
Meadowbrook Cl SL3 69 C3
Meadowbrook Montessori Sch RG42 91 C2
Meadowcroft Rd RG2 113 B4
Meadowlea Cl UB7 70 B4
Meadows Cty Comb Sch The HP10 3 C4
Meadows The
Flackwell Heath HP10 3 A4
Sandhurst GU47 150 C3
Meadowside RG31 57 A1
Meadowside Rd RG8 56 B3
Meadowsweet Cl RG18 106 C2
Meadowview TW19 69 C1
Meads The 4 SL4 67 A3
Meadway Ashford TW15 98 A2
Frimley GU16 151 C1
Staines TW18 97 A1
Meadway Cl TW18 97 A1
Meadway Comp Sch RG30 84 C4
Meadway Prec RG30 85 A3
Meadway The RG30 84 C4
Meare Est HP10 3 C4
Mearings The RG30 111 C3
Measham Way RG6 87 B1
Meashill Way OX11 9 C4
Meavy Gdns RG2 86 A1
Medallion Pl SL6 40 A4
Mede Cl TW19 95 B4
Mede Ct TW18 96 C3
Medina Cl RG41 115 C4
Medlake Rd TW20 96 B1
Medlar Dr GU17 150 C2
Medway Cl
Thatcham RG18 106 A3
Wokingham RG41 115 C4
Medway Ct RG30 85 B3
Melbourne Ave Slough SL1 42 B4
Winnersh RG41 88 B1
Melbury Cl KT16 124 A1
Meldreth Way RG6 87 B1
Meldrum Cl RG14 130 B3
Melford Gn RG4 59 C3
Melksham Cl RG6 113 C4
Melling Cl RG6 87 C2
Mellor Wlk 27 RG1 86 A3
Melody Cl RG41 88 B2
Melrose RG12 118 A1
Melrose Ave RG6 87 A3
Melrose Gdns RG2 114 C1
Melton Ct SL6 39 C3
Melville Ave GU16 151 C1
Membury Wlk RG12 118 C3
Memorial Ave RG9 35 C1
Mendip Cl Charvil RG10 61 A2
Harlington UB3 71 B4
Slough SL3 44 A1
Mendip Dr RG31 84 A3
Mendip Rd RG12 118 C2
Menpes Rd RG31 57 B2
Meon Cl RG26 135 A1
Merchants Pl RG1 86 A4
Mercia Rd SL6 39 B2
Mercian Way SL1 41 B3
Mercury Ave RG41 115 C3
Mere Cl SL7 1 C1
Mere Rd
Shepperton TW17 125 A2
Slough SL1 42 C2
Mereoak La RG7 112 C2
Meridian Ct SL5 120 A1
Merlewood RG12 118 B2
Merlin Cl SL3 69 A4
Merlin Clove RG42 92 A1
Merlin Ct Frimley GU16 151 B1
Maidenhead SL6 39 A4
Mermaid Cl RG41 88 A1
Merrifield Cl RG6 114 B4
Merrivale Gdns RG2 86 A1
Merron Cl GU46 149 B3
Merryhill Green Hill RG41 88 B2
Merryhill Rd RG42 118 A4
Merryman Dr RG45 143 A4
Merryweather Cl RG40 115 C1
Merrywood Pk GU15 151 C2
Mersey Way RG18 106 A3
Merthyr Vale RG4 59 A3
Merton Cl Maidenhead SL6 39 B2
Sandhurst GU47 143 C1
Merton Rd SL1 43 A2
Merton Rd N RG2 86 A1
Merton Rd S RG2 86 A1
Mervyn Rd TW17 125 B1
Merwin Way SL4 66 B2
Metcalf Rd TW15 98 A2
Meteor Cl RG5 88 A4
Meteorological Off (HQ) RG12 118 B4
Meteorological Office Coll RG2 113 B4
Metro Ctr The RG41 89 A1
Mews The Newbury RG14 104 C1
Reading RG1 86 C3
Swallowfield RG7 140 B4
Mey Cl RG31 84 B3
Meyrick Dr RG14 130 B3
Mezel Hill Cotts SL4 94 B2
Michael Rd SL6 39 B3
Michaelmas Cl GU46 149 B2
Micheldever Way RG12 118 C2
Michelet Cl GU18 146 A1
Micklands Prim Sch RG4 59 B2
Micklands Rd RG4 59 C2
Mickle Hill GU47 143 A1
Micro Ctr The RG2 86 A1
Midcroft SL2 22 A1
Middle Cl Frimley GU15 152 B3
Newbury RG14 130 B4
Middle Gn Slough SL3 43 C3
Staines TW18 97 B1
Middle Gordon Rd GU15 151 B3
Middle Hill TW20 95 B2
Middle Walk SL1 21 B1
Middlefields RG10 61 C3
Middlegreen Rd SL3 43 B3
Middlegreen Trad Est SL3 43 B2
Middlemoor Rd GU16 151 C1
Middleton Ct RG14 105 C3
Middleton Rd GU15 151 C4
Middletons Cl RG17 100 C4
Midsummer Mdw RG4 58 C3
Midway Ave
Chertsey KT16 124 A3
Thorpe TW20 123 A3
Midway Cl TW18 97 A3
Midwinter Cl RG30 84 C4
Milbanke Ct RG12 117 C4
Milbanke Way RG12 117 C4
Mildenhall Cl RG6 87 B1
Mildenhall Rd SL1 42 C4
Mile Elm SL7 2 A2
Miles Pl GU18 152 C4
Miles Way RG5 88 A4
Milestone Ave
Charvil RG10 61 A3
Sonning RG4 60 C2
Milestone Cres RG10 61 A2
Milestone View Ct RG4 59 C2
Milestone Way RG4 59 B3
Milford Ct SL1 43 A2
Milford Rd RG1 58 C1
Milkhouse Rd RG20 103 B2
Mill Bank RG17 102 A2
Mill Cl Bagshot GU19 145 B2
Wokingham RG41 116 A4
Mill Ct SL3 69 B2
Mill End RG9 16 B4
Mill Farm Ave TW16 98 C1
Mill Field GU19 145 B2
Mill Gn Binfield RG42 90 C1
Caversham RG4 59 B1
Mill Hall Sch RG20 131 B4
Mill House La KT16 123 A3
Mill La Ascot SL5 121 A4
Bracknell RG12 117 C3
Cookham SL6 20 B4
Earley RG6 87 C2
Earley, Sindlesham RG6 87 C1
Henley-on-T RG9 35 C4
Horton SL3 69 B2
Hurley SL6 17 C2
Lambourn RG17 25 B1
Newbury RG14 105 A2
Padworth RG7 109 B1
Reading RG1 86 A4
Reading, Horncastle RG31 84 C2
Shiplake RG9 36 A1
Taplow SL6 40 B4
Thorpe TW20 123 B3
Windsor SL4 67 A4
Mill La *continued*
Winnersh RG41 87 C1
Yateley GU46 149 B4
Mill Mead TW18 96 C2
Mill Pl SL3 68 B3
Mill Pond Rd GU20 146 A3
Mill Rd
Burghfield Common RG30 84 C1
Caversham RG4 59 B1
Goring RG8 34 B4
Marlow SL7 1 C1
Shiplake RG9 36 A2
Mill Reef Cl RG19 105 C2
Mill Ride SL5 119 B4
Mill St Colnbrook SL3 69 B4
Slough SL2 42 C3
Millbank SL7 1 C1
Millbank Cres RG5 87 C3
Millboard Rd SL8 3 A2
Millbridge Rd GU46 149 A4
Millbrook Way SL3 69 C3
Milldown Ave RG8 34 B4
Milldown Rd RG8 34 B4
Miller's Ct TW20 96 B1
Miller's La SL4 68 A1
Millers Cl Goring RG8 34 A4
Staines TW18 97 A2
Millers Ct RG4 59 B1
Millers Field RG17 48 A2
Millers Gr RG31 84 C2
Milley La RG10 62 A4
Milley Rd RG10 62 C3
Millfield Charlton TW16 125 B4
Lambourn RG17 25 A1
Millgreen La RG19 132 C1
Millholme Wlk GU15 152 B2
Millins Cl GU47 143 C1
Millmead RG41 116 A4
Millmere GU46 149 B4
Mills Spur SL4 95 A4
Millside SL8 3 B2
Millstream Ho RG14 105 B2
Millstream La SL1 41 C3
Millstream Way HP10 3 C4
Millworth La RG2 113 C2
Milman Cl RG12 119 A4
Milman Rd RG2 86 A3
Milner Rd SL1 41 A4
Milsom Cl RG2 113 C3
Milton Cl Bracknell RG12 118 A2
Henley-on-T RG9 15 B1
Horton SL3 69 A2
Milton Ct RG40 116 A4
Milton Dr Littleton TW17 124 C3
Wokingham RG40 116 A4
Milton Gdns
Stanwell TW19 97 C4
Wokingham RG40 116 A3
Milton Rd Earley RG6 87 A4
Egham TW20 95 C2
Slough SL2 22 B1
Wokingham RG40, RG41 116 A3
Milton Way RG10 61 C3
Milverton Cl SL6 39 A2
Milward Gdns RG12 117 B4
Mina Ave SL3 43 B2
Minchin Gn RG42 90 B2
Minden Cl RG41 115 C3
Minerva Cl TW19 70 A1
Ministry Rd RG19 132 A3
Minley Rd GU17 149 C1
Minniecroft Rd SL1 21 A1
Minorca Ave GU16 152 C1
Minorca Rd GU16 152 C1
Minstead Cl RG12 118 C3
Minstead Dr GU46 149 B3
Minster Ct
Camberley GU15 151 B4
Camberley, York Town GU15 150 C2
Minster St RG1 86 A4
Minster Way SL3 43 C2
Minsterley Ave TW16, TW17 125 C3
Mint Cl RG6 86 C1
Minter Ct RG26 134 C1
Minton Cl RG30 84 C4
Minton Rise SL6 41 A4
Mirador Cres SL2 43 B3
Mire La RG10 62 B2
Misbourne Ct SL3 44 A1
Missenden Cl TW14 98 C4
Missenden Gdns SL1 41 A4
Mistletoe Rd GU46 149 B2
Mitcham Cl RG2 86 A3
Mitcham Rd GU15 145 A1
Mitchell Cl SL1 42 A2
Mitchell Way RG5 88 A4
Mitford Cl RG2 113 B4
Mitre Cl TW17 125 B2
Mitre Pl RG42 91 A1
Mixnams La KT16 124 A3
Moat Dr SL2 43 B4
Modbury Gdns RG2 86 B1
Moffatts Cl GU47 150 A4
Moffy Hill SL6 19 C1
Mohawk Way RG5 88 A4
Mole Rd RG41 114 C3
Moles Cl RG40 116 B3
Mollison Cl RG5 88 A4
Molly Millar Bridge RG41 116 A2
Molly Millar's La RG41 116 A2
Molly Millars Cl RG40 116 A2
Molyneux Rd GU20 146 B2
Molyns Mews 1 SL1 41 C3
Monarch Cl TW14 98 C4
Monck Ct 7 RG30 85 B3
Mondial Way UB3 71 B4
Moneyrow Gn SL6 65 A4
Monkey Island La
Holyport SL6 65 C4
Maidenhead SL6 40 C1
Monkley Ct 5 RG4 59 B1
Monks Cl SL5 120 A2
Monks Dr SL5 120 A2
Monks Hollow SL7 1 C3
Monks La RG14 130 C4
Monks Rd
Virginia Water GU25 122 B3
Windsor SL4 66 B3
Monks Way
Harmondsworth UB7 70 C4
Reading RG30 85 B3
Staines TW18 97 B1
Monks Wlk SL5 120 A2
Monksbarn RG2 86 B1
Monksfield Way SL2 22 A1
Monkshood Cl RG40 116 C4
Monkswood Cl RG14 130 C4
Monkswood Ct 6 SL7 1 C1
Monktons La RG7 137 B3
Monmouth Ct 5 RG1 59 A1
Mons Cl RG41 115 C3
Mons Wlk TW20 95 B2
Monsell Gdns TW18 96 C2
Montacute Dr RG19 106 C1
Montagu Rd SL3 68 A3
Montague Cl
Camberley GU15 151 A3
Lightwater GU18 146 A1
Wokingham RG40 116 C4
Montague Ho (Coll) RG40 115 B3
Montague Rd SL1 42 C3
Montague St
Caversham RG4 59 B1
Reading RG1 85 B4
Montague Terr RG14 131 A4
Monteagle La
Yateley GU46 149 A3
Yateley GU46 149 B3
Montem Inf Sch The SL1 42 A2
Montem La SL1 42 B2
Montgomery Cl GU47 150 A4
Montgomery Dr RG7 113 A1
Montgomery Pl SL2 43 B4
Montgomery Rd RG14 130 C4
Montpelier Ct SL4 67 B3
Montpelier Dr RG4 59 B3
Montrose Ave Datchet SL3 68 B4
Slough SL1 42 A4
Montrose Cl Ashford TW15 98 B2
Frimley GU16 151 C1
Montrose Dr SL6 39 A3
Montrose Ho 2 RG1 86 A4
Montrose Rd TW14 71 B1
Montrose Way SL3 68 B4
Montrose Wlk RG31 84 C2
Monument Cl RG14 130 B4
Monycrower Dr SL6 39 C4
Moor Cl Sandhurst GU47 143 C1
Wokingham RG40 141 C4
Moor Copse Cl RG6 87 A2
Moor End SL6 40 B1
Moor Furlong SL1 41 C3
Moor La
Harmondsworth UB7 70 B4
Maidenhead SL6 19 C1
Newbury RG14 104 C2
Staines TW18, TW19 96 B3
Moor Park Ho RG12 117 C2
Moor Pl GU20 146 A3
Moorbridge Rd SL6 40 A4
Moordale Ave RG42 90 C1
Moore Cl SL1 42 A2
Moore Grove Cres TW20 95 C1
Moores Gn RG40 116 C4
Moores La SL4 41 C1
Moores Pl RG17 100 B3
Moorfield Terr SL6 40 A4
Moorfields Cl TW18 123 C4
Moorhayes Dr TW18 124 B3
Moorhen Dr RG6 87 A1
Moorings The SL4 95 B4
Moorland Rd UB7 70 B4
Moorlands Dr SL6 38 C4
Moorlands Pl GU15 151 A3
Moorlands Prim Sch RG30 84 C4
Moorlands Rd GU15 151 A2
Moormede Cres TW18 96 C2
Moors The Pangbourne RG8 56 B3
Thatcham RG19 106 B1
Moorside HP10 3 C4
Moorside Cl
Farnborough (Hants) GU14 151 A1
Maidenhead SL6 19 C1
Moorstown Ct 7 SL1 42 C2
Moray Ave GU47 150 B4
Moray Dr SL2 43 A4
Mordaunt Dr RG45 143 A2
Morden Cl RG12 118 C3
Moreau Wlk SL3 43 C4
Morecambe Ave RG4 58 C3
Moreland Ave SL3 69 B4
Moreland Cl SL3 69 B4
Moreleigh Ct RG2 113 A4
Morella Cl GU25 122 B3
Morello Dr SL3 43 C3
Moreton Ct RG1 86 B3
Moreton Way SL1 41 B3
Morgan Ct TW15 98 A2
Morgan Rd RG1 86 B3
Moriston Cl RG30 85 A4
Morlais RG4 59 A3

Morlands Ave RG30 85 A3
Morley Cl Slough SL3 43 C2
Yateley GU46 149 A3
Morley Ct SL5 120 C2
Morley Pl RG17 100 B3
Mornington Ave RG40 141 C4
Mornington Cl RG26 134 C1
Mornington Rd TW15 98 B2
Morpeth Cl RG2 86 B2
Morrell Ct TW18 97 A2
Morrice Cl SL3 44 A1
Morris Ct SL4 66 C3
Morris Pl 5 SL7 1 B1
Morriss Ct 14 RG1 86 B4
Mortaine Rd TW15 97 B3
Mortimer Cl RG2 113 B4
Mortimer La RG7 137 B4
Mortimer Rd SL3 43 B2
Mortimer Sta RG7 137 C3
Morton Pl RG7 83 C2
Moss Cl RG4 59 B2
Mossy Vale SL6 19 B1
Mostyn Ho RG42 91 A1
Moulsford Prep Sch OX10 14 A3
Moulsham Copse La GU46 149 A4
Moulsham La GU46 149 A4
Moundsfield Way SL1 41 C2
Mount Cl
Farnham Common SL2 22 B4
Newbury RG14 105 A1
Mount Cl The GU25 122 B2
Mount Felix KT12 125 C1
Mount La Bracknell RG12 118 B4
Chaddleworth RG20 49 A4
Mount Lee TW20 95 C2
Mount Pleasant
Bracknell RG12 118 B3
Reading RG1 86 A3
Sandhurst GU47 143 A1
Tadley RG26 135 A1
Wokingham RG41 116 A3
Mount Pleasant Cl GU18 146 A1
Mount Pleasant Cotts
15 Bourne End SL8 3 A2
Englefield Green TW20 95 B1
Mount Pleasant Gr RG1 86 A3
Mount Rd RG18 106 C2
Mount St RG2 86 A3
Mount The Caversham RG4 58 C2
Reading RG1 86 B3
Wentworth GU25 122 B2
Mount View RG9 15 B1
Mount View Ct RG9 15 B1
Mountain Ash SL7 1 B3
Mountbatten Cl
Newbury RG14 105 B3
6 Slough SL1 43 A2
Mountbatten Rise GU47 142 C1
Mountbatten Sq 8 SL4 67 B3
Mountfield RG8 34 B4
Mounts Hill SL4, SL5 93 B2
Mountsfield Cl TW19 70 A1
Mowbray Cres TW20 96 A2
Mowbray Dr RG30 85 A4
Mower Cl RG40 116 C4
Moyleen Rise SL7 1 B1
Muckhatch La TW20 123 A4
Mud La
Finchampstead RG27 140 C1
Peasemore RG20 50 B3
Muirfield Cl RG1 86 B4
Muirfield Ho RG12 117 C2
Mulberry Ave TW19 97 C4
Mulberry Bsns Pk RG41 116 A2
Mulberry Cl
Crowthorne RG45 143 B2
1 Sandhurst GU47 150 B4
Woodley RG5 87 C3
Mulberry Ct
1 Bracknell RG12 118 C2
Newbury RG14 104 C2
Wokingham RG40 116 B3
Mulberry Dr SL3 43 C1
Mulberry Ho RG42 91 A1
Mulberry Trees TW17 125 B1
Mulberry Way RG7 83 C2
Mulberry Wlk SL6 39 B4
Mulfords Hill RG26 135 A1
Mulgrave Rd GU15 151 C1
Mullens Rd TW20 96 B2
Mullion Ct 22 RG1 85 C4
Mulroy Dr GU15 152 A3
Mumbery Hill RG10 36 C1
Muncaster Cl TW15 98 A2
Muncaster Rd TW15 98 A2
Munces Rd SL7 1 B3
Munday Ct RG42 90 C1
Mundaydean La SL7 1 A2
Mundesley Spur SL1 42 C4
Mundesley St RG1 86 A3
Munkle Marsh RG19 107 A2
Munnings Dr GU47 150 C3
Munro Ave RG5 87 C2
Murdoch Cl TW18 97 A2
Murdoch Rd RG40 116 B3
Murray Ct SL5 120 B2
Murray Ho RG41 116 A3
Murray Rd RG41 116 A3
Murrellhill La RG42 117 B4
Murrells La GU15 151 A2
Murrin Rd SL6 39 B4
Mus of Berkshire Aviation The RG5 88 A3
Mus of English Rural Life RG2 86 C2
Mus of Reading RG1 86 A4
Mushroom Castle La RG42 92 A1
Mustard La RG4 60 C1
Mustard Mill Rd TW18 96 C2
Muswell Cl RG7 83 C2
Mutton Oaks RG12 117 B4
Myers Way GU16 152 B1
Mylne Sq RG40 116 B3
Mylum Cl RG2 113 B3
Myrke The SL3 42 C1
Myrtle Ave TW14 71 C1
Myrtle Cl
Burghfield Common RG7 111 A2
Lightwater GU18 153 A4
Poyle SL3 69 C3
Purley on T RG31 57 B2
Myrtle Cres SL2 42 C3
Myrtle Dr GU17 150 B3
Myton Wlk RG7 83 C2

N

Nabbs Hill Cl RG31 84 B3
Nairn Cl GU16 151 C1
Nalderhill Rd RG20 103 A3
Napier Cl RG45 143 B3
Napier Dr GU15 152 A4
Napier Lodge TW15 98 B1
Napier Rd Ashford TW15 98 B1
Crowthorne RG45 143 B2
Harmondsworth TW6 70 B3
Maidenhead SL6 39 A3
Reading RG1 86 B4
Napier Wlk TW15 98 B1
Napper Cl SL5 119 B4
Narromine Dr RG31 84 C2
Naseby RG12 118 A1
Naseby Rise RG14 105 B3
Nash Cl RG6 87 A2
Nash Gdns SL5 119 C4
Nash Grove La RG40 115 C1
Nash Pk RG42 90 A1
Nash Rd SL3 44 A1
Nashdom La SL1 21 A3
Natalie Cl TW14 98 B4
Nathan Ct 20 RG1 85 C4
Naylors The RG7 139 B3
Neath Gdns RG30 84 C4
Needham Cl SL4 66 C3
Neil Cl TW15 98 B2
Nell Gwynn Ave TW17 125 B2
Nell Gwynne Ave SL5 120 B3
Nell Gwynne Cl SL5 120 B3
Nelson Cl Bracknell RG12 118 C4
East Bedfont TW14 98 C4
Slough SL3 43 B1
Nelson Ct KT16 124 A1
Nelson Rd Ashford TW15 97 C2
Caversham RG4 59 B1
Harmondsworth TW6 70 C3
Windsor SL4 66 C2
Nelson Terr 22 RG1 86 A3
Nelson Way GU15 150 C2
Nelson's La RG10 89 A3
Nene Rd TW6, UB7 71 A3
Neptune Cl RG41 115 C3
Neptune Rd TW6 71 B3
Neptune Way SL1 41 C2
Netherton RG12 118 A3
Netley Cl RG4 59 C3
Nettlecombe RG12 118 B2
Nettleton Rd TW6 71 A3
Neve Ho SL6 39 C4
Nevelle Cl RG42 117 B4
Neville Cl Stoke Poges SL2 22 C3
Waltham St Lawrence RG10 62 C3
Neville Ct SL1 21 B1
Neville Dr RG19 106 C2
Nevis Rd RG31 57 B2
New Bath Rd RG10 61 B3
New Bldgs RG7 81 B2
New Bright St 5 RG1 86 A3
New Christ Church CE Prim Sch RG1 86 A3
New Cl RG9 16 A4
New Ct SL7 1 B1
New Forest Ride RG12 118 C2
New Greenham Pk RG19 131 C3
New Hill RG8 57 B3
New Lane Hill RG30 84 C3
New Mdw SL5 119 B4
New Mile Rd SL5 120 B4
New Mill La RG27 140 C1
New Mill Rd RG27 140 C2
New Par TW15 97 C2
New Park Rd TW15 98 B2
New Rd Bagshot GU19 145 C2
Blackwater GU17 150 C2
Bourne End SL8 3 A2
Bracknell RG12 118 B4
Burghfield Common RG7 111 C1
Cookham SL6 19 C4
Crowthorne RG45 143 B3
Datchet SL3 68 B3
East Bedfont TW14 71 B1
Egham TW18 96 B2
Harlington UB3 71 B4
Holyport SL6 65 A4
Hurley SL6 17 C2
Littleton TW17 125 A3
Marlow Bottom SL7 1 B3
Newbury RG14 105 B1
North Ascot SL5 92 C1
Reading RG1 86 B3
Sandhurst GU47 150 A4
Shiplake RG9 36 A2
Slough SL3 44 A2
New Rd *continued*
Twyford RG10 61 B4
Twyford, Ruscombe RG10 61 C3
Windlesham GU19,GU20 146 A2
Wokingham RG41 115 A4
New Road Hill RG7 108 A2
New Scotland Hill Prim Sch GU47 143 A1
New Sq East Bedfont TW14 98 B4
Slough SL1 42 C2
New St Beech Hill RG7 138 A1
Henley-on-T RG9 15 C1
Staines TW18 97 A2
New Town Prim Sch RG1 86 B4
New Way RG7 82 A1
New Wickham La TW20 96 A1
New Wokingham Rd RG45 143 A3
New Zealand Ave KT12 125 C1
Newall Rd TW6 71 B3
Newalls Rise RG10 36 C1
Newark Rd GU20 146 A3
Newark St RG1 86 A3
Newberry Cres SL4 66 B3
Newbery Cl RG31 57 B1
Newbery Way SL1 42 B2
Newbold Coll RG42 90 B1
Newbold Rd RG14 104 B3
Newbold Sch RG42 90 B1
Newbolt Cl RG18 106 B3
Newbury Cl RG10 61 A2
Newbury Coll RG14 104 C2
Newbury District Hospl RG14 104 C1
Newbury District Mus RG14 105 A2
Newbury Dr SL6 40 A3
Newbury Hill RG18 52 C3
Newbury La RG20 31 B2
Newbury Rd
Great Shefford RG17 48 A1
Harmondsworth TW6 70 C3
Hermitage RG18 79 A3
Lambourn RG17 25 B1
Newbury Ret Pk RG14 131 A4
Newbury St
Kintbury RG17 102 A1
Lambourn RG17 25 A1
Newbury Sta RG14 105 A1
Newcastle Rd RG2 86 B2
Newchurch Rd Slough SL2 41 C4
Tadley RG26 135 A1
Newell Gn RG42 91 B2
Newfield Gdns SL7 1 C2
Newfield Rd SL7 1 C2
Newfield Way SL7 1 C1
Newhaven Cres TW15 98 B2
Newhaven Spur SL2 22 A1
Newhurst Gdns RG42 91 B2
Newlands Ave RG4 59 A2
Newlands Cl GU46 149 B3
Newlands Cty Prim Sch GU46 149 B3
Newlands Dr
Maidenhead SL6 39 A4
Poyle SL3 69 C2
Newlands Rd GU15 151 A1
Newlands Sch SL6 39 A4
Newlyn Gdns RG2 86 A1
Newmarket Cl 10 RG6 87 B1
Newport Cl 11 RG14 105 A2
Newport Dr RG42 91 A1
Newport Rd
Harmondsworth TW6 71 A3
Newbury RG14 105 A2
Reading RG1 59 A1
Slough SL2 21 C1
Newquay Dr RG6 87 A1
Newstead Rise RG2 86 C1
Newton Ave RG4 59 B3
Newton Cl SL3 43 C2
Newton Ct SL4 68 A1
Newton La SL4 68 A1
Newton Side Orch SL4 68 A1
Newtonside SL4 68 A1
Newtown RG26 135 A1
Newtown Gdns RG9 35 C4
Newtown Rd
Henley-on-T RG9 35 C4
Marlow SL7 1 C2
Newbury RG14 & RG20 131 A3
Sandhurst GU47 150 A4
Niagara Rd RG9 35 C4
Nicholas Ct 23 RG1 85 C4
Nicholas Gdns SL1 41 C3
Nicholas Rd RG9 35 A4
Nicholls SL4 66 B2
Nicholls Wlk SL4 66 B2
Nicholson Wlk 3 TW20 96 A2
Nicholsons Ctr 5 SL6 39 C4
Nicholsons La SL6 39 C4
Nideggen Cl RG19 106 B2
Nightingale Cres RG12 118 B2
Nightingale Gdns GU47 150 A4
Nightingale Ho 3 RG1 85 C3
Nightingale La
Maidenhead SL6 19 B2
Mortimer RG7 137 B3
Nightingale Pk SL2 21 C3
Nightingale Pl SL6 19 C4
Nightingale Rd RG5 87 B2
Nightingale Wlk SL4 67 B2
Nightingales The
Newbury RG14 131 A4
Stanwell TW19 97 C4
Nimrod Cl RG5 88 A4
Nimrod Way RG2 86 A3
Nine Acres SL1 41 C3
Nine Elms Cl TW14 98 C4
Nine Mile Ride
Bracknell RG12, RG40 117 C1
Crowthorne RG40 142 B4
Nine Mile Ride Prim Sch RG40 141 C3
Nire Rd RG4 59 C1
Nixey Cl SL1 43 A2
No 4 RG30 85 B3
Noakes Hill RG8 54 A4
Nobel Dr UB3 71 C4
Noble Rd RG9 35 C4
Nobles Way TW20 95 C1
Nodmore RG20 49 A4
Norcot Rd RG30 84 C4
Norden Cl SL6 39 B2
Norden Mdws SL6 39 B3
Norden Rd SL6 39 B3
Nores Rd RG2 113 B4
Norfolk Ave SL1 42 B4
Norfolk Chase RG42 91 C1
Norfolk Cl RG41 115 C3
Norfolk Park Cotts SL6 39 C4
Norfolk Rd Maidenhead SL6 39 C4
Reading RG30 85 B4
Norland Dr HP10 3 B4
Norland Nursery Training Coll RG17 101 B4
Norlands RG18 106 B3
Norlands La TW18, TW20 123 C4
Norman Ave RG9 15 C1
Norman Ct TW18 97 A2
Norman Ho TW17 125 A1
Norman Keep RG42 118 C4
Norman Pl RG1 59 A1
Norman Rd Ashford TW15 98 B1
Caversham RG4 59 B2
Normandy Wlk TW20 96 B2
Normanhurst TW15 98 A2
Normans The SL2 43 A4
Normanstead Rd RG31 84 B4
Normay Rise RG14 130 B3
Normoor Rd RG7 110 C1
Norreys Ave RG40 116 B4
Norreys Dr SL6 39 B2
Norris Field RG20 49 A4
Norris Ho SL6 39 C4
Norris La RG20 49 A4
Norris Rd Reading RG6 87 A3
Staines TW18 96 C2
North Burnham Cl SL1 21 A2
North Cl East Bedfont TW14 71 B1
Medmenham SL7 17 B4
Windsor SL4 66 C3
North Cotts SL2 22 B1
North Croft HP10 3 C3
North Dr Sulhamstead RG7 110 B4
Wentworth GU25 121 C2
North End La SL5 121 A1
North Farm Cl RG17 25 B2
North Fryerne GU46 149 B4
North Gn Bracknell RG12 118 B4
3 Maidenhead SL6 19 C1
Slough SL1 42 C3
North Gr KT16 123 C2
North Hatton Rd TW6 71 B3
North Links Rd HP10 3 A4
North Lodge Dr SL5 119 B4
North Lodge Mews RG30 85 B2
North Pk SL0 44 B2
North Rd
East Bedfont TW14 71 B1
Maidenhead SL6 39 C4
Moulsford OX10 13 C2
Winkfield SL5 119 A4
North Row SL3 23 C4
North St Caversham RG4 59 A1
Egham TW20 95 C1
Reading RG1 85 C4
Winkfield SL4 93 A3
North Standen Rd RG17 100 A2
North Star La SL6 39 B3
North Town Cl 1 SL6 19 C1
North Town Mead 4 SL6 19 C1
North Town Moor SL6 19 C1
North Town Rd SL6 19 C1
North View Gdns 8 RG14 105 A2
North Wlk RG7 83 C2
Northam Cl RG6 87 C2
Northampton Ave SL1 42 B4
Northampton Cl RG12 118 C3
Northborough Rd SL2 22 A1
Northbourne Cl RG6 87 A1
Northbrook Copse RG12 118 C2
Northbrook Pl RG14 105 A2
Northbrook Rd RG4 59 B3
Northbrook St RG14 105 A2
Northbury Ave RG10 61 C3
Northbury La RG10 61 C3
Northcott RG12 118 A1
Northcourt Ave RG2 86 B2
Northcroft SL2 22 A1
Northcroft Cl TW20 95 A2
Northcroft Gdns TW20 95 A2
Northcroft La RG14 104 C2
Northcroft Rd TW20 95 A2
Northcroft Terr RG14 104 C2
Northcroft Villas TW20 95 A2
Northdean 5 SL6 19 C1
Northend Cl HP10 3 B4
Northern Ave RG14 105 A3
Northern Hts SL8 3 A3
Northern Perimeter Rd TW6 71 B3
Northern Perimeter Road (W) TW6 70 B3
Northern Rd SL2 22 B1
Northern Way RG2 85 C1
Northern Woods HP10 3 B4
Northfield GU18 153 A4
Northfield Ave RG9 36 A2
Northfield Ct
Henley-on-T RG9 15 B2
Staines TW18 124 A4
Northfield End RG9 15 B2
Northfield Rd Eton SL4 41 C1
Maidenhead SL6 19 C1
Reading RG1 59 A1
Shiplake RG9 36 A2
Staines TW18 124 A4
Thatcham RG18 106 A2
Northfields Chieveley RG20 51 A2
Lambourn RG17 25 A2
Northfields Terr RG17 25 B2
Northgate Dr GU15 152 A4
Northington Cl RG12 118 C2
Northlands Dr SL1 21 B2
Northmead Rd SL2 41 C4
Northolt Rd TW6 70 C3
Northrop Rd TW6 71 C3
Northumberland Ave RG2 86 B2
Northumberland Cl
Bracknell RG42 91 C1
Stanwell TW19 70 C1
Northumberland Cres TW14 71 C1
Northumbria Rd SL6 39 A2
Northview RG17 100 B3
Northview Hts RG17 100 B3
Northway Newbury RG14 105 A1
Thatcham RG18 106 B3
Wokingham RG41 115 C4
Northwood Dr RG14 105 B2
Northwood Rd TW6 70 B3
Norton Cl RG14 130 B3
Norton Pk SL5 120 B2
Norton Rd Frimley GU15 152 B2
Reading RG1 86 C4
Swallowfield RG7 139 B2
Wokingham RG40 116 B3
Woodley RG5 87 C3
Norway Dr SL2 43 A4
Norwich Ave GU15 151 C2
Norwich Dr RG5 87 B4
Norwich Ho SL6 39 C4
Norwood Cres TW6 71 B3
Norwood Rd RG1 86 C4
Notley End TW20 95 B1
Notton Way RG6 113 C4
Nuffield Dr GU47 143 C1
Nuffield Rd Barkham, Arborfield Garrison RG2 140 C4
Barkham, Langley Common RG2 141 A4
Nugee Ct RG45 143 A3
Nugent Ct SL7 1 C2
Nuneaton RG12 118 C2
Nunhide La RG8,RG31 83 C3
Nuns Acre RG8 34 A4
Nuns Wlk GU25 122 B2
Nuptown La RG42 91 C4
Nursery Cl Hurst RG10 88 C4
Shiplake RG9 36 A2
Nursery Gdns
Purley on T RG8 57 A3
Staines TW18 97 A1
Sunbury TW16 125 C4
Nursery La
North Ascot SL5 119 C4
Slough SL3 43 B3
Nursery Rd Burnham SL6 41 A4
Sunbury TW16 125 C4
Nursery Way TW19 68 B1
Nursery Wlk SL7 1 A1
Nut La RG10 62 C3
Nutbean La RG7 139 C3
Nutbourne Ct TW18 96 C1
Nutfield Ct GU15 151 B4
Nuthatch Dr RG6 87 A2
Nuthurst RG12 118 C2
Nutley RG12 118 A1
Nutley Cl GU46 149 B3
Nutmeg Cl RG6 86 C1
Nutter's La RG2 140 A4
Nuttingtons RG20 49 C3
Nutty La TW17 125 B3

O

O' Bee Gdns RG26 134 C1
Oak Ave Egham TW20 96 B1
Sandhurst GU47 143 B1
Oak Dr
Burghfield Common RG7 110 C1
Newbury RG14 104 C1
Woodley RG5 88 A3
Oak End Way RG7 109 B2
Oak Farm Cl GU17 150 B3
Oak Gn RG2 113 B4
Oak Grove Cres GU15 150 C3
Oak Hill SN8 99 B2
Oak La
Englefield Green TW20 95 B3
Windsor SL4 67 A3
Oak Leaf Ct SL5 119 B4
Oak Lo 8 TW16 98 C1
Oak Lodge RG45 143 B3
Oak Stubbs La SL4 40 C2
Oak Tree Ave SL7 1 B2
Oak Tree Cl Marlow SL7 1 B2
Tadley RG26 135 A1

Oak Tree Cl *continued*
Wentworth GU25 ....122 B2
Oak Tree Copse RG31 .....57 C2
Oak Tree Dr TW20 ....95 B2
Oak Tree Rd Marlow SL7 .....1 B2
Reading RG31 ....57 C1
Thatcham RG19 ....106 C1
Oak Tree Wlk RG8 ....57 B3
Oak View RG31 ....84 B4
Oak Way
East Bedfont TW14 ....98 C4
Woodley RG5 ....87 B2
Oakdale RG12 ....118 B2
Oakdale Cl RG31 ....84 B4
Oakdale Wlk RG5 ....88 A4
Oakdene
Burghfield Common RG7 ...111 A1
Sunningdale SL5 ....120 C2
Oaken Copse GU15 ....152 B4
Oaken Gr Maidenhead SL6 ..19 B1
Newbury RG14 ....130 B4
Oakengates RG12 ....118 A1
Oakes Ct RG17 ....100 B3
Oakfield RG1 ....86 B3
Oakfield Ave SL1 ....42 A3
Oakfield Ct RG41 ....116 A3
Oakfield Cty Fst Sch SL4 ..67 A3
Oakfield Rd Ashford TW15 ..98 A2
Blackwater GU17 ....150 C2
Bourne End SL8 ....3 A2
Silchester RG26 ....135 C1
Oakfields GU15 ....151 A3
Oakhall Ct TW16 ....98 C2
Oakhall Dr TW16 ....98 C2
Oakham Cl RG31 ....57 B1
Oakhurst SL6 ....20 A2
Oaklands Reading RG1 .....86 B3
Yateley GU46 ....149 B3
Oaklands Cl SL5 ....92 C1
Oaklands Cty Jun Sch
RG45 ....143 A3
Oaklands Dr
North Ascot SL5 ....92 C1
Wokingham RG41 ....116 A3
Wokingham RG41 ....116 A3
Oaklands Inf Sch RG45 ...143 A3
Oaklands La RG45 ....143 A4
Oaklands Pk RG41 ....116 A2
Oaklea Dr RG27 ....140 C1
Oakleigh GU18 ....153 B4
Oakley HP10 ....3 C4
Oakley Cres SL1 ....42 C3
Oakley Green Rd SL4 .....66 A3
Oakley Rd
Camberley GU15 ....151 A2
Caversham RG4 ....58 C2
Newbury RG14 ....105 B2
Oakmede Pl RG42 ....90 B1
Oakridge GU24 ....153 C3
Oaks Rd Shiplake RG9 .....36 A2
Stanwell TW19 ....70 B1
Oaks The Bracknell RG12 ..118 B4
Staines TW18 ....96 C2
Yateley GU46 ....149 B3
Oakside Way RG2 ....113 C4
Oaktree Way GU47 ....143 A1
Oakview RG40 ....116 A2
Oakway Dr GU16 ....151 C1
Oakwood Rd
Bracknell RG12 ....118 C4
Virginia Water GU25 .....122 B2
Windlesham GU20 ....146 C2
Oareborough RG12 ....118 C2
Oast Ct TW18 ....96 C2
Oast House Cl TW19 ......95 C4
Oatlands Dr Slough SL1 ...42 B4
Walton-on-T KT13 ....125 C1
Oatlands Rd RG2 ....113 C3
Oban Ct SL1 ....42 B2
Oban Gdns RG5 ....87 C2
Obelisk Way GU15 ....151 B3
Oberon Way TW17 ....124 C3
Ockwells Rd SL6 ....39 B1
Octavia RG12 ....118 A1
Octavia Way TW18 ....97 A1
Oddfellows Rd RG14 .....104 C1
Odell Cl RG6 ....114 A4
Odencroft Rd SL2 ....22 A1
Odiham Ave RG4 ....59 C3
Odiham Rd RG7 ....139 B1
Odney La SL6 ....20 A4
Ogmore Cl RG30 ....84 C4
Okingham Cl GU47 ....143 B1
Old Acre La RG10 ....61 A3
Old Barn Cl RG4 ....59 A3
Old Bath Rd Charvil RG10 ..61 A3
Newbury RG14 ....104 C2
Sonning RG4 ....60 B1
Old Bisley Rd GU16 ......152 B2
Old Bothampstead Rd
RG20 ....51 B3
Old Bracknell Cl RG12 ...118 A3
Old Bracknell La E RG12 .118 A3
Old Bracknell La W
RG12 ....118 A3
Old Charlton Rd TW17 ...125 B2
Old Court Cl SL6 ....39 A2
Old Crown 11 SL1 ....42 C2
Old Dean Rd GU15 ....151 B4
Old Elm Dr RG30 ....84 B4
Old Farm Cres RG31 ......57 B1
Old Farm Dr RG12 ....91 B1
Old Ferry Dr TW19 ....68 B1
Old Fives Ct SL1 ....21 A1
Old Forest Rd RG41 ....88 C1
Old Forge Cl SL6 ....40 A2
Old Forge Cres TW17 ....125 A2
Old Forge End GU47 .....150 A4
Old Green La GU15 ......151 B4
Old Hayward La RG17 .....73 B1
Old House Ct SL3 ....43 B4
Old Kennels Ct RG30 ......85 A3
Old Kiln Rd HP10 ....3 A4
Old La
Hamstead Marshall RG20 ..102 C1
Headley RG19 ....133 C1
Old La The RG1 ....85 C3
Old Lands Hill RG12 .....118 B4
Old Marsh La SL6 ....40 C2
Old Mill Ct RG10 ....61 B3
Old Mill La SL6 ....40 B2
Old Moor La HP10 ....3 C4
Old Newtown Rd RG14 ....104 C1
Old Nursery Pl TW15 ......98 A2
Old Orchard The RG31 ....84 C2
Old Palace Ct SL3 ....69 B3
Old Pasture Rd
GU16, GU15 ....151 C2
Old Pharmacy Ct RG45 ...143 B2
Old Pond Cl GU15 ....151 B1
Old Portsmouth Rd
GU15 ....152 A3
Old Post Office La 10 SL6 .39 C4
Old Priory La RG42 ....91 B1
Old Sawmill La RG45 .....143 B3
Old Sawmills The RG17 ...127 C3
Old School Ct TW19 ....95 C4
Old School La GU46 .....149 B3
Old School The
Hampstead Norreys RG18 ...52 C3
Wooburn Green HP10 ....3 B2
Old School Yd The RG17 ..25 A1
Old Slade La SL0 ....44 C1
Old St Chieveley RG18 .....51 C1
Chieveley, Beedon
Common RG20 ....51 B3
Hermitage RG18 ....78 C4
Old Station Bsns Pk RG20 .31 C2
Old Station Way HP10 ......3 C3
Old Station Yd The RG17 ..25 A1
Old Vicarage Way HP10 .....3 B2
Old Watery La HP10 ....3 C4
Old Well Ct RG4 ....60 B2
Old Welmore GU46 ....149 C3
Old Whitley Wood La
RG2 ....113 B3
Old Wokingham Rd
RG40,RG45 ....143 B4
Old Woosehill La RG41 ..115 C4
Oldacre GU24 ....153 C4
Oldacres SL6 ....40 A4
Oldbury RG12 ....117 C3
Oldbury Rd KT16 ....123 C1
Oldcorne Hollow GU46 ...149 A3
Olde Farm Dr GU17 ......150 A3
Oldean Cl RG31 ....57 B1
Oldershaw Mews SL6 ......39 A4
Oldfield Cl RG6 ....87 A4
Oldfield Prim Sch SL6 .....40 A3
Oldfield Rd SL6 ....40 A4
Oldfield Rd Ind Est SL6 ...40 A4
Oldhouse La GU18 ....146 B1
Oldstead RG12 ....118 B2
Oldway La SL1 ....41 B3
Oleander Cl RG45 ....143 A4
Oliver Dr RG31 ....84 B3
Oliver Rd SL5 ....120 A3
Oliver's Paddock SL7 ......1 B3
Ollerton RG12 ....118 A1
Omega Way TW20 ....123 B4
Omer's Rise RG7 ....110 C2
One Pin La SL2 ....22 B4
Onslow Dr SL5 ....93 A1
Onslow Gdns RG4 ....59 B2
Onslow Lodge TW18 ....96 C1
Onslow Mews KT16 ....124 A2
Onslow Rd SL5 ....121 A1
Opal Ct SL3 ....23 B1
Opal Way RG41 ....115 C4
Opendale Rd SL1 ....41 A4
Opladen Way RG12 ....118 C2
Oracle Ctr RG12 ....118 B4
Oracle Ctr The RG1 ....86 A4
Oracle Parkway
Reading RG6 ....86 C4
Sonning RG6 ....60 A1
Orbit Cl RG40 ....141 C3
Orchard Ave Ashford TW15 .98 B1
Hatton TW14 ....71 B1
Slough SL1 ....41 B4
Windsor SL4 ....67 A3
Orchard Chase RG10 ......88 C4
Orchard Cl Ashford TW15 ...98 B1
Farnborough (Hants) GU17 .150 C1
Henley-on-T RG9 ....15 C1
Hermitage RG18 ....79 B4
Maidenhead SL6 ....40 A2
Newbury RG14 ....105 B3
Purley on T RG31 ....57 B2
Shinfield RG7 ....113 A1
Shiplake RG9 ....35 C1
West End GU24 ....153 B3
Wokingham RG40 ....116 B3
Woolhampton RG7 ....108 B1
Orchard Ct
Bracknell RG12 ....118 B4
Harmondsworth UB7 ....70 B4
Reading RG2 ....113 B4
Thatcham RG19 ....106 C2
Walton-on-T KT12 ....125 C1
Orchard Dr Sunbury TW17 .125 C3
Wooburn Green HP10 ....3 B2
Orchard Est RG10 ....61 C3
Orchard Gate
Farnham Common SL2 ......22 B4
Sandhurst GU47 ....150 A4
Orchard Gr Caversham RG4 .59 C2
Flackwell Heath HP10 ....3 A4
Maidenhead SL6 ....39 B4
Orchard Hill Bourne End SL8 .3 A1
Windlesham GU20 ....146 B2
Orchard Ho 6 SL8 ....3 A2
Orchard Park Cl RG17 ...100 B2
Orchard Pl RG40 ....116 B3
Orchard Rd Hurst RG10 ....88 C4
Mortimer RG7 ....137 A3
Old Windsor SL4 ....68 A1
Orchard St RG1 ....86 A3
Orchard The
Flackwell Heath HP10 ....3 A4
Lightwater GU18 ....153 A4
Marlow SL7 ....1 C2
Theale RG7 ....83 C2
Virginia Water GU25 .....122 C2
Orchard Way
Ashford TW15 ....97 C3
Camberley GU15 ....151 A1
Slough SL3 ....43 C3
Orchardene RG14 ....105 A2
Orchards The TW15 ....98 B2
Orchardville SL1 ....21 A1
Orchids The OX11 ....10 B4
Oregon Ave RG31 ....57 B2
Oregon Wlk RG40 ....141 C4
Oriel Hill GU15 ....151 B2
Oriental Rd SL5 ....120 B3
Orion RG12 ....118 A1
Orkney Cl RG31 ....84 C2
Orkney Ct SL6 ....20 C3
Ormathwaites Cnr RG42 ...91 C1
Ormonde Rd RG41 ....116 A3
Ormsby St RG1 ....85 C4
Orrin Cl RG30 ....85 A4
Orts Rd Newbury RG14 ....105 A1
Reading RG1 ....86 B4
Orville Cl RG5 ....88 A4
Orwell Cl Caversham RG4 ..58 C2
Windsor SL4 ....67 B2
Osborne Ave TW19 ....97 C4
Osborne Dr GU18 ....153 A4
Osborne La RG42 ....91 B2
Osborne Mews SL4 ....67 B3
Osborne Rd Egham TW20 ...95 C1
Reading RG30 ....85 A4
Windsor SL4 ....67 B2
Wokingham RG40 ....116 B3
Osborne St SL1 ....42 C2
Osbourne Ct SL4 ....67 B3
Osier Pl TW20 ....96 B1
Osman's Cl RG42 ....92 A1
Osnaburgh Hill GU15 .....151 A3
Osney Rd SL6 ....19 C1
Osprey Ct 4 RG1 ....86 B4
Osterley Cl RG40 ....116 C3
Osterley Dr RG4 ....59 C3
Ostler Gate SL6 ....19 B1
Oswald Cl RG42 ....91 B1
Othello Gr RG42 ....118 C4
Otter Cl RG45 ....143 A4
Our Lady of Peace
RC Inf Sch SL1 ....41 B4
Our Lady of Peace
RC Mid Sch SL1 ....41 B4
Our Lady of the Rosary
RC Sch TW18 ....97 A1
Our Lady's Prep Sch
RG45 ....143 A3
Ouseley Lodge TW19 ......95 B4
Ouseley Rd TW19 ....95 B4
Overbridge Sq RG14 ......105 C2
Overbury Ave RG41 ....88 C1
Overdale Rise GU16 ......151 C2
Overdown Rd RG31 ....57 B2
Overlanders End RG31 ....57 C2
Overlord Cl GU15 ....151 B4
Owen Rd Newbury RG14 ...105 A3
Windlesham GU20 ....146 B3
Owl Cl RG41 ....115 C3
Owlsmoor Cty Prim Sch
GU47 ....143 C1
Owlsmoor Rd GU47 ....143 B1
Owston RG6 ....87 B1
Oxenhope RG12 ....118 A3
Oxford Ave Burnham SL1 ...21 A2
Harlington UB3 ....71 C4
Slough SL1 ....41 C4
Oxford Cl TW15 ....98 B1
Oxford Rd Marlow SL7 ......1 B1
Newbury RG14 ....104 C3
Reading RG30 ....58 A1
Sandhurst GU47 ....143 C1
Windsor SL4 ....67 B3
Wokingham RG41 ....116 A3
Oxford Rd E SL4 ....67 B3
Oxford Road Prim Sch
RG1 ....85 C4
Oxford St Caversham RG4 ..59 A1
Hungerford RG17 ....100 C4
Lambourn RG17 ....25 A2
Newbury RG14 ....104 C2

P

Pacific Cl TW14 ....98 C4
Pack & Prime La RG9 .....15 B1
Packman Dr RG10 ....61 B3
Padbury Cl TW14 ....98 B4
Padbury Oaks UB7 ....70 A3
Paddick Cl RG4 ....60 C2
Paddick Dr RG6 ....87 B1
Paddock Cl
Camberley GU15 ....152 A3
Maidenhead SL6 ....39 A1
Paddock Cotts SL6 ....39 A1
Paddock Hts RG10 ....61 C2
Paddock Rd
Caversham RG4 ....59 B1
Newbury RG14 ....130 C4
Paddock The
Bracknell RG12 ....118 B3
Crowthorne RG45 ....143 A3
Datchet SL3 ....68 A3
Maidenhead SL6 ....19 B1
Newbury RG14 ....105 B1
Paddocks The HP10 ....3 A4
Paddocks Way KT16 ......124 A1
Padley Ct 7 RG1 ....86 B4
Padstow Cl SL3 ....43 C2
Padstow Gdns RG2 ....86 A1
Padstow Wlk TW14 ....98 C4
Padworth La RG7 ....109 C2
Padworth Prep Sch RG7 .109 C1
Padworth Rd RG7 ....136 B4
Page Rd TW14 ....71 B1
Page's Croft RG40 ....116 B3
Paget Cl Camberley GU15 .152 A4
Marlow SL7 ....1 C2
Paget Dr SL6 ....39 A2
Paget Rd SL3 ....43 C1
Pagoda The SL6 ....20 A1
Paice Gn RG40 ....116 B4
Paices Hill RG7 ....135 A3
Pakenham Rd RG12 ......118 B1
Palace Cl SL1 ....41 C3
Paley St SL6 ....64 A3
Palmer CE Jun Sch The
RG40 ....116 B4
Palmer Cl
Crowthorne RG40 ....143 A4
Peasemore RG20 ....50 B4
Palmer Park Ave RG6 .....87 A3
Palmer School Rd RG40 .116 B3
Palmera Ave RG31 ....84 B2
Palmers Cl SL6 ....39 A2
Palmers Hill RG8 ....54 B3
Palmers La
Burghfield Common RG7 ...111 A1
Burghfield Common,
Poundgreen RG7 ....112 A2
Palmerston Ave SL3 ....43 A2
Palmerstone Rd RG6 ......87 A3
Pamber Heath Rd RG26 ..135 C1
Pamber Rd RG7 ....136 A1
Pamela Row SL6 ....65 A4
Pan's Gdns GU15 ....151 C2
Panbourne Hill RG8 ....56 B3
Pangbourne Coll RG8 .....56 A2
Pangbourne Prim Sch
RG8 ....56 C3
Pangbourne Rd RG8 ....55 B2
Pangbourne St 2 RG30 ....85 A4
Pangbourne Sta RG8 ....56 B3
Pankhurst Dr RG12 ....118 B2
Pannells Cl KT16 ....123 C1
Pantile Row SL3 ....44 A1
Papist Way OX10 ....13 C4
Papplewick Sch SL5 ......120 A1
Paprika Cl RG6 ....86 C1
Par The SL2 ....22 B3
Parade The Ashford TW16 ..98 C1
Bourne End SL8 ....3 A2
Earley RG6 ....87 A2
Egham TW18 ....96 B2
Reading RG30 ....85 B3
Tadley RG26 ....135 A1
Wentworth GU25 ....122 B2
Windsor SL4 ....66 B3
Woodley RG5 ....87 C4
Paradise Mews RG9 ....15 B1
Paradise Rd RG9 ....15 B1
Paradise Way RG7 ....108 B4
Park Ave Camberley GU15 .151 B2
Egham TW20 ....96 B1
Staines TW18 ....97 A1
Thatcham RG18 ....106 B2
Upper Halliford TW17 ....125 C3
Wokingham RG40 ....116 A3
Wraysbury TW19 ....68 B2
Park Cl SL4 ....67 B3
Park Close Cotts TW20 ....94 C2
Park Cnr SL4 ....66 C2
Park Cres Reading RG30 ....85 A3
Sunningdale SL5 ....120 C2
Park Dr SL5 ....120 C2
Park End RG14 ....105 A2
Park Farm Ind Est GU15 ..151 B1
Park Gr RG30 ....85 A3
Park Ho SL6 ....39 C3
Park House Sch RG14 ....130 C3
Park La Barkham RG40 ....141 A3
Beech Hill RG7 ....137 B1
Binfield RG42 ....90 C1
Burnham SL1 ....21 C4
Camberley GU15 ....151 B3
Charvil RG10 ....61 A2
Horton SL3 ....69 A2
Newbury RG14 ....105 A2
Reading RG31 ....84 B4
Slough SL3 ....43 A2
Stockcross RG20 ....103 A1
Thatcham RG18 ....106 B2
Winkfield SL4 ....93 A4
Park Lane Prim Sch RG31 .84 B4
Park Lane Prim Sch
Annexe RG31 ....84 B4
Park Lawn SL2 ....22 B1
Park Mews TW19 ....97 C4
Park Rd Ashford TW15 .....98 A2
Park Rd *continued*
Bracknell RG12 ....113 B4
Camberley GU15 ....151 B2
Egham TW20 ....95 A2
Henley-on-T RG9 ....15 C1
Lower Halliford TW17 ....125 A1
Sandhurst GU47 ....150 B4
Stanwell TW19 ....70 B1
Stoke Poges SL2 ....22 C2
Wokingham RG40 ....115 A3
Park St Bagshot GU19 ....145 C2
Camberley GU15 ....151 B3
Hungerford RG17 ....100 B3
Maidenhead SL6 ....39 C4
Newbury RG14 ....105 A2
Poyle SL3 ....69 B3
Slough SL1 ....42 C2
Windsor SL4 ....67 B3
Park Terr RG14 ....105 A2
Park The RG17 ....25 A2
Park View Bagshot GU19 ..145 B2
Beech Hill RG7 ....138 B3
Park View Dr N RG10 ......61 A3
Park View Dr S RG10 ......61 A2
Park Wall La RG8 ....34 B1
Park Way
Hungerford RG17 ....100 C2
Newbury RG14 ....105 A2
Park Wlk RG8 ....57 B3
Parkcorner La RG41 .....114 C3
Parker's La RG42 ....92 A3
Parkers Ct GU19 ....145 C2
Parkgate SL1 ....21 B1
Parkhill Cl GU17 ....150 B2
Parkhill Dr RG31 ....57 B1
Parkhill Rd GU17 ....150 B2
Parkhouse La RG30 ....85 B3
Parkhouse Mews 9 RG30 ..85 B3
Parkhurst 20 RG30 ....85 B3
Parkland Ave SL3 ....43 B1
Parkland Dr RG12 ....118 C4
Parkland Gr TW15 ....98 A2
Parkland Rd TW15 ....98 A2
Parkside Henley-on-T RG9 ...15 B1
Maidenhead SL6 ....19 B1
Parkside Rd Reading RG30 .85 B3
Sunningdale SL5 ....121 A2
Thatcham RG18 ....106 B3
Parkside Wlk SL1 ....43 A2
Parkstone Dr GU15 ......151 B2
Parkview
Flackwell Heath HP10 ....3 A4
Maidenhead SL6 ....39 C4
Parkview Chase SL1 ....41 C4
Parkway Camberley GU15 ..151 B2
Crowthorne RG45 ....143 A3
Marlow SL7 ....2 A2
Parkway Dr RG4 ....60 C2
Parlaunt Park Comb Sch
SL3 ....44 A2
Parlaunt Rd SL3 ....44 A1
Parliament La SL6 ....20 C3
Parnham Ave GU18 ....153 B4
Parry Gn N SL3 ....43 C1
Parry Gn S SL3 ....44 A1
Parsley Cl RG6 ....86 C1
Parson's Wood La SL2 ....22 B3
Parsonage Gdns SL7 ......1 C1
Parsonage La
Farnham Common SL2 ......22 B2
Hungerford RG17 ....100 B3
Lambourn RG17 ....25 A2
Windsor SL4 ....67 A3
Parsonage Pl RG17 ....25 A2
Parsonage Rd TW20 ....95 B2
Parsonage Way GU16 ....151 C1
Parsons Cl Barkham RG2 ..141 A4
Newbury RG14 ....104 C1
Parsons Down
Jun & Inf Schs RG19 ....106 A2
Parsons Field GU47 ......150 A4
Part La RG7 ....139 C2
Parthia Cl RG1 ....86 A3
Partridge Ave GU46 ......149 A3
Partridge Cl GU16 ....151 C1
Partridge Dr RG31 ....84 B3
Partridge Mead SL6 ....19 C1
Paschal Rd GU15 ....151 C4
Pasture Cl RG6 ....114 A4
Patches Field SL7 ....1 C3
Paterson Cl GU16 ....152 B2
Pates Manor Dr TW14 .....98 B4
Patricia Cl SL1 ....41 C3
Patrick Gdns RG42 ....91 C1
Patrick Rd RG4 ....59 A1
Patriot Pl RG1 ....86 B4
Patten Ash Dr RG40 ......116 C4
Patten Ave GU46 ....149 B3
Pavenham Cl RG6 ....114 A4
Pavilion Gdns TW18 ....97 A1
Pavilions End The GU15 ..151 B2
Pavy Cl RG19 ....106 C1
Paxton Ave SL1 ....42 B2
Payley Dr RG40 ....116 C4
Paynesdown Rd RG19 ....106 A2
Peace La SL6 ....19 C3
Peach St RG40 ....116 B3
Peachy Dr RG19 ....106 C1
Peacock Ave TW14 ....98 B4
Peacock Cotts RG12 ......117 B3
Peacock La RG12 ....117 B3
Peacock Rd SL7 ....2 A2
Pear Ave TW17 ....125 C3
Pear Tree Ct GU15 ....152 A4
Pear Tree La RG14 ....105 B3
Pear Tree Rd TW15 ....98 B2
Pearce Cl SL6 ....19 C1
Pearce Dr SL6 ....19 C4

Pearce Rd SL6 ... 19 C1
Pearces Orch RG9 ... 15 B2
Pearl Gdns SL1 ... 42 A3
Pearmain Cl TW17 ... 125 A2
Pearmans Glade RG2 ... 113 C4
Pearson Rd RG4 ... 60 B2
Pearson Way RG5 ... 87 C3
Peartree Cl SL1 ... 41 C3
Peascod Pl 21 SL4 ... 67 B3
Peascod St SL4 ... 67 B3
Pease Hill RG7 ... 107 C4
Peasemore Hill RG20 ... 50 A4
Pebble Hill RG17 ... 128 A3
Peckmoor Dr RG19 ... 131 B4
Peddlars Gr GU46 ... 149 C3
Peel Cl Caversham RG4 ... 59 B1
Windsor SL4 ... 67 A2
Woodley RG5 ... 88 A4
Peel Ct SL1 ... 42 A4
Peel Ctr The RG12 ... 118 A4
Peel Ho TW20 ... 95 C1
Pegasus Cl RG19 ... 106 A2
Pegasus Ct RG31 ... 84 B4
Peggotty Pl GU47 ... 143 C1
Pegs Green Cl RG30 ... 85 A3
Peket Cl TW18 ... 123 C4
Pelham Ct Maidenhead SL6 ... 39 C4
12 Reading RG30 ... 85 B3
Staines TW18 ... 97 A2
Pelican La RG14 ... 105 A2
Pelican Rd RG26 ... 135 C1
Pell St RG1 ... 86 A3
Pelling Hill SL4 ... 95 A4
Pemberton Gdns RG31 ... 84 B2
Pemberton Rd SL2 ... 21 C1
Pembroke RG12 ... 118 A1
Pembroke Broadway
GU15 ... 151 B3
Pembroke Cl Ascot SL5 ... 120 B2
Burghfield Common RG7 ... 111 B2
Pembroke Ho 3 RG4 ... 59 B1
Pembroke Mews SL5 ... 120 B2
Pembroke Pl RG4 ... 59 B2
Pembroke Rd 22 RG14 ... 105 A2
Pembury Ct UB3 ... 71 B4
Pendals Cl RG18 ... 52 C3
Pendeen Ct SL1 ... 42 A3
Pendell Ave UB3 ... 71 C4
Pendennis Ave RG4 ... 59 C3
Pendine Pl RG12 ... 118 A2
Pendlebury RG12 ... 118 A1
Pendragon Ct RG30 ... 85 B3
Pendragon Way GU15 ... 152 B2
Pendred Rd RG2 ... 113 B3
Peninsular Cl GU15 ... 152 A4
Peninsular Cl TW14 ... 71 C1
Penling Cl SL6 ... 19 C3
Penn Cl RG4 ... 59 A3
Penn Ct 8 SL7 ... 1 C1
Penn Mdw SL2 ... 22 C2
Penn Rd Newbury RG14 ... 104 B3
Slough SL2 ... 22 B1
Pennfields RG10 ... 61 C3
Pennine Cl RG31 ... 84 A3
Pennine Rd SL2 ... 42 A4
Pennine Way Charvil RG10 ... 61 A2
Harlington UB3 ... 71 B4
Penny La TW17 ... 125 C1
Pennylets Gn SL2 ... 23 A3
Pennypiece RG8 ... 34 B4
Pennyroyal Ct RG1 ... 86 A3
Penroath Ave RG30 ... 85 B3
Penrose Ave RG5 ... 87 C3
Penrose Cl RG14 ... 104 C3
Penrose Ct TW20 ... 95 B1
Pensford Cl RG45 ... 143 A4
Penshurst Rd SL6 ... 39 B3
Pentangle The 13 RG14 ... 105 A2
Pentland Ave TW17 ... 125 A2
Pentland Cl RG30 ... 84 C3
Pentland Pl RG19 ... 106 B1
Pentland Rd SL2 ... 42 A4
Pentlands The RG17 ... 102 B1
Penton Ave TW18 ... 123 C4
Penton Ct TW18 ... 96 C1
Penton Hall TW18 ... 124 A4
Penton Hall Dr TW18 ... 124 A4
Penton Hook Marina
Chertsey KT16 ... 124 A3
Egham TW18 ... 123 C4
Penton Hook Rd TW18 ... 124 A4
Penton Rd TW18 ... 96 C1
Penwood Ct SL6 ... 39 A4
Penwood Gdns RG12 ... 117 B2
Penwood La SL7 ... 1 B1
Penwood Rd RG20 ... 130 B2
Penyston Rd SL6 ... 39 B4
Penzance Spur SL2 ... 22 A1
Peppard La RG9 ... 35 C4
Peppard Rd RG4 ... 59 B4
Pepper La RG2 ... 86 C2
Pepys Cl SL3 ... 69 A4
Perch Cl SL7 ... 18 B4
Percival Rd TW13 ... 98 C3
Percy Ave TW15 ... 98 A2
Percy Bryant Rd TW16 ... 98 C1
Percy Pl SL3 ... 68 A3
Peregrine Cl
Bracknell RG12 ... 118 A2
Wokingham RG41 ... 115 C3
Peregrine Rd TW16 ... 125 C4
Periam Cl RG9 ... 35 B4
Perkins Ct TW15 ... 97 C2
Perkins Way RG41 ... 116 A3
Perrin Cl TW15 ... 97 C2
Perry Ho SL1 ... 21 A1
Perry Oaks RG12 ... 118 C4
Perry Oaks Dr TW6, UB7 ... 70 B3
Perry Way Bracknell RG12 ... 118 C4
Lightwater GU18 ... 152 C4
Perrycroft SL4 ... 66 C2
Perryfields Way SL1 ... 21 A1
Perryhill Dr GU47 ... 142 C1
Perryman Way SL2 ... 21 C1
Perserverance Hill RG9 ... 35 A3
Perth Ave SL1 ... 42 A4
Perth Cl RG5 ... 61 A1
Perth Trad Est SL1 ... 42 A4
Peterhead Mews SL3 ... 44 A1
Peterhouse Cl GU47 ... 143 C1
Petersfield Ave Slough SL2 ... 43 A3
Staines TW18 ... 97 B1
Petersfield Rd TW18 ... 97 B2
Petrel Cl RG41 ... 115 C3
Petts La TW17 ... 125 A3
Petty Pl SL6 ... 39 B2
Petworth Ave RG30 ... 84 C2
Petworth Ct Reading RG1 ... 85 C3
Windsor SL4 ... 67 A3
Pevensey Ave RG4 ... 59 C3
Pevensey Ct RG2 ... 86 C1
Pevensey Rd SL2 ... 42 A4
Pewsey Vale RG12 ... 118 C2
Pheasant Cl RG41 ... 88 B1
Pheasant La RG20 ... 131 C2
Pheasants Croft SL6 ... 39 A2
Pheasants Ridge SL7 ... 1 B4
Philbye Mews SL1 ... 41 C2
Philip Dr HP10 ... 3 B4
Philip Rd TW18 ... 97 B1
Phillimore Rd RG4 ... 59 B4
Phillips Cl RG5 ... 61 A1
Phipps Cl SL6 ... 39 A1
Phipps Rd SL1 ... 41 C4
Phoebe Ct RG1 ... 86 A3
Phoenix Bsns Pk RG12 ... 117 B4
Phoenix Cl RG41 ... 115 C3
Phoenix Ct SL6 ... 39 B2
Phoenix Pl TW18 ... 97 A2
Phoenix Wlk RG14 ... 130 B3
Phyllis Court Dr RG9 ... 15 C2
Pickering RG12 ... 118 A3
Picket Post Cl RG12 ... 118 C3
Picketts La RG8 ... 55 C2
Pickford Dr SL3 ... 43 C3
Pickins Piece SL3 ... 69 A3
Pickwell Cl RG6 ... 87 B1
Pickwick Gdns GU15 ... 152 A2
Picton Cl GU15 ... 152 A4
Picton Way RG4 ... 59 A2
Piercefield RG31 ... 84 B2
Pierces Hill RG31 ... 57 B1
Pierson Rd SL4 ... 66 B3
Pigeonhouse La SL4, SL5 ... 92 C2
Pigeons Farm Rd RG19 ... 131 B4
Piggott Sch The RG10 ... 61 B4
Piggotts Rd 4 RG4 ... 59 B1
Pightle The RG7 ... 111 C2
Pigott Ct RG40 ... 116 B3
Pigott Rd RG40 ... 116 C4
Pike Cl SL7 ... 18 B4
Pike St RG14 ... 105 A2
Pikeshaw Way RG31 ... 57 B1
Pimento Dr RG6 ... 86 C1
Pimpernel Pl RG18 ... 106 C2
Pincents Kiln Ind Est
RG31 ... 84 A2
Pincents La RG31 ... 84 A3
Pinchcut RG7 ... 111 A2
Pinchington La
RG14 & RG19 ... 131 A4
Pindar Pl RG14 ... 105 C3
Pine Ave GU15 ... 151 B2
Pine Cl Maidenhead SL6 ... 39 A4
Sandhurst GU15 ... 150 C4
Pine Croft Rd RG41 ... 116 A1
Pine Ct RG12 ... 118 C3
Pine Dr Blackwater GU17 ... 150 C2
Mortimer RG7 ... 136 C3
Wokingham RG40 ... 142 A4
Pine Gr Twyford RG10 ... 61 B3
Windlesham GU20 ... 146 B2
Pine Mount Rd GU15 ... 151 B2
Pine Ridge RG14 ... 105 B3
Pine Ridge Golf Ctr
GU16 ... 152 B1
Pine Ridge Rd RG7 ... 111 A2
Pine Trees Bsns Pk TW18 ... 96 C2
Pine Way TW20 ... 95 A1
Pinecote Dr SL5 ... 120 C1
Pinecroft SL7 ... 1 B2
Pinefields Cl RG45 ... 143 A2
Pinehill Rd RG45 ... 143 B2
Pinehill Rise GU47 ... 150 B4
Pinehurst SL5 ... 120 B2
Pinel Cl GU25 ... 122 C3
Piner Cotts SL4 ... 66 C2
Pineridge Cty Inf Sch
GU15 ... 145 A1
Pineridge Gdns 10 RG30 ... 85 B3
Pines Cty Inf Sch RG12 ... 118 A1
Pines Cty Jun Sch RG12 ... 118 A1
Pines The
Camberley GU15 ... 151 C4
Twyford RG10 ... 61 C4
Pinetree Ct RG4 ... 59 A3
Pinewood Ave RG45 ... 143 B3
Pinewood Cl RG26 ... 134 B1
Pinewood Dr
Caversham RG4 ... 58 C3
Newtown RG20 ... 131 A1
Staines TW18 ... 97 A2
Pinewood Gdns GU19 ... 145 B2
Pinewood Mews TW19 ... 70 B1
Pinewood Rd GU25 ... 122 A3
Pingewood Cl RG30 ... 85 A1
Pingewood Rd RG30 ... 85 A1
Pingewood Rd S
RG7,RG30 ... 112 B4
Pinglestone Cl TW6, UB7 ... 70 C4
Pink La SL1 ... 21 A2
Pinkneys Dr SL6 ... 38 C4
Pinkneys Rd SL6 ... 39 A4
Pinks La RG26 ... 134 C1
Piper's End GU25 ... 122 B3
Pipers Cl SL1 ... 21 B1
Pipers Ct Burnham SL1 ... 21 B1
Thatcham RG19 ... 107 A1
Pipers Way RG19 ... 107 A1
Pipit Cl RG19 ... 106 A2
Pippins Ct TW15 ... 98 A1
Pippins The SL3 ... 43 C3
Pipsons Cl GU46 ... 149 B3
Pitch Pl RG42 ... 90 B2
Pitcroft Ave RG6 ... 87 A3
Pitfield La RG7 ... 137 B2
Pitford Rd RG5 ... 88 A4
Pitts Cl RG42 ... 90 B1
Pitts La RG6 ... 87 A4
Pitts Rd SL1 ... 42 B3
Plackett Way SL1 ... 41 B3
Plaines Cl SL1 ... 41 C3
Plaitinson Rd RG2 ... 113 B3
Planes The KT16 ... 124 B1
Plantagenet Pk RG42 ... 118 C4
Plantation Cl RG18 ... 78 C3
Plantation Rd Chilton OX12 ... 9 C4
Tadley RG26 ... 134 C1
Plantation Row GU15 ... 151 A3
Platt Ct RG17 ... 100 C2
Platt La RG17 ... 45 B3
Play Platt RG7 ... 83 B2
Players Gn RG5 ... 87 C3
Playhatch Rd RG4 ... 60 A3
Plough La Shiplake RG9 ... 35 C1
Stoke Poges SL2 ... 23 A2
Wokingham RG40 ... 116 C3
Plough Rd GU46 ... 149 C4
Ploughlands RG42 ... 117 C4
Ploughlees La SL1 ... 42 C3
Plover Cl Staines TW18 ... 96 C3
Wokingham RG41 ... 115 C3
Plover La RG27 ... 140 C1
Plowden Way RG9 ... 35 C1
Plummery The 1 RG1 ... 86 B4
Plumpton Rd RG14 ... 105 B1
Plumtrees RG6 ... 87 A1
Pluto Cl SL1 ... 41 C2
Pluto Rd OX11 ... 9 C4
Plymouth Ave RG5 ... 87 B3
Plymouth Rd SL1 ... 41 C4
Plympton Cl RG6 ... 87 C2
Pocket Cl RG12 ... 117 B4
Pococks La SL4 ... 42 C1
Poffley Pl RG19 ... 107 A2
Point (L Ctr) The RG12 ... 118 A4
Point Royal RG12 ... 118 A2
Pointers Cl RG20 ... 51 A1
Points The SL6 ... 39 A2
Polehampton CE Inf Sch
RG10 ... 61 B3
Polehampton Cl RG10 ... 61 B2
Polehampton Jun Sch
RG10 ... 61 C3
Pollard Cl SL4 ... 68 A1
Pollard Gr GU15 ... 152 B2
Pollardrow Ave RG42 ... 117 C4
Pollards Way RG31 ... 84 B2
Polsted Rd RG31 ... 57 B1
Polyanthus Way RG45 ... 143 A4
Polygon Bsns Ctr SL3 ... 69 C3
Pond Cl RG14 ... 130 B4
Pond Croft GU46 ... 149 C3
Pond Head La RG6 ... 87 B2
Pond La Hermitage RG18 ... 79 B4
Mapledurham RG4 ... 58 A3
Pond Moor Rd RG12 ... 118 A2
Pond Rd TW20 ... 96 B1
Pondside Cl UB3 ... 71 B4
Pool End Cl TW17 ... 125 A2
Pool La Slough SL1 ... 42 C3
Waltham St Lawrence RG10 ... 63 A3
Poole Cl RG30 ... 85 A4
Pooley Ave TW20 ... 96 A2
Pooley Green Cl TW20 ... 96 B2
Pooley Green Rd TW20 ... 96 B2
Poolmans Rd SL4 ... 66 B2
Pope Cl TW14 ... 98 C4
Popes Cl SL3 ... 69 B4
Popes La SL6 ... 19 B4
Popeswood Rd RG42 ... 117 B4
Popham Cl RG12 ... 118 C2
Poplar Ave Reading RG30 ... 84 C3
Windlesham GU20 ... 146 A3
Poplar Cl SL3 ... 69 C3
Poplar Gdns RG2 ... 86 C1
Poplar Ho SL3 ... 43 C1
Poplar La Hurst RG10 ... 62 A1
Winnersh RG41 ... 88 B2
Poplar Pl RG14 ... 105 A3
Poplar Rd TW15 ... 98 B2
Poplars Gr SL6 ... 20 A1
Poplars The SL5 ... 120 A2
Poppy Dr RG18 ... 106 C2
Poppy Pl RG40 ... 116 A3
Poppy Way RG31 ... 84 B3
Poppyhills Rd GU15 ... 151 C4
Porchester SL5 ... 120 A3
Porchester Rd RG14 ... 105 A1
Porchfield Cl RG6 ... 87 A1
Porlock Cl RG19 ... 106 B1
Porlock Pl RG31 ... 84 B2
Port Down RG17 ... 100 C3
Porter Cl RG6 ... 114 B4
Porter End RG14 ... 131 A4
Portesbery Hill Dr GU15 ... 151 C3
Portesbery Rd GU15 ... 151 C3
Portesbery Sch GU15 ... 151 B3
Portia Gr RG42 ... 118 C4
Portland Bsns Ctr SL3 ... 68 A3
Portland Cl SL2 ... 21 B1
Portland Cres TW13 ... 98 B2
Portland Gdns RG30 ... 84 B4
Portland Rd TW15 ... 97 C3
Portlands SL7 ... 1 B1
Portlands Mews 8 SL7 ... 1 B1
Portlock Rd SL6 ... 39 B4
Portman Cl 5 RG42 ... 118 A4
Portman Rd RG30 ... 58 B1
Portmeirion Gdns RG30 ... 57 C1
Portnall Dr GU25 ... 121 C2
Portnall Rd GU25 ... 121 C2
Portnall Rise GU25 ... 121 C2
Portrush Rd RG5 ... 87 B3
Portsmouth Ct SL1 ... 42 C3
Portsmouth Rd GU15 ... 152 A4
Portway Swallowfield RG7 ... 139 B1
Tadley RG26 ... 134 C1
Portway Cl RG1 ... 85 C3
Post Horn Pl RG31 ... 84 C2
Post Office Cotts SL2 ... 23 A3
Post Office La
Burghfield Common RG30 ... 111 B3
Slough SL3 ... 43 B4
Post Office Rd RG17 ... 127 C3
Posting House Mews
RG14 ... 104 C2
Potley Hill Cty Prim Sch
GU46 ... 150 A3
Potley Hill Rd GU46 ... 149 C3
Pottery La RG17 ... 127 C3
Pottery Rd RG30 ... 57 C1
Poulcott TW19 ... 68 C1
Pound Cres SL7 ... 1 B1
Pound La Hurst RG10 ... 89 A3
Little Marlow SL7 ... 2 B2
Marlow SL7 ... 1 B1
Newbury RG20 ... 104 B2
Sonning RG4 ... 60 C1
Thatcham RG19 ... 106 A2
Windlesham GU20 ... 146 B2
Pound Piece RG17 ... 100 B3
Pound Rd KT16 ... 124 A1
Pound St RG14 ... 104 C1
Pound The Cookham SL6 ... 19 C4
Slough SL1 ... 21 B1
Poundfield La SL6 ... 19 C4
Poundfield Way RG10 ... 61 C2
Powis Cl SL6 ... 39 A2
Powney Rd SL6 ... 39 B4
Poyle 14 Trad Est SL3 ... 69 C2
Poyle Cty Fst Sch SL3 ... 69 C3
Poyle Gdns RG12 ... 118 B4
Poyle La SL1 ... 21 A2
Poyle New Cotts SL3 ... 69 C3
Poyle Rd SL3 ... 69 C3
Poyle Tech Ctr The SL3 ... 69 C3
Poynings SL0 ... 44 C1
Prancing Horse Cl RG19 ... 106 C2
Precinct The TW20 ... 96 A2
Precincts The SL1 ... 21 B1
Prescott RG12 ... 117 C1
Prescott Rd SL3 ... 69 C3
Presentation Coll RG30 ... 85 B3
Preston Pl RG14 ... 105 B3
Preston Rd Littleton TW17 ... 125 A2
Reading RG2 ... 86 A3
Slough SL2 ... 43 B3
Prestwick Ct 36 RG1 ... 86 B4
Prestwood SL2 ... 43 A4
Pretoria Rd KT16 ... 123 C1
Price Gdns RG42 ... 91 A1
Prides Crossing SL5 ... 93 A1
Priest Ave RG40 ... 116 C3
Priest Hill Caversham RG4 ... 59 A2
Englefield Green TW19, SL4 ... 95 B3
Priest La GU24 ... 153 B3
Priestwood Ave RG42 ... 117 C4
Priestwood Court Rd
RG42 ... 118 A4
Priestwood Sq 1 RG42 ... 118 A4
Primrose Cl RG8 ... 57 B3
Primrose La RG41 ... 88 B2
Primrose Walk GU46 ... 149 A3
Primrose Way GU47 ... 143 A1
Primrose Wlk RG12 ... 118 B2
Prince Albert Dr SL5 ... 119 B2
Prince Andrew Cl SL6 ... 20 A1
Prince Andrew Rd SL6 ... 20 A1
Prince Andrew Way SL5 ... 119 B4
Prince Consort Cotts SL4 ... 67 B3
Prince Consort Dr SL5 ... 119 B3
Prince Consort's Dr
Old Windsor SL4 ... 94 A3
Winkfield SL4 ... 93 C2
Prince Dr GU47 ... 143 A1
Prince Hold Rd RG19 ... 106 A2
Prince of Wales Ave RG30 ... 85 B4
Prince of Wales Wlk 1
GU15 ... 151 B3
Prince William Ct TW15 ... 97 C2
Prince William Dr RG31 ... 57 B1
Princes Cl Bagshot GU19 ... 145 C1
Eton SL4 ... 41 C1
Princes Ct SL8 ... 3 B2
Princes La RG20 ... 50 B3
Princes Rd Ashford TW15 ... 97 C2
Bourne End SL8 ... 3 B2
Egham TW20 ... 95 C1
Feltham TW13 ... 98 C3
Princes St Reading RG1 ... 86 B4
Slough SL1 ... 43 A2
Princess Ave SL4 ... 67 A2
Princess Christians Hospl
SL4 ... 67 B3
Princess Margaret Hospl
The SL4 ... 67 B3
Princess Margaret Royal
Free Sch The SL4 ... 67 B2
Princess Marina Dr
Barkham, Arborfield
Garrison RG2 ... 140 C4
Barkham, Langley
Common RG2 ... 115 A1
Princess Sq RG12 ... 118 A4
Princess St SL6 ... 39 C3
Princess Way GU15 ... 151 B3
Prior Croft Cl GU15 ... 152 A2
Prior End GU15 ... 152 A3
Prior Heath Cty Inf Sch
GU15 ... 152 A3
Prior Rd GU15 ... 152 A3
Prior's La GU17 ... 150 A3
Priors Cl Maidenhead SL6 ... 40 A1
5 Slough SL1 ... 43 A2
Priors Court Rd RG18 ... 78 C4
Priors Court Specl Sch
RG18 ... 78 B4
Priors Ct 21 RG1 ... 86 A3
Priors Rd Tadley RG26 ... 135 A1
Windsor SL4 ... 66 B2
Priors Way SL6 ... 40 A1
Priors Way Ind Est SL6 ... 40 A1
Priors Wood RG45 ... 142 B2
Priory Ave Caversham RG4 ... 59 A1
Hungerford RG17 ... 100 B2
Priory Cl Hungerford RG17 ... 100 B2
Sunningdale SL5 ... 121 A1
Priory Ct Camberley GU15 ... 150 C3
Caversham RG4 ... 59 A1
Egham TW20 ... 96 B1
Winnersh RG41 ... 88 B2
Priory Cty Jun & Inf Sch
SL1 ... 41 B4
Priory Gn TW18 ... 97 A2
Priory La RG42 ... 91 B1
Priory Mews TW18 ... 97 A2
Priory Pl Greenham RG19 ... 131 A3
Hungerford RG17 ... 100 B2
Priory Rd Burnham SL1 ... 41 B4
Hungerford RG17 ... 100 B2
Newbury RG14 ... 105 A1
Sunningdale SL5 ... 121 A1
Winkfield SL5 ... 119 A4
Priory The RG41 ... 88 B2
Priory Way Datchet SL3 ... 68 A4
Harmondsworth UB7 ... 70 C4
Priory Wlk RG12 ... 118 C3
Priscilla Ho 13 TW16 ... 98 C1
Pritchard Cl RG19 ... 131 B4
Privet Cl RG6 ... 87 A1
Proctors Rd RG40 ... 116 C3
Progress Bsns Ctr SL1 ... 41 B4
Promenade SL4 ... 67 B4
Promenade Rd RG4 ... 59 A1
Prospect Cotts RG42 ... 117 B4
Prospect Ct RG30 ... 85 A3
Prospect La TW20 ... 95 A2
Prospect Pl Hurley SL6 ... 17 C2
Newbury RG14 ... 105 A1
Staines TW18 ... 96 C2
3 Windsor SL4 ... 67 B2
Prospect Rd
Hungerford RG17 ... 100 B3
Marlow SL7 ... 1 B1
Prospect Sch RG30 ... 85 A3
Prospect St
Caversham RG4 ... 59 A1
Reading RG1 ... 85 C4
Providence Ho GU19 ... 145 C2
Providence La UB3 ... 71 B4
Providence Pl SL6 ... 39 C4
Prudential Bldgs 8 SL1 ... 42 C2
Prune Hill TW20 ... 95 C1
Prunus Cl GU24 ... 153 C3
Pudding Hill RG10 ... 37 B3
Pudding La RG20 ... 28 C1
Puffers Way RG14 ... 104 C1
Pullmans Pl TW18 ... 97 A2
Pump La Ascot SL5 ... 120 C4
Shinfield RG7 ... 112 B1
Pump La N SL7 ... 1 C3
Pump La S SL7 ... 2 A2
Pumpkin Hill SL1 ... 21 C3
Pundles La SL6 ... 63 B3
Purbrook Ct RG12 ... 118 C2
Purcell Rd RG45 ... 143 A4
Purfield Dr RG10 ... 36 C1
Purley CE Inf Sch RG8 ... 57 B3
Purley La RG8 ... 57 B3
Purley Rise RG8 ... 56 C3
Purley Village RG8 ... 57 B3
Purley Way RG8 ... 56 C3
Pursers Farm RG7 ... 113 A2
Purslane RG40 ... 116 B3
Purssell Cl SL6 ... 39 A2
Purton Ct SL2 ... 22 B3
Purton La SL2 ... 22 B3
Putman Pl RG9 ... 15 C1
Pycroft Ct KT16 ... 123 C1
Pyegrove Chase RG12 ... 118 C1
Pyke Cl RG40 ... 116 B3
Pykes Hill RG8 ... 54 B2
Pyle Hill RG14 ... 105 A1
Pyrcroft Grange
Prim Sch KT16 ... 123 C2
Pyrcroft Rd KT16 ... 123 C1

Q

R

Robinson Cl OX11 12 A4
Robinson Ct RG6 87 A1
Roby Dr RG12 118 B1
Rochester Ave
Feltham TW13 98 C3
Woodley RG5 60 C1
Rochester Rd TW20 96 B1
Rochford Way SL6 41 A4
Rochfords Gdns SL2 43 B3
Rockall Ct SL3 44 A2
Rockbourne Gdns RG30 58 A1
Rockfel Rd RG17 25 A1
Rockfield Way 7 GU47 150 B4
Rockingham Rd RG14 104 C1
Rockmoor La SP11 147 A1
Rodd Est TW17 125 B2
Rodney Ct 11 RG1 86 A3
Rodney Way SL3 69 C3
Rodway Rd RG30 57 C1
Roebuck Est RG42 90 B1
Roebuck Gn SL1 41 C3
Roebuck Rise RG31 57 B2
Roebuts Cl RG14 130 C4
Rogers La SL2 22 C2
Rogers's La RG17 47 B3
Rogosa Rd GU24 153 C3
Rokeby Cl Bracknell RG12 118 B4
Newbury RG14 131 A4
Rokeby Dr RG4 58 B4
Rokes Pl GU46 149 A3
Rokesby Rd SL2 21 C1
Rolls La SL6 64 C4
Roman Field RG7 136 A1
Roman Lea SL6 19 C4
Roman Ride RG45 142 B3
Roman Way Bourne End SL8 3 A2
Earley RG6 87 B2
Thatcham RG18 106 A2
Winkfield RG42 118 C4
Romana Ct TW13 97 A2
Romano Ct 9 RG14 105 A1
Romans Gate RG26 135 C1
Romany Cl RG30 58 A1
Romany La RG30 58 A1
Romeo Hill RG42 118 C4
Romney Cl TW15 98 B2
Romney Ct 11 SL7 1 C2
Romney Ho RG12 118 C3
Romney Lock Rd SL4 67 B4
Romsey Cl
Blackwater GU17 150 B3
Slough SL3 43 C2
Romsey Rd RG30 58 A1
Rona Ct RG30 85 A4
Ronaldsay Spur SL1 42 C4
Ronita Ct RG1 86 C3
Rood Hill RG20 76 B2
Rook Cl RG41 115 C3
Rook Rd HP10 3 B2
Rookery Ct SL7 1 B1
Rookery Rd TW13 97 A2
Rookery The RG20 50 B4
Rooksfield RG20 132 A1
Rooksmead Rd TW16 125 C4
Rooksnest La RG17 128 A3
Rookswood Bracknell RG42 91 A1
Stockcross RG20 103 C3
Rookwood Ave GU47 143 C1
Rope Wlk RG19 106 B2
Rosa Ave TW15 98 A2
Rosary Gdns Ashford TW15 98 A2
Yateley GU46 149 B3
Rose Cl RG5 88 A4
Rose Cotts SL6 39 B2
Rose Ct RG40 116 B3
Rose Gdns TW19 97 B4
Rose Hill Binfield RG42 90 B2
Burnham SL1 21 A3
Rose Ind Est
Bourne End SL8 3 A2
Marlow Bottom SL7 1 B3
Rose Kiln La RG1 & RG2 86 A2
Rose La Hurley RG9 17 A1
Knowl Hill RG10 37 A4
Rose St RG40 116 B3
Rose Wlk Reading RG1 86 A4
Slough SL2 42 A4
Roseacre Cl TW17 125 A2
Rosebank Cl SL6 19 C4
Rosebay RG40 116 C4
Rosebery Rd RG4 58 B4
Rosecroft Way RG2 113 C3
Rosedale RG42 90 B2
Rosedale Cres RG6 87 A4
Rosedale Gdns
Bracknell RG12 118 A2
Thatcham RG19 106 B1
Rosedene La GU47 150 B4
Rosefield Rd TW18 97 A2
Rosehill Ct SL1 43 A2
Rosehill Ho RG4 59 B4
Rosehill Pk RG4 59 B4
Roseleigh Cl SL6 39 A4
Rosemary Ave RG6 86 C1
Rosemary Gdns GU17 150 B3
Rosemary La
Blackwater GU17 150 B3
Thorpe TW20 123 A3
Rosemary Terr RG14 104 C1
Rosemead KT16 124 A1
Rosemead Ave
Feltham TW13 98 C3
Purley on T RG31 57 A2
Rosen Ct RG19 106 C2
Rosery The SL8 3 A2
Roses La SL4 66 B3
Rosewood RG5 87 B2
Rosewood Dr TW17 124 C2
Rosewood Way
Farnham Common SL2 22 B4
West End GU24 153 C3
Rosier Cl RG19 106 C1
Rosken Gr SL2 22 A2
Roslyn Rd RG5 87 B3
Ross Ho 2 RG30 85 B3
Ross Rd Maidenhead SL6 39 C2
Reading RG1 59 A1
Rossendale Rd RG4 59 B2
Rossett Cl RG12 118 A3
Rossey Pl SL4 42 B1
Rossington Pl RG2 113 B4
Rossiter Cl SL3 43 C1
Rosslea GU20 146 A3
Rosslyn Cl TW16 98 C1
Rothbury Wlk GU15 152 B2
Rother Cl GU47 150 B4
Rotherfield Ave RG41 116 A4
Rotherfield Cl RG7 83 C2
Rotherfield Rd RG9 35 C4
Rotherfield Way RG4 59 A2
Rothwell Gdns RG5 61 A1
Rothwell Ho RG45 143 B2
Rothwell Wlk RG4 59 B1
Rotten Row Hill RG7 81 C2
Roughgrove Copse RG42 90 A1
Rounce La GU24 153 B3
Round Cl GU46 149 C3
Round End RG14 130 B3
Roundabout La RG41 115 B4
Roundfield RG7 107 A3
Roundhead Rd RG7 83 B2
Roundshead Dr RG12 118 B4
Roundway Egham TW20 96 B2
Frimley GU15 152 B3
Roundway Cl GU15 152 B3
Routh Ct TW14 98 B4
Routh La RG30 84 C3
Row La RG4 59 C4
Rowallan Cl RG4 59 B3
Rowan 2 RG12 118 C2
Rowan Ave TW20 96 B2
Rowan Cl Camberley GU15 151 C4
Wokingham RG41 115 C3
Rowan Ct RG6 87 A1
Rowan Dr
Crowthorne RG45 143 B3
Newbury RG14 105 A3
Woodley RG5 87 C4
Rowan Ho 1 SL8 3 A2
Rowan Way
Burghfield Common RG30 111 A3
Slough SL2 42 A4
Rowanhurst Dr SL2 22 B4
Rowans Cl GU14 150 C1
Rowans The TW16 98 C2
Rowcroft Rd RG2 140 C4
Rowdell Dr RG2 86 B1
Rowdown RG17 24 C3
Rowe Ct RG30 85 A4
Rowland Cl SL4 66 B2
Rowland Hill
Almshouses TW15 98 A2
Rowland Way Earley RG6 86 C1
Littleton TW15 98 B1
Rowland's Cl RG7 136 B3
Rowles Paddock RG20 10 A1
Rowley Cl RG12 118 C3
Rowley La SL3 23 B2
Rowley Rd RG2 86 A2
Roxborough Way SL6 38 C2
Roxburgh Cl GU15 152 B2
Roxeth Ct TW15 98 A2
Roxford Cl TW17 125 C2
Roxwell Cl SL1 41 C3
Roy Cl RG18 78 C3
Royal Ascot Golf Club
SL5 120 A4
Royal Ave RG31 84 B3
Royal Berkshire Hospl The
RG1 86 B3
Royal Cotts SL6 19 B4
Royal Ct 10 RG1 86 B4
Royal Free Ct 22 SL4 67 B3
Royal Holloway Univ
of London TW20 95 B1
Royal Hunt Ho SL5 119 B4
Royal Mans RG9 15 C1
Royal Military Acad
GU15 150 C3
Royal Military Acad
Hospl GU15 151 A4
Royal Oak Cl GU46 149 C3
Royal Oak Dr RG45 143 A4
Royal Prim Sch The SL4 94 B2
Royal Victoria Gdns SL5 120 A2
Royal Way RG2 112 C4
Royal Windsor Race Course
SL4 66 C4
Roycroft La RG40 141 C4
Royston Cl RG30 84 C4
Royston Way SL1 41 B4
Rubus Cl GU24 153 C3
Ruby Cl Slough SL1 42 A2
Wokingham RG41 115 C4
Rudd Hall Rise GU15 151 C2
Ruddlesway SL4 66 B3
Rudland Cl RG19 106 B1
Rudsworth Cl SL3 69 B4
Rufus Isaacs Rd RG4 59 A1
Rugby Cl GU47 143 C1
Ruggles-Brise Rd TW15 97 B2
Rumseys La OX11 12 A4
Runnemede Rd TW20 96 A2
Runnymede Cotts TW19 96 B4
Runnymede Ct TW20 96 A2
Runnymede Rdbt TW20 96 A2
Rupert Cl RG9 15 C2
Rupert House Sch RG9 15 C1
Rupert Rd RG14 130 C4
Rupert Sq 19 RG1 86 B4
Rupert St RG1 86 B4
Rupert Wlk 17 RG1 86 B4
Rupert's La RG9 15 C2
Ruscombe Gdns SL3 68 A4
Ruscombe La RG10 61 C3
Ruscombe Pk RG10 61 C3
Ruscombe Rd RG10 61 C3
Ruscombe Way TW14 98 C4
Rushall Cl RG6 113 C4
Rusham Park Ave TW20 96 A1
Rusham Rd TW20 95 C1
Rushbrook Rd RG5 87 B4
Rushburn HP10 3 C3
Rushden Dr RG2 86 C1
Rushes The
Maidenhead SL6 40 B3
Marlow SL7 18 B4
Rushey Way RG6 87 B1
Rushington Ave SL6 39 C3
Rushmere Pl TW20 95 C2
Rushmoor Gdns RG31 84 A2
Rushy Ho 7 RG12 118 C3
Ruskin Ave TW14 71 C1
Ruskin Ct RG45 142 C2
Ruskin Rd TW18 96 C1
Ruskin Way RG41 115 B3
Russel Cl RG12 118 B1
Russell Ct
Blackwater GU17 150 B3
Maidenhead SL6 39 C4
Russell Dr TW19 70 B1
Russell Ho 3 SL8 3 A2
Russell Rd
Lower Halliford TW17 125 B1
Mapledurham RG4 58 B4
Newbury RG14 104 C1
Russell St Reading RG1 85 C4
Windsor SL4 67 B3
Russell Way RG41 88 A1
Russet Ave TW16, TW17 125 C3
Russet Cl TW19 69 C1
Russet Gdns GU15 151 B2
Russet Glade
Burghfield Common RG7 111 A1
Caversham RG4 59 B4
Russet Rd SL6 39 B2
Russington Rd TW17 125 B2
Russley Gn RG40 116 A1
Rustington Cl 5 RG6 87 A1
Ruston Way SL5 119 C4
Rutherford Cl SL4 66 C3
Rutherford Wlk RG31 84 A4
Rutherwyk Rd KT16 123 C1
Rutland Ave SL1 42 B4
Rutland Gate SL6 39 B3
Rutland Pl SL6 39 B3
Rutland Rd Maidenhead SL6 39 B3
Reading RG30 85 B4
Ruxbury Ct TW15 97 C3
Ruxbury Rd KT16 123 B2
Ryan Mount GU47 150 A4
Ryans Mount SL7 1 B1
Rycroft SL4 66 C2
Rydal Ave RG30 57 C1
Rydal Cl GU15 152 B3
Rydal Dr RG19 106 A2
Rydal Pl GU18 153 A4
Rydal Way TW20 96 A1
Ryde Gdns GU46 149 A3
Ryde The TW18 124 A4
Rydings SL4 66 C2
Rye Cl Maidenhead SL6 39 A2
Newell Green RG12 91 B1
Winkfield RG12 118 B4
Rye Ct 1 SL1 43 A2
Rye Gr GU18,GU20 146 C1
Ryecroft Cl Wargrave RG10 36 C1
Woodley RG5 60 C1
Ryecroft Gdns GU17 150 C2
Ryehurst La RG42 90 C3
Ryeish Green Comp Sch
RG7 113 B2
Ryeish La RG7 113 B2
Ryemead La RG42, SL4 92 B3
Ryhill Way RG6 113 C4
Ryland Cl TW13 98 C2
Rylstone Cl SL6 39 B2
Rylstone Rd RG30 85 B4
Ryvers End SL3 43 C2
Ryvers Rd SL3 43 C2
Ryvers Sch SL3 43 B2

S

Sabah Ct TW15 98 A2
Sackville St RG1 86 A4
Sacred Heart Coll SL5 121 B2
Sacred Heart
RC Prim Sch The RG9 15 B1
Saddleback Rd GU15 151 C4
Saddlebrook Pk TW16 98 C1
Saddler Cnr GU47 150 A4
Saddlewood GU15 151 B2
Sadlers Ct RG41 88 B1
Sadlers End RG41 115 B4
Sadlers La RG41 115 B4
Sadlers Mews SL6 40 A4
Sadlers Rd RG17 127 A3
Saffron Cl Datchet SL3 68 A3
Earley RG6 87 B2
Newbury RG14 104 C2
Saffron Ct TW14 98 B4
Saffron Rd RG12 118 A3
Sage Cl RG6 87 A1
Sage Rd RG31 57 B2
Sage Wlk RG42 91 B1
Sagecroft Rd RG18 106 B3
Sailing Club Rd SL8 3 A2
Sainsbury Ctr The KT16 124 A1
St Adrian's Cl SL6 39 A2
St Agnes Mews RG2 86 B1
St Agnes Terr RG17 25 A1
St Alban's St SL4 67 B3
St Albans Cl 10 SL4 67 B3
St Andrew's Ave SL4 66 C3
St Andrew's Cl
Old Windsor SL4 68 A1
Upper Halliford TW17 125 B3
Wraysbury TW19 68 C1
St Andrew's Cres SL4 66 C3
St Andrew's Sch RG8 55 B1
St Andrew's Way SL1 41 B3
St Andrews RG12 117 C2
St Andrews Cl
Bradfield RG7 82 B3
Crowthorne RG45 142 C3
St Andrews Cotts 1 SL4 67 A3
St Andrews Ct Ascot SL5 120 B2
Colnbrook SL3 69 B4
35 Reading RG1 86 B4
28 Slough SL1 42 C2
St Andrews Rd
Caversham RG4 58 C2
Henley-on-T RG9 35 B4
St Ann's Cl KT16 123 C2
St Ann's Heath
Cty Mid Sch GU25 122 C2
St Ann's Hill Rd KT16 123 B2
St Ann's Rd KT16 123 C2
St Anne's Ave TW19 97 B4
St Anne's Cl RG9 15 B1
St Anne's Prim Sch TW19 97 C4
St Anne's RC Prim Sch
Caversham RG4 59 A1
Chertsey KT16 124 A1
St Annes Glade GU19 145 B2
St Annes Rd RG4 59 A1
St Anthony's RC Prim Sch
SL2 22 B1
St Anthony's Way TW14 71 C2
St Anthonys Cl RG42 118 A4
St Augustine's
RC Prim Sch GU16 151 C1
St Barnabas Rd
Caversham RG4 59 A3
Earley RG2 86 C1
St Bartholomew's Sch
RG14 104 C1
St Bartholomews Rd RG1 86 C4
St Bernard's Convent Sch
SL3 43 B2
St Bernard's Prep Sch
SL1 43 A2
St Bernards Rd SL3 43 B2
St Birinus Rd RG31 84 B3
St Catherine's Sch GU15 151 B2
St Catherines Cl RG41 88 A1
St Catherines Ct
Staines TW18 97 A2
3 Windsor SL4 67 A3
St Catherines Hill RG7 136 C3
St Catherines Rd GU16 152 A1
St Cecelia Ct RG2 86 B2
St Chad's Rd SL6 39 A2
St Christophers Gdns
SL5 119 B4
St Clements Cl RG6 87 B1
St Columba's Cl SL6 39 A2
St Crispin's Comp Sch
RG40 116 C3
St Cuthbert's Cl TW20 95 B1
St Cuthbert's RC Prim Sch
TW20 95 B1
St David's Cl SL6 39 A2
St David's Jun Sch TW15 97 C3
St David's Rd RG14 104 C1
St Davids Cl RG4 58 C3
St Davids Dr TW20 95 B1
St Dominic Savio
RC Prim Sch RG5 87 B4
St Donats Pl RG14 105 A1
St Dunstan's Rd TW13 98 C3
St Edmund Campion
RC Prim Sch SL6 39 A3
St Edward's RC Sch
Reading RG30 85 B4
Windsor SL4 67 A3
St Edward's Royal Free
Ecumenical Mid Sch
Reading RG30 85 B4
Windsor SL4 67 A3
St Edwards Rd RG6 87 A3
St Elizabeth Cl RG2 113 A4
St Elmo Cl SL2 22 B1
St Elmo Cres SL2 22 B1
St Ethelbert's RC Sch SL2 43 A4
St Finian's RC Prim Sch
RG18 106 B4
St Francis RC Sch SL5 120 A2
St Gabriel's Sch RG20 131 A3
St George's Ave RG14 104 C1
St George's Cl SL4 66 C3
St George's Cres SL1 41 B3
St George's La SL5 120 A3
St George's Rd GU15 151 B3
St George's Sch
Ascot SL5 120 A3
Windsor SL4 67 B4
St Georges Ct GU47 143 C1
St Georges Ind Est GU15 151 A2
St Georges Rd RG30 85 B4
St Georges Terr RG30 85 A4
St Giles Cl RG1 86 A3
St Giles Ct 14 RG1 86 A3
St Helens Cres GU47 150 A4
St Helier Cl RG41 116 A2
St Hilda's Ave TW15 97 C2
St Ives Cl RG7 83 B1
St Ives Rd SL6 40 A4
St James Cl
Pangbourne RG8 56 B3
Twyford RG10 61 C3
St James Ctyd 4 SL7 1 C1
St James Pl SL1 41 B4
St James Rd RG40 141 C4
St James Wlk SL0 44 C2
St John the Evangelist
CE Sch RG14 104 C1
St John's Beamont
Prep Sch SL4 95 A3
St John's CE Prim Sch
RG1 86 B4
St John's Gdns RG14 104 C1
St John's Rd
North Ascot SL5 92 C1
Sandhurst GU47 150 B4
St Johns Cl RG5 87 C4
St Johns Ct TW20 96 A2
St Johns Dr SL4 67 A3
St Johns Hill RG1 86 B4
St Johns Inf Sch RG7 137 A3
St Johns Rd
Caversham RG4 59 B1
Mortimer RG7 137 A3
Newbury RG14 105 A1
Reading RG1 86 B4
Slough SL2 43 A3
Thatcham RG19 106 B2
Windsor SL4 67 A3
St Johns St
Crowthorne RG45 143 A2
Reading RG1 86 B4
St Johns Way KT16 124 A1
St Joseph's Convent Sch
RG1 86 C3
St Joseph's Convent Sch
Prep Sch RG1 86 C3
St Joseph's Ct 7 RG14 105 A2
St Joseph's RC Prim Sch
Bracknell RG12 118 B4
Newbury RG14 105 A2
St Joseph's RC Sec Sch
SL2 43 A4
St Jude's CE Sch TW20 95 B1
St Jude's Cl TW20 95 B2
St Jude's Cotts TW20 95 B2
St Jude's Rd TW20 95 B2
St Katherines Rd RG9 35 B4
St Laurence Way SL1 43 A2
St Lawrence Sq RG17 100 B3
St Leger Ct RG14 104 C2
St Leonard's Ave 29 SL4 67 B3
St Leonard's Rd
Windsor SL4 67 B2
Windsor, Clewer Green SL4 66 B1
St Leonards Hill SL4 66 C2
St Leonards Wlk SL0 44 C2
St Luke's CE Prim Sch
SL6 39 C4
St Luke's Rd
Maidenhead SL6 39 C4
Old Windsor SL4 68 A1
St Lukes Ct RG4 59 A2
St Lukes Way RG4 59 A3
St Margaret Clitherow
RC Prim Sch RG12 117 C1
St Margaret's Rd SL6 39 A4
St Margarets Ave TW15 98 A2
St Mark's Cl RG7 83 A3
St Mark's Cres SL6 39 A4
St Mark's Hospl SL6 39 B4
St Mark's Pl SL4 67 B3
St Mark's Rd
Binfield RG42 117 B4
Henley-on-T RG9 15 C1
Maidenhead SL6 39 B4
Windsor SL4 67 B3
St Marks Cl RG19 106 B2
St Marks Rd Binfield RG42 90 B1
Henley-on-T RG9 35 B4
St Martin's Ct TW15 97 B2
St Martins Cl 3 RG6 87 B1
St Martins RC Prim Sch
RG4 59 C3
St Mary's All Saints
CE Prim Sch RG1 85 C3
St Mary's Ave TW19 97 B4
St Mary's CE Comb Sch
SL3 68 A3
St Mary's CE Jun Sch
RG18 106 B2
St Mary's CE Prim Sch
Kintbury RG17 102 A1
Slough SL1 43 A2
Winkfield RG42 92 A2
St Mary's CE Sch TW19 97 C4
St Mary's Cl
Maidenhead SL6 40 A4
Stanwell TW19 97 B4
St Mary's Cres TW19 97 B4
St Mary's Ct 6 RG14 105 A2
St Mary's Dr TW14 98 B4
St Mary's Gdns GU19 145 C2
St Mary's Hill SL5 120 B2
St Mary's Jun Sch RG7 137 B3

St Mary's Pl [14] RG14 . . . .105 A2
St Mary's RC Prim Sch
SL6 . . . . .19 C1
St Mary's Rd Ascot SL5 . .120 A2
Camberley GU15 . . . . .151 B3
Slough SL3 . . . . .43 C2
St Mary's Sch SL5 . . . . . . .120 A1
St Mary's Wlk SL6 . . . . . . .39 C4
St Marys Ave RG8 . . . . .57 B3
St Marys Butts RG1 . . . . . . .86 A4
St Marys Cl
Henley-on-T RG9 . . . . .35 A4
Sandhurst GU47 . . . . .150 B4
St Marys La SL4 . . . . .92 B3
St Marys Rd
Mortimer RG7 . . . . .137 A3
Newbury RG14 . . . . .105 A2
Wokingham RG41 . . . . .88 A1
St Marys Way RG7 . . . . . . .111 A2
St Matthew's Ct TW15 . . . . .98 A2
St Michael's CE Prim Sch
RG12 . . . . .118 A2
St Michael's Ct SL2 . . . . . . .21 B1
St Michael's RC Prim Sch
TW15 . . . . .98 A2
St Michael's Rd
Newbury RG14 . . . . .104 C1
Reading RG30 . . . . .84 B4
St Michaels CE Prim Sch
GU47 . . . . .149 C4
St Michaels Cl RG17 . . . . . .25 A1
St Michaels Cotts RG40 . .143 B4
St Michaels Ct RG10 . . . . . .61 C3
St Michaels Rd
Ashford TW15 . . . . .98 A2
Camberley GU15 . . . . .151 A3
Sandhurst GU47 . . . . .149 C4
St Micheal's CE Sch SL5 .120 B2
St Nazaire Cl TW20 . . . . . . .96 B2
St Nicholas CE Comb Sch
SL6 . . . . .20 C1
St Nicholas CE Prim Sch
Hurst RG10 . . . . .88 C4
Shepperton TW17 . . . . . . .125 A2
St Nicholas Dr TW17 . . . . .125 A1
St Nicholas' Rd RG14 . . . .104 C1
St Nicolas CE Jun Sch
RG14 . . . . .105 A1
St Olave's Cl TW18 . . . . . . .96 C1
St Patrick's Ave RG10 . . . . .61 A3
St Patrick's Cl SL6 . . . . . . .39 A2
St Paul's CE Comb Sch
HP10 . . . . .3 B2
St Paul's CE Jun Sch
RG41 . . . . .116 A3
St Paul's Cl TW15 . . . . .98 B2
St Paul's Ct SL6 . . . . .39 C3
St Paul's Gate RG41 . . . . .116 A3
St Paul's RC Prim Sch
RG31 . . . . .84 B4
St Paul's Rd TW18 . . . . . . .96 B1
St Pauls Ave SL2 . . . . .43 A3
St Pauls Ct RG1 . . . . .86 A3
St Peter St SL7 . . . . .1 C1
St Peter's CE Comb Sch
SL1 . . . . .21 A1
St Peter's CE Mid Sch
SL4 . . . . .67 C1
St Peter's CE Prim Sch
RG6 . . . . .87 A3
St Peter's Cl Burnham SL1 . .21 A1
Old Windsor SL4 . . . . .68 A1
Staines TW18 . . . . .96 C1
St Peter's RC Comb Sch
SL7 .1 B2
St Peter's Rd SL6 . . . . .19 B1
St Peters Ave RG4 . . . . .58 C2
St Peters Gdns GU46 . . . . .149 B3
St Peters Hill RG4 . . . . .58 C2
St Peters Rd RG6 . . . . .87 A3
St Pinnock Ave TW18 . . . . .124 A4
St Pirans Ind Day Sch
SL6 . . . . .19 C1
St Richards Rd RG14 . . . . .105 A2
St Ronans Rd RG30 . . . . . . .85 A4
St Saviour's Terr [9] RG1 . . .86 A3
St Saviours Rd RG1 . . . . . . .85 C3
St Sebastian Cl RG40 . . . . .142 C4
St Stephens Cl RG4 . . . . . . .59 A1
St Swithins Cl RG20 . . . . . . .75 B2
St Swithuns Ct RG10 . . . . . .61 B2
St Theresa's RC Prim Sch
RG40 . . . . .116 B3
St Theresa's Rd TW14 . . . . .71 C2
St Thomas Ct RG18 . . . . . .106 C2
St Thomas Wlk SL3 . . . . . . .69 B4
St-Cloud Way SL6 . . . . .40 A4
Salamanca RG45 . . . . .142 C3
Salcombe Dr RG6 . . . . .87 A2
Salcombe Rd
Ashford TW15 . . . . .97 C3
Newbury RG14 . . . . .104 C1
Reading RG2 . . . . .86 B2
Sale Garden Cotts RG40 .116 B3
Saleby Cl RG6 . . . . .87 C1
Salesian Gdns KT16 . . . . .124 A1
Salesian Sch KT16 . . . . . .124 A1
Salford Cl RG2 . . . . .113 B4
Salisbury Ave SL2 . . . . .42 B4
Salisbury Cl RG41 . . . . . . .116 A1
Salisbury Ct SL6 . . . . .39 C3
Salisbury Mews SL2 . . . . . .22 B1
Salisbury Rd
Blackwater GU17 . . . . . . .150 B3
Harlington TW6 . . . . .71 B1
Salisbury Rd *continued*
Hungerford RG17 . . . . .100 B2
Reading RG30 . . . . .85 C4
Salmon Cl RG7 . . . . .113 A1
Salmond Rd RG2 . . . . .113 B3
Salt Hill Ave SL1 . . . . .42 B3
Salt Hill Dr SL1 . . . . .42 B3
Salt Hill Mans SL1 . . . . .42 B3
Salt Hill Way SL1 . . . . .42 B3
Salters Cl SL6 . . . . .40 A4
Salters Rd SL6 . . . . .40 A4
Saltersgate Cl RG6 . . . . . . .87 B1
Saltire Gdns [2] RG42 . . . .118 A4
Salva Ct [6] RG1 . . . . .86 B3
Salwey Cl RG12 . . . . .118 A2
Samarkand Cl GU15 . . . . .152 A2
Samian Pl RG42 . . . . .90 C1
Sampage Cl RG2 . . . . .113 B3
Sampson Bsns Pk GU15 .151 A2
Sampson Ct TW17 . . . . . . .125 B2
Sampson Pk RG42 . . . . . . .117 B4
Sampsons Gn SL2 . . . . .21 C1
Sanctuary Cl RG30 . . . . . . .84 C4
Sanctuary Rd TW19, TW6 . .71 A1
Sandcroft Rd RG4 . . . . .58 C3
Sanden Cl RG17 . . . . .100 B3
Sandford Down RG12 . . . .118 C2
Sandford Dr RG5 . . . . .60 C1
Sandford La RG5, RG10 . . . .88 B3
Sandgate Ave RG30 . . . . . . .57 C1
Sandhills Ct GU25 . . . . . . .122 C2
Sandhills La GU25, TW20 .122 C2
Sandhills Mdw TW17 . . . . .125 B1
Sandhills Way RG31 . . . . . .84 C2
Sandhurst La GU17 . . . . . .150 A3
Sandhurst Rd
Crowthorne RG45 . . . . . . .143 A2
Wokingham RG40 . . . . . . .142 A4
Yateley GU46 . . . . .149 C4
Sandhurst Sch GU47 . . . . .150 B4
Sandhurst Sta GU47 . . . . .150 A4
Sandisplatt Rd SL6 . . . . . . .39 A3
Sandleford Cl RG2 . . . . . . .113 B3
Sandleford Hospl RG14 . . .131 A4
Sandleford Rise RG14 . . . .131 A4
Sandlers End SL2 . . . . .22 A1
Sandown Ave RG31 . . . . . . .84 A2
Sandown Cl GU17 . . . . . . .150 B3
Sandown Dr GU16 . . . . . . .151 C1
Sandown Rd SL2 . . . . .41 C4
Sandown Way RG14 . . . . . .105 B1
Sandpit Hill RG14,RG20 . . .130 B2
Sandpit La RG7 . . . . .140 A3
Sandringham Ct SL1 . . . . . .41 B4
Sandringham Dr TW15 . . . .97 B2
Sandringham Rd
Maidenhead SL6 . . . . .19 C1
Stanwell TW19, TW6 . . . . . .70 C1
Sandringham Way RG31 . .84 A2
Sands Farm Dr SL1 . . . . . . .21 B1
Sandstone Cl RG41 . . . . . . .88 B1
Sandy Cl RG18 . . . . .79 A2
Sandy Dr TW14 . . . . .98 C4
Sandy La Bracknell RG12 . .118 B4
Camberley GU15 . . . . .151 C3
Hermitage RG18 . . . . .78 C2
North Ascot SL5 . . . . .119 B4
Sandhurst GU47 . . . . .143 A1
Sunningdale SL5 . . . . .121 A2
Virginia Water GU25 . . . . .122 C3
Wokingham RG41 . . . . . . .115 B2
Sandy Lane Inf Sch RG42 . .91 B1
Sandy Lane Jun Sch RG42 .91 B1
Sandy Mead SL6 . . . . .40 B1
Sandy Ride SL5 . . . . .120 C3
Sandy Way KT12 . . . . .125 C1
Sandygate Cl SL7 . . . . .1 B2
Sandygate Rd SL7 . . . . .1 B2
Sapgood Cl RG19 . . . . .106 C1
Sapphire Cl RG41 . . . . . . .115 C4
Sarsby Dr TW19 . . . . .96 A3
Sarum RG12 . . . . .117 C1
Sarum Cres RG40 . . . . . . .116 B4
Sarum Ct [1] RG30 . . . . .85 B3
Sarum Rd RG26 . . . . .135 A1
Sarum Way RG17 . . . . .100 B2
Satis Ho SL3 . . . . .68 B4
Saturn Cl RG41 . . . . .115 C3
Saturn Croft RG42 . . . . .92 A1
Saunders Cl RG10 . . . . .61 C2
Saunders Ct RG8 . . . . .57 A3
Saunton Ave UB3 . . . . .71 C4
Savernake Cl RG30 . . . . . . .84 C4
Savernake Way RG12 . . . .118 C2
Savill Gardens The TW20 . .94 C1
Savill Way SL7 . . . . .1 C1
Saville Cres TW15 . . . . .98 B1
Saville Gdns GU15 . . . . . . .152 A3
Savory Wlk RG42 . . . . .90 B1
Savoy Gr GU17 . . . . .150 B2
Sawmill Rd RG18 . . . . .79 A2
Sawpit Rd RG10 . . . . .88 C4
Sawtry Cl RG6 . . . . .87 C1
Sawyer's Cl SL4 . . . . .66 C4
Sawyers Cl SL6 . . . . .39 A1
Sawyers Cres SL6 . . . . .39 A1
Saxby Cl RG7 . . . . .111 A2
Saxon Cl SL3 . . . . .43 C2
Saxon Ct [22] Reading RG1 . . .86 B4
Stanwell TW19 . . . . .70 A1
Thatcham RG19 . . . . .106 A2
Saxon Cty Jun Sch
TW17 . . . . .125 A2
Saxon Dr RG42 . . . . .118 C4
Saxon Gdns SL6 . . . . .20 B1
Saxon Rd TW15 . . . . .98 B1
Saxon Way
Harmondsworth UB7 . . . . . . .70 B4
Saxon Way *continued*
Old Windsor SL4 . . . . .68 A1
Saxons Acre RG20 . . . . .28 B2
Sayers Cl RG14 . . . . .131 A4
Scafell Cl RG31 . . . . .57 A1
Scafell Rd SL2 . . . . .41 C4
Scampton Rd TW6 . . . . .70 C1
Scania Wlk RG42 . . . . .92 A1
Scarborough Rd TW6 . . . . .71 B1
Scarborough Way SL1 . . . .42 A2
Scarlet Oaks GU15 . . . . . .151 C2
Scarletts La RG10 . . . . .37 B1
Sch of Electronic
Engineering RG2 . . . . . . .114 C1
Scholars Cl Caversham RG4 .58 C2
Great Shefford RG17 . . . . . .48 A2
School Cl GU24 . . . . .153 C2
School Hill
Crowthorne RG45 . . . . . . .143 B2
Sandhurst GU47 . . . . .143 A1
Wargrave RG10 . . . . .36 B1
Woolhampton RG7 . . . . . . .107 C2
School Ho TW19 . . . . .70 B1
School La Bagshot GU19 . .145 C1
Boxford RG20 . . . . .76 C2
Burghfield Common RG7 . . .111 A1
Caversham RG4 . . . . .59 A1
Caversham, Emmer
Green RG4 . . . . .59 A3
Cookham SL6 . . . . .20 A4
Cookham, Cookham
Dean SL6 . . . . .19 A4
East Garston RG17 . . . . .47 B3
Egham TW20 . . . . .96 A2
Froxfield SN8 . . . . .99 A1
Little Marlow SL7 . . . . .2 B3
Littlewick Green SL6 . . . . . .38 A2
Lower Halliford TW17 . . . .125 A1
Maidenhead SL6 . . . . .19 C1
Medmenham SL7 . . . . .17 A3
Silchester RG7 . . . . .136 A1
Stoke Poges SL2 . . . . .23 A2
Swallowfield RG7 . . . . . . .139 C2
Wargrave RG10 . . . . .36 B1
Windlesham GU20 . . . . . . .146 B2
Yateley GU46 . . . . .149 A3
School of Military Survey
RG18 . . . . .78 C4
School Rd Arborfield RG2 . .114 C1
Ascot SL5 . . . . .120 B2
Ashford TW15 . . . . .98 A1
Burghfield Common RG30 . .111 B3
Chieveley RG20 . . . . .78 A4
Compton RG20 . . . . .31 C2
Harmondsworth UB7 . . . . . . .70 B4
Hurst RG10 . . . . .88 C4
Padworth RG7 . . . . .109 C1
Reading RG31 . . . . .84 B4
Swallowfield RG7 . . . . . . .139 C2
Waltham St Lawrence RG10 .62 C2
Windlesham GU20 . . . . . . .146 A3
Wokingham RG40 . . . . . . .116 B3
Wooburn Green HP10 . . . . . .3 C3
School Terr RG1 . . . . .86 C4
Schroder Ct TW20 . . . . .95 A2
Scotland Hill GU47 . . . . . .150 A4
Scotlands Dr SL2 . . . . .22 A3
Scots Cl TW19 . . . . .97 B4
Scots Dr RG41 . . . . .115 C4
Scott Cl Caversham RG4 . . . .59 A3
Farnham Common SL2 . . . . .22 B4
Woodley RG5 . . . . .88 A4
Scott Terr RG12 . . . . .118 C4
Scott's Ave TW16 . . . . .98 C1
Scott's Way TW16 . . . . .98 C1
Scottalls La RG18 . . . . .52 C3
Scours La RG30 . . . . .58 A1
Scratchface La RG7 . . . . . .81 C3
Scrivens Mead RG19 . . . .106 C2
Scylla Cres TW6&TW14 . . . .98 A4
Scylla Rd TW14, TW6 . . . . . .71 A1
Seacourt Rd SL3 . . . . .44 A1
Seafield Ct [26] RG1 . . . . . . .85 C4
Seaford Gdns RG5 . . . . .87 C3
Seaford Rd
Stanwell TW19, TW6 . . . . . .70 B1
Wokingham RG40 . . . . . . .116 B3
Sealand Rd TW6 . . . . .71 A1
Searing Way RG26 . . . . . . .135 A1
Searles Farm La RG30 . . . .85 A1
Seaton Dr TW15 . . . . .97 C3
Seaton Gdns RG2 . . . . .86 B1
Seaton Rd GU15 . . . . .151 A3
Second Ave RG7 . . . . .135 B1
Second Cres SL1 . . . . .42 B4
Second St E RG19 . . . . . . .132 A3
Second St W RG19 . . . . . . .131 C2
Seddon Hill RG42 . . . . .91 A1
Sedge Gr RG18 . . . . .106 C2
Sedgefield Rd RG14 . . . . . .131 B4
Sedgmoor Cl HP10 . . . . .3 A4
Sedgmoor Gdns HP10 . . . . . .3 A4
Sedgmoor La HP10 . . . . .3 A4
Sedgmoor Rd HP10 . . . . .3 A4
Seebys Oak GU47 . . . . . . .150 C3
Sefton Cl Stoke Poges SL2 . .22 C2
West End GU24 . . . . .153 C3
Sefton Paddock SL2 . . . . . .23 A3
Sefton Park Cotts SL2 . . . . .23 A2
Segsbury Gr RG12 . . . . . . .118 C3
Selborne Cl GU17 . . . . . . .150 B3
Selborne Ct [2] RG1 . . . . . . .86 B4
Selborne Gdns RG30 . . . . . .58 A1
Selby Rd TW15 . . . . .98 B1
Selcourt Cl RG5 . . . . .87 B4
Sellafield Way RG6 . . . . . . .87 B1
Selsdon Ave RG5 . . . . .87 C4
Selsey Way RG6 . . . . .114 A4
Selwood Cl TW19 . . . . .70 B1
Selwood Gdns TW19 . . . . . .70 B1
Selwyn Cl SL4 . . . . .66 C3
Selwyn Dr GU46 . . . . .149 A3
Selwyn Pl [2] SL1 . . . . .41 C3
Sen Cl RG42 . . . . .91 B1
Send Rd RG4 . . . . .59 B1
Servite Ho SL6 . . . . .40 A4
Setley Way RG12 . . . . .118 C3
Seton Dr RG31 . . . . .84 C3
Sett The GU46 . . . . .149 A3
Sevenoaks Dr RG7 . . . . . .113 A2
Sevenoaks Rd RG6 . . . . .87 A2
Seventh St RG19 . . . . .131 C3
Severalls The SN8 . . . . . . .126 B2
Severn Cl Sandhurst GU47 .150 B4
Thatcham RG18 . . . . .106 A3
Severn Cres SL3 . . . . .69 A4
Severn Way RG30 . . . . .84 C3
Sewell Ave RG41 . . . . .116 A4
Sewell Cl RG18 . . . . .79 A1
Seymour Ave RG2 . . . . . . .113 C3
Seymour Cl SL6 . . . . .39 A2
Seymour Court La SL7 . . . . .1 A3
Seymour Court Rd SL7 . . . . .1 B2
Seymour Dr GU15 . . . . . . .152 A4
Seymour Ho SL3 . . . . .43 C2
Seymour Park Rd SL7 . . . . . .1 B2
Seymour Plain SL7 . . . . .1 B3
Seymour Rd SL1 . . . . .42 B2
Seymour Way TW16 . . . . . .98 C1
Shackleton Ct [6] TW19 . . .70 C1
Shackleton Rd SL1 . . . . .42 C3
Shackleton Way RG5 . . . . .88 A4
Shafer Ct RG14 . . . . .105 A1
Shaftesbury Cl RG12 . . . . .118 B2
Shaftesbury Cres TW18 . . .97 B1
Shaftesbury Ct
Maidenhead SL6 . . . . .39 C3
[6] Slough SL1 . . . . .42 C2
Wokingham RG40 . . . . . . .116 B4
Shaftesbury Mount
GU17 . . . . .150 B2
Shaftesbury Rd
Bisley GU24 . . . . .153 C2
Reading RG30 . . . . .85 A4
Shaggy Calf La SL2 . . . . . . .43 A3
Shakespeare Cl RG4 . . . . . .59 B3
Shakespeare Rd RG18 . . . .106 B2
Shakespeare Way RG42 . .118 C4
Shalbourne Cl RG17 . . . . .100 A3
Shalbourne Rise GU15 . . .151 B3
Sharney Ave SL3 . . . . .44 A2
Sharnwood Dr RG31 . . . . . .84 C3
Sharonelle Ct RG40 . . . . . .116 A3
Sharpethorpe Cl [2] RG6 . . .87 A1
Shaw Ct SL4 . . . . .68 A1
Shaw Farm Rd RG14 . . . . .105 A3
Shaw Hill RG14 . . . . .105 A3
Shaw Mill RG14 . . . . .105 A3
Shaw Pk RG45 . . . . .143 A2
Shaw Rd Newbury RG14 . . .105 A2
Reading RG1 . . . . .85 C3
Shaw The SL6 . . . . .19 C3
Shaw-Cum-Donnington
Parochial Prim Sch
RG14 . . . . .105 A3
Shears Ct TW16 . . . . .98 C1
Sheehy Way SL2 . . . . .43 A3
Sheep Fair Way RG17 . . . . .25 A1
Sheep Leaze La RG20 . . . . .29 B1
Sheep Wlk RG4 . . . . .59 A2
Sheepcote La
Bourne End SL1 . . . . .3 C1
Holyport SL6 . . . . .64 B2
Sheepcote Rd Eton SL4 . . . .42 A1
Windsor SL4 . . . . .66 C3
Sheepdrove Rd RG17 . . . . .25 B2
Sheephouse Rd SL6 . . . . . .20 A1
Sheephouse Way RG20 . . .49 A3
Sheepridge La SL7,HP10 . . .2 C4
Sheeps Ditch Cl TW18 . . . .97 A1
Sheepwalk Littleton TW17 .125 A2
Shepperton TW17 . . . . . . .124 C2
Sheepwash RG20 . . . . . . .131 A1
Sheepways La RG4 . . . . . . .58 A4
Sheerlands Rd RG2 . . . . . .140 C4
Sheet St SL4 . . . . .67 B3
Sheet Street Rd SL4 . . . . . .94 A4
Sheffield Rd
Harlington TW14, TW6 . . . . .71 B1
Slough SL1 . . . . .42 B4
Sheffield Way TW14, TW6 . .71 B1
Shefford CE Sch RG17 . . . .48 A2
Shefford Cres RG40 . . . . . .116 B4
Shefford Lodge [5] RG14 . .105 A1
Sheldon Gdns RG2 . . . . . . .86 B1
Shelgate Wlk RG5 . . . . .87 B4
Shelley Ave RG12 . . . . . . .118 C4
Shelley Cl Medmenham SL7 .17 B4
Slough SL3 . . . . .43 C1
Wooburn Green HP10 . . . . . .3 C4
Woodley RG5 . . . . .87 C2
Shelley Ct
Camberley GU15 . . . . .151 B3
[28] Reading RG1 . . . . .86 B4
Shelley Rd [12] Marlow SL7 . . .1 C2
Thatcham RG18 . . . . .106 B2
Shelley Walk GU46 . . . . . .149 A3
Shelson Ave TW13 . . . . .98 C2
Shelton Ct SL3 . . . . .43 B2
Shenstone Cl RG40 . . . . . .142 A4
Shenstone Dr SL1 . . . . .21 B1
Shenstone Pk SL5 . . . . . . .120 C3
Shenstone Rd RG2 . . . . .86 A2
Shephards La RG42 . . . . . . .91 A1
Shepherd's Hill RG20 . . . . .76 C2
Shepherds Ave RG6 . . . . . .87 A4
Shepherds Chase GU19 . .145 C1
Shepherds Cl Hurley SL6 . . .17 C2
Shepperton TW17 . . . . . . .125 A2
Shepherds Ct SL4 . . . . .66 C3
Shepherds Hill
Bracknell RG12 . . . . .118 B4
Compton RG20 . . . . .31 C2
Earley RG6 . . . . .87 B4
Woodley RG5 . . . . .60 B1
Shepherds House La RG6 .87 A4
Shepherds La
Caversham RG4 . . . . .58 B3
Hurley SL6 . . . . .17 C2
Shepherds Mount RG20 . . .31 C2
Shepherds Rise RG20 . . . . .31 C2
Shepherds Way RG45 . . . .142 C2
Shepherds Wlk RG6 . . . . . .87 B4
Shepley Dr Reading RG30 . . .85 B2
Wentworth SL5 . . . . .121 B2
Shepley End SL5 . . . . .121 B2
Shepperton Bsns Pk
TW17 . . . . .125 B2
Shepperton Court Dr
TW17 . . . . .125 A2
Shepperton Ct TW17 . . . . .125 A2
Shepperton Rd
TW17, TW18 . . . . .124 B3
Shepperton Sta TW17 . . .125 B2
Shepperton Studios
TW17 . . . . .124 C3
Sheraton Cl GU17 . . . . . . .150 C2
Sheraton Dr RG31 . . . . .57 A1
Sherborne Cl SL3 . . . . .69 C3
Sherborne Ct SL6 . . . . .39 C3
Sherborne Rd TW14 . . . . . .98 B4
Sherbourne Dr
Maidenhead SL6 . . . . .39 B2
Wentworth SL5 . . . . .121 B2
Windsor SL4 . . . . .66 C2
Woodley RG5 . . . . .87 C4
Sherbourne Gdns TW17 .125 C1
Sherbourne Wlk SL2 . . . . . .22 B4
Sherfield Cl RG2 . . . . .86 B2
Sherfield Dr RG2 . . . . .86 B2
Shergold Way SL6 . . . . .19 C3
Sheridan Ave RG4 . . . . .59 A2
Sheridan Cres RG26 . . . . .134 C1
Sheridan Ct
Maidenhead SL6 . . . . .40 A4
Newbury RG14 . . . . .105 B2
[1] Slough SL1 . . . . .41 C3
Sheridan Way RG41 . . . . .115 C3
Sheringham Ct [9] RG1 . . . .86 B3
Sherman Rd Reading RG1 . .86 A3
Slough SL1 . . . . .42 C4
Sherrardmead RG14 . . . . .105 A3
Sherring Cl RG42 . . . . .91 B1
Sherwood Cl
Bracknell RG12 . . . . .119 A4
Slough SL3 . . . . .43 C2
Sherwood Ct
Colnbrook SL3 . . . . .69 B4
Slough SL3 . . . . .43 C1
Sherwood Dr SL6 . . . . .39 A3
Sherwood Gdns RG9 . . . . .35 B4
Sherwood Ho [11] RG1 . . . . .85 C3
Sherwood Pl RG8 . . . . .57 A2
Sherwood Rd RG41 . . . . . . .88 B1
Sherwood Rise RG8 . . . . . .57 A3
Sherwood St RG30 . . . . . . .85 B4
Shield Rd TW15 . . . . .98 B2
Shifford Cres SL6 . . . . .19 C2
Shildon Cl GU15 . . . . .152 B2
Shilling Cl RG30 . . . . .85 A3
Shinfield CE Jun Sch
RG2 . . . . .113 C2
Shinfield Cty Inf Sch
RG2 . . . . .113 C2
Shinfield Rd RG2 . . . . .86 C2
Shinfield Rise RG2 . . . . . . .86 C1
Shiplake Coll RG9 . . . . . . .35 C1
Shiplake Ho Bourne End SL8 .3 A2
Bracknell RG12 . . . . .118 C3
Shiplake Sta RG9 . . . . .36 A2
Shipley Cl RG5 . . . . .61 A1
Shipton Cl RG31 . . . . .57 B1
Shire Cl GU19 . . . . .145 C1
Shire's Head Cl RG30 . . . . .85 B3
Shires The RG41 . . . . .115 B2
Shires Way GU46 . . . . . . .149 B4
Shirley Ave Reading RG2 . .113 B4
Windsor SL4 . . . . .66 C3
Shirley Rd SL6 . . . . .39 B3
Shoesmiths Ct [4] RG1 . . . .86 A4
Sholto Rd TW6 . . . . .71 A1
Shooters Hill RG8 . . . . .56 B3
Shooters Way RG2 . . . . . .112 C4
Shop La
Leckhampstead RG20 . . . . .49 C3
Newbury RG14 . . . . .104 C3
Shoppenhanger's Rd SL6 .39 C2
Shoreham Rd (E) TW6 . . . .70 C1
Shoreham Rd (W) TW6 . . .70 C1
Shoreham Rise SL2 . . . . . . .21 B1
Shorland Oaks RG42 . . . . . .91 B1
Short La TW15, TW19 . . . . .97 C4
Short Rd TW19 . . . . .70 C1
Short St Caversham RG4 . . . .59 A1
Pangbourne RG8 . . . . .56 B3
Reading RG1 . . . . .86 A3
Short The RG8 . . . . .57 B3
Shortfern SL2 . . . . .43 B4
Shortheath La RG7 . . . . . .110 C2
Shortlands UB3 . . . . .71 B4
Shortlands Hill OX10 . . . . .13 B2
Shortwood Ave TW18 . . . . .97 A3
Shortwood Cty Inf Sch
TW18 . . . . .97 A3

Shrewsbury Terr RG14 ....104 C1
Shrewsbury Rd
TW14, TW6 ....71 B1
Shrivenham Cl 3 GU47 ..150 B4
Shropshire Gdns RG42 ....91 C1
Shrubbs Hill La SL5 ....121 B2
Shrubland Dr RG30 ....85 A2
Shrublands Dr GU18 ....153 A4
Shute End RG40, 41 ....116 A3
Shyshack La RG26 ....134 C1
Sibley Park Rd RG6 ....87 A1
Sibson RG6 ....87 B1
Sidbury Cl SL5 ....121 A2
Sidestrand Rd RG14 ....130 C4
Sidings The TW18 ....97 A2
Sidmouth Ct 5 RG1 ....86 B4
Sidmouth Grange Cl RG6 .87 A4
Sidmouth Grange Rd RG6 .87 A4
Sidmouth St RG1 ....86 B4
Sidney Rd Staines TW18 ....97 A2
Windsor SL4 ....66 B2
Silbury Cl RG31 ....84 A2
Silchester CE Prim Sch
RG7 ....136 A1
Silchester Ct TW15 ....97 C3
Silchester Ho SL6 ....40 A4
Silchester House Sch SL6 .40 B4
Silchester Rd
Reading RG30 ....85 B2
Tadley RG26 ....135 B1
Silco Dr SL6 ....39 C3
Silk La RG10 ....61 B2
Silver Birches RG41 ....115 B2
Silver Cl SL6 ....39 A3
Silver Dr GU16 ....152 B2
Silver Fox Cres RG5 ....87 B3
Silver Hill GU47 ....150 C4
Silver La RG7 ....136 A4
Silver St RG1 ....86 A3
Silver Street Flats 23 RG1 .86 A3
Silverdale Rd Earley RG6 ...87 B2
Tadley RG26 ....135 A1
Wargrave RG10 ....36 C1
Silverglades GU46 ....149 B2
Silverthorne Dr RG4 ....58 C3
Silvertrees Dr SL6 ....39 A3
Silverwood Dr GU15 ....152 A4
Silwood RG12 ....117 C1
Silwood Cl SL5 ....120 B4
Silwood Pk
(Imperial Coll) SL5 ....120 C3
Silwood Rd SL5 ....120 C3
Simkins Cl RG42 ....92 A1
Simmonds Cl RG42 ....117 C4
Simmonds St RG1 ....86 A4
Simmons Cl SL3 ....44 A1
Simmons Field RG18 ....106 C2
Simmons Fields RG10 ....61 A2
Simmons Pl TW18 ....96 C2
Simmons Rd RG9 ....15 B2
Simms Farm La RG7 ....136 C2
Simod Ct RG30 ....85 B4
Simons Cl RG31 ....57 B2
Simons La RG41 ....115 B4
Simons Wlk TW20 ....95 B1
Simpson Cl SL6 ....40 A4
Sindle Cl RG41 ....88 A1
Sindlesham Rd RG2 ....114 C2
Sindlesham Specl Sch
RG41 ....114 C4
Singer La RG9 ....15 C1
Singers Cl RG9 ....35 C4
Singers La RG9 ....35 C4
Sinhurst Rd GU15 ....151 A2
Sipson Cl UB7 ....71 A4
Sipson La UB3, UB7 ....71 A4
Sipson Rd UB7 ....71 A4
Sipson Way UB7 ....71 A4
Sir Sydney Camm Ho SL4 .67 A3
Sir William Borlase's
Gram Sch SL7 ....1 B1
Sir William Perkin's Ind
Sch for Girls KT16 ....123 C1
Sirius Cl RG41 ....115 C3
Sirl Cotts SL5 ....120 B3
Six Acre La RG17 ....126 A3
Sixth St RG19 ....131 C3
Skarries View RG4 ....58 B4
Skeffling Cl RG6 ....87 C1
Skelmerdale Way RG6 ....87 C2
Skelton Fields RG42 ....91 B1
Skerries Ct SL3 ....44 A1
Skerrit Way RG8 ....57 B2
Skillman Dr RG19 ....106 C2
Skilton Rd RG31 ....57 B2
Skimpedhill La RG12 ....118 A4
Skinners Green La RG14 .130 A4
Skippons Cl RG14 ....130 B3
Sky Bsns Pk TW20 ....123 B4
Skydmore Path SL2 ....21 C1
Skye Cl RG31 ....84 C2
Skyes Dr TW18 ....97 A2
Skylings RG14 ....105 B2
Skyport Dr UB7 ....70 B4
Skyway 14 Trad Est SL3 ....69 C2
Slade Hill Gdns RG20 ....129 C1
Slaidburn Gn RG12 ....118 C1
Slanting Hill RG18 ....79 A2
Sledmere Ct TW14 ....98 C4
Slim Rd GU15 ....151 B4
Sloan Ct RG8 ....34 B3
Slopes The RG4 ....59 B1
Slough & Eton CE Sec Sch
SL1 ....42 B2
Slough Gram Sch SL3 ....43 A2
Slough Mus SL1 ....43 A2
Slough Rd Datchet SL3 ....68 A4
Eton SL4 ....42 C1
Slough Sta SL1 ....42 C3
Slough Trad Est SL1 ....42 A4
Smallmead Rd
Burghfield Common RG2 ....85 B1
Reading RG2 ....86 A1
Smallridge RG14 ....130 B2
Smith Hospl RG9 ....15 A3
Smith Sq RG12 ....118 B4
Smith's La SL4 ....66 C3
Smitham Bridge Rd
RG17 ....100 B3
Smithfield Cl SL6 ....38 C2
Smithfield Rd SL6 ....39 A2
Smiths Hill OX12 ....6 C3
Smithy's Gn GU20 ....146 B2
Snake La RG20 ....104 A4
Snape Spur SL1 ....42 C4
Snelsmore Common
Ctry Pk RG18 ....77 C1
Snipe La RG20 ....131 C1
Snowball Hill
Maidenhead SL6 ....39 A1
White Waltham SL6 ....64 A4
Snowberry Cl RG41 ....115 C3
Snowden Cl SL4 ....66 B2
Snowden Dr RG31 ....84 A3
Snowdon Cl RG19 ....106 B1
Snowdon Rd TW6 ....71 B1
Snowdrop Copse RG18 ..106 C2
Snowdrop Gr RG41 ....88 B2
Snows Paddock GU20 ....146 A4
Snows Ride GU20 ....146 A3
Soane End RG4 ....59 A4
Soham Cl RG6 ....114 B4
Soho Cres HP10 ....3 B2
Soho Mills Ind Est HP10 ....3 B2
Soke Rd RG7 ....135 C2
Soldiers Rise RG40 ....142 B4
Solent Ct 15 RG1 ....86 A3
Solent Rd TW6 ....70 C1
Somerford Cl SL6 ....40 A4
Somersby Cres SL6 ....39 C2
Somerset Cl
Hungerford RG17 ....100 B3
Wokingham RG41 ....115 B3
Somerset Gr RG42 ....91 C1
Somerset Hospital SN8 ....99 A3
Somerset Lodge 3 SL6 ....39 C3
Somerset Way SL0 ....44 C2
Somerset Wlk RG31 ....84 A3
Somerton Gdns RG6 ....87 A1
Somerton Gr RG19 ....106 B1
Somerville Cres GU46 ....149 C3
Somerville Gr RG41 ....115 B2
Somerville Rd SL4 ....42 B1
Sonning CE Prim Sch
RG4 ....60 B2
Sonning La RG4 ....60 B1
Sonning Mdws RG4 ....60 B1
Sonninge Cl GU47 ....150 B4
Sopwith Cl RG5 ....88 A4
Sorrel Cl
Burghfield Common RG7 ...111 A2
Newbury RG14 ....105 B3
Wokingham RG40 ....116 C4
Sorrel Dr GU18 ....152 C4
Sospel Ct SL2 ....22 B2
South Ave Egham TW20 ....96 B1
Henley-on-T RG9 ....35 C4
South Bank RG8 ....14 B2
South Cl Burnham SL1 ....41 B3
Medmenham SL7 ....17 B4
Wokingham RG40 ....116 B2
South Dr Reading RG2 ....86 C1
Sonning RG4 ....60 B1
Sulhamstead RG7 ....110 B4
Wentworth GU25 ....122 A1
Wokingham RG40 ....116 B3
South End Rd RG7 ....82 A1
South Farm La GU19 ....146 A1
South Field Cl SL4 ....41 B2
South Gate Ave TW13 ....98 B2
South Gn SL1 ....42 C3
South Gr KT16 ....123 C2
South Groves RG17 ....73 A1
South Hill Pk RG12 ....118 B1
South Hill Rd RG12 ....118 A2
South Lake Cres RG5 ....87 C3
South Lake Inf Sch RG5 ....87 C3
South Lake Jun Sch RG5 ....87 B3
South Lynn Cres RG12 ...118 A2
South Mdw RG45 ....143 B2
South Meadow La SL4 ....67 B4
South Oak Way RG2,RG7 .112 C4
South Path SL4 ....67 B3
South Pl Marlow SL7 ....1 C1
Wokingham RG40 ....116 B3
South Rd Bisley GU24 ....153 C2
Bracknell RG40, RG12 ....117 C1
Crowthorne RG45 ....143 C2
Englefield Green TW20 ....95 B1
Maidenhead SL6 ....39 C3
South Row Chilton OX11 ....10 B4
Fulmer SL3 ....23 C4
South St Blewbury OX11 ....12 A4
Caversham RG4 ....59 A1
Reading RG1 ....86 B4
Staines TW18 ....96 C2
South Stoke Cty Prim Sch
RG8 ....14 A2
South View Cookham SL6 ....19 C4
Hungerford RG17 ....100 B3
Wooburn Green HP10 ....3 C4
South View Ave RG4 ....59 B1
South View Gdns 9
RG14 ....105 A2
South View Pk RG4 ....59 B1
Southampton Cl GU17 ....150 B3
Southampton Rd
TW19, TW6 ....70 C1
Southampton St RG1 ....86 A3
Southbank Gdns RG17 ....25 B1
Southbourne Dr SL8 ....3 A2
Southbury La RG10 ....61 C3
Southcote Dr GU15 ....152 A3
Southcote Farm La RG30 ..85 B2
Southcote La RG30 ....85 B2
Southcote Lodge RG30 ....85 A2
Southcote Prim Sch RG30 .85 B2
Southcote Rd RG30 ....85 B3
Southcroft
Englefield Green TW20 ....95 A2
Slough SL2 ....22 A1
Southdown Rd
Caversham RG4 ....59 A3
Tadley RG26 ....135 A1
Thatcham RG19 ....105 C2
Southend RG18 ....106 B3
Southern Cotts TW19 ....70 A1
Southern Ct 19 RG1 ....86 A4
Southern Hill RG1 ....86 B3
Southern Ind Area RG12 .117 C3
Southern Perimeter Rd
East Bedfont TW6 ....71 A1
Hatton TW14, TW6 ....71 B1
Stanwell TW19, TW6 ....70 B1
Southern Rd GU15 ....151 B3
Southerndene Cl RG31 ....57 B1
Southfield Gdns SL1 ....41 A4
Southfields Boxford RG20 ..76 B2
Chieveley RG20 ....78 A4
Southfields Ave TW15 ....98 A1
Southfields Sch RG40 ....116 B3
Southgate Ho SL6 ....39 C4
Southglade RG2 ....113 B4
Southlake Ct RG5 ....87 B3
Southlands Cl RG40 ....116 B3
Southlands Rd RG40 ....116 B2
Southlea Rd SL3 ....68 A3
Southview Cl RG10 ....61 C3
Southview Rd SL7 ....1 C2
Southville Cl TW14 ....98 C4
Southville Cres TW14 ....98 C4
Southville Jun & Inf Schs
TW14 ....98 C4
Southville Rd TW14 ....98 C4
Southwark Cl GU46 ....149 B3
Southway GU15 ....151 A2
Southwell Park Rd GU15 .151 B3
Southwick GU19 ....145 C1
Southwick Ct RG12 ....118 C2
Southwold RG12 ....117 C1
Southwold Cl RG6 ....87 B1
Southwold Spur SL3 ....44 B2
Southwood RG40 ....116 B2
Southwood Gdns
Burghfield Common RG7 ...111 A2
Cookham SL6 ....19 C3
Southwood Rd SL6 ....19 C3
Sovereign Dr GU15 ....152 A4
Sovereign Ho TW15 ....97 C2
Sovereign Way RG31 ....84 B3
Sowbury Bank RG20 ....78 A4
Spackman Cl RG19 ....106 B1
Spackmans Way SL1 ....42 B2
Spade Oak Mdw SL8 ....2 C2
Span Hill RG4 ....60 A4
Sparrow Cl RG41 ....115 C3
Sparrowbill RG20 ....28 C1
Sparvell Way GU15 ....151 B3
Speedbird Way UB7 ....70 B4
Speedwell Way RG18 ....106 C2
Speen Hill Cl RG14 ....104 C2
Speen La RG14 ....104 B2
Speen Lodge Ct RG14 ....104 C2
Speen Pl RG14 ....104 C2
Speenhamland Ct 5
RG14 ....105 A2
Speenhamland Prim Sch
RG14 ....104 C2
Spelthorne Coll TW15 ....97 C2
Spelthorne Cty Inf Sch
TW15 ....98 C1
Spelthorne Gr TW16 ....98 C1
Spelthorne La
TW15, TW17 ....125 B4
Spelthorne Mus TW18 ....96 C2
Spelthorne Sports Club
TW15 ....98 B1
Spencer Cl
Silchester RG26 ....135 C1
Wokingham RG41 ....115 B3
Spencer Gdns TW20 ....95 B2
Spencer Rd
Bracknell RG42 ....117 C4
Newbury RG14 ....130 B3
Reading RG2 ....113 A4
Slough SL3 ....43 C2
Spencers Cl SL6 ....39 B4
Spencers La SL6 ....19 C3
Spencers Rd SL6 ....39 B4
Spenwood Cl RG7 ....113 A1
Sperling Rd SL6 ....19 C1
Spey Rd RG30 ....85 A4
Spinfield Cty Comb Sch
SL7 ....1 A1
Spinfield La W SL7 ....1 B1
Spinfield Mount SL7 ....1 A1
Spinfield Pk SL7 ....1 B1
Spinis RG12 ....117 C1
Spinner Gn RG12 ....118 A2
Spinners Wlk Marlow SL7 ....1 B1
Windsor SL4 ....67 B3
Spinney SL1 ....42 A3
Spinney Cl RG4 ....59 A4
Spinney Dr TW14 ....98 B4
Spinney La SL4 ....93 A4
Spinney The Ascot SL5 ...120 C2
Frimley GU15 ....152 B3
Reading RG31 ....84 C2
Wokingham RG40 ....141 C4
Yateley GU46 ....149 B4
Spinningwheel La RG42 ....90 B4
Spitfire Way RG5 ....88 A4
Spittal St SL7 ....1 B1
Splash The RG42 ....91 A1
Spode Cl RG30 ....84 C4
Spout La TW19 ....70 A2
Spout La N TW19 ....70 A2
Spray La RG20 ....28 B1
Spray Rd Ham SN8 ....126 C2
Inkpen RG17 ....127 A2
Spriggs Cl RG19 ....106 B1
Spring Ave TW20 ....95 C1
Spring Cl Maidenhead SL6 ..19 C1
Pangbourne RG8 ....55 B3
Spring Cnr TW13 ....98 C3
Spring Gdns Ascot SL5 ...120 A3
Bourne End SL8 ....3 A2
Frimley GU15 ....152 A3
Marlow SL7 ....1 C2
Shinfield RG7 ....113 A1
Wooburn Green HP10 ....3 C4
Spring Gr RG1 ....86 A3
Spring Hill SL6 ....39 C2
Spring Ho SL7 ....1 C2
Spring La
Aldermaston RG7 ....135 B4
Aston Tirrold OX11 ....12 C4
Caversham RG4 ....60 A3
Cold Ash RG18 ....106 B4
Cookham SL6 ....19 B3
Farnham Common SL2 ....22 B3
Mortimer RG7 ....137 A3
Slough SL1 ....41 C3
Swallowfield RG7 ....139 A2
Spring Mdw RG12 ....118 B4
Spring Mdws RG17 ....48 A2
Spring Rd TW13 ....98 C3
Spring Rise TW20 ....95 C1
Spring Terr 29 RG1 ....86 A3
Spring Wlk RG10 ....36 B1
Spring Wood La RG7 ....111 A1
Spring Woods
Sandhurst GU47 ....143 B1
Virginia Water GU25 ....122 A3
Springate Field SL3 ....43 C2
Springcross Ave GU17 ...150 B2
Springdale Earley RG6 ....87 A1
Wokingham RG40 ....141 C4
Springfield
Lightwater GU18 ....153 B4
Slough SL1 ....43 A2
Springfield Cl SL4 ....67 A3
Springfield Ct SL6 ....40 A4
Springfield Cty Prim Schs
TW16 ....125 C4
Springfield End RG8 ....34 B4
Springfield La Marlow SL7 ..1 A1
Newbury RG14 ....131 A4
Springfield Mews RG4 ....59 A2
Springfield Pk
Maidenhead SL6 ....40 B1
Twyford RG10 ....61 C2
Springfield Prim Sch
RG31 ....84 A4
Springfield Rd
Ashford TW15 ....97 C2
Bracknell RG12 ....117 B4
Brands Hill SL3 ....69 A4
Frimley GU15 ....152 A3
Silchester RG26 ....135 C1
Windsor SL4 ....67 A3
Springfields Cl KT16 ....124 A1
Springhill Ct RG12 ....118 A3
Springhill Rd RG8 ....34 B4
Springmead Ct GU47 ....143 C1
Spruce Ct 26 SL1 ....42 C2
Spruce Dr GU18 ....153 A4
Spruce Rd RG5 ....88 A3
Spur The Slough SL1 ....41 B4
Wargrave RG10 ....36 C2
Spurcroft Prim Sch
RG19 ....106 B1
Spurcroft Rd RG19 ....106 B1
Square The Bagshot GU19 .145 C2
Bracknell RG12 ....118 C3
Earley RG6 ....114 A4
Harmondsworth TW6 ....70 A3
Lightwater GU18 ....146 B1
Pangbourne RG8 ....56 B3
Shinfield RG7 ....113 A1
Squire's Bridge Rd
TW17 ....125 A3
Squire's Rd TW17 ....125 A3
Squires Bridge Rd KT17 .124 C3
Squires Ct
Camberley GU15 ....151 B2
Chertsey KT16 ....124 A1
Squires Wlk TW15 ....98 B1
Squirrel Cl GU47 ....150 A4
Squirrel Dr SL4 ....93 A4
Squirrel Rise SL7 ....1 B3
Squirrels Drey RG45 ....142 C3
Squirrels Way RG6 ....87 A1
Stable Cl RG7 ....111 A2
Stable Cotts SL7 ....18 B3
Stable Croft GU19 ....145 B1
Stable Ct RG14 ....105 A3
Stable View GU46 ....149 B4
Stables Ct SL7 ....1 A1
Stacey's Ind Est RG26 ....135 B1
Staddlestone Cl RG31 ....57 B1
Stadium Way RG30 ....58 A1
Staff Coll GU15 ....151 B4
Staff College Rd GU15 ....151 A3
Stafferton Way SL6 ....40 A3
Stafford Ave SL2 ....22 B1
Stafford Cl Burnham SL6 ....41 A4
Woodley RG5 ....87 C4
Stafford Lake GU21,GU24 .153 C1
Staffordshire Cl RG30 ....84 C4
Staffordshire Croft RG42 ..91 C1
Stag Hill RG17 ....73 A1
Stainash Cres TW18 ....97 A2
Stainash Par TW18 ....97 A2
Staines By-Pass
TW15, TW18 ....97 B2
Staines Central Trad Est
TW18 ....96 C2
Staines La KT16 ....124 A2
Staines Lane Cl KT16 ....123 C2
Staines Prep Sch The
TW18 ....97 A2
Staines Rd Chertsey KT16 .124 B3
East Bedfont TW14 ....98 B4
Laleham TW18 ....124 A4
Wraysbury TW19 ....95 C4
Staines Rd W TW15,TW16 ..98 B1
Staines Sta TW18 ....97 A2
Stainford Cl TW15 ....98 B2
Stamford Ave GU16 ....151 C1
Stamford Rd SL6 ....39 B3
Stanbrook Cl RG7 ....82 A1
Stanbury Gate RG7 ....113 A2
Stanfield RG26 ....135 A1
Stanford Dingley
Circular Wlks RG18 ....80 C4
Stanham Rd RG30 ....84 C4
Stanhope Heath TW19 ....70 B1
Stanhope Rd
Camberley GU15 ....150 C2
Reading RG2 ....86 B2
Slough SL1 ....41 B4
Stanhope Way TW19 ....70 B1
Stanlake La RG10 ....61 C2
Stanley Cl SL7 ....1 C2
Stanley Cotts SL2 ....42 C3
Stanley Gn E SL3 ....43 C1
Stanley Gn W SL3 ....43 C1
Stanley Gr 5 RG1 ....85 C4
Stanley Ho SL4 ....68 A1
Stanley Rd Ashford TW15 ..97 C2
Newbury RG14 ....105 A1
Wokingham RG40 ....116 C3
Stanley St RG1 ....85 C4
Stanmore Cl SL5 ....120 A3
Stanmore Gdns RG7 ....136 C3
Stanmore Rd Beedon RG20 .30 B1
East Ilsley RG20 ....30 C3
Stanshawe Rd RG1 ....86 A4
Stansted Rd TW6 ....70 C1
Stanton Cl RG6 ....87 B2
Stanton Way SL3 ....43 C1
Stanway Cotts
7 Chertsey KT16 ....124 A1
Reading RG1 ....86 C3
Stanwell Cl TW19 ....70 B1
Stanwell Gdns TW19 ....70 B1
Stanwell Moor Rd
TW19, TW6, UB7 ....70 A2
Stanwell New Rd
TW18, TW19 ....97 A3
Stanwell Rd Ashford TW15 .97 C2
East Bedfont TW14,
TW19, TW6 ....98 A4
Horton SL3, TW19 ....69 B2
Stapleford Rd RG30 ....85 B2
Staplehurst RG12 ....117 C1
Stapleton Cl Marlow SL7 ....1 C2
Newbury RG14 ....130 B3
Star La Knowl Hill RG10 ....37 C2
Reading RG1 ....86 A4
Star Post Rd GU15 ....151 C4
Star Rd RG4 ....59 B1
Starling Cl RG41 ....115 C3
Starlings Dr RG31 ....84 A3
Starmead Dr RG40 ....116 C3
Starting Gates RG14 ....105 B1
Startins La SL6 ....19 B4
Starwood Ct SL3 ....43 B2
Statham Ct RG42 ....117 C4
Station App Ashford TW15 ..97 C2
Maidenhead SL6 ....39 C3
Marlow SL7 ....1 C1
Reading RG1 ....86 A4
Shepperton TW17 ....125 B2
Staines TW18 ....97 A2
Virginia Water GU25 ....122 B3
Station Cres TW15 ....97 C2
Station Flats SL5 ....121 A1
Station Hill Ascot SL5 ....120 A3
Cookham SL6 ....19 C4
Hampstead Norreys RG18 ..52 C3
Reading RG1 ....86 A4
Station Ind Est RG40 ....116 A3
Station Par Ashford TW15 ..97 C2
Cookham SL6 ....19 C3
Sunningdale SL5 ....121 A1
Virginia Water GU25 ....122 C2
Station Path TW18 ....96 C2
Station Rd Ashford TW15 ....97 C2
Bagshot GU19 ....145 C2
Ball Hill RG20 ....130 A2
Bourne End SL8 ....3 A2
Bracknell RG12 ....118 A4
Chertsey KT16 ....124 A1
Cookham SL6 ....19 C4
Earley RG6 ....87 B2

Viburnum Ct GU24 ...153 C3
Vicarage Ave TW20 ...96 A2
Vicarage Cl Cookham SL6 ...20 A4
 Wokingham RG40 ...141 C3
Vicarage Cres TW20 ...96 A2
Vicarage Ct
 East Bedfont TW14 ...98 B4
 Egham TW20 ...96 A1
Vicarage Dr SL6 ...40 B2
Vicarage Flats SL4 ...67 B4
Vicarage Gdns Ascot SL5 ...120 A2
 White Waltham SL6 ...63 C4
Vicarage La
 Cold Ash RG18 ...106 B4
 Laleham TW18 ...124 B3
 Wraysbury TW19 ...95 C4
 Yateley GU46 ...149 B4
Vicarage Rd Ashford TW16 ...98 C1
 Bagshot GU19 ...145 B2
 Blackwater GU17 ...150 C2
 Egham TW20 ...96 A2
 Henley-on-T RG9 ...35 C4
 Maidenhead SL6 ...39 C4
 Reading RG2 ...86 B3
 Staines TW18 ...96 C3
 Yateley GU46 ...149 B4
Vicarage Way SL3 ...69 B4
Vicarage Wlk SL6 ...40 B2
Vicarage Wood Way
 RG31 ...57 A1
Vickers Cl Shinfield RG2 ...113 C2
 Woodley RG5 ...88 A4
Vickers Ct 9 TW19 ...70 C1
Victor Cl SL6 ...39 A4
Victor Rd Thatcham RG19 ...106 C2
 Windsor SL4 ...67 B2
Victor Way RG5 ...88 A4
Victoria Ave GU15 ...151 A3
Victoria Ct Bagshot GU19 ...145 C1
 Henley-on-T RG9 ...15 C1
 2 Marlow SL7 ...1 C1
 Slough SL1 ...42 C3
Victoria Dr GU17 ...150 B2
Victoria Gdns RG14 ...105 A2
Victoria Ho SL4 ...68 A1
Victoria La UB3 ...71 B4
Victoria Mews RG30 ...85 B4
Victoria Rd Ascot SL5 ...120 A2
 Caversham RG4 ...59 A2
 Eton SL4 ...41 C1
 Farnham Common SL2 ...22 B3
 Marlow SL7 ...1 C1
 Mortimer RG7 ...136 C3
 Reading RG31 ...84 B4
 Sandhurst GU47 ...143 C1
 Slough SL2 ...43 A3
 Staines TW18 ...96 C3
 Wargrave RG10 ...36 C1
Victoria St
 Englefield Green TW20 ...95 B1
 Reading RG1 ...86 B4
 18 Slough SL1 ...42 C2
 Windsor SL4 ...67 B3
Victoria Way 16 RG1 ...86 B4
Victory Rd KT16 ...124 A1
Vigo La GU46 ...149 B2
Viking RG12 ...117 C2
Villa Mews RG1 ...86 C4
Village Cl RG2 ...113 A3
Village Ct SL5 ...120 B2
Village Gate TW17 ...125 A2
Village Rd Dorney SL4 ...41 A2
 Thorpe TW20 ...123 B3
Village Sh Ctr The 13 SL1 ...42 C2
Village The
 Finchampstead RG40 ...141 C2
 Old Windsor SL4 ...94 A3
Village Way Ashford TW15 ...98 A2
 Yateley GU46 ...149 B4
Villiers Ct SL4 ...67 A4
Villiers Mead RG41 ...116 A3
Villiers Rd SL2 ...42 B4
Villiers Way RG14 ...130 B3
Villiers Wlk RG14 ...130 B3
Vincent Cl Chertsey KT16 ...123 C1
 Harmondsworth UB7 ...71 A4
 Woodley RG5 ...87 C3
Vincent Dr TW17 ...125 C3
Vincent Ho 10 RG1 ...85 C4
Vincent Rd Chertsey KT16 ...123 C1
 Thatcham RG18 ...106 C2
Vincent Rise RG12 ...118 C3
Vine Cl TW19 ...70 A1
Vine Cres RG30 ...85 A2
Vine Ct Newbury RG14 ...105 A1
 Stoke Poges SL2 ...23 A3
Vine Rd SL2 ...22 C3
Vineries Cl UB7 ...71 A4
Vinery The RG10 ...36 B1
Vines The RG41 ...115 B2
Vineyard Dr SL8 ...3 A3
Vinter Ct TW17 ...125 A2
Viola Ave TW19 ...97 C4
Viola Croft RG42 ...118 C4
Violet Gr RG18 ...106 C3
Virginia Ave GU25 ...122 B2
Virginia Beeches GU25 ...122 B3
Virginia Cl TW18 ...124 B3
Virginia Ct Ashford TW15 ...97 C2
 Virginia Water GU25 ...122 B3
Virginia Dr GU25 ...122 B3
Virginia Water SL5 ...121 C3
Virginia Water Prep Sch
 GU25 ...122 B3
Virginia Water Sta GU25 ...122 C2
Virginia Way RG30 ...85 A3
Viscount Ct 37 SL4 ...67 B3
Viscount Ind Est SL3 ...69 C2
Viscount Rd TW19 ...97 C4
Viscount Way Hatton TW6 ...71 C2
 Woodley RG5 ...88 A4
Vivien Cl SL6 ...19 C3
Vivienne Ho TW18 ...97 A2
Vo-Tec Ctr RG14 ...105 C1
Voller Dr RG31 ...84 B3
Volunteer Rd RG7 ...83 B1
Vulcan Cl Sandhurst GU47 ...150 A4
 Woodley RG5 ...61 A1
Vulcan Way GU47 ...150 A4

W

Waborne Rd SL8 ...3 A2
Wade Dr SL1 ...42 A3
Wadham GU47 ...143 C1
Wadham Cl TW17 ...125 B1
Wagbullock Rise RG12 ...118 B2
Waggoners Hollow
 GU19 ...145 C1
Wagner Cl SL6 ...38 C2
Wagtail Cl RG10 ...61 C2
Waingel's Copse Sch
 RG10 ...61 A1
Waingels Rd RG5, RG10 ...61 A1
Wainscot SL5 ...120 C2
Wakefield Cres SL2 ...22 C3
Wakeford Cl RG26 ...135 C1
Wakeford Ct RG26 ...135 C1
Wakelins End SL6 ...19 C4
Wakeman Rd SL8 ...3 A2
Wakemans RG8 ...55 B2
Walbury RG12 ...118 C3
Waldeck Rd SL6 ...40 A4
Waldeck St RG1 ...86 A3
Waldegrave Pl RG14 ...105 A2
Walden Ave RG2 ...114 B2
Waldens Cl SL8 ...3 A2
Waldorf Hts GU17 ...150 B2
Waldron Hill RG12 ...118 C4
Waldrons The RG17 ...47 B3
Waleys Pl 7 RG4 ...59 B1
Walgrove Gdns SL6 ...63 C4
Walk The Ashford TW16 ...98 C1
 Eton SL4 ...42 A1
Walker Cl TW14 ...98 C4
Walker Rd SL6 ...40 A2
Walker's Ridge GU15 ...151 C3
Walkers La RG17 ...25 A2
Walkers Pl RG30 ...85 B4
Wall La RG7 ...136 B1
Wallace Cl Marlow SL7 ...1 C2
 Upper Halliford TW17 ...125 B3
 Woodley RG5 ...87 B3
Wallace Wlk SL4 ...42 C1
Wallcroft Cl RG42 ...90 C1
Walled Gdn The RG10 ...36 B1
Waller Ct RG4 ...59 A1
Waller Dr RG14 ...105 C3
Wallingford Cl RG12 ...118 C3
Wallingford Rd
 Compton RG20 ...31 C3
 Goring RG8 ...34 B4
 South Stoke RG8 & OX10 ...14 B3
Wallington Rd GU15 ...145 A1
Wallington's Rd RG17 ...101 C1
Wallis Ct SL1 ...43 A2
Wallner Way RG40 ...116 C3
Walmer Cl
 Crowthorne RG45 ...143 B3
 Reading RG30 ...85 A3
Walmer Rd RG5 ...60 C1
Walnut Cl
 Wokingham RG41 ...115 C3
 Yateley GU46 ...149 B2
Walnut Tree Cl
 Bourne End SL8 ...3 A1
 Twyford RG10 ...61 C3
Walnut Tree Ct RG8 ...34 B3
Walnut Tree Ho TW20 ...95 C2
Walnut Tree Rd TW17 ...125 B4
Walnut Way Bourne End SL8 ...3 A1
 Reading RG30 ...84 B4
Walpole Rd
 Old Windsor SL4 ...95 A4
 Slough SL1 ...41 B4
Walrus Cl RG5 ...88 A4
Walsh Ave RG42 ...91 C1
Walter Inf Sch RG41 ...116 A3
Walter Rd RG41 ...115 C4
Walters Cl RG18 ...106 B4
Waltham Cl
 Maidenhead SL6 ...38 C1
 Sandhurst GU47 ...143 B1
Waltham Rd
 Twyford RG10 ...62 A3
 White Waltham SL6 ...38 C1
Waltham St Lawrence
 Cty Prim Sch RG10 ...62 C2
Walton Ave RG9 ...35 C4
Walton Bridge Rd
 KT12, TW17 ...125 C1
Walton Cl RG5 ...87 B4
Walton Dr SL5 ...119 C4
Walton Gdns TW13 ...98 C2
Walton La Burnham SL2 ...21 C2
 Lower Halliford KT13,TW17 ...125 B1
 Walton-on-T TW17 ...125 C1
Walton Way RG14 ...105 B2
Wandhope Way RG31 ...57 B1
Wansey Gdns RG14 ...105 B3
Wanstraw Gr RG12 ...118 C1
Wantage Cl RG12 ...118 C2
Wantage Rd
 Great Shefford RG17 ...48 B3
 Lambourn RG17 ...25 B3
 Reading RG30 ...85 B4
 Sandhurst GU47 ...150 B4
 Streatley RG8 ...33 C4
Wapshott Rd TW18 ...96 C2
War Memorial Pl RG9 ...35 C4
Waram Cl RG17 ...100 C4
Warbler Cl RG31 ...84 A3
Warbler Dr RG6 ...87 A1
Warborough Ave RG31 ...84 A4
Warborough Rd OX12 ...7 A4
Warbreck Dr RG31 ...57 A2
Warbrook La RG27 ...141 A1
Ward Cl Iver SL0 ...44 C4
 Wokingham RG40 ...116 B4
Ward Gdns SL1 ...41 C3
Ward Royal 6 SL4 ...67 B3
Ward Royal Par 3 SL4 ...67 B3
Wardle Ave RG31 ...57 B1
Wardle Cl GU19 ...145 C2
Wards Pl TW20 ...96 B1
Wards Stone Pk RG12 ...118 C1
Wareham Rd RG12 ...118 C2
Warehouse Rd RG19 ...131 C3
Warfield CE Prim Sch
 RG42 ...91 C1
Warfield Rd
 Bracknell RG12 & RG42 ...91 B1
 East Bedfont TW14 ...98 C4
Warfield St RG42 ...91 B2
Wargrave Hill RG10 ...36 B1
Wargrave Rd
 Remenham Hill RG9 ...15 C1
 Twyford RG10 ...61 B3
Wargrave Sta RG10 ...36 B1
Wargrove Dr GU47 ...150 B4
Waring Cl RG6 ...114 B4
Warings The RG7 ...109 A4
Warley Rise RG31 ...57 B2
Warner Cl Harlington UB3 ...71 B4
 Slough SL1 ...41 C3
Warners Hill SL6 ...19 B4
Warnford Rd RG30 ...84 C4
Warnsham Cl 1 RG6 ...87 A1
Warren Cl
 Burghfield Common RG7 ...111 A2
 Sandhurst GU47 ...150 A4
 Slough SL3 ...43 C2
Warren Ct 7 SL2 ...22 B4
Warren Down RG42 ...117 C4
Warren House Rd RG40 ...116 B4
Warren La RG40 ...141 C3
Warren Rd Ashford TW15 ...98 C1
 Newbury RG14 ...130 B3
 Woodley RG4,RG5 ...60 B1
Warren Rise GU16 ...151 C2
Warren Row SL5 ...119 B4
Warren Row Rd RG10 ...37 B3
Warren The RG4 ...58 B2
Warrington Ave SL1 ...42 B4
Warrington Spur SL4 ...95 A4
Warwick RG12 ...118 C2
Warwick Ave Slough SL2 ...22 B1
 Staines TW18 ...97 B1
 Thorpe Lea TW20 ...123 B4
Warwick Cl Frimley GU15 ...152 A2
 Maidenhead SL6 ...39 A2
Warwick Ct 34 SL4 ...67 B3
Warwick Dr RG14 ...105 A1
Warwick Ho RG2 ...86 B2
Warwick Rd Ashford TW15 ...97 C2
 Reading RG2 ...86 B2
Warwick Villas TW20 ...123 B4
Wasdale Cl GU47 ...143 B1
Wash Hill HP10 ...3 C2
Wash Hill Lea HP10 ...3 C2
Wash Water RG20 ...130 A2
Washbury Ho RG14 ...130 C4
Washington Ct SL7 ...2 A2
Washington Dr Slough SL1 ...41 B3
 Windsor SL4 ...66 C2
Washington Gdns RG40 ...142 A4
Washington Rd RG4 ...59 A1
Wasing La RG7 ...134 B3
Watchetts Cty Jun Sch
 The GU15 ...151 A1
Watchetts Dr GU15 ...151 B1
Watchetts Lake Cl GU15 ...151 B2
Watchetts Rd GU15 ...151 A2
Watchmoor Pk GU15 ...151 A2
Watchmoor Rd GU15 ...151 A2
Watchmoor Trade Ctr
 GU15 ...151 A2
Water La RG19 ...131 B4
Water Rd RG30 ...85 A4
Water Splash La SL5 ...120 C4
Water St RG18 ...52 C3
Waterbeach Cl SL1 ...42 B4
Waterbeach Rd SL1 ...42 B4
Waterfall Cl GU25 ...122 A3
Waterford Way RG40 ...116 B3
Waterham Rd RG12 ...118 A2
Waterhouse Mead
 GU47 ...150 B4
Waterloo Cl
 Camberley GU15 ...152 A4
 East Bedfont TW14 ...98 C4
 Moulsford OX10 ...14 A4
Waterloo Cres RG40 ...116 C2
Waterloo Rd
 Crowthorne RG45 ...143 A2
 Reading RG2 ...86 A3
 Wokingham RG40 ...116 C3
Waterloo Rise RG2 ...86 A2
Waterman Ct 5 SL1 ...41 C3
Waterman Pl RG1 ...59 A1
Watermans Bsns Pk The
 TW18 ...96 C2
Watermans Rd RG9 ...35 C4
Watermans Way RG10 ...36 B1
Watermead TW14 ...98 C4
Watermeadows The
 RG14 ...105 A2
Watermill Ct RG7 ...108 B1
Waters Dr TW18 ...96 C2
Watersfield Ct 4 RG6 ...87 A1
Waterside HP10 ...3 C4
Waterside Ct RG14 ...105 B2
Waterside Dr
 Purley on T RG8 ...57 B3
 Slough SL3 ...44 A2
 Theale RG7 ...83 C2
Waterside Gdns 9 RG1 ...86 A4
Watersplash La RG42 ...91 A1
Watersplash Rd TW17 ...125 A3
Watery La Kintbury RG20 ...128 C3
 Wooburn Green HP10 ...3 C4
Watkins Cl RG40 ...141 C4
Watlington St RG1 ...86 B4
Watmore La RG41 ...88 B1
Watson Cl RG40 ...115 C1
Watts La OX11 ...12 A4
Wavell Cl RG2 ...86 C1
Wavell Gdns SL2 ...21 C1
Wavell Rd SL6 ...39 A3
Wavendene Ave TW20 ...96 B1
Waverley RG12 ...117 C2
Waverley Cl GU15 ...151 C2
Waverley Ct 18 RG30 ...85 B3
Waverley Dr
 Camberley GU15 ...151 C3
 Virginia Water GU25 ...122 A3
Waverley Rd
 Bagshot GU19 ...145 C2
 Reading RG30 ...85 B4
 Slough SL1 ...42 B4
Waverley Sch RG40 ...115 C1
Waverley Way RG40 ...115 C1
Waverleys The RG18 ...106 B2
Waybrook Cres RG1 ...86 C3
Wayland Cl RG12 ...118 C3
Waylands TW19 ...68 C1
Waylands Cl RG7 ...82 B2
Waylen St RG1 ...85 C4
Ways End GU15 ...151 C2
Wayside Mews SL6 ...39 C4
WC Lee's Resthouses
 GU20 ...146 B2
Weald Rise RG30 ...57 C1
Wealden Way RG30 ...84 C4
Weardale Cl RG2 ...86 B2
Weaver Moss GU47 ...150 A4
Weavers Ct 37 RG1 ...86 B4
Weavers La RG17 ...127 B3
Weavers Way RG10 ...61 B2
Weavers Wlk 20 RG14 ...105 A2
Webb Cl Bagshot GU19 ...145 C1
 Binfield RG42 ...90 C1
 Slough SL3 ...43 B1
Webb Ct RG40 ...116 C4
Webb's Cl RG1 ...85 C3
Webbs Acre RG19 ...106 C1
Webbs La RG7 ...109 A4
Webster Cl SL6 ...39 A3
Wedderburn Cl RG41 ...88 B1
Wedgewood Way RG30 ...57 C1
Weekes Dr SL1 ...42 A2
Weighbridge Row RG1 ...58 C1
Weir Cl RG31 ...84 C2
Weir Pl TW18 ...123 C4
Weir Rd KT16 ...124 A1
Weirside Ct 13 RG1 ...86 B4
Welbeck RG12 ...117 C2
Welbeck Rd SL6 ...39 B3
Welby Cl SL6 ...39 A2
Welby Cres RG41 ...88 A1
Weldale St RG1 ...85 C4
Welden SL2 ...43 B4
Welford Pk RG20 ...75 C4
Welford Rd RG5 ...88 A4
Welford & Wickham
 CE Prim Sch RG20 ...75 B2
Well Cl GU15 ...151 A2
Well House La RG27 ...140 A2
Well Mdw RG14 ...105 A3
Welland Cl Brands Hill SL3 ...69 A4
 Reading RG31 ...57 B1
Wellbank SL6 ...20 C1
Wellburn Cl GU47 ...150 A4
Wellcroft Rd SL1 ...42 A3
Weller Dr Barkham RG40 ...141 A3
 Camberley GU15 ...151 B2
Wellers La RG42 ...91 B4
Wellesley Ave SL0 ...44 C2
Wellesley Cl GU19 ...145 B2
Wellesley Ct SL0 ...44 C2
Wellesley Dr RG45 ...142 C3
Wellesley Path SL1 ...43 A2
Wellesley Rd SL1 ...43 A2
Welley Ave TW19 ...68 C2
Welley Rd TW19 ...68 C1
Wellfield Cl RG31 ...84 B4
Wellhill Rd OX12 ...27 B3
Wellhouse La RG18 ...79 C3
Wellhouse Rd SL6 ...19 C1
Wellington Ave
 Reading RG2 ...86 B2
 Virginia Water GU25 ...122 A2
Wellington Bsns Pk
 RG45 ...142 C2
Wellington Cl
 Newbury RG14 ...105 B3
 Sandhurst GU47 ...150 B4
 Walton-on-T KT12 ...125 C1
Wellington Coll RG45 ...143 A2
Wellington Cotts
 Ball Hill RG20 ...129 A1
 Knowl Hill RG10 ...37 B3
Wellington Cres RG26 ...134 B1
Wellington Ct
 Ashford TW15 ...97 C2
 Shinfield RG7 ...113 A2
 Stanwell TW19 ...97 C4
Wellington Ctry Pk RG7 ...139 B1
Wellington Dr RG12 ...118 C2
Wellington Gdns RG7 ...82 A1
Wellington Rd
 Ashford TW15 ...97 C2
 Crowthorne RG45 ...143 B2
 Hatton TW14 ...71 C1
 Maidenhead SL6 ...39 B4
 Sandhurst GU47 ...150 B4
 Wokingham RG40 ...116 A3
Wellington St SL1 ...43 A2
Wellington Terr GU47 ...150 B4
Wellingtonia Ave
 RG45,RG40 ...142 B2
Wells Cl SL4 ...67 A4
Wells La SL5 ...120 A3
Welsh La RG7, RG7 ...139 A1
Welshmans Rd RG7 ...136 A3
Welwick Cl RG6 ...87 C1
Welwyn Ave TW14 ...71 C1
Wendan Rd RG14 ...130 C4
Wendover Ct TW18 ...96 B2
Wendover Dr GU16 ...152 B2
Wendover Pl TW18 ...96 B2
Wendover Rd
 Bourne End SL8 ...3 A3
 Burnham SL1 ...41 A4
 Egham TW18, TW20 ...96 B2
Wendover Way RG30 ...84 B4
Wenlock Edge RG10 ...61 A2
Wenlock Way RG19 ...106 B1
Wensley Cl RG10 ...61 B3
Wensley Rd RG1 ...85 C3
Wensleydale Dr GU15 ...152 B3
Wentworth Ave
 North Ascot SL5 ...119 B4
 Reading RG2 ...113 B4
 Slough SL2 ...22 A1
Wentworth Cl
 Ashford TW15 ...98 A2
 Crowthorne RG45 ...142 C3
 Yateley GU46 ...149 B3
Wentworth Club GU25 ...122 A2
Wentworth Cres SL6 ...39 B3
Wentworth Ct RG14 ...105 A1
Wentworth Dr GU25 ...121 C3
Wentworth Way SL5 ...119 B4
Wescott Inf Sch RG40 ...116 B3
Wescott Rd RG40 ...116 B3
Wesley Dr TW20 ...96 A1
Wesley Pl SL4 ...93 A3
Wessex Cl RG17 ...100 B3
Wessex Ct 4 TW19 ...70 C1
Wessex Gdns RG10 ...61 C2
Wessex Inf Sch SL6 ...39 A2
Wessex Jun Sch SL6 ...39 A2
Wessex Rd Bourne End SL8 ...3 A1
 Harmondsworth TW19, TW6 ...70 C2
Wessex Road Ind Est
 SL8 ...3 A1
Wessex Way SL6 ...39 A2
Wessons Hill SL6 ...19 B4
West Cl Ashford TW15 ...97 C2
 Medmenham SL7 ...17 B4
West Cres SL4 ...66 C3
West Ct RG4 ...60 C1
West Dean SL6 ...39 C4
West Dr Reading RG31 ...84 C3
 Sonning RG4 ...60 B1
 Wentworth GU25 ...121 C1
West End Ct SL2 ...22 C2
West End La
 Harlington UB3 ...71 B4
 Newell Green RG42 ...91 A2
 Stoke Poges SL2 ...22 C2
West End Rd RG7 ...136 C3
West Fryerne GU46 ...149 B4
West Gn GU46 ...149 A4
West Green Ct RG1 ...85 C3
West Hill RG1 ...86 A3
West Ilsley Ho RG20 ...10 A1
West La RG9 ...15 B1
West Mead SL6 ...19 C1
West Mead Sch RG40 ...116 C3
West Mills RG14 ...104 C2
West Mills Yd RG14 ...104 C2
West Point SL1 ...41 B3
West Ramp TW6 ...71 A3
West Rd Bracknell RG40 ...117 B1
 Camberley GU15 ...151 B3
 East Bedfont TW14 ...98 B4
 Maidenhead SL6 ...39 C4
West Ridge SL8 ...3 A2
West Sq SL0 ...44 C4
West St Henley-on-T RG9 ...15 B1
 Maidenhead SL6 ...39 C4
 Marlow SL7 ...1 B1
 Newbury RG14 ...104 C2
 Reading RG1 ...86 A4
West Surrey Est TW15 ...125 B4
West View
 East Bedfont TW14 ...98 B4
 Peasemore RG20 ...50 B4
West View Cotts RG18 ...52 C3
West Way TW17 ...125 B2
Westacott Bsns Ctr SL6 ...38 C1
Westacott Way SL6 ...38 B2
Westborough Ct SL6 ...39 B3
Westborough Rd SL6 ...39 B3

Westbourne Rd
Feltham TW13 ....98 C3
Sandhurst GU47 ....150 C4
Staines TW18 ....97 A1
Westbourne Terr
3 Newbury RG14 ....105 A2
Reading RG30 ....85 B4
Westbrook SL6 ....40 C1
Westbrook Cl RG17 ....100 B3
Westbrook Gdns RG12 ....118 B4
Westbrook Gn OX11 ....11 C4
Westbrook Rd
Reading RG30 ....58 B1
Staines TW18 ....96 C2
Westbrook St OX11 ....11 C4
Westbury Cl
Crowthorne RG45 ....143 A3
Shepperton TW17 ....125 A2
Westbury La RG8 ....57 A3
Westcombe Cl RG12 ....118 C1
Westcote Rd RG30 ....85 B3
Westcotts Gn RG42 ....91 B1
Westcroft SL2 ....22 A1
Westdene Cres RG4 ....58 C2
Westende RG40 ....116 B3
Westende Jun Sch RG40 ....116 B3
Westerdale RG19 ....106 B2
Westerdale Dr GU16 ....152 A2
Westerham Wlk 33 RG1 ....86 A3
Western Ave
Chertsey KT16 ....124 A3
Henley-on-T RG9 ....35 C4
Newbury RG14 ....104 C2
Thorpe TW20 ....123 A3
Woodley RG5 ....60 C1
Western Cl KT16 ....124 A3
Western Ctr The RG12 ....117 C4
Western Dr
Shepperton TW17 ....125 B2
Wooburn Green HP10 ....3 C3
Western Elms Ave RG30 ....85 C4
Western End RG14 ....104 C1
Western House Inf Sch
SL1 ....41 C3
Western Ind Area RG12 ....117 C4
Western Oaks RG31 ....57 C1
Western Perimeter Rd
TW19, TW6, UB7 ....70 A3
Western Perimeter Rd
Rdbt TW19 ....70 B1
Western Rd
Bracknell RG12 ....117 C4
Henley-on-T RG9 ....35 C4
Reading RG1 ....85 C3
Westfield Bglws SL7 ....16 C3
Westfield Cotts SL7 ....16 C3
Westfield Cres
Shiplake RG9 ....36 A2
Thatcham RG18 ....106 A2
Westfield Inf Sch SL8 ....3 A2
Westfield Rd
Camberley GU15 ....151 A1
Caversham RG4 ....59 A1
Cholsey OX10 ....13 B3
Maidenhead SL6 ....39 A4
Slough SL2 ....22 A1
Thatcham RG18 ....106 A3
Winnersh RG41 ....88 A1
Westfield Way RG14 ....104 C1
Westfields RG20 ....31 B2
Westfields Inf Sch GU46 ....149 A3
Westgate Cres SL1 ....41 C3
Westgate Ct RG14 ....104 C1
Westgate Cty Sec Sch
SL1 ....42 A3
Westgate Rd RG14 ....104 C1
Westhatch Cnr RG42 ....91 B3
Westhatch La RG42 ....91 B3
Westhead Dr RG14 ....131 A4
Westhorpe Rd SL7 ....1 C2
Westland RG18 ....106 A2
Westland Cl TW19 ....70 C1
Westlands Ave Earley RG2 ....86 C1
Slough SL1 ....41 B4
Westlands Cl SL1 ....41 B4
Westlands Rd RG14 ....131 A4
Westley Mill Binfield RG42 ....90 C4
Holyport RG42 ....63 C1
Westlyn Rd RG26 ....135 C1
Westmacott Dr TW14 ....98 C4
Westmead SL4 ....67 A2
Westmead Dr RG14 ....130 C4
Westminster Way RG6 ....87 B1
Westmorland Cl RG41 ....115 B3
Westmorland Dr
Bracknell RG42 ....91 C1
Frimley GU15 ....152 A2
Westmorland Rd SL6 ....39 B3
Weston Gr GU19 ....145 C1
Weston Rd SL1 ....41 C4
Westonbirt Dr RG4 ....58 C2
Westons RG20 ....51 B4
Westridge Ave RG8 ....57 B3
Westview Dr RG10 ....61 C3
Westward Rd RG41 ....115 C4
Westwates Cl RG12 ....118 B4
Westway RG8 ....34 B4
Westwood Farm Jun & Inf Schs RG31 ....57 B2
Westwood Glen RG31 ....57 B1
Westwood Gn SL6 ....19 C3
Westwood Rd Marlow SL7 ....1 B1
Newbury RG14 ....105 B1
Reading RG31 ....57 B1
Windlesham GU20 ....146 C3
Westwood Row RG31 ....57 B1
Wetherby Cl RG4 ....59 B3
Wetherby Ho GU15 ....151 B4
Wethered Dr SL1 ....41 A4
Wethered Pk SL7 ....1 B1
Wethered Rd SL7 ....1 B1
Wetton Pl TW20 ....95 C2
Wexford Ct SL6 ....40 A4
Wexham Court Comb Sch
SL2 ....43 B4
Wexham Cty Sec Sch SL2 ....43 B4
Wexham Park Hospl SL3 ....23 B1
Wexham Park La SL3 ....23 B1
Wexham Pl SL2 ....23 B3
Wexham Rd SL1, SL2 ....43 A3
Wexham St SL3 ....23 A2
Wexham Woods SL3 ....43 B4
Wey Ave KT16 ....124 A3
Wey Cl GU15 ....151 A3
Weybridge Mead GU46 ....149 C4
Weycrofts RG42 ....90 C1
Weymead Cl KT16 ....124 B1
Whaley Rd RG40 ....116 B4
Wharf La Bourne End SL8 ....3 A2
Henley-on-T RG9 ....15 C1
Wharf Rd Newbury RG14 ....105 A2
Wraysbury TW19 ....95 B4
Wharf St RG14 ....105 A2
Wharf The Newbury RG14 ....105 A2
Taplow SL6 ....40 B4
Wharfedale Rd RG41 ....88 A2
Wharfside RG7 ....109 B2
Whatley Gn RG12 ....118 A2
Whatmore Cl TW19 ....70 A1
Wheatash Rd KT15 ....124 A1
Wheatbutts The SL4 ....41 C1
Wheatfield Cl SL6 ....39 A2
Wheatfields Rd RG2 ....113 C3
Wheatlands Cl RG31 ....84 C2
Wheatlands La RG14 ....130 A3
Wheatlands Rd SL3 ....43 B2
Wheatley RG12 ....117 C2
Wheatley Cl RG2 ....86 C1
Wheatsheaf La
Newbury RG14 ....105 A2
Staines TW18 ....96 C1
Wheatsheaf Par SL4 ....68 A1
Wheble Dr RG5 ....87 B4
Wheeler Cl
Burghfield Common RG7 ....111 A2
Wokingham RG41 ....115 C3
Wheeler Ct RG31 ....57 C1
Wheelers Green Way
RG19 ....106 C1
Wheelton Cl RG6 ....87 C2
Wheelwrights Pl SL3 ....69 B4
Whins Cl GU15 ....151 A2
Whins Dr GU15 ....151 A2
Whinshill Ct SL5 ....121 A1
Whistler Gr GU47 ....150 B3
Whistlers La RG7 ....136 A1
Whistley Cl RG12 ....118 C3
Whitakers Cl RG18 ....106 A2
Whitamore Row RG9 ....35 C4
Whitby Ct RG4 ....59 B3
Whitby Dr 7 RG1 ....86 B3
Whitby Gn RG4 ....59 B3
Whitby Rd SL1 ....42 B3
Whitchurch Cl SL6 ....19 C2
Whitchurch Prim Sch
RG8 ....56 C4
Whitchurch Rd RG8 ....56 B3
White Bridge Cl TW14 ....71 C1
White City RG45 ....143 B3
White Cl Hermitage RG18 ....78 C3
Slough SL1 ....42 B3
White Gates RG20 ....75 B3
White Hart Ind Est GU17 ....150 C2
White Hart Rd
2 Maidenhead SL6 ....39 C4
Slough SL1 ....42 B2
White Hart Row 3 KT16 ....124 A1
White Hill
Remenham Hill RG9 ....16 A1
Shiplake RG9 ....35 A3
Windlesham GU20 ....146 A3
Wooburn Moor HP9 ....3 C4
White Horse La RG40 ....141 B3
White Horse Rd SL4 ....66 B3
White House Gdns GU46 ....149 B4
White House Prep Sch
RG41 ....116 A2
White House Rd OX10 ....14 C4
White Lilies Island SL4 ....67 A4
White Lion Way GU46 ....149 B2
White Lodge Cl
Marlow Bottom SL7 ....1 B3
Purley on T RG31 ....57 A2
White Paddock SL6 ....39 A1
White Rd Chilton OX11 ....10 B4
Sandhurst GU15 ....150 C3
White Rock SL6 ....20 A1
White Shoot OX11 ....12 A3
White Waltham
CE Prim Sch SL6 ....63 B4
Whiteacres Dr SL6 ....40 A1
Whitebeam Cl RG41 ....115 B2
Whiteford Rd SL2 ....42 C4
Whitegates La RG6 ....87 A4
Whitegrove Prim Sch
RG42 ....91 C1
Whitehall SL6 ....20 A1
Whitehall Dr RG2 ....140 C4
Whitehall Farm La GU25 ....122 C3
Whitehall La Egham TW20 ....95 C1
Horton TW19 ....69 A1
Whitehaven SL1 ....42 C3
Whitehill Cl GU15 ....151 B4
Whitehill Pl GU25 ....122 C2
Whitehills Cl SL7 ....1 B3
Whitehills Gn RG8 ....34 B3
Whitehouse Way SL3 ....43 B2
Whiteknights Prim Sch
RG6 ....86 C1
Whiteknights Rd RG6 ....86 C3
Whitelands Dr SL5 ....119 B4
Whitelands Park Prim Sch
RG18 ....106 B3
Whitelands Rd RG18 ....106 B2
Whiteley SL4 ....66 C4
Whitelocke Inf Sch
RG40 ....116 B4
Whitelocks Piece RG17 ....73 A1
Whitemoor La
Lower Basildon RG8 ....34 B1
Upper Basildon RG8 ....54 C3
Whitepit La HP10 ....3 B4
Whites Hill RG7 ....110 B3
Whites La Beenham RG7 ....109 A4
Datchet SL3 ....68 A4
Whitestone Cl RG6 ....87 C2
Whitewalls Cl RG20 ....31 C3
Whiteways Ct TW18 ....97 A1
Whitewell Cl RG2 ....114 C1
Whitley Cl TW19 ....70 C1
Whitley Park Inf Sch RG2 ....86 A1
Whitley Park Jun Sch
RG2 ....86 A1
Whitley Park La RG2 ....86 B2
Whitley Rd GU46 ....149 B2
Whitley St RG2 ....86 A3
Whitley Wood La RG2 ....113 B4
Whitley Wood Rd RG2 ....113 B4
Whitmoor Rd GU19 ....145 C1
Whitmore Cl GU47 ....143 B1
Whitmore La SL5 ....121 A3
Whitstone Gdns RG2 ....86 B1
Whittaker Rd SL2 ....21 C1
Whittenham Cl SL2 ....43 A3
Whittle Cl
Sandhurst GU47 ....143 A1
Wokingham RG40 ....141 C4
Whittle Parkway SL1 ....41 B4
Whitton Cl 6 RG6 ....87 B1
Whitton Rd RG12 ....118 C3
Whitworth Rd RG2 ....141 A4
Whurley Way SL6 ....19 C1
Whynstones Rd SL5 ....120 A2
Whyteladyes La SL6 ....19 C3
Wick Hill La RG40 ....142 A3
Wick La TW20 ....94 C2
Wick Rd TW20 ....95 A1
Wickets The
Ashford TW15 ....97 C2
Maidenhead SL6 ....39 B4
Wickford Way RG6 ....113 C4
Wickham La TW20 ....96 A1
Wickham Rd
Camberley GU15 ....151 C4
Earley RG6 ....87 C1
Wickham Vale RG12 ....117 C2
Wickhurst Cotts SL6 ....38 A3
Wicks Gn RG42 ....90 A2
Widbrook Rd SL6 ....20 A2
Widecroft Rd SL0 ....44 C4
Widmere La SL7 ....1 A3
Wield Ct RG6 ....87 C1
Wiggett Gr RG42 ....90 B1
Wigmore La Reading RG30 ....58 A1
Reading RG30 ....58 B1
Theale RG7 ....83 B1
Wigmore Rd RG26 ....134 C1
Wilberforce Mews SL6 ....39 C4
Wilberforce Way RG12 ....118 B2
Wilcox Gdns TW17 ....124 C3
Wild Briar RG40 ....141 C4
Wild Cl RG6 ....114 B4
Wildcroft Dr RG40 ....116 A1
Wilde Theatre RG12 ....118 B1
Wilder Ave RG8 ....56 C3
Wilderness Ct RG6 ....87 A2
Wilderness Rd Earley RG6 ....87 A2
Frimley GU16 ....151 C1
Wilders Cl Bracknell RG42 ....91 A1
Frimley GU16 ....151 C2
Wildgreen N SL3 ....44 A1
Wildgreen S SL3 ....44 A1
Wildridings Cty Prim Sch
RG12 ....118 A3
Wildridings Rd RG12 ....118 A3
Wildridings Sq RG12 ....118 A3
Wildwood Dr RG26 ....134 B1
Wildwood Gdns GU46 ....149 B2
Wilford Rd SL3 ....43 C1
Wilfred Way RG19 ....107 A2
Wilfrids Wood Cl HP10 ....3 A3
Willats Cl KT16 ....124 A2
William Byrd Sch UB3 ....71 B4
William Cl RG19 ....106 B1
William Ellis Cl SL4 ....68 A1
William Gray Cty Inf Sch
The RG5 ....87 B4
William Gray Cty Jun Sch
The RG5 ....87 B3
William Penn Comb Sch
SL2 ....22 B1
William Sim Wood RG42 ....92 A1
William St Reading RG1 ....85 C4
Slough SL1 ....42 C3
Windsor SL4 ....67 B3
Williant Cl SL6 ....38 C1
Willington Cl GU15 ....151 A3
Willink Sch The RG7 ....110 C1
Willis Cl RG18 ....79 A2
Willoners SL2 ....42 A4
Willoughby Rd
Bracknell RG12 ....117 C3
Slough SL3 ....44 A2
Willow Bank SL7 ....1 B3
Willow Bank Jun & Inf Schs
RG5 ....60 C1
Willow Cl
Burghfield Common RG30 ....111 A3
Colnbrook SL3 ....69 B4
Flackwell Heath HP10 ....3 B3
Newbury RG14 ....104 C1
Willow Cotts OX10 ....13 C3
Willow Court La OX10 ....13 C3
Willow Ct 2 Charlton TW16 ....98 C1
Frimley GU16 ....151 B1
Wokingham RG41 ....116 A3
Willow Dr Bracknell RG12 ....118 B4
Maidenhead SL6 ....40 A1
Twyford RG10 ....61 B3
Willow Gdns
Purley on T RG31 ....57 A1
Reading RG2 ....86 C1
Willow Gn GU24 ....153 C3
Willow Gr SL4 ....67 A2
Willow La
Blackwater GU17 ....150 B2
Wargrave RG10 ....36 B2
Willow Lo 10 TW16 ....98 C1
Willow Par SL3 ....44 A2
Willow Pk SL2 ....23 A3
Willow Pl SL4 ....67 B4
Willow Rd Newtown RG20 ....131 C1
Poyle SL3 ....69 C3
Willow St 3 RG1 ....86 A3
Willow Tree Glade RG31 ....84 B2
Willow Way GU47 ....142 C1
Willow Wlk
Chertsey KT16 ....124 A1
Englefield Green TW20 ....95 B2
Willow Wood Cl SL1 ....21 A2
Willowbrock SL4 ....42 B1
Willowbrock Rd TW19 ....97 C3
Willowdale RG40 ....141 C4
Willowford GU46 ....149 B3
Willowherb Cl RG40 ....116 C4
Willowmead TW18 ....124 A4
Willowmead Cl 10
Marlow SL7 ....1 C2
Newbury RG14 ....130 B3
Willowmead Gdns SL7 ....1 C2
Willowmead Rd 8 SL7 ....1 C2
Willowmead Sq 9 SL7 ....1 C2
Willows Ct RG8 ....56 B3
Willows End GU47 ....150 A4
Willows Rd SL8 ....3 A2
Willows The
14 Bourne End SL8 ....3 A2
9 Bracknell RG12 ....118 C3
Caversham RG4 ....59 A1
Lightwater GU18 ....146 B1
Windsor SL4 ....66 B4
Willowside RG5 ....60 C1
Willson Rd TW20 ....95 A2
Wilmington Cl RG5 ....87 C4
Wilmot Cl RG42 ....90 B1
Wilmot Rd SL1 ....21 A1
Wilmot Way GU15 ....151 C2
Wilmot Wlk RG14 ....130 B3
Wilsford Cl RG6 ....113 C4
Wilson Ave RG9 ....35 C4
Wilson Cl RG20 ....31 C2
Wilson Ct RG41 ....88 A1
Wilson Prim Sch RG30 ....85 B4
Wilson Rd RG30 ....85 B4
Wilson Valkenburg Ct
RG14 ....104 C2
Wilstrode Ave RG42 ....90 C1
Wilton Cl UB7 ....70 B4
Wilton Cres SL4 ....66 B2
Wilton Rd
Camberley GU15 ....151 A2
Reading RG30 ....85 B4
Wiltshire Ave
Crowthorne RG45 ....143 A3
Slough SL2 ....22 B1
Wiltshire Cl RG17 ....100 B3
Wiltshire Dr RG40 ....116 B4
Wiltshire Gr RG42 ....91 C1
Wiltshire Lodge 2 SL6 ....39 C3
Wiltshire Rd Marlow SL7 ....2 A2
Wokingham RG40 ....116 B4
Wiltshire Wlk RG31 ....84 A3
Wilwood Rd RG42 ....117 C4
Wilwyne Cl RG4 ....59 B2
Wimbledon Cl GU15 ....144 C1
Wimbledon Rd GU15 ....144 C1
Wimblington Dr RG6 ....114 B4
Wimbourne Gdns RG30 ....58 A1
Wimbushes RG40 ....141 B3
Winbury Ct SL6 ....39 C4
Winbury Sch SL6 ....40 A2
Wincanton Rd RG2 ....113 B4
Winch Cl RG42 ....90 B2
Winchbottom La SL7, HP10 ....2 A4
Winchcombe Cty
Jun & Inf Schs RG14 ....105 A2
Winchcombe Rd
Newbury RG14 ....105 A1
Twyford RG10 ....61 C2
Winchester Cl SL3 ....69 C3
Winchester Dr SL6 ....39 A2
Winchester Ho 12 RG14 ....105 A1
Winchester Rd
Harlington UB3 ....71 C4
Reading RG2 ....86 A2
Winchester Way GU17 ....150 B3
Winchgrove Rd RG42 ....91 A1
Winchstone Cl TW17 ....124 C3
Wincroft Rd RG4 ....58 C3
Windermere Cl
East Bedfont TW14 ....98 C4
Stanwell TW19 ....97 B3
Windermere Cl *continued*
Thorpe Lea TW20 ....96 A1
Winnersh RG41 ....88 B2
Windermere Rd
Lightwater GU18 ....146 A1
Reading RG2 ....86 B2
Windermere Way
Slough SL1 ....41 B4
Thatcham RG19 ....106 A2
Windermere Wlk GU15 ....152 B3
Winding Wood Dr GU15 ....152 A2
Windle Cl GU20 ....146 B2
Windlebrook Gn 3 RG42 ....118 A4
Windlemere Golf Ctr
GU24 ....153 C4
Windlesham Ct GU20 ....146 B3
Windlesham Rd
Bracknell RG42 ....117 C4
West End GU24 ....153 C4
Windlesham Village
Cty Inf Sch GU20 ....146 A3
Windmill Ave RG41 ....115 C4
Windmill Bsns Village
TW16 ....125 C4
Windmill Cl Charlton TW16 ....98 C1
Windsor SL4 ....67 A3
Wokingham RG41 ....115 C4
Windmill Cnr RG7 ....137 A3
Windmill Ct RG7 ....137 A3
Windmill Field GU20 ....146 B2
Windmill La RG7 ....108 A3
Windmill Lodge TW16 ....125 C4
Windmill Rd
Bracknell RG42 ....118 A4
Charlton TW16 ....125 C4
Cookham SL6 ....19 C3
Fulmer SL3 ....23 B4
Mortimer RG7 ....137 A3
Slough SL1 ....42 B3
Windmill Rd W TW16 ....125 C4
Windmill Terr TW17 ....125 C1
Windmill Trad Est TW16 ....125 C4
Windrush Ave SL3 ....44 A2
Windrush Ct 8 RG30 ....85 A4
Windrush Ho SL8 ....3 A2
Windrush Hts GU47 ....150 A4
Windrush Way
Maidenhead SL6 ....39 C4
Reading RG30 ....85 A4
Windsor Boys Sch SL4 ....67 A3
Windsor Bsns Ctr The
SL4 ....67 B4
Windsor Castle SL4 ....67 C4
Windsor Cl SL1 ....21 B1
Windsor Ct 16 RG1 ....85 C4
Windsor Dr TW15 ....97 B2
Windsor & Eton
Central Sta SL4 ....67 B3
Windsor & Eton
Riverside Sta SL4 ....67 B4
Windsor Forest Ct SL5 ....119 B4
Windsor Girls Sch SL4 ....67 A2
Windsor Great Pk SL4 ....94 B2
Windsor Hill HP10 ....3 C3
Windsor Ho RG9 ....35 C4
Windsor L Ctr SL4 ....67 A4
Windsor La SL1 ....21 B1
Windsor Park Rd UB3 ....71 C4
Windsor Pl KT16 ....124 A2
Windsor Rd Datchet SL3 ....68 A4
Englefield Green
TW19, TW20 ....95 C3
Fulmer SL2 ....23 A4
Holyport SL6 ....40 B1
North Ascot SL5 ....120 A4
Slough SL1 ....42 C2
Wraysbury TW19 ....68 C1
Windsor Ride
Bracknell SL5 ....119 B2
Sandhurst GU15 ....151 A4
Wokingham RG40 ....142 A4
Windsor Rise RG14 ....131 B4
Windsor Sq 24 RG1 ....86 A3
Windsor St KT16 ....124 A2
Windsor Way RG31 ....84 A2
Windsor Youth Hostel
SL4 ....67 A4
Wing Cl SL7 ....1 B1
Wingate Rd RG5 ....87 C3
Wingfield Gdns GU16 ....152 B2
Wingrove Rd RG30 ....85 B3
Winkfield Cl RG41 ....116 A2
Winkfield La
Oakley Green SL4 ....66 A1
Winkfield SL4 ....92 B4
Winkfield Rd Ascot SL5 ....120 A4
Windsor SL4 ....66 C1
Winkfield Row RG42 ....92 A2
Winkfield St SL4 ....92 B3
Winkworth La RG7 ....135 B1
Winnersh Gate RG41 ....88 B1
Winnersh Gr RG41 ....88 B1
Winnersh Prim Sch RG41 ....88 B2
Winnersh Sta RG41 ....88 B1
Winnersh Triangle Ind Est
RG41 ....88 A2
Winnersh Triangle Sta
RG41 ....88 A2
Winscombe RG12 ....117 C2
Winser Dr RG30 ....85 B3
Winston Cl RG7 ....113 B1
Winston Way
Purley on T RG8 ....57 A3
Thatcham RG19 ....105 C2
Winter Hill SL6 ....2 B1